# Python Automation Cookbook

Third Edition



100+ new and updated recipes for scalable workflows, MCP integrations, and AI-powered automation

**Jaime Buelta**

<packt>

# Python Automation Cookbook

Third Edition



**Portfolio Director:** Kunal Chaudhari
**Relationship Lead:** Denim Pinto
**Project Manager:** Ankit Maroli
**Content Engineers:** Alexander Powell, Deepayan Bhattacharjee
**Technical Editor:** Irfa Ansari
**Indexer:** Manju Arasan
**Production Designer:** Shantanu Zagade

First published: September 2018
Second edition: May 2020
Third edition: June 2026

Production reference: 1290626

Published by Packt Publishing Ltd.
Grosvenor House
11 St Paul's Square
Birmingham
B3 1RB, UK.

ISBN 978-1-80670-289-3
www.packtpub.com

*To my grandfather Joaquín, who taught me how difficult and rewarding it is to write a book*

*– Jaime Buelta*

# Contributors

## About the author

**Jaime Buelta** has been a professional programmer for more than two decades, with the majority of that time spent working in Python. His career spans many different industries, including aerospace, networking, industrial systems, video game online services, finance, cybersecurity and AI. Across these roles, he has worked closely with non-technical areas such as marketing, management, sales and game design. A committed advocate of automating everything, so that computers or AI handle the heavy lifting and people can focus on what really makes them unique, he is the author of several books since 2018, including this one, *Hands-On Docker for Microservices with Python*, and *Python Architecture Patterns*. He currently lives in Dublin, Ireland, where he works as a Principal Software Engineer and is a long-time participant at PyCon Ireland.

*Writing a book is a far from solo endeavor. I want to thank the reviewers and the team at Packt, whose comments and feedback have greatly improved this new edition. I also want to thank the whole Python developer community, which is so welcoming and supportive and has created the best all-around programming language. But most importantly, I could not have done it without the support and patience of my beloved wife, Dana.*

# About the reviewers

**Miklós Prisznyák** is a software engineer with a research background and a technology entrepreneur based in Edinburgh. A physicist by training, he has over twenty years of experience across finance, media, and scientific computing. Since moving to the UK in 2018, he has worked as a senior Python developer for major institutions: a first role in Cambridge at an engineering company, several years in Glasgow at JP Morgan Chase, remote work on trading systems for Bank of America, and AWS serverless backends for Sky in Edinburgh.

More recently his focus has moved to AI. He worked with the Tanzanian Communications Regulatory Authority to build Big Data capability. He advised a public sector client in Tanzania and helped CRDB, Tanzania's largest commercial bank, with daily reconciliation of over USD 2 million in ATM transactions and with cash forecasting. He is co-founder and CEO of ADB Technology, which builds sovereign AI technology for African governments and enterprises, including the AISee media intelligence platform, bilingual English and Swahili voice agents, and clinical AI; he also co-founded Voith AI, building an AI clinical assistant.

Miklós likes to travel and read, and he is interested in the sciences, mathematics, linguistics, history, politics, chess, and go (the board game). He still reads physics for pleasure, and enjoys a good cup of coffee. Above all, he values time with his son Zsombor, who is studying Computer Science in Edinburgh.

**Ricardo Bánffy** is a software engineer and architect based in Dublin, Ireland, with 25+ years of building things in Python and a long list of other languages picked up along the way. He works as a senior engineer and technical leader, wrangling cloud platforms and automating workflows to help teams ship cleaner code faster. He's contributed to open-source projects like Debian, Fedora, Sysdig, and tmux. He also created the 3270font, a version of the classic IBM terminal typeface for modern computers. When he's not automating something, he's usually necromancing an old computer back to life.

# Table of Contents

## Chapter 4: Searching and Reading Local Files 133



## Chapter 5: Generating Fantastic Reports 179

# Preface

We all spend too much time at work on manual tasks that add relatively little value. Scanning through information sources for a few relevant bits of data, updating the same spreadsheet graph with fresh data over and over, or opening files one by one to find the data we need. Many of these tasks can be automated so that the computer performs most of the work, but perhaps you don't yet feel capable of doing it.

The good news is that now is the best moment to start. The Python language and its ecosystem have grown ever more powerful while remaining approachable. The environment continues to improve, with stronger integrations, richer libraries, and with a vibrant community behind it all.

But the most impactful change since the previous editions of this book has been the rise of AI tools, which have become astonishingly capable within a very short space of time. Their progress over the past year in particular has been remarkable. AI tools can now help you create code, accelerate your learning, and even handle tasks independently.

AI, however, is a multiplier. If your knowledge is solid, it will greatly amplify your abilities. But without clear direction, results will be scattered and unfocused. We will start the book by building our foundation, by way of small, clear recipes that can be adapted to your needs. These building blocks will gradually combine into more complex workflows. While we will note where AI can help us, we will focus first on the capabilities of Python, ensuring predictable, deterministic results. Among other recipes, you will learn to automate common tasks like scraping the web for opportunities, generating spreadsheet reports with graphs, sending automatic emails, receiving text notifications, and running tasks in the background, all while you focus on more important work. Don't underestimate this part! You will be achieving genuinely impressive results.

Then we will build on this foundation by showing you how to work directly with AI models and create your own AI agents that combine some of the earlier recipes. The automations that result are powerful, but we don't shy away from discussing their limitations, caveats, and risks.

Throughout the book we introduce many of the excellent third-party tool options to be found in the rich Python ecosystem. This will inspire your imagination and plant ideas for tackling a wide range of projects by leveraging the available libraries, even those not covered here. There are plenty to choose from!

Although familiarity with Python is helpful, this book is designed for non-programmers. It offers clear, practical recipes, guiding you towards greater proficiency while keeping the focus on real, everyday goals.

# Who this book is for

This book is for Python beginners, not necessarily developers, who want to use and expand their knowledge in order to automate tasks and learn how to do so with the help of AI. Most of the examples in the book are aimed at marketing, sales, and other non-tech areas. However, if you have already learnt a little about the Python language, such as its basic concepts, then so much the better.

# What this book covers

*Chapter 1, Let's Begin Our Automation Journey*, presents some content that will be used all through the book. It addresses the 'vibe coding' idea, and explains how to install and manage third-party tools, how to perform effective string manipulation, and how to use command-line arguments. It also introduces you to regular expressions and other methods of text processing.

*Chapter 2, Automating Tasks Made Easy*, shows how to prepare and automatically run tasks. It covers how to program tasks to be executed when they should, instead of running them manually; how to be notified with the result of a task that's run automatically; and how to be notified if there has been an error in an automated process.

*Chapter 3, Building Your First Web Scraping Applications*, explores sending web requests to communicate with external websites, including via raw HTML content, structured feeds, and RESTful APIs; and looks at automating a browser to execute steps without manual intervention. It also covers how to process results to extract relevant information.

*Chapter 4, Searching and Reading Local Files*, explains how to search through local files and directories and analyze the information stored there. You will learn how to filter through relevant files in different encodings and read files in several common formats, such as CSVs, PDFs, Word documents, and even images.

*Chapter 5, Generating Fantastic Reports*, looks at how to display information given in text format in multiple formats. This includes creating templates to produce text files, as well as creating richly formatted and properly styled Word and PDF documents.

*Chapter 6, Fun with Spreadsheets*, explores how to read and write spreadsheets in the CSV format, and in Microsoft Excel, including with formatting and charts and using Python inside Excel.

*Chapter 7, Cleaning and Processing Data,* presents techniques to deal with multiple sources of information and clean up data before processing it. You will learn how to batch-process to speed up working with large amounts of data, including using specific data analysis libraries like Pandas.

*Chapter 8, Developing Stunning Graphs,* explains how to produce beautiful charts, including common examples such as pie, line, and bar charts, as well as other advanced cases, such as stacked bars and even maps. It also explains how multiple graphs can be combined and styled to generate rich graphics and show relevant information in an understandable format.

*Chapter 9, Dealing with Communication Channels,* explains how to send messages via multiple channels, using external tools to do the most of the heavy lifting. This chapter goes into sending and receiving emails individually as well as en masse, communicating through SMS messages, and creating a bot in Telegram.

*Chapter 10, Why Not Automate Your Marketing Campaign?,* combines the different recipes included in previous chapters to generate a full marketing campaign, including steps such as detecting an opportunity, generation of promotions, communication to potential customers, and analyzing and reporting sales produced by promotions. This chapter shows how to combine different elements to create powerful systems.

*Chapter 11, Calling AI Models,* shows you how to integrate an AI model to work with text and images into your code, both from an externally hosted provider as well as using a local model.

*Chapter 12, Adding Tools to GenAI,* discusses how to enhance AI models' abilities to interact with different tools, including the definition of MCP servers to multiply the capacities of the models by making them able to perform specific actions.

*Chapter 13, Building AI Agents for Business Automation,* explores the ReAct architecture to create AI Agents capable of executing complex tasks by combining multiple tools.

*Chapter 14, Real-World AI Example,* combines all the techniques and lessons from the previous chapters to generate a full example of an agent to perform a complex task, and discusses the implications in terms of security, performance, costs, and others. These are important elements for real work!

*Chapter 15, Automatic Testing Routines,* explores the write and execute tests to verify that code is behaving as expected. The pytest framework is presented and common scenarios for working effectively with tests are discussed.

*Chapter 16*, *Debugging Techniques*, features different methods and tips for helping with the debugging process to ensure the quality of your software. It leverages the great introspection capabilities of Python and its out-of-the-box debugging tools for fixing problems and producing solid automated software.

# To get the most out of this book

- Before reading this book, readers need to know the basics of the Python language. We do not assume that the reader is an expert in the language.
- The reader needs to know how to input commands in the command line (Terminal, Bash, or equivalent).
- To understand the code in this book you need a text editor, which will enable you to read and edit the code. Use an IDE that supports the Python language, such as PyCharm.

## Download the example code files

The code bundle for the book is hosted on GitHub at `https://github.com/PacktPublishing/Python-Automation-Cookbook-Third-Edition`. We also have other code bundles from our rich catalog of books and videos available at `https://github.com/PacktPublishing`. Check them out!

## Download the color images

We also provide a PDF file that has color images of the screenshots/diagrams used in this book. You can download it here: `https://packt.link/gbp/9781806702893`.

## Conventions used

There are a number of text conventions used throughout this book.

`CodeInText`: Indicates code words in text, database table names, folder names, filenames, file extensions, pathnames, dummy URLs, user input, and Twitter handles. For example: "Finally, the `meeting_preparation_agent.py` script is the one that orchestrates everything."

A block of code is set as follows:

```
def main(base_url, to_search):
    checked_links = set()
    to_check = [base_url]
    max_checks = 10
```

Any command-line input or output is written as follows:

```
>>> result = requests.get('https://jsonplaceholder.typicode.com/posts')
```

**Bold**: Indicates a new term, an important word, or words that you see on the screen. For instance, words in menus or dialog boxes appear in the text like this. For example: "This is the specification of the **standard output** (**stdout**)"

Note

Warnings or important notes appear like this.

Tip

Tips and tricks appear like this.

# Get in touch

Feedback from our readers is always welcome.

**General feedback**: If you have questions about any aspect of this book or have any general feedback, please email us at `customercare@packt.com` and mention the book's title in the subject of your message.

**Errata**: Although we have taken every care to ensure the accuracy of our content, mistakes do happen. If you have found a mistake in this book, we would be grateful if you reported this to us. Please visit `http://www.packt.com/submit-errata`, click **Submit Errata**, and fill in the form.

**Piracy**: If you come across any illegal copies of our works in any form on the internet, we would be grateful if you would provide us with the location address or website name. Please contact us at `copyright@packt.com` with a link to the material.

**If you are interested in becoming an author**: If there is a topic that you have expertise in and you are interested in either writing or contributing to a book, please visit `http://authors.packt.com/`.

## Share your thoughts

Once you've read *Python Automation Cookbook, Third Edition*, we'd love to hear your thoughts! Scan the QR code below to go straight to the Amazon review page for this book and share your feedback.

https://packt.link/r/1806702894

Your review is important to us and the tech community and will help us make sure we're delivering excellent quality content.

# Free benefits with your book

This book comes with free benefits to support your learning. Activate them now for instant access (see the "*How to Unlock*" section for instructions).

Here's a quick overview of what you can instantly unlock with your purchase:

**DRM-Free PDF Version**

Download DRM-free PDF and ePub copies of this book.

**7-Day Packt Library Access**

Get 7-day unlimited access to 8,000+ books and videos. No credit card required.

Available for first-time Packt+ trial users only.

**Next-Gen Reader Access**

Read this book on Packt Reader with progress sync, dark mode and note-taking.

## How to Unlock

Scan the QR code (or go to `packtpub.com/unlock`). Search for this book by name, confirm the edition, and then follow the steps on the page.

UNLOCK NOW

*Note: Keep your invoice handy. Purchases made directly from Packt don't require one*

# 1

# Let's Begin Our Automation Journey

The objective of this chapter is to lay down some of the basic techniques that will be useful throughout the whole book. The main idea is to create a good Python environment in which to run the automation tasks that follow and be able to parse text inputs into structured data.

We will introduce generative artificial intelligence (GenAI) tools. Throughout the book we will looking at how they can help us in our automation projects. In this chapter we will get a taste of that, and consider some of their limitations.

Python has a good number of tools installed by default, but it also makes it easy to install third-party tools that can simplify many common operations. We'll see how to import modules from external sources and use them to leverage the full potential of Python.

We will install and use tools to help process texts. The ability to structure input data is critical in any automation task. Most of the data that we will process in this book will come from unformatted sources such as web pages or text files. As the old computer adage says, *garbage in, garbage out*, making the sanitizing of inputs a very important task.

In this chapter, we'll cover the following topics:

- The elephant in the room: vibe coding
- Working with multiple Python versions and virtual environments through uv
- Installing third-party packages
- Creating strings with formatted values
- Manipulating strings
- Extracting data from structured strings

- Using a third-party tool—parse
- Introducing regular expressions
- Going deeper into regular expressions
- Adding command-line arguments

> Note
>
> **Your purchase includes a free PDF copy + exclusive extras**
>
> Your purchase includes a DRM-free PDF copy of this book, 7-day trial to the Packt+ library (no credit card required), and additional exclusive extras. See the *Free benefits with your book* section in the *Preface* to unlock them instantly and maximize your learning.

# Technical requirements

Python requirements are as set out in the *Preface*, and we shall also be using the uv tool, installation of which is described in the next section but one.

The code presented in this chapter can be found in the book's GitHub repository, at `https://github.com/PacktPublishing/Python-Automation-Cookbook-Third-Edition/tree/main/ch01`.

# The elephant in the room: vibe coding

Since the introduction of ChatGPT and other related tools, the coding world has been living an ongoing revolution where we can generate code with the help of generative artificial intelligence (GenAI). These tools, based on what are called large language models (LLMs), allow users to describe in plain language a piece of required code, and the computer then returns the code itself, along with some comments and explanation.

> Note
>
> For the majority of the book, we will predominantly be using ChatGPT, as it's the most commonly available tool. You can create a free account at `https://chatgpt.com/`.
>
> Other alternatives include Anthropic's Claude (`https://claude.ai/`), Google's Gemini (`https://gemini.google.com/`) or Microsoft's Copilot (`https://copilot.microsoft.com`).

These instructions that we give the GenAI tool are known as *prompts*. For example, to perform a very simple operation in Python:

*Figure 1.1: ChatGPT conversation*

If we copy the code, save it to a file named `simple_script.py` and execute it, we see the expected result:

```
$ python3 simple_script.py
First number: 60
Second number: 81
Sum: 141
```

While this is a very simple example, you can complicate the instructions and keep iterating on the result to create quite complex pieces of code, with only a minimal amount of coding knowledge. The fact that with GenAI you have your own expert coder that you can ask, in your own words, to generate code at a fast pace is truly revolutionary, and it's empowering a great many people to upscale their coding capacities.

At the same time, it's not without its risks and limitations:

- You have a pretty capable artificial developer at your disposal, but, at the same time, it can be very obtuse: it tends to understand what you *say*, but not what you really *want*. Any good developer will push back and ask insightful clarifying questions to understand the real problem to fix, and not just blindly do what they are asked to do.
- It works well for small, well-defined problems, but the amount of data that a particular LLM can deal with at the same time is limited. This is known as *context*. When the context is full, the LLM is way less effective. While current tools are getting better at automatically handling this context behind the scenes, you may have experienced issues in long conversations with ChatGPT, for example, where the longer a conversation runs, the weirder it gets. This creates problems as codebases grow bigger, and requires methods capable of working with that scale.
- They can generate code at such a fast pace that it exceeds the capacity to absorb and understand it. When you are doing your own coding, you develop an intimate knowledge of the code, and that's not present when you delegate the writing of code. Fully delegating to an AI tool means that, ultimately, no one has that deep knowledge of the code produced. That can create a liability and make the code very difficult to understand and maintain, making it prone to bugs or unexpected behaviors.
- There are also risks related to the security of the code generated. LLMs can be tricked into producing bad effects, making it very difficult to verify that the code will be safe to use.

But tools are getting better and better, and LLMs are also improving all the time. That has led to a process that has been called *vibe coding*. The term itself was initially described by Andrej Karpathy in a tweet:

> *There's a new kind of coding I call "vibe coding", where you fully give in to the vibes, embrace exponentials, and forget that the code even exists. It's possible because the LLMs ... are getting too good. ...When I get error messages I just copy paste them in with no comment, usually that fixes it. The code grows beyond my usual comprehension, I'd have to really read through it for a while. Sometimes the LLMs can't fix a bug so I just work around it or ask for random changes until it goes away. It's not too bad for throwaway weekend projects, but still quite amusing. I'm building a project or webapp, but it's not really coding - I just see stuff, say stuff, run stuff, and copy paste stuff, and it mostly works.*

While the term can be interpreted in different ways, it normally understood to mean working with code without actually coding, instead iterating through a tool to perform code changes, not caring unduly about the resulting code, but only about its results.

While this is not suitable for all coding work, it can be effective for small, controlled projects. Which may be the case for many of the recipes that we describe in this book! Just be wary about delegating everything to the tool.

> **Tip**
>
> As important as generating code, GenAI is also a fantastic tool to explain code. You can learn a lot by using it to explain what is going on in some piece of code that you don't understand completely.

After that brief introduction to the new vistas in software development opened by the advent of GenAI, we now turn to a slightly more mundane, but no less important, topic: using virtual environments to prepare our project to run the proper Python version and libraries.

# Working with multiple Python versions and virtual environments through uv

As a first step when working with Python, it is a good practice to explicitly define the working environment.

This helps you to detach from the operating system interpreter and environment and properly define the dependencies that will be used. Not doing so tends to generate chaotic scenarios. Remember, *explicit is better than implicit!*

*Explicit is better than implicit* is one of the most quoted parts of the *Zen of Python*. The *Zen of Python* is a list of general guidelines for Python programming, intended to provide clarity on what is considered Pythonic. The full *Zen of Python* can be invoked from the Python interpreter by calling `import this`.

This explicitness is especially important in two scenarios:

- When dealing with multiple projects on the same computer, as they can have different dependencies that may clash at some point. For example, two versions of the same module cannot be installed in the same environment.
- When working on a project that will be used on a different computer, for example when developing some code on a personal laptop that will ultimately run in a remote server.

A common joke among developers is responding to a bug with 'it runs on my machine', meaning that it appears to work on their laptop but not on the production servers. Although a huge number of factors can produce this error, a good practice is to produce an automatically replicable environment, reducing uncertainty over what dependencies are really being used.

In Python 3 the `venv` module, which sets up a local virtual environment, is included as part of the standard library. (This was not the case in the previous version, where you had to install the external `virtualenv` package.) Using the `venv` module, none of the installed dependencies will be shared with the Python interpreter installed on the machine, creating an isolated environment.

In recent years a new tool has simplified the use of environments, installation of third-party modules and running them: `uv`. This tool is quickly being adopted by the Python community as it simplifies the work and is much quicker than the previous alternatives!

> **Note**
>
> The command `pip`, included in Python, is used to install dependencies. When using it with an active virtual environment, it installs the required packages in it. `uv` simplifies the operation by managing automatically what virtual environment to use, based on the working directory, and where to install the packages.

## Getting ready

Install `uv` if not already installed. The easiest way is to install it through the standard `pip` command:

```
$ pip install uv
Collecting uv
...
Installing collected packages: uv
Successfully installed uv-0.9.9
```

Before creating a virtual environment, check what Python binary you are calling:

```
$ uv run python -c "import sys; print(sys.executable)"
/usr/local/opt/python@3.14/bin/python3.14
```

## How to do it...

You can create your local environment by calling `uv venv`:

```
$ uv venv
Using CPython 3.14.0 interpreter at: /usr/local/opt/python@3.14/bin/python3.14
Creating virtual environment at: .venv
Activate with: source .venv/bin/activate
```

You can see that now calling uv run returns the Python interpreter in your virtual environment instead of the interpreter in your system:

```
$ uv run python -c "import sys; print(sys.executable)"
/your/local/path/.venv/bin/python3
```

So far, this is a wrapper to create a `virtualenv`, but note that if we use uv we don't need to activate the virtual environment, we can just call it through uv run and it will run inside the environment:

```
$ uv run
Provide a command or script to invoke with `uv run <command>` or `uv run
<script>.py`.

The following commands are available in the environment:

- python
- python3
- python3.14

See `uv run --help` for more information.
```

When running scripts inside uv run, it automatically uses any virtual environment in the directory. Previously you needed to manually enter the virtual environment and leave it.

It's also more explicit with the version of Python that you are using, and you can use a different version if necessary.

To force the version of Python to use, you can use the uv pin command:

```
$ uv python pin 3.14
Pinned `.python-version` to `3.14`
$ uv python pin
3.14
$ uv run python
Python 3.14.0 (main, Oct  7 2025, 09:34:52) [Clang 17.0.0 (clang-1700.3.19.1)] on
Darwin
>>> exit()
$ "license" for more information.
```

If you want to use a different version of Python, uv will download it if necessary:

```
$ uv python pin 3.15.0a1
Updated `.python-version` from `3.14` -> `3.15a1`
$ uv run python
Python 3.15.0a1 (main, Oct 31 2025, 23:15:40) [Clang 21.1.4 ] on darwin
Type "help", "copyright", "credits" or "license" for more information.
>>> exit()
```

The specific version is stored in a file called `.python-version`

> **Note**
>
> Be careful with discrepancies between the virtual environment and the Python version! If the Python version doesn't match the version on the virtual environment, it will use the pinned version. You may need to recreate the virtual environment by calling `uv venv` again.

To be sure that we use the Python 3.14 version, the last one fully released at the time of writing, pin it back again:

```
$ uv python pin 3.14
Pinned `.python-version` to `3.14`
Jaimes-iMac-24:chapter01 jaime$ uv run python -c "import sys;
print(sys.executable)"
/your/local/path/.venv/bin/python3
```

## How it works

`uv` simplifies the workflow by using the defined virtual environment. The virtual environment can contain its own version, third-party packages, etc.

The virtual environment contains all the Python data in the `.venv` directory. The best thing about it is that it can be deleted and recreated very easily, removing the fear of experimenting in a self-contained sandbox.

By default `uv` will use the `.venv` name for the subdirectory, but this can be overwritten by using the `-directory` argument.

Once created, the `.venv` works as a regular virtual environment in Python as well, and you can activate it manually, which will show it active by default with the name of the directory:

```
$ pwd
/your/local/path/.
$ source .venv/bin/activate
(path) $ which python
/your/local/path/.venv/bin/python3
(path) $ deactivate
$ which python3
/usr/local/bin/python3
```

This name can be changed with use of `-prompt` when creating the virtual environment.

## There's more

`uv` is a pretty powerful tool and we have barely scratched the surface. The most important use case throughout the book will be to install third-party packages, as we will see in the next recipe, but take a look at the full documentation at `https://docs.astral.sh/uv/` for others.

> **Note**
>
> `uv` has an important use case for defining complex projects and handling dependencies, build packages, etc. While this is pretty powerful, it can only be confusing for the automation projects that are the focus of this book as it can be, frankly, a bit too much of an overhead. My recommendation is to use `uv` as a tool for creating virtual environments, installing packages and running scripts, unless you have a clear power use around packaging.

## See also

- The *Installing third-party packages* recipe, coming next.
- The *Using a third-party tool—parse* recipe, later in the chapter.

# Installing third-party packages

One of the strongest capabilities of Python is the ability to use an impressive catalog of third-party packages that cover an amazing amount of ground in different areas, from modules specialized in performing numerical operations, machine learning, and network communications, to command-line convenience tools, database access, image processing, and much more!

Most of them are available on the official Python Package Index (`https://pypi.org/`), which has more than 200,000 packages ready to use. In this book, we'll install some of them. In general, it's worth spending a little time researching external tools when trying to solve a problem. It's very likely that someone else has already created a tool that solves all, or at least part, of the problem.

More important than finding and installing a package is keeping track of which packages are being used. This greatly helps with **replicability**, meaning the ability to start the whole environment from scratch in any situation.

## Getting ready

The starting point is to find a package that will be of use in our project.

A great one is `requests`, a module that deals with HTTP requests and is known for its easy and intuitive interface, as well as its great documentation. Take a look at the documentation, which can be found here:`https://requests.readthedocs.io/en/latest/`.

We'll use `requests` throughout this book when dealing with HTTP connections.

The next step will be to choose the version to use. In this case, the latest (2.32.5, at the time of writing) will be perfect. If the version of the module is not specified, by default it will install the latest version, which can lead to inconsistencies in different environments as newer versions are released.

We'll also use the great `pendulum` module for time handling (version 3.2.0: `https://pendulum.eustace.io`).

## How to do it...

Create a `requirements.txt` file in our main directory, which will specify all the requirements for our project. Let's start with `pendulum` and `requests`:

```
pendulum==3.2.0
requests==2.32.5
```

Install all the requirements with the `uv pip` command:

```
$ uv pip install -r requirements.txt
Resolved 10 packages in 385ms
Installed 10 packages in 55ms
 + certifi==2026.5.20
 + charset-normalizer==3.4.7
 + idna==3.18
```

```
 + parse==1.20.2
 + pendulum==3.2.0
 + python-dateutil==2.9.0.post0
 + requests==2.32.5
 + six==1.17.0
 + tzdata==2026.2
 + urllib3==2.7.0
```

**Note**

If you have previously used `pip` to install packages, you may be finding out that using `uv` is much faster.

Show the available modules installed using `uv pip list`:

```
$ uv pip list
Package            Version
------------------ -----------
certifi            2026.5.20
charset-normalizer 3.4.7
idna               3.18
parse              1.20.2
pendulum           3.2.0
python-dateutil    2.9.0.post0
requests           2.32.5
six                1.17.0
tzdata             2026.2
urllib3            2.7.0
```

You can now use both modules when using the virtual environment:

```
$ uv run python
Python 3.14.0 (main, Oct  7 2025, 09:34:52) [Clang 17.0.0 (clang-1700.3.19.1)] on
darwin
Type "help", "copyright", "credits" or "license" for more information.
>>> import pendulum
>>> import requests
>>>
```

## How it works...

The `requirements.txt` file specifies the module and version, and `uv pip` performs a search on `pypi.org`.

Note that creating a new virtual environment from scratch and running the following will completely recreate your environment, which makes replicability very straightforward:

```
$ uv pip install -r requirements.txt
```

Note that *step 2* of the *How to do it...* section automatically installs other modules that are dependencies, such as `urllib3`.

## There's more...

If any of the modules need to be changed to a different version because a new version is available, change them using requirements and run the `install` command again:

```
$ uv pip install -r requirements.txt
```

This is also applicable when a new module needs to be included.

At any point, the `pipfreeze` command can be used to display all of the installed modules. `freeze` returns the modules in a format compatible with `requirements.txt`, making it possible to generate a file with our current environment:

```
$ uv pip freeze > requirements.txt
```

This will include dependencies, so expect a lot more modules in the file.

Finding great third-party modules is sometimes not easy. Searching for specific functionality can work well, but sometimes there are great modules that are a surprise because they do things you never thought of. A great curated list is Awesome Python (`https://github.com/vinta/awesome-python`), which covers a lot of great tools for common Python use cases, such as cryptography, database access, date and time handling, and more.

> **Tip**
>
> GenAI can help with finding a suitable module for a particular use case.
>
> Generally, it will be knowledgeable and direct you towards using common packages, such as `requests`. But you can ask about specific use cases and recommendations.
>
> Don't take a GenAI recommendation at face value, however: check the project itself and verify that it's what you need. A common problem from GenAI is that it will use an

> stablished older package that perhaps is not the best for your specific usage, for example, because there's a newer package that will get you better results. GenAI can help with the search, but not take the decision for you.

In some cases, installing packages may require additional tools, such as compilers or a specific library that supports specific functionality (for example, a particular database driver). If that's the case, the documentation will explain the dependencies.

## See also

- The *Working with multiple Python versions and virtual environments with uv* recipe, earlier in this chapter.
- The *Using a third-party tool—parse recipe*, later in this chapter, to learn how to use one installed third-party module.

# Creating strings with formatted values

One of the basic abilities when creating text and documents is to be able to properly format values into structured strings. Python is smart at presenting good defaults, such as properly rendering a number, but there are a lot of options and possibilities.

We'll discuss some of the common options when creating formatted text using the example of a table.

## Getting ready

The main tool to format strings in Python is the `format` method. It works with a defined mini-language to render variables this way:

```
result = template.format(*parameters)
```

The `template` is a string that is interpreted based on the mini-language. At its simplest, templating replaces the values between the curly brackets with the parameters. Here are a couple of examples:

```
>>> 'Put the value of the string here: {}'.format('STRING')
"Put the value of the string here: STRING"
>>> 'It can be any type ({}) and more than one ({})'.format(1.23, 'STRING')
"It can be any type (1.23) and more than one (STRING)"
>>> 'Specify the order: {1}, {0}'.format('first', 'second')
'Specify the order: second, first'
```

```
>>> 'Or name parameters: {first}, {second}'.format(second='SECOND', first='FIRST')
'Or name parameters: FIRST, SECOND'
```

In 95% of cases, this formatting will be all that's required; keeping things simple is great! But for complicated times, such as when aligning strings automatically and creating good looking text tables, the mini-language `format` has more options.

## How to do it...

Write the following script, `recipe_format_strings_step1.py`, to print an aligned table:

```
# INPUT DATA
data = [
    (1000, 10),
    (2000, 17),
    (2500, 170),
    (2500, -170),
]
# Print the header for reference
print('REVENUE | PROFIT | PERCENT')
# This template aligns and displays the data in the proper format
TEMPLATE = '{revenue:>7,} | {profit:>+6} | {percent:>7.2%}'
# Print the data rows
for revenue, profit in data:
    row = TEMPLATE.format(revenue=revenue, profit=profit, percent=profit /
revenue)
    print(row)
```

Run it to display the following aligned table. Note that `PERCENT` is correctly displayed as a percentage:

```
$ uv run recipe_format_strings_step1.py
REVENUE | PROFIT | PERCENT
  1,000 |    +10 |   1.00%
  2,000 |    +17 |   0.85%
  2,500 |   +170 |   6.80%
  2,500 |   -170 |  -6.80%
```

## How it works...

The `TEMPLATE` constant defines three columns, each one defined by a parameter named `revenue`, `profit`, and `percent` respectively. This makes it explicit and straightforward to apply the template to the `format` call.

After the name of the parameter there's a colon that separates the format definition. Note that everything is inside the curly brackets. In all columns, the format specification sets the width to seven characters, to make sure all the columns have the same width, and aligns the values to the right with the > symbol:

- `revenue` adds a thousands separator with the `,` symbol – `[{revenue:>7,}]`.
- `profit` adds a + sign for positive values. A minus sign (`-`) for negatives is added automatically – `[{profit:>+7}]`.
- `percent` displays a percent value with a precision of two decimal places – `[{percent:>7.2%}]`. This is done through `.2` (precision) and adding a `%` symbol for the percentage.

## There's more...

You may have also seen the Python formatting available with the `%` operator. While it works for simple formatting, it is less flexible than the formatting mini-language, and it is not recommended that you use it.

A great new feature since Python 3.6 is to use f-strings, which perform a format action using defined variables:

```
>>> param1 = 'first'
>>> param2 = 'second'
>>> f'Parameters {param1}:{param2}'
'Parameters first:second'
```

This simplifies a lot of the code and allows us to create very descriptive and readable code.

Be careful when using f-strings to ensure that the string is replaced at the proper time. A common problem is that the variable defined to be rendered is not yet defined. For example, `TEMPLATE`, defined previously, won't be defined as an f-string, as revenue and the rest of the parameters are not available at that point. All variables defined at the scope of the string definition will be available, both local and global.

If you need to write a curly bracket, you'll need to repeat it twice. Note that each duplication will be displayed as a single curly bracket, plus a curly bracket for the value replacement, making a total of three brackets:

```
>> value = 'VALUE'
>>> f'This is the value, in curly brackets {{{value}}}'
'This is the value, in curly brackets {VALUE}'
```

This allows us to create meta templates – templates that produce templates. In some cases this will be useful, but they get complicated very quickly. Use with care, as it's easy to produce code that will be difficult to read.

> Tip
>
> Representing characters that have a special meaning usually requires some sort of special way to specify them, for example, by duplicating the curly bracket as we see here. This is called 'escaping' and it's a common process in any code representation.

The Python Format Specification mini-language has more options than the ones shown here.

As the language tries to be quite concise, sometimes it can be difficult to determine the position of the symbols. You may sometimes ask yourself questions, like *'is the + symbol before or after the width parameters?'* Read the documentation with care and remember to always include a colon before the format specification – or, alternatively, ask the GenAI the proper formatting:

> Tip
>
> **Prompt example**:
>
> How can I display in Python a number formatted so that it has a thousands separator, two decimal places and fits in a column of 9 rows, left aligned
>
> Summarized example response:
>
> `f"{num:<9,.2f}"`

Please refer to the full documentation and examples on the Python website: `https://docs.python.org/3/library/string.html#formatspec` or at the fantastic web page at `https://pyformat.info`, which shows lots of examples.

## See also

- The *Template Reports* recipe in *Chapter 5, Generating Fantastic Reports*, to learn more advanced template techniques.
- The *Manipulating strings* recipe, later in this chapter, to learn more about working with text.

# Manipulating strings

When dealing with text, it's often necessary to manipulate and process it; that is, to be able to join it, split it into regular chunks, or change it to uppercase or lowercase. We'll discuss more advanced methods for parsing text and separating it later; however, in lots of cases, it is useful to divide a paragraph into lines, sentences, or even words. Other times, words will require some characters to be removed or a word will need to be replaced with a canonical version to be able to compare it with a predetermined value.

## Getting ready

We'll define a basic piece of text and transform it into its main components; then we'll reconstruct it. As an example, imagine a report needs to be transformed into a new format to be sent via email.

The input format we'll use in this example will be this:

```
AFTER THE CLOSE OF THE SECOND QUARTER, OUR COMPANY, CASTAÑACORP
HAS ACHIEVED A GROWTH IN THE REVENUE OF 7.47%. THIS IS IN LINE
WITH THE OBJECTIVES FOR THE YEAR. THE MAIN DRIVER OF THE SALES HAS BEEN
THE NEW PACKAGE DESIGNED UNDER THE SUPERVISION OF OUR MARKETING DEPARTMENT.
OUR EXPENSES HAS BEEN CONTAINED, INCREASING ONLY BY 0.7%, THOUGH THE BOARD
CONSIDERS IT NEEDS TO BE FURTHER REDUCED. THE EVALUATION IS SATISFACTORY
AND THE FORECAST FOR THE NEXT QUARTER IS OPTIMISTIC. THE BOARD EXPECTS
AN INCREASE IN PROFIT OF AT LEAST 2 MILLION DOLLARS.
```

We need to redact the text to eliminate any references to numbers. It needs to be properly formatted by adding a new line after each period, justified with 80 characters, and transformed into ASCII for compatibility reasons.

The text will be stored in the `INPUT_TEXT` variable in the interpreter.

## How to do it...

1. After entering the text, split it into individual words:

```
>>> INPUT_TEXT = '''
...     AFTER THE CLOSE OF THE SECOND QUARTER, OUR COMPANY, CASTAÑACORP
...     HAS ACHIEVED A GROWTH IN THE REVENUE OF 7.47%. THIS IS IN LINE
...
'''
>>> words = INPUT_TEXT.split()
```

2. Replace any numerical digits with an 'X' character:

```
>>> redacted = [''.join('X' if w.isdigit() else w for w in word) for word
in words]
```

3. Transform the text into pure ASCII (note that the name of the company contains the letter ñ, which is not ASCII):

```
>>> ascii_text = [word.encode('ascii', errors='replace').decode('ascii')
...               for word in redacted]
```

4. Textwrap into 80-character lines:

```
>>> newlines = [word + '\n' if word.endswith('.') else word for word in
ascii_text]
>>> LINE_SIZE = 80
>>> lines = []
>>> line = ''
>>> for word in newlines:
...     if line.endswith('\n') or len(line) + len(word) + 1 > LINE_SIZE:
...         lines.append(line)
...         line = ''
...     line = line + ' ' + word
```

5. Format all of the lines as titles and join them as a single piece of text:

```
>>> lines = [line.title() for line in lines]
>>> result = '\n'.join(lines)
```

6. Print the result:

```
>>> print(result)
 After The Close Of The Second Quarter, Our Company, Casta?Acorp Has
Achieved A Growth In The Revenue Of X.Xx%. This Is In Line With The
Objectives For The Year. The Main Driver Of The Sales Has Been The New
Package Designed Under The Supervision Of Our Marketing Department. Our
Expenses Has Been Contained, Increasing Only By X.X%, Though The Board
Considers It Needs To Be Further Reduced. The Evaluation Is Satisfactory
And The Forecast For The Next Quarter Is Optimistic.
```

## How it works...

Each step performs a specific transformation of the text:

- The first step splits the text into the default separators, whitespaces, and new lines. This splits it into individual words with no lines or multiple spaces for separation.
- To replace the digits, we go through every character of each word. For each one, if it's a digit, an `'X'` is returned instead. This is done with two list comprehensions, one to run on the list, and another on each word, replacing them only if there's a digit—`['X' if w.isdigit() else w for w in word]`. Note that the words are joined together again.
- Each of the words is encoded into an ASCII byte sequence and decoded back again into the Python string type. Note the use of the errors parameter to force the replacement of unknown characters such as ñ.

> **Note**
>
> The difference between strings and bytes is not very intuitive at first, especially if you never have to worry about multiple languages or encoding transformations. Strings only exist in Python, as long as the information leaves the interpreter (for example, to be written in a file) is converted into bytes. In Python 3, there's a strong separation between internal strings and bytes. So, most of the tools applicable to strings won't be available in byte objects. Unless you have a good idea of why you need a byte object, always work with Python strings. If you need to perform transformations like the one in this task, encode and decode in the same line so that you keep your objects within the

> comfortable realm of Python strings. If you are interested in learning more about encodings you could refer to the brief article at `https://eli.thegreenplace.net/2012/01/30/the-bytesstr-dichotomy-in-python-3`, as well as the longer and more detailed one at `http://www.diveintopython3.net/strings.html`.

- The next step adds an extra newline character (the `\n` character) for all words ending with a period. This marks the different paragraphs. After that, it creates a line and adds the words one by one. If an extra word will make it go over 80 characters, it finishes the line and starts a new one. If the line already ends with a new line, it finishes it and starts another one as well. Note that there's an extra space added to separate the words.
- Finally, each of the lines is capitalized as a Title (the first letter of each word is uppercased) and all the lines are joined through new lines.

## There's more...

Some other useful operations that can be performed on strings are as follows:

1. Strings can be sliced like any other list. This means that `"word"[0:2]` will return `"wo"`.
2. Use `.splitlines()` to separate lines with a newline character.
3. There are `.upper()` and `.lower()` methods, which return a copy with all of the characters set to uppercase or lowercase. Their use is very similar to `.title()`:

```
>>> 'UPPERCASE'.lower()
'uppercase'
```

4. For easy replacements (for example, changing all *As to Bs or changing mine \ to ours*), use `.replace()`. This method is useful for very simple cases, but replacements can get tricky easily. Be careful with the order of replacements to avoid collisions and case sensitivity issues. Note the wrong replacement in the following example:

```
>>> 'One ring to rule them all, one ring to find them, One ring to bring
them all and in the darkness bind them.'.replace('ring', 'necklace')
'One necklace to rule them all, one necklace to find them, One necklace to
bnecklace them all and in the darkness bind them.'
```

This is similar to the issues we'll encounter with regular expressions matching unexpected parts of your code. There are more examples to follow later. Refer to the regular expressions recipes for more information.

> **Tip**
>
> To wrap text lines you can use the `textwrap` module included in the standard library, instead of manually counting characters. View the documentation here: `https://docs.python.org/3/library/textwrap.html`.

If you work with multiple languages, or with any kind of non-English input, it is very useful to learn the basics of Unicode and encodings. In a nutshell, given the vast amount of characters in all the different languages in the world, including alphabets not related to the Latin one, such as Chinese or Arabic, Unicode provides a standard to try and cover all of them so that computers can properly understand them. Python 3 greatly improved this situation, making sure that the internal objects of the strings can deal with all of those characters. The default encoding that Python uses, and the most common and compatible one, is currently UTF-8.

A good article to learn about the basics of UTF-8 is this blog post: `https://www.joelonsoftware.com/2003/10/08/the-absolute-minimum-every-software-developer-absolutely-positively-must-know-about-unicode-and-character-sets-no-excuses/`.

Dealing with encodings is still relevant when reading from external files that can be encoded in different encodings (for example, CP-1252 or windows-1252, which is a common encoding produced by legacy Microsoft systems, or ISO 8859-15, which is the industry standard).

## See also

- The previous recipe, *Creating strings with formatted values* recipe, to learn the basics of string creation.
- The *Introducing regular expressions* recipe, covered later in the chapter, to learn how to detect and extract patterns in text.
- The *Going deeper into regular expressions* recipe, covered later in the chapter, to further your knowledge of regular expressions.
- The Dealing with encodings recipe in *Chapter 4, Searching and Reading Local Files*, to learn about different kinds of encodings.

# Extracting data from structured strings

In a lot of automated tasks, we'll need to treat input text structured in a known format and extract the relevant information. For example, a spreadsheet may mention a percentage in a piece of text (such as 37.4%) and we want to retrieve it in a numerical format to apply it later (0.374, as a float).

In this recipe, we'll learn how to process sale logs that contain inline information about a product, such as whether it has been sold, its price, profit made, and other information.

## Getting ready

Imagine that we need to parse information stored in sales logs. We'll use a sales log with the following structure:

```
[<Timestamp in iso format>] - SALE - PRODUCT: <product id> - PRICE: $<price of the sale>
```

For example, a specific log may look like this:

```
[2018-05-05T10:58:41.504054] - SALE - PRODUCT: 1345 - PRICE: $09.99
```

Note that the price has a leading zero. All prices will have two digits for the dollars and two for the cents.

> **Note**
>
> The standard ISO 8601 defines standard ways of representing the time and date. It is widely used in the computing world and can be parsed and generated by virtually any computer language.

## How to do it...

1. In the Python interpreter, make the following imports. Remember to run `uv run python`, which will use your `virtualenv`, as described in the section *Working with multiple Python versions and virtual environments with uv*:

    ```
    >>> import pendulum
    >>> from decimal import Decimal
    ```

> **Note**
>
> We will use `Decimal` type to keep precision at all times. More information later in the recipe

2. Enter the log to parse:

```
>>> log = '[2025-05-05T11:07:12.267897] - SALE - PRODUCT: 1345 - PRICE:
$09.99'
```

3. Split the log into its parts, which are divided by - (note the space before and after the dash). We ignore the `SALE` part as it doesn't add any relevant information:

```
>>> divide_it = log.split(' - ')
>>> timestamp_string, _, product_string, price_string = divide_it
```

4. Parse the timestamp into a datetime object:

```
>>> timestamp = pendulum.parse(timestamp_string.strip('[]'))
```

5. Parse the `product_id` into an integer:

```
>>> product_id = int(product_string.split(':')[-1])
```

6. Parse the price into a `Decimal` type:

```
>>> price = Decimal(price_string.split('$')[-1])
```

7. Now you have all of the values in native Python format:

```
>>> timestamp, product_id, price
(DateTime(2025, 5, 5, 11, 7, 12, 267897, tzinfo=Timezone('UTC')), 1345,
Decimal('9.99'))
```

## How it works...

The basic working of this is to isolate each of the elements and then parse them into the proper type. The first step is to split the full log into smaller parts. The - (dash) string is a good divider, as it splits it into four parts—a timestamp one, one with just the word SALE, the product, and the price.

In the case of the timestamp, we need to isolate the ISO format, which is in brackets in the log. That's why the timestamp has the brackets stripped from it. We use the pendulum module (introduced earlier) to parse it into a DateTime object.

The word SALE is ignored. There's no relevant information there.

To isolate the product ID, we split the product part at the colon. Then we parse the last element as an integer:

```
>>> product_string.split(':')
['PRODUCT', ' 1345']
>>> int(' 1345')
1345
```

To divide the price, we use the dollar sign as a separator, and parse it as a Decimal character:

```
>>> price_string.split('$')
['PRICE: ', '09.99']
>>> Decimal('09.99')
Decimal('9.99')
```

As described in the next section, do not parse this value into a float type, as it will change the precision.

## There's more...

These log elements can be combined together into a single object, helping to parse and aggregate them. For example, we could define a class in Python code in the following way:

```
class PriceLog(object):
  def __init__(self, timestamp, product_id, price):
    self.timestamp = timestamp
    self.product_id = product_id
    self.price = price
  def __repr__(self):
    return '<PriceLog ({}, {}, {})>'.format(self.timestamp,
                                            self.product_id,
                                            self.price)

  @classmethod
  def parse(cls, text_log):
```

```
    '''
    Parse from a text log with the format
    [<Timestamp>] - SALE - PRODUCT: <product id> - PRICE: $<price>
    to a PriceLog object
    '''
    divide_it = text_log.split(' - ')
    tmp_string, _, product_string, price_string = divide_it
    timestamp = pendulum.parse(tmp_string.strip('[]'))
    product_id = int(product_string.split(':')[-1])
    price = Decimal(price_string.split('$')[-1])
    return cls(timestamp=timestamp, product_id=product_id, price=price)
```

So, the parsing can be done as follows:

```
>>> log = '[2018-05-05T12:58:59.998903] - SALE - PRODUCT: 897 - PRICE: $17.99'
>>> PriceLog.parse(log)
<PriceLog (2018-05-05 12:58:59.998903+00:00, 897, 17.99)>
```

Avoid using float types for prices. Floats have precision problems that may produce strange errors when aggregating multiple prices, for example:

```
>>> 0.1 + 0.1 + 0.1
0.30000000000000004
```

Try these two options to avoid any problems:

- **Use integer cents as the base unit**: This means multiplying currency inputs by 100 and transforming them into `Integers` (or whatever fractional unit is correct for the currency used). You may still want to change the base when displaying them.
- **Parse into the decimal type**: The `Decimal` type keeps the fixed precision and works as you'd expect. You can find further information about the `Decimal` type in the Python documentation at `https://docs.python.org/3.8/library/decimal.html`.

If you use the `Decimal` type, parse the results directly into `Decimal` from the string. If transforming it first into a float, you can carry the precision errors to the new type.

Tip

Parsing data is also something where GenAI can help, but be sure to confirm that the results are as expected. In my experience GenAI tools will try to use regular expressions and not convert the types into the proper ones (e.g. not transforming prices into `Decimal`, but instead keeping them as strings or transforming them into float values)

## See also

- The *Creating a virtual environment recipe*, covered earlier in the chapter, to learn how to start a virtual environment with installed modules.
- The next recipe, *Using a third-party tool—parse*, to further your knowledge of how to use third-party tools to deal with text.
- The *Introducing regular expressions* recipe, later in the chapter, to learn how to detect and extract patterns from text.
- The *Going deeper into regular expressions* recipe, later in the chapter, to further your knowledge of regular expressions.

# Using a third-party tool—parse

While manually parsing data works very well for small strings, as seen in the previous recipe, it can be very laborious to tweak the exact formula to work with a variety of inputs. What if the input has an extra dash sometimes? Or if it has a variable length header depending on the size of one of the fields?

A more advanced option is to use regular expressions, as we'll see in the next recipe. But there's a great module in Python called parse (`https://github.com/r1chardj0n3s/parse`), which allows us to reverse format strings. It is a fantastic tool that's powerful, easy to use, and greatly improves the readability of code.

## Getting ready

Add the `parse` module to the `requirements.txt` file in our virtual environment and reinstall the dependencies, as shown in the *Creating a virtual environment* recipe.

The `requirements.txt` file should look like this:

```
pendulum==3.2.0
requests== 2.32.5
parse==1.20.2
```

Then, reinstall the modules in the virtual environment:

```
$ uv pip install -r requirements.txt
Resolved 13 packages in 349ms
Prepared 1 package in 45ms
Installed 1 package in 4ms
 + parse==1.20.2
```

# How to do it...

1. Import the parse function:

```
>>> from parse import parse
```

2. Define the log to parse, in the same format as in the *Extracting data from structured strings* recipe:

```
>>> LOG = '[2025-10-06T12:58:00.714611] - SALE - PRODUCT: 1345 - PRICE:
$09.99'
```

3. Analyze it and describe it as you would do when trying to print it, like this:

```
>>> FORMAT = '[{date}] - SALE - PRODUCT: {product} - PRICE: ${price}'
```

4. Run parse and check the results:

```
>>> result = parse(FORMAT, LOG)
>>> result
<Result () {'date': '2025-10-06T12:58:00.714611', 'product': '1345',
'price': '09.99'}>
>>> result['date']
'2025-10-06T12:58:00.714611'
>>> result['product']
'1345'
>>> result['price']
'09.99'
```

5. Note the results are all strings. Define the types to be parsed:

```
>>> FORMAT = '[{date:ti}] - SALE - PRODUCT: {product:d} - PRICE: ${price:
05.2f}'
```

6. Parse once again, noticing that the types now match the defined ones:

```
>>> result = parse(FORMAT, LOG)
>>> result['date']
datetime.datetime(2025, 10, 6, 12, 58, 0, 714611)
>>> result['product']
1345
>>> result['price']
9.99
```

Define a custom type for the price to avoid issues with the float type:

```
>>> from decimal import Decimal
>>> def price(string):
...     return Decimal(string)
...
>>> FORMAT = '[{date:ti}] - SALE - PRODUCT: {product:d} - PRICE: ${price:price}'
>>> parse(FORMAT, LOG, {'price': price})
<Result () {'date': datetime.datetime(2025, 10, 6, 12, 58, 0, 714611), 'product':
1345, 'price': Decimal('9.99')}>
```

Notice that now the `price` field is defined as `Decimal`.

## How it works...

The `parse` module allows us to define a format, as a string, that reverses the `format` method when parsing values. A lot of the concepts that we discussed when creating strings apply here —put values in brackets, define the type after a colon, and so on.

By default, as seen initially, the values are parsed as strings. This is a good starting point when analyzing text. The values can be parsed into more useful native types, as shown next. Please note that while most of the parsing types are the same as the ones in the Python Format Specification mini-language, some others are available, such as `ti` for timestamps in ISO format.

**Tip**

Though we are using timestamp in this book in a more liberal way as a replacement for "Date and time," in the strictest sense, it should only be used for numeric formats, such as *Unix timestamp* or *epoch*, defined as the number of seconds since a particular time.

The usage of a timestamp that includes other formats is common anyway as it's a clear and understandable concept, but be sure to agree on formats when sharing information with others.

If native types are not enough, our own parsing can be defined, as demonstrated in the last step. Note that the definition of the price function gets a string and returns the proper format, which in this case a `Decimal` type.

All the issues about floats and price information described in the *There's more...* section of the *Extracting data from structured strings* recipe apply here as well.

## There's more...

The timestamp can also be translated into a `pendulum` object for consistency. Also, `pendulum` objects carry over time zone information. Adding the same structure as in the previous recipe gives the following object, which is capable of parsing logs:

```
import parse
from decimal import Decimal
import pendulum
class PriceLog(object):
  def __init__(self, timestamp, product_id, price):
    self.timestamp = timestamp
    self.product_id = product_id
    self.price = price
  def __repr__(self):
    return '<PriceLog ({}, {}, {})>'.format(self.timestamp,
                                           self.product_id,
                                           self.price)

  @classmethod
  def parse(cls, text_log):
    '''
    Parse from a text log with the format
    [<Timestamp>] - SALE - PRODUCT: <product id> - PRICE: $<price>    to a
PriceLog object
```

```
    '''
    def price(string):
      return Decimal(string)
    def isodate(string):
      return pendulum.parse(string)

    FORMAT = ('[{timestamp:isodate}] - SALE - PRODUCT: {product:d} - '
              'PRICE: ${price:price}')
    formats = {'price': price, 'isodate': isodate}
    result = parse.parse(FORMAT, text_log, formats)
    return cls(timestamp=result['timestamp'],
               product_id=result['product'],
               price=result['price'])
```

So, parsing it returns similar results:

```
>>> log = '[2025-10-06T14:58:59.051545] - SALE - PRODUCT: 827 - PRICE: $22.25'
>>> PriceLog.parse(log)
<PriceLog (2025-10-06 14:58:59.051545+00:00, 827, 22.25)>
```

This code is contained in the GitHub file, `https://github.com/PacktPublishing/Python-Automation-Cookbook-Third-Edition/blob/main/ch01/price_log.py`

All supported parse types can be found in the documentation at `https://github.com/r1chardj0n3s/parse#format-specification`.

> **Tip**
>
> Typically, GenAI tries to use regexes, which we will see in the next two recipes, to parse values. That works in some cases, but it can overcomplicate things. We will see some of the problems of regexes later. Having an easier way to parse regular values is very valuable and should not be underestimated.

## See also

- The *Extracting data from structured strings* recipe, earlier in this chapter, to learn how to use simple processes to get information from text.

- The next recipe, *Introducing regular expressions*, to learn how to detect and extract patterns from text.
- The *Going deeper into regular expressions* recipe, later in this chapter, to further your knowledge of regular expressions.

# Introducing regular expressions

A **regular expression**, or **regex**, is a pattern to *match* text. In other words, it allows us to define an **abstract string** (typically, the definition of a structured kind of text) to check against other strings to see if they match or not.

It is better to describe them with an example. Think of defining a pattern of text, such as *a word that starts with an uppercase A and contains only lowercase 'n's and 'a's after that.* Let's show some possible comparisons and results:

| **Text to compare** | **Result** |
|---|---|
| Anna | Match |
| Bob | No match (No initial A) |
| Alice | No match (l is not n or a after initial A) |
| James | No match (No initial A) |
| Aaan | Match |
| Ana | Match |
| Annnn | Match |
| Aaaan | Match |
| ANNA | No match (N is not n or a) |

*Table 1.1: A pattern matching example*

If this sounds complicated, that's because it is. Regexes can, notoriously, be complicated, intricate and difficult to follow. But they are also very useful because they allow us to perform incredibly powerful pattern matching.

Some common uses of regexes are:

- **Validating input data**: For example, a phone number consisting only of numbers, dashes, and brackets.
- **String parsing**: Retrieve data from structured strings, such as logs or URLs. Typically, capture some section of the full string. This is similar to what's described in the previous recipe.
- **Scraping**: Find the occurrences of something in a long piece of text. For example, find all the email addresses in a web page.
- **Replacement**: Find and replace a word or words with others. For example, replace *the owner* with *John Smith*.

## Getting ready

The Python module to deal with regexes is called `re`. The main function we'll cover is `re.search()`, which returns a match object with information about what matched the pattern.

> **Note**
>
> As regex patterns are also defined as strings, we'll differentiate them by prefixing them with an `r`, such as `r'pattern'`. This is the Python way of labeling a text as raw string literals, meaning that the string within is taken literally, without any escaping. This means that a "\" is used as a backslash instead of an escaping sequence. For example, without the `r` prefix, `\n` means a newline character.

Some characters are special and refer to concepts such as *the end of the string, any digit, any character, any whitespace character*, and so on.

The simplest form is just a literal string. For example, the regex pattern `r'LOG'` matches the string `'LOGS'`, but not the string `'NOT A MATCH'`. If there's no match, `re.search` returns `None`. If there is, it returns a special `Match` object:

```
>>> import re
>>> re.search(r'LOG', 'LOGS')
<_sre.SRE_Match object; span=(0, 3), match='LOG'>
>>> re.search(r'LOG', 'NOT A MATCH')
>>>
```

## How to do it...

1. Import the re module:

```
>>> import re
```

2. Then, to match a pattern that is not at the start of the string:

```
>>> re.search(r'LOG', 'SOME LOGS')
<_sre.SRE_Match object; span=(5, 8), match='LOG'>
```

3. Match a pattern that is only at the start of the string. Note the ^ character at the start of the pattern:

```
>>> re.search(r'^LOG', 'LOGS')
<_sre.SRE_Match object; span=(0, 3), match='LOG'>
>>> re.search(r'^LOG', 'SOME LOGS')
>>>
```

4. Match a pattern only at the end of the string. Note the `$` character at the end:

```
>>> re.search(r'LOG$', 'SOME LOG')
<_sre.SRE_Match object; span=(5, 8), match='LOG'>
>>> re.search(r'LOG$', 'SOME LOGS')
>>>
```

5. Match the word `'thing'` (not excluding `things`), but not `something` or `anything`. Note the `\b` at the start of the second pattern:

```
>>> STRING = 'something in the things she shows me'
>>> match = re.search(r'thing', STRING)
>>> STRING[:match.start()], STRING[match.start():match.end()],
STRING[match.end():]
('some', 'thing', ' in the things she shows me')
>>> match = re.search(r'\bthing', STRING)
>>> STRING[:match.start()], STRING[match.start():match.end()],
STRING[match.end():]
('something in the ', 'thing', 's she shows me')
```

6. Match a pattern that's only numbers and dashes (for example, a phone number). Retrieve the matched string:

```
>>> re.search(r'[0123456789-]+', 'the phone number is 1234-567-890')
<_sre.SRE_Match object; span=(20, 32), match='1234-567-890'>
>>> re.search(r'[0123456789-]+', 'the phone number is
1234-567-890').group()
'1234-567-890'
```

7. Match an email address naively:

```
>>> re.search(r'\S+@\S+', 'my email is email.123@test.com').group() 'email.
123@test.com'
```

## How it works...

The `re.search` function matches a pattern, no matter its position in the string. As explained previously, this will return `None` if the pattern is not found, or a `Match` object.

The following special characters are used:

- `^`: Marks the start of the string
- `$`: Marks the end of the string
- `\b`: Marks the start or end of a word
- `\S`: Marks any character that's not a whitespace, including characters like * or $

More special characters are shown in the next recipe, *Going deeper into regular expressions*.

In *step 6* of the *How to do it...* section, the `r'[0123456789-]+'` pattern is composed of two parts. The first is between square brackets, and matches any single character between `0` and `9` (any number) and the dash (`-`) character. The `+` sign after that means that this character can be present one or more times. This is called a **quantifier** in regexes. This makes a match on any combination of numbers and dashes, no matter how long it is.

*Step 7* again uses the `+` sign to match as many characters as necessary before the `@` and again after it. In this case, the character match is `\S`, which matches any non-whitespace character.

> **Tip**
>
> Please note that the naive pattern for emails described here is *very* naive, as it will match invalid emails such as `john@smith@test.com`. A better regex for most uses is

> r"(^[a-zA-Z0-9_.+-]+@[a-zA-Z0-9-]+\.[a-zA-Z0-9-.]+$)". You can go to http://emailregex.com/ to find it, along with links to further information.
>
> Note that parsing a valid email including corner cases is actually a difficult and challenging problem. The previous regex should be fine for most uses covered in this book, but specific tools like specific the library email-validator (https://github.com/JoshData/python-email-validator) or tools in a general framework project such as Django, are better options to handle emails.

The resulting matching object returns the position where the matched pattern starts and ends (using the start and end methods), as shown in *step 5*, which splits the string into matched parts, showing the distinction between the two matching patterns.

> **Note**
>
> The difference displayed in *step 5* is a very common one. Trying to capture GP (as in General Practitioner, for a medical doctor) can end up capturing eggplant and bagpipe! Similarly, thing\b won't capture things. Be sure to test and make the proper adjustments, such as capturing \bGP\b for just the word GP.

The specific matched pattern can be retrieved by calling group(), as shown in *step 6*. Note that the result will always be a string. It can be further processed using any of the methods we've seen previously, such as by splitting the phone number into groups by dashes, for example:

```
>>> match = re.search(r'[0123456789-]+', 'the phone number is 1234-567-890')
>>> [int(n) for n in match.group().split('-')]
[1234, 567, 890]
```

The captured string will include all characters, like the dashes in this case. Note how we remove them by using .split()

## There's more...

Dealing with regexes can be difficult and complex. Please allow time to test your matches and be sure that they work as you expect in order to avoid nasty surprises.

> *"Some people, when confronted with a problem, think "I know, I'll use regular expressions." Now they have two problems."*

*–Jamie Zawinski*

Regular expressions are at their best when they are kept very simple. In general, if there is a specific tool to do it, prefer it over regexes. A very clear example of this is with HTML parsing; refer to *Chapter 3, Building Your First Web Scraping Application*, for better tools to achieve this.

> **Tip**
>
> Some text editors allow us to search using regexes as well. While most are editors aimed at writing code, such as Vim, BBEdit, or Notepad++, they're also present in more general tools, such as MS Office, Open Office, or Google Documents. But be careful, as the particular syntax may be slightly different.

You can check your regexes interactively. A good one that's freely available online is `https://regex101.com/`, which displays each of the elements and explains the regex. Double-check that you're using the Python flavor:

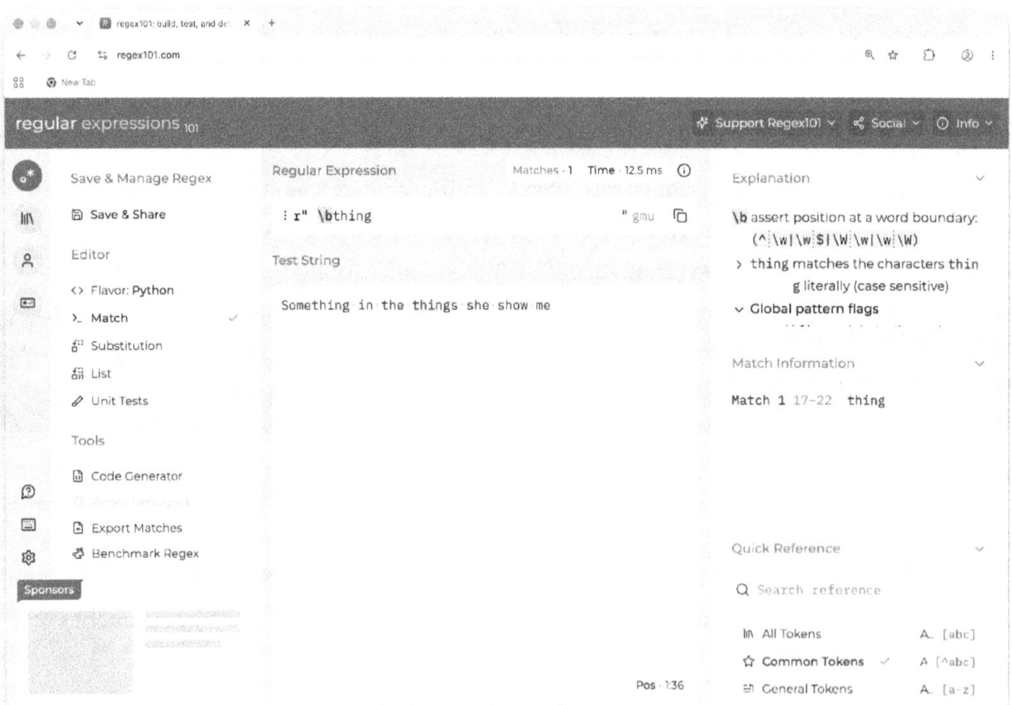


*Figure 1.2: An example using RegEx101*

Note that the **EXPLANATION** box in the preceding image describes that `\b` matches a word boundary (the start or end of a word), and that *thing* matches literally these characters.

Regexes, in some cases, can be very slow, or even susceptible to what's called a **regex denial-of-service attack**, a string created to confuse a particular regex so that it takes an enormous amount of time. In the worst-case scenario, it can even block the computer. While automating tasks probably won't get you into those problems, keep an eye out in case a regex takes too long to process.

> **Tip**
>
> GenAI is quite keen on regexes and it will try to parse most text with regexes. This is generally a problem and it's a good idea to critically analyze any regex and double check if there's a simpler way to retrieve the same information. There are many tools that allow simpler parsing of common elements that can produce safer, more understandable code.
>
> At the same time, GenAI can be very useful when producing regex if that's what's required.
>
> The bottom line is that regexes can be difficult to maintain and to test that they produce the required effect. Take care with them.

## See also

- The *Extracting data from structured strings* recipe, earlier in the chapter, to learn simple techniques to extract information from text.
- The *Using a third-party tool—parse* recipe, earlier in the chapter, to use a third-party tool to extract information from text.
- The *Going deeper into regular expressions* recipe, covered next, to further your knowledge of regular expressions.

# Going deeper into regular expressions

In this recipe, we'll learn more about how to deal with regular expressions. After introducing the basics, we will dig a little deeper into pattern elements, introduce groups as a better way to retrieve and parse strings, learn how to search for multiple occurrences of the same string, and deal with longer texts.

## How to do it...

1. Import re:

```
>>> import re
```

2. Match a phone pattern as part of a group (in brackets). Note the use of \d as a special character for any digit:

```
>>> match = re.search(r'the phone number is ([\d-]+)', '37: the phone
number is 1234-567-890')
>>> match.group()
'the phone number is 1234-567-890'
>>> match.group(1)
'1234-567-890'
```

3. Compile a pattern and capture a case-insensitive pattern with a yes|no option:

```
>>> pattern = re.compile(r'The answer to question (\w+) is (yes|no)',
re.IGNORECASE)
>>> pattern.search('Naturally, the answer to question 3b is YES')
<_sre.SRE_Match object; span=(10, 42), match='the answer to question 3b is
YES' >
>>> pattern.search('Naturally, the answer to question 3b is YES').groups()
('3b', 'YES')
```

4. Match all the occurrences of cities and state abbreviations in the text. Note that they are separated by a single character, and the name of the city always starts with an uppercase letter. Only four states are matched for simplicity:

```
>>> PATTERN = re.compile(r'([A-Z][\w\s]+?).(TX|OR|OH|MI)')
>>> TEXT ='the jackalopes are the team of Odessa,TX while the knights are
native of Corvallis OR and the mud hens come from Toledo.OH; the whitecaps
have their base in Grand Rapids,MI'
>>> list(PATTERN.finditer(TEXT))
[<_sre.SRE_Match object; span=(31, 40), match='Odessa,TX'>, <_sre.SRE_Match
object; span=(73, 85), match='Corvallis OR'>, <_sre.SRE_Match object;
span=(113, 122), match='Toledo.OH'>, <_sre.SRE_Match object; span=(157,
172), match='Grand Rapids,MI'>]
>>> _[0].groups() ('Odessa', 'TX')
```

## How it works...

The new special characters that were introduced are as follows:

- `\d`: Matches any digit (0 to 9).
- `\s`: Matches any character that's a whitespace, including tabs and other whitespace special characters. Note that this is the reverse of `\S`, which was introduced in the previous recipe.
- `\w`: Matches any letter (this includes digits, but excludes characters such as periods).
- `.`: (dot): Matches any character.

> **Note**
>
> Note that the same letter in uppercase or lowercase means the opposite match, for example, `\d` matches a digit, while `\D` matches a non-digit.

To define groups, put them in parentheses. A group can be retrieved individually, making it perfect for matching a bigger pattern that contains a variable part to be processed in the next step, as demonstrated in *step 2*. Note the difference from the *step 6* pattern in the previous recipe. In this case, the pattern is not only the number, but it includes the prefix text, even if we then extract only the number:

```
>>> re.search(r'the phone number is ([\d-]+)', '37: the phone number is 
1234-567-890')
<_sre.SRE_Match object; span=(4, 36), match='the phone number is 1234-567-890'>
>>> _.group(1)
'1234-567-890'
>>> re.search(r'[0123456789-]+', '37: the phone number is 1234-567-890')
<_sre.SRE_Match object; span=(0, 2), match='37'>
>>> _.group()
'37'
```

Remember that group 0 (`.group()` or `.group(0)`) is always the whole match. The rest of the groups are ordered as they appear.

Patterns can be compiled as well. This saves some time if the pattern needs to be matched over and over. To use it that way, compile the pattern and then use the compiled object to perform searches, as shown in *steps 3* and *4*. Some extra flags can be added, such as making the pattern case insensitive.

*Step 4*'s pattern requires a little bit of explanation. It's composed of two groups, separated by a single character. The special character "." (dot) means it matches everything. In our example, it matches a period, a whitespace, and a comma. The second group is a straightforward selection of defined options, in this case, US state abbreviations.

The first group starts with an uppercase letter (`[A-Z]`) and accepts any combination of letters or spaces (`[\w\s]+?`), but not punctuation marks such as periods or commas. This matches the cities, including those that are composed of more than one word.

The final `+?` makes the match of letters *non-greedy*, matching as few characters as possible. This avoids some problems such as when there are no punctuation symbols between the cities. Take a look at the result where we don't include the *non-greedy* qualifier for the second match and how it includes two elements:

```
>>> PATTERN = re.compile(r'([A-Z][\w\s]+).(TX|OR|OH|MI)')
>>> TEXT ='the jackalopes are the team of Odessa,TX while the knights are native
of Corvallis OR and the mud hens come from Toledo.OH; the whitecaps have their
base in Grand Rapids,MI'
>>> list(PATTERN.finditer(TEXT))[1]
<re.Match object; span=(73, 122), match='Corvallis OR and the mud hens come from
Toledo.OH>
```

Note that this pattern starts on any uppercase letter and keeps matching until it finds a state, unless separated by a punctuation mark, which may not be what's expected, for example:

```
>>> re.search(r'([A-Z][\w\s]+?).(TX|OR|OH|MI)', 'This is a test, Escanaba MI')
<_sre.SRE_Match object; span=(16, 27), match='Escanaba MI'>
>>> re.search(r'([A-Z][\w\s]+?).(TX|OR|OH|MI)', 'This is a test with Escanaba MI')
<_sre.SRE_Match object; span=(0, 31), match='This is a test with Escanaba MI'>
```

*Step 4* also shows you how to find more than one occurrence in a long text. While the `.findall()` method exists, it doesn't return the full match object, while `.finditer()` does. As is common now in Python 3, `.finditer()` returns an iterator that can be used in a *for* loop or list comprehension. Note that `.search()` returns only the first occurrence of the pattern, even if more matches appear:

```
>>> PATTERN.search(TEXT)
<_sre.SRE_Match object; span=(31, 40), match='Odessa,TX'>
>>> PATTERN.findall(TEXT)
[('Odessa', 'TX'), ('Corvallis', 'OR'), ('Toledo', 'OH'), ('Grand Rapids', 'MI')]
```

## There's more...

The special characters can be reversed if they are case swapped. For example, the reverse of the ones we used are as follows:

- **\D**: Marks any non-digit.
- **\W**: Marks any non-letter.
- **\B**: Marks a position that's *not* at the start or end of a word. For example, `r'thing\B'` will match *things* but not *thing*.

> **Note**
>
> The most commonly used special characters are typically `\d` (digits) and `\w` (letters and digits), as they match digits and letters, which are normally what you want.

Groups can be assigned names as well. This makes them more explicit at the expense of making the group more verbose in the following way— `(?P<groupname>PATTERN)`. Groups can be referred to by name with `.group(groupname)` or by calling `.groupdict()` while maintaining its numeric position.

For example, the *step 4* pattern can be described as follows:

```
>>> PATTERN = re.compile(r'(?P<city>[A-Z][\w\s]+?).(?P<state>TX|OR|OH|MN)')
>>> match = PATTERN.search(TEXT)
>>> match.groupdict()
{'city': 'Odessa', 'state': 'TX'}
>>> match.group('city')
'Odessa'
>>> match.group('state')
'TX'
>>> match.group(1), match.group(2)
('Odessa', 'TX')
```

As perhaps you have by now come to suspect, regular expressions are a very extensive topic. They can be notoriously deep, and there are whole technical books devoted to them, like *Mastering Python Regular Expressions* by Lopez and Romero. The Python documentation is also a good reference to use (`https://docs.python.org/3/library/re.html`) and to learn more.

Tip

GenAI is your friend here! GenAI loves regexes and will explain in great detail how an existing regex works and how to change it if there's an unexpected effect.

**Prompt example**:

Explain this regex `r'(?P<city>[A-Z][\w\s]+?).(?P<state>TX|OR|OH|MN)'`

Summarized example response:

`(?P<city>[A-Z][\w\s]+?) This is a named captured book named city. It should start with a capital letter.`

`. A literal dot. It captures a single character. If the intent was to match a literal period, it should be written as "\."`

`(?P<state>TX|OR|OH|MN)` This is another named capturing group called state.

It matches exactly one of these state abbreviations: TX, OR, OH or MN

Potential gotchas:

The dot will match any character and not just a literal dot.

Cities with punctuation (like St. Paul) may not work correctly

If you feel a little intimidated at the start, it's a perfectly natural feeling. Starting by asking GenAI. It will analyze the patterns with care, and they will start to make sense. You can keep asking the AI about it. In addition, don't be afraid to run a regex interactive analyzer!

While regexes can be really powerful and generic, they may not be the proper tool for what you are trying to achieve. We've seen some caveats already, and patterns that have subtleties. As a rule of thumb, if a pattern starts to feel complicated, it's time to search for a different tool. That's a common experience with GenAI code, where the tool will likely try to overuse regexes. Remember the previous recipes too and the options they presented, such as `parse`.

## See also

- The *Introducing regular expressions* recipe, earlier in the chapter, to learn the basics of using regular expressions.
- The *Using a third-party tool—parse* recipe, earlier in the chapter, to learn a different technique to extract information from text.

# Adding command-line arguments

Often a solution is best structured as a command-line interface that accepts different parameters to change the way it works, for example, scraping a web page from a provided URL or other URL. Python includes a powerful `argparse` module in the standard library to create rich command-line argument parsing with minimal effort.

> **Note**
>
> `argparse` is included in the standard library, and it is a solid choice for common line scripts. But great third-party tools are also available, like `click` (`https://click.palletsprojects.com/en/stable/`) and `typer` (`https://typer.tiangolo.com`) that are worth exploring. They offer additional features for more sophisticated CLI interfaces.

## Getting ready

The basic use of `argparse` in a script can be shown in three steps:

1. Define the arguments that your script is going to accept, generating a new parser.
2. Call the defined parser, returning an object with all of the resulting arguments.
3. Use the arguments to call the entry point of your script, which will apply the defined behavior.

Try to use the following general structure for your scripts:

```
IMPORTS
def main(main parameters):
  DO THINGS
if __name__ == '__main__':
    DEFINE ARGUMENT PARSER
    PARSE ARGS
    VALIDATE OR MANIPULATE ARGS, IF NEEDED
    main(arguments)
```

The `main` function makes it easy to know what the entry point for the code is. The section under the `if` statement is only executed if the file is called directly, but not if it's imported. We'll follow this for all the steps.

## How to do it...

1. Create a script that will accept a single integer as a positional argument, and will print a hash symbol that number of times. The `recipe_cli_step1.py` script is as follows, but note that we are following the structure presented previously, and the main function is just printing the argument:

```
import argparse
def main(number):
    print('#' * number)
if __name__ == '__main__':
    parser = argparse.ArgumentParser()
    parser.add_argument('number', type=int, help='A number')
    args = parser.parse_args()

    main(args.number)
```

2. Call the script and check how the parameter is presented. Calling the script with no arguments displays the automatic help. Use the automatic argument `-h` to display the extended help:

```
$ uv run recipe_cli_step1.py
usage: recipe_cli_step1.py [-h] number
recipe_cli_step1.py: error: the following arguments are required: number
$ uv run recipe_cli_step1.py -h
usage: recipe_cli_step1.py [-h] number

positional arguments:
  number                A number

options:
  -h, --help            show this help message and exit
```

3. Calling the script with the extra parameters work as expected

```
$ uv run recipe_cli_step1.py 4
####
$ uv run recipe_cli_step1.py not_a_number
usage: recipe_cli_step1.py [-h] number
```

```
recipe_cli_step1.py: error: argument number: invalid int value:
'not_a_number'
```

4. Change the script to accept an optional argument for the character to print. The default will be "#". The `recipe_cli_step2.py` script will look like this:

```
import argparse
def main(character, number):
    print(character * number)
if __name__ == '__main__':
    parser = argparse.ArgumentParser()
    parser.add_argument('number', type=int, help='A number')
    parser.add_argument('-c', type=str, help='Character to print',
                        default='#')
args = parser.parse_args()
main(args.c, args.number)
```

5. The help is updated, and using the `-c` flag allows us to print different characters:

```
$ uv run recipe_cli_step2.py -h
usage: recipe_cli_step2.py [-h] [-c C] number

positional arguments:
  number                A number

options:
  -h, --help            show this help message and exit
  -c C                  Character to print
$ uv run recipe_cli_step2.py 4
####
$ uv run recipe_cli_step2.py 5 -c m
mmmmm
```

6. Add a flag that changes the behavior when present. The `recipe_cli_step3.py` script is as follows:

```
import argparse
def main(character, number):
    print(character * number)
if __name__ == '__main__':
```

```
    parser = argparse.ArgumentParser()
    parser.add_argument('number', type=int, help='A number')
    parser.add_argument('-c', type=str, help='Character to print',
                        default='#')
    parser.add_argument('-U', action='store_true', default=False,
                        dest='uppercase',
                        help='Uppercase the character')
    args = parser.parse_args()
    if args.uppercase:
        args.c = args.c.upper()
    main(args.c, args.number)
```

7. Calling it uppercases the character if the `-U` flag is added:

```
$ uv run recipe_cli_step3.py 4
####
$ uv run recipe_cli_step3.py 4 -c f
ffff
$ uv run recipe_cli_step3.py 4 -c f -U
FFFF
```

## How it works...

As described in *step 1* of the *How to do it...* section, the arguments are added to the parser through `.add_arguments`. Once all of the arguments are defined, calling `parse_args()` returns an object that contains the results (or exits if there's an error).

Each argument should add a help description, but their behavior can change greatly depending on the details:

- If an argument starts with a `-`, it is considered an optional parameter, like the `-c` argument in *step 4*. If not, it's a positional argument, like the number argument in *step 1*.
- For clarity, always define a default value for optional parameters. It will be `None` if you don't, but this may be confusing. It's a good idea to add `default=None` to be explicit.
- Remember to always add a `help` parameter with a description of the parameter; help is automatically generated, as shown in *step 2*.
- If a `type` is present, it will be validated, for example, `number` in *step 3*. By default, the type will be a string.

- The actions `store_true` and `store_false` can be used to generate flags, arguments that don't require any extra parameters. Set the corresponding default value to be the opposite Boolean. This is demonstrated in the `U` argument in *steps 6* and *7*.
- The name of the property in the `args` object will be, by default, the name of the argument (without the dash, if it's present). You can change it with `dest`. For example, in *step 6*, the command-line argument `-U` is described as `uppercase`.

> **Tip**
>
> Changing the name of an argument for internal usage is very useful when using short arguments, such as single letters. A good command-line interface will use `-c`, but, internally, it's probably a good idea to use a more verbose label, such as `configuration_file`. Remember, explicit is better than implicit!

Some arguments can work in coordination with others, as shown in *step 3*. Prepare the parameters to pass to the `main` function so they are clear. For example, in *step 3*, only two parameters are passed, but one may have been modified.

## There's more...

You can create long arguments as well with double dashes, for example:

```
parser.add_argument('-v', '--verbose', action='store_true', default=False,
    help='Enable verbose output')
```

This will accept both `-v` and `--verbose`, and it will store the name verbose.

Adding long names is a good way of making the interface more intuitive and easier to remember.

The main inconvenience when dealing with command-line arguments is that you may end up with too many of them. This creates confusion. Try to make your arguments as independent as possible and don't make too many dependencies between them; otherwise, handling the combinations can be tricky.

In particular, try to not create more than a couple of positional arguments, as they won't have mnemonics. Positional arguments also accept default values, but most of the time, that won't be the expected behavior.

Note

GenAI can help you produce a complex interface if necessary, or speed up its production by defining the expected use case. But keep in mind that a complex interface is likely an indication of trying to perform a complex operation with too many parameters, and that a rethink is needed. Do you really need all those parameters? Can it be simplified?

To simplify the usage of the command-line interface, but still allow further customization, you can use environment variables to set default values – as for example in this code (`recipe_cli_env.py`):

```
import argparse
import os

default_character = os.environ.get('DEFAULT_CHAR', '#')


def main(character, number):
    print(character * number)


if __name__ == '__main__':
    parser = argparse.ArgumentParser()
    parser.add_argument('number', type=int, help='A number')
    help_msg = f'Character to print (default "{default_character}"). Set with env
DEFAULT_CHAR'
    parser.add_argument('-c', type=str, help=help_msg,
                        default=default_character)
    args = parser.parse_args()
    main(args.c, args.number)
```

Notice how we use the dictionary `os.environ` to retrieve a value in the environment variable `DEFAULT_CHAR`. If not present, it will use the value '#'. We store it into `default_character`, which we use to define the default value in the parser. We include extra information in the `help` command to make clear how to use the parameters and environment variables.

Because it uses the environment variable, which can be defined in the shell, the need to always specify the character to use when we run it is removed:

```
$ uv run recipe_cli_env.py 4
####
$ DEFAULT_CHAR=* uv run recipe_cli_env.py 4
****
$ DEFAULT_CHAR=* uv run recipe_cli_env.py -c ^ 5
^^^^^
```

This pattern is common in command-line utilities and can be used to simplify the call, while allowing for flexibility.

For advanced details on `argparse`, refer to the Python documentation (`https://docs.python.org/3/library/argparse.html`).

## See also

- The *Creating a virtual environment* recipe, earlier in this chapter, to learn how to create an environment installing third-party modules.
- The *Installing third-party packages* recipe, earlier in this chapter, to learn how to install and use external modules in the virtual environment.

## Get this book's PDF version and more

Scan the QR code (or go to `packtpub.com/unlock`). Search for this book by name, confirm the edition, and then follow the steps on the page.

UNLOCK NOW

*Note: Keep your invoice handy. Purchases made directly from Packt don't require an invoice.*

# 2

# Automating Tasks Made Easy

To properly automate tasks, we need a way to make them execute automatically at the correct times. A task that needs to be started manually is not fully automated.

However, to be able to leave them running in the background while worrying about more pressing issues, the task will need to be adequate to run in *fire-and-forget* mode. We should be able to monitor that it executes correctly, be sure that we capture relevant information (such as receiving notifications if something interesting arises), and know whether there have been any errors while running it.

Ensuring that a piece of software runs consistently with high reliability is actually a very big deal. It is one area that, in order to be done properly, requires specialized knowledge and staff, who typically go by the names of sysadmin, operations, or **SRE** (**Site Reliability Engineering**). Big operations, such as Amazon and Google, but also more traditional ones like banks, invest heavily in ensuring that everything works reliably 24/7.

The objective for this book is rather more modest than that, as much software doesn't require this kind of high availability. Designing systems with downtimes of less than a few seconds per year is challenging and may even require specialized hardware, but executing a task with reasonable reliability is a much easier thing to do. However, be aware that there's maintenance to be done, and plan accordingly.

In this chapter, we'll cover the following recipes:

- Preparing a task
- Setting up a cron job
- Capturing errors and problems
- Sending email notifications

# Technical requirements

You can check the code presented in the chapter in the GitHub URL `https://github.com/PacktPublishing/Python-Automation-Cookbook-Third-Edition/tree/main/ch02`.

# Preparing a task

It all starts with defining precisely the work that needs to be executed and designing it in a way that doesn't require human intervention to run.

Some ideal characteristic points are as follows:

1. **Single, clear entry point**: No confusion about how to start the task.
2. **Clear parameters**: If there are any parameters, they should be as explicit as possible.
3. **No interactivity**: Stopping execution to request information from the user is not possible.
4. **The results should be stored, typically on a file**: So it's possible to check them at a time other than when it runs.
5. **Clear result**: When we oversee the execution of a program ourselves, we can accept more verbose results, such as unlabeled data or extra debugging information. However, for an automated task the final result should be as concise and to the point as possible.
6. **Errors should be logged**: To analyze what went wrong.

As we saw in the previous chapter, a command-line program has a lot of those characteristics already. It always has a clear entry point, with defined parameters, and the result can be stored, even if just in text format. And, from the previous recipes in *Chapter 1*, it can be improved by implementing a config file that more explicitly states the parameters, plus by directing the output to a file.

> Note
>
> Note that fulfilling point 6 is the objective of the *Capturing errors and problems* recipe in this chapter and will be covered there.

To avoid interactivity, do not use any function that waits for user input, such as `input`. And remember to delete any debugger breakpoints!

## Getting ready

We'll start by following a structure in which a `main` function will serve as the entry point, and all parameters are supplied to it.

This is the same basic structure that was presented in the *Adding command-line arguments* recipe in *Chapter 1, Let's Begin Our Automation Journey*.

The definition of a `main` function with all the explicit arguments covers points 1 (single, clear entry point) and 2 (clear parameters). Point 3 (no interactivity) is not difficult to achieve.

To improve points 2 (clear parameters) and 5 (clear result), we'll look at retrieving the configuration from a file and storing the result in another file, instead of displaying the text in the console. Another option is to send a notification, such as an email, which will be covered later in this chapter.

## How to do it...

1. Prepare the following command-line program for multiplying two numbers, and save it as `prepare_task_step1.py`:

```
import argparse
def main(number, other_number):
    result = number * other_number
    print(f'The result is {result}')
if __name__ == '__main__':
    parser = argparse.ArgumentParser()
    parser.add_argument('-n1', type=int, help='A number', default=1)
    parser.add_argument('-n2', type=int, help='Another number', default=1)
    args = parser.parse_args()
    main(args.n1, args.n2)
```

2. Run `prepare_task_step1.py` to multiply two numbers:

```
$ uv run prepare_task_step1.py -n1 3 -n2 7
The result is 21
```

3. Update the file to define a config file that contains both arguments, and save it as `prepare_task_step3.py`. Note that defining a config file overwrites any command-line parameters:

```
import argparse
import configparser
def main(number, other_number):
    result = number * other_number
    print(f'The result is {result}')
if __name__ == '__main__':
```

```
    parser = argparse.ArgumentParser()
    parser.add_argument('-n1', type=int, help='A number', default=1)
    parser.add_argument('-n2', type=int, help='Another number', default=1)
    parser.add_argument('--config', '-c', type=argparse.FileType('r'),
                        help='config file')
    args = parser.parse_args()
    if args.config:
        config = configparser.ConfigParser()
        config.read_file(args.config)
        # Transforming values into integers
        args.n1 = int(config['ARGUMENTS']['n1'])
        args.n2 = int(config['ARGUMENTS']['n2'])
    main(args.n1, args.n2)
```

4. Create the config file `config.ini`. See the `ARGUMENTS` section and the `n1` and `n2` values:

```
[ARGUMENTS]
n1=5
n2=7
```

5. Run the command with the config file. Note that the config file overwrites the command-line parameters, as described in *step 2*:

```
$ uv run prepare_task_step3.py -c config.ini
The result is 35
$ uv run prepare_task_step3.py -c config.ini -n1 2 -n2 3
The result is 35
```

6. Add a parameter to store the result in a file, and save it as `prepare_task_step6.py`:

```
import argparse
import sys
import configparser
def main(number, other_number, output):
    result = number * other_number
    print(f'The result is {result}', file=output)
if __name__ == '__main__':
    parser = argparse.ArgumentParser()
    parser.add_argument('-n1', type=int, help='A number', default=1)
    parser.add_argument('-n2', type=int, help='Another number', default=1)
    parser.add_argument('--config', '-c', type=argparse.FileType('r'),
```

```
                        help='config file')
parser.add_argument('-o', dest='output', type=argparse.FileType('w'),
                        help='output file',
                        default=sys.stdout)
args = parser.parse_args()
if args.config:
    config = configparser.ConfigParser()
    config.read_file(args.config)
    # Transforming values into integers
    args.n1 = int(config['ARGUMENTS']['n1'])
    args.n2 = int(config['ARGUMENTS']['n2'])
main(args.n1, args.n2, args.output)
```

7. Run the result to check that the program is sending the output to the defined file. Note that there's no output outside the result files:

```
$ uv run prepare_task_step6.py  -n1 3 -n2 5 -o result.txt
$ cat result.txt
The result is 15
$ uv run prepare_task_step6.py  -c config.ini -o result.txt
$ cat result.txt
The result is 35
```

## How it works...

The `argparse` module allows us to define files as parameters, with the `argparse.FileType` type, and opens them automatically. This is very handy and will raise an error if the file path leads to an invalid location.

Remember to open the file in the correct mode. In *step 5*, the config file is opened in read mode (`r`) and the output file in write mode (`w`), which will overwrite the file if it exists.

Another option that you may find useful is the append mode (a), which will add the next piece of data to the end of an existing file.

The `configparser` module, included in Python standard library, allows us to use config files with ease. As demonstrated in *step 2*, the parsing of the file is simple, as follows:

```
config = configparser.ConfigParser()
config.read_file(file)
```

The config will then be accessible as a dictionary. This has the sections of the config file as the keys, and inside another dictionary with each of the config values. So the value `n2` in the `ARGUMENTS` section is accessed as `config['ARGUMENTS']['n2']`.

Note that the values are always stored as strings, which if necessary are required to be transformed in code into other types, such as integers.

> **Tip**
>
> Remember what we discussed in *Chapter 1, Adding command line parameters* about environment variables. The values in the config file work in a similar way. Both alternatives are available and can be combined, but for automated processes a config file is typically more explicit and simpler, as you'll keep all required configuration in a file that can be source-controlled.

If you need to obtain Boolean values, do not perform `value = bool(config[raw_value])`. Any non-empty string will be transformed into `True` no matter what; for instance, the string `'False'` is a true string, as it's not empty. Using an empty string is a bad option as well, as it's confusing. Use the `.getboolean` method instead, for example, `value = config.getboolean(raw_value)`. There are similar `.getint()` and `.getfloat()` methods for integers and float values.

Python 3 allows us to pass a file parameter to the `print` function, which will write to that file. *Step 5* shows the usage to redirect all the printed information to a file.

Note that the default parameter is `sys.stdout` (standard output), which will print the value to the terminal (standard output). This means that calling the script without an `-o` parameter will display the information on the screen, which is helpful when developing and debugging the script:

```
$ uv run prepare_task_step6.py -c config.ini
The result is 35
$ uv run prepare_task_step6.py -c config.ini -o result.txt
$ cat result.txt
The result is 35
```

## There's more...

Please refer to the full documentation of `configparser` in the official Python documentation: `https://docs.python.org/3/library/configparser.html`.

In most cases this configuration parser should be good enough, but if more power is needed you can use YAML files as configuration files.

YAML files (`https://learn.getgrav.org/advanced/yaml`) are very common as configuration files in multiple software projects. They are well-structured and can be parsed directly, taking into account directly different data types.

1. To use YAML files we need to use a third-party module. Add PyYAML to the requirements.txt file:

    ```
    pyyaml==6.0.3
    ```

2. Install the requirements in our `uv`-handled virtual environment:

    ```
    $ uv pip install -r requirements.txt
    ```

3. Create the `prepare_task_yaml.py` file:

    ```
    import yaml
    import argparse
    import sys
    def main(number, other_number, output):
        result = number * other_number
        print(f'The result is {result}', file=output)
    if __name__ == '__main__':
        parser = argparse.ArgumentParser()
        parser.add_argument('-n1', type=int, help='A number', default=1)
        parser.add_argument('-n2', type=int, help='Another number', default=1)
        parser.add_argument('-c', dest='config', type=argparse.FileType('r'),
     help='config file in YAML format',
     default=None)
        parser.add_argument('-o', dest='output', type=argparse.FileType('w'),
                            help='output file',
                            default=sys.stdout)
        args = parser.parse_args()
        if args.config:
            config = yaml.load(args.config, Loader= yaml.SafeLoader)
            # No need to transform values
            args.n1 = config['ARGUMENTS']['n1']
            args.n2 = config['ARGUMENTS']['n2']
        main(args.n1, args.n2, args.output)
    ```

> **Note**
>
> Note that the `PyYAMLyaml.load()` function requires a `Loader` parameter. This is to avoid arbitrary code execution if the YAML file comes from an untrusted source. Always use `yaml.SafeLoader` unless you need a set of YAML language features. And **never** use loaders other than `yaml.SafeLoader` if any part of the config coming from a YAML file comes from an untrusted source (for example, user input). Refer to this article for more information: `https://github.com/yaml/pyyaml/wiki/PyYAML-yaml.load(input)-Deprecation`.

4. Define the config file, `config.yaml`:

```
ARGUMENTS:
    n1: 7
    n2: 4
```

5. Then run the following:

```
$ uv run prepare_task_yaml.py -c config.yaml
The result is 28
```

There's also the possibility of setting a default config file, as well as a default output file. This can be handy to create a task that requires no input parameters when running automatically.

As a general rule, try to avoid creating too many input and configuration parameters if the task has a very specific objective in mind. Limit the input parameters to different executions of the task. A parameter that never changes is probably fine being defined as a **constant**. A high number of parameters will make config files or command-line arguments complicated and will create more maintenance in the long run. On the other hand, if your objective is to create a very flexible tool to be used in very different situations, then creating more parameters is probably a good idea. Try to find your own proper balance!

## See also

- The *Command-line arguments* recipe in *Chapter 1, Let's Begin Our Automation Journey*, for more information about command-line arguments.

- The *Sending email notifications* recipe, covered later in this chapter, to see a more fleshed-out example of an automated task.
- The *Debugging with breakpoints* recipe in *Chapter 13*, *Debugging Techniques*, to learn how to debug the code before executing it automatically.

# Setting up a cron job

Cron is an old-fashioned but reliable way of executing commands. It has been around since the 1970s in Unix, and it's an old favorite in system administration to perform maintenance tasks such as freeing up disk space, rotating log files, making backups, and many other common, repetitive operations.

> **Note**
>
> This recipe is specific to Unix and Unix-like operating systems, so it will work in Linux and macOS. While it's possible to schedule a task in Windows, it's very different and uses Task Scheduler, which won't be described here. If you have access to a Linux server, this can be a good way of scheduling periodic tasks.
>
> Another alternative is to install locally in a Windows computer a Linux distribution through WLS (`https://learn.microsoft.com/en-us/windows/wsl/install`)

The main advantages are as follows:

- It's present in virtually all Unix and Linux systems and configured to run automatically.
- It's easy to use, although a little deceptive at first.
- It's well known. Almost anyone involved with admin tasks will have a general idea of how to use it.
- It allows for easy periodic commands, with good precision on when to run.

However, it also has some disadvantages, including the following:

- By default, it may not give much feedback. Retrieving the output, logging execution, and errors are critical.
- The task should be as self-contained as possible to avoid problems with environment variables (such as using the wrong Python interpreter), or with what path should execute.
- As we mentioned before, it is Unix(-like) specific.

- Only fixed periodic times are available. E.g. *run every 3 minutes on Mondays*, but not *run at sunset every day*, as sunset changes over the year; or *run in the last business day of the month*, as it can depend on details like bank holidays.

  > **Note**
  >
  > You can work through this problem by running a periodic task often and then determine dynamically in your code if now is the right moment to do the whole processing or just finalize.
  >
  > For example, run every day and decide if it's a working day or not, taking into account a calendar of bank holidays.

- It doesn't control how many tasks run at the same time. Each time the countdown goes off, it creates a new task, it cannot configure *run 10 minutes after the previous execution finishes*. For example, a task that takes 1 hour to complete, and that is scheduled to run once every 45 minutes, will have 15 minutes of overlap where two tasks will be running.

> **Tip**
>
> Don't underestimate the importance of the last effect. Running multiple expensive tasks at the same time can have a bad effect on performance. Having expensive tasks overlapping may result in a race condition where each task blocks the others from ever finishing! Allow ample time for your tasks to finish, and keep an eye on them. Keep in mind that any other programs running on the same host may have their performance affected, and that can include any service, such as web servers, databases, and email. To avoid surprises, check how loaded the host where the task will be executed is.
>
> In case that your program neeed to figure out there is another copy of itself running to avoid classes, a time-honored way is to create a file under `/var/lock/[program-name]` containing its `pid`. A program just started checks if the file is there, which means either another copy is running, of that the previous copy crashed without deleting the file.

While there are alternatives to cron, the fact is that it remains a really useful and simple entry point, based on a readily understandable concept: a description of when to run and what program to execute, including all required arguments.

## Getting ready

We will produce a script, called `cron.py`:

```
import argparse
import sys
from datetime import datetime, UTC
import configparser
def main(number, other_number, output):
    result = number * other_number
    print(f'[{datetime.now(UTC).isoformat()}] The result is {result}',
          file=output)
if __name__ == '__main__':
    parser =
argparse.ArgumentParser(formatter_class=argparse.ArgumentDefaultsHelpFormatter)
    parser.add_argument('--config', '-c', type=argparse.FileType('r'),
                        help='config file',
                        default='/etc/automate.ini')
    parser.add_argument('-o', dest='output', type=argparse.FileType('a'),
                        help='output file',
                        default=sys.stdout)
    args = parser.parse_args()
    if args.config:
        config = configparser.ConfigParser()
        config.read_file(args.config)
        # Transforming values into integers
        args.n1 = int(config['ARGUMENTS']['n1'])
        args.n2 = int(config['ARGUMENTS']['n2'])
    main(args.n1, args.n2, args.output)
```

Note the following details:

1. The config file is, by default, `/etc/automate.ini`. Reuse `config.ini` from the previous recipe.
2. A timestamp has been added to the output. This will make it explicit *when* the task is run.
3. The result is being appended to the file, as shown with the a mode when the file is opened.
4. The `ArgumentDefaultsHelpFormatter` parameter automatically adds information about default values when printing the help using the `-h` argument.

Check that the task is producing the expected result and that you can log to a known file:

```
$ uv run cron.py
[2025-11-25T21:49:26.687405+00:00]The result is 35
$ uv run cron.py -o /path/automate.log
$ cat /path/automate.log
[2025-11-25T21:49:50.507122+00:00]The result is 35
```

## How to do it...

We need to be sure that we run our script from the proper environment. For that, we need to use the Python interpreter in the virtual environment:

```
$ pwd
/your/path/
$ /your/path/.venv/bin/python cron.py
```

Prepare the cron job to be executed. Get the full path and check that it can be executed without any problems. Execute it a couple of times:

```
$ /your/path/.venv/bin/python /your/path/cron.py -o /path/automate.log
$ /your/path/.venv/bin/python /your/path/cron.py -o /path/automate.log
```

Check that the result is being added correctly to the result file:

```
$ cat /path/automate.log
[2025-11-25T21:58:39.865606+00:00] The result is 35
[2025-11-25T21:58:40.805463+00:00] The result is 35
```

Edit the crontab file to run the task once every 5 minutes:

```
$ crontab -e
*/5 * * * * your/path/.venv/bin/python /your/path/cron.py -o /path/automate.log
```

Note that this opens an editing terminal with your default command-line editor.

> **Note**
>
> If you haven't set up your default command-line editor, then by default it is likely to be Vim. This can be disconcerting if you don't have experience with Vim. Press `i` to start inserting text and `Esc` when you're done. Then, exit after saving the file with `:wq`. For more information about Vim, refer to this introduction: `https://null-`

> byte.wonderhowto.com/how-to/intro-vim-unix-text-editor-every-hacker-should-be-familiar-with-0174674.
>
> For information on how to change the default command-line editor, refer to the following link: https://www.a2hosting.com/kb/developer-corner/linux/setting-the-default-text-editor-in-linux.

Check the crontab contents. Note that this displays the crontab contents but doesn't set it to edit:

```
$ crontab -l
*/5 * * * * your/path/.venv/bin/python /your/path/cron.py -o /path/automate.log
```

Wait and check the result file to see how the task is being executed:

```
$ tail -F /path/automate.log
[2025-11-25T22:20:00.443924+00:00] The result is 35
[2025-11-25T22:25:01.062576+00:00] The result is 35
[2025-11-25T22:30:00.889056+00:00] The result is 35
```

## How it works...

The crontab line consists of a line describing how often to run the task (the first six elements), plus the task. Each of the initial five elements means a different unit of time to execute. Most of them are stars, meaning *any*:

```
* * * * *
| | | | |
| | | | +---- Day of the Week   (range: 1-7, 1 standing for Monday)
| | | +------ Month of the Year (range: 1-12)
| | +-------- Day of the Month  (range: 1-31)
| +---------- Hour              (range: 0-23)
+------------ Minute            (range: 0-59)
```

Therefore the line `*/5 * * * *` means *every time the minute is divisible by 5, in all hours, all days, all months, all days of the week.*

Here are some more examples:

```
30  15 * * * means "every day at 15:30"
30   * * * * means "every hour, at 30 minutes"
0,30 * * * * means "every hour, at 0 minutes and 30 minutes"
*/30 * * * * means "every half hour"
0    0 * * 1 means "every Monday at 00:00"
```

> **Tip**
>
> Try not to guess too much. Use a cheat sheet such as `https://crontab.guru/` for examples and tweaks. Most of the common usages will be described there directly. You can also edit a formula and get a descriptive piece of text on how it's going to run. Or, alternatively, ask a GenAI about your needs.

After the description of how to run the cron job, include the line to execute the task, as prepared in *step 2* of the *How to do it...* section.

Note that the task is described with the full paths for every related file – the interpreter, the script, and the output file. This removes all ambiguities related to paths and reduces the chance of possible errors. A very common error is for cron not to be able to determine one or more of those three elements.

> **Tip**
>
> While we are using `uv` most commonly to run our scripts, for this recipe it adds an extra layer of complexity because it also needs to be properly configured to use the proper virtual env. Instead, is better to directly call the Python interpreter inside the virtual environment.

## There's more...

The default output can be a bit verbose. When calling `uv run cron.py -h`, it gets displayed as:

```
-o OUTPUT   output file (default: <_io.TextIOWrapper name='<stdout>' mode='w'
encoding='utf-8'>)
```

This is the specification of the **standard output** (**stdout**). The format of the `output` parameter can be changed using the `formatter_class` argument in the `ArgumentParser`. This means that you can use a custom formatter inheriting from the available default ones to tweak how the values of the parameter are displayed. Refer to the documentation at `https://docs.python.org/3/library/argparse.html#formatter-class`.

If there's any problem in the execution of the crontab, you should receive a system mail. This will show up as a message in the terminal like this:

```
You have mail.
$
This can be read with mail:
$ mail
Mail version 8.1 6/6/93. Type ? for help.
"/var/mail/user": 1 message 1 new
>N 1 user@host Fri Jun 17 21:15 20/914 "Cron <user@host"
? 1
Message 1:
...
/usr/local/Cellar/python/3.14/Frameworks/Python.framework/Versions/3.14/Resources/
Python.app/Contents/MacOS/Python: can't open file 'cron.py': [Errno 2] No such
file or directory
```

In the next recipe, we will explore methods to capture the errors independently so that the task can run smoothly.

## See also

- The *Adding command-line options* recipe in *Chapter 1, Let's Begin Our Automation Journey*, to understand the basic concepts of command-line options.
- The *Capturing errors and problems* recipe, next in this chapter, to learn how to store events that occur during execution.

# Capturing errors and problems

An automated task's main characteristic is its *fire-and-forget* quality. We are not actively looking at the result, but making it run in the background.

On top of the problems and bugs of any program, most of the recipes in this book deal with external information, such as web pages or other reports. External information is inherently more varied and can contain unanticipated elements, increasing the likelihood of finding an unexpected problem when running. This recipe will present an automated task that safely stores unexpected behaviors in a log file that can be checked afterward.

## Getting ready

As a starting point our task will be to divide two numbers, as described in the command line.

This task is very similar to the one presented in *step 5* of *How it works...* for the *Preparing a task* recipe earlier in this chapter, except that instead of multiplying two numbers we'll divide them.

## How to do it...

1. Create the `task_with_error_handling_step1.py` file, as follows:

```
import argparse
import sys
def main(number, other_number, output):
    result = number / other_number
    print(f'The result is {result}', file=output)
if __name__ == '__main__':
    parser = argparse.ArgumentParser()
    parser.add_argument('-n1', type=int, help='A number', default=1)
    parser.add_argument('-n2', type=int, help='Another number',
default=1)
    parser.add_argument('-o', dest='output', type=argparse.FileType('w'),
                        help='output file', default=sys.stdout)
    args = parser.parse_args()
    main(args.n1, args.n2, args.output)
```

2. Execute it a couple of times to see that it divides two numbers:

```
$ uv run task_with_error_handling_step1.py -n1 3 -n2 2
The result is 1.5
$ uv run task_with_error_handling_step1.py -n1 25 -n2 5
The result is 5.0
```

3. Check that dividing by 0 produces an error, and that the error is not logged on the result file:

```
$ uv run task_with_error_handling_step1.py -n1 5 -n2 1 -o result.txt
$ cat result.txt
The result is 5.0
$ uv run task_with_error_handling_step1.py -n1 5 -n2 0 -o result.txt
Traceback (most recent call last):
```

```
  File "task_with_error_handling_step1.py", line 20, in <module>
  main(args.n1, args.n2, args.output)
  File "task_with_error_handling_step1.py", line 6, in main
    result = number / other_number
             ~~~~~~~^~~~~~~~~~~~~
ZeroDivisionError: division by zero
$ cat result.txt
```

4. Create the `task_with_error_handling_step4.py` file:

```
import argparse
import sys
import logging
LOG_FORMAT = '%(asctime)s %(name)s %(levelname)s %(message)s'
LOG_LEVEL = logging.DEBUG
def main(number, other_number, output):
    logging.info(f'Dividing {number} between {other_number}')
    result = number / other_number
    print(f'The result is {result}', file=output)
if __name__ == '__main__':
    parser = argparse.ArgumentParser()
    parser.add_argument('-n1', type=int, help='A number', default=1)
    parser.add_argument('-n2', type=int, help='Another number', default=1)
    parser.add_argument('-o', dest='output', type=argparse.FileType('w'),
                        help='output file', default=sys.stdout)
    parser.add_argument('-l', dest='log', type=str, help='log file',
                        default=None)
    args = parser.parse_args()
    if args.log:
        logging.basicConfig(format=LOG_FORMAT, filename=args.log,
                            level=LOG_LEVEL)
    else:
        logging.basicConfig(format=LOG_FORMAT, level=LOG_LEVEL)
    try:
        main(args.n1, args.n2, args.output)
    except Exception as exc:
```

```
        logging.exception(f"Error running task: {exc}")
        exit(1)
```

5. Run it to check that it displays the proper `INFO` and `ERROR` logs, and that it stores them in the log file:

```
$ uv run task_with_error_handling_step4.py -n1 5 -n2 0
2025-12-01 18:07:30,946 root INFO Dividing 5 between 0
2025-12-01 18:07:30,946 root ERROR Error running task
Traceback (most recent call last):
  File "task_with_error_handling_step4.py", line 31, in <module>
    main(args.n1, args.n2, args.output)
  File "task_with_error_handling_step4.py", line 10, in main
    result = number / other_number
             ~~~~~~~^~~~~~~~~~~~~~
ZeroDivisionError: division by zero
$ uv run task_with_error_handling_step4.py -n1 5 -n2 0 -l error.log
$ cat error.log
2025-12-01 18:08:40,292 root INFO Dividing 5 between 0
2025-12-01 18:08:40,292 root ERROR Error running task
Traceback (most recent call last):
  File "task_with_error_handling_step4.py", line 33, in <module>
    main(args.n1, args.n2, args.output)
  File "task_with_error_handling_step4.py", line 11, in main
    result = number / other_number
             ~~~~~~~^~~~~~~~~~~~~~
ZeroDivisionError: division by zero
```

## How it works...

To properly capture any unexpected exceptions, the `main` function should be wrapped in a `try`–`except` block, as implemented in *step 4* of the *How to do it...* section. Compare this to how *step 1* does not wrap the code:

```
try:
    main(...)
except Exception as exc:
    # Something went wrong
    logging.exception(f"Error running task: {exc}")
    exit(1)
```

Note that capturing information about the specific exception that produced the problem is important for getting information on what went wrong.

This kind of exception capture, using any `Exception`, is nicknamed 'Pokémon Exception' because it's *gonna catch 'em all.* It will capture any unexpected error. This capture should only be used at the highest level of code, as a safeguard against something totally unexpected, since capturing everything can hide other kinds of error that can be tied to more specific parts of the code. For example, an exception with a `ZeroDivisionError` can be captured specifically and dealt with specific handling.

As a bare minimum, any unexpected exception should be logged in detail to allow for further analysis.

The extra step, to exit with status 1 by using the `exit(1)` call, stops the program altogether and informs the operating system that something went wrong with our script.

The `logging` module allows us to log. Note the basic configuration, which includes an optional file to store the logs, the format, and the level of the logs to display.

The available levels for logs are – from less critical to more critical – `DEBUG`, `INFO`, `WARNING`, `ERROR`, and `CRITICAL`. The logging level sets the minimum severity required to log the message. For example, an `INFO` log won't be stored if the severity is set to `WARNING`.

> **Tip**
>
> The minimum severity level can be configured dynamically, producing cases where a higher number of lower-level logs are created or avoided. This is useful to adjust the number of logs that are produced in regular operation or when you are trying to track down a problem. Dealing with a high number of logs can be tricky!

Creating logs is easy: call the `logging.<logging level>` method (where the logging level is `debug`, `info`, and so on). For example:

```
>>> import logging
>>> logging.basicConfig(level=logging.INFO)
>>> logging.warning('a warning message')
WARNING:root:a warning message
>>> logging.info('an info message')
INFO:root:an info message
>>> logging.debug('a debug message')
>>>
```

Note how logs with a severity lower than `INFO` are not displayed. Use the level definition to tweak how much information to display. For example, `DEBUG` logs may be displayed only while developing the task to deal with low-level details. But when running the task in normal operation they should be avoided, as they produce too much noise. Notice that `task_with_error_handling_step4.py` specifies the logging level to be `DEBUG`, by default.

Good definition of log levels is key to displaying relevant information while reducing noise. It is not always easy to set up, but especially if more than one person is involved, try to agree on exactly what `WARNING` versus `ERROR` means in order to avoid misinterpretations.

`logging.exception()` is a special case that will create an `ERROR` log, but it will also include information about the exception, such as the **stack trace**.

Remember to check logs to discover errors. If the log file is different from the results file, it is useful to add a reminder for the user, like this:

```
try:
    main(args.n1, args.n2, args.output)
except Exception as exc:
    logging.exception(f'Unexpected error {exc}')
    print('There has been an error. Check the logs', file=args.output)
```

## There's more...

The Python `logging` module has many capabilities, including the following:

- It provides many options to format the log, for example, automatically including the file and line number of the log that was produced.
- It defines different `logger` objects, each with its own configuration, such as logging level and format. This allows us to publish logs to different systems in different ways, though a single logger object is normally used to keep things simple.
- It can send logs to multiple places, such as to both the standard output and file, or even to a remote logger.
- It automatically 'rotates' logs, creating new log files after a certain time or size. This is handy for keeping logs organized by day or week. It also allows for the compression or removal of old logs. Logs take up space when they accumulate.
- It reads standard logging configurations from files.

Instead of creating complex rules on what to log, try to log extensively using the proper level on each individual log, and then filter by level.

Note

When using GenAI tools, you can request log creation, but be sure to review them, as it tends to create many logs. Finding the proper balance in logs, both in number and amount of detail, is important, and it is worth experimenting with different options.

Too much information can lead to noise. You can always delete a log you (or GenAI) created, if you think it was adding relevant information at one point but it's no longer doing so.

For comprehensive details, refer to the Python logging module documentation at`https://docs.python.org/3/library/logging.html`, or the tutorial at`https://docs.python.org/3/howto/logging.html`.

## See also

- The *Adding command-line options* recipe in *Chapter 1, Let's Begin Our Automation Journey*, to describe the basic elements of the command-line options.
- The *Preparing a task* recipe, earlier in this chapter, to learn about the strategy to follow when designing an automated task.

# Sending email notifications

Email is still an inescapable tool for everyday use. It's arguably the best place to send a notification if an automated task has detected something. On the other hand, email inboxes are already too full of spam messages, so be careful.

Tip

Spam filters are a reality. Be careful about who emails are sent to, and about the number of emails sent. An email server or address can be labeled as a spam source, and all emails may be quietly dropped by the internet.

This is common in addresses from Internet providers, meaning that setting up your own mail server without special consideration is futile, as all their emails will be immediately dropped.

This recipe shows you how to send a single email using an existing email account. This approach is viable for sending a few emails to a couple of people (e.g. yourself), as a result of an automated task, but no more than that. Refer to *Chapter 9, Dealing with Communication*

*Channels*, for more ideas on sending emails, including groups and other communication channels like chats or messages.

## Getting ready

For this recipe we require a valid email account set up, which includes the following:

- A valid email server using SMTP (Simple Mail Transfer Protocol). SMTP is the (old, but still valid) standard for email communication
- A port to connect to
- An email address
- A password

These four elements should be enough to be able to send an email.

> **Note**
>
> Some email services, for example Gmail, will encourage you to set up 2FA (two-factor authentication), meaning that a password is not enough to send an email. Typically they'll allow you to create a specific password for apps to use, bypassing the 2FA request. If you are logged in, accessing this page `https://myaccount.google.com/apppasswords` will allow you to create access with a specific password. Please note that this password method is less secure than the usual access, so use it with extra care.
>
> Check your email provider's information for options.

The email service you use should indicate what the SMTP server is and what port to use in their documentation. This information can be retrieved from email clients using SMTP as well, as they use the same parameters. Check your provider documentation. In the following example, we will use a Gmail account.

## How to do it...

1. Create the `email_task.py` file, as follows:

```
import argparse
import configparser
import smtplib
from email.message import EmailMessage
def main(to_email, server, port, from_email, password):
    print(f'With love, from {from_email} to {to_email}')
    # Create the message
    subject = 'With love, from ME to YOU'
```

```
        text = '''This is an example test'''
        msg = EmailMessage()
        msg.set_content(text)
        msg['Subject'] = subject
        msg['From'] = from_email
        msg['To'] = to_email
        # Open communication and send
        with smtplib.SMTP_SSL(server, port) as smtp:
            smtp.login(from_email, password)
            smtp.send_message(msg)
    if __name__ == '__main__':
        parser = argparse.ArgumentParser()
        parser.add_argument('email', type=str, help='destination email')
        parser.add_argument('-c', dest='config', type=argparse.FileType('r'),
                            help='config file', default=None)
        args = parser.parse_args()
        if not args.config:
            print('Error, a config file is required')
            parser.print_help()
            exit(1)
        config = configparser.ConfigParser()
        config.read_file(args.config)
        main(args.email,
             server=config['DEFAULT']['server'],
             port=config['DEFAULT']['port'],
             from_email=config['DEFAULT']['email'],
             password=config['DEFAULT']['password'])
```

2. Create a configuration file called `email_conf.ini` with the specifics of your email account. For example, for a Gmail account, fill in the following template. (The template is available in GitHub at `https://github.com/PacktPublishing/Python-Automation-Cookbook-Third-Edition/blob/master/ch02/email_conf.ini` but be sure to fill it in with your data.)

```
[DEFAULT]
email = EMAIL@gmail.com
server = smtp.gmail.com
port = 465
password = PASSWORD
```

3. Ensure that the file cannot be read or written to by other users of the system, by setting the file permissions to allow only our user. '600' permissions mean read and write access for the file owner, and no access to anyone else:

```
$ chmod 600 email_conf.ini
```

4. Run the script to send a test email:

```
$ uv run email_task.py -c email_conf.ini destination_email@server.com
```

5. Check the inbox of the destination email account; an email should be received with the subject 'With love, from ME to YOU'.

## How it works...

There are two key steps in the preceding scripts: the generation of the message and the sending.

The message needs to contain `To` and `From` email addresses, as well as the `Subject`. If the content is pure text, as in this case, calling `.set_content()` is enough. The whole message can then be sent.

It is technically possible to send an email that is tagged as coming from a different email address than the one you used to send it. This is discouraged, though, as it can be considered by your email provider as an attempt to impersonate a different email. You can use the `reply-to` header to allow answering to a different account.

Sending the email requires you to connect to the specified server and start an SMTP connection.

The steps are quite straightforward – configure the server, log in to it, send the prepared message, and quit. (If you need to send more than one message, you can log in, send multiple emails, and then quit, instead of connecting each time.)

## There's more...

If the objective is a bigger operation, such as a marketing campaign, or even production emails (e.g. to confirm a user's email address), please refer to *Chapter 9, Dealing with Communication Channels*.

The email message content used in this recipe is very simple, but emails can be much more complicated than that.

The `To` field can contain multiple recipients. Separate them with commas, like this:

```
message['To'] = ','.join(recipients)
```

Emails can be defined in HTML, with plain text as an alternative, and may have attachments. The basic operation is to set up a `MIMEMultipart` and then attach each of the MIME parts that compose the email:

```
from email.mime.multipart import MIMEMultipart
from email.mime.text import MIMEText
from email.mime.image import MIMEImage
message = MIMEMultipart()
part1 = MIMEText('some text', 'plain')
message.attach(part1)
with open('path/image', 'rb') as image:
    part2 = MIMEImage(image.read())
message.attach(part2)
```

> **Tip**
>
> GenAI can help you craft a particular email the right way. Multipart emails can be difficult and laborious to create, requiring trial and error, but GenAI can help speed the process up.

The most common SMTP connection is `SMTP_SSL`, which is more secure than plain SMTP, as all communication with the server is encrypted and login and password are always required. However, plain, unauthenticated SMTP exists – check your email provider's documentation.

Remember that this recipe is aimed at simple notifications. Emails can grow quite complex if information is attached. If your objective is an email for customers or any general group, try to use the ideas in *Chapter 9, Dealing with Communication Channels.*

Email providers can also expose specific APIs for accessing their services. For example, there's a Google Gmail-specific API. Some features might be accessible only through their own APIs, rather than via a standard mechanism like SMTP. Documentation on using the Gmail API can be found here `https://developers.google.com/workspace/gmail/api/quickstart/python`.

> **Tip**
>
> Migrating the script to use specific APIs from your provider can be an excellent use of GenAI, where it can help you with the authentication specified by the provider.

## See also

- The *Adding command-line options* recipe in *Chapter 1, Let's Begin Our Automation Journey*, to understand the basic concepts of command-line options.
- The *Preparing a task* recipe, earlier in this chapter, to learn about the strategy to follow when designing an automated task.

# 3

# Building Your First Web Scraping Application

The internet, and the **World Wide Web** (**WWW**), is probably the most prominent source of information today. Most of that information is retrievable through the HTTP protocol. HTTP was invented originally to share pages of hypertext (hence the name **HyperText Transfer Protocol**), which started the WWW.

The HTTP protocol is used behind the scenes every time we manually request a web page, in a process familiar to almost everyone. But we can also use the HTTP protocol to trigger requests programmatically to retrieve and process information. Python has an HTTP client included in its standard library, but the fantastic `requests` module makes obtaining web pages very easy. When that's not enough, we can use Playwright to automate a full browser. In this chapter, we will see how.

In this chapter we're going to cover the following main recipes:

- Downloading web pages
- Parsing HTML
- Crawling the web
- Subscribing to feeds
- Accessing web APIs
- Interacting with forms
- Using Playwright for advanced interaction
- Accessing password-protected pages with basic auth

- Accessing websites with browser cookies
- Speeding up web scraping

# Technical requirements

You will find the code presented in this chapter in the book's GitHub repository at `https://github.com/PacktPublishing/Python-Automation-Cookbook-Third-Edition/tree/main/ch03`.

# Downloading web pages

The basic ability to download a web page involves making an HTTP `GET` request against a URL. This is the basic operation of any web browser.

Let's quickly recap the different parts of this operation, as it has three distinct elements:

1. Using the HTTP protocol. This deals with the way the request is structured.
2. Using the `GET` method, which is the most common HTTP method. We'll see more in the *Accessing web APIs* recipe.
3. A full URL describing the address of the page, including the server (for example: `mypage.com`) and the path (for example: `/page`).

The request will be routed to the server by the Internet and processed by the server, and then a response will be sent back. This response contains a numerical **status code**, typically 200 if everything has gone fine, and a *body* containing the result, which will normally be text with an HTML page.

> Note
>
> The Internet is quite complex and this is a simplification of what happens, but it's useful for our purposes.

Most of this is handled automatically by the HTTP client used to perform the request. We'll see in this recipe how to make a simple request to obtain a web page.

> Note
>
> HTTP requests and responses can also contain *headers*. A header contains important information about the request itself, such as the total size of the request, the format of the content, the date of the request, and what browser or server is used.

## Getting ready

Using the `requests` module, getting web pages is super-simple. Install the module:

```
$ echo " requests==2.32.5" >> requirements.txt
$ uv venv
…
$ uv pip install -r requirements.txt
…
```

We'll download the page `https://www.cs.vu.nl/~ast/` because it is a straightforward HTML page that is easy to read in text mode.

> **Note**
>
> Note that the URL starts with `https://`, the 's' indicating that we are using the secure version of HTTP protocol. We will discuss this protocol later.

## How to do it...

1. Import the `requests` module:

```
>>> import requests
```

2. Make a request to the server using the following URL, which will take a second or two:

```
>>> url = 'https://www.cs.vu.nl/~ast/'
>>> response = requests.get(url)
```

3. Check the returned object status code:

```
>>> response.status_code
200
```

4. Check the content of the result:

```
>>> response.text
'<!DOCTYPE HTML PUBLIC "-//W3C//DTD HTML 4.01 Transitional//
EN">\n<html>\n<head>\n
...
FULL BODY
```

```
...
</html>\n'
```

5. Check the ongoing and returned headers:

```
>>> response.request.headers
{'User-Agent': 'python-requests/2.32.5', 'Accept-Encoding': 'gzip,
deflate', 'Accept': '*/*', 'Connection': 'keep-alive'}
>>> response.headers
{'Server': 'nginx', 'Date': 'Thu, 04 Dec 2025 18:39:43 GMT', 'Content-
Type': 'text/html; charset=UTF-8', 'Content-Length': '15600', 'Connection':
'keep-alive', 'Last-Modified': 'Tue, 09 Sep 2025 15:30:29 GMT', 'ETag':
'"3cf0-63e5ffbe570d2"', 'Accept-Ranges': 'bytes'}
```

## How it works...

The operation of `requests` is very simple: perform the request, using the `GET` method in this case, over the URL. This returns a result object that can be analyzed. The main elements are the `.status_code` and the body content, which can be presented as `.text`.

The full request can be inspected in the `.request` attribute:

```
>>> response.request
<PreparedRequest [GET]>
>>> response.request.url
'https://www.cs.vu.nl/~ast/'
```

The full requests module documentation can be found here: `https://requests.readthedocs.io/en/master/`.

Over the course of the chapter, we'll be showing more features of the `requests` library.

## There's more...

All the HTTP status codes are listed and explained at this web page: `https://developer.mozilla.org/en-US/docs/Web/HTTP/Reference/Status`. In Python they are also described internally in the `http.HTTPStatus` enum using convenient constant names, such as `OK`, `NOT_FOUND`, or `FORBIDDEN`.

Note

The most famous error status code is arguably 404, which is returned when the resource described by a URL is not found. Try it out by doing `requests.get("https://www.cs.vu.nl/~ast/invalid")`.

The general structure of the status codes is:

- **1XX** – Information on protocol specifics.
- **2XX** – Success.
- **3XX** – Redirection. For example: The URL is no longer valid and is available somewhere else. The new URL should be included in the response.
- **4XX** – Client error. There's some error in the information sent to the server (like a problem in the format of the request) or in the client (for example, authentication is required in order to access the requested URL).
- **5XX** – Server error. There's an error on the server side; for example, the server might be unavailable or there might be a bug processing the request.

These days, a request should use the **HTTPS** (**secure HTTP**) protocol. It is the same as HTTP but ensures that the contents of the request and response are encrypted and remain private between the client and the server. `requests` handles this protocol transparently.

Tip

Any website that handles any private information should use HTTPS to ensure that the information does not leak out, HTTP being vulnerable to eavesdropping. HTTPS is now the de-facto standard when communicating over the WWW, and use of plain HTTP is discouraged.

## See also

- The *Installing third-party packages* recipe in *Chapter 1, Let's Begin Our Automation Journey*, to learn the basics of installing external modules.
- The next recipe in this chapter, *Parsing HTML*, to find out how to treat the information returned from the server.

# Parsing HTML

While downloading raw text or a binary file is always available, the main language of the web is HTML.

HTML is a structured language, defining different parts of a document such as headings and paragraphs. HTML is also hierarchical, defining sub-elements. The ability to parse raw text into a structured document basically gives us the ability to extract information automatically from a web page. For example, some text might be relevant to us if it's enclosed by certain HTML element tags, such as a class `div` or after a heading `h3` tag.

> **Tip**
>
> This recipe will help you when you need to systematize accessing web pages, but if it's something that you need to do once, is very likely that GenAI can help you! GenAI tools capable of accessing the Internet are great at scraping elements of web pages, and searching and extracting information. But they won't be consistent, which is something that this recipe will allow you to be. For example, checking over and over to understand whether the data in a particular web page has changed.

## Getting ready

We'll use the excellent **Beautiful Soup** module to parse HTML text into a memory object that can be analyzed. We need to use the latest version of the `beautifulsoup4` package to be compatible with Python 3. Add the package to your `requirements.txt` and install the dependencies in the virtual environment:

```
$ echo "beautifulsoup4==4.14.3" >> requirements.txt
$ uv pip install -r requirements.txt
```

## How to do it...

1. Import BeautifulSoup and `requests`:

   ```
   >>> import requests
   >>> from bs4 import BeautifulSoup
   ```

2. Set up the URL of the page to download and retrieve it:

```
>>> URL = 'https://www.cs.vu.nl/~ast/'
>>> response = requests.get(URL)
>>> response
<Response [200]>
```

3. Parse the downloaded page:

```
>>> page = BeautifulSoup(response.text, 'html.parser')
```

4. Obtain the title of the page. See that it is the same as what's displayed in the browser:

```
>>> page.title
<title>Andrew S Tanenbaum, Professor at the Vrije Universiteit</title>
>>> page.title.string
'Andrew S Tanenbaum, Professor at the Vrije Universiteit'
```

> **Note**
>
> Professor Tanenbaum is a well-known author of networking and operating system books from the 1970s onwards, notable for the creation of the MINIX operating system and discussions with Linus Torvalds at the early days of Linux.

5. Find all the h3 elements in the page, to determine the existing sections:

```
>>> page.find_all('h3')
[<h3>Professor of Computer Science</h3>, <h3><img align="middle" alt=""
src="home/images/envelope.gif"/>
       Address:</h3>, <h3> PERSONAL INFORMATION</h3>, <h3> BOOKS</h3>,
<h3>  PAPERS</h3>, <h3> SOFTWARE</h3>, <h3> TEACHING</h3>, <h3> HONORS</
h3>, <h3> PH.D. THESES SUPERVISED:</h3>, <h3> COLLEAGUES</h3>, <h3>KEN
BROWN INCIDENT</h3>, <h3>RFID VIRUS STORY</h3>, <h3> PHOTOS</h3>, <h3>
```

```
STEGANOGRAPHY DEMO</h3>, <h3> MESSAGE TO DUTCH HIGH SCHOOL (VWO) STUDENTS</
h3>]
```

6. Extract the whole text on the section for 'BOOKS'. Stop when you reach the next `<h3>` tag:

```
>>> books_section = [tag for tag in page.find_all('h3') if 'BOOKS' in
tag.text][0]
>>> section = []
>>> for element in books_section.next_elements:
...     if element.name == 'h3':
...         break
...     section.append(element.string or '')
...
>>> result = ''.join(section)
>>> result
' BOOKS\n\n Photos of the covers of my booksPhotos of the covers of my
books \nTranslations of my booksTranslations of my books \n  Structured
Computer Organization, 6th ed. Structured Computer Organization, 6th ed. \n
Computer Networks, 6th ed.Computer Networks, 6th ed. \n Operating Systems
Design and Implementation, 3rd ed.Operating Systems Design and
Implementation, 3rd ed. \n Modern Operating Systems, 5th ed.Modern
Operating Systems, 5th ed.\n Distributed Systems, 3rd ed.Distributed
Systems, 3rd ed. \nHow to Prepare Your InputHow to Prepare Your InputHow to
Prepare Your Input\n\n  '
```

Notice that all the raw text is displayed, including the `\n` newline characters.

## How it works...

The first step is to download the page. Then, the raw text can be parsed, as in *step 3*. The resulting page object contains the parsed information.

> **Note**
>
> The `html.parser` parser is the default one, but there are some operations where it struggles. For example, for big pages it can be slow, and it can have issues rendering highly dynamic web pages. For such tasks you can use other parsers, such as `lxml`, which is much faster, or `html5lib`, which operates closer to how a browser operates. They are external modules that will need to be added to the `requirements.txt` file.

`BeautifulSoup` allows us to search for specific HTML elements. It can search for the first occurrence of an HTML element with `.find()` or return a list with `.find_all()`. In *step 5* it searched for all `<h3>` tags and kept only the one that contained the title 'BOOKS'.

> **Tip**
>
> While attributes are not included in our example page, it is possible to search for attributes, such as `id`, in HTML tags by adding the parameter `attrs` in the find call. For example, :`.find(attrs={'id': 'my_id'})`
>
> You can get help from your preferred GenAI tool to determine the best way to capture a specific element in the page.

After that, in *Section 5*, it kept iterating on `.next_elements` until it found the next `h3` tag, which marks the end of the section.

In *Section 6*, the text of each element is extracted and finally composed into a single text. Note the line `section.append(element.string or '')`, where the `or` avoids storing `None`, returned when an `element` has no text. Instead, it stores an empty string, which can be joined correctly with the rest of strings.

> **Note**
>
> HTML is highly versatile and can be used to define an essentially limitless variety of document structures. The case presented in this recipe is common, but there are many ways of structuring a web page, like including grouping related sections inside a big `<div>` container element, while at the less structured end of the spectrum there may be raw unstructured text. Some experimentation and perhaps consultation with GenAI may be required to tweak the process to extract the juicy bits on a web page. Don't be afraid to try!

## There's more...

Regexes can be used as input in the `.find()` and `.find_all()` methods. For example, this search uses the `h2` and `h3` tags:

```
>>> page.find_all(re.compile('^h(2|3)'))
[<h2>Andrew S. Tanenbaum's Home Page </h2>, <h3>Professor of Computer Science</
h3>, <h3><img align="middle" alt="" src="home/images/envelope.gif"/>
       Address:</h3>, <h3> PERSONAL INFORMATION</h3>, <h3> BOOKS</h3>, <h3>
PAPERS</h3>, <h3> SOFTWARE</h3>, <h3> TEACHING</h3>, <h3> HONORS</h3>, <h3> PH.D.
THESES SUPERVISED:</h3>, <h3> COLLEAGUES</h3>, <h3>KEN BROWN INCIDENT</h3>,
<h3>RFID VIRUS STORY</h3>, <h3> PHOTOS</h3>, <h3> STEGANOGRAPHY DEMO</h3>, <h3>
MESSAGE TO DUTCH HIGH SCHOOL (VWO) STUDENTS</h3>]
```

Another useful `.find()` trick is to specify the CSS class with the `class_` parameter. This will be shown later in the book.

The full Beautiful Soup documentation can be found here: `https://www.crummy.com/software/BeautifulSoup/bs4/doc/`.

## See also

- The *Installing third-party packages* recipe in *Chapter 1, Let's Begin Our Automation Journey*, to learn about installing external modules.
- The *Downloading web pages* recipe, earlier in this chapter, to learn the basics of requesting web pages.

# Crawling the web

Given the nature of hyperlink pages, starting from a known place and following links to other pages is a very important tool in your arsenal when scraping the web.

To do so, we crawl a page looking for a short phrase, and we print any paragraph that contains it. We will search only in pages that belong to a single site, for example: only URLs starting with `www.somesite.com`. We won't follow links to external sites.

> **Tip**
>
> This recipe talks about consistent crawling of a site, which can be relevant when we are interested, for example, to know whether something on a page has changed by crawling it once a day. For example, we may be interested in what offers are available or in the evolution of prices. Crawling can also be used to download full information, for example, collecting all the reviews for a movie on a movie review site.
>
> Right now GenAI can be very useful for crawling and condensing parts of the web to collect information in a less strict, but faster and more flexible way. For example, instead of our having to download all the reviews of a movie and then process the data, GenAI can provide a *summary* of the reception of a movie. Depending on your goals, this may or may not be enough.

## Getting ready

This recipe builds on the concepts introduced so far, and will involve downloading and parsing pages to search for links and then continue downloading.

> **Tip**
>
> When crawling the web, remember to set limits when downloading. It's very easy to crawl over too many pages. As any Wikipedia reader can confirm, the internet is potentially limitless.

We'll use a prepared example, available in the GitHub repo at `https://github.com/PacktPublishing/Python-Automation-Cookbook-Third-Edition/tree/main/ch03/test_site`. Download the whole site and run the included script:

```
$ uv run simple_delay_server.py
```

This serves the site at the URL http://localhost:8000. You can find this in a browser. It's a simple blog with three entries.

Most of it is uninteresting, but I've added a couple of paragraphs that contain the keyword `python`:

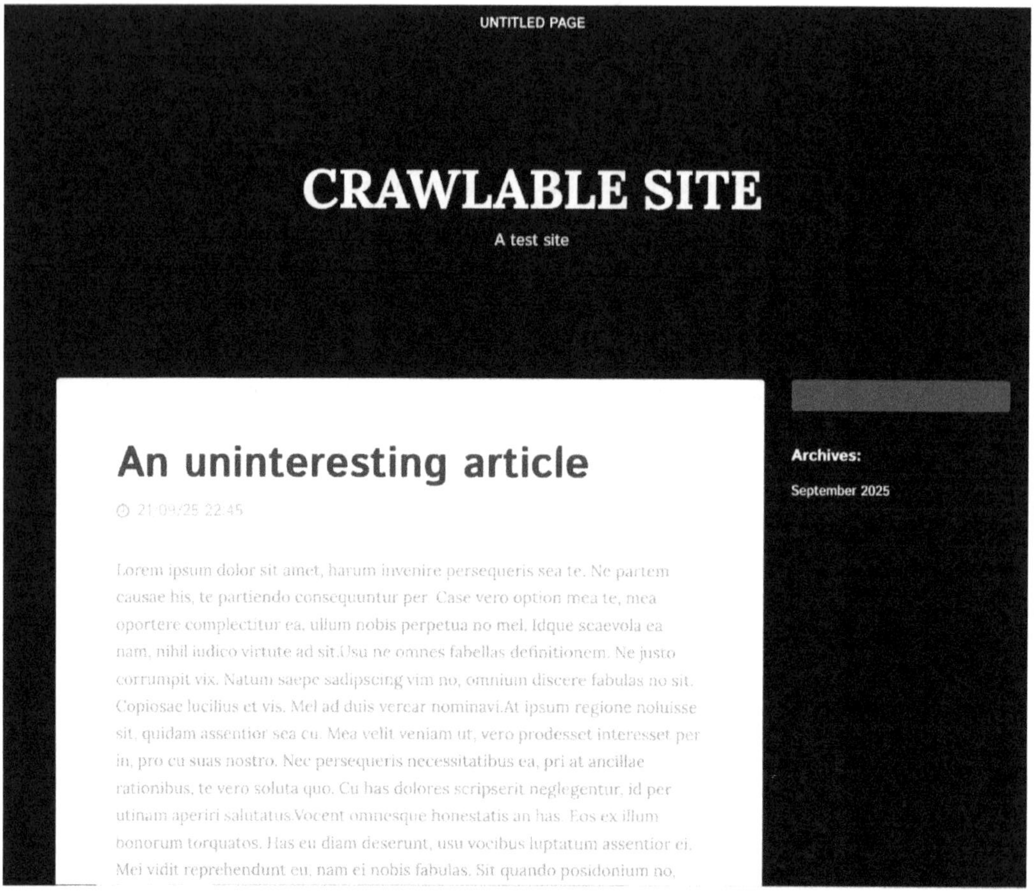


*Figure 3.1: A screenshot of the blog*

## How to do it...

1. The full script, `crawling_web_step1.py`, is available on GitHub at the following link: `https://github.com/PacktPublishing/Python-Automation-Cookbook-Third-Edition/blob/main/ch03/crawling_web_step1.py`. The most relevant bits are displayed here:

```
...
def process_link(source_link, text):
    logging.info(f'Extracting links from {source_link}')
    parsed_source = urlparse(source_link)
    result = requests.get(source_link)
    # Error handling. See GitHub for details
```

```
    ...
    page = BeautifulSoup(result.text, 'html.parser')
    search_text(source_link, page, text)
    return get_links(parsed_source, page)
def get_links(parsed_source, page):
    '''Retrieve the links on the page'''
    links = []
    for element in page.find_all('a'):
        link = element.get('href')
        # Validate is a valid link. See GitHub for details
        ...
        links.append(link)
    return links
```

2. Search for references to 'python' to return a list of the URLs that contain it and the paragraph in question. Notice there are a couple of errors because of broken links:

```
$ uv run crawling_web_step1.py http://localhost:8000/ -p python
Link http://localhost:8000/: --> A smaller article , that contains a
reference to Python
WARNING:root:Ignoring external link https://google.com
Link http://localhost:8000/files/5eabef23f63024c20389c34b94dee593-1.html:
--> A smaller article , that contains a reference to Python
Link http://localhost:8000/files/33714fc865e02aeda2dabb9a42a787b2-0.html:
--> This is the actual bit with a python reference that we are interested
in.
Link http://localhost:8000/files/archive-september-2025.html: --> A smaller
article , that contains a reference to Python
Link http://localhost:8000/index.html: --> A smaller article , that
contains a reference to Python
```

3. Another good search term is 'crocodile'. Try it out:

```
$ uv run crawling_web_step1.py http://localhost:8000/ -p crocodile
```

## How it works...

Let's see each of the components of the script:

1. A loop that goes through all the found links, in the `main` function:

```
def main(base_url, to_search):
    checked_links = set()
    to_check = [base_url]
    max_checks = 10
    while to_check and max_checks:
        link = to_check.pop(0)
        links = process_link(link, text=to_search)
        checked_links.add(link)
        for link in links:
            if link not in checked_links:
                checked_links.add(link)
                to_check.append(link)
        max_checks -= 1
```

   Note that there's a retrieval limit of 10 pages, and the code here is checking that any new link to be added has not been added already.

   > **Note**
   >
   > Note that these two elements act as limits for the script. We won't download the same link twice and we'll stop at some point.

2. Downloading and parsing the link, in the `process_link` function:

```
def process_link(source_link, text):
    logging.info(f'Extracting links from {source_link}')
    parsed_source = urlparse(source_link)
    result = requests.get(source_link)
    if result.status_code != http.client.OK:
        logging.error(f'Error retrieving {source_link}: {result}')
        return []
    if 'html' not in result.headers['Content-type']:
        logging.info(f'Link {source_link} is not an HTML page')
        return []
    page = BeautifulSoup(result.text, 'html.parser')
```

```
        search_text(source_link, page, text)
        return get_links(parsed_source, page)
```

The code here downloads the file and checks that the status is correct, to skip errors such as broken links. This code also checks that the type (as described in `Content-Type`) is an HTML page, to skip PDFs and other formats. Finally it parses the raw HTML into a `BeautifulSoup` object.

The code also parses the source link using `urlparse` so that later, in *step 4*, it can skip all the references to external sources. `urlparse` divides a URL into its constituent elements:

```
>>> from urllib.parse import urlparse
>>> urlparse('http://localhost:8000/files/
b93bec5d9681df87e6e8d5703ed7cd81-2.html')
ParseResult(scheme='http', netloc='localhost:8000', path='/files/
b93bec5d9681df87e6e8d5703ed7cd81-2.html', params='', query='', fragment='')
```

The code searches for the text we wish to find, in the `search_text` function:

```
def search_text(source_link, page, text):
    '''Search for an element with the searched text and print it'''
    for element in page.find_all(string=re.compile(text, flags=re.IGNORECASE)):
        print(f'Link {source_link}: --> {element}')
```

This searches the parsed object for the specified text. Note that the search is performed as a regex, and only in the text of the page. It prints the resulting matches, including `source_link`, and references the URL where the match was found:

```
for element in page.find_all(string=re.compile(text)):
    print(f'Link {source_link}: --> {element}')
```

The `get_links` function retrieves all links on a page:

```
def get_links(parsed_source, page):
    '''Retrieve the links on the page'''
    links = []
    for element in page.find_all('a'):
        link = element.get('href')
        if not link:
            continue
```

```
            # Avoid internal, same page links
            if link.startswith('#'):
                continue
            if link.startswith('mailto:'):
                # Ignore other links like mailto
                # More cases like ftp or similar may be included here
                continue
            # Always accept local links
            if not link.startswith('http'):
                netloc = parsed_source.netloc
                scheme = parsed_source.scheme
                path = urljoin(parsed_source.path, link)
                link = f'{scheme}://{netloc}{path}'
            # Only parse links in the same domain
            if parsed_source.netloc not in link:
                logging.warning(f'Ignoring external link {link}')
                continue
            links.append(link)
        return links
```

This searches in the parsed page for all `<a>` tags and retrieves the `href` attributes, but focuses on tags that have such an `href` attribute where the value is a fully qualified URL (starting with `http`) or a local link. This removes links that are not URLs, such as '#' links that are internal to the page.

> **Tip**
>
> Keep in mind that some references could have other effects, for example, the `mailto:` scheme. There is a check to avoid `mailto:` schemes, but there could be cases like `ftp` or `irc`, though they are very rare to see in practice. Even `mailto:` is less and less common as time goes by.

An extra check is done to check that the links have the same source as the original link; only then are they registered as valid links. The `netloc` attribute detects whether a link comes from the same URL domain as the parsed URL generated in *step 2*.

Note

We won't follow links that point to addresses in different domains from the source document (for example, a reference link to `http://www.google.com`), but a `WARNING` displaying these links will be produced.

Finally, the links are returned, where they'll be added to the loop described in *step 1*.

## There's more...

Further filters could be enforced; for example, all links that end in `.pdf` could be discarded, as they likely refer to PDF files:

```
# In get_links
if link.endswith('pdf'):
  continue
```

The use of `Content-Type` can also be determined, so as to parse the returned object in different ways. Keep in mind that `Content-Type` won't be available without making the request, which means the code cannot skip links without requesting them first. A PDF result (`Content-Type: application/pdf`) won't have a valid `response.text` object to be parsed, but a PDF result can be parsed in other ways. The same goes for other types, such as CSV files (`Content-Type: text/csv`), or a ZIP file that may need to be decompressed (`Content-Type: application/zip`). We'll see how to deal with those later.

## See also

- The *Downloading web pages* recipe, earlier in this chapter, to learn the basics of requesting web pages.
- The previous recipe, *Parsing HTML*, to learn how to parse elements in HTML.

# Subscribing to feeds

**RSS** (**Really Simple Syndication**) is probably the biggest secret of the internet. Its time in the spotlight seemed to be during the early 2000s, and it enables easy subscription to websites. It is present in lots of websites and is incredibly useful.

At its core, RSS is a way of presenting a succession of ordered references (typically articles, but also other elements such as podcast episodes or YouTube publications) and when they were published. This makes for a very natural way of learning what articles are new since the last check, as well as presenting some structured data about them, such as the title and a summary.

In this recipe, we will present the `feedparser` module and determine how to obtain data from an RSS feed.

> **Note**
>
> RSS is not the only available feed format. There's also a format called Atom, but Atom and RSS are very similar. `feedparser` is also capable of parsing Atom, so both formats can be processed in the same way.

## Getting ready

We need to add the `feedparser` dependency to our `requirements.txt` file and check that we install the module:

```
$ echo "feedparser==6.0.12" >> requirements.txt
$ uv pip install -r requirements.txt
```

We will use `pendulum` as well for this recipe. Be sure that it's included in your `requirements.txt` file.

Feed URLs can be found on almost all pages that deal with publications, including blogs, news, podcasts, and so on. Sometimes they are very easy to find, but sometimes they are a little bit hidden. Search for text like 'feed' or 'RSS'. GenAI can also provide suggestions, for example: "*Find me the RSS link for the web page X*".

Most newspapers and news agencies divide their RSS feeds thematically. For our example, we'll parse main page feed of *The New York Times*, a generalist news publication, http://rss.nytimes.com/services/xml/rss/nyt/HomePage.xml.

> **Note**
>
> Please note that this feed changes quite often, meaning that the linked entries will be different from the examples in this book.

## How to do it...

1. Import the `feedparser` module, as well as `datetime`, `pendulum`, and `requests`:

```
>>> import feedparser
>>> import datetime
>>> import pendulum
>>> import requests
```

2. Parse the feed (it will be downloaded automatically) and check when it was last updated. Feed information, like the title of the feed, can be obtained in the feed attribute:

```
>>> rss = feedparser.parse('http://rss.nytimes.com/services/xml/rss/nyt/
HomePage.xml')
>>> rss.feed.updated
'Sat, 06 Dec 2025 14:37:06 +0000'
```

3. Get the entries that are less than or equal to 6 hours old:

```
>>> time_limit = pendulum.parse(rss.feed.updated, strict=False) -
datetime.timedelta(hours=6)
>>> entries = [entry for entry in rss.entries if
pendulum.parse(entry.published, strict=False) > time_limit]
```

4. Some of the returned entries will be older than 6 hours:

```
>>> len(entries)
14
>>> len(rss.entries)
21
```

5. Retrieve information about the `entries`, such as the title. The full entry URL is available as `link`. Explore the available information in this particular feed, for example, we use `entries[13]`. The information will vary with the information obtained from the feed when you pull from it.

```
>>> entries[13]['title']
'Sweet Season'
>>> entries[13]['link']
```

```
'https://www.nytimes.com/2025/12/06/briefing/sweet-season.html'
>>> entries[13]['summary']
'Rejoice: NYT Cooking's holiday cookie extravaganza has returned.'
```

## How it works...

The parsed feed object contains the information from the entries, as well as general information about the feed itself, such as when it was updated. The feed information can be found in the feed attribute:

```
>>> rss.feed.title
'NYT > Top Stories'
```

Each of the entries works as a dictionary, so the fields are easy to retrieve. They can also be accessed as attributes, but treating them as keys allows us to get all the available fields:

```
>>> entries[13].keys()
dict_keys(['title', 'title_detail', 'links', 'link', 'id', 'guidislink',
'summary', 'summary_detail', 'authors', 'author', 'author_detail', 'published',
'published_parsed', 'tags', 'media_content', 'media_credit', 'credit'])
```

The basic strategy when dealing with feeds is to parse them and go through the entries, performing a quick check on whether they are interesting or not, for example, by checking the *description* or *summary* fields. If the entry seems interesting, it can be fully downloaded through the link field. Then, to avoid rechecking entries, store the latest publication date, and next time check only newer entries.

> **Note**
>
> By default `pendulum` parses only a few common formats. Using the `strict=False` parameter fallback to allow more formats before raising an exception. If you need to specify a particular non-default format, use the `.from_format()` helper. Check the `pendulum` documentation for more info. https://pendulum.eustace.io/docs/#parsing

## There's more...

The full `feedparser` documentation can be found here: `https://pythonhosted.org/feedparser/`.

The information available can differ from feed to feed. In the *New York Times* example, there's a `tags` field with categorization information (topics, subjects, etc), but this is not standard. As a minimum, entries will have a `title`, a `description`, and a `link`.

> **Tip**
>
> RSS feeds are also a great way of curating your own selection of news sources. There are great feed readers for that, like Feedly, Feedbin or Feeder.

Be careful when trying to retrieve information programmatically from new sites and similar sources. The level of web scraping has been increasing in recent years, leading websites to put protections in place to avoid bot activity. For example, if you follow the link in the article we extracted above in *step 6*, you'll get an error 403 code, meaning that bot access is `Forbidden`.

```
>>> response = requests.get(entries[13]['link'])
>>> response.status_code
403
```

Checking the page directly, you can see that it's paywalled and requires a login to access it.

## See also

- The *Installing third-party packages* recipe in *Chapter 1, Let's Begin Our Automation Journey*, to learn the basics of installing external modules.
- The *Downloading web pages* recipe, earlier in this chapter, to learn more about making requests and obtaining remote pages.
- The *Using Playwright for advanced interaction* recipe, later in this chapter, for interactions where a full browser needs to be rendered.

# Accessing web APIs

Web technologies are not only capable of creating interactive UIs for human consumption. Rich interfaces usable by programs also can be created, allowing powerful interactions through HTTP. The most common interface of this kind is through RESTful APIs using JSON. These text-based interfaces are easy to understand and to program, and use common technologies that are **language-agnostic**, meaning they can be accessed in any programming language that has an HTTP client module – including, of course, Python.

Note

Formats other than JSON are also sometimes used, such as XML. But JSON is a very simple and readable format that translates very well into Python dictionaries (and other language equivalents). JSON is by far the most common format for RESTful APIs at the moment. Learn more about JSON here: `https://www.json.org/`.

The strict definition of RESTful would require mentioning a number of specific characteristics, but an informal definition of RESTful is a system that describes resources through HTTP URLs. This means each URL represents a particular resource, such as an article in a newspaper or a property on a real estate site. Resources can then be manipulated through HTTP methods (`GET` to view, `POST` to create, `PUT`/`PATCH` to edit, and `DELETE` to delete).

Note

You can read more about the meaning of RESTful at `https://codewords.recurse.com/issues/five/what-restful-actually-means`.

Using requests is very easy with RESTful interfaces, as they include native JSON support.

## Getting ready

To demonstrate how to operate RESTful APIs we'll use the example site `https://jsonplaceholder.typicode.com/`. It simulates a typical case and features posts, comments, and other common resources. We will use posts and comments. The URLs we'll use will be as follows:

```
# The collection of all posts
/posts
# A single post. X is the ID of the post
/posts/X
# The comments of post X
/posts/X/comments
```

The site returns the correct result for each of them. Pretty handy!

Note

Because it is a test site, data won't be created, but the site will return all the correct responses.

## How to do it...

1. Import requests:

```
>>> import requests
```

2. Get a list of all posts and display the latest post:

```
>>> result = requests.get('https://jsonplaceholder.typicode.com/posts')
>>> result
<Response [200]>
>>> result.json()
# List of 100 posts NOT DISPLAYED HERE
>>> result.json()[-1]
{'userId': 10, 'id': 100, 'title': 'at nam consequatur ea labore ea harum',
'body': 'cupiditate quo est a modi nesciunt soluta\nipsa voluptas error
itaque dicta in\nautem qui minus magnam et distinctio eum\naccusamus
ratione error aut'}
```

3. Create a new post. See the URL of the newly created resource. The call also returns the resource:

```
>>> new_post = {'userId': 10, 'title': 'a title', 'body': 'something
something'}
>>> result = requests.post('https://jsonplaceholder.typicode.com/posts',
              json=new_post)
>>> result
<Response [201]>
>>> result.json()
{'userId': 10, 'title': 'a title', 'body': 'something something', 'id':
101}
>>> result.headers['Location']
'http://jsonplaceholder.typicode.com/posts/101'
```

   Notice that the `POST` request to create the resource returns `201`, which is the proper status for created.

4. Fetch an existing post with `GET`:

```
>>> result = requests.get('https://jsonplaceholder.typicode.com/posts/2')
>>> result
```

```
<Response [200]>
>>> result.json()
{'userId': 1, 'id': 2, 'title': 'qui est esse', 'body': 'est rerum tempore
vitae\nsequi sint nihil reprehenderit dolor beatae ea dolores neque\nfugiat
blanditiis voluptate porro vel nihil molestiae ut reiciendis\nqui aperiam
non debitis possimus qui neque nisi nulla'}
```

5. Use `PATCH` to update partially the values. Check the returned resource:

```
>>> update = {'body': 'new body'}
>>> result = requests.patch('https://jsonplaceholder.typicode.com/posts/2',
json=update)
>>> result
<Response [200]>
>>> result.json()
{'userId': 1, 'id': 2, 'title': 'qui est esse', 'body': 'new body'}
```

## How it works...

Two kinds of resource are typically accessed – single resources (`https://jsonplaceholder.typicode.com/posts/X`) and collections (`https://jsonplaceholder.typicode.com/posts`).

- Collections accept `GET` to retrieve all the members of the collection and `POST` to create a new resource
- Single elements accept `GET` to retrieve the element, `PUT` and `PATCH` to edit, and `DELETE` to remove the element

> **Note**
>
> The difference between `PUT` and `PATCH` is that `PUT` replaces the whole object while `PATCH` can update it partially. For more details, see `https://developer.mozilla.org/en-US/docs/Web/HTTP/Reference/Methods/PATCH` and `https://developer.mozilla.org/en-US/docs/Web/HTTP/Reference/Methods/PUT`, but keep in mind that the `PATCH` behaviour can be different depending of the implementation, making it safer, if the object is retrieved, to replace part and then submit the whole object with a `PUT`.

All the available HTTP methods can be called using `requests`. In the previous recipes, we used `.get()`, but `.post()`, `.patch()`, `.put()`, and `.delete()` are available.

The returned response object has a `.json()` method that decodes the result from JSON.

Equally, to send information, a `json` argument is available. This encodes a dictionary into JSON and sends it to the server. The data needs to follow the format of the resource, or an error may be raised.

> **Note**
>
> `GET` and `DELETE` don't require data, while `PATCH`, `PUT`, and `POST` require data to be sent through the payload of the request body.

The `referred-to` resource will be returned, and its URL is available in the header. This is useful when creating a new resource, as its URL is likely not known beforehand.

> **Tip**
>
> The difference between `PATCH` and `PUT` is that the latter replaces the whole resource, while the former does a partial update.

## There's more...

RESTful APIs are very powerful but also have huge variability. Please check the documentation of the specific API to learn about its details and how it's supposed to be used.

## See also

- The *Downloading web pages* recipe, earlier in this chapter, to learn the basics of requesting web pages
- The *Installing third-party packages* recipe in *Chapter 1, Let's Begin Our Automation Journey*, to learn the basics of installing external modules

# Interacting with forms

Many web pages contain forms. Forms are a way of sending values to a web page, for example, to create a new comment on a blog post, or to submit an order.

Browsers present forms into which you can enter values and send them in a single action after pressing the submit button or equivalent. We'll see how to create this action programmatically in this recipe.

> **Tip**
>
> Be aware that sending data to a site is normally a more delicate matter than receiving data from it. For example, sending automatic comments to a website is very much the definition of **spam**. This means that it can be more difficult to automate as it involves considering security measures implemented by the web service. Double-check that what you're trying to achieve is a valid, ethical use case.

## Getting ready

We'll work against the test server `https://httpbin.org/forms/post`, which allows us to send a test form and sends back the submitted information.

> **Note**
>
> Note that the URL `https://httpbin.org/forms/post` renders the form, but internally calls the URL `https://httpbin.org/post` to send the information. We'll use both URLs during this recipe.

The following is an example form to order a pizza:

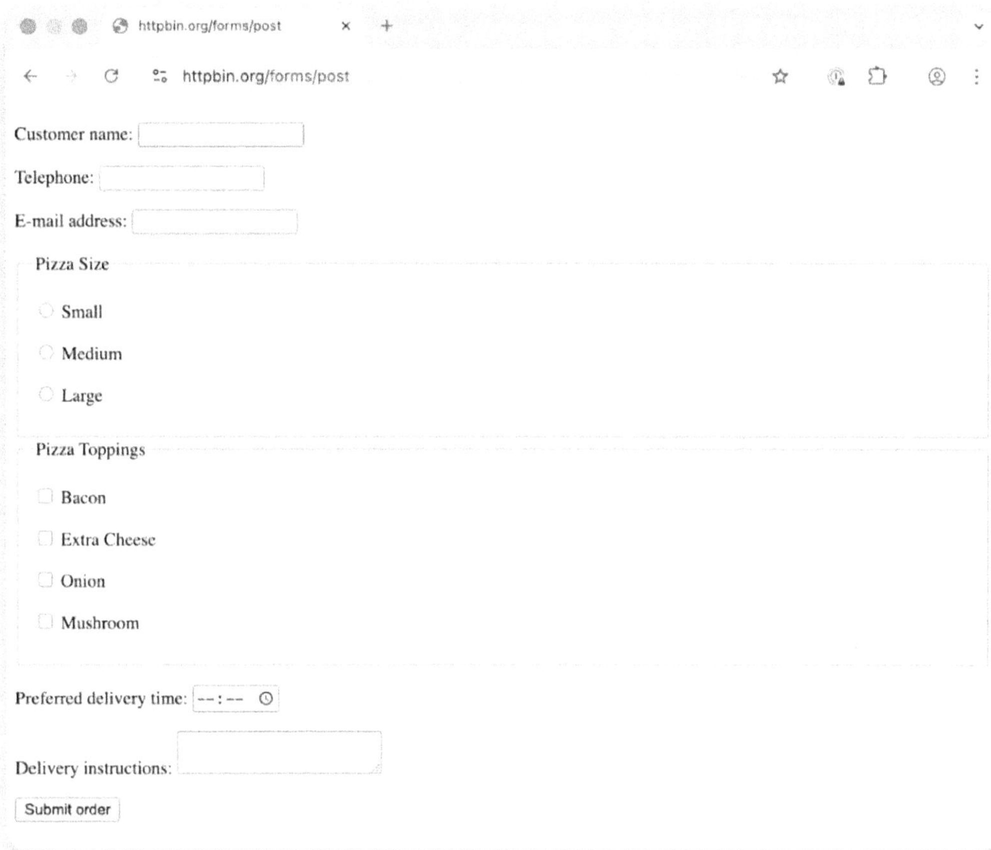


*Figure 3.2: Rendered form*

You can fill the form in manually and see it return the information in JSON format, including extra information such as the browser being used.

The following is the frontend of the web form that is generated:

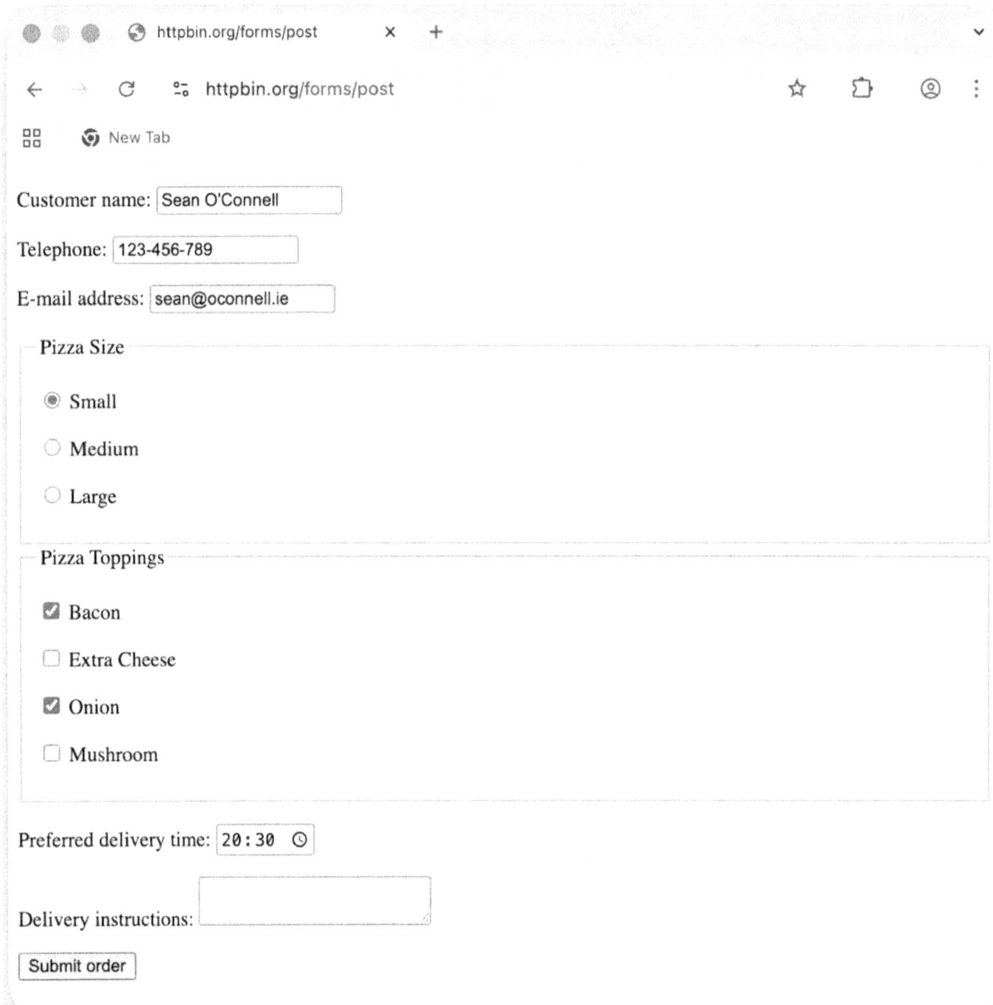


*Figure 3.3: Filled-in form*

The following screenshot shows the backend of the web form that is generated:

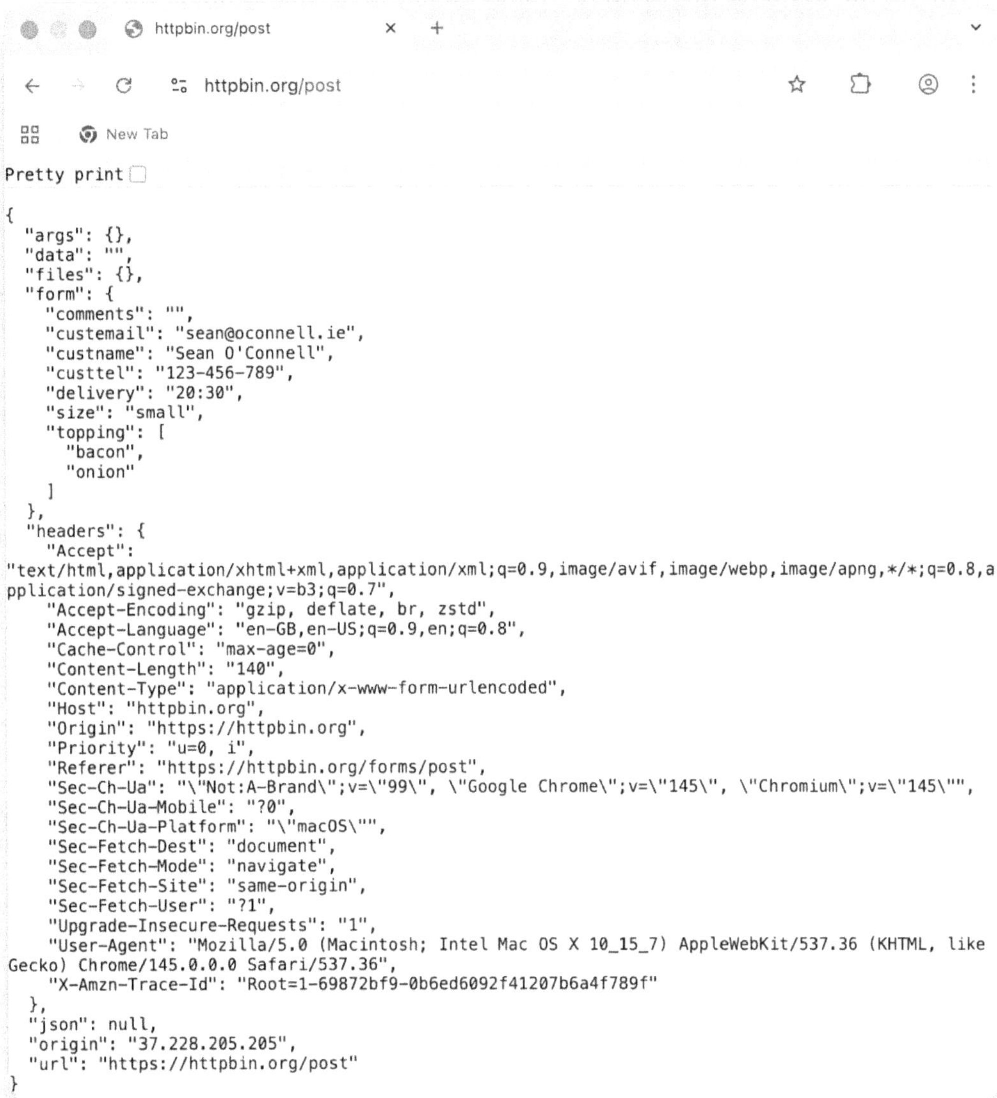


*Figure 3.4: Returned JSON content*

We need to analyze the HTML to see the accepted data in the form. The source code is as follows:

```
<!DOCTYPE html>
<html>
```

```
  <head>
  </head>
  <body>
  <!-- Example form from HTML5 spec http://www.w3.org/TR/html5/forms.html#writing-
a-form's-user-interface -->
  <form method="post" action="/post">
   <p><label>Customer name: <input name="custname"></label></p>
   <p><label>Telephone: <input type=tel name="custtel"></label></p>
   <p><label>E-mail address: <input type=email name="custemail"></label></p>
   <fieldset>
    <legend> Pizza Size </legend>
    <p><label> <input type=radio name=size value="small"> Small </label></p>
    <p><label> <input type=radio name=size value="medium"> Medium </label></p>
    <p><label> <input type=radio name=size value="large"> Large </label></p>
   </fieldset>
   <fieldset>
    <legend> Pizza Toppings </legend>
    <p><label> <input type=checkbox name="topping" value="bacon"> Bacon </label></
p>
    <p><label> <input type=checkbox name="topping" value="cheese"> Extra Cheese </
label></p>
    <p><label> <input type=checkbox name="topping" value="onion"> Onion </label></
p>
    <p><label> <input type=checkbox name="topping" value="mushroom"> Mushroom </
label></p>
   </fieldset>
   <p><label>Preferred delivery time: <input type=time min="11:00" max="21:00"
step="900" name="delivery"></label></p>
   <p><label>Delivery instructions: <textarea name="comments"></textarea></
label></p>
   <p><button>Submit order</button></p>
  </form>
  </body>
</html>
```

Check the names of the inputs, `custname`, `custtel`, `custemail`, `size` (a radio option), `topping` (a multiselection checkbox), `delivery` (time), and `comments`.

## How to do it...

1. Import the `requests`, `BeautifulSoup`, and `re` modules:

```
>>> import requests
>>> from bs4 import BeautifulSoup
>>> import re
```

2. Retrieve the form page, parse it, and print the input fields. Check that the posting URL is `/post` (not `/forms/post`):

```
>>> response = requests.get('https://httpbin.org/forms/post')
>>> page = BeautifulSoup(response.text)
>>> form = page.find('form')
>>> {field.get('name') for field in form.find_all(re.compile('input|
textarea'))}
{'delivery', 'topping', 'size', 'custemail', 'comments', 'custtel',
'custname'}
```

Note that `textarea` is a valid input and is defined in the HTML format.

3. Prepare the data to be posted as a dictionary. Check that the values are as defined in the form:

```
>>> data = {'custname': "Sean O'Connell", 'custtel': '123-456-789',
'custemail': 'sean@oconnell.ie', 'size': 'small', 'topping': ['bacon',
'onion'], 'delivery': '20:30', 'comments': ''}
```

4. Post the values and check that the response is the same as returned in the browser:

```
>>> response = requests.post('https://httpbin.org/post', data)
>>> response
<Response [200]>
>>> response.json()
{'args': {}, 'data': '', 'files': {}, 'form': {'comments': '', 'custemail':
'sean@oconnell.ie', 'custname': "Sean O'Connell", 'custtel': '123-456-789',
'delivery': '20:30', 'size': 'small', 'topping': ['bacon', 'onion']},
'headers': {'Accept': '*/*', 'Accept-Encoding': 'gzip, deflate, zstd',
'Content-Length': '140', 'Content-Type': 'application/x-www-form-
urlencoded', 'Host': 'httpbin.org', 'User-Agent': 'python-requests/2.32.5',
```

```
'X-Amzn-Trace-Id': 'Root=1-6934508c-364a5a155320f02273d7c9a6'}, 'json':
None, 'origin': '79.117.195.58', 'url': 'https://httpbin.org/post'}
```

## How it works...

The `requests` module directly encodes and sends data in the configured format. By default, it sends POST data in the `application/x-www-form-urlencoded` format.

> Note
>
> Compare the action of `requests` with the *Accessing web APIs* recipe, where the data is explicitly sent in JSON format using the argument `json`. This means that the `Content-Type` is `application/json` instead of `application/x-www-form-urlencoded`.

The key aspect here is to respect the format of the form. If there's an error with the format or values submitted, the server should return a 4XX status code and error message which can be analyzed to understand the error and fix any errors.

## There's more...

Other than following the format of forms and inputting valid values, the main problem when working with forms is the multiple ways of preventing spam and abusive behavior.

You will often have to ensure that you have downloaded a form before submitting it, to avoid submitting multiple forms or being suspected of attempting a **Cross-Site Request Forgery** (**CSRF**) attack.

> Note
>
> CSRF, which means producing a malicious call from one page to a different one, taking advantage of the fact that your browser is authenticated, is a serious problem. For example, you might think you are entering a site about adorable puppies, when in fact advantage is taken of you being logged into your bank page to perform financial operations on your behalf, such as transferring your savings to a distant account. Here is a good description of CSRF: `https://stackoverflow.com/a/33829607`. New techniques in browsers help with these CSRF issues by default.

To obtain the specific CSRF token, you need to first download the form, as shown in the recipe, obtain the value of the CSRF token, and resubmit it. Note that the token can have different names; this is just an example:

```
>>> form.find(attrs={'name': 'token'}).get('value')
'ABCEDF12345'
```

## See also

- The *Downloading web pages* recipe, earlier in this chapter, to learn the basics of requesting web pages.
- The *Parsing HTML* recipe, earlier in this chapter, to follow up on parsing the information returned from the server.

# Using Playwright for advanced interaction

Over time the complexity of web sites has grown tremendously, and there are many instances of web sites needing to render a complicated interface, perhaps created by iteration of multiple JS modules. Sometimes, nothing short of the real thing will work and trying to automate with a tool like `requests` feels deficient.

There have been projects to automate web browsers directly in the past, but **Playwright** is a new project aimed at that goal. It's conceived as a way of automatic testing, but it also can be used to automate interactions with a site.

Playwright can control most common browsers, including Safari, Chrome, Firefox, and Microsoft Edge. For our example, we will use Chrome.

## Getting ready

Be sure to have Chrome installed – `https://www.google.com/chrome/`.

Add the `playwright` module to `requirements.txt` and install it:

```
$ echo " playwright==1.56.0" >> requirements.txt
$ uv pip install -r requirements.txt
```

To install playwright drivers, etc., run its install procedure:

```
$ uv run playwright install
```

# How to do it...

1. Import playwright in non-headless mode, which will start a browser and load the form page:

```
>>> from playwright.sync_api import sync_playwright
>>> playwright = sync_playwright().start()
>>> browser = playwright.chromium.launch(headless=False)
>>> page = browser.new_page()
>>> page.goto('https://httpbin.org/forms/post')
<Response url='https://httpbin.org/forms/post' request=<Request
url='https://httpbin.org/forms/post' method='GET'>>
```

   You'll see that a Chromium page has opened and it displays the form.

2. Add a value in the **Customer name** field. Remember that the input value it is called `custname`:

```
>>> page.locator("input[name='custname']").clear()
>>> page.locator("input[name='custname']").fill("Sean  O'Connell")
```

   The form will update:

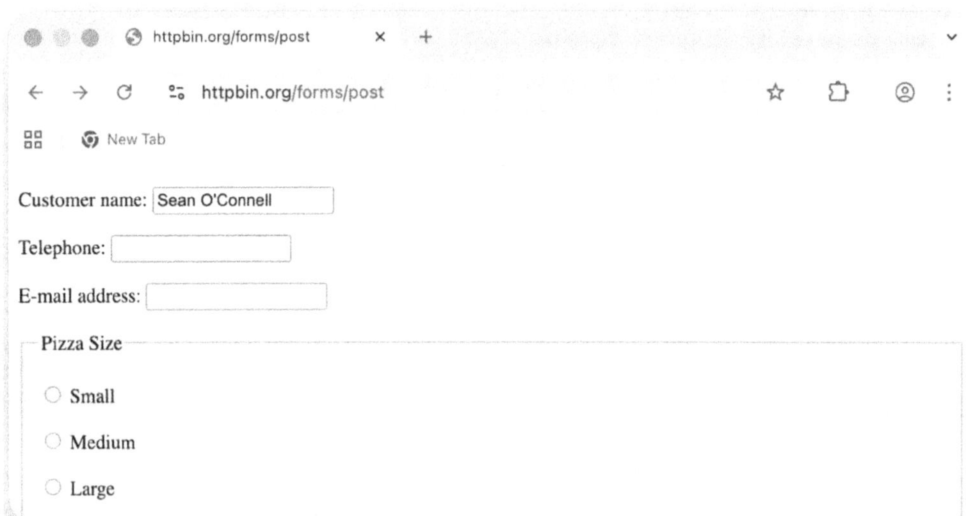


*Figure 3.5: Form being filled automatically*

3. Set the pizza size to medium:

```
>>> page.locator("input[name='size'][value='medium']").check()
```

   This will set the **Pizza Size** radio button.

4. You can also read text from the form

```
>>> toppings = page.locator('fieldset').filter(has_text='Toppings')
>>> for i in range(toppings.locator('label').count()):
...     option = toppings.locator('label').nth(i)
...     print(option.inner_text())
...
 Bacon
 Extra Cheese
 Onion
 Mushroom
```

5. Add bacon and cheese:

```
>>> page.get_by_role('checkbox', name='Bacon').check()
>>> page.get_by_role('checkbox', name='Extra Cheese').check()
```

   Finally, the checkboxes will appear as marked:

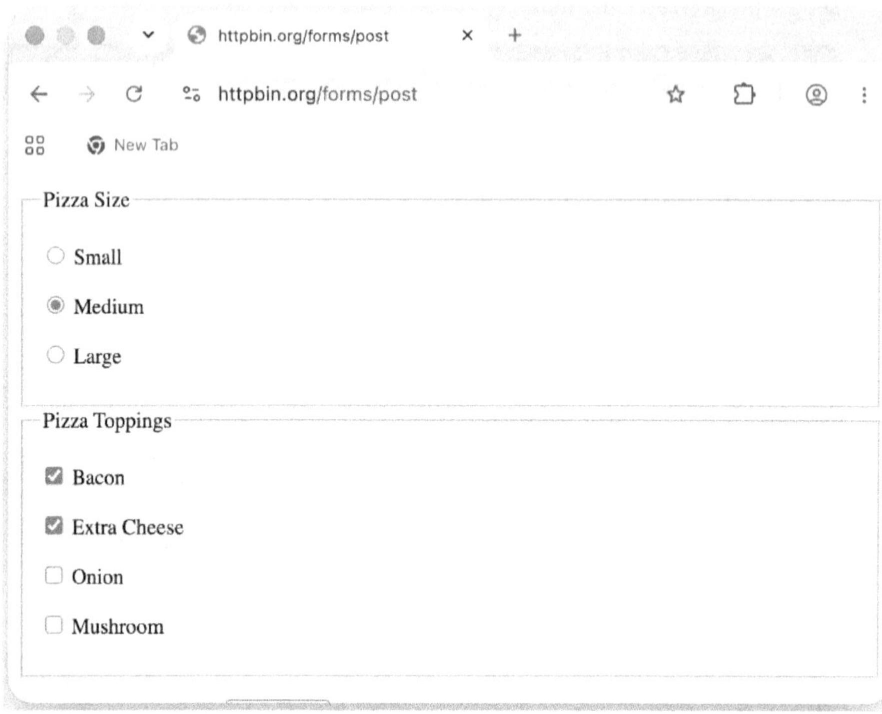


*Figure 3.6: Form with checked boxes*

6. Submit the form. The page will load with the result will be displayed:

```
>>> page.get_by_role("button", name="Submit").click()
```


```
{
  "args": {},
  "data": "",
  "files": {},
  "form": {
    "comments": "",
    "custemail": "",
    "custname": "Sean  O'Connell",
    "custtel": "",
    "delivery": "",
    "size": "medium",
    "topping": [
      "bacon",
      "cheese"
```

```
    ]
  },
  "headers": {
    "Accept": "text/html,application/xhtml+xml,application/xml;q=0.9,image/
avif,image/webp,image/apng,*/*;q=0.8,application/signed-
exchange;v=b3;q=0.7",
    "Accept-Encoding": "gzip, deflate, br, zstd",
    "Accept-Language": "en-GB,en;q=0.9",
    "Cache-Control": "max-age=0",
    "Content-Length": "107",
    "Content-Type": "application/x-www-form-urlencoded",
    "Host": "httpbin.org",
    "Origin": "https://httpbin.org",
    "Priority": "u=0, i",
    "Referer": "https://httpbin.org/forms/post",
    "Sec-Ch-Ua": "\"Chromium\";v=\"141\", \"Not?A_Brand\";v=\"8\"",
    "Sec-Ch-Ua-Mobile": "?0",
    "Sec-Ch-Ua-Platform": "\"macOS\"",
    "Sec-Fetch-Dest": "document",
    "Sec-Fetch-Mode": "navigate",
    "Sec-Fetch-Site": "same-origin",
    "Sec-Fetch-User": "?1",
    "Upgrade-Insecure-Requests": "1",
    "User-Agent": "Mozilla/5.0 (Macintosh; Intel Mac OS X 10_15_7)
AppleWebKit/537.36 (KHTML, like Gecko) Chrome/141.0.0.0 Safari/537.36",
    "X-Amzn-Trace-Id": "Root=1-6a306056-565187af3dea4003659cb864"
  },
  "json": null,
  "origin": "37.228.205.205",
  "url": "https://httpbin.org/post"
}
```

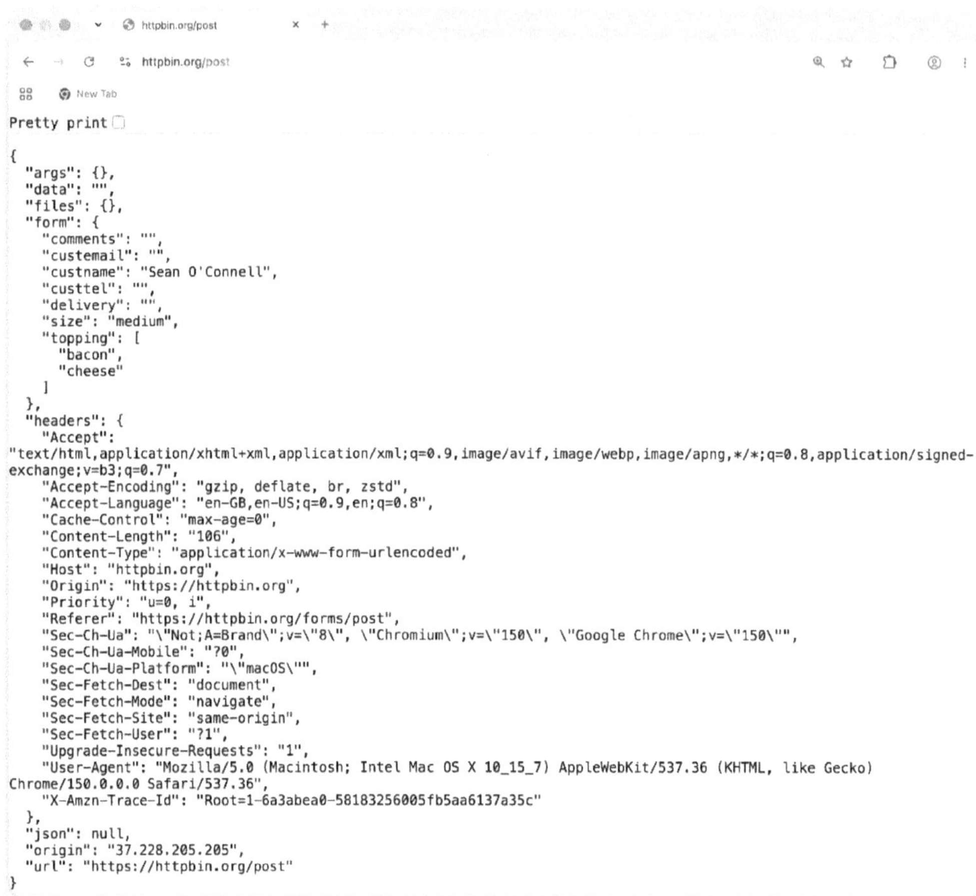


*Figure 3.7: Returned JSON information*

7. Close the browser:

```
>>> browser.close()
```

## How it works...

*Step 1* in the *How to do it...* section shows how to create a playwright page (equivalent to a browser tab) and go to a particular URL.

Playwright works in a similar way to Beautiful Soup: you select an element and then manipulate it. The selectors in playwright are also compatible with selectors available in JavaScript.

Using the `.locator` method you can use any CSS selector and it will return the proper DOM element(s).

In *Step 2* we have seen how the selector `input[name=<name>]` selects, from an `<input>` HTML tag, the values that have the desired name.

Once we have selected a single element, we can interact with it. In step 2, we `.clear` and `.type` into a text box. The first removes any text elements and the second works as manual typing would, inputting one character at a time.

> **Tip**
>
> Alternatively, the `.fill` method can be used to fill the text in a single action. This comes with the risk that some planned behavior, like autocomplete the input while writing one character at a time, can interact badly and provoke an unexpected reaction on the UI if the full data is input in a single go.

In *Step 3* we require a more precise selection. Using just `locator(input[name='size'])` returns all the sizes, so we need to add a qualifier to `input[name='size'][value='medium']`. Once we select a single element, we can use `.click` to simulate a click, selecting the element.

We need to show how the HTML code is structured for *Step 4*.

```
<fieldset>
 <legend> Pizza Toppings </legend>
 <p><label> <input type=checkbox name="topping" value="bacon"> Bacon </label></
p>
 <p><label> <input type=checkbox name="topping" value="cheese"> Extra Cheese </
label></p>
 <p><label> <input type=checkbox name="topping" value="onion"> Onion </label></
p>
 <p><label> <input type=checkbox name="topping" value="mushroom"> Mushroom </
label></p>
</fieldset>
```

We want first to select the right fieldset, and then iterate throught the different options. Note that the `label` elements are the ones containing the text we are interested in, not the `input` elements.

We combine the different locators to first select the `fieldset` section which contains the text `Toppings`:

```
>>> toppings = page.locator('fieldset').filter(has_text='Toppings')
```

Then we find out how many checkboxes are in this section:

```
>>> toppings.get_by_role('checkbox').count()
4
```

And iterate through them using the `.nth` method:

```
... option = toppings.locator('label').nth(i)
```

Finally, we retrieve the `inner_text` inside the `label` element:

```
...print(option.inner_text())
```

We use for the next *Step 5* a different way of selecting elements, using `.get_by_role`, which works in an analogous way.

Finally, *step 7* closes the browser.

## There's more...

Finding the right selector to use in the `locator` is a key aspect and one that is highly dependent on how the specific page is structured. Some common ways to select elements are

- `tag` for tags. For example, `p` for a `p` HTML tag or `input`.
- `#<id>` for an `id` attribute
- `.<class>` for a `class` attribute
- `[attribute=value]` for attributes of the tag

These can be combined, allowing us to match a `div` tag with a `class` attribute value of `myclass` and a `style` attribute value of `mystyle` with `div.myclass[style="mystyle"]`.

If you use a selector that retrieves more than one element, you will need to keep filtering. You can use further filters either by again using `.locator` with the elements to filter, or with the `.filter` method with options like containing text, being visible, etc. as we saw in *Step 4*. If you have a list of elements, you can iterate through them with the `.nth` method, or can use the convenient `.first` and `.last` attributes.

See the Playwright documentation for all the filtering options: `https://playwright.dev/python/docs/api/class-locator#locator-filter`.

> **Tip**
>
> Using GenAI to get help on the creation of the proper selectors or code can be very useful! Copying the HTML code you want to work with and explaining what you are trying to achieve will help you get good results.
>
> For example, if you want to select the answers in a FAQ style page, you could use the prompt: "*In this HTML code, show me the best selector to use in Playwright to choose all the text responses from the questions. <copy HTML code>*". The GenAI tool will return selectors, including alternatives and reasons why they could be better or worse. You can continue iterating until finding the best one for your objective.

Playwright error messages in Python are quite good at alerting you to the nature of problems encountered. For example, trying to perform a click on all input elements, you get the following error:

```
>>> page.locator('input').click()
…
playwright._impl._errors.Error: Locator.click: Error: strict mode violation:
locator("input") resolved to 11 elements:
    1) <input name="custname"/> aka get_by_role("textbox", name="Customer name:")
    2) <input type="tel" name="custtel"/> aka get_by_role("textbox",
name="Telephone:")
    3) <input type="email" name="custemail"/> aka get_by_role("textbox", name="E-
mail address:")
    4) <input name="size" type="radio" value="small"/> aka get_by_role("radio",
name="Small")
    5) <input name="size" type="radio" value="medium"/> aka get_by_role("radio",
name="Medium")
    6) <input name="size" type="radio" value="large"/> aka get_by_role("radio",
name="Large")
…
```

You can see the suggestions in the error code to use specific calls to `get_by_role`. This function works in a similar way to `locator`. You have several alternatives available, like `get_by_role`, `get_by_text`, `get_by_label`, etc. Check the playwright documentation for more details.

Sometimes, opening a browser can be inconvenient. By default, Playwright starts the browser in headless mode and manipulates it from there, like this:

```
>>> from playwright.sync_api import sync_playwright
>>> playwright = sync_playwright().start()
>>> page = browser.new_page()
>>> page.goto('https://httpbin.org/forms/post')
```

The page won't be displayed externally, but Playwright has an internal representation. A 'screenshot' can be saved anyway with the following line:

```
>>> img = page.screenshot(path='screenshot.png')
```

To illustrate the difference, there's a prepared script in the GitHub repo at `https://github.com/PacktPublishing/Python-Automation-Cookbook-Third-Edition/blob/main/ch03/playwright_form.py`, which can be checked with

```
$ uv run playwright_form.py
$ uv run playwright_form.py --headless
```

To better allow the changes to be seen, there's a delay of a few seconds introduced in non-headless mode.

Here is the full Python Playwright documentation: `https://playwright.dev/python/`.

## See also

- The *Parsing HTML* recipe, earlier in this chapter, to learn how to parse elements in HTML.
- The *Interacting with forms* recipe, earlier in this chapter, to see an alternative way to work with forms.

# Accessing password-protected pages with basic authentication

Sometimes a web page is not open to the public but is protected in some way. The simplest form of protection is to use basic HTTP authentication, which is integrated into virtually every web server and implements a user/password schema.

## Getting ready

We can test this kind of authentication in `https://httpbin.org`.

It has a path, `/basic-auth/{user}/{password}`, which forces authentication with the user and password stated. This is very handy for understanding how authentication works.

## How to do it...

1. Import `requests`:

```
>>> import requests
```

2. Make a GET request to the URL with the correct credentials. Notice that we set the credentials on the URL to be 'user' and 'psswd':

```
>>> requests.get('https://httpbin.org/basic-auth/user/psswd',
                 auth=('user', 'psswd'))
<Response [200]>
```

3. Use the wrong credentials to return a 401 status code (unauthorized):

```
>>> requests.get('https://httpbin.org/basic-auth/user/psswd',
                 auth=('user', 'wrong'))
<Response [401]>
```

The credentials can also be passed directly as part of the URL, separated by a colon and an `@` symbol before the server, like this:

```
>>> requests.get('https://user:psswd@httpbin.org/basic-auth/user/psswd')
<Response [200]>
>>> requests.get('https://user:wrong@httpbin.org/basic-auth/user/psswd')
<Response [401]>
```

## How it works...

As HTTP basic authentication is supported everywhere, support from `requests` is very easy.

*Steps 2* and *4* in the *How to do it...* section show how to provide the proper password. *Step 3* shows what happens when the password is wrong.

> **Note**
>
> Remember to **always use HTTPS** to ensure that the sending of the password is kept secret. If you use HTTP, the password will be sent in the open over the internet, allowing it to be captured by listening parties.

## There's more...

Adding the user and password to the URL works on the browser as well. Try to access the page directly to see a box asking for the username and password:

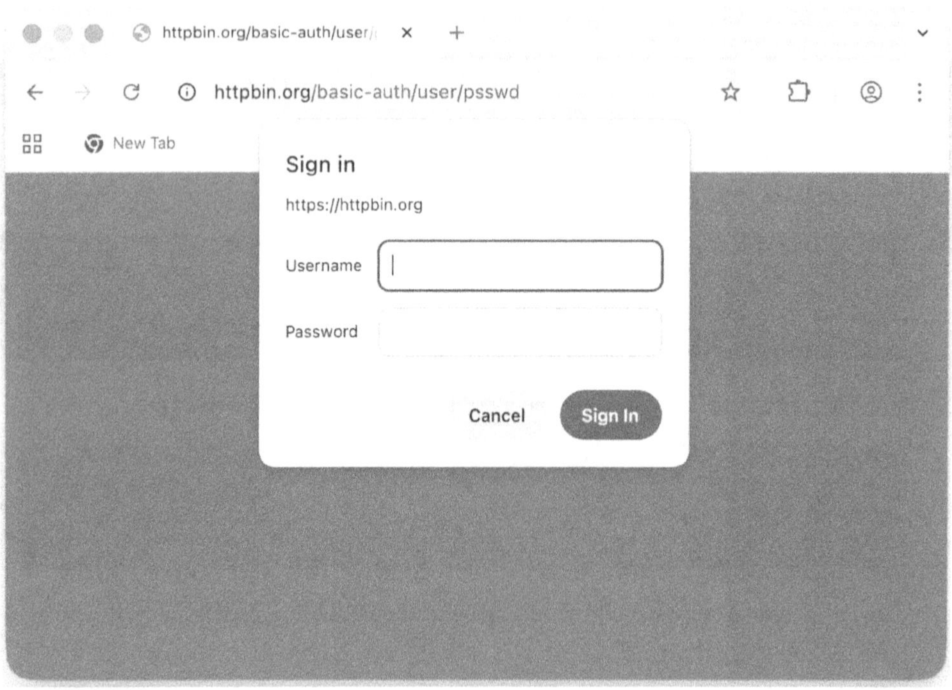


*Figure 3.8: User credentials page*

When using a URL containing the username and password, such as `https://user:psswd@httpbin.org/basic-auth/user/psswd`, the dialog does not appear and authentication occurs automatically.

If you need to access multiple pages, you can create a session in `requests` and set the authentication parameters to avoid having to input them everywhere:

```
>>> s = requests.Session()
>>> s.auth = ('user', 'psswd')
>>> s.get('https://httpbin.org/basic-auth/user/psswd')
<Response [200]>
```

## See also

- The *Downloading web pages* recipe, earlier in this chapter, to learn the basics of requesting web pages.
- The *Accessing web APIs* recipe, earlier in this chapter, to learn how to access APIs that are behind an authentication wall.
- The *Accessing websites with browser cookies* recipe, coming up next, for programmatically accessing websites with more complex authentication processes.

# Accessing websites with browser cookies

Many web pages may have more complicated login procedures than basic auth. Perhaps they have a login and password, but don't allow basic auth. Or the login procedure is more complicated and includes features like **multifactor authentication** (**MFA**).

Sessions in web pages are essentially controlled by storing a cookie with a session token, which the browser can send to the web server in all their communications. Setting this session token can require multiple procedures, but once the browser has it, it can be used to authenticate the access.

Instead of preparing our program to perform the login, we can instead retrieve this session cookie and use it.

> Note
>
> Importantly, this will authenticate our program as ourselves when making requests. While powerful, this is also dangerous as it can perform actions that could affect our account if there's any problem. Be careful and understand the risks, especially for big web sites that may have sophisticated methods of controlling abuse.

## Getting ready

Add the `browser_cookie3` module to `requirements.txt` and install it:

```
$ echo " browser_cookie3==0.20.1" >> requirements.txt
$ uv pip install -r requirements.txt
```

We will access the main GitHub page (`https://github.com`), so first ensure that you have an account. Notice that when you're not logged into the page, there's no top header with your notifications:

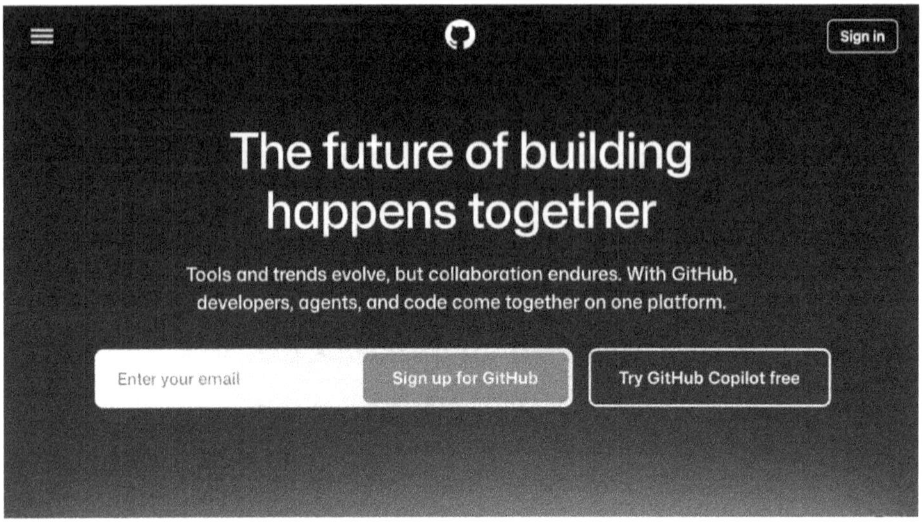


*Figure 3.9: Login page for GitHub*

When you're logged in, however, there's a visible header bearing your personal notifications. Notice the top right inbox icon, with a blue dot, next to your avatar:

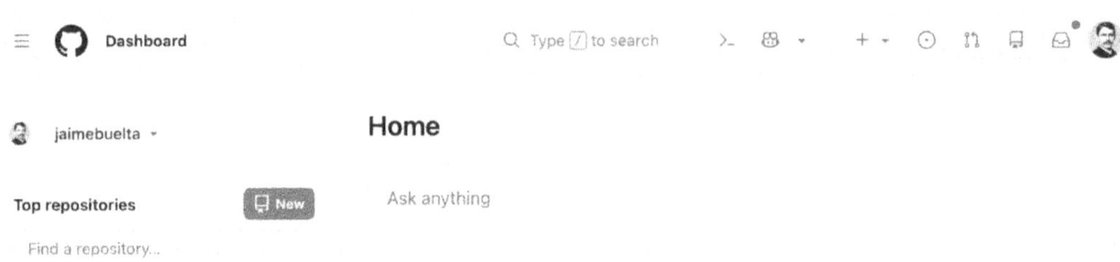


*Figure 3.10: Top of GitHub logged page*

We will search for the element `<tool-tip id="notification-indicator-tooltip">`

Before starting, verify that you're logged into GitHub in your browser. We will assume it's Chrome.

## How to do it...

1. Import `requests` and `BeautifulSoup` modules:

```
>>> import requests
>>> from bs4 import BeautifulSoup
```

2. Retrieve the main GitHub URL:

```
>>> response = requests.get('https://github.com')
>>> content = BeautifulSoup(response.text, 'html.parser')
```

3. Search for the tooltip `<tool-tip id="notification-indicator-tooltip">` and see it's not there:

```
>>> content.find_all('tool-tip', id='notification-indicator-tooltip')
[]
```

4. Import browser_cookie3:

```
>>> import browser_cookie3
```

5. Obtain the cookies from Chrome. You may need to grant permission in your OS.

```
>>> cookies = browser_cookie3.chrome()
```

6. Call again to GitHub, this time using the cookies, and parse again:

```
>>> response = requests.get('https://github.com', cookies=cookies)
>>> content = BeautifulSoup(response.text, 'html.parser')
```

7. Search for the tooltip again. This time it's present:

```
>>> content.find_all('tool-tip', id='notification-indicator-tooltip')
[<tool-tip class="sr-only position-absolute" data-direction="s" data-
target="notification-indicator.tooltip" data-type="label" data-view-
component="true" for="AppHeader-notifications-button" id="notification-
indicator-tooltip" popover="manual">Notifications</tool-tip>]
```

## How it works...

*Steps 1* to *3* are straightforward and retrieve the main page, but at that point the GitHub user is not logged in, as we are accessing the site from a new session.

In *Step 5*, using the `browser_cookie3` package, we obtain the cookies from our Chrome browser, which is logged into the page. We use the cookies as a parameter to retrieve the page again in the next step. This time, we carry over the session from the one open in the browser and then retrieve the response, since we are logged in.

## There's more...

It is a good practice to retrieve only the minimum number of cookies that we require, for the specific domain that we need.

```
>>> cookies2 = browser_cookie3.chrome(domain_name='github.com')
```

This is safer, as we retrieve only the minimum necessary cookies. If `domain_name` is not specified, more cookies can be imported. This allows the request to access more domains than expected, which can present a security problem.

> **Tip**
>
> For example, you may also be logged into your email, making it possible for your script to access it even if was not designed to do so. Or even worse, your bank! Always retrieve the minimum amount of information. Cookies are very sensible!

If you need to carry out multiple requests, instead of passing the cookies you can set up a `Session` in `requests` which will carry over any cookies set up and changes (overwrite cookies, clean up, etc) .

```
>>> with requests.Session() as s:
...     response = s.get(url, cookies=cookies)
...     response2 = s.get(url)  # This second request will use the cookies
```

Check the requests documentation for more information on using `Sessions` and cookies, at `https://docs.python-requests.org/en/latest/user/advanced/`.

You can retrieve cookies from different browsers, and it is worth checking the documentation for specific information on supported browsers.

You can also use the cookies in Playwright to produce a full browser experience, though the format of the cookies will need to be tweaked. Check out the following script `playwright_github.py`:

```
from playwright.sync_api import sync_playwright
import time
import browser_cookie3

def cookie_to_playwright(c):
    """Convert browser_cookie3 cookie to Playwright cookie format."""
```

```
    cookie = {
        "name": c.name,
        "value": c.value,
        "domain": c.domain,
        "path": c.path,
        "httpOnly": c._rest.get("HttpOnly", False),
        "secure": bool(c.secure),
        # Map sameSite if available
        "sameSite": (
            "Strict" if c._rest.get("SameSite") == "Strict"
            else "Lax" if c._rest.get("SameSite") == "Lax"
            else "None"
        ),
    }
    if c.expires is not None:
        cookie["expires"] = c.expires

    return cookie


def main():
    cookies = browser_cookie3.chrome(domain_name='github.com')

    playwright = sync_playwright().start()
    browser = playwright.chromium.launch(headless=False)
    context = browser.new_context()
    pw_cookies = [cookie_to_playwright(c) for c in cookies]
    context.add_cookies(pw_cookies)
    page = context.new_page()
    page.goto('https://github.com')
    time.sleep(10)

if __name__ == "__main__":
    main()
```

Note that we are adding the cookies to a new context. A context is an isolated environment inside a browser instance, similar to an incognito window. We create a new page in this context, which now contains all the cookie information.

> **Tip**
>
> We can create multiple contexts at the same time to provide different cookie information in each context. For example, to work with two independent users.

The full documentation on `browser_cookie3` can be found here: `https://github.com/borisbabic/browser_cookie3`.

## See also

- The *Downloading web pages* recipe, earlier in this chapter, to learn the basics of requesting web pages.
- The *Parsing HTML* recipe, earlier in this chapter, for more information on how to use `BeautifulSoup` to parse HTML.
- The *Accessing password-protected pages with basic auth* recipe, earlier in this chapter, for web sites that use basic auth for simpler access.
- The *Using Playwright for advanced interaction* recipe, earlier in this chapter, with the basics on how to use Playwright for using a browser programmatically.

# Speeding up web scraping

Most of the time spent downloading information from web pages is usually spent waiting. A request goes from our computer to the remote server, gets processed, and then we must wait until the response is composed and comes back to our computer.

During execution of the recipes in the book, you'll notice there's a wait involved in calls to requests, normally of around one to two seconds. But computers can do other stuff while waiting, including making more requests at the same time. In this recipe, we will see how to download a list of pages in parallel and wait until they are all ready. We will use an intentionally slow server to show why it's worth getting this right.

> **Note**
>
> Be aware that many web sites on the Internet have methods in place to try to limit how fast you can extract information from them. A large number of bots and scrapers are abusing sites, and because of that you may find that a web page returns errors and rate-limits you if you ask for too many requests in quick succession. The right HTTP status code for that is `429 Too Many Requests`, although it may not be returned in all situations. It may be necessary to implement a cool-down time between requests.
>
> Be responsible and try to limit the amount of info you download from open sites.

## Getting ready

We'll look at code to crawl and search for keywords, making use of the futures capabilities of Python 3 to download multiple pages at the same time.

A **future** is an object that represents the promise of a value. This means that you immediately receive an object while the code is being executed in the background – only, when specifically requesting its `.result()`, the code waits until the result is available.

> **Note**
>
> If the result is already available when you call `result()`, it returns immediately, which makes it faster. Think of the operation as putting something in the washing machine while doing other tasks. There's a chance that the laundry will be done by the time we finish the rest of our chores.

To generate a future, you need a background engine, called an **executor**. Once created, submit a function with its parameters to retrieve a future. Rretrieval of the result can be delayed as long as necessary, allowing the generation of several futures in a row; then we can wait until all are finished and execute them in parallel. This is an alternative to creating one, waiting until it finishes, creating another, and so on.

There are several ways to create an executor, but in this recipe we'll use `ThreadPoolExecutor`, which uses threads.

We'll use a prepared example, available at the following GitHub repo: `https://github.com/PacktPublishing/Python-Automation-Cookbook-Third-Edition/tree/main/ch03/test_site`. Download the whole site and run the included script:

```
$ uv run simple_delay_server.py -d 2
```

This serves the site at the URL `http://localhost:8000`. You can view it in a browser. It's a simple blog with three entries. Most of it is uninteresting, but we've added a couple of paragraphs that contain the keyword 'python'. The parameter `-d 2` makes the server intentionally slow, simulating a bad connection.

## How to do it...

1. Write the following script, `speed_up_step1.py`. The full code is available on GitHub it the Chapter03 directory (`https://github.com/PacktPublishing/Python-Automation-Cookbook-Third-Edition/blob/main/ch03/speed_up_step1.py`). Here are shown only the most relevant parts. It is based on `crawling_web_step1.py`:

```
...
def process_link(source_link, text):
    ...
    return source_link, get_links(parsed_source, page)
...
def main(base_url, to_search, workers):
    checked_links = set()
    to_check = [base_url]
    max_checks = 10
    with concurrent.futures.ThreadPoolExecutor(max_workers=workers) as
executor:
        while to_check:
            futures = [executor.submit(process_link, url, to_search)
                       for url in to_check]
            to_check = []
            for data in concurrent.futures.as_completed(futures):
                link, new_links = data.result()
                checked_links.add(link)
                for link in new_links:
                    if link not in checked_links and link not in to_check:
                        to_check.append(link)
                max_checks -= 1
```

```
                if not max_checks:
                    return
if __name__ == '__main__':
    parser = argparse.ArgumentParser()
    ...
    parser.add_argument('-w', type=int, help='Number of workers',
                        default=4)
    args = parser.parse_args()
    main(args.u, args.p, args.w)
```

Notice the differences in the `main` function. Also, there's an extra parameter added (number of concurrent workers), and the function `process_link` now returns the source link.

2. Run the script `crawling_web_step1.py` to get a time baseline. Notice that the output has been removed here for clarity:

```
$ time uv run crawling_web_step1.py http://localhost:8000/
... REMOVED OUTPUT
uv run crawling_web_step1.py http://localhost:8000/  0.19s user 0.08s
system 2% cpu 12.495 total
```

3. Run the new script with one worker, which will make it slower than the original one:

```
$ time uv run speed_up_step1.py -w 1
... REMOVED OUTPUT
uv run speed_up_step1.py -w 1  0.21s user 0.08s system 1% cpu 16.507 total
```

4. Increase the number of workers:

```
$ time uv run speed_up_step1.py -w 2
... REMOVED OUTPUT
uv run speed_up_step1.py -w 2  0.20s user 0.08s system 3% cpu 8.478 total
```

5. Adding more workers decreases the time:

```
$ time uv run speed_up_step1.py -w 5
... REMOVED OUTPUT
uv run speed_up_step1.py -w 5  0.22s user 0.08s system 4% cpu 6.476 total
```

## How it works...

The main engine to create the concurrent requests is the `main` function. Notice that the rest of the code is basically untouched (other than returning the source link in the `process_link` function).

> **Note**
>
> This change is actually quite common when adapting for concurrency. Concurrent tasks need to return all the relevant data, as they cannot rely on an ordered context.

This is the relevant part of the code that handles the concurrent engine:

```
with concurrent.futures.ThreadPoolExecutor(max_workers=workers) as executor:
    while to_check:
        futures = [executor.submit(process_link, url, to_search)
                   for url in to_check]
        to_check = []
        for data in concurrent.futures.as_completed(futures):
            link, new_links = data.result()
            checked_links.add(link)
            for link in new_links:
                if link not in checked_links and link not in to_check:
                    to_check.append(link)
             max_checks -= 1
             if not max_checks:
                return
```

The `with` context creates a pool of workers, specifying how many. Inside, a list of futures containing all the URLs to retrieve is created. The `.as_completed()` function returns the futures that are finished, and then there's some work to do to obtain newly found links and check whether they need to be added to be retrieved or not. This process is similar to the one presented in the *Crawling the web* recipe.

The process starts again until enough links have been retrieved or there are no links to retrieve. Note that the links are retrieved in batches. The first time, the base link is processed and all links are retrieved, while in the second iteration all retrieved links will be requested. Once they have all been downloaded, a new batch will be processed.

> **Note**
>
> When dealing with concurrent requests, keep in mind that they can change order between two executions. If a request takes a little more or a little less time, that can affect the ordering of the retrieved information.

## There's more...

While in this example we used the `ThreadPoolExecutor`, it's not the only option. Python can execute the background tasks in different processes using `ProcessPoolExecutor`, or in different interpreter threads with the new (in Python 3.14) `InterpreterPoolExecutor`.

They provide better isolation of tasks and allow the use of more of the machine's resources, but they are heavier. You can think of interpreters as an intermediate stage between threads and processes.

> **Tip**
>
> Feel free to experiment with `ProcessPoolExecutor` and `InterpreterPoolExecutor`, but they are typically useful when you have heavy tasks that require more CPU power. For I/O-bound tasks like scraping the web, it's not likely that you'll be able to get better performance than by using just threads. But, again, this is highly dependent on many parameters.

The full futures documentation (including a detailed description of the different executors) in Python can be found here: `https://docs.python.org/3/library/concurrent.futures.html`.

> **Tip**
>
> As you can see in *steps 4* and *5* of the *How to do it...* section, properly determining the optimal number of workers can require that some tests be carried out. Some numbers can make the process slower, due to the increase in management. Do not be afraid to experiment!

In the Python world, there are other ways to make concurrent HTTP requests besides those already discussed. There's a native request module that allows us to work with futures, called `requests-futures`. It can be found here: `https://github.com/ross/requests-futures`.

Another alternative is to use **asynchronous programming**. This way of working can be very efficient in situations that involve dealing with many concurrent calls, but the approach to coding it demands is different from the traditional way and requires some time to get used to. It also has pros and cons, depending on the situation. Python includes the `asyncio` module to work asynchronously, and there's a good module called `aiohttp` to work with HTTP requests. You can find more information about `aiohttp` here: `https://aiohttp.readthedocs.io/en/stable/client_quickstart.html`, while a good introduction to asynchronous programming is this article: `https://djangostars.com/blog/asynchronous-programming-in-python-asyncio/`.

## See also

- The *Crawling the web* recipe, earlier in this chapter, for the less efficient alternative to this recipe.
- The *Downloading web pages* recipe, earlier in this chapter, to learn the basics of requesting web pages.

# Get this book's PDF version and more

Scan the QR code (or go to `packtpub.com/unlock`). Search for this book by name, confirm the edition, and then follow the steps on the page.

UNLOCK NOW

*Note: Keep your invoice handy. Purchases made directly from Packt don't require an invoice.*

# 4

# Searching and Reading Local Files

In this chapter we will introduce the basic operations for reading information from files, starting with searching and opening files stored in different directories and subdirectories. Then we'll describe some of the most common file types and how to read them, including raw text files, PDFs, and Word documents.

The last recipe will search for a word inside different kinds of file, working recursively on a directory tree.

In this chapter, we'll cover the following recipes:

- Crawling and searching directories
- Reading text files
- Dealing with encodings
- Reading CSV files
- Reading log files
- Reading file metadata
- Reading images
- Reading PDF files
- Reading Word documents
- Scanning documents for a keyword

# Technical requirements

You can check the code presented in the chapter in the book's GitHub repository, at `https://github.com/PacktPublishing/Python-Automation-Cookbook-Third-Edition/tree/main/ch04`.

# Crawling and searching directories

In this recipe we'll learn how to scan a directory recursively to get all the files contained there. That will include all the files in subdirectories. The matched files can be of a particular kind, like text files, or every single one of them.

This is normally a starting operation when dealing with files, to detect all the existing ones.

## Getting ready

Let's start by creating a test directory with some file information:

```
$ mkdir dir
$ touch dir/file1.txt
$ touch dir/file2.txt
$ mkdir dir/subdir
$ touch dir/subdir/file3.txt
$ touch dir/subdir/file4.txt
$ touch dir/subdir/file5.pdf
$ touch dir/file6.pdf
```

All the files will be empty; we will use them in this recipe only to discover them. Notice there are four files that have a `.txt` extension, and two that have a `.pdf` extension.

> **Note**
>
> The files are also available in the GitHub repository here: `https://github.com/PacktPublishing/Python-Automation-Cookbook-Third-Edition/tree/main/ch04/documents/dir`.

Enter the created `dir` directory:

```
$ cd dir
```

## How to do it...

1. Print all the filenames in the current directory and subdirectories:

```
>>> from pathlib import Path
>>> for root, dirs, files in Path('.').walk():
...     for file in files:
...         print(file)
...
file2.txt
file1.txt
file6.pdf
file3.txt
file4.txt
file5.pdf
```

2. Print the full path of the files, joining with the root:

```
>>> for root, dirs, files in Path('.').walk():
...     for file in files:
...         full_file_path = root / file
...         print(full_file_path)
...
file2.txt
file1.txt
file6.pdf
subdir/file3.txt
subdir/file4.txt
subdir/file5.pdf
```

3. Walk the files using a *glob* (a file matching pattern)

```
>>> for path in Path('.').rglob('*'):
...     if path.is_file():
...         print(path)
...
file2.txt
file1.txt
file6.pdf
subdir/file3.txt
```

```
subdir/file4.txt
subdir/file5.pdf
```

4. Print only the `.pdf` files using `.walk()`:

```
>>> for root, dirs, files in Path('.').walk():
...   for file in files:
...     if file.endswith('.pdf'):
...       full_file_path = root / file
...       print(full_file_path)
...
file6.pdf
subdir/file5.pdf
```

5. Print `.pdf` files using a *glob*

```
>>> for path in Path('.').rglob('*.pdf'):
...   if path.is_file():
...     print(path)
...
file6.pdf
subdir/file5.pdf
```

6. Print only files that contain an odd number:

```
>>> import re
>>> for root, dirs, files in Path('.').walk():
...   for file in files:
...     if re.search(r'[13579]', file):
...       full_file_path = root / file
...       print(full_file_path)
...
file1.txt
subdir/file3.txt
subdir/file5.pdf
```

## How it works...

`Path('.').walk()` goes through a whole directory and all subdirectories under it, returning all the files. For each directory, it returns a tuple with the directory, any subdirectories under it, and all the files. If you are in in the `dir` subdirectory:

```
>>> for root, dirs, files in Path('.').walk():
...     print(root, dirs, files)
...
. ['subdir'] ['file2.txt', 'file1.txt', 'file6.pdf']
./subdir [] ['file3.txt', 'file4.txt', 'file5.pdf']
```

The retuned paths, such as the base path and the file, can be joined directly through the / operator.

The returned paths are compatible with strings, any kind of filtering can be performed on them, as in *step 3*. In *step 6* the full power of regular expressions can be used to filter. The / operator also allow you to mix pure strings, allowing expressions like

```
>>> root / "myfile.txt"
PosixPath('subdir/myfile.txt')
```

Alternatively to use .walk, using `.rglob` allow for a more straightforward searching for files. This uses a glob, a pattern matching files. The leading `r` means that it does so recursively, covering all subdirectories from the base one. As seen in steps 3 and 5, it returns the whole subdirectory and file name in a single Path object. Depending on your use case, you may prefer to use `walk` or `rglob`.

> **Note**
>
> See more about how to define globs in the documentation `https://docs.python.org/3/library/glob.html`

In the next recipe we'll deal with the content of the files, not just the filename.

## There's more...

In this recipe the returned files are not opened or modified in any way. This operation is read-only. Files can be opened as described in the following recipes.

Tip

Be aware that changing the structure of the directory while walking over it may affect the results. If you need to carry out some file maintenance while walking through the tree, like copying or moving a file, it's a good idea to store the resulting files in a different directory to avoid problems on the walking loop.

That way, you make a difference between the input (the directory being walked) and the output (the other directory) and avoid mixing them in case you need to repeat the process.

The `Path` objects has multiple elements to deal with the paths, like:

- `.absolute()`, which returns the absolute path of a file.
- `.stem`, and .suffix which shows the final part without the suffix (extension) and the suffix:

```
>>> Path('file.txt').stem
'file'
>>> Path('file.txt').suffix
'.txt'
```

- `.exists()`, to return whether a file exists or not on the filesystem.

The full documentation about `pathlib` can be found at `https://docs.python.org/3/library/pathlib.html`.

As demonstrated in *step 4*, multiple ways of filtering can be used. All string manipulations and tips shown in *Chapter 1, Let's Begin Our Automation Journey*, can be applied here as well.

## See also

- The *Introducing regular expressions* recipe in *Chapter 1, Let's Begin Our Automation Journey*, to learn how to filter using regular expressions.
- The *Reading text files* recipe, later in this chapter, to open the found files and read their context.

# Reading text files

After searching for a particular file, a typical next action is to open it and read its content. Text files are very simple yet very powerful files. They store data in plain text, without using complicated binary formats.

Text file support is provided natively in Python, and it's easy to understand a text file as a collection of lines that can be represented as Python strings.

## Getting ready

We'll read the `zen_of_python.txt` file, containing *The Zen of Python* by Tim Peters, which is a collection of aphorisms that very well describe the design principles behind Python. It is available in the GitHub repository here: `https://github.com/PacktPublishing/Python-Automation-Cookbook-Third-Edition/blob/main/ch04/documents/zen_of_python.txt`, and reads as follows:

```
Beautiful is better than ugly.
Explicit is better than implicit.
Simple is better than complex.
Complex is better than complicated.
Flat is better than nested.
Sparse is better than dense.
Readability counts.
Special cases aren't special enough to break the rules.
Although practicality beats purity.
Errors should never pass silently.
Unless explicitly silenced.
In the face of ambiguity, refuse the temptation to guess.
There should be one-- and preferably only one --obvious way to do it.
Although that way may not be obvious at first unless you're Dutch.
Now is better than never.
Although never is often better than *right* now.
If the implementation is hard to explain, it's a bad idea.
If the implementation is easy to explain, it may be a good idea.
Namespaces are one honking great idea -- let's do more of those!
```

*The Zen of Python* is described in PEP-20 here: `https://www.python.org/dev/peps/pep-0020/`.

> **Note**
>
> *The Zen of Python* will be displayed on any Python interpreter by typing `import this`.

## How to do it...

1. Open and print the whole file, line by line (the result is not displayed):

```
>>> with open('zen_of_python.txt') as file:
...     for line in file:
...         print(line)
...
[RESULT NOT DISPLAYED]
```

2. Open the file and print any line containing the string 'should':

```
>>> with open('zen_of_python.txt', 'r') as file:
...     for line in file:
...         if 'should' in line.lower():
...             print(line)
...
Errors should never pass silently.
There should be one-- and preferably only one --obvious way to do it.
```

3. Open the file and print the first line containing the word 'better':

```
>>> with open('zen_of_python.txt', 'rt') as file:
...     for line in file:
...         if 'better' in line.lower():
..            print(line)
...             break
...
Beautiful is better than ugly.
```

## How it works...

To open a file, use the `open()` function. This returns a file object that then can be iterated over to return it line by line, as shown in *step 1* of the *How to do it...* section. Note it opens the file in text mode.

The `with` context manager is a very convenient way of dealing with files. It will close the file after finishing its use (leaving the block), and will do so even if an exception has been raised.

*Step 2* shows how to iterate and filter the lines based on what lines are applicable for our tasks. The lines are returned as strings that can be filtered in multiple ways, as described in the recipes in *Chapter 1, Let's Begin Our Automation Journey and Chapter 3, Building Your First Web Scraping Application*.

Reading the whole file may not be required, as shown in *step 3*. Because iterating through the file line by line will be reading the file as you go, you can stop at any time and avoid reading the rest of the file. For a small file, such as our example, that's not very relevant, but for long files it can reduce memory use and time.

## There's more...

The `with` context manager is the preferred way of dealing with files, but it's not the only one. You can also open and close them manually, like this:

```
>>> file = open('zen_of_python.txt')
>>> content = file.read()
>>> file.close()
```

Note the `.close()` method, to ensure that the file is closed and to free resources related to opening a file. The `.read()` method reads the whole file in one go, instead of line by line.

> **Note**
>
> The `.read()` method also accepts a size parameter in bytes that limits the size of the data read. For example, `file.read(1024)` will return up to 1KB of information. The next call to `.read()` will continue from that point. If you want to skip parts, you can use the `.seek()` method to position the reading cursor.
>
> This is useful for big files where reading them all is not ideal.
>
> For more information on streams (file objects), check the Python documentation `https://docs.python.org/3/library/io.html`

Files are opened in a particular mode. Modes define a combination of read or write, as well as whether to treat the data as text or binary data. By default, files are opened in read-only and text mode, which are described as just `"r"` (*step 2*) or as `"rt"` (*step 3*). Note that both these have the same effect, since text mode is the default.

More modes will be explored in other recipes.

## See also

- The *Crawling and searching directories* recipe, earlier in this chapter, to find files that will be read later.
- The *Dealing with encodings* recipe, later in this chapter, to learn how to deal with files encoded in a non-standard way.

# Dealing with encodings

Text files can be created using different encodings. An encoding transforms the bytes stored in the file to a set of characters. For example, using ASCII encoding, a sequence of four bytes with the numbers `[108, 111, 118, 101]` is converted into the word "*love*".

Going a step deeper, files really are a collection of bits: 1s and 0s. The number 108 is stored in 8 bits: `01101100`. ASCII covers the characters mostly used in English language, but in real life we need to cover other languages, from adding a few extra characters to similar languages, such as accents in French (e.g. *é*), to requiring a large number of characters for languages that use a complete different set of characters, such as Japanese (e.g ひ). We also need to represent a variety of other characters, such as punctuation and mathematical symbols.

For various historical and technical reasons, multiple systems were designed in ways that were not necessarily compatible. In recent years, with the introduction of Unicode, a widely supported standard that aims to cover all characters, the situation has greatly improved, but compatibility problems may still be encountered when working with different systems, as not all files use the most common Unicode encoding, UTF-8.

> Note
>
> As we suggested above, there's a difference between raw data in a file and a string object in Python, once opened and decoded. In Python, a string object is transformed from whatever encoding the file contained it into a native Unicode string. Once it is in this format it may be stored in different encodings. By default, Python works with the encoding defined by the OS, which in modern operating systems is UTF-8. This is a highly compatible encoding, but you may need to save files in a different one, depending on your specific requirements.

## Getting ready

We prepared two files in the GitHub repository that store the string '20£' in two different encodings: one in the usual UTF-8 and another in ISO 8859-1, a different common encoding. These prepared files are available in GitHub under the `ch04/documents` directory, with the names example_iso.txt and example_utf8.txt: https://github.com/PacktPublishing/Python-Automation-Cookbook-Third-Edition/tree/main/ch04/documents.

We'll use the BeautifulSoup module, presented previously in the *Parsing HTML* recipe in *Chapter 3, Building Your First Web Scraping Application*, to guess the encoding of a file.

## How to do it...

1. Open the example_utf8.txt file and display its content:

```
>>> with open('example_utf8.txt') as file:
...     print(file.read())
..
20£
```

2. Try to open the example_iso.txt file, which will raise an exception:

```
>>> with open('example_iso.txt') as file:
...     print(file.read())
...
Traceback (most recent call last):
  ...
UnicodeDecodeError: 'utf-8' codec can't decode byte 0xa3 in position 2:
invalid start byte
```

3. Open the example_iso.txt file with the proper encoding:

```
>>> with open('example_iso.txt', encoding='iso-8859-1') as file:
...     print(file.read())
...
20£
```

4. Open the utf8 file and save its content in an iso-8859-1 file:

```
>>> with open('example_utf8.txt') as file:
...     content = file.read()
>>> with open('example_output_iso.txt', 'w', encoding='iso-8859-1') as
file:
...     file.write(content)
```

```
...
4
```

5. Finally, read from the new file in the proper format to ensure it is correctly saved:

```
>>> with open('example_output_iso.txt', 'r',encoding='iso-8859-1') as file:
...     print(file.read())
...
20£
```

## How it works...

*Step 1* and *step 2* in the *How to do it...* section are very straightforward. In *step 3* we add an extra parameter, `encoding`, to specify that the file needs to be opened in something other than `UTF-8`.

> **Note**
>
> Python accepts a lot of standard encodings right out of the box. Check here for all of them and their aliases: `https://docs.python.org/3/library/codecs.html#standard-encodings`.

In *step 4* we create a new file in `ISO-8859-1` and write to it as usual. Notice the `"w"` parameter, which specifies to open it for writing and in text mode.

*Step 5* is a confirmation that the file is properly saved. Note that we are reading it using the `"r"` mode.

## There's more...

This recipe assumes that we know what encoding a file uses. But sometimes we might not be sure about that, and here GenAI can help:

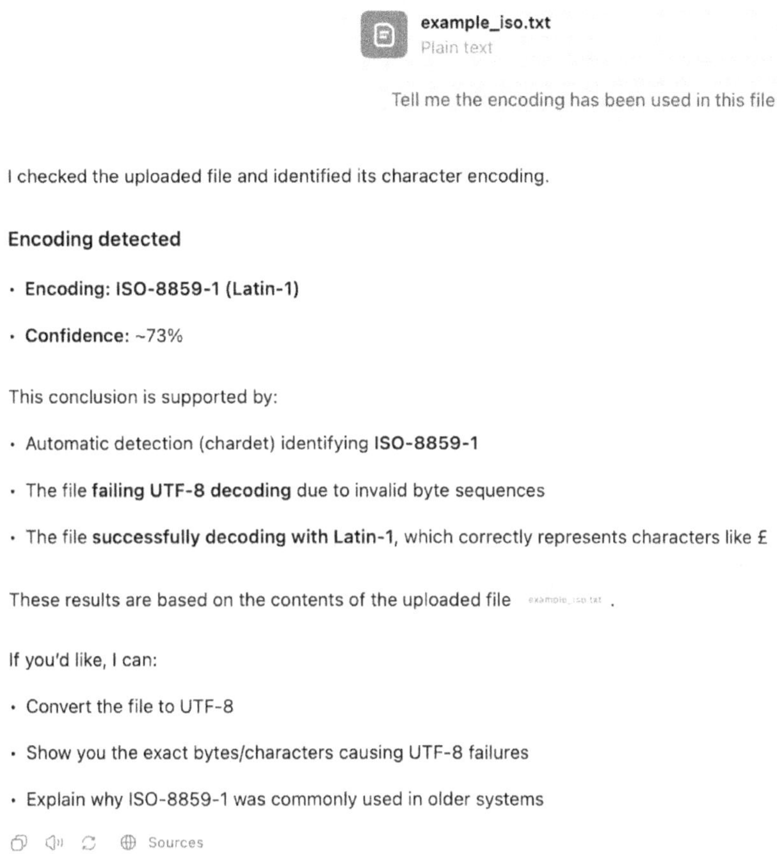


*Figure 4.1: Asking ChatGPT to get the encoding used for a file*

In this example, it is correct, and produces a high confidence, but it's good to verify it and double check. Note that it suggests converting the file to `UTF-8`. Using GenAI to detect the encoding can be acceptable, but you may need to perform a programmatic check in Python. For example, you may receive files regularly without knowing the encoding. Also, keep in mind that GenAI may hallucinate a more common encoding than the one that is actually used, or give a low level of confidence.

A programmatic alternative is to use `BeautifulSoup`, a module used to parse HTML, which can try to detect what encoding a particular file has.

Tip

Automatically detecting what encoding a file has may be theoretically impossible, in that there is potentially an infinite number of encodings! But typically, a subset of the usual encodings should cover 90% of real-world cases. In some cases a file can be understood using a different, but similar, encoding to the one actually used, as we will see in the next example. The easiest way of knowing for sure is to just ask whoever created the file in the first place.

Remember to have `BeautifulSoup` installed. We'll need to open the file to read in binary format with the `'rb'` parameter and then pass the binary content to the `UnicodeDammit` module of Beautiful Soup, like this:

```
>>> from bs4 import UnicodeDammit
>>> with open('example_output_iso.txt', 'rb') as file:
...     content = file.read()
...
>>> suggestion = UnicodeDammit(content)
>>> suggestion.original_encoding
'windows-1252'
>>> suggestion.unicode_markup
'20£'
```

The encoding can then be inferred. Note that here `'windows-1252'` is returned instead of `'iso-8859-1'`. This has happened because these two encodings are very similar, and for this particular file they are identical. So they are equivalent in practice for these files, but this showcases the problems with multiple encodings.

Though `.unicode_markup` returns the decoded string, it's better to use this suggestion just to obtain the encoding, and then reopen the file in text mode with the proper encoding. This makes the code more readable and helps in treating the file as text. For example, to treat it line by line.

```
>>> with open('example_iso.txt', encoding='windows-1252') as file:
...     print(file.read())
...
20£
```

Tip

When dealing with different operating systems, there are also other changes that may not be directly related with the encoding, but it can produce differences. For example, in Windows machines new lines are declared with two characters (CR LF) and in Unix and Unix-like systems with a single LF, even if the encoding is the same!

## See also

- The *Manipulating strings* recipe in *Chapter 1, Let's Begin Our Automation Journey*, to learn more about how to edit strings.
- The *Parsing HTML* recipe in *Chapter 3, Building Your First Web Scraping Application*, to learn more about Beautiful Soup.

# Reading CSV files

Some text files contain tabular data separated by commas. This is a convenient way of creating structured data, instead of using more complex binary formats such as Excel. These files are called **Comma Separated Values** or **CSV** files, and most spreadsheet packages allow us to work directly with them.

## Getting ready

We've prepared a CSV file using the data for the top 10 movies by theatre attendance, as described by this page: `http://www.mrob.com/pub/film-video/topadj.html`.

We copied the first 10 elements of the table into a spreadsheet program (Numbers) and exported the file as a CSV. The file is available in the GitHub repository in the `ch04/documents` directory as `top_films.csv`

top_films

| Rank | Admissions (millions) | Title (year) (studio) | Director(s) |
|---|---|---|---|
| 1 | 225.7 | Gone With the Wind (1939) (MGM) | Victor Fleming, George Cukor, Sam Wood |
| 2 | 194.4 | Star Wars (Ep. IV: A New Hope) (1977) (Fox) | George Lucas |
| 3 | 156.4 | The Sound of Music (1965) (Fox) | Robert Wise |
| 4 | 148.4 | ET: The Extra-Terrestrial (1982) (Univ) | Steven Spielberg |
| 5 | 130.0 | The Ten Commandments (1956) (Para) | Cecil B. DeMille |
| 7 | 126.3 | Snow White and the Seven Dwarfs (1937) (BV) | David Hand |
| 6 | 121.7 | Titanic (1997) (Fox) | James Cameron |
| 8 | 120.7 | Jaws (1975) (Univ) | Steven Spielberg |
| 9 | 120.1 | Doctor Zhivago (1965) (MGM) | David Lean |
| 10 | 117.1 | 101 Dalmatians (1961) (BV) | Clyde Geronimi, Hamilton Luske, Wolfgang Reitherman |

*Figure 4.2: Content of the CSV file*

## How to do it...

1. Import the csv module:

```
>>> import csv
```

2. Open the file, create a reader, and iterate through it to show the tabular data of all rows (only three rows are shown):

```
>>> import csv
>>> with open('top_films.csv') as file:
...     data = csv.reader(file)
...     for row in data:
...         print(row)
...
['Rank', 'Admissions\n(millions)', 'Title (year) (studio)', 'Director(s)']
['1', '225.7', 'Gone With the Wind (1939) (MGM)', 'Victor Fleming, George
Cukor, Sam Wood']
['2', '194.4', 'Star Wars (Ep. IV: A New Hope) (1977) (Fox)', 'George
Lucas']
...
```

```
['10', '117.1', '101 Dalmatians (1961)\xa0(BV)', 'Clyde Geronimi, Hamilton
Luske, Wolfgang Reitherman']
```

3. Open the file and use `DictReader` to structure the data, including the header:

```
>>> with open('top_films.csv') as file:
...     data = csv.DictReader(file)
...     structured_data = [row for row in data]
...
>>> structured_data[0]
{'Rank': '1', 'Admissions\n(millions)': '225.7', 'Title (year) (studio)':
'Gone With the Wind (1939) (MGM)', 'Director(s)': 'Victor Fleming, George
Cukor, Sam Wood'}
```

4. Each of the items in `structured_data` is a full dictionary that contains each of the values:

```
>>> structured_data[0].keys()
dict_keys(['Rank', 'Admissions\n(millions)', 'Title (year) (studio)',
'Director(s)'])
>>> structured_data[0]['Rank']
'1'
>>> structured_data[0]['Director(s)']
'Victor Fleming, George Cukor, Sam Wood'
```

## How it works...

Notice that the file needs to be read and that we use a `with` context block. This ensures that the file is closed at the end of the block.

As shown in *step 2* of the *How to do it...* section, the `csv.reader` class allows us to structure the returning lines of code by subdividing them as lists, following the format of the table data. Notice how all the values are described as strings. `csv.reader` does not understand whether the first line is a header or not.

For a more structured read of the file, in *step 3* we used `csv.DictReader`. By default it reads the first row as a header defining the applicable fields and then converts each of the rows into dictionaries with those fields.

> **Tip**
>
> Sometimes, as in this case, the field names used in the file can be a little verbose. Don't be afraid to translate the dictionary as an extra step to obtain more manageable field names.

## There's more...

A CSV has a very loosely defined file structure specification. There are several ways that the data can be stored, which are represented in the csv module as **dialects**. For example, the field values can be delimited by commas, semicolons, or tabs. The list of default accepted dialects can be displayed by calling `csv.list_dialect()`.

> **Note**
>
> By default, the dialect will be Excel, which is the most common one. Even other spreadsheets will commonly use it.

Dialects can also be inferred from the file itself, through the `Sniffer` class.

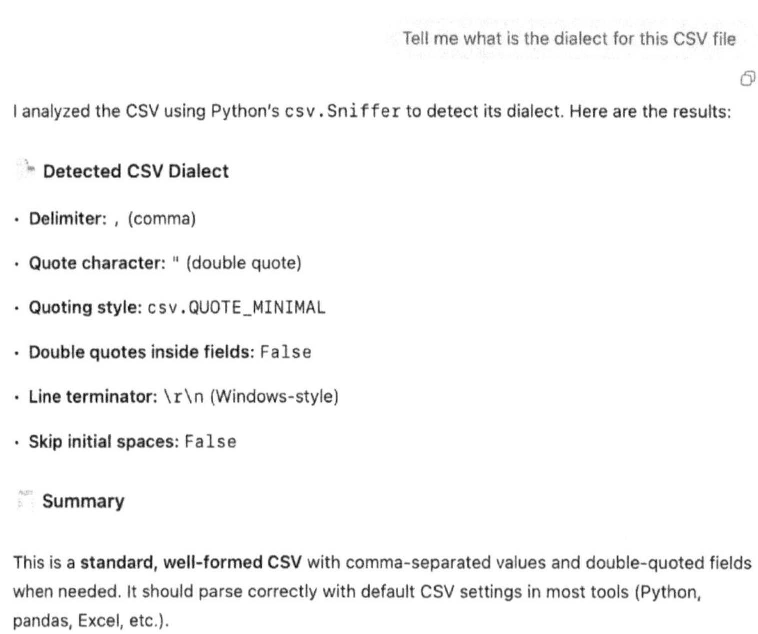


*Figure 4.3: ChatGPT using the Sniffer class to infer the CSV dialect.*

As you can see in *Figure 4.3*, we can use GenAI, but it uses Python code itself. And from the Sniffer class we can directly use its output, as we will see.

The `Sniffer` class analyzes a sample of the file (or the whole file) and returns a dialect object to allow reading in the proper way.

Notice that the file is opened with no new lines, to not make any assumptions about how newline characters are represented, or even whether they are present:

```
>>> with open('top_films.csv', newline='') as file:
...     dialect = csv.Sniffer().sniff(file.read())
```

The dialect can then be used when opening the reader. Note the newline again, as the dialect will split the lines correctly:

```
>>> with open('top_films.csv', newline='') as file:
...     reader = csv.reader(file, dialect)
...     for row in reader:
...         print(row)
```

The full csv module documentation can be found here: `https://docs.python.org/3/library/csv.html`.

## See also

- The *Dealing with encodings* recipe, earlier in this chapter, to learn how to deal with encodings.
- The *Reading text files* recipe, earlier in this chapter, to learn more about opening and reading files.

# Reading log files

Another common structured text file format is used in **log files**. These consist of rows of log data, which are lines of text having a particular format suited to describing events.

> Note
>
> Different applications can generate very different log formats and there's no common structure or syntax for them

Typically, each log entry will have a time when the event occurred, so the file is an ordered collection of event entries.

## Getting ready

The `example_log.log` file, containing five sales logs, can be obtained from the GitHub repository here: `https://github.com/PacktPublishing/Python-Automation-Cookbook-Third-Edition/blob/main/ch04/documents/example_logs.log`.

The format in this case is:

```
[<Timestamp in iso format>] - SALE - PRODUCT: <product id> - PRICE: $<price of the sale>
```

We'll use the `ch01/price_log.py` file, introduced in *Chapter 1*, to process each log into an object. There's a copy in the `ch04/documents` directory to simplify the import process.

Be sure to have available the `parse` and `delorean` modules, as they are dependencies for the `price_log.py` file. You can use the included `ch04/requirements.txt` file for that.

## How to do it...

1. Import `PriceLog`:

```
>>> from price_log import PriceLog
```

2. Open the log file and parse all logs:

```
>>> with open('example_logs.log') as file:
...     logs = [PriceLog.parse(log) for log in file]
...
>>> len(logs)
5
>>> logs[0]
<PriceLog (Delorean(datetime=datetime.datetime(2025, 6, 17, 22, 11, 50, 268396), timezone='UTC'), 1489, 9.99)>
```

3. Determine the total income by all sales:

```
>>> total = sum(log.price for log in logs)
>>> total
Decimal('47.82')
```

4. Determine how many units have been sold of each `product_id`:

```
>>> from collections import Counter
>>> counter = Counter(log.product_id for log in logs)
>>> counter
Counter({1489: 2, 4508: 1, 8597: 1, 3086: 1})
```

5. Filter the logs to find all occurrences of selling product ID 1489:

```
>>> product_1489 = [log for log in logs if log.product_id == 1489]
>>> len(logs)
5
>>> product_1489[0].product_id, product_1489[0].timestamp
(1489, Delorean(datetime=datetime.datetime(2025, 6, 17, 22, 11, 50,
268396), timezone='UTC'))
>>> product_1489[1].product_id, product_1489[1].timestamp
(1489, Delorean(datetime=datetime.datetime(2025, 6, 17, 22, 11, 50,
268468), timezone='UTC'))
```

## How it works...

As each entry is a single line, we open the file and go one by one, parsing each of them. The parsing code is available in `price_log.py`. Check it for more details on the parsing process.

In *step 2* of the *How to do it...* section we open the file and process each of the lines to create a log list with all our processed logs. Then we can perform aggregation operations, as in the next steps.

*Step 3* shows how to aggregate all values. In this case, that means summing the price of all items sold over the log file to get the total revenue.

*Step 4* uses `Counter` to determine the amount of each item in the file log. This returns a dictionary-like object with the values to count and the number of times they appear.

Filtering can also be done using a line-by-line approach, as shown in *step 5*. This is similar to the other filtering we've done in this chapter's recipes.

## There's more...

Remember that you can stop processing a file as soon as you have all the data you need. This may be a good strategy if the file is very big, as is often the case with log files.

`Counter` is a great tool to quickly count a list. See the Python documentation here for more details: `https://docs.python.org/3/library/collections.html#counter-objects`. You can get the ordered items by calling the following:

```
>>> counter.most_common()
[(1489, 2), (4508, 1), (8597, 1), (3086, 1)]
```

## See also

- The *Using a third-party tool—parse* recipe in *Chapter 1, Let's Begin Our Automation Journey*.
- The *Reading text files* recipe, earlier in this chapter, to learn more about opening and reading files.

# Reading file metadata

File metadata is everything associated with a particular file that is not the data content itself. The most obvious piece of metadata is the file name, but others include the size of the file, the creation date, and its permissions.

Browsing through that data may be important, for example, to filter files older than a date, or to find all files bigger than a value in kilobytes. In this recipe, we'll see how to access the file metadata in Python.

## Getting ready

We'll use the `zen_of_python.txt` file, available in the GitHub repository (`https://github.com/PacktPublishing/Python-Automation-Cookbook-Third-Edition/blob/main/ch04/documents/zen_of_python.txt`). Using the `ls` command, you can see that the file takes up 823 bytes, and that, in this example, it was created on December 15th:

```
$ ls -lrt zen_of_python.txt
-rw-r--r--@ 1 jaimebuelta  staff  823 15 Dec 15:43 zen_of_python.txt
```

(On your computer, the dates may vary, depending on when you downloaded the code.)

## How to do it...

1. Import os and `datetime`:

```
>>> import os
>>> from datetime import datetime
```

2. Retrieve the stats of the `zen_of_python.txt` file:

```
>>> stats = os.stat('zen_of_python.txt')
>>> stats
os.stat_result(st_mode=33188, st_ino=225410994, st_dev=16777234,
st_nlink=1, st_uid=502, st_gid=20, st_size=823, st_atime=1765811416,
st_mtime=1765809824, st_ctime=1765809830)
```

3. Get the size of the file, in bytes:

```
>>> stats.st_size
823
```

4. Find out when the file was last modified:

```
>>> datetime.fromtimestamp(stats.st_mtime)
datetime.datetime(2025, 12, 15, 15, 43, 44, 918240)
```

5. Find out when the file was last accessed:

```
>>> datetime.fromtimestamp(stats.st_atime)
datetime.datetime(2025, 12, 15, 16, 10, 16, 921395)
```

## How it works...

`os.stats` returns a `stats` object that represents the metadata stored in the filesystem. The metadata includes:

- The size of the file in bytes, as shown in *step 3* in the *How to do it...* section, using `st_size`.
- When the file content was last modified, as shown in *step 4*, using `st_mtime`.
- When the file was last read (accessed), as shown in *step 5*, using `st_atime`.

The times are returned as timestamps, so in *step 4* and *step 5* we create a `datetime` object from the timestamps to better access the data.

All these values can be used to filter the files and access the ones of interest.

Tip

Notice that you don't need to open the file with `open()` to read its metadata. Detecting whether a file was changed after a known time by reading its modification time will be quicker than comparing its contents, so you can take advantage of that for comparison.

## There's more...

To obtain the stats one by one, convenience functions are available in `os.path`, which follow the pattern `get<value>`:

```
>>> os.path.getsize('zen_of_python.txt')
823
>>> os.path.getmtime('zen_of_python.txt')
1765809824.9182403
>>> os.path.getatime('zen_of_python.txt')
1765811416.9213953
```

The value is specified in the UNIX timestamp format (seconds since January 1, 1970).

Tip

Note that calling all three of these functions will be slower than making a single call to `os.stats` and processing the results. Also, returned stats can be inspected to detect the available metadata.

The metadata fields described in this recipe are available for all filesystems, but there are more fields that can be used, depending on the particular platform.

For example, to obtain the creation date of a file, you can use the `st_birthtime` parameter for macOS or `st_mtime` in Windows.

Note

`st_mtime` is always available, but its meaning changes between systems. In Unix systems, it will change when the content is modified, so it's not a reliable way to obtain the time when the file was created.

`os.stat` will follow symbolic links. If you want to get the stats of a symbolic link itself, use `os.lstat()`.

> **Note**
>
> A symbolic link is a file or directory that refers to another one. It's a way to have multiple files or directories pointing to the same one. Check out this article for a more in-depth description: `https://www.komprise.com/glossary_terms/symbolic-link/`.

You can check the full documentation about all available stats here: `https://docs.python.org/3/library/os.html#os.stat_result`.

## See also

- The *Reading text files* recipe, earlier in this chapter, to learn the basics of opening and reading files.
- The *Reading images* recipe, coming next, to learn how to read and process image files.

# Reading images

Probably the most common form of data that is not text is image data. Images have their own set of specific metadata that can be read and used to filter values or perform other operations.

The main challenge is dealing with multiple image formats and different metadata specifications. We'll show in this recipe how to get information from both JPEG and PNG files, and see how the same information can be encoded differently.

## Getting ready

The best general toolkit for dealing with images in Python is, arguably, `Pillow`. This library allows you to easily read files in the most common formats, as well as perform operations on them. `Pillow` started as a fork of **PIL** (**Python Imaging Library**), a previous module that became stagnant some years ago.

We will also use the `xmltodict` module to transform some data from XML into a more convenient dictionary. We will add both modules to `requirements.txt` and reinstall them in the virtual environment:

```
$ echo "Pillow==12.0.0" >> requirements.txt
$ echo "xmltodict==1.0.2" >> requirements.txt
$ uv pip install -r requirements.txt
```

The metadata information in photo files is defined in the **EXIF** (**Exchangeable Image File**) format. EXIF is a standard for storing information about pictures, including things like what camera took the picture, when it was taken, the exposure and focal length settings, color info, GPS information describing the location, and so on.

> **Tip**
>
> You can get a good summary here: `https://www.slrphotographyguide.com/what-is-exif-metadata/`. All the information is optional, but virtually all digital cameras and processing software will store some data. Because of privacy concerns, parts of it, like the exact location, can be disabled.

The following images will be used for this recipe, and are available to download in the GitHub repository (`https://github.com/PacktPublishing/Python-Automation-Cookbook-Third-Edition/tree/main/ch04/images`):

- `photo-dublin-a1.jpg`
- `photo-dublin-a2.png`
- `photo-dublin-b.png`

Two of them, `photo-dublin-a1.jpg` and `photo-dublin-a2.png`, are the same scene, but while the first is the untouched picture, the second has been retouched to slightly alter the colors and it has also been scaled. Notice that one is in JPEG format and the other in PNG. The other image, `photo-dublin-b.png`, is a picture of a different scene. Both pictures were taken in Dublin, with the same phone camera, on two different days.

While Pillow understands how JPG files store the EXIF info directly, PNG files store XMP info, which is a more generic standard that can contain EXIF data.

> **Tip**
>
> More information about XMP can be obtained here: `https://www.adobe.com/devnet/xmp.html`. For the most part, it defines an XML tree structure that's relatively readable in raw.

To further complicate matters, XMP is encoded using RDF, which is a standard describing how to encode an XML tree.

Tip

If EXIF, XMP, and RDF sound confusing, well, it's because they are. XMP stores the EXIF information using RDF. Ultimately, the differences between them are not very relevant, and the best approach is to find out the interesting bits and pieces. We can inspect the specifics of the object attributes and methods using Python introspection tools and check exactly how the data is structured, and what the name of the parameter we are looking for is.

As the GPS information is stored in different formats, we've included in the GitHub repository a file called `gps_conversion.py`: `https://github.com/PacktPublishing/Python-Automation-Cookbook-Third-Edition/blob/main/ch04/gps_conversion.py`. This includes the functions `exif_to_decimal` and `rdf_to_decimal`, which will transform both formats into decimals to enable them to be compared.

## How to do it...

1. Import the modules and functions needed in this recipe:

```
>>> from PIL import Image
>>> from PIL.ExifTags import TAGS, GPSTAGS
>>> import xmltodict
>>> from gps_conversion import exif_to_decimal, rdf_to_decimal
```

2. Open the first photo:

```
>>> image1 = Image.open('images/photo-dublin-a1.jpg')
```

3. Get the width, height, and format of the file:

```
>>> image1.height
3024
>>> image1.width
4032
>>> image1.format
'JPEG'
```

4. Retrieve the EXIF information of the image and transform it into a convenient dictionary. Show the camera, the lens used, and when it was taken:

```
>>> exif_info_1 = {TAGS.get(tag, tag): value
        for tag, value in image1._getexif().items()}
>>> exif_info_1['Model']
'iPhone X'
>>> exif_info_1['LensModel']
'iPhone X back dual camera 4mm f/1.8'
>>> exif_info_1['DateTimeOriginal']
'2018:04:21 12:07:55'
```

5. Open the second image and obtain the XMP info:

```
>>> image2 = Image.open('images/photo-dublin-a2.png')
>>> image2.height
1512
>>> image2.width
2016
>>> image2.format
'PNG'
>>> xmp_info = xmltodict.parse(image2.info['XML:com.adobe.xmp'])
```

6. Obtain the RDF description field, which contains all the values we are looking for. Retrieve the model (a TIFF value), the lens model (an EXIF value), and the creation date (an XMP value). Check the values are the same as in *step 4*, even if the file is different:

```
>>> rdf_info_2 = xmp_info['x:xmpmeta']['rdf:RDF']['rdf:Description']
>>> rdf_info_2['tiff:Model']
'iPhone X'
>>> rdf_info_2['exifEX:LensModel']
'iPhone X back dual camera 4mm f/1.8'
>>> rdf_info_2['xmp:CreateDate']
'2018-04-21T12:07:55'
```

7. Obtain the GPS information in both pictures, transform into an equivalent format, and check that they are the same. Notice that the resolution is not the same, but they match up to the fourth decimal point:

```
>>> gps_info_1 = {GPSTAGS.get(tag, tag): value
        for tag, value in exif_info_1['GPSInfo'].items()}
>>> exif_to_decimal(gps_info_1)
('N53.34690555555556', 'W6.247797222222222')
>>> rdf_to_decimal(rdf_info_2)
('N53.346905', 'W6.247796666666667')
```

8. Open the third image and obtain the creation date and GPS info, and check it doesn't match the other photo, although it is close (the second and third decimals are not the same):

```
>>> image3 = Image.open('images/photo-dublin-b.png')
>>> xmp_info = xmltodict.parse(image3.info['XML:com.adobe.xmp'])
>>> rdf_info_3 = xmp_info['x:xmpmeta']['rdf:RDF']['rdf:Description']
>>> rdf_info_3['xmp:CreateDate']
'2018-03-08T18:16:58.253'
>>> rdf_to_decimal(rdf_info_3)
('N53.34984166666667', 'W6.260388333333333')
```

## How it works...

Pillow is able to interpret files in most common image formats, as shown in *step 2* of the *How to do it...* section.

The `Image` object contains basic information about the size and format of the file and is displayed in *step 3*. The info property contains information that is dependent on the format.

The EXIF metadata for JPG files can be parsed with the `.getexif()` method, but then it needs to be translated properly, as it uses the raw binary definition. For example, the number 42,036 corresponds to the `LensModel` property. Fortunately, there's a definition of all tags in the `PIL.ExifTags` module. We translate the dictionary into readable tags in *step 4* to obtain a more readable dictionary.

*Step 5* opens a PNG file, which has the same properties related to size, but now the metadata is stored in XML/RDF format and needs to be parsed with the help of `xmltodict`. *Step 6* shows how to navigate this metadata to extract the same information that's in the JPG file. The data is the same, as both files come from the same original picture, even if the images are different.

> **Tip**
>
> `Xmltodict` has some issues when trying to parse data that's not in XML format. Check that the input is valid XML.

*Step 7* extracts the GPS information for both images, which is stored in different ways, and shows that the coordinates are the same (although the precision is different because of the way it is encoded).

> **Tip**
>
> Not every image will necessarily have location information or other metadata. This information can be changed or removed, or stored differently, depending on the format and the camera generating the file.

*Step 8* shows the information for the third photo.

## There's more...

`Pillow` also has extensive functionality around modifying pictures. It is very easy to resize or make simple modifications to a file, such as rotating it, resizing it, or transforming it from one format to another. The module also facilitates various more complex operations, like cropping the image, applying color filters, or generating animated GIFs. If you're interested in image processing using Python, it is definitely the module to master. You can find the complete `Pillow` documentation here: `https://pillow.readthedocs.io`.

The GPS coordinates in the recipe are stated in **DMS** (**degrees**, **minutes**, **seconds**) and **DDM** (**degrees**, **decimal**, **minutes**), and transformed into **DD** (**decimal**, **degrees**). You can find out more about the different GPS formats here: `http://www.ubergizmo.com/how-to/read-gps-coordinates/`. You'll also find out how to search the exact locations of the pictures there, in case you're curious.

> **Tip**
>
> Navigating through the different parameters and structure of the image metadata can be difficult. This is an area when you can get clear help from GenAI to parse the data in the format you need and make the right transformations and conversions.

A more advanced use of reading image files is to try to process them for **OCR** (**Optical Character Recognition**). This means automatically detecting text in an image and extracting and processing it. The open source module `tesseract` allows you to do this, and it can be used with Python and `Pillow`.

You need to install `tesseract` on your system (`https://github.com/tesseract-ocr/tesseract/wiki`), as well as the `pytesseract` Python module (using `uv pip install pytesseract`).

You can download a file with clear text, called `photo-text.jpg`, from the GitHub repository at `https://github.com/PacktPublishing/Python-Automation-Cookbook-Third-Edition/blob/main/ch04/images/photo-text.jpg`:

```
>>> from PIL import Image
>>> import pytesseract
>>> pytesseract.image_to_string(Image.open('images/photo-text.jpg'))
'Automate!\n'
```

OCR can be difficult if the text is not very clear in the image, or it is mixed with images, or it uses a distinctive font. There's an example of that in the `photo-dublin-a-text.jpg` file, (available in the GitHub repository at `https://github.com/PacktPublishing/Python-Automation-Cookbook-Third-Edition/blob/main/ch04/images/photo-dublin-a-text.jpg`), which includes text over the picture:

```
>>> pytesseract.image_to_string(Image.open('photo-dublin-a-text.jpg'))
'oe ee KM\n\n'
```

Not great!

Note

More information about Tesseract is available via the following links:

`https://github.com/tesseract-ocr/tesseract`

`https://github.com/madmaze/pytesseract`

Other available OCR options, like easyOCR, can sometimes produce better results. To use it, install it with `uv pip install easyocr`:

```
>>> import easyocr
>>> reader = easyocr.Reader(['en']). # Load the English module(s)
...
```

```
>>> reader.readtext('images/photo-text.jpg', detail=0)
['Automatel']
```

While not perfect (it understood `'Automatel'` instead of `'Automate'`) it produced a better result in the presence of mixed images and text.

When reading with `detail=0`, it simplifies the result. But without it, it will also return the position of text and assigned confidence.

> Note
>
> More information about easyOCR is available in the documentation at `https://github.com/jaidedai/easyocr`.
>
> Note that easyOCR supports many languages.

Getting the best results from OCR may require initial image processing. Image processing is out of scope for this book, but it's worth mentioning the OpenCV package, which is more powerful than `Pillow`. You can process a file and then open it with Pillow: `http://opencv-python-tutroals.readthedocs.io/en/latest/py_tutorials/py_tutorials.html`.

## See also

- The *Reading text files* recipe, earlier in this chapter, to learn the basics of opening and reading files.
- The *Reading file metadata* recipe, earlier in this chapter, to learn how to get extra information from files.
- The *Crawling and searching directories* recipe, earlier in this chapter, to learn how to search and find files in directories.

# Reading PDF files

A common format for documents is **PDF** (**Portable Document Format**). It started as a format to describe a document so that any printer would print it in the same way, so PDF is a format that ensures that the document will be printed exactly as shown. It has become a de-facto standard for sharing documents, especially documents that are final and intended to be read-only.

## Getting ready

For this recipe, we are going to use the `pypdf` module. We need to add it to our virtual environment:

```
$ echo "pypdf==6.6.2" >> requirements.txt
$ pip install -r requirements.txt
```

In the GitHub directory `ch04/documents` we have prepared two documents, `document-1.pdf` and `document-2.pdf`, to use in this recipe. Note they contain mostly Lorem Ipsum text, which is just placeholder.

> **Note**
>
> Lorem Ipsum text is commonly used in design to show text without needing to create the content before the design. You can learn more about it here: `https://loremipsum.io/`.

They are both the same test document, but the second one can only be opened with a password. The password is `automate`.

## How to do it...

1. Import the module:

```
>>> from pypdf import PdfReader
```

2. Open the `document-1.pdf` file and create a PDF document object. Notice that the file needs to be open for the whole reading:

```
>>> file = open('document-1.pdf', 'rb')
>>> document = PdfReader(file)
```

3. Get the number of pages of the document and check it is not encrypted:

```
>>> len(document.pages)
3
>>> document.is_encrypted
False
```

4. Get the creation date from the document info (2018-Jun-24 11:15:18) and discover that it has been created with a Mac Quartz PDFContext:

```
>>> document.metadata['/CreationDate']
"D:20180624111518Z00'00'"
>>> document.metadata['/Producer']
'Mac OS X 10.13.5 Quartz PDFContext'
```

5. Get the first page and read the text on it:

```
>>> document.pages[0].extract_text()
'\nA VERY IMPORTANT DOCUMENT By James McCormac CEO Loose Seal Inc \n'
```

6. Do the same operation for the second page (redacted here):

```
>>> document.pages[1].extract_text()
'"!This is an example of a test document that is stored in PDF format. It
contains some \nsentences to describe what it is and the it has lore ipsum
text.\n!"\nLorem ipsum dolor sit amet, consectetur adipiscing elit. ...$'
```

7. Close the file and open `document-2.pdf`:

```
>>> file.close()
>>> file = open('document-2.pdf', 'rb')
>>> document = PdfReader(file)
```

8. Check the document is encrypted (it requires a password) and raise an error if we try to access its content:

```
>>> document.is_encrypted
True
>>> len(document.pages)
...
PyPDF2.errors.FileNotDecryptedError: File has not been decrypted
```

9. Decrypt the file with the password and access its content:

```
>>> document.decrypt('automate')
<PasswordType.OWNER_PASSWORD: 2>
>>> len(document.pages)
3
```

```
>>> document.pages[0].extract_text()
'\nA VERY IMPORTANT DOCUMENT By James McCormac CEO Loose Seal Inc \n'
```

10. Close the file to clean up:

```
>>> file.close()
```

## How it works...

Once the document is open, as shown in *step 1* and *step 2* of the *How to do it...* section, the document object provides access to the document.

> Note
>
> We open and close manually the file with `open` and `.close` to allow us to describe different steps and results interactively. The file needs to be open while we perform all the operations. Generally, is a better idea to use a `with` block instead, as we've seen earlier in the chapter.

The pages of the document are available in `.pages`, which can be accessed like a list.

Other data that's accessible is stored in `.metadata`, which stores information on the creator, when it was created, etc.

> Note
>
> The information in `.metadata` is optional and sometimes not up to date. It depends greatly on the tool used to generate the PDF.

Each of the page objects can get its text by calling `.extract_text()`, which will return all the text contained in the page, as in *step 5* and *step 6*. This method tries to extract all text, but it has some limitations. For well-structured texts, such as our example, it works quite well, and the resulting text can be processed cleanly. Text in multiple columns or other more complex layouts may require more extensive processing.

> Tip
>
> Note that the PDF file needs to be open for the whole operation, so be careful if you use a `with` context operator. After leaving the with block, the file is closed.

*Step 8* and *step 9* show how to deal with encrypted files. You can detect whether a file is encrypted or not with `.is_encrypted`, and then decrypt it using the `.decrypt` method, providing the correct password.

## There's more...

PDF is such a flexible format that it is widely used for a variety of purposes, but that also means that it can be difficult to parse and process.

While most PDF files contain textual content, it is not uncommon for them to contain images of text. This happens when a document has been scanned. In this case, the information is stored as a collection of images instead of as text. This makes it difficult to extract the textual data; we may end up having to resort to methods such as OCR to parse the images into text.

PyPDF2 does not provide a good interface to deal with images. You may need to transform the PDF into a collection of images and then process the images with other tools like Pillow. See the *Reading images* recipe for ideas about OCR and the use of Pillow. Most PDF readers can do it, or you can use a command-line tool such as `pdftoppm` (`https://linux.die.net/man/1/pdftoppm`) or QPDF (see the following).

Some methods of encrypting files may not be understood by PyPDF2. It will generate `NotImplementedError`: only algorithm code 1 and 2 are supported. If that happens, you need to decrypt the PDF externally and open it once it is decrypted. You can use QPDF to create a copy without the password, as follows:

```
$ qpdf --decrypt --password=PASSWORD encrypted.pdf output-decrypted.pdf
```

The full documentation for QPDF is available here: `http://qpdf.sourceforge.net/files/qpdf-manual.html`. QPDF is available in most package managers as well.

QPDF is capable of performing numerous transformations and analyzing PDFs in depth. There are also bindings in Python to a library called `pikepdf` (`https://pikepdf.readthedocs.io/en/stable/`). This package is more complicated to use than PyPDF2 and it's not as straightforward for text extraction, but it can be useful for other operations such as extracting images from a PDF.

## See also

- The *Reading text files* recipe, earlier in this chapter, to learn the basics of opening and reading files.
- The *Crawling and searching directories* recipe, earlier in this chapter, to learn how to search and find files in directories.

# Reading Word documents

Word documents (`.docx`) are another common document type for storing mainly text. They are typically generated with Microsoft Office, but other tools can also be used to produce compatible files. Word files are probably the most common means of sharing documents that need to be editable, but they are also common for distributing documents.

We'll see in this recipe how to extract text content from a Word document.

## Getting ready

We'll use the `python-docx` module to read and process Word documents:

```
$ echo "python-docx==1.2.0" >> requirements.txt
$ pip install -r requirements.txt
```

We have prepared a test file, available in the GitHub `ch04/documents` directory, called `document-1.docx`, which we'll use in this recipe. Note that this document follows the same Lorem Ipsum pattern that was described in the test document for the *Reading PDF files* recipe.

## How to do it...

1. Import `python-docx`:

```
>>> import docx
```

2. Open the `document-1.docx` file:

```
>>> doc = docx.Document('document-1.docx')
```

3. Check some of the metadata properties stored in `core_properties`:

```
>>> doc.core_properties.title
'A very important document'
>>> doc.core_properties.keywords
'lorem ipsum'
>>> doc.core_properties.modified
datetime.datetime(2025, 12, 16, 16, 33, tzinfo=datetime.timezone.utc)
```

4. Check the number of paragraphs:

```
>>> len(doc.paragraphs)
58
```

5. Walk through the paragraphs to detect the ones that contain text. Note that not all text is displayed here:

```
>>> for index, paragraph in enumerate(doc.paragraphs):
...     if paragraph.text:
...         print(index, paragraph.text)
...
30 A VERY IMPORTANT DOCUMENT
31 By James McCormac
32 CEO Loose Seal Inc
34
...
56 TITLE 2
57 ...
```

6. Obtain the text for paragraphs 30 and 31, which correspond to the title and subtitle on the first page:

```
>>> doc.paragraphs[30].text
'A VERY IMPORTANT DOCUMENT'
>>> doc.paragraphs[31].text
'By James McCormac'
```

7. Each of the paragraphs has runs, which are sections of the text with different properties. Check that the first text paragraph and run is in bold and the second is in italics:

```
>>> doc.paragraphs[30].runs[0].text
'A VERY IMPORTANT DOCUMENT'
>>> doc.paragraphs[30].runs[0].italic
>>> doc.paragraphs[30].runs[0].bold
True
>>> doc.paragraphs[31].runs[0].text
'By James McCormac'
>>> doc.paragraphs[31].runs[0].italic
```

```
True
>>> doc.paragraphs[31].runs[0].bold
```

8. In this document, most of the paragraphs have only one run, but we have a good example of different runs in paragraph 48. Display its text and the different styles. For example, the word `Word` is in bold, and ipsum is in italics:

```
>>> [run.text for run in doc.paragraphs[48].runs]
['This is an example of a test document that is stored in ', 'Word format',
'. It contains some ', 'sentences', ' to describe what it is and it has ',
'lorem ipsum', ' text.']
>>> run1 = doc.paragraphs[48].runs[1]
>>> run1.text
'Word format'
>>> run1.bold
True
>>> run2 = doc.paragraphs[48].runs[5]
>>> run2.text
'lorem ipsum'
>>> run2.italic
True
```

## How it works...

The most important peculiarity of Word documents is that the data is structured in paragraphs, instead of in pages. The size of the font, line size, and other factors may make the number of pages change.

Most of the paragraphs are also typically empty, or contain only new lines, tabs, or other whitespace characters. It is a good idea to check when a paragraph is empty and skip it.

In the *How to do it...* section, *step 2* opens the file and *step 3* shows how to access the core properties. These are properties that are defined in Word as document metadata, such as the author or creation date.

> **Note**
>
> Word metadata needs to be taken with a grain of salt, as tools that produce Word documents (but not Microsoft Office) won't necessarily complete it. Double-check before attempting to use Word metadata.

The paragraphs of the document can be iterated and have their text extracted in raw format, as shown in *step 6*. This is information that doesn't include styling information, so raw is typically the most useful format for processing the data automatically.

If the styling information is required, the runs can be used as in *step 7* and *step 8*. Each paragraph can contain one or more runs, which are smaller text units that share the same styling. For example, if a sentence is *Word1* **word2**, there will be two runs, one with italicized text (*Word1*) and another with bold (**word2**). Furthermore, there can be intermediate runs with regular text that contain just whitespace characters, making in this case a total of three runs. The styling can be detected individually for properties such as bold, italic, or underline.

> Tip
>
> The division in runs can be quite complicated. Due to the way editors work, it is not uncommon to have half-words, a word split into two runs, sometimes with the same properties. Do not rely on the number of runs when analyzing the content. In particular, double-check if you're trying to check whether a part with a particular style is divided in two or more runs.

Be aware that because Word documents are produced not only by Microsoft Word but also by other text processors (e.g. LibreOffice Writer or Google Docs), some properties may not be defined, it being left to the text processor to optionally specify them. For example, it is very common to keep the default font, which may mean that the font information on runs is left empty.

## There's more...

Further style information, such as `small_caps` or `size`, can be found under the font attribute:

```
>>> run2.font.cs_italic
True
>>> run2.font.size
152400
>>> run2.font.small_caps
```

Normally, focusing on the raw text, without paying attention to the style information, is the correct way of parsing. But sometimes a bold word in a paragraph will have special significance. It may be the header or some particularly meaningful text. Because it's highlighted, it likely is what you're looking for! Keep that in mind when analyzing documents.

You can find the complete `python-docx` documentation here: `https://python-docx.readthedocs.io/en/latest/`.

## See also

- The *Reading text files* recipe, earlier in this chapter, to learn the basics of opening and reading text files.
- The *Reading PDF files* recipe, earlier in this chapter, to learn how to process other kinds of document files.

# Scanning documents for a keyword

In this recipe we will apply all the lessons from the previous recipes as we search all the files in a directory for a particular keyword. This is a recap of the rest of the recipes in this chapter and includes a script that searches different kinds of file.

## Getting ready

Be sure to include the following modules in the requirements.txt file and install them into your virtual environment:

```
beautifulsoup4==4.14.3
Pillow==12.0.0
PyPDF2==3.0.1
python-docx==1.2.0
```

Check that the directory to search has the following files (all are available in `https://github.com/PacktPublishing/Python-Automation-Cookbook-Third-Edition/tree/main/ch04/documents/`). Note that `file5.pdf` and `file6.pdf` are copies of `document-1.pdf`, for simplicity. `file1.txt` to `file4.txt` are empty files:

```
├── dir
│   ├── file1.txt
│   ├── file2.txt
│   ├── file6.pdf
│   └── subdir
│       ├── file3.txt
│       ├── file4.txt
│       └── file5.pdf
├── document-1.docx
├── document-1.pdf
├── document-2-1.pdf
```

```
├── document-2.pdf
├── example_iso.txt
├── example_output_iso.txt
├── example_utf8.txt
├── top_films.csv
└── zen_of_python.txt
```

We've prepared a script, `scan.py`, that will search for a word in all the `.txt`, `.csv`, `.pdf`, and `.docx` files. The script is available in the `ch04` directory of the GitHub repository.

## How to do it...

1. Refer to `help -h` for how to use the `scan.py` script:

```
$ uv run scan.py -h
usage: scan.py [-h] [-w W] directory

positional arguments:
  directory   Directory to scan

options:
  -h, --help  show this help message and exit
  -w W        Word to search
```

2. Search for the word 'the', which is present in most of the files:

```
$ uv run scan.py documents -w the
>>> Word found in ./documents/top_films.csv
>>> Word found in ./documents/zen_of_python.txt
>>> Word found in ./documents/document-1.pdf
>>> Word found in ./documents/dir/file6.pdf
>>> Word found in ./documents/dir/subdir/file5.pdf
```

3. Search for the word 'lorem', only present in the `.pdf` and `.docx` files:

```
$ uv run scan.py documents -w lorem
>>> Word found in ./documents/document-1.pdf
>>> Word found in ./documents/document-1.docx
>>> Word found in ./documents/dir/file6.pdf
>>> Word found in ./documents/dir/subdir/file5.pdf
```

4. Search for the word '20£', only present in the two ISO files, with different encodings, and in the UTF-8 file:

```
$ python scan.py -w 20£
>>> Word found in ./documents/example_iso.txt
>>> Word found in ./documents/example_output_iso.txt
>>> Word found in ./documents/example_utf8.txt
```

5. The search is case-insensitive. Search for the word 'BETTER', only present in the `zen_of_python.txt` file:

```
$ python scan.py -w BETTER
>>> Word found in ./documents/zen_of_python.txt
```

## How it works...

The `scan.py` script has the following elements:

- An entry point that parses the input parameters and creates the help for the command line.
- A `main` function that walks through the directory and analyzes each of the files found. Based on their extension, it decides whether there's an available function to process and search it.
- An `EXTENSION` dictionary, which pairs the extensions with the function to search them.
- The `search_txt`, `search_csv`, `search_pdf`, and `search_docx` functions, which process and search for the required word for each kind of file.

Keep in mind that file extensions are just file name endings and provide only a hint of the format of a file. So, they should be taken with a grain of salt. The Python standard library includes the function `mimetypes.guess_type`, which can make an educated guess as to a file's type. Check out the Python documentation here: https://docs.python.org/3/library/mimetypes.html.

The comparison is case-insensitive, so the search word is transformed into lowercase, and in all comparisons the text is transformed into lowercase.

Each of the search functions has its own peculiarities:

- `search_txt` first tries to open the file in UTF-8, and if that fails it guesses the encoding using `UnicodeDammit` and then opens the file and reads it line by line. As soon as the word is found, it stops and returns success.

- Because we open the file, read, and then read again, we need to position the reading cursor to the start with `.seek(0)`. We also use a `finally` block to ensure that we close the file at the end, even in the event of an exception.
- `search_csv` opens the file in CSV, and iterates not only line by line but also column by column. As soon as the word is found, it returns.
- `search_pdf` opens the file and exits if it is encrypted. If not, it goes page by page, extracting the text and comparing it with the word. It returns as soon as it finds a match.
- `search_docx` opens the file and iterates through all its paragraphs for a match. As soon as a match is found, the function returns.

## There's more...

Here are some extra ideas that could be implemented:

- More search functions for different formats could be added. In this chapter we went through log files and images, as well as text files.
- A similar structure could work for searching only in the 10 most recently written files, checking their metadata. This can be useful to avoid noise from older files if we are looking for fresh information.
- `search_csv` is not sniffing to detect the dialect. This could be added as well.
- Reading is quite sequential. It should be possible to read the files in parallel, analyzing them for faster returns. Be aware that reading files in parallel can lead to sorting issues, as the files won't always be processed in the same order.

> **Tip**
>
> To analyze specific file formats, GenAI can help in determining the right module to parse and extract information. In my experience, it is better to do some research to find the right third-party module to parse the data correctly and then create the code. Just asking the GenAI tool to parse a particular format sometimes creates bad results, as it may try to use suboptimal modules or try to parse it itself, adding a lot of code in the process.
>
> Instead, ask what modules are available, give them a quick try, and then integrate them into your task.
>
> Remember that you can transform files from some format to text files first (by using external applications or GenAI) and then search through them more easily. Sometimes GenAI can do the transformation itself, simplifying the operation.

## See also

- The *Crawling and searching directories* recipe, earlier in this chapter, to learn how to search and find files in directories.
- The *Reading text files* recipe, earlier in this chapter, to learn the basics of opening and reading basic text files.
- The *Dealing with encodings* recipe, earlier in this chapter, to learn how to open files with different encodings.
- The *Reading CSV files* recipe, earlier in this chapter, to learn how to read CSV files.
- The *Reading PDF files* recipe, earlier in this chapter, to learn how to open and read PDF documents.
- The *Reading Word documents* recipe, earlier in this chapter, to learn the basics of reading Word documents.

# 5

# Generating Fantastic Reports

We'll see in this chapter how to write automated documents and perform associated operations, such as dealing with templates in different formats. We will cover simple options like plain text and options that include richer possibilities, such as Markdown. We'll also cover standard formats such as Word and PDF. These two formats are arguably the most common way of sharing documents and reports across the globe.

> **Note**
>
> For this chapter we will talk more about how to format and present content. With GenAI tools we are now able to generate much of the content automatically. We will find out more about how to use those tools to deal with content in *Chapter 11*.

In this chapter, we will cover the following recipes:

- Creating a simple report in plain text
- Using templates for reports
- Formatting text in Markdown
- Writing a basic Word document
- Styling a Word document
- Generating structure in Word documents
- Adding pictures to Word documents
- Writing a simple PDF document
- Structuring a PDF
- Aggregating PDF reports
- Watermarking and encrypting a PDF

We will start our report generation with a minimal text one.

# Technical requirements

You can check the code presented in the chapter in the GitHub repository at `https://github.com/PacktPublishing/Python-Automation-Cookbook-Third-Edition/tree/main/ch05`.

# Creating a simple report in plain text

The simplest possible way to create a report is to generate plain text and store it in a file. Though this may seem trivial in comparison with some of the other formats we will look at later, don't underestimate its utility. Plain text is the easiest format to share as it will work in virtually all environments, and it can go a long way in representing information.

> **Tip**
>
> Plain text is also the easiest to use with GenAI, being its native language. (Or Markdown, as we will see later.)

## Getting ready

For this recipe we will generate a brief report in text format about the number of movies watched in the last month and the total duration of all those movies. Internally, the data to be represented will be in the form of a Python dictionary. The report will include the generation date as well, for reference.

## How to do it...

1. Import `datetime`:

```
>>> import datetime
```

2. Create the template with the report in text format:

```
>>> TEMPLATE = '''
Movies report
-------------
Date: {date}
Movies seen in the last 30 days: {num_movies}
Total minutes: {total_minutes}
'''
```

3. Create a dictionary with the values to store. Note that this is the data to be presented in the report:

```
>>> data = {
    'date': datetime.datetime.now(datetime.UTC),
    'num_movies': 3,
    'total_minutes': 376,
}
```

4. Compose the text of the report, adding the data to the template:

```
>>> report = TEMPLATE.format(**data)
```

5. Create a new file with the current date and store the report:

```
>>> FILENAME_TMPL = "{date}_report.txt"
>>> filename = FILENAME_TMPL.format(date=data['date'].strftime('%Y-%m-%d'))
>>> filename
'2026-01-17_report.txt'
>>> with open(filename, 'w') as file:
...     file.write(report)
```

6. Check the newly created report:

```
$ cat 2026-01-17_report.txt

Movies report
-------------
Date: 2026-01-17 15:58:37.721316+00:00
Movies seen in the last 30 days: 3
Total minutes: 376
```

## How it works...

*Step 2* and *step 3* in the *How to do it...* section set up a simple template and add a dictionary with all the data. Then, in *step 4*, the two are combined into the specific report.

> **Note**
>
> In *step 4*, the dictionary is combined with a template. Notice that the keys of the dictionary correspond to the parameters of the template. The trick here is to use the

> double star in the format call to unpack the dictionary, passing each of the keys as a parameter to `format()`.

In *step 5*, the resulting report, a string, is stored in a newly created file. We use the `with` context manager paired with `open()`, as introduced in previous chapters. In this case we generate a new file to write the data. After closing the `with` block the file is properly closed and the data is stored on the disk.

> **Tip**
>
> The open modes determine how to open a file, whether we want read or write access, and whether the file is text or binary. The `w` mode opens the file to write it, overwriting it if it already exists. Be careful not to delete an existing file by mistake!

*Step 6* checks that the file has been created with the proper data.

## There's more...

The filename is created with a dynamic date to minimize the probability of overwriting existing files. The date format starting with the year and ending with the day has been selected so that the files are sorted in the correct order.

> **Tip**
>
> The format YYYY-MM-DD for dates is covered in the ISO 8601 standard, which describes different ways to format dates and times. It is a standard format that's easily parsed and is supported in Python. Conveniently it's also sorted by time by default.

The `with` context manager will close the file even if there's an exception. In case of an error, the write call will raise an `IOError` exception.

> **Note**
>
> Some of the common problems when writing to disk include problems with permissions, no space being left on the hard drive, or a path problem (for instance, trying to write in a non-existent directory).

Note that a file may not be fully committed to disk until it is closed or explicitly flushed. Generally, the operating system will take care of things, but keep this in mind if you're trying to open a file twice, once for read and once for write operations.

> Tip
>
> Not closing the file properly can produce an error if the program ends abruptly before being able to flush the data to the hard drive, making data apparently disappear. If required, call `file.flush()` to force the data to be committed to disk. This is useful when writing several times into the same file. Note that at the end of the `with` block, the file will be flushed and closed automatically.

## See also

- The *Using templates for reports* recipe, later in this chapter, to learn about HTML templates.
- The *Formatting text in Markdown* recipe, later in this chapter, to learn about Markdown.
- The *Aggregating PDF reports* recipe, later in this chapter, to learn how to produce PDF reports.

# Using templates for reports

While plain text can convey a lot of information, to generate better reports we need a system where styling can be added to the text. Details such as bold text, bullet points, and images can make a difference. As all browsers work with HTML, generating reports in this format is a good option. Everyone is familiar with a browser rendering text.

HTML is a very flexible format that can be used to render rich text and reports. While an HTML file can be understood as pure plain text, and can be written directly from Python, doing so is very error prone and tedious. There are modules like Jinja or Mako that allow you handle structured text markup more easily and define HTML syntax-aware templates.

> Note
>
> GenAI tools will understand HTML formatting, but you'll get better results using Markdown, which we will show in the next recipe.

This also detaches the template containing how data will be represented from the code, separating the generation of the data from the representation of that data. The styling of the template can be done separately by specialized designers, to make it look great.

A more graphical example: If you want to represent a list of movies in an HTML page, there's some HTML markup always involved, no matter the movies presented. An HTML table, the CSS styling defining the fonts and colors to use, perhaps a header or a footer. The data to represent is the movies themselves.

## Getting ready

The tool used in this recipe, **Jinja**, reads a file that contains the template and applies the context to it. The context contains the data to be displayed.

> Note
>
> Because version 2 of Jinja made some backwards-incompatible changes, the package is called jinja2, and sometimes the whole is referred as *Jinja2*. But the latest version is 3, which remained compatible with version 2. We will use the name *Jinja*, though you'll see that the package is called `jinja2`.

We should start by installing the module:

```
$ echo "jinja2==3.1.6" >> requirements.txt
$ uv pip install -r requirements.txt
```

Jinja uses its own syntax, which is a mixture of HTML and Python. It is aimed at HTML documents, so it easily performs operations such as correctly escaping special characters.

In the GitHub repository, at `https://github.com/PacktPublishing/Python-Automation-Cookbook-Third-Edition/tree/main/ch05`, we've included a template file called `jinja_template.html` with the template to use.

## How to do it...

1. Import the Jinja template and datetime:

```
>>> from jinja2 import Template
>>> from datetime import datetime
```

2. Read the template from the files into memory:

```
>>> with open('jinja_template.html') as file:
...     template = Template(file.read())
```

3. Create a context with the data to be displayed:

```
>>> context = {
...     'date': datetime.now(),
...     'movies': ['Casablanca', 'The Sound of Music', 'Vertigo'],
...     'total_minutes': 404,
...     }
```

4. Render the template and write a new file, `report.html`, with the following result:

```
>>> with open('report.html', 'w') as file:
...     file.write(template.render(context))
```

5. Exit the Python interpreter and open the `report.html` file in a browser:

*Figure 5.1: The rendered report.html*

## How it works...

*Steps 2* and *4* in the *How to do it...* section are very straightforward: they read the template and render and save the resulting report.

As seen in *steps 3* and *4*, the main task is to create a context dictionary with the information to be displayed. The template then renders that information, as shown in *step 5*. Let's take a look at `jinja_template.html`:

```
<!DOCTYPE html>
<html lang="en">
<head>
    <title> Movies Report</title>
</head>
<body>
    <h1>Movies Report</h1>
    <p>Date {{date}}</p>
    <p>Movies seen in the last 30 days: {{movies|length}}</p>
    <ol>
        {% for movie in movies %}
        <li>{{movie}}</li>
        {% endfor %}
    </ol>
    <p>Total minutes: {{total_minutes}} </p>
</body>
</html>
```

Most of it is replacing the context values defined between curly brackets, such as `{{total_minutes}}`.

Note the tag pair, `{% for ... %}` / `{% endfor %}`, which defines a loop. This allows for a very Pythonic way of generating multiple rows or elements in a list.

Filters can be applied to the variables to modify them. In this case, the length filter is applied to the movies list to obtain the size using the pipe symbol, as shown in `{{movies|length}}`.

## There's more...

Other than the `{% for %}` tag, there's also an `{% if %}` tag, allowing it to display conditionally:

```
{% if movies|length > 5 %}
  Wow, so many movies this month!
{% else %}
  Regular number of movies
{% endif %}
```

A good number of filters are defined already (see the list here: `https://jinja.palletsprojects.com/en/stable/templates/#list-of-builtin-filters`), and it is also possible to define custom filters.

> **Tip**
>
> Note that you can add a lot of processing and logic to the template using filters. While a little bit is fine, try to limit the amount of logic in the template. Most of the calculations for data to be displayed should be done beforehand, leaving the template to just display values. This makes the context very straightforward and simplifies the template, making change management more painless.

When dealing with HTML files, it is a good idea to auto-escape the variables. Because some characters have meaning in HTML syntax, they need to be transformed into their proper counterpart so that HTML displays them correctly. For example, to display correctly the < character, you'll need to replace it with < . In order to do this automatically you can escape the text, meaning that Jinja will transform it correctly to keep the resulting text as you'd expect. To escape the text, create the template with the `autoescape` parameter. Check the difference here:

```
>>> Template('{{variable}}', autoescape=False).render({'variable': '<'})
'<'
>>> Template('{{variable}}', autoescape=True).render({'variable': '<'})
'<'
```

Escaping can be applied to each variable independently with the e filter (meaning *escape*) and unapplied with the `safe` filter (meaning it is safe to render as it is).

```
>>> Template('{{variable|e}}').render({'variable': '<'})
'<'
>>> Template('{{variable|safe}}').render({'variable': '<'})
'<'
```

Jinja2 templates are extensible, meaning that you can create a `base_template.html` file and then extend it, changing some of the elements. You can include other files as well, partitioning and separating different sections. Refer to the full documentation for further details.

Note

Jinja2 is very powerful and allows us to create complex HTML templates, and also in other formats such as LaTeX or JavaScript, though this requires configuring. I encourage you to read the whole documentation and have a look at all its capabilities!

The whole Jinja2 documentation can be found here: `https://jinja.palletsprojects.com/en/stable/`.

## See also

- The *Creating a simple report in plain text* recipe, earlier in this chapter, to learn the basics of creating plain text reports.
- The *Formatting text in Markdown* recipe, coming up next, to learn Markdown, an alternative template format.

# Formatting text in Markdown

**Markdown** is a very popular markup language used to create plain text that can be converted into styled HTML. It is a good way of structuring documents in such a way that they are still easy to read in plain text format, while including enough structural information to allow them to be styled in HTML.

Note

Another advantage of Markdown is that it is very natural for GenAI to read and write the format, to the point that it's likely that it will return text in Markdown. It is very popular among developers, and that probably influenced the training of the AI models.

In this recipe we'll see how to transform a Markdown document into styled HTML using Python.

## Getting ready

We should start by installing the `mistune` module, which will compile Markdown documents into HTML:

```
$ echo "mistune==3.2.0" >> requirements.txt
$ uv pip install -r requirements.txt
```

In the GitHub repository is a template file called `markdown_template.md`, which is a template of the report to generate.

## How to do it...

1. Import `mistune` and `datetime`:

```
>>> import mistune
>>> from datetime import datetime
```

2. Read the template from the file:

```
>>> with open('markdown_template.md') as file:
...     template = file.read()
```

3. Set up the context of the data to be included in the report:

```
>>> context = {
...    'date': datetime.now(),
...    'pmovies': ['Casablanca', 'The Sound of Music', 'Vertigo'],
...    'total_minutes': 404,
... }
```

4. As movies need to be displayed as bullet points, we will transform the list into a suitable Markdown bulleted list. We will also store the number of movies:

```
>>> context['num_movies'] = len(context['pmovies'])
>>> context['movies'] = '\n'.join('* {}'.format(movie) for movie in
context['pmovies'])
```

5. Render the template and compile the resulting Markdown into HTML:

```
>>> md_report = template.format(**context)
>>> report = mistune.markdown(md_report)
```

6. Finally, store the resulting report in the `report.html` file:

```
>>> with open('report.html', 'w') as file:
...    file.write(report)
```

7. Open the `report.html` file in a browser to check the result:

*Figure 5.2: The rendered report, as seen in a browser*

## How it works...

*Steps 2* and *3* in the *How do it...* section prepare the template and the data to be displayed. In *step 4*, extra information is produced – the number of movies, derived from the `pmovies` element. The `pmovies` list is then transformed into a valid Markdown element from a Python list. Note the newlines and the initial `*`, which will be rendered as a bullet point:

```
>>> '\n'.join('* {}'.format(movie) for movie in context['pmovies'])
'* Casablanca\n* The Sound of Music\n* Vertigo'
```

In *step 5*, the template is generated in Markdown format. The format is very readable in this raw form, which is the strong point of Markdown:

```
Movies Report
=======


Date: 2026-01-17 16:39:40.845144
```

```
Movies seen in the last 30 days: 3

* Casablanca
* The Sound of Music
* Vertigo

Total minutes: 404
```

Then, using `mistune`, the report is transformed into HTML and stored in a file in *step 6*.

## There's more...

Learning Markdown is extremely useful, as it is supported by many common websites as a way of enabling text input that is easy to read and write and which can be rendered to a styled format. Some examples are GitHub, Stack Overflow, and most blogging platforms.

> **Note**
>
> There is more than one kind of Markdown. This is because the official definition was limited and ambiguous, and there was little interest in clarifying or extending it. This led to several implementations that are slightly different, such as GitHub Flavored Markdown, CommonMark or MultiMarkdown (which has extra capabilities).

Markdown can normally be rendered as HTML, but other formats are also possible. For example, `mistune` can render a Markdown file as RST, a similar format that's used in Python projects.

The text in Markdown is quite readable in its raw form, but you may want to see interactively how it will look. There are many tools available these days, including text editors from IDEs like VS code, but you can use the Dillinger online editor at `https://dillinger.io/`.

Note

Markdown text will look different depending on the rendering tool, as the fonts, text size, theme, etc. may be different. Some flavours of Markdown can accept some features, like tables, that others won't support. Check the specific tool you're using to understand all the details.

The full docs for Mistune are available here: `http://mistune.readthedocs.io/en/latest/`.

The original Markdown syntax can be found at `https://daringfireball.net/projects/markdown/syntax`, and a good cheat sheet with the most frequently used elements is to be found at `https://www.markdownguide.org/cheat-sheet/`.

## See also

- The *Creating a simple report in pain text* recipe, earlier in this chapter, to learn the basics of creating plain text reports.
- The *Using templates for reports* recipe, earlier in this chapter, to learn how to create templates directly in HTML.

# Writing a basic Word document

**Microsoft (MS) Office** is one of the most common pieces of software, and MS Word in particular is almost the de facto standard for editable documents. Generating `.docx` documents is possible using automated scripts, which can help to distribute reports in a format that's easily shared in many businesses.

In this recipe, we will learn how to generate a full Word document programmatically.

## Getting ready

We'll use the `python-docx` module to process Word documents:

```
$ echo "python-docx==1.2.0" >> requirements.txt
$ pip install -r requirements.txt
```

## How to do it...

1. Import python-docx and datetime:

```
>>> import docx
>>> from datetime import datetime
```

2. Define the context with the data to be stored in the report:

```
>>> context = {
...     'date': datetime.now(),
...     'movies': ['Casablanca', 'The Sound of Music', 'Vertigo'],
...     'total_minutes': 404,
... }
```

Create a new .docx document and include a heading, 'Movies Report':

```
>>> document = docx.Document()
>>> document.add_heading('Movies Report', 0)
<docx.text.paragraph.Paragraph object at 0x10b8246e0>
```

1. Add a paragraph describing the date, with the date in italics:

```
>>> paragraph = document.add_paragraph('Date: ')
>>> paragraph.add_run(str(context['date'])).italic = True
```

2. In a different paragraph, add information about the number of movies seen:

```
>>> paragraph = document.add_paragraph('Movies see in the last 30 days: ')
>>> paragraph.add_run(str(len(context['movies']))).italic = True
```

3. Add each of the movies as a bullet point:

```
>>> for movie in context['movies']:
...     document.add_paragraph(movie, style='List Bullet')
...
<docx.text.paragraph.Paragraph object at 0x10b74ad70>
<docx.text.paragraph.Paragraph object at 0x10b74bce0>
<docx.text.paragraph.Paragraph object at 0x10b80c830>
```

4. Add the total minutes and save the file, as follows:

```
>>> paragraph = document.add_paragraph('Total minutes: ')
>>> paragraph.add_run(str(context['total_minutes'])).italic = True
>>> document.save('word-report.docx')
```

5. Close the interpreter and open the `word-report.docx` file to check it:

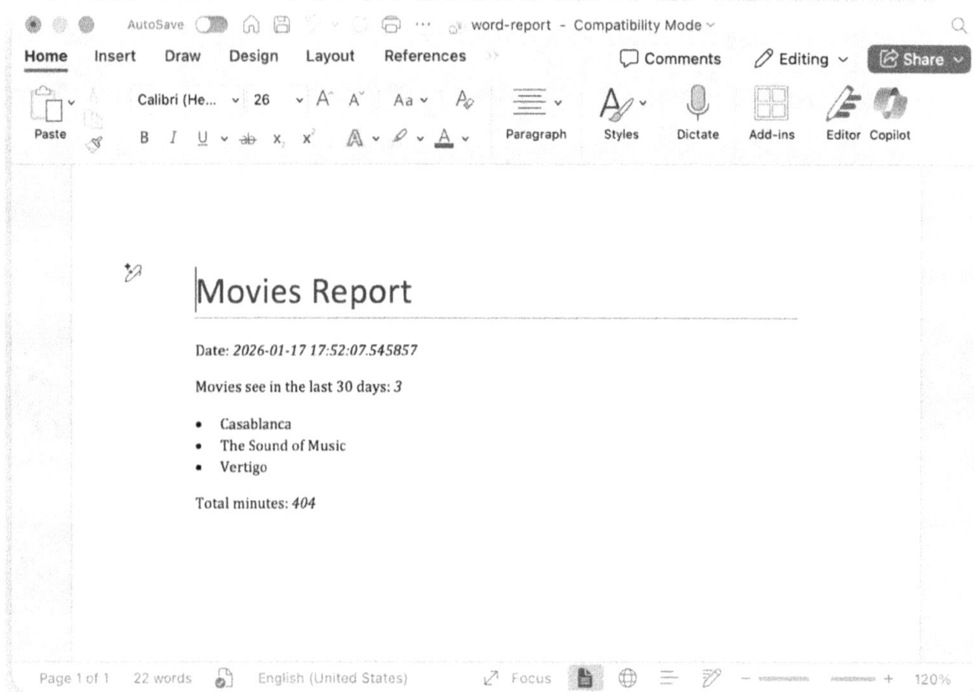


*Figure 5.3: The content of word-report.docx*

## How it works...

The basics of a Word document is that it is divided into *paragraphs*, and each of the paragraphs is divided into *runs*. A run is a part of a paragraph that shares the same style.

*Steps 1* and *2* in the *How to do it...* section are preparation for importing and defining the data that's going to be stored in the report.

In *step 3*, the document is created and a heading with the proper title is added. This automatically styles the text.

Dealing with paragraphs is introduced in *step 4*. A new paragraph is created based on the text with the default style, but new runs can be added to change it. Here, we added the first run with the text 'Date:', but another run is added after that with the specific time and the format changed to *italics*.

In *steps 5* and *6*, we can see information about the movies. The first part stores the number of movies, in a similar format to *step 4*. After that, the movies are added to the report one by one, and the style set up to be bullet points with the style 'List Bullet'.

Finally, *step 7* stores the total run time of all movies, in a similar way to *step 4*, and finally stores the document in a file.

## There's more...

If you need to introduce extra lines in the document for formatting purposes, add empty paragraphs.

Due to the way that the `.docx` format works, there's no easy way to determine how many pages a document will have, or what page a paragraph is located on: they are determined at rendering time. You may need to run some tests on sizes, especially if you're generating dynamic documents.

> **Tip**
>
> Even if you generate `.docx` files, having MS Office is not necessary. There are other applications that can open and handle these files, including free alternatives such as LibreOffice.

The whole `python-docx` documentation is available here: `https://python-docx.readthedocs.io/en/latest/`.

## See also

- The *Styling a Word document* recipe, coming up next, to learn how format a document.
- The *Generating structure in Word documents* recipe, later in this chapter, to learn how to create sections and other separators in Word documents.

# Styling a Word document

A Word document can contain text with almost no formatting, but we can also add styling to enhance the displayed content's intelligibility. Word has a set of predefined styles that can be applied to the document and used to highlight the important parts of it.

## Getting ready

We'll use the `python-docx` module to process Word documents, so be sure to have it available in your environment:

```
$ echo "python-docx==1.2.0" >> requirements.txt
$ uv pip install -r requirements.txt
```

## How to do it...

1. Import the `python-docx` module:

   ```
   >>> import docx
   ```

2. Create a new document:

   ```
   >>> document = docx.Document()
   ```

3. Add a paragraph that highlights some words in different ways (italics, bold, and underline):

   ```
   >>> p = document.add_paragraph('This shows different kinds of emphasis: ')
   >>> p.add_run('bold').bold = True
   >>> p.add_run(', ')
   <docx.text.run.Run object at 0x10b8604b0>
   >>> p.add_run('italics').italic = True
   >>> p.add_run(' and ')
   <docx.text.run.Run object at 0x10b717e10>
   >>> p.add_run('underline').underline = True
   >>> p.add_run('.')
   <docx.text.run.Run object at 0x10b8c2d50>
   ```

4. Create some paragraphs and style them with default styles, such as `ListBullet`, `List Number`, or `Quote`:

```
>>> document.add_paragraph('a few', style='List Bullet')
<docx.text.paragraph.Paragraph object at 0x10b83dd50>
>>> document.add_paragraph('bullet', style='List Bullet')
<docx.text.paragraph.Paragraph object at 0x10b830250>
>>> document.add_paragraph('points', style='List Bullet')
<docx.text.paragraph.Paragraph object at 0x10b82d400>
>>> document.add_paragraph('Or numbered', style='List Number')
<docx.text.paragraph.Paragraph object at 0x10b82d310>
>>> document.add_paragraph('that will', style='List Number')
<docx.text.paragraph.Paragraph object at 0x10b860f30>
>>> document.add_paragraph('that keep', style='List Number')
<docx.text.paragraph.Paragraph object at 0x10b860bb0>
>>> document.add_paragraph('count', style='List Number')
<docx.text.paragraph.Paragraph object at 0x10b8bcc80>
>>> document.add_paragraph('And finish with a quote', style='Quote')
<docx.text.paragraph.Paragraph object at 0x10b8c2bd0>
```

5. Create a paragraph in a different font and size. We'll use the Arial font and a point size of 25. The paragraph will be aligned to the right:

```
>>> from docx.shared import Pt
>>> from docx.enum.text import WD_ALIGN_PARAGRAPH
>>> p = document.add_paragraph('This paragraph will have a manual styling
and right alignment')
>>> p.runs[0].font.name = 'Arial'
>>> p.runs[0].font.size = Pt(25)
>>> p.alignment = WD_ALIGN_PARAGRAPH.RIGHT
```

6. Save the document:

```
>>> document.save('word-report-style.docx')
```

Open the `word-report-style.docx` document to verify its content:

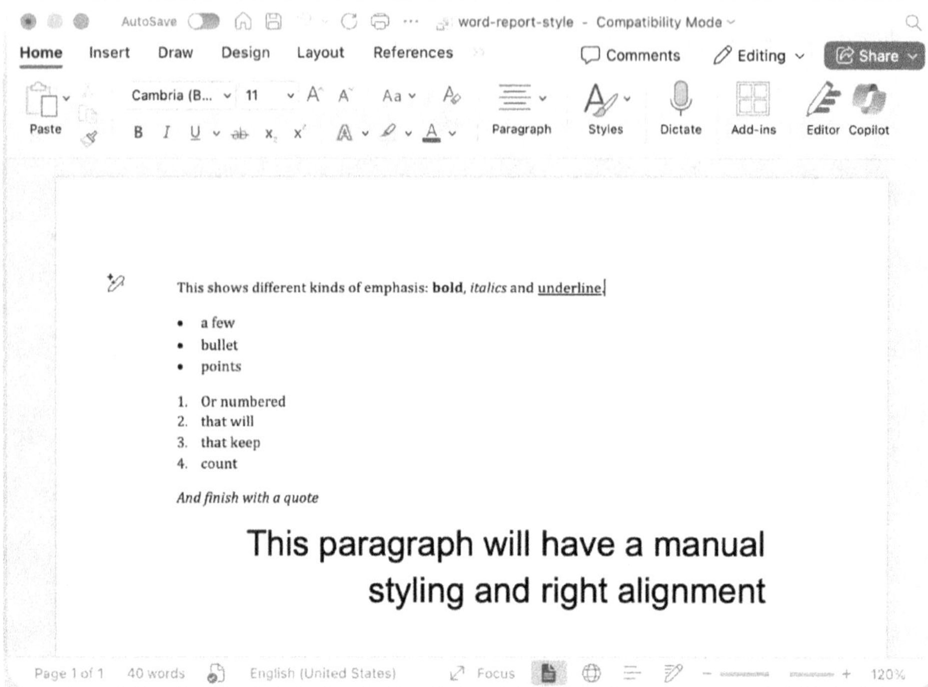


*Figure 5.4: The final word-report-style.docx document*

## How it works...

After creating the document in *step 1*, *step 2* from the *How to do it...* section adds a paragraph with several runs. In Word, a paragraph can contain multiple runs, which are smaller portions of text that may have different styles applied. In general, any format change related to individual words will be applied to a run, while a change that affects the whole paragraph will be applied to the paragraph object.

Each of the runs is created, by default, with the Normal style. Any attribute of `.bold`, `.italic`, or `.underline` can be changed to `True` to set up whether the run should be in a single style or some combination of these. A value of `False` will deactivate it, while a `None` value will apply the configured default.

**Tip**

Note that the correct word in this protocol is *italic*, not *italics*. Setting the property to 'italics' won't have any effect but won't display an error either. This is due the dynamic nature of Python, allowing the creation of new attributes in objects.

*Step 4* shows how to apply some of the default styles for paragraphs; in this case, to show bullet points, numbered lists, and quotes. There are more included styles, which can be found here: `https://python-docx.readthedocs.io/en/latest/user/styles-understanding.html?highlight=List%20Bullet#paragraph-styles-in-default-template`. Find out which ones work best for your document. Using predefined styles simplifies the styling of the document.

The `.font` property of a run is shown in *step 5*. This allows you to manually set up a specific font and size. Note that the size needs to be specified using the proper `Pt` (points) object.

> **Tip**
>
> The point is a standard typographic unit used for expressing text size. Point sizes are common on regular Word documents, but it can be difficult to know the exact size which will be presented on screen or when printed on a sheet of paper. Don't be afraid to perform some tests and experiment with them.

The alignment of the paragraph is set in the paragraph object and uses a constant to define whether it is left, right, center, or justified. There are different options too for justification. The full alignment options can be found here: `https://python-docx.readthedocs.io/en/latest/api/enum/WdAlignParagraph.html`.

Finally, *step 7* saves the file to the filesystem.

## There's more...

The `font` attribute can also be used to set additional text properties, such as small caps, shadow, emboss, or strikethrough. The whole range of possibilities is shown in the following documentation: `https://python-docx.readthedocs.io/en/latest/api/text.html#font-objects`.

Another available option is to change the color of the text:

```
>>> from docx.shared import RGBColor
>>> DARK_BLUE = RGBColor.from_string('1b3866')
>>> run.font.color.rgb = DARK_BLUE
```

The color can be described in the usual hex format using a string. Try to define all the colors as named constants to ensure they are consistent, and limit yourself to a maximum of three colors in a report so as not to distract from the content.

You can use an online color picker, such as this one: `https://www.w3schools.com/colors/colors_picker.asp`. Remember to not use the # symbol at the beginning. If you need to generate a palette, it's a good idea to use tools such as `https://coolors.co/` to generate good combinations.

> **Tip**
>
> Alternatively, asking to GenAI for a color in hex format or recommendation for a palette is also a possibility. For example, try this prompt: *Show me a palette of colors in hex format with a green tint. They should be readable for a word document.*

The complete `python-docx` documentation is available at `https://python-docx.readthedocs.io/en/latest/`.

## See also

- The *Writing a basic Word document* recipe, earlier in this chapter, to learn the basics of creating a Word document.
- The *Generating structure in Word documents* recipe, next, to learn how to create sections and other separators in Word documents.

# Generating structure in Word documents

To create professional reports, they need to be properly structured. An MS Word document doesn't have the concept of *a page*, as it works in paragraphs. But we can introduce breaks and sections to properly divide a document.

We'll see in this recipe how to create a structured Word document, introducing breaks to create sections.

## Getting ready

We'll use the `python-docx` module to process Word documents. Be sure that it's added to your environment:

```
$ echo "python-docx==1.2.0" >> requirements.txt
$ uv pip install -r requirements.txt
```

## How to do it...

1. Import the `python-docx` module:

    ```
    >>> import docx
    ```

2. Create a new document:

```
>>> document = docx.Document()
```

3. Create a paragraph that has a line break:

```
>>> p = document.add_paragraph('This is the start of the paragraph')
>>> run = p.add_run()
>>> run.add_break(docx.text.run.WD_BREAK.LINE)
>>> p.add_run('And now this in a different line')
<docx.text.run.Run object at 0x10b8b4de0>
>>> p.add_run('And now this in a different line')
<docx.text.run.Run object at 0x10b8b4e50>
```

4. Create a page break and write a paragraph:

```
>>> document.add_page_break()
<docx.text.paragraph.Paragraph object at 0x10b801440>
>>> document.add_paragraph('This appears in a new page')
<docx.text.paragraph.Paragraph object at 0x10a82e8f0>
```

5. Create a new section, which will be on landscape pages:

```
>>> section = document.add_section( docx.enum.section.WD_SECTION.NEW_PAGE)
>>> section.orientation = docx.enum.section.WD_ORIENT.LANDSCAPE
>>> section.page_height, section.page_width = section.page_width,
section.page_height
>>> document.add_paragraph('This is part of a new landscape section')
<docx.text.paragraph.Paragraph object at 0x10b865770>
```

6. Create another section, reverting to portrait orientation:

```
>>> section = document.add_section( docx.enum.section.WD_SECTION.NEW_PAGE)
>>> section.orientation = docx.enum.section.WD_ORIENT.PORTRAIT
>>> section.page_height, section.page_width = section.page_width,
section.page_height
>>> document.add_paragraph('In this section, recover the portrait
orientation')
<docx.text.paragraph.Paragraph object at 0x10b7a4710>
```

7. Save the document:

```
>>> document.save('word-report-structure.docx')
```

8. Check the result by opening the document and checking the resulting sections:

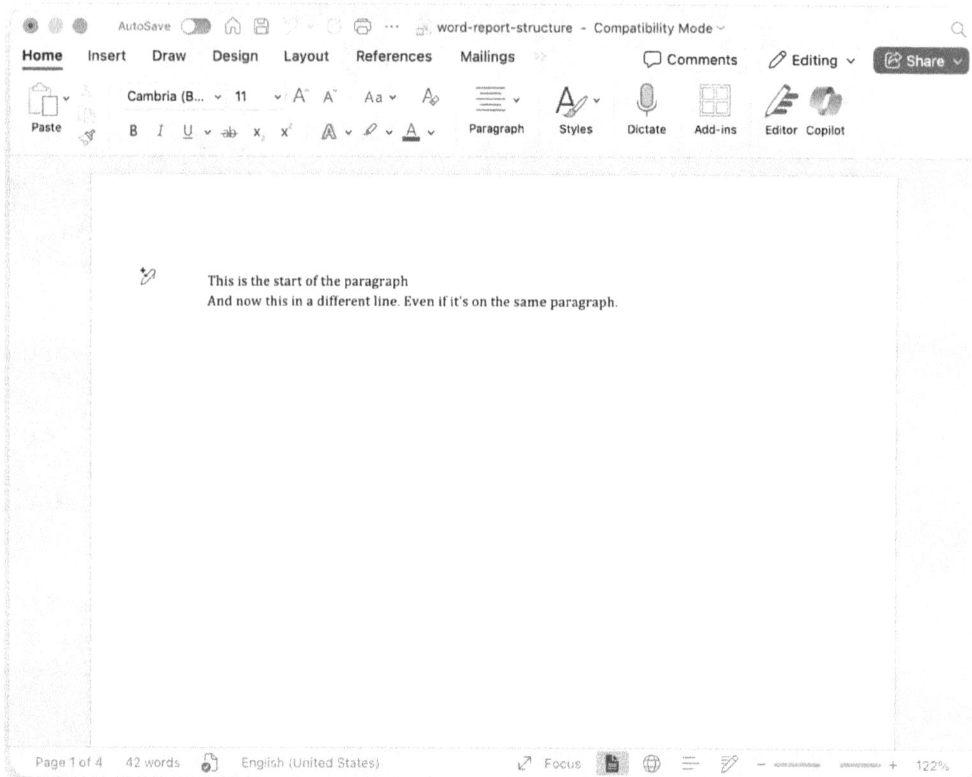


*Figure 5.5: The rendered first page*

Check the new page:

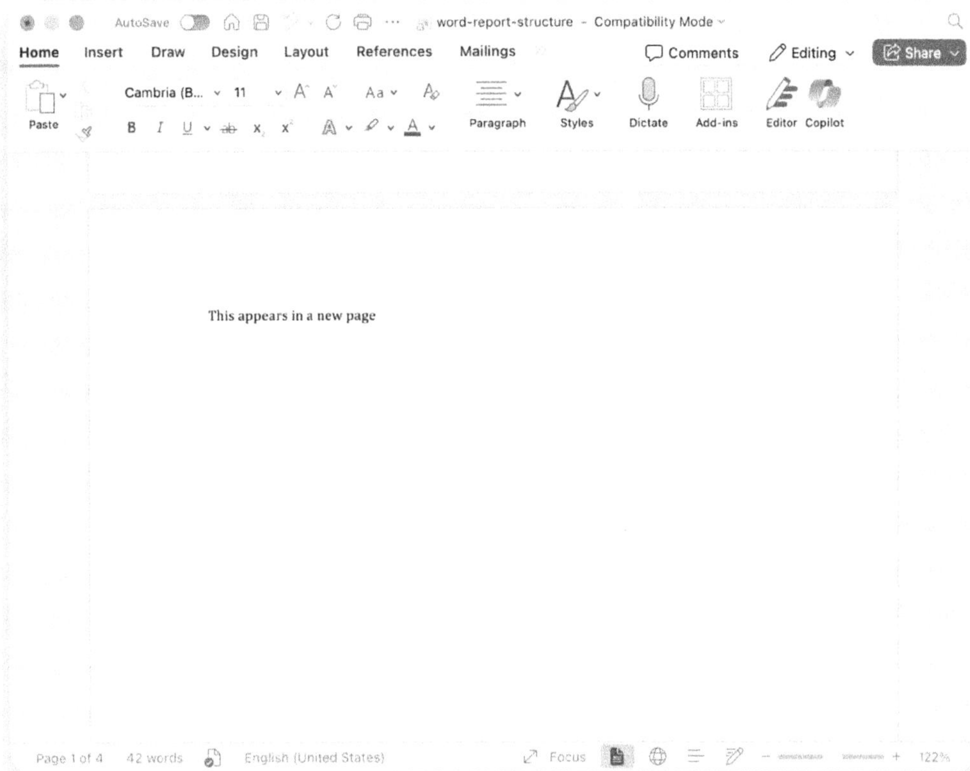


*Figure 5.6: The rendered new file*

Check for a landscape section:

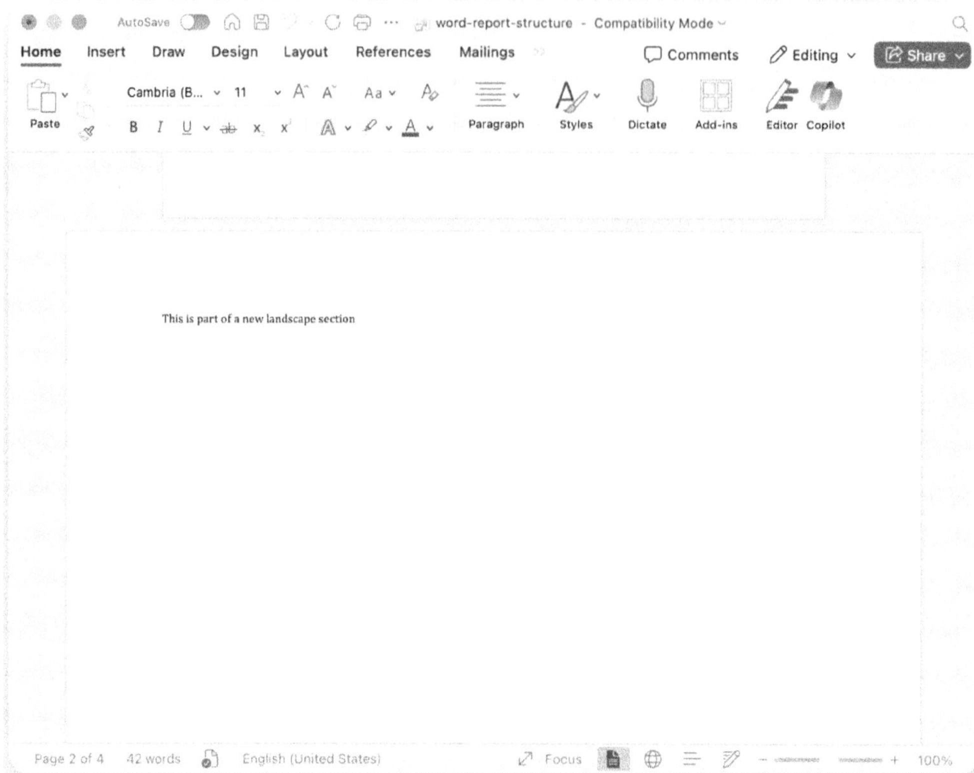


*Figure 5.7: The rendered landscape section*

Then, go back to portrait orientation:

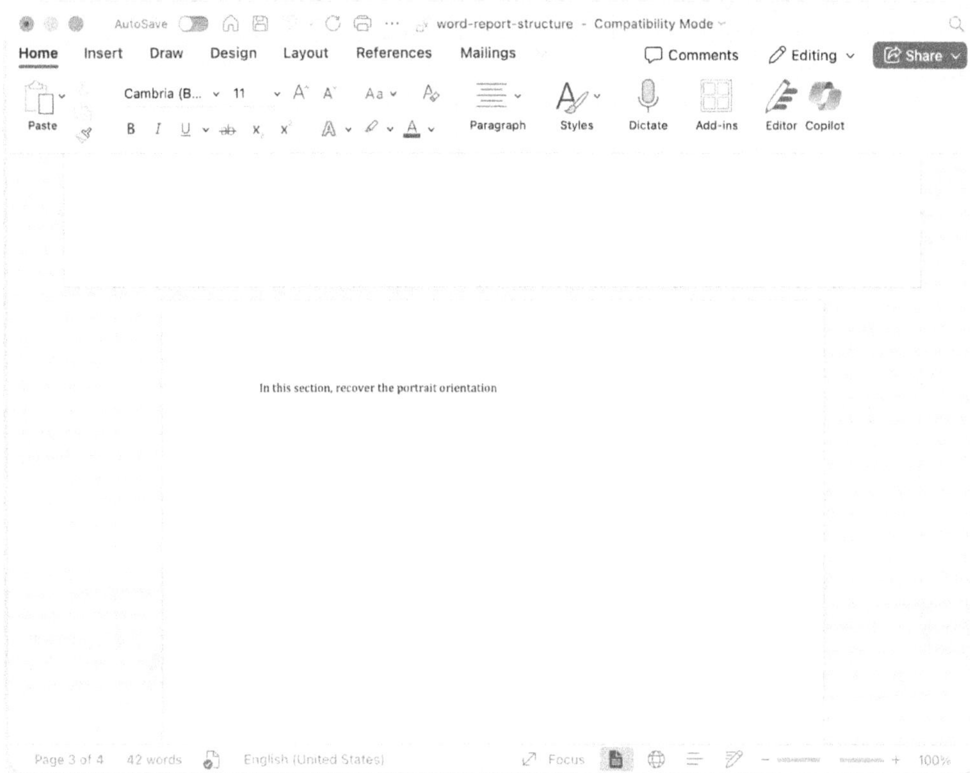


*Figure 5.8: The new page, after going back to portrait orientation*

## How it works...

After creating the document in *step 2* in the *How to do it...* section, we add a paragraph for the first section. Notice that the document starts with a section. The paragraph introduces a line break in the middle of the paragraph by adding a `WD_BREAK.LINE` break.

> **Tip**
>
> There is a small difference between a line break in a paragraph and a new paragraph – vertical separation between the lines either side of a line break is smaller than the separation when breaking to a new paragraph. For most uses, though, it is quite similar. Try to experiment with them.

A page break is introduced in *step 3*, without changing the section.

*Step 4* creates a new section on a new page. *Step 5* also changes the orientation of the page to landscape in the section. In *step 6*, a new section is introduced, and the orientation reverts to portrait.

> **Note**
>
> Note that when changing the orientation, we also need to swap the width and height. Each new section inherits the properties from the previous one, so this swapping needs to happen in *step 6* as well.

Finally, the document is saved in *step 7*.

## There's more...

Each section can define its own page composition, including the orientation, size of the page and margins. Page dimensions can be changed using the relevant section parameters, and defined in inches or centimeters (Cm), like this

```
>>> from docx.shared import Inches, Cm
>>> section.page_height = Inches(10)
>>> section.page_width = Cm(20)
```

Page margins can be defined in the same way:

```
>>> section.left_margin = Inches(1.5)
>>> section.right_margin = Cm(2.81)
>>> section.top_margin = Inches(1)
>>> section.bottom_margin = Cm(2.54)
```

Sections can also be forced to start not only on the next page, but on the next odd page, which will look better when printing on two sides:

```
>>> document.add_section( docx.enum.section.WD_SECTION.ODD_PAGE)
```

The complete `python-docx` documentation is available here: `https://python-docx.readthedocs.io/en/latest/`.

## See also

- The *Writing a basic Word document* recipe, earlier in this chapter, to learn the basics of how to create a Word document.
- The previous recipe, *Styling a Word document*, to learn how to add format to the document.

# Adding pictures to Word documents

Word documents can include images to show graphs or other kinds of pictorial information. Adding an image is a great way of creating rich reports.

> **Tip**
>
> Any experienced Word user will know how frustrating it can be to properly position an image, as the surrounding environment can make the position change. Keep in mind that while positioning the image programmatically can help, as it will be included in a specific place, changing the surrounding paragraphs can change how it gets rendered. For example, an image may move to the next page if the preceding paragraph becomes longer.

In this recipe, we'll learn how to attach an existing image file to a Word document.

## Getting ready

We'll use the `python-docx` module to process Word documents. Be sure to have it installed in your environment:

```
$ echo "python-docx==1.2.0" >> requirements.txt
$ uv pip install -r requirements.txt
```

We need to prepare an image to include in the document. We'll use the file in the GitHub repo at `https://github.com/PacktPublishing/Python-Automation-Cookbook-Third-Edition/blob/main/ch04/images/photo-dublin-a1.jpg`, which shows a view of Dublin. Download the file and make it available in your working directory.

## How to do it...

1. Import the `python-docx` module:

```
>>> import docx
```

2. Create a new document:

```
>>> document = docx.Document()
```

3. Create a paragraph with some text:

```
>>> document.add_paragraph('This is a document that includes a picture
taken in Dublin')
```

4. Add the image:

```
>>> image = document.add_picture('photo-dublin-a1.jpg')
```

Scale the image properly to fit on the page (14 x 10 cm):

```
>>> from docx.shared import Cm
>>> image.width = Cm(14)
>>> image.height = Cm(10)
```

5. The image has been added to a new paragraph. Align it to the center and add descriptive text:

```
>>> paragraph = document.paragraphs[-1]
>>> from docx.enum.text import WD_ALIGN_PARAGRAPH
>>> paragraph.alignment = WD_ALIGN_PARAGRAPH.CENTER
>>> paragraph.add_run().add_break()
>>> paragraph.add_run('A picture of Dublin')
```

6. Add a new paragraph with extra text, and save the document:

```
>>> document.add_paragraph('Keep adding text after the image')
<docx.text.paragraph.Paragraph object at 0x10ee4cf30>
>>> document.save(word-image.docx')
```

7. Check the result:

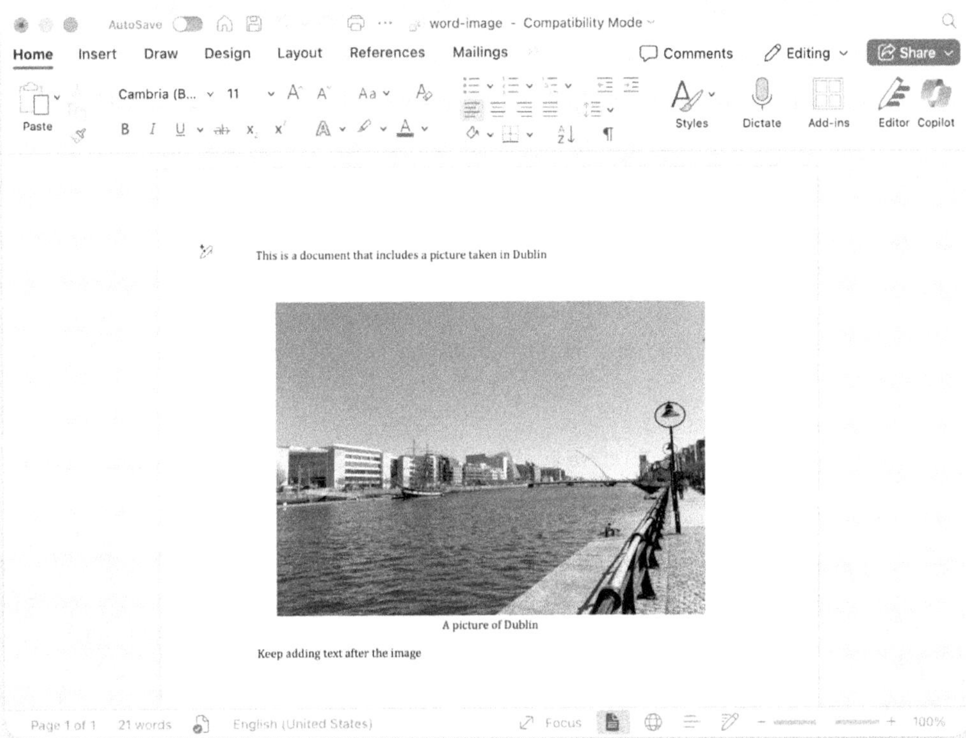


*Figure 5.9: The report.docx document with a picture*

## How it works...

The first few steps (*steps 1* to *3* in the *How to do it...* section) create the document and add some text.

*Step 4* adds the image from the file, while *step 5* resizes it to a manageable size. (By default, the image is too big.)

> **Tip**
>
> Keep in mind the proportion of the image when resizing. Note that you can also use other measures such as *Inches*, which is defined in *shared* as well.

Inserting the image also creates a new paragraph, so the paragraph can be styled to align the image or to add more text, such as a reference or description. The paragraph is obtained in *step 6* through the `document.paragraph` property. The last paragraph is obtained and styled properly, aligning it to the center. A new line and a run with descriptive text are added.

*Step 7* adds extra text after the image and saves the document.

## There's more...

The size of the image can be changed, but as we saw previously, the aspect ratio of the image needs to be calculated if it changes. The resizing may end up not being perfect if done by approximation, as in *step 5* from the *How to do it...* section.

> **Tip**
>
> Notice that the image does not have a perfect aspect ratio of 10:14. Instead, it is 10:13.33, so the image is slightly distorted. For a photograph, that may be good enough, but for images sensitive to proportion changes, such as charts, extra care may be required.

To obtain the proper ratio for a precise adjustment, divide the height by the width and then scale properly:

```
>>> image = document.add_picture('photo-dublin-a1.jpg')
>>> image.height / image.width
0.75
>>> RELATION = image.height / image.width
>>> image.width = Cm(12)
>>> image.height = Cm(12 * RELATION)
```

If you need to transform the values to a particular size, you can use the `cm`, `inches`, `mm`, or `pt` attributes:

```
>>> image.width.cm
12.0
>>> image.width.mm
120.0
>>> image.width.inches
4.724409448818897
>>> image.width.pt
340.15748031496065
```

The full `python-docx` documentation is available here: `https://python-docx.readthedocs.io/en/latest/`.

## See also

- The *Writing a basic Word document* recipe, earlier in this chapter, to learn the basics of working with Word documents.
- The *Styling a Word document* recipe, earlier in this chapter, to learn how to add rich format to the document.
- The previous recipe, *Generating structure in Word documents*, to learn how to add sections and other separators to the documents.

# Writing a simple PDF document

PDF is a widely used format for many kinds of document, including shared reports, brochures, ebooks, academic articles and many others. It's a ubiquitous format! The main characteristic of PDF documents is that they define exactly how the document is going to look when printed, and they are read-only after being produced. This makes them very convenient for transmitting information while preserving the appearance and layout.

In this recipe, we'll see how to write a simple PDF report using Python.

## Getting ready

We'll use the `fpdf` module to create PDF documents, which in its latest version is imported from the module `fpdf2`

```
$ echo "fpdf2==2.8.5" >> requirements.txt
$ pip install -r requirements.txt
```

## How to do it...

1. Import the `fpdf` module:

```
>>> import fpdf
```

2. Create a document:

```
>>> document = fpdf.FPDF()
```

3. Define the font and color for a title, and add the first page:

```
>>> document.set_font('Times', 'B', 14)
>>> document.set_text_color(19, 83, 173)
>>> document.add_page()
```

4. Write the title of the document:

```
>>> document.cell(0, 5, 'PDF test document')
False
>>> document.ln()
```

5. Write a long paragraph:

```
>>> document.set_font('Times', '', 12)
>>> document.set_text_color(0)
>>> document.multi_cell(0, 5, 'This is an example of a long paragraph. ' *
10)
False
>>> document.ln()
```

6. Write another long paragraph:

```
>>> document.multi_cell(0, 5, 'Another long paragraph. Lorem ipsum dolor
sit amet, consectetur adipiscing elit.' * 20)
False
```

7. Save the document:

```
>>> document.output('pdf-report.pdf')
''
```

8. Check the `pdf-report.pdf` document:

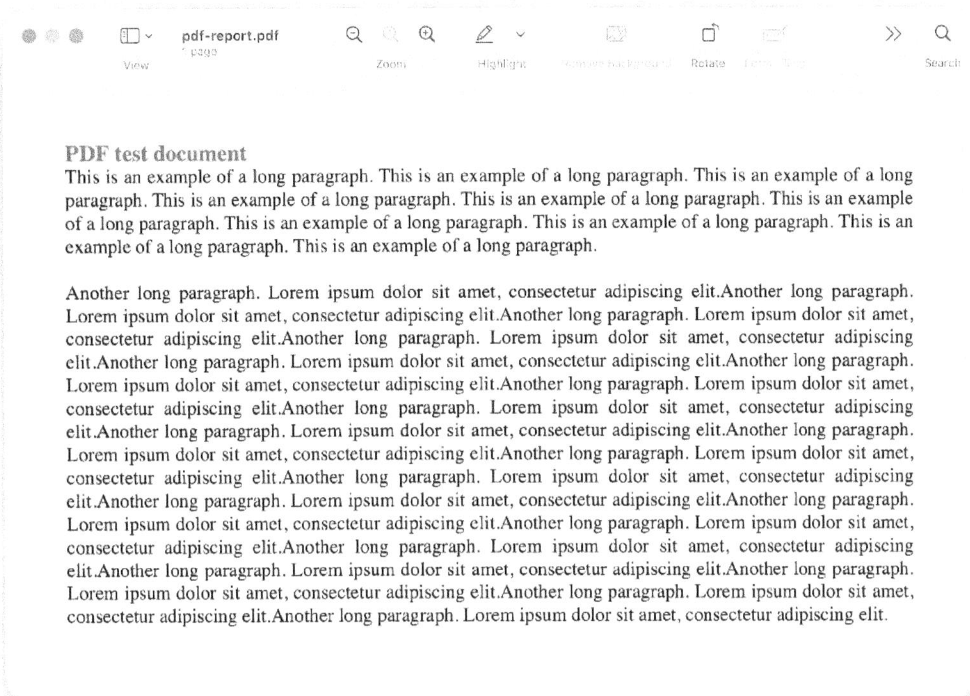


PDF test document

This is an example of a long paragraph. This is an example of a long paragraph. This is an example of a long paragraph. This is an example of a long paragraph. This is an example of a long paragraph. This is an example of a long paragraph. This is an example of a long paragraph. This is an example of a long paragraph. This is an example of a long paragraph. This is an example of a long paragraph.

Another long paragraph. Lorem ipsum dolor sit amet, consectetur adipiscing elit.Another long paragraph. Lorem ipsum dolor sit amet, consectetur adipiscing elit.Another long paragraph. Lorem ipsum dolor sit amet, consectetur adipiscing elit.Another long paragraph. Lorem ipsum dolor sit amet, consectetur adipiscing elit.Another long paragraph. Lorem ipsum dolor sit amet, consectetur adipiscing elit.Another long paragraph. Lorem ipsum dolor sit amet, consectetur adipiscing elit.Another long paragraph. Lorem ipsum dolor sit amet, consectetur adipiscing elit.Another long paragraph. Lorem ipsum dolor sit amet, consectetur adipiscing elit.Another long paragraph. Lorem ipsum dolor sit amet, consectetur adipiscing elit.Another long paragraph. Lorem ipsum dolor sit amet, consectetur adipiscing elit.Another long paragraph. Lorem ipsum dolor sit amet, consectetur adipiscing elit.Another long paragraph. Lorem ipsum dolor sit amet, consectetur adipiscing elit.Another long paragraph. Lorem ipsum dolor sit amet, consectetur adipiscing elit.Another long paragraph. Lorem ipsum dolor sit amet, consectetur adipiscing elit.Another long paragraph. Lorem ipsum dolor sit amet, consectetur adipiscing elit.Another long paragraph. Lorem ipsum dolor sit amet, consectetur adipiscing elit.Another long paragraph. Lorem ipsum dolor sit amet, consectetur adipiscing elit.Another long paragraph. Lorem ipsum dolor sit amet, consectetur adipiscing elit.

*Figure 5.10: The content of pdf-report.pdf*

## How it works...

The `fpdf` module creates a PDF document and allows us to write in it.

The first operations are to specify the font and size to use and then add the first page. This is done in *step 3*. The first font is in bold (second argument, `'B'`) and in a bigger font than the rest of the document. This makes it a title. The color is also set up with `.set_text_color`, in terms of RGB components.

> **Tip**
>
> The text can also be styled in italics with `I` and underlined with `U`. You can combine them, so `BI` will produce text in both bold and italic.
>
> To determine the color in RGB components you can use a color picker like `https://www.w3schools.com/colors/colors_picker.asp`. Alternatively you can ask GenAI to find components for descriptive colors, for example, with the prompt: *Get me in RGB*

> *components the value for a professional strong orange to be used as the color of a font for titles on a report.*

The `.cell` call creates a text box containing the specified text. The first couple of parameters are the width and height. Width 0 uses the whole space up to the right margin. Height 5 (mm) is adequate for a size 12 font. The call to `.ln` introduces a new line.

To write a multiline paragraph we use the `.multi_cell` method. Its parameters are the same as `.cell`. Two paragraphs are written in *steps 5* and *6*. Notice the change in font previously, to distinguish the title from the body of the report. `set_text_color` is called with a single argument to set up the color in grayscale. In this case, it is set to black using 0.

> **Tip**
>
> Using `.cell` for long text will make it go over the margin and off the page. Use it only for text that will fit in a single line. To find out wheter a string will fit in a line calculate `max_width = document.w - document.l_margin - document.r_margin` and compare it with the size of the string to be written with `document.get_string_width(string)`.

The document is saved to disk in *step 7*.

## There's more...

Pages are added automatically if a `multi_cell` operation occupies all space available in a page. Calling `.add_page` will move to a new page, producing a line break.

You can use any of the default fonts (Courier, Helvetica, and Times), or add an extra font using `.add_font`. Check the documentation for more details: `https://py-pdf.github.io/fpdf2/Unicode.html#built-in-fonts-vs-unicode-fonts`.

The Symbol and ZapfDingbats fonts are also available, but they represent symbols. This could be useful if you need to display special characters but be sure to test the result before using them. The rest of the default fonts should include your necessities for serif, sans serif, and fixed-width cases. In PDFs, the fonts used will be embedded in the document, so they'll always be displayed correctly.

The default fonts don't have great Unicode support. In case you want to write in languages that require it, add a more capable font. `fpdf` has a collection of Unicode-enabled free fonts in its documentation `https://py-pdf.github.io/fpdf2/Unicode.html#free-font-pack`. Keep the height consistent throughout the document, at least between text of the same size. Define a constant you're comfortable with, and use it for all the content:

```
>>> BODY_TEXT_HEIGHT = 5
>>> document.multi_cell(0, BODY_TEXT_HEIGHT, text)
```

By default, the text will be justified, but that can be changed. Use the align argument with `J` (justified), `C` (center), `R` (right), or `L` (left) either as characters or as a definition (e.g. `fpdf.Align.J`). For example, these equivalent lines produces text aligned to the left:

```
>>> document.multi_cell(0, BODY_TEXT_HEIGHT, text, align='L')
>>> document.multi_cell(0, BODY_TEXT_HEIGHT, text, align=fpdf.Align.L)
```

The full FPDF documentation can be found here: `https://py-pdf.github.io/fpdf2/`.

## See also

- *Structuring a PDF*, next, to learn how to add separators to a PDF document.
- *Aggregating PDF reports*, later in this chapter, to learn how to merge different PDF documents into one.
- *Watermarking and encrypting a PDF*, later in this chapter, to learn how to add security measures to the document.

# Structuring a PDF

Some elements can be automatically generated when creating a PDF to add a better look and structure to your elements. In this recipe, we'll see how to add a header and footer, and how to create links to other parts of the document.

## Getting ready

We'll use the `fpdf` module to create PDF documents, which in its latest version is imported from the module `fpdf2`. We will also use the module `lorem_text` to generate placeholder text.

```
$ echo "fpdf2==2.8.5" >> requirements.txt
$ echo "lorem-text==3.0" >> requirements.txt
$ uv pip install -r requirements.txt
```

## How to do it...

The `structuring_pdf.py` script is available in GitHub, here: `https://github.com/PacktPublishing/Python-Automation-Cookbook-Third-Edition/blob/main/ch05/structuring_pdf.py`. The most relevant bits are displayed here:

```
import fpdf
from random import randint
from lorem_text import lorem

class StructuredPDF(fpdf.FPDF):
    LINE_HEIGHT = 5
    def footer(self):
        self.set_y(-15)
        self.set_font('Times', 'I', 8)
        page_number = 'Page {number}/{{nb}}'.format(number=self.page_no())
        self.cell(0, self.LINE_HEIGHT, page_number, 0, align='R')
    def chapter(self, title, paragraphs):
        self.add_page()
        link = self.title_text(title)
        page = self.page_no()
        for paragraph in paragraphs:
            self.multi_cell(0, self.LINE_HEIGHT, paragraph)
            self.ln()
        return link, page
    def title_text(self, title):
        self.set_font('Times', 'B', 15)
        self.cell(0, self.LINE_HEIGHT, title)
        self.set_font('Times', '', 12)
        self.line(10, 17, 110, 17)
        link = self.add_link()
        self.set_link(link)
```

```
        self.ln()
        self.ln()
        return link
    def get_full_line(self, head, tail, fill):
        ...
    def toc(self, links):
        self.add_page()
        self.title_text('Table of contents')
        self.set_font('Times', 'I', 12)
        for title, page, link in links:
            line = self.get_full_line(title, page, '.')
            self.cell(0, self.LINE_HEIGHT, line, link=link)
            self.ln()
def main():
    document = StructuredPDF()
    document.alias_nb_pages()
    links = []
    num_chapters = randint(5, 40)
    for index in range(1, num_chapters):
        chapter_title = 'Chapter {}'.format(index)
        num_paragraphs = randint(10, 15)
        paragraphs = [lorem.paragraph() for _ in range(num_paragraphs)]
        link, page = document.chapter(chapter_title, paragraphs)
        links.append((chapter_title, page, link))
    document.toc(links)
    document.output('structure-pdf-report.pdf')
```

1. Run the script. It will generate the `structure-pdf-report.pdf` file, which contains some chapters and a table of contents. Note that the specific content it generates is somewhat random, so the specific numbers will vary each time you run it:

```
$ uv run structuring_pdf.py
```

2. Check the result. Here is a sample:

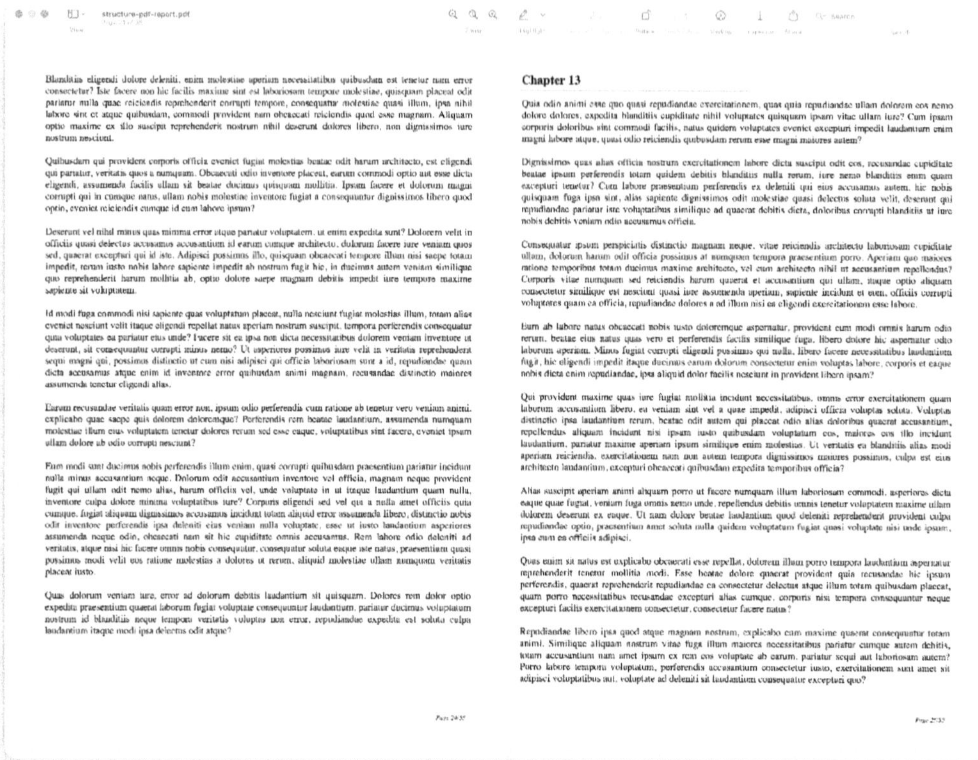


*Figure 5.11: Two pages inside structure-pdf-report.pdf*

3. Check the table of contents at the end:

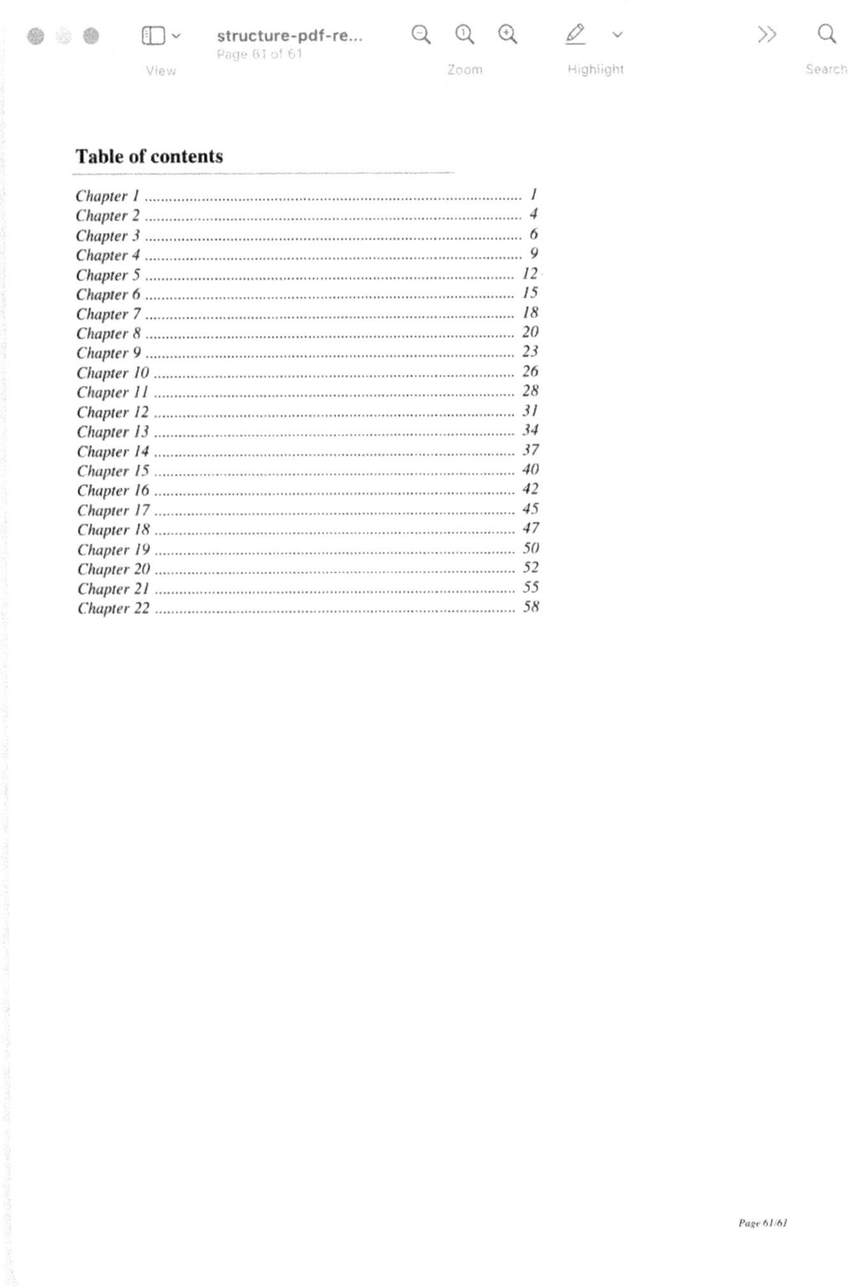


**Table of contents**

*Chapter 1* .......... *1*
*Chapter 2* .......... *4*
*Chapter 3* .......... *6*
*Chapter 4* .......... *9*
*Chapter 5* .......... *12*
*Chapter 6* .......... *15*
*Chapter 7* .......... *18*
*Chapter 8* .......... *20*
*Chapter 9* .......... *23*
*Chapter 10* .......... *26*
*Chapter 11* .......... *28*
*Chapter 12* .......... *31*
*Chapter 13* .......... *34*
*Chapter 14* .......... *37*
*Chapter 15* .......... *40*
*Chapter 16* .......... *42*
*Chapter 17* .......... *45*
*Chapter 18* .......... *47*
*Chapter 19* .......... *50*
*Chapter 20* .......... *52*
*Chapter 21* .......... *55*
*Chapter 22* .......... *58*

*Page 61/61*

*Figure 5.12: The table of contents at the end of report.pdf*

## How it works...

Let's take a look at each of the elements of the script.

The class `StructuredPDF` inherits from the `FPDF` class. This is useful for overwriting the footer method, which creates a footer for each of the pages at generation time. It also helps simplify the code in `main`.

The `main` function creates the document. It starts a new empty document and adds each of the chapters, collecting their link information. Finally, it calls the `.toc` method to generate a table of contents using the link information.

> **Note**
>
> The text to be stored is generated by the module `lorem_text`, which generates placeholder "lorem ipsum" text. Check its full documentation at https://lorem-text.readthedocs.io/en/latest/

The `.chapter` method first prints a title section and then adds each of the paragraphs. It collects the page number the chapter starts on, and the link returned by the `.title_text` method to collect all of them in the `links` list.

The `.title_text` method writes the text in bigger and bolder text. Then it adds a line to separate the title from the body of the chapter. It generates and sets a `link` object pointing to the current page (the start of the chapter), in the following lines:

```
link = self.add_link()
self.set_link(link)
```

This link will be used in the table of contents to add a clickable element that points to this chapter.

The content of the chapter is added with `.multi_cell` for each of the defined paragraphs, with a new line between them using the `.ln` method.

The `footer` method in the `StructuredPDF` class automatically adds a footer to each page. It sets a smaller font, and it adds text with the current page (obtained through `page_no`) and uses `{nb}`, which will be replaced with the total number of pages.

> **Note**
>
> The call to `.alias_nb_pages()` in `main` ensures that `{nb}` is replaced when the document is generated.

Finally, the table of contents is generated in the `.toc` method. It writes the title and adds all the referenced links that have been collected in the form of link, page, and chapter name, which is all the info required.

## There's more...

Notice the use of `randint` to add a bit of randomness to the document. This call, available in Python's standard library, returns a random number between the specified maximum and minimum (both inclusive) .

The `.get_full_line` method generates a correctly sized line for the table of contents. It takes a start (the name of the chapter) and end (the page number), and adds the number of fill characters (dots) needed to fill the line to the defined width (120 mm).

To calculate the width of the text, the script calls `.get_string_width`, which takes into account the font and its size.

Link objects can be used to point to a specific page, instead of the current one, and not necessarily to the start of the page. To tweak the call, use `.set_link(link, y=place, page=num_page)`. Check the documentation at `https://py-pdf.github.io/fpdf2/fpdf/fpdf.html#fpdf.fpdf.FPDF.set_link`.

Adjusting some of the elements can take a certain amount of trial and error; for example, to position the line. A slightly longer or shorter line can be a matter of taste. Don't be afraid to experiment and check until you obtain the desired effect.

You can also create more types of links, such as hyperlinks to public URLs. For more details, check the link documentation here `https://py-pdf.github.io/fpdf2/Links.html`.

The full `fpdf` documentation can be found here: `https://py-pdf.github.io/fpdf2/`.

## See also

- The previous recipe, *Writing a simple PDF document*, to learn the basics of how to work with PDF documents.

- The *Aggregating PDF reports* recipe, coming next, to learn how to merge multiple documents into a single one.
- The *Watermarking and encrypting a PDF* recipe, later in this chapter, to learn how to add security measures to the document.

# Aggregating PDF reports

In this recipe, we'll see how to combine two PDFs into one. We will append the pages of one report to the end of the other.

## Getting ready

We'll use the `pypdf` module, installing it in the usual way:

```
$ echo " pypdf==6.6.0" >> requirements.txt
$ uv pip install -r requirements.txt
```

We need two PDFs to combine. For this recipe, we'll use two PDFs produced in previous recipes:

- `pdf-report.pdf`, as seen in *Writing a simple PDF recipe*
- `structure-pdf-report.pdf`, as seen in *Structuring a PDF*

But these two are just examples; feel free to use whatever two PDFs suit you.

## How to do it...

1. Import `pypdf` and create the output PDF:

```
>>> import pypdf
>>> output_pdf = pypdf.PdfWriter()
```

2. Read the first file and create a reader:

```
>>> file1 = open('pdf-report.pdf', 'rb')
>>> pdf1 = pypdf.PdfReader(file1)
```

3. Append all pages to the output PDF:

```
>>> output_pdf.append_pages_from_reader(pdf1)
```

4. Open the second file, create a reader, and append the pages to the output PDF:

```
>>> file2 = open('structure-pdf-report.pdf', 'rb')
>>> pdf2 = pypdf.PdfReader(file2)
>>> output_pdf.append_pages_from_reader(pdf2)
```

5. Create the output file and save it:

```
>>> with open('pdf-result.pdf', 'wb') as out_file:
...     output_pdf.write(out_file)
(False, <_io.BufferedWriter name='pdf-result.pdf'>)
```

6. Close both source files:

```
>>> file1.close()
>>> file2.close()
```

Check the output file and confirm that it contains both PDF pages.

## How it works...

`pypdf` allows us to create a reader for each source file and add all their pages to a newly created PDF writer. Note that the files are opened in binary mode (`rb`).

> **Tip**
>
> The input files need to remain open until the result is saved. This is due to the way the copying of the pages works. If the files are closed, the resulting file may be stored as an empty file.

The PDF writer finally saves the resulting content to the new file `pdf-result.pdf`. Note that the file needs to be open to write in binary mode (`wb`).

## There's more...

`.append_pages_from_reader` is very convenient for adding all pages, but it's also possible to add specific pages one by one with `.add_page`. For example, to add the third page, the code would look like this:

```
>>> page = pdf1.pages[3]
>>> output_pdf.add_page(page)
```

While fpdf is the more capable package, there are some operations that are handled more naturally with pypdf, like merging or splitting documents. You can pass a fpdf document to pypdf in the following way:

```
>>> import io
>>> pypdf_reader = pypdf.PdfReader(io.BytesIO(fpdf_document.output()))
```

The full documentation for pypdf can be found here: https://pypdf.readthedocs.io/en/stable/.

## See also

- The *Writing a simple PDF document* recipe, earlier in this chapter, to learn the basics of how to work with PDF documents.
- The previous recipe, *Structuring a PDF*, to learn how to add separators to a PDF document.
- The *Watermarking and encrypting a PDF* recipe, coming next, to learn how to add security measures to the document.

# Watermarking and encrypting a PDF

PDF files have some interesting security measures to help limit their distribution and protect their contents. We can encrypt the content, requiring users to input a password in order to read it. We'll also see how to add a watermark to label the document clearly as not for public distribution and, if leaked, for its origin to be known.

## Getting ready

We'll use pypdf, so ensure that it's installed in your environment. We will also use pdf2image, to transform Pillow images into PDF format. pdf2image also install Pillow as a dependency, which we will use to create the watermark image.

```
$ echo "pypdf==6.6.0" >> requirements.txt
$ echo "pdf2image==1.17.0" >> requirements.txt
$ echo "Pillow==12.0.0" >> requirements.txt
$ pip install -r requirements.txt
```

We also need a PDF file to watermark and encrypt. We'll use a structure-pdf-report.pdf file generated by the structuring_pdf.py script, described in the *Structuring a PDF* recipe, which is available on GitHub: https://github.com/PacktPublishing/Python-Automation-Cookbook-Third-Edition/blob/master/ch05/structuring_pdf.py.

## How to do it...

1. The script, `watermarking_pdf.py`, is available on GitHub here: `https://github.com/PacktPublishing/Python-Automation-Cookbook-Third-Edition/blob/main/ch05/watermarking_pdf.py`. The most relevant bits are displayed here:

```
def encrypt(out_pdf, password):
    output_pdf = pypdf.PdfWriter()
    in_file = open(out_pdf, "rb")
    input_pdf = pypdf.PdfReader(in_file)
    output_pdf.append_pages_from_reader(input_pdf)
    output_pdf.encrypt(password)
    # Intermediate file
    with open(INTERMEDIATE_ENCRYPT_FILE, "wb") as out_file:
        output_pdf.write(out_file)
    in_file.close()
    # Rename the intermediate file
    os.rename(INTERMEDIATE_ENCRYPT_FILE, out_pdf)
def create_watermark(watermarked_by):
    mask = Image.new('L', WATERMARK_SIZE, 0)
    draw = ImageDraw.Draw(mask)
    font = ImageFont.load_default()
    text = 'WATERMARKED BY {}\n{}'.format(watermarked_by, datetime.now())
    draw.multiline_text((0, 100), text, 55, font=font)
    watermark = Image.new('RGB', WATERMARK_SIZE)
    watermark.putalpha(mask)
    watermark = watermark.resize((1950, 1950))
    watermark = watermark.rotate(45)
    # Crop to only the watermark
    bbox = watermark.getbbox()
    watermark = watermark.crop(bbox)
    return watermark
def apply_watermark(watermark, in_pdf, out_pdf):
    # Transform from PDF to images
    images = convert_from_path(in_pdf)
    ...
    # Paste the watermark in each page
    for image in images:
        image.paste(watermark, position, watermark)
```

```
    # Save the resulting PDF
    images[0].save(out_pdf, save_all=True, append_images=images[1:])
```

2. Watermark the PDF file with the following command:

```
$ uv run watermarking_pdf.py structure-pdf-report.pdf -u automate_user -o out.pdf
Creating a watermark
Watermarking the document
```

3. Check that the document added a watermark with `automate_user` and a timestamp to all the pages of `out.pdf`:

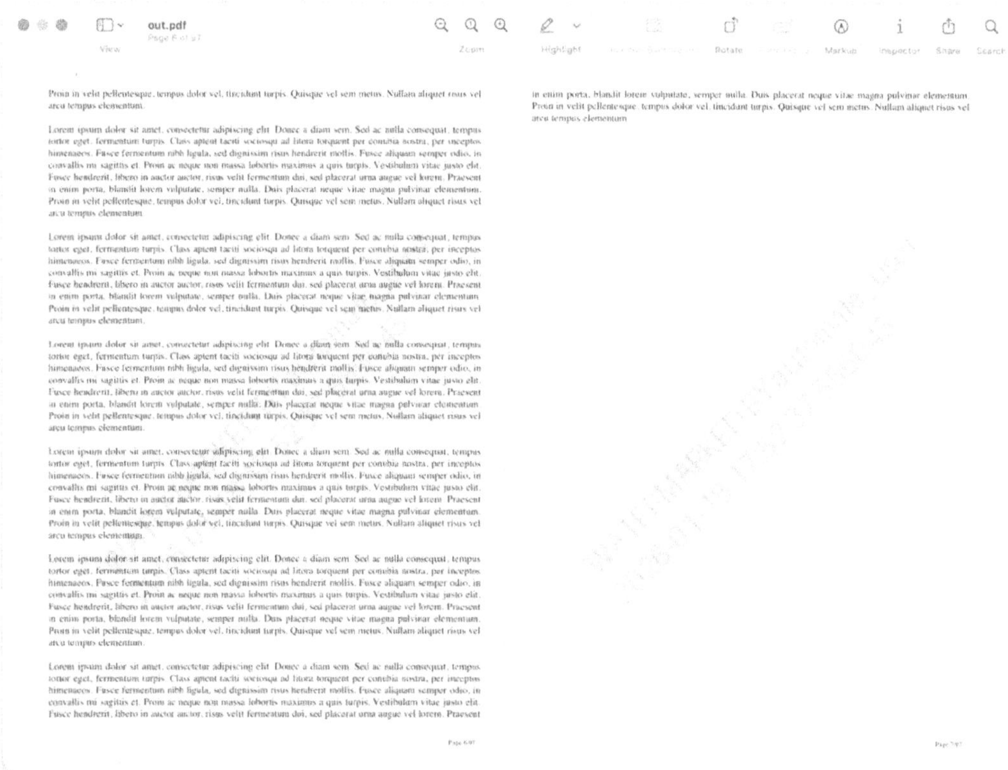


*Figure 5.13: Watermarked content of out.pdf*

4. Watermark and encrypt with the following command. Note that encrypting the file may take a little bit of time:

```
$ uv run watermarking_pdf.py report.pdf -u automate_user -o out.pdf -p
secretpassword
Creating a watermark
Watermarking the document
Encrypting the document
```

5. Open the resulting file, `out.pdf`, and check that it requires you to input the `secretpassword` password. The timestamp will also be new.

## How it works...

The `watermarking_pdf.py` script first obtains the parameters from the command line using `argparse`, and then passes it to a `main` function that calls the other three functions: `create_watermark`, `apply_watermark`, and, if a password is used, `encrypt`.

`create_watermark` generates an image with the watermark. It uses the `Pillow Image` class to create a gray image (mode L) and draw the text. Then this image gets applied as an alpha channel to a new image, making the image semi-transparent so that it will show the text to watermark.

> **Note**
>
> The alpha channel makes fully transparent anything in white (color 0) and fully opaque anything in black (color 255). In this case, the background is white (fully transparent) and the color of the text is 55, making it semi-transparent.

The image is then rotated 45 degrees and cropped to reduce the transparent background that may have appeared. This centers the image and allows for better positioning.

In the next step, `apply_watermark` transforms the PDF into a sequence of `Pillow Images` using the `pdf2image` module. It calculates the position to apply the watermark and then pastes the watermark.

> **Note**
>
> We need to perform a calculation to position the watermark image in the center of the page. The position for image insertion is referenced by its top-left corner, which means that we need to shift vertically and horizontally by half the difference in height and width respectively between the watermark and the full page. In Pillow, the reference is

in the top-left corner of the image. Note that the script assumes that all the pages of the document have the same size.

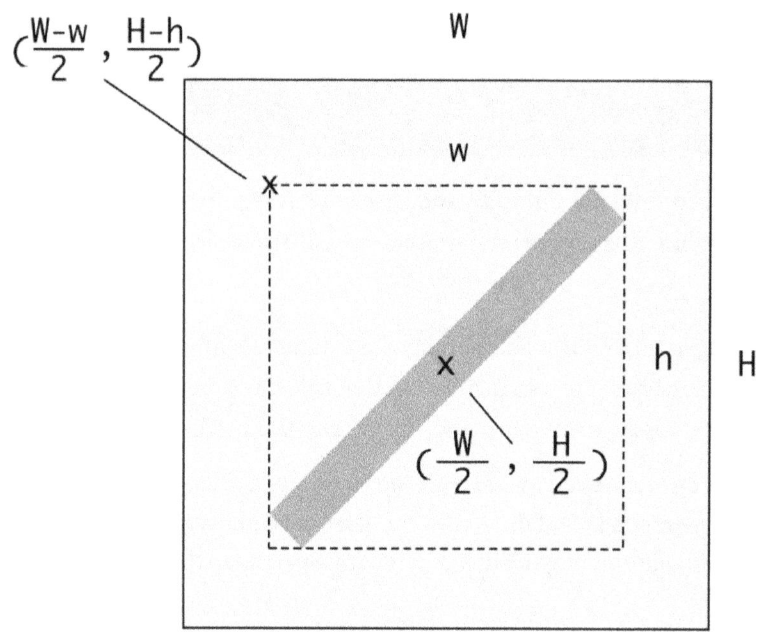


Figure 5.14 Positioning of the watermark

Finally, the result is saved to a PDF file. Notice the `save_all` parameter, which allows us to save a multipage PDF.

If a password is especified, the `encrypt` function is called. It opens the output PDF using `PdfReader` and creates a new intermediate PDF with `PdfWriter`. All the pages of the output PDF are added to the new PDF, the PDF is encrypted, and then the intermediate PDF is renamed as the output PDF using `os.rename`.

## There's more...

As part of the watermarking process, notice that the pages are transformed from text into image. This adds extra protection as the text won't be extractable directly as text. When protecting a file, this is a good idea, as it will stop copying/pasting directly.

> **Tip**
>
> The transformation of pages from text to image form is not a huge security measure as the text may be extracted through OCR tools, as we've seen in *Chapter 4*. But it protects against casual extraction of the text. The output file size is also much bigger, about 30 MB, which also makes it slower to encrypt and decrypt.

The default font from Pillow can be a little rough. Another font, if the TrueType or OpenType file is available, can be added and used by calling the following:

```
font = ImageFont.truetype('my_font.ttf', SIZE)
```

Note that this may require installing the `FreeType` libraries, normally available as part of the `libfreetype` package. Further documentation is available at `https://www.freetype.org/`. Depending on the font and size, you may need to adjust the sizes.

The full `pdf2image` documentation can be found at `https://github.com/Belval/pdf2image`, the full documentation for PyPDF2 at `https://pypdf.readthedocs.io/en/stable/`, and that for Pillow at `https://pillow.readthedocs.io/en/stable/`.

## See also

- The *Writing a simple PDF document* recipe, earlier in this chapter, to learn the basics of how to work with PDF documents.
- The *Structuring a PDF* recipe, earlier in this chapter, to learn how to add separators to a PDF document.
- The previous recipe, *Aggregating PDF reports*, to learn how to merge multiple documents into a single one.

# Get this book's PDF version and more

Scan the QR code (or go to `packtpub.com/unlock`). Search for this book by name, confirm the edition, and then follow the steps on the page.

UNLOCK NOW

*Note: Keep your invoice handy. Purchases made directly from Packt don't require an invoice.*

# 6

# Fun with Spreadsheets

Spreadsheets are one of the most versatile and omnipresent tools in the world of computing. Their intuitive approach of sheets and cells is used by virtually everyone who uses a computer as part of their day-to-day work. But they also allow you to perform very complex operations, perhaps exploiting a powerful macro language. Indeed it's become a running joke that entire businesses are managed from and described by a single spreadsheet. In other words they are incredibly powerful tools, and much valuable information is stored there. This makes the ability to automate reading from and writing to spreadsheets so interesting.

But spreadsheets have their problems, some major, like:

- Intrinsic problems with the format itself. Spreadsheets silently change data types, they don't version-diff cleanly, formulas and data are tangled together with no separation between code and inputs, and errors propagate without any test coverage.
  Python presents an advantage here where the code is stricter and the logic can be implemented in a clearer way. Python is also more versatile than custom tools like VBA, which only work on a single suite of applications. Python also allows use of a vast collection of third-party libraries to perform operations, notable in terms of both its breadth (including, for example, statistical and other specialized mathematical libraries) and the performance that highly optimized modules can provide.
- Misuse of the 'if you have a hammer, everything looks like a nail' sort. Excel is the tool everyone knows, so businesses end up running important production logic inside spreadsheets that should really be using different tools, such as a database, a ticketing system, a bespoke application, or a pipeline.

- Python allows greater interoperability, utilization of its big library allowing connection to many other services.
- Data can start in a spreadsheet and be communicated somewhere else through Python, or vice versa.

In this chapter we'll see how to process spreadsheets, mainly in the most common format, Microsoft Excel.

> **Tip**
>
> On top of the advantages described above, in Python the code is readable and easy to understand compared to other alternatives. In *Chapter 7, Cleaning and Processing Data*, we'll go through some techniques that can help increase your productivity when dealing with spreadsheet files and processes.

As you might expect, GenAI tools are supercharging spreadsheets, making it easier than ever to generate powerful formulas and produce capable spreadsheets. Over the course of the chapter we will include various tips and suggestions for using GenAI tools to work with spreadsheets.

In this chapter, we will cover the following recipes:

- Writing a CSV file
- Updating CSV files
- Reading an Excel spreadsheet
- Updating an Excel spreadsheet
- Creating new sheets in an Excel spreadsheet
- Creating charts in Excel
- Working with cell formats in Excel
- Using Python in Excel

Let's start by taking a look at CSV files.

# Technical requirements

You can check the code presented in the chapter in the GitHub URL `https://github.com/PacktPublishing/Python-Automation-Cookbook-Third-Edition/tree/main/ch06`.

# Writing a CSV file

CSV files can be used as simple spreadsheets in a format understandable by a wide variety of tools. They are text files with tabular data separated by commas (hence the name *Comma-*

*Separated Values*), in a simple table format. CSV files can be created using Python's standard library and can be read by all kinds of spreadsheet software. Even operating systems will typically have a way to work with CSV files included by default.

## Getting ready

For this recipe, only the standard library of Python is required. Everything is ready out of the box!

For visualization we will use LibreOffice (`https://www.libreoffice.org/`), but it's likely that your OS already has some way of opening the files (e.g. you may have installed Microsoft Excel, and macOS comes preinstalled with Numbers, another spreadsheet package).

## How to do it...

1. Import the `csv` module:

```
>>> import csv
```

2. Define the header with how the data will be ordered and with the data to store:

```
>>> HEADER = ('Admissions', 'Name', 'Year')
>>> DATA = [
... (225.7, 'Gone With the Wind', 1939),
... (194.4, 'Star Wars', 1977),
... (156.4, 'The Sound of Music', 1965)
... ]
```

3. Write the data to a CSV file:

```
>>> with open('movies.csv', 'w',  newline='') as csvfile:
...     movies = csv.writer(csvfile)
...     movies.writerow(HEADER)
...     for row in DATA:
...         movies.writerow(row)
```

4. Check the resulting CSV file in a spreadsheet. In the following screenshot the file is displayed using LibreOffice:

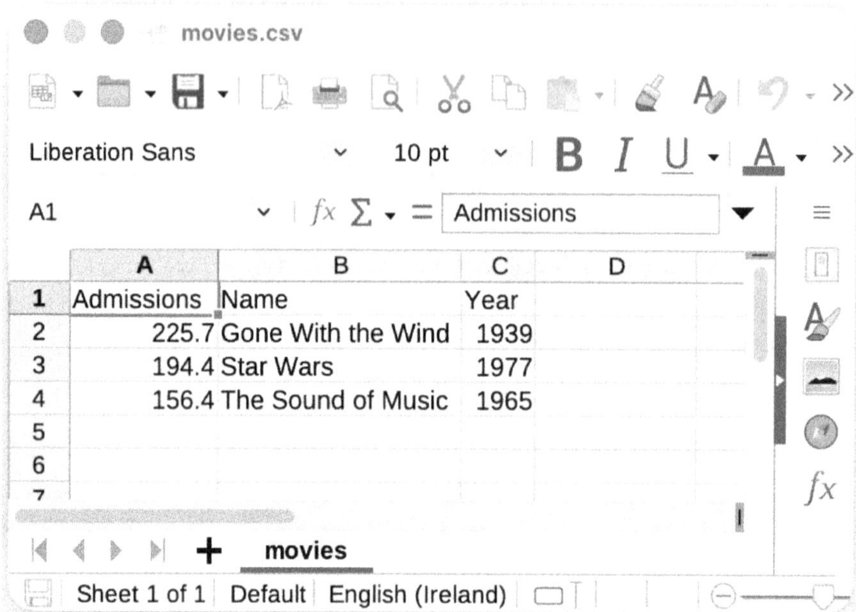


*Figure 6.1: Contents of the movies.csv file*

## How it works...

After the preparation work in *steps 1* and *2* in the *How to do it...* section, *step 3* is the part that saves the `movies.csv` file.

It opens a new file, `movies.csv`, in write (`w`) mode. The file handle object in `csvfile` references the file, which the `CSV.writer()` function uses to create the CSV file. All this happens in a `with` block, so it closes the file when the block is complete.

> **Tip**
>
> Note the `newline=''` parameter. This is done to ensure that the `writer` is in control of the newline format and to avoid incompatibility issues, such as adding a newline twice. This won't normally be a problem, but sometimes the CSV format requires the newline to be a specific character, different from the default one. This can happen, for example, if working with a file to be used on a different operating system. It's better to handle it explicitly in the CSV configuration.

The `writer` writes the elements row by row using the `.writerow()` method. The first row is the `HEADER`, and the remaining rows are the lines of data.

## There's more...

The code presented stores the data in the default CSV dialect. The CSV dialect defines what character divides the data on each row (commas or other characters), how to escape characters, newline characters (also known as line terminators) defining a new entry, and so on.

> **Note**
>
> Escaping is the process of storing characters that could be interpreted as part of the syntax, for example when handling text that includes a comma or a quote. The dialect will determine how to store it in that case; for example surrounding by double quotes text that contains verbatim commas, for example.

In case the dialect needs to be tweaked, each of these parameters can be defined in the writer call. Refer to the following link for a list of all the parameters that can be defined: `https://docs.python.org/3/library/csv.html#dialects-and-formatting-parameters`.

> **Tip**
>
> CSV files are better when simple. If the data to be stored is complicated, maybe the best alternative is not a CSV file. But CSV files are extremely useful when dealing with tabular data. They can be understood by virtually all programs, which makes them very portable, and even dealing with them at a low level is easy.

The full csv module documentation can be found here: `https://docs.python.org/3/library/csv.html`.

## See also

- The *Reading CSV files* recipe in *Chapter 4, Searching and Reading Local Files*.
- The *Updating CSV files* recipe in the following section.

# Updating CSV files

Given that CSV files are simple text files, the best solution to update their content is to read them, process them into internal Python objects, make the changes, and then overwrite the result back in the same format. In this recipe, we will see how to do this.

## Getting ready

In this recipe, we will use the `movies.csv` file that is available on GitHub at `https://github.com/PacktPublishing/Python-Automation-Cookbook-Third-Edition/blob/main/ch06/movies.csv`. It contains the following data:

| **Admissions** | **Name** | **Year** |
|---|---|---|
| 225.7 | Gone With the Wind | 1939 |
| 194.4 | Star Wars | 1968 |
| 156.4 | The Sound of Music | 1965 |

*Table 6.1: Movie data*

Notice that the Year given for *Star Wars* is incorrect (the movie was released in 1977). We'll change it in this recipe.

## How to do it...

1. Import the `csv` module and define the filename:

```
>>> import csv
>>> FILENAME = 'movies.csv'
```

2. Read the contents of the file using `DictReader` and transform it into a list of ordered rows:

```
>>> with open(FILENAME, newline='') as file:
...     data = [row for row in csv.DictReader(file)]
```

3. Check the obtained data. Change the proper value from 1968 to 1977:

```
>>> data
[{'Admissions': '225.7', 'Name': 'Gone With the Wind', 'Year': '1939'},
{'Admissions': '194.4', 'Name': 'Star Wars', 'Year': '1968'},
{'Admissions': '156.4', 'Name': 'The Sound of Music', 'Year': '1965'}]
>>> data[1]['Year']
'1968'
>>> data[1]['Year'] = '1977'
```

4. Open the file again and store the values:

```
>>> HEADER = data[0].keys()
>>> with open(FILENAME, 'w', newline='') as file:
...     writer = csv.DictWriter(file, fieldnames=HEADER)
...     writer.writeheader()
...     writer.writerows(data)
```

5. Check the result in spreadsheet software. The result is similar to that displayed in *step 4* of the *Writing a CSV spreadsheet* recipe.

## How it works...

After importing the `csv` module in *step 2* of the *How to do it...* section, we extract all the data from the file. The file is opened in a `with` block. `DictReader` conveniently transforms it into a list of dictionaries, with the headers as keys and the cell content as values.

The conveniently formatted data can then be manipulated and modified. We changed the data to fix the Year problem in *step 3*.

> **Tip**
>
> In this recipe, we change the value by directly accessing a row number, but searching for the specific row or rows to change may be required in a more general case.

*Step 4* overwrites the file and, using `DictWriter`, stores the data. `DictWriter` requires us to define the fields on the columns by requiring the fieldnames. To obtain them, we retrieve the keys of one of the rows and store them in `HEADER`.

The file is opened again in `w` mode to overwrite it. `DictWriter` first stores the header with `.writeheader` and then stores all the rows with a single call to `.writerows()`.

> **Note**
>
> The rows can also be added one-by-one by calling the `.writerow()` method.

After closing the `with` block, the file is stored and can be checked to verify that it's correct.

## There's more...

For familiar data sources, the dialect of the CSV file is typically known, but this may not always be the case, especially if the file comes from an unknown source. In that case, the `Sniffer` class can help. It analyzes a sample of the file (or the whole file) and returns a guessed dialect object:

```
>>> with open(FILENAME, newline='') as file:
...     dialect = csv.Sniffer().sniff(file.read())
```

The `dialect` object can then be passed to the `DictReader` class when opening the file. The file will need to be opened twice for reading. Remember to use the dialect on the `DictWriter` class as well to save the file in the same format.

> Tip
>
> You can also specify the dialect as one of the named dialects available in `csv.list_dialects()`, if you know it. You can ask a GenAI tool for the dialect as well, to get a good guess.

The full documentation for the csv module can be found here: `https://docs.python.org/3/library/csv.html`.

## See also

- The *Reading CSV files* recipe in *Chapter 4, Searching and Reading Local Files.*
- The previous recipe in this chapter, *Writing a CSV spreadsheet.*

# Reading an Excel spreadsheet

MS Office is by far the most common office suite software, making its formats pretty much the dominant standard. MS Excel is probably the most common spreadsheet application, and the Excel format is the most common spreadsheet format, forcing many other spreadsheet applications to understand the format.

In this recipe, we'll see how to obtain information from an Excel spreadsheet using the `openpyxl` module in Python.

## Getting ready

We will use the `openpyxl` module. We should install the module, adding it to our `requirements.txt` file as follows:

```
$ echo "openpyxl==3.1.5" >> requirements.txt
$ uv pip install -r requirements.txt
```

In the GitHub repository there's an Excel spreadsheet named `movies.xlsx` that contains information on the top 10 movies by attendance. The file can be found here: `https://github.com/PacktPublishing/Python-Automation-Cookbook-Third-Edition/blob/master/ch06/movies.xlsx`.

(The source of the information is: `http://www.mrob.com/pub/film-video/topadj.html`.)

## How to do it...

1. Import the `openpyxl` module:

```
>>> import openpyxl
```

2. Load the file into memory:

```
>>> xlsfile = openpyxl.load_workbook('movies.xlsx')
```

3. List all sheets and get the first one, which is the only one that contains data:

```
>>> xlsfile.sheetnames
['Sheet1']
>>> sheet = xlsfile['Sheet1']
```

4. Obtain the values of cells `B5` and `D5` (admissions and director of E.T.):

```
>>> sheet['B5'].value
161
```

```
>>> sheet['D5'].value
'Steven Spielberg'
```

5. Obtain the size in rows and columns. Any cell out of that range will return `None` as a value:

```
>>> sheet.max_row
11
>>> sheet.max_column
4
>>> sheet['A12'].value is None
True
>>> sheet['E1'].value is None
True
```

## How it works...

After importing the module in *step 1*, *step 2* in the *How to do it...* section loads the file into memory in a `Workbook` object. Each workbook can contain one or more sheets, each of them containing cells.

To determine the available sheets, in *step 3* we obtain all the sheet names (there's a single sheet in this example) and then access the sheet like a dictionary to retrieve a `Worksheet` object. We use the name `sheet`.

`sheet` can then access all the cells directly by their names, such as `A4orC3`. Each of them will return a `Cell` object. The `.value` attribute stores the value in the cell.

> **Tip**
>
> In the rest of the recipes in this chapter, we will see more attributes of `Cell` objects. Keep reading!

Obtaining the area where the data is stored is possible with `max_columns` and `max_rows`. This allows us to search within the limits of the data.

> **Tip**
>
> Excel defines the columns as letters (A, B, C, and so on) and rows as numbers (1, 2, 3, ... ). Remember to always set the column, and then the row (`D1`, and not `1D`), or an error will be raised.

Cells outside the boundaries are accessible but won't return data. They are available to write new data.

## There's more...

Cells can also be retrieved with `sheet.cell(column, row)`. Both elements start their index at 1.

All the cells within the data area iterate from the sheet, for example:

```
>>> for row in sheet:
...     for cell in row:
...         # Do stuff with cell
```

> **Note**
>
> This will return a list of lists with all cells, row by row: `A1`, `B1`, `C1` ... `A2`, `B2`, `C2`, and so on.
>
> You can retrieve the cell's column with columns iterating through `sheet.columns`: `A1`, `A2`, `A3`.. and then `B1`, `B2`, `B3`..., and so on.

When retrieving a cell, you can find its position with `.coordinate`, `.row`, and `.column (for the column as an number index) and .column_letter (for the letter column)`:

```
>>> cell.coordinate
'D4'
>>> cell.column_letter
'D'
>>> cell.row
4
```

The full `openpyxl` documentation can be found here: `https://openpyxl.readthedocs.io/en/stable/index.html`.

## See also

- The *Updating an Excel spreadsheet* recipe in the next section.
- The *Creating new sheets in an Excel spreadsheet* recipe later in this chapter.
- The *Creating charts in Excel* recipe later in the chapter.
- The *Working with cell formats in Excel* recipe later in the chapter.

# Updating an Excel spreadsheet

In this recipe, we'll see how to update an existing Excel spreadsheet. This will include changing raw values in cells and setting up formulas that will be evaluated when the spreadsheet is open. We'll also see how to add comments to cells.

## Getting ready

We will use the openpyxl module. We should install the module, adding it to our requirements.txt file as follows:

```
$ echo "openpyxl==3.1.5" >> requirements.txt
$ uv pip install -r requirements.txt
```

In the GitHub repository, there's an Excel spreadsheet named movies.xlsx that contains information on the top 10 movies by attendance.

The file can be found here: https://github.com/PacktPublishing/Python-Automation-Cookbook-Third-Edition/blob/main/ch06/movies.xlsx.

## How to do it...

1. Import the openpyxl module and the Comment class:

```
>>> import openpyxl
>>> from openpyxl.comments import Comment
```

2. Load the file into memory and get the sheet:

```
>>> xlsfile = openpyxl.load_workbook('movies.xlsx')
>>> sheet = xlsfile['Sheet1']
```

3. Obtain the value of cell D5 (director of E.T):

```
>>> sheet['D5'].value
'Steven Spielberg'
```

4. Change the value to just Spielberg:

```
>>> sheet['D5'].value = 'Spielberg'
```

5. Add a comment to that cell:

```
>>> sheet['D5'].comment = Comment('Changed text automatically', 'User')
```

6. Add a new element that obtains the total of all values in the Admissions column:

```
>>> sheet['B12'] = '=SUM(B2:B11)'
```

7. Save the spreadsheet to the `movies_comment.xlsx` file:

```
>>> xlsfile.save('movies_comment.xlsx')
```

8. Check the resulting file, which includes the comment and the calculation of the total of column B in `B12`:

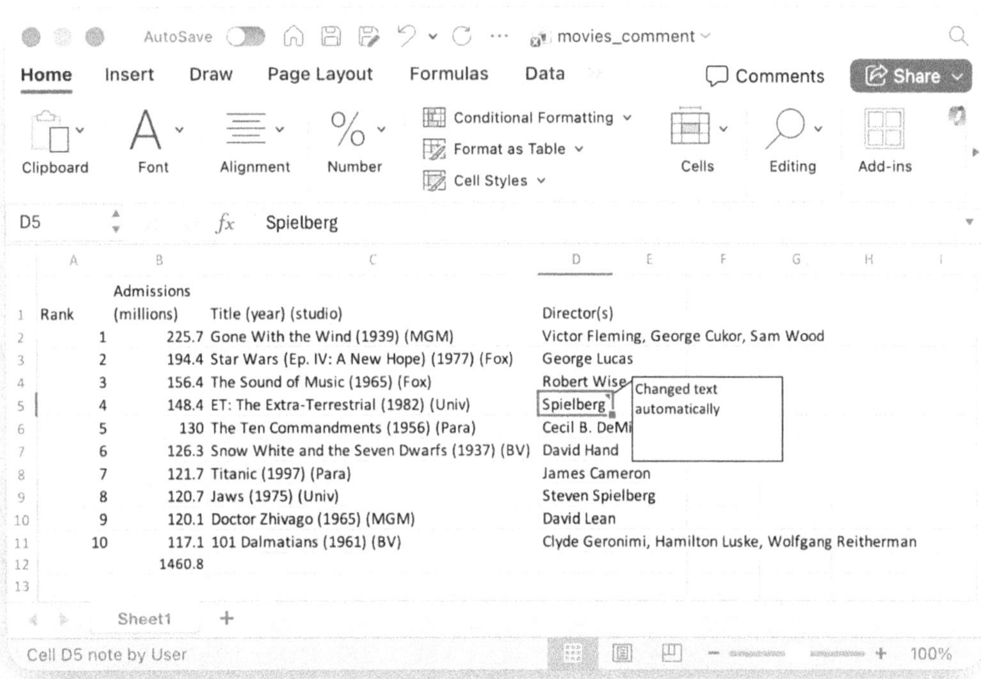


*Figure 6.2: The cell now shows a comment*

## How it works...

In the *How to do it...* section, after making the imports in *step 1* and reading the spreadsheet in *step 2*, we select the cell to be changed in *step 3*.

Updating the value is done in *step 4* with an assignment. A comment in the cell is added, overwriting the `.comment` attribute with a new `Comment` class instance. Note that the name of the user making the comment is required.

Values can also include descriptions of formulas. In *step 6* we add a new formula to cell *B12*. The value is calculated and displayed when the file is opened in *step 8*.

> **Note**
>
> The value of a formula is not calculated in Python, but in Excel. This means that the formula could contain errors or display unexpected results through bugs in the resulting spreadsheet. Be sure to double-check that the formulas are correct.
>
> GenAI is fantastic helping you to determine what formula to use to achieve the effect you want. For example, you can prompt "*Write a formula that calculates the average values in column C*". MS Excel is integrating Copilot, their own GenAI tool, directly into Excel, so you can ask questions and get suggestions directly in the tool.

Finally, in *step 7*, the spreadsheet is saved to disk by calling the `.save` method of the XLSX file object. The name of the resulting file can be the same as the input file, so as to overwrite it.

The comment and values can be viewed by externally accessing the file.

## There's more...

You can store data in each cell using native Python data types, and they will be translated into the proper types for Excel when you write the file. For example, storing a `datetime` object will store time data in the proper date format. The same is true with float or other numeric formats.

If you don't need to change any value in the spreadsheet, you can open it in read-only mode:

```
>>> xlsfile = openpyxl.load_workbook('movies.xlsx', read_only=True)
>>> xlsfile['Sheet1']['A1'].value = '37%'
...
AttributeError: Cell is read only
```

Adding comments to automatically generated cells can help review the resulting file, making it clear how each specific value was generated.

While it is possible to add formulas to automatically generate Excel files, debugging the results can be tricky. If you don't expect the spreadsheet to change after being generated , it's better to make the calculations in Python and store the result in a raw format, meaning that no Excel formula is applied. This makes the spreadsheet simpler and can be stored without changes not only in Excel format, but in other formats, like CSV.

To achieve this effect when loading a spreadsheet, you can use the `data_only` parameter for `load_workbook`. This will load all the cells with their last value, instead of a dynamic formula.

The full `openpyxl` documentation can be found here: `https://openpyxl.readthedocs.io/en/stable/index.html`.

## See also

- The previous recipe, *Reading an Excel spreadsheet.*
- The *Creating new sheets in an Excel spreadsheet* recipe, in the following section.
- The *Creating charts in Excel* recipe later in the chapter.
- The *Working with cell formats in Excel* recipe later in the chapter.

# Creating new sheets in an Excel spreadsheet

In this recipe, we'll demonstrate how to create a new Excel spreadsheet from scratch and then deal with multiple sheets within that spreadsheet, including creating them.

## Getting ready

We will use the `openpyxl` module. We should install the module, adding it to our `requirements.txt` file as follows:

```
$ echo "openpyxl==3.1.5" >> requirements.txt
$ uv pip install -r requirements.txt
```

For this recipe, we'll create a new file with historic information about the movies with the most attendance. The source data is extracted from here: `http://www.mrob.com/pub/film-video/topadj.html`.

## How to do it...

1. Import the `openpyxl` module:

```
>>> import openpyxl
```

2. Create a new Excel file. This creates a default sheet, called Sheet:

```
>>> xlsfile = openpyxl.Workbook()
>>> xlsfile.sheetnames
```

```
['Sheet']
>>> sheet = xlsfile['Sheet']
```

3. Add data about the number of attendees to this sheet from the source. For simplicity only the first three entries are added:

```
>>> data = [
...     (225.7, 'Gone With the Wind', 'Victor Fleming'),
...     (194.4, 'Star Wars', 'George Lucas'),
...     (156.4, 'The Sound of Music', 'Robert Wise')
...     ]
>>> for row, (admissions, name, director) in enumerate(data, 1):
...     sheet[f'A{row}'].value = admissions
...     sheet[f'B{row}'].value = name
```

4. Create a new sheet:

```
>>> sheet = xlsfile.create_sheet("Directors")
>>> sheet
<Worksheet "Directors">
>>> xlsfile.sheetnames
['Sheet', 'Directors']
```

5. Add the name of the director for each movie:

```
>>> for row, (admissions, name, director) in enumerate(data, 1):
...     sheet[f'A{row}'].value = director
...     sheet[f'B{row}'].value = name
```

6. Save the file as `movie_sheets.xlsx`:

```
>>> xlsfile.save('movie_sheets.xlsx')
```

7. Open the `movie_sheets.xlsx` file to check that it has two sheets which contain the expected information, as shown in the following screenshot:

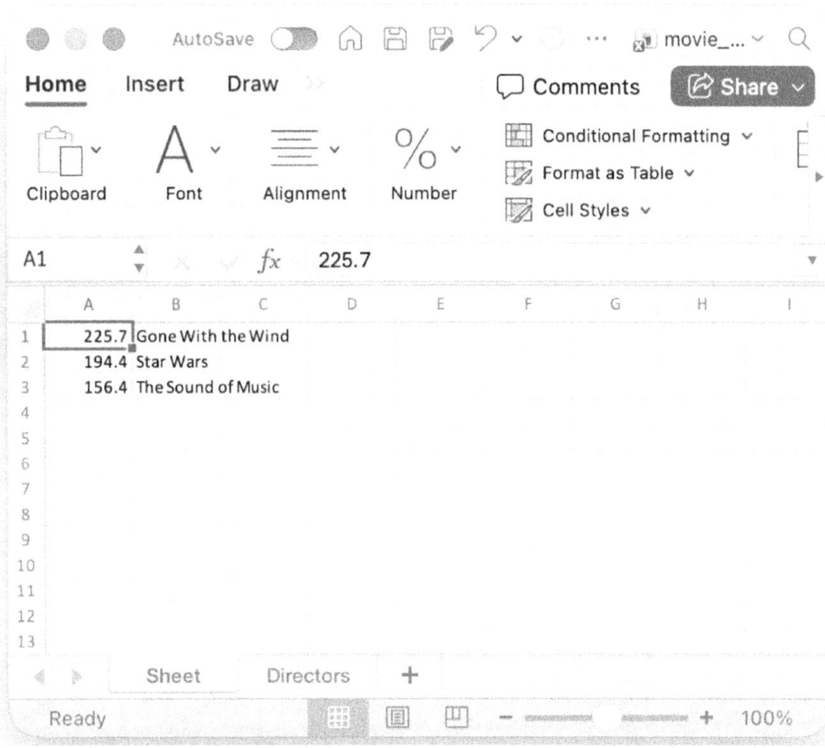


*Figure 6.3: Content of movie_sheets.xlsx*

# How it works...

In the *How to do it...* section, after importing the module in *step 1*, we create a new spreadsheet in *step 2*. This is a new spreadsheet that contains just the default sheet.

The data to be stored is defined in *step 3*. Note that it contains information that will go on both sheets (name in both; the admissions in the first sheet and the director's name in the second). In this step, the first sheet is filled.

> **Note**
>
> Note how the value is stored. The proper cell is defined as column A or B and the proper row (rows start at 1). The `enumerate` function returns a tuple with the first element as the index and the second as the enumerated parameter (in this case, a tuple with three values).

After that, the new sheet is created in *step 4*, using the name `Directors`. `.create_sheet` returns the new sheet.

The information in the `Directors` sheet is stored in *step 5* and the file is saved in *step 6*.

## There's more...

The name of an existing sheet can be changed through the `.title` property:

```
>>> sheet = xlsfile['Sheet']
>>> sheet.title = 'Admissions'
>>> xlsfile.sheetnames
['Admissions', 'Directors']
```

Be careful, as it won't be possible to access the sheet with `xlsfile['Sheet']`. That name doesn't exist anymore!

The active sheet, the sheet that will be displayed when the file is opened, can be obtained through the `.active` property and changed assigning the index. The index starts at 0 for the first sheet:

```
>>> xlsfile.active
<Worksheet "Admissions">
>>> xlsfile.active = 1
>>> xlsfile.active
<Worksheet "Directors">
>>> xlsfile.active = 0
>>> xlsfile.active
<Worksheet "Admissions">
```

The sheet can also be copied using `.copy_worksheet`. Be aware that some data, for example, charts, won't be carried over. All the cell data will be duplicated:

```
>>> new_copied_sheet = xlsfile.copy_worksheet(source_sheet)
```

Copying sheets is typically done when wanting to process the same source data in multiple ways, so this limitation makes sense. But if you need to copy a chart directly, keep in mind that you can replicate it by code, multiple times if necessary.

The full openpyxl documentation can be found here: https://openpyxl.readthedocs.io/en/stable/index.html.

## See also

- The *Reading an Excel spreadsheet* recipe earlier in the chapter.
- The *Updating an Excel spreadsheet* recipe earlier in the chapter.
- The *Creating charts in Excel* recipe in the following section.
- The *Working with cell formats in Excel* recipe later in the chapter.

# Creating charts in Excel

Spreadsheets include many tools for dealing with data, including presenting the data in colorful charts. Let's see how to append a chart programmatically to an Excel spreadsheet.

## Getting ready

We will use the openpyxl module. We should also install the module, adding it to our requirements.txt file as follows:

```
$ echo "openpyxl==3.1.5" >> requirements.txt
$ uv pip install -r requirements.txt
```

As part of the recipe, we will create a new file with historic information about the movies with most attendance. The data is extracted from here: http://www.mrob.com/pub/film-video/topadj.html.

## How to do it...

1. Import the openpyxl module and create a new Excel file:

   ```
   >>> import openpyxl
   >>> from openpyxl.chart import BarChart, Reference
   >>> xlsfile = openpyxl.Workbook()
   ```

2. Add data about the number of attendees in this sheet from the source. Only the first three entries are added for simplicity:

```
>>> data = [
... ('Name', 'Admissions'),
... ('Gone With the Wind', 225.7),
... ('Star Wars', 194.4),
... ('The Sound of Music', 156.4)
... ]
>>> sheet = xlsfile['Sheet']
>>> for row in data:
...     sheet.append(row)
```

3. Create a `BarChart` object and fill it with basic information:

```
>>> chart = BarChart()
>>> chart.title = "Admissions per movie"
>>> chart.y_axis.title = 'Millions'
```

4. Create a reference to the data and append the data to the chart:

```
>>> data = Reference(sheet, min_row=2, max_row=4, min_col=1, max_col=2)
>>> chart.add_data(data, from_rows=True, titles_from_data=True)
```

5. Set the legend to not overlay. That means that the legend will appear outside of the chart.

```
>>> chart.legend.overlay = False
```

6. Add the chart to the sheet and save the file:

```
>>> sheet.add_chart(chart, "A6")
>>> xlsfile.save('movie_chart.xlsx')
```

7. Check the resulting chart in the spreadsheet, as shown in the following screenshot:

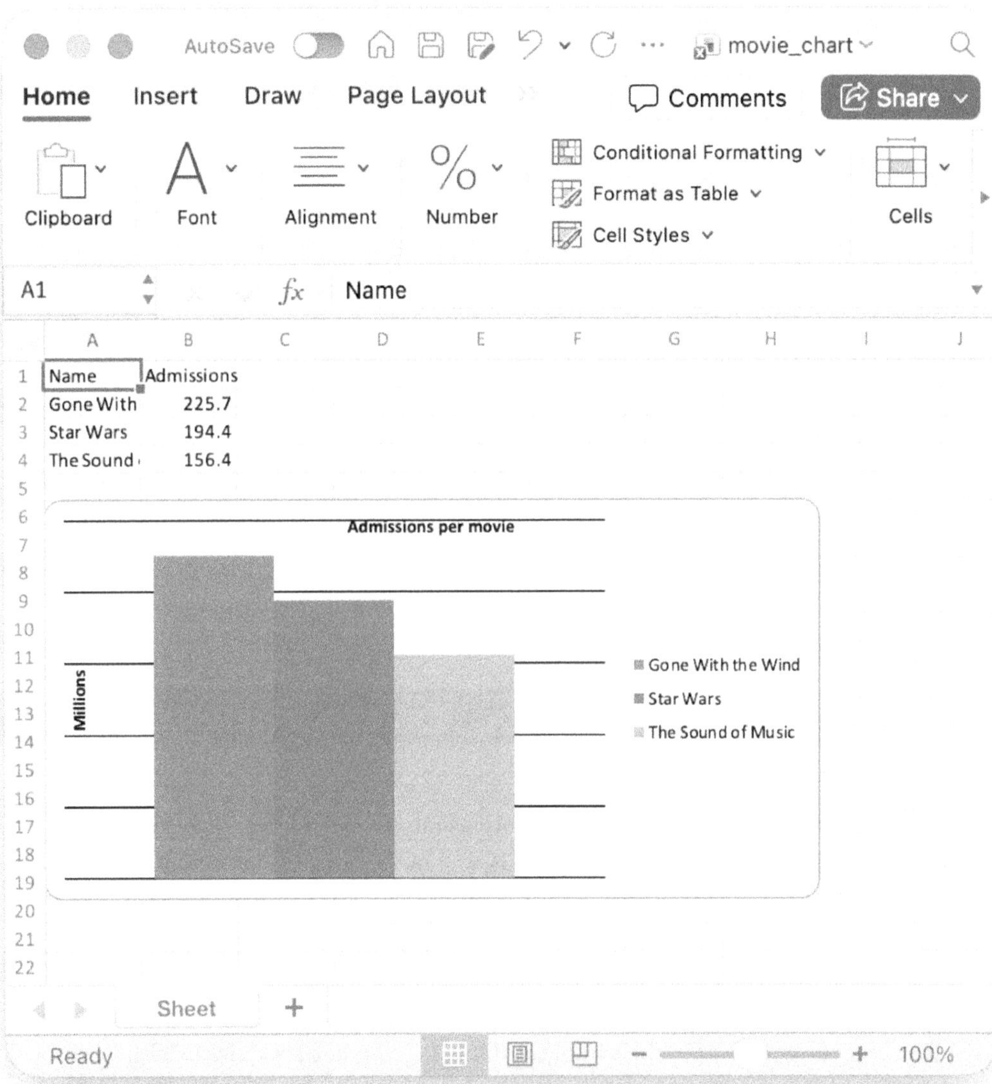


*Figure 6.4: Displayed chart*

## How it works...

In the *How to do it...* section, after preparing the data in *steps 1* and *2*, the data is ready in the range `A1:B4`. Note that `A1` and `B1` both contain a header that should not be used in the chart.

In *step 3*, we set up the new chart and include the basic data, such as a title and the units of the *y-axis*.

*Step 4* creates a reference box through a `Reference` object, from row 2 column 1 to row 4 column 2, which is the area where our data lives, excluding the header. This corresponds to `A2:B4` The data is added to the chart with the `.add_data()` method. The `from_rows` argument makes each row a different data series. Another argument, `titles_from_data`, uses the first column to name the series.

We stop the legend overlaying in *step 5*. You can experiment with this value, but putting the legend outside of the chart area makes it clearer in this case.

The chart is added to cell `A6` in *step 6* and saved to disk.

## There's more...

Numerous charts can be created, including bar charts, line charts, area charts (line charts that fill the area between the line and the axis), pie charts, or scatter charts (XY charts where one value is plotted against the other). Each kind of chart has an equivalent class, for example, `PieChart` or `LineChart`.

Each one, at the same time, can have different types. For example, the default type for `BarChart` is column, printing the bars vertically, but they can also be printed horizontally by selecting a different type:

```
>>> chart.type = 'bar'
```

> **Tip**
>
> This is an area where GenAI can be immensely useful. You can ask the GenAI tool about the best way of representing some data and how to translate it into an Excel chart, or even ask it to generate Python code for `openpyxl`. You can also check the `openpyxl` documentation to see all available possibilities for defining charts.

Instead of extracting the *x-axis* labels from the data, they can be set explicitly with `set_categories`. For example, compare *step 4* with the following code:

```
data = Reference(sheet, min_row=2, max_row=4, min_col=2, max_col=2)
labels = Reference(sheet, min_row=2, max_row=4, min_col=1, max_col=1)
chart.add_data(data, from_rows=False, titles_from_data=False)
chart.set_categories(labels)
```

The range, instead of using a `Reference` object, can also be input with text labels describing the region:

```
chart.add_data('Sheet!B2:B4', from_rows=False, titles_from_data=False)
chart.set_categories('Sheet!A2:A4')
```

This way of describing it may be more difficult to deal with if the range of data needs to be created programmatically.

> **Tip**
>
> Defining charts in Excel correctly can be difficult sometimes. The way Excel extracts the data from a particular range can be baffling. Remember to allow time for trial and error, and to deal with different ways of plotting the data. For example, in *step 4*, we defined three series with one data point, while in the preceding code, we defined a single series with three data points. Most of those differences are subtle. Finally, the most important point is how the resulting chart looks. Try different chart types and learn the differences. Once again, GenAI can be very helpful in providing insight and ideas on how to display information. Ultimately, however, trust your instincts about how the chart displays the data so that it can be readily understood. That's the objective of a good chart.

The full `openpyxl` documentation can be found here: `https://openpyxl.readthedocs.io/en/stable/index.html`.

## See also

- The *Reading an Excel spreadsheet* recipe earlier in the chapter.
- The *Updating an Excel spreadsheet* recipe earlier in the chapter.
- The *Creating new sheets in an Excel spreadsheet* recipe in the previous section.
- The *Working with cell formats in Excel* recipe in the following section.

# Working with cell formats in Excel

Presenting information in spreadsheets is not just a matter of organizing it into cells or displaying it graphically in charts. It also involves changing the format to highlight the important details. In this recipe, we'll see how to manipulate the format of cells to enhance the results and present data in the best possible way.

## Getting ready

We will use the `openpyxl` module. We should install the module, adding it to our `requirements.txt` file as follows:

```
$ echo "openpyxl==3.1.5" >> requirements.txt
$ uv pip install -r requirements.txt
```

As part of the recipe, we will create a new file with historic information about the movies with the most attendance. The data is extracted from here: `http://www.mrob.com/pub/film-video/topadj.html`.

## How to do it...

1. Import the `openpyxl` module and create a new Excel file:

```
>>> import openpyxl
>>> from openpyxl.styles import Font, PatternFill, Border, Side
>>> xlsfile = openpyxl.Workbook()
```

2. Add data about the number of attendees in this sheet from the source. Only the first four entries are added, for simplicity:

```
>>> data = [
...     ('Name', 'Admissions'),
...     ('Gone With the Wind', 225.7),
...     ('Star Wars', 194.4),
...     ('The Sound of Music', 156.4),
...     ('ET: The Extra-Terrestrial', 148.44),
... ]
>>> sheet = xlsfile['Sheet']
>>> for row in data:
...     sheet.append(row)
```

3. Define the colors to use for styling the spreadsheet:

```
>>> BLUE = '2F5D8A'
>>> LIGHT_BLUE = 'E8F1FA'
>>> WHITE = 'FFFFFF'
```

4. Define the header in a blue background and a white font:

```
>>> header_font = Font(name='Tahoma', size=14, color=WHITE)
>>> header_fill = PatternFill("solid", fgColor=BLUE)
>>> for row in sheet['A1:B1']:
...     for cell in row:
...         cell.font = header_font
...         cell.fill = header_fill
```

5. Define an alternate pattern for the columns and a border on each row after the header:

```
>>> white_side = Side(border_style='thin', color=WHITE)
>>> blue_side = Side(border_style='thin', color=BLUE)
>>> alternate_fill = PatternFill("solid", fgColor=LIGHT_BLUE)
>>> border = Border(bottom=blue_side, left=white_side, right=white_side)
>>> for row_index, row in enumerate(sheet['A2:B5']):
...     for cell in row:
...         cell.border = border
...         if row_index % 2:
...             cell.fill = alternate_fill
```

6. Adjust the column width

```
>>> sheet.column_dimensions['A'].width = 20
>>> sheet.column_dimensions['B'].width = 12
```

7. Save the file as `movies_format.xlsx`:

```
>>> xlsfile.save('movies_format.xlsx')
```

8. Check the resulting file:

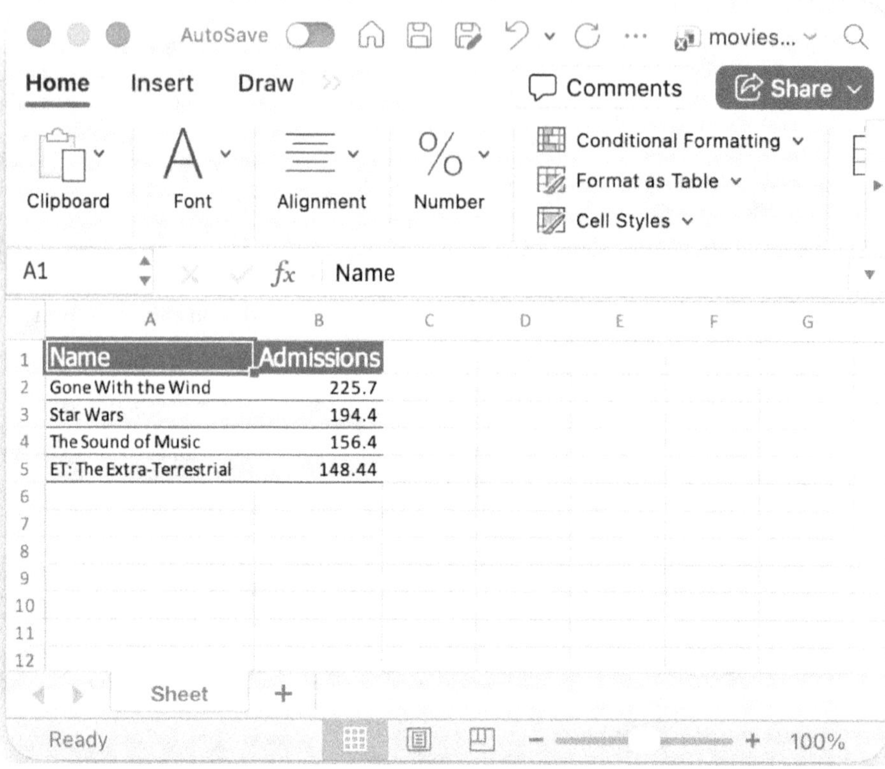


Figure 6.5: Formatted movie data spreadsheet

## How it works...

In the *How to do it...* section, in *step 1*, we import the `openpyxl` module and create a new Excel file. In *step 2* we add the data to the first sheet. *Step 3* is also a preparation step to define the colors to be used. The colors are defined in hex format, which is common in the web design world.

> **Tip**
>
> To find the color definitions, there are plenty of color pickers online or even embedded in the OS. A tool like `https://coolors.co/` can be useful to define a palette to work with. Alternatively, you can ask GenAI about colors to use. For example, try the prompt '*Get me two blue colors, one of them light, that look good for the background in a spreadsheet. They should look professional. Return them in hex format*'.

In *step 4* we prepare the format to define the header. The header will have a different font (Tahoma), a bigger size (14pt), and it will be white on a blue background. To achieve this, we prepare a `Font` object with the font, size, and foreground color, and a `PatternFill` with the background color.

The loop after creating `header_font` and `header_fill` applies the font and fill to the proper cells.

> **Note**
>
> Note that iterating over a range always returns the row, and then cells, even if only one row is involved.

In *step 5*, a border to the rows and an alternate background is applied. The border is defined with blue bottom and white left and right. The fill is created in a similar way to *step 4*, but in a light blue. The background is only applied to even rows.

> **Note**
>
> Note that the top border of a cell is the bottom of the one above, and vice versa. This means that it's possible to overwrite the border in a loop. Also that our effect to set the bottom in blue also applies to the top of the next row.

In step 6 we adjust the width of the columns to show all values. This allows us to display all the contents of the columns.

> **Tip**
>
> There's no way in `openpyxl` to automatically choose the column size so that it fits its content. But you can iterate through all the cells in the column to find the maximum length of content (i.e. find the width in characters of the cell using `len(str(cell.value))`) and define the width based on that.

The file is finally saved in *step 7*.

## There's more...

There are many options available to style the text, such as bold, italic, strikeout, or underline. Define the font and reassign it if you need to change any of its elements. And remember to check that the font is available in the system.

There are also various ways of creating a fill. `PatternFill` accepts several patterns, but the most useful one is solid. `GradientFill` can be used to apply a two-color gradient.

> **Tip**
>
> It's best to limit yourself to solid fills using `PatternFill`. You can tweak the color to best represent what you want. Remember to include `style='solid'`, or the color may not appear.
>
> GenAI is your friend when deciding on colors! You can ask for palettes for multiple elements.

It's also possible to define conditional formatting, but for an automatically generated spreadsheet it's less complicated to try to define the logic in Python and then apply the proper static formatting based on the result.

Number formatting can be set up properly, for example:

```
cell.style = 'Percent'
```

This will display the value `0.37` as `37%`.

> **Tip**
>
> Ultimately, formatting a spreadsheet is about deciding how to present the data in a way that's best for the reader to understand it. Don't be afraid to experiment and analyze the results.
>
> GenAI is a great tool for that, helping you with recommendations and ideas on how to format the data for the best effect. But ultimately, it comes down to your decision on what looks clearer.

The full `openpyxl` documentation can be found here: `https://openpyxl.readthedocs.io/en/stable/index.html`.

## See also

- The *Reading an Excel spreadsheet* recipe earlier in the chapter.
- The *Updating an Excel spreadsheet* recipe earlier in the chapter.
- The *Creating new sheets in an Excel spreadsheet* recipe earlier in the chapter.
- The *Creating charts in Excel* recipe in the previous section.

# Using Python in Excel

Though Excel has its own language to perform calculations, recent versions have included the possibility of using Python as an alternative.

This makes it possible to take advantage of our Python skills and apply them directly in Excel spreadsheets.

> Note
>
> Unfortunately, running Python in Excel executes the results in the Microsoft Cloud, which requires a working Internet connection.

## Getting ready

You need to have a working copy of Excel that has Python in Excel. Running Python in Excel is not available in all subscriptions – generally you need to have a Microsoft 365 Business or Enterprise account. More information is available here: `https://techcommunity.microsoft.com/blog/excelblog/python-in-excel-%e2%80%93-available-now/4240212`.

In this recipe, we will use the `movies.xlsx` file available on GitHub at `https://github.com/PacktPublishing/Python-Automation-Cookbook-Third-Edition/blob/main/ch06/movies.xlsx`. It contains the top ten movies from the list in `http://www.mrob.com/pub/film-video/topadj.html`.

# How to do it...

1. Open the file `movies.xlsx` in Excel

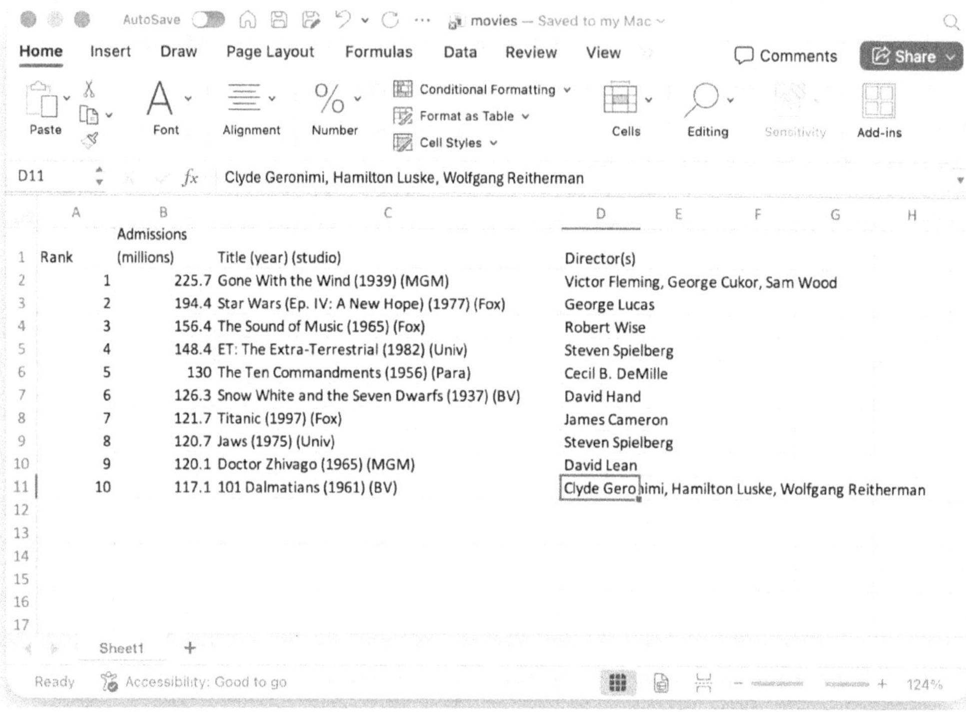


*Figure 6.6: Spreadsheet with movies*

2. Select cell B12, and write `=PY(` , which will select this cell as a Python function

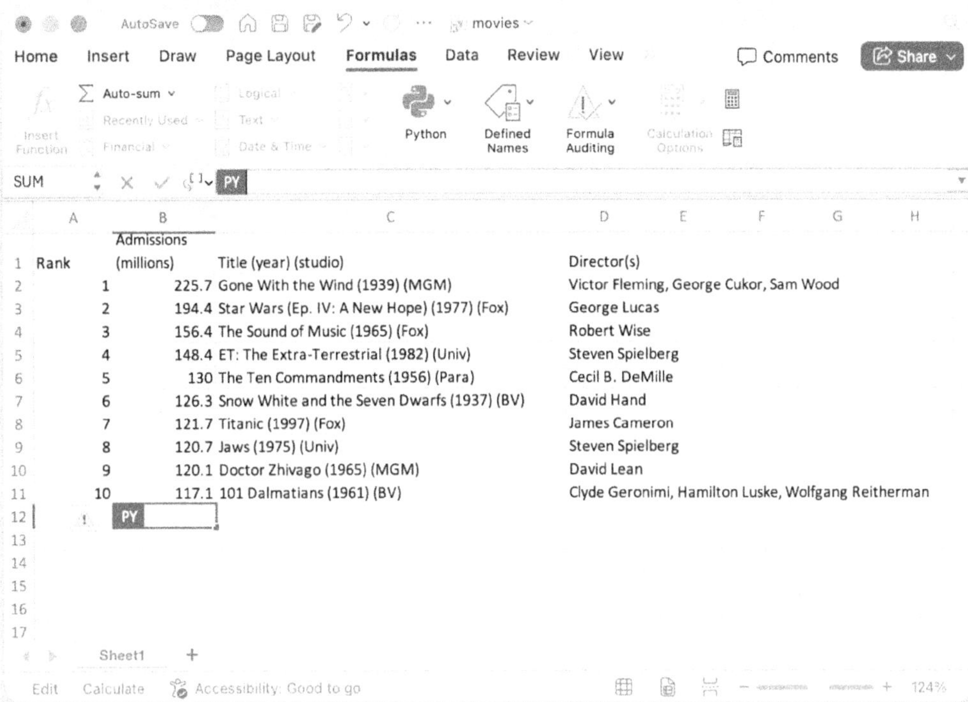


*Figure 6.7: Adding a Python function*

**Note**

Note that the formulas section has a Python element. It will only be present if your Excel subscription allows you to use Python in Excel.

3. Introduce the following code into the cell:

```
result = 0
for row in data['Admissions\n(millions)']:
    result += row

result
```

> **Tip**
>
> This is easier if you open the editor by clicking in the button just next to the Python logo in the ribbon.

4. Run the code by pressing `CTRL + ENTER`. The result will appear in the cell.

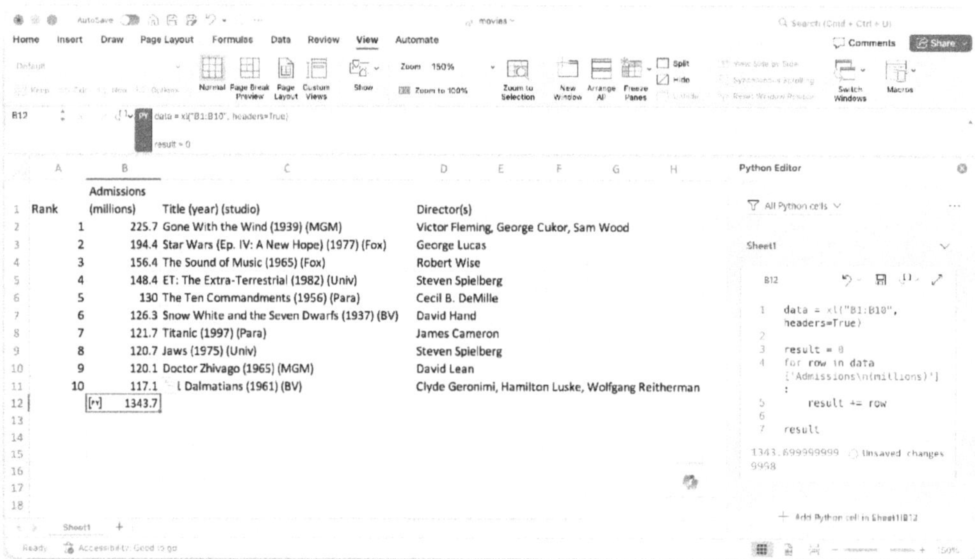


*Figure 6.8: Result being displayed, computed in Python*

## How it works...

In the *How to do it...* section, in *step 2*, we mark the cell to be a Python function.

The code to calculate the sum of all values in *step 3* includes the first part that retrieves the data from the spreadsheet with the xl function:

```
data = xl("B1:B10", headers=True)
```

We use `headers=True` to mark that the first selected row (`B1`) is the header of the data, which makes for more convenient way to access the data, as we see in the next loop:

```
result = 0
for row in data['Admissions\n(millions)']:
    result += row
```

Here we go through the rows in the column defined for its header name, `Admissions\n(millions)`. Note the `\n`, as the column has a newline.

On the final line, we select the variable `result`, which will be used as the value to display on the cell.

The code is executed in *step 4*. Note the py label in the `B12` cell.

## There's more...

The data that gets returned by `xl` is a Pandas `DataFrame` object. This allows us to perform many operations in a native way. For example, instead of iterating through the cells you can add them directly with

```
data = xl("B1:B10", headers=True)
data['Admissions\n(millions)'].sum()
```

> **Note**
>
> Pandas is extensively used in data analysis and is an incredibly powerful tool for that. Its programming interface facilitate thinking in array processing and other forms of parallel computing. It's worth becoming proficient with it all by itself.
>
> We will talk more about Pandas and `DataFrame` objects in *Chapter 7*

You can also create charts in Python, using MatplotLib which is included automatically.

For example, this code

```
data = xl("B1:C10", headers=True)

data.plot(x="Title (year) (studio)", kind="bar")
```

selects the two first columns, so we select to plot the admissions with the movie title in the X axis as a bar chart. After running the code, Excel will ask you to right-click over the cell and select 'Display plot over cells' to fully display the image.

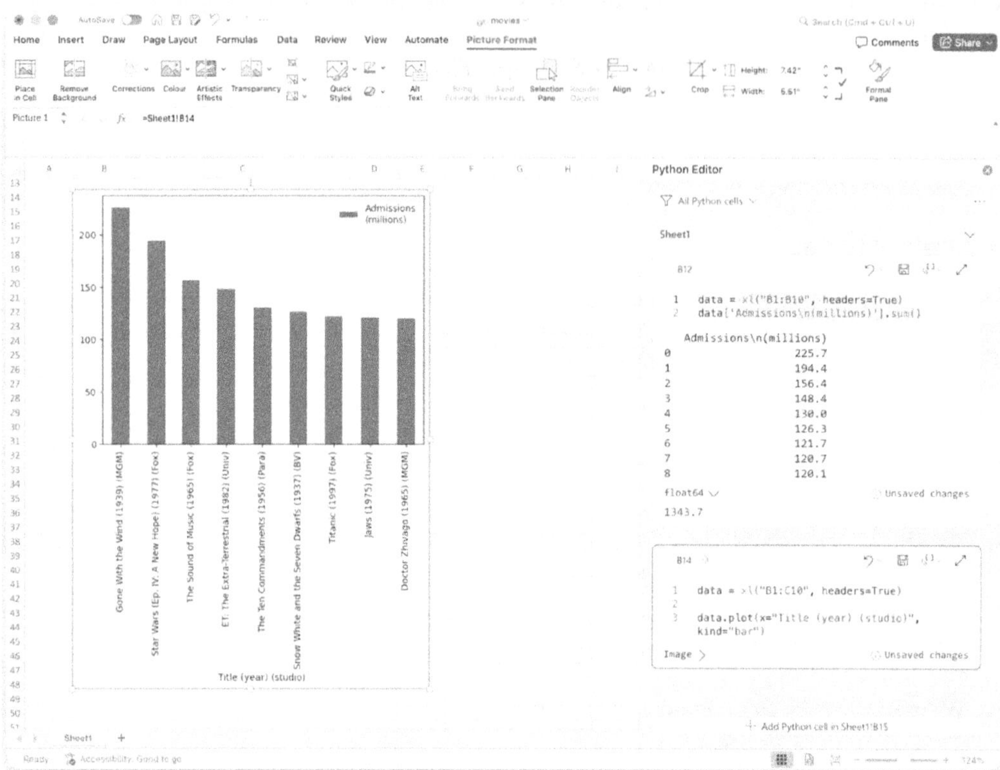


*Figure 6.9: Displaying a chart created in Python*

> **Note**
>
> We will talk more about how to make plots using MatplotLib in *Chapter 8*

In addition to `Matplotlib` and `Pandas`, Excel can also explicitly import standard libraries in the usual way with `import` statements. There's a list of third party packages that are available, including modules we talk about in this book like `Pillow` and `beautifulsoup4`, at `https://support.microsoft.com/en-gb/office/open-source-libraries-and-python-in-excel-c817c897-41db-40a1-b9f3-d5ffe6d1bf3e`.

For example, if you want to make a hash from a value in cell `D3`, using `hashlib` (included in the standard library), you can do it with

```
import hashlib

m = hashlib.sha256()
m.update(xl("D3").encode())

m.hexdigest()
```

Remember that the value returned by the last line will be the one displayed in the cell. (In this case, the hexdigest.)

Check the full documentation on Python in Excel on the Microsoft website: `https://support.microsoft.com/en-us/office/introduction-to-python-in-excel-55643c2e-ff56-4168-b1ce-9428c8308545`.

## See also

- The *Processing data with Pandas* recipe in *Chapter 7*.
- The *Plotting a simple sales graph* recipe in *Chapter 8*.

# 7

# Cleaning and Processing Data

Some automated tasks will require dealing with large amounts of data. As data grows, two new and distinct problems appear: processing takes too long and input data quality issues cause more problems.

Both problems are well known in the realm of data science when dealing with large quantities of data, but the problems can appear even at a smaller scale.

The quality of input data is highly related to the number of sources of the data. In general, data from a single source will be more consistent, but using a single source is limiting. And even if the data comes from the same source, it can still contain inconsistencies or errors.

> **Note**
>
> Examples of differences include regional differences, such as different date formats or currencies, extra information, different names for the same concept (including spelling differences), typos, generally poor data quality including errors... The list is long!

To compare apples with apples, the input data will probably need to be cleaned. This can be a difficult task that requires multiple iterations until the cleaning process is refined, particularly if the data changes over time. We will look at a variety of relevant techniques.

For some automated cases, time is not a problem. For an automated background emailer that composes and sends a daily update email during the night, to be read at the start of the day, it doesn't matter if it takes two hours or two minutes. But if someone is actively waiting for results, a process taking too long can be highly inefficient.

While code development and testing are ongoing, waiting for the completion of data processing is critical as it will not only use up time that could be spent on developing features but also destroys focus and concentration, which are key to the development process.

There are several tips and techniques for speeding up code execution. The main two are: avoid performing the same operation multiple times; and parallelize the task by dividing it into smaller chunks that can be run at the same time.

> **Tip**
>
> The best general advice on how to reduce the time taken by your computer tasks is to learn computer science, in particular, algorithms and data structures. This is out of scope for this book, and it can be a long journey. GenAI is there to help, but don't be afraid to ask a fellow programmer for help! Even online!

*Chapter 3, Building Your First Web Scraping Application*, introduced parallelization of code as part of the *Speeding up web scraping* recipe. We will continue with the concept during this chapter.

In this chapter, we will cover the following recipes:

- Preparing a CSV spreadsheet
- Appending currency based on location
- Standardizing the date format
- Transforming and validating data in JSON
- Aggregating results
- Processing data in parallel
- Processing data with Pandas

Let's start by getting the base information ready in a tabular file.

# Technical requirements

You can check the code presented in this chapter in the GitHub repo at `https://github.com/PacktPublishing/Python-Automation-Cookbook-Third-Edition/tree/main/ch07`.

# Preparing a CSV spreadsheet

As we saw in the previous chapter, CSV files are files containing tabular data defined as a collection of rows with defined columns, separated by commas. They are a very common format for all kinds of data. We will see in this recipe how to extract data from log files and store the information in a CSV file.

## Getting ready

We will use a similar log format as the one introduced in the *Extracting data from structured strings* recipe in *Chapter 1, Let's Begin Our Automation Journey*:

```
[<Timestamp>] - SALE - PRODUCT: <product id> - PRICE: <price>
```

Each line will represent a sale log.

We will use an adapted parser for logs based on the `price_log.py` file created in the *Extracting data from structured strings* recipe. As requisites we have the `parse` module. We should install the module, adding it to our `requirements.txt` file as follows:

```
$ echo "parse==1.20.2" >> requirements.txt
$ uv pip install -r requirements.txt
```

In the GitHub repository there are some log files to process which have the following structure:

```
sale_logs/
  OH
    logs.txt
  ON
    logs.txt
```

The code can be found in the GitHub repository at `https://github.com/PacktPublishing/Python-Automation-Cookbook-Third-Edition/tree/main/ch07`.

## How to do it...

1. Check the contents of the `sale_logs/OH/logs.txt` file:

```
$ head sale_logs/OH/logs.txt
[08-27-2025 18:39:41] - SALE - PRODUCT: 12346 - PRICE: 02.99
[08-27-2025 19:39:41] - SALE - PRODUCT: 12346 - PRICE: 02.99
[08-27-2025 20:39:41] - SALE - PRODUCT: 12346 - PRICE: 02.99
[08-27-2025 21:39:41] - SALE - PRODUCT: 12346 - PRICE: 02.99
[08-27-2025 22:39:41] - SALE - PRODUCT: 12345 - PRICE: 09.99
[08-27-2025 23:39:41] - SALE - PRODUCT: 12345 - PRICE: 07.99
[08-28-2025 00:39:41] - SALE - PRODUCT: 12346 - PRICE: 02.99
[08-28-2025 01:39:41] - SALE - PRODUCT: 12346 - PRICE: 02.99
```

```
[08-28-2025 02:39:41] - SALE - PRODUCT: 12346 - PRICE: 02.99
[08-28-2025 03:39:41] - SALE - PRODUCT: 12346 - PRICE: 02.99
```

2. Import the data and transform it into a CSV file using the `logs_to_csv.py` script. The script takes the location as input:

```
$ uv run logs_to_csv.py sale_logs/OH/logs.txt output_1_OH.csv -l OH
```

3. Check the resulting CSV file in a spreadsheet. In the following screenshot, the file is displayed using the LibreOffice software:

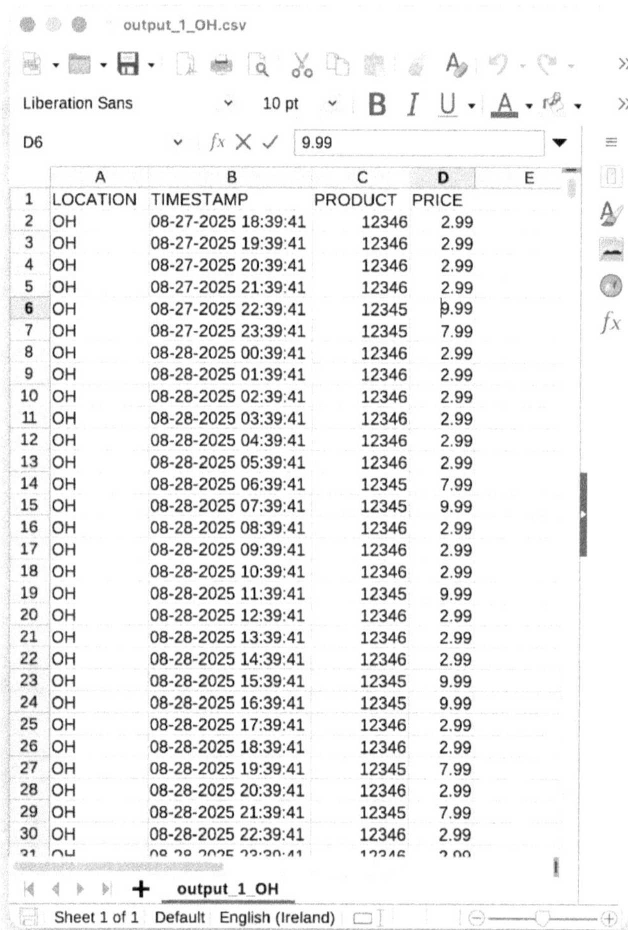


| | A | B | C | D | E |
|---|---|---|---|---|---|
| 1 | LOCATION | TIMESTAMP | PRODUCT | PRICE | |
| 2 | OH | 08-27-2025 18:39:41 | 12346 | 2.99 | |
| 3 | OH | 08-27-2025 19:39:41 | 12346 | 2.99 | |
| 4 | OH | 08-27-2025 20:39:41 | 12346 | 2.99 | |
| 5 | OH | 08-27-2025 21:39:41 | 12346 | 2.99 | |
| 6 | OH | 08-27-2025 22:39:41 | 12345 | 9.99 | |
| 7 | OH | 08-27-2025 23:39:41 | 12345 | 7.99 | |
| 8 | OH | 08-28-2025 00:39:41 | 12346 | 2.99 | |
| 9 | OH | 08-28-2025 01:39:41 | 12346 | 2.99 | |
| 10 | OH | 08-28-2025 02:39:41 | 12346 | 2.99 | |
| 11 | OH | 08-28-2025 03:39:41 | 12346 | 2.99 | |
| 12 | OH | 08-28-2025 04:39:41 | 12346 | 2.99 | |
| 13 | OH | 08-28-2025 05:39:41 | 12346 | 2.99 | |
| 14 | OH | 08-28-2025 06:39:41 | 12345 | 7.99 | |
| 15 | OH | 08-28-2025 07:39:41 | 12345 | 9.99 | |
| 16 | OH | 08-28-2025 08:39:41 | 12346 | 2.99 | |
| 17 | OH | 08-28-2025 09:39:41 | 12346 | 2.99 | |
| 18 | OH | 08-28-2025 10:39:41 | 12346 | 2.99 | |
| 19 | OH | 08-28-2025 11:39:41 | 12345 | 9.99 | |
| 20 | OH | 08-28-2025 12:39:41 | 12346 | 2.99 | |
| 21 | OH | 08-28-2025 13:39:41 | 12346 | 2.99 | |
| 22 | OH | 08-28-2025 14:39:41 | 12346 | 2.99 | |
| 23 | OH | 08-28-2025 15:39:41 | 12345 | 9.99 | |
| 24 | OH | 08-28-2025 16:39:41 | 12345 | 9.99 | |
| 25 | OH | 08-28-2025 17:39:41 | 12346 | 2.99 | |
| 26 | OH | 08-28-2025 18:39:41 | 12346 | 2.99 | |
| 27 | OH | 08-28-2025 19:39:41 | 12345 | 7.99 | |
| 28 | OH | 08-28-2025 20:39:41 | 12346 | 2.99 | |
| 29 | OH | 08-28-2025 21:39:41 | 12345 | 7.99 | |
| 30 | OH | 08-28-2025 22:39:41 | 12346 | 2.99 | |

*Figure 7.1: Screenshot of product data*

Notice how the CSV includes the location, which is stated as `OH`. Notice also the format of the timestamp, which replicates the one in the source data. A later recipe in this chapter will process and standardize the timestamp.

## How it works...

Let's take a look at the `logs_to_csv.py` script used in *step 2*.

It imports from the `price_log.py` file, which contains the parsing of the logs. This is code based on the *Extracting data from structured strings* recipe in *Chapter 1*. The code adds a header with all the rows and adds a location column. Let's take a look:

```
class PriceLog:
    def __init__(self, location, timestamp, product_id, price):
        self.timestamp = timestamp
        self.product_id = product_id
        self.price = price
        self.location = location
    @classmethod
    def parse(cls, location, text_log):
        '''
        Parse from a text log with the format
        [<Timestamp>] - SALE - PRODUCT: <product id> - PRICE: <price>
        to a PriceLog object
        It requires a location
        '''
        def price(string):
            return Decimal(string)
        FORMAT = ('[{timestamp}] - SALE - PRODUCT: {product:d} - '
                  'PRICE: {price:price}')
        formats = {'price': price}
        result = parse.parse(FORMAT, text_log, formats)
        return cls(location=location, timestamp=result['timestamp'],
                   product_id=result['product'], price=result['price'])
    @classmethod
    def header(cls):
        return ['LOCATION', 'TIMESTAMP', 'PRODUCT', 'PRICE']
    def row(self):
        return [self.location, self.timestamp, self.product_id, self.price]
```

The file is converted into CSV format by the `log_to_csv` function in the `logs_to_csv.py` file:

```
def log_to_csv(input_file, output_file, location):
    logs = [PriceLog.parse(location, line) for line in input_file]
    # Save into csv format
    writer = csv.writer(output_file)
    writer.writerow(PriceLog.header())
    writer.writerows(l.row() for l in logs)
```

The rest of `logs_to_csv.py` deals with the parsing of arguments, which was described in detail in *Chapter 2, Automating Tasks Made Easy*.

The resulting file contains the same information, but CSV is an easier format to understand, process, and add extra information to, as we will see in the following recipes.

## There's more...

The main objective in this recipe is to import data from a text file into a CSV without imposing any formatting restrictions on the raw data. For example, the date is in a particular format. The timestamp format will change from file to file, as we will see in the following recipes.

The description of the location is also left deliberately open, as we will use it to set different kinds of locations in the following recipes.

If the log files are very big, reading the whole file and then saving it could be memory inefficient. In that case, you can process one line at a time, in the following way:

```
def log_to_csv(input_file, output_file, location):
    writer = csv.writer(output_file)
    writer.writerow(PriceLog.header())
    # Read and save line by line
    for line in input_file:
         log = PriceLog.parse(location, line)
         writer.writerow(log.row())
```

This approach can also be done in batches, reading and writing several lines at a time. This can increase the throughput, though a bit of experimentation could be required to find the optimal solution.

## See also

- The *Reading CSV files* recipe in *Chapter 4, Searching and Reading Local Files*.

- The *Extracting data from structured strings* recipe from *Chapter 1, Let's Begin Our Automation Journey*.
- The *Preparing a task* recipe in *Chapter 2, Automating Tasks Made Easy*.

# Appending currency based on location

The resulting CSV file from the previous recipe doesn't contain currency information, even though the location can indicate different places with different currencies. In this recipe, we will process a CSV file to add extra information: the currency the prices are in, and a conversion into US dollars.

## Getting ready

We will use the CSV file resulting from the previous recipe that receives and transforms logs to the following format:

```
[<Timestamp>] - SALE - PRODUCT: <product id> - PRICE: <price>
```

Each line will represent a sale log.

We will use the `parse` module, so we should install it by adding it to our `requirements.txt` file as follows:

```
$ echo "parse==1.20.2" >> requirements.txt
$ uv pip install -r requirements.txt
```

The GitHub repository contains some log files to process which have the following structure:

```
sale_logs/
  OH
    logs.txt
  ON
    logs.txt
```

The logs represent regional sales, one in the US state of Ohio (OH) and one in the Canadian province of Ontario (ON)

The code can be found in the GitHub repository, at `https://github.com/PacktPublishing/Python-Automation-Cookbook-Third-Edition/tree/main/ch07`.

## How to do it...

1. Import the data and transform it into a CSV file using the `logs_to_csv.py` script. The script adds the location as input. Create the files for both the `OH` and `ON` logs:

```
$ uv run logs_to_csv.py sale_logs/OH/logs.txt output_1_OH.csv -l OH
$ uv run logs_to_csv.py sale_logs/ON/logs.txt output_1_ON.csv -l ON
```

2. Process both resulting files using the `location_price.py` script:

```
$ uv run location_price.py output_1_OH.csv output_2_OH.csv
$ uv run location_price.py output_1_ON.csv output_2_ON.csv
```

3. Check the resulting CSV files in a spreadsheet application. In the following screenshots, the files are displayed using the LibreOffice software:

| | A | B | C | D | E | F | G |
|---|---|---|---|---|---|---|---|
| 1 | LOCATION | TIMESTAMP | PRODUCT | PRICE | COUNTRY | CURRENCY | USD |
| 2 | ON | 2018-08-27 19:05:55+00:00 | 12346 | 3.99 | CANADA | CAD | 3 |
| 3 | ON | 2018-08-27 20:05:55+00:00 | 12346 | 3.99 | CANADA | CAD | 3 |
| 4 | ON | 2018-08-27 21:05:55+00:00 | 12346 | 3.99 | CANADA | CAD | 3 |
| 5 | ON | 2018-08-27 22:05:55+00:00 | 12345 | 10.5 | CANADA | CAD | 8 |
| 6 | ON | 2018-08-27 23:05:55+00:00 | 12346 | 3.99 | CANADA | CAD | 3 |
| 7 | ON | 2018-08-28 00:05:55+00:00 | 12346 | 3.99 | CANADA | CAD | 3 |
| 8 | ON | 2018-08-28 01:05:55+00:00 | 12346 | 3.99 | CANADA | CAD | 3 |
| 9 | ON | 2018-08-28 02:05:55+00:00 | 12346 | 3.99 | CANADA | CAD | 3 |
| 10 | ON | 2018-08-28 03:05:55+00:00 | 12346 | 3.99 | CANADA | CAD | 3 |
| 11 | ON | 2018-08-28 04:05:55+00:00 | 12346 | 3.99 | CANADA | CAD | 3 |
| 12 | ON | 2018-08-28 05:05:55+00:00 | 12345 | 10.5 | CANADA | CAD | 8 |
| 13 | ON | 2018-08-28 06:05:55+00:00 | 12346 | 3.99 | CANADA | CAD | 3 |
| 14 | ON | 2018-08-28 07:05:55+00:00 | 12346 | 3.99 | CANADA | CAD | 3 |
| 15 | ON | 2018-08-28 08:05:55+00:00 | 12345 | 13.5 | CANADA | CAD | 10 |
| 16 | ON | 2018-08-28 09:05:55+00:00 | 12346 | 3.99 | CANADA | CAD | 3 |
| 17 | ON | 2018-08-28 10:05:55+00:00 | 12345 | 10.5 | CANADA | CAD | 8 |
| 18 | ON | 2018-08-28 11:05:55+00:00 | 12346 | 3.99 | CANADA | CAD | 3 |
| 19 | ON | 2018-08-28 12:05:55+00:00 | 12346 | 3.99 | CANADA | CAD | 3 |
| 20 | ON | 2018-08-28 13:05:55+00:00 | 12346 | 3.99 | CANADA | CAD | 3 |
| 21 | ON | 2018-08-28 14:05:55+00:00 | 12346 | 3.99 | CANADA | CAD | 3 |
| 22 | ON | 2018-08-28 15:05:55+00:00 | 12346 | 3.99 | CANADA | CAD | 3 |
| 23 | ON | 2018-08-28 16:05:55+00:00 | 12346 | 3.99 | CANADA | CAD | 3 |
| 24 | ON | 2018-08-28 17:05:55+00:00 | 12346 | 3.99 | CANADA | CAD | 3 |
| 25 | ON | 2018-08-28 18:05:55+00:00 | 12345 | 13.5 | CANADA | CAD | 10 |
| 26 | ON | 2018-08-28 19:05:55+00:00 | 12346 | 3.99 | CANADA | CAD | 3 |
| 27 | ON | 2018-08-28 20:05:55+00:00 | 12346 | 3.99 | CANADA | CAD | 3 |

*Figure 7.2a: Screenshot of Canadian product data*

| | A | B | C | D | E | F | G |
|---|---|---|---|---|---|---|---|
| 1 | LOCATION | TIMESTAMP | PRODUCT | PRICE | COUNTRY | CURRENCY | USD |
| 2 | OH | 08-27-2025 18:39:41 | 12346 | 2.99 | USA | USD | 2.99 |
| 3 | OH | 08-27-2025 19:39:41 | 12346 | 2.99 | USA | USD | 2.99 |
| 4 | OH | 08-27-2025 20:39:41 | 12346 | 2.99 | USA | USD | 2.99 |
| 5 | OH | 08-27-2025 21:39:41 | 12346 | 2.99 | USA | USD | 2.99 |
| 6 | OH | 08-27-2025 22:39:41 | 12345 | 9.99 | USA | USD | 9.99 |
| 7 | OH | 08-27-2025 23:39:41 | 12345 | 7.99 | USA | USD | 7.99 |
| 8 | OH | 08-28-2025 00:39:41 | 12346 | 2.99 | USA | USD | 2.99 |
| 9 | OH | 08-28-2025 01:39:41 | 12346 | 2.99 | USA | USD | 2.99 |
| 10 | OH | 08-28-2025 02:39:41 | 12346 | 2.99 | USA | USD | 2.99 |
| 11 | OH | 08-28-2025 03:39:41 | 12346 | 2.99 | USA | USD | 2.99 |
| 12 | OH | 08-28-2025 04:39:41 | 12346 | 2.99 | USA | USD | 2.99 |
| 13 | OH | 08-28-2025 05:39:41 | 12346 | 2.99 | USA | USD | 2.99 |
| 14 | OH | 08-28-2025 06:39:41 | 12345 | 7.99 | USA | USD | 7.99 |
| 15 | OH | 08-28-2025 07:39:41 | 12345 | 9.99 | USA | USD | 9.99 |
| 16 | OH | 08-28-2025 08:39:41 | 12346 | 2.99 | USA | USD | 2.99 |
| 17 | OH | 08-28-2025 09:39:41 | 12346 | 2.99 | USA | USD | 2.99 |
| 18 | OH | 08-28-2025 10:39:41 | 12346 | 2.99 | USA | USD | 2.99 |
| 19 | OH | 08-28-2025 11:39:41 | 12345 | 9.99 | USA | USD | 9.99 |
| 20 | OH | 08-28-2025 12:39:41 | 12346 | 2.99 | USA | USD | 2.99 |
| 21 | OH | 08-28-2025 13:39:41 | 12346 | 2.99 | USA | USD | 2.99 |
| 22 | OH | 08-28-2025 14:39:41 | 12346 | 2.99 | USA | USD | 2.99 |
| 23 | OH | 08-28-2025 15:39:41 | 12345 | 9.99 | USA | USD | 9.99 |
| 24 | OH | 08-28-2025 16:39:41 | 12345 | 9.99 | USA | USD | 9.99 |
| 25 | OH | 08-28-2025 17:39:41 | 12346 | 2.99 | USA | USD | 2.99 |
| 26 | OH | 08-28-2025 18:39:41 | 12346 | 2.99 | USA | USD | 2.99 |
| 27 | OH | 08-28-2025 19:39:41 | 12345 | 7.99 | USA | USD | 7.99 |

*Figure 7.2b: Screenshot of US product data*

Notice how the currency changes depending on the location where the product was sold, either Ohio (US) or Ontario (Canada). In both cases, the prices are displayed in their equivalent US Dollar value for comparison.

## How it works...

Let's take a look at the `location_price.py` script, used in *step 2*.

The end of the script file deals with the parsing of arguments, which was described in detail in *Chapter 2, Automating Tasks Made Easy*.

The main function reads the input CSV and calls the `add_price_by_location` function for each of the rows. It then saves the file:

```
def main(input_file, output_file):
    reader = csv.DictReader(input_file)
```

```
        result = [add_price_by_location(row) for row in reader]
        # Save into csv format
        header = result[0].keys()
        writer = csv.DictWriter(output_file, fieldnames=header)
        writer.writeheader()
        writer.writerows(result)
```

It uses the CSV `DictReader` class to transform each of the rows into a dictionary, and the dictionary is then passed for processing. The resulting rows are stored in the output CSV file using a `DictWriter` class. The header for the fields of the output file is obtained from the keys in the dictionary entry for the first output row.

The usage of `DictReader` and `DictWriter` was described in *Chapter 6, Fun with Spreadsheets*.

The most interesting code is in `add_price_by_location`. This code will detect the country (USA or Canada) based on location code. Let's take a look:

```
US_LOCATIONS = ['AL', 'AK', …, 'WY', 'DC']
CAD_LOCATIONS = ['AB', 'BC', … , 'NU', 'YT']
CAD_TO_USD = Decimal('0.76')
def add_price_by_location(row):
    location = row['LOCATION']
    if location in US_LOCATIONS:
        row['COUNTRY'] = 'USA'
        row['CURRENCY'] = 'USD'
        row['USD'] = Decimal(row['PRICE'])
    elif location in CAD_LOCATIONS:
        row['COUNTRY'] = 'CANADA'
        row['CURRENCY'] = 'CAD'
        row['USD'] = Decimal(row['PRICE']) * CAD_TO_USD
    else:
        raise ValueError (f'Location not found: {location}')
    return row
```

Based on the location, it derives the currency. Note that the two-letter codes for Canadian provinces and territories and for US states are described in two lists. The full descriptions of each are stored in the `CAD_LOCATIONS` and `US_LOCATIONS` arrays. If the detected location is a US state, the currency is set to US dollars, and it's set to Canadian dollars for all the provinces and territories in Canada.

> **Note**
>
> It's very convenient that US states and Canadian provinces have different unique codes, making them easy to distinguish. In other systems, things may be more complicated.

It adds a new key to the dictionary for the country, the currency, and the US dollar equivalent of the price. These three keys are then added as columns to the output CSV.

> **Note**
>
> Python dictionaries keep the insertion order. This means that the last added key to the dictionary will be retrieved last when keys are presented. We take advantage of this behavior regarding the generation of the header, as any new element introduced will be stored as a new column at the end, retaining the order of the older elements.

The resulting file provides information on each sale log in a common currency, making comparisons easier.

## There's more...

As we commented before, processing and distinguishing location and currency may not always be as straightforward as presented here. Different countries may have different ways of representing places, and in some cases the codes used to represent locations from different countries will overlap.

The country is added as a column to be available later.

The currency exchange rate is defined as a constant, but that's only an approximation. It may be necessary to obtain it from an external source as it is likely to change daily. For example, `www.exchangerate-api.com` offers a free API to integrate exchange rate conversions, as follows:

```
>>> import requests
>>> result = requests.get('https://open.er-api.com/v6/latest/CAD')
>>> result.json()['rates']['USD']
0.755081
```

More complicated setups may require access to specific exchange rate sources or the ability to retrieve the historic information on rates.

> **Tip**
>
> Most exchange rate sources impose a limit on the number of calls, or charge per access. Be sure to avoid constantly polling for data, and store the rates for local use.

## See also

- The *Preparing a CSV spreadsheet* recipe from the previous section.
- The *Reading CSV files* recipe in *Chapter 4, Searching and Reading Local Files*.
- The *Preparing a task* recipe in *Chapter 2, Automating Tasks Made Easy*.

# Standardizing the date format

The date time format in the logs differs depending on the location. In the Canadian logs, the format is the standard ISO 8601 in the format `YYYY-MM-DD`. The logs coming from the USA use the format `MM-DD-YYYY`.

> **Tip**
>
> The format `YYYY-MM-DD` is the programmer's notion of a perfect date, as sorting them alphabetically also sort them as dates.

In this recipe, we will append a new column with a standard format to unify both dates.

## Getting ready

We will use the CSV file resulting from the previous recipe that receives and transforms logs in the following format:

```
[<Timestamp>] - SALE - PRODUCT: <product id> - PRICE: <price>
```

Each line will represent a sale log.

We will use the parse and pendulum modules, installing them by adding them to our requirements.txt file as follows:

```
$ echo "parse==1.20.2" >> requirements.txt
$ echo "pendulum==3.2.0" >> requirements.txt
$ uv pip install -r requirements.txt
```

In the GitHub repository are some log files to process, which have the following structure:

```
sale_logs/
  OH
    logs.txt
  ON
    logs.txt
```

The code can be found in the GitHub repository at https://github.com/PacktPublishing/Python-Automation-Cookbook-Third-Edition/tree/main/ch07.

## How to do it...

1. Import the data and transform it into a CSV file using the logs_to_csv.py script. The script adds the location as input. Create the files for both the OH and OT logs:

   ```
   $ uv run logs_to_csv.py sale_logs/OH/logs.txt output_1_OH.csv -l OH
   $ uv run logs_to_csv.py sale_logs/ON/logs.txt output_1_ON.csv -l ON
   ```

2. Process both resulting files using the location_price.py script:

   ```
   $ uv run location_price.py output_1_OH.csv output_2_OH.csv
   $ uv run location_price.py output_1_ON.csv output_2_ON.csv
   ```

3. Process both files using the `standard_date.py` script:

```
$ uv run standard_date.py output_2_OH.csv output_3_OH.csv
$ uv run standard_date.py output_2_ON.csv output_3_ON.csv
```

4. Check the resulting CSV files in a spreadsheet application. In the following screenshots, the files are displayed using the LibreOffice software:

| | A | B | C | D | E | F | G | H |
|---|---|---|---|---|---|---|---|---|
| 1 | LOCATION | TIMESTAMP | PRODUCT | PRICE | COUNTRY | CURRENCY | USD | STD_TIMESTAMP |
| 2 | OH | 08-27-2025 18:39:41 | 12346 | 2.99 | USA | USD | 2.99 | 2025-08-27T17:39:41+00:00 |
| 3 | OH | 08-27-2025 19:39:41 | 12346 | 2.99 | USA | USD | 2.99 | 2025-08-27T18:39:41+00:00 |
| 4 | OH | 08-27-2025 20:39:41 | 12346 | 2.99 | USA | USD | 2.99 | 2025-08-27T19:39:41+00:00 |
| 5 | OH | 08-27-2025 21:39:41 | 12346 | 2.99 | USA | USD | 2.99 | 2025-08-27T20:39:41+00:00 |
| 6 | OH | 08-27-2025 22:39:41 | 12345 | 9.99 | USA | USD | 9.99 | 2025-08-27T21:39:41+00:00 |
| 7 | OH | 08-27-2025 23:39:41 | 12345 | 7.99 | USA | USD | 7.99 | 2025-08-27T22:39:41+00:00 |
| 8 | OH | 08-28-2025 00:39:41 | 12346 | 2.99 | USA | USD | 2.99 | 2025-08-27T23:39:41+00:00 |
| 9 | OH | 08-28-2025 01:39:41 | 12346 | 2.99 | USA | USD | 2.99 | 2025-08-28T00:39:41+00:00 |
| 10 | OH | 08-28-2025 02:39:41 | 12346 | 2.99 | USA | USD | 2.99 | 2025-08-28T01:39:41+00:00 |
| 11 | OH | 08-28-2025 03:39:41 | 12346 | 2.99 | USA | USD | 2.99 | 2025-08-28T02:39:41+00:00 |
| 12 | OH | 08-28-2025 04:39:41 | 12346 | 2.99 | USA | USD | 2.99 | 2025-08-28T03:39:41+00:00 |
| 13 | OH | 08-28-2025 05:39:41 | 12346 | 2.99 | USA | USD | 2.99 | 2025-08-28T04:39:41+00:00 |
| 14 | OH | 08-28-2025 06:39:41 | 12345 | 7.99 | USA | USD | 7.99 | 2025-08-28T05:39:41+00:00 |
| 15 | OH | 08-28-2025 07:39:41 | 12345 | 9.99 | USA | USD | 9.99 | 2025-08-28T06:39:41+00:00 |
| 16 | OH | 08-28-2025 08:39:41 | 12346 | 2.99 | USA | USD | 2.99 | 2025-08-28T07:39:41+00:00 |
| 17 | OH | 08-28-2025 09:39:41 | 12346 | 2.99 | USA | USD | 2.99 | 2025-08-28T08:39:41+00:00 |
| 18 | OH | 08-28-2025 10:39:41 | 12346 | 2.99 | USA | USD | 2.99 | 2025-08-28T09:39:41+00:00 |
| 19 | OH | 08-28-2025 11:39:41 | 12345 | 9.99 | USA | USD | 9.99 | 2025-08-28T10:39:41+00:00 |
| 20 | OH | 08-28-2025 12:39:41 | 12346 | 2.99 | USA | USD | 2.99 | 2025-08-28T11:39:41+00:00 |
| 21 | OH | 08-28-2025 13:39:41 | 12346 | 2.99 | USA | USD | 2.99 | 2025-08-28T12:39:41+00:00 |
| 22 | OH | 08-28-2025 14:39:41 | 12346 | 2.99 | USA | USD | 2.99 | 2025-08-28T13:39:41+00:00 |
| 23 | OH | 08-28-2025 15:39:41 | 12345 | 9.99 | USA | USD | 9.99 | 2025-08-28T14:39:41+00:00 |
| 24 | OH | 08-28-2025 16:39:41 | 12345 | 9.99 | USA | USD | 9.99 | 2025-08-28T15:39:41+00:00 |
| 25 | OH | 08-28-2025 17:39:41 | 12346 | 2.99 | USA | USD | 2.99 | 2025-08-28T16:39:41+00:00 |
| 26 | OH | 08-28-2025 18:39:41 | 12346 | 2.99 | USA | USD | 2.99 | 2025-08-28T17:39:41+00:00 |
| 27 | OH | 08-28-2025 19:39:41 | 12345 | 7.99 | USA | USD | 7.99 | 2025-08-28T18:39:41+00:00 |
| 28 | OH | 08-28-2025 20:39:41 | 12346 | 2.99 | USA | USD | 2.99 | 2025-08-28T19:39:41+00:00 |
| 29 | OH | 08-28-2025 21:39:41 | 12345 | 7.99 | USA | USD | 7.99 | 2025-08-28T20:39:41+00:00 |
| 30 | OH | 08-28-2025 22:39:41 | 12346 | 2.99 | USA | USD | 2.99 | 2025-08-28T21:39:41+00:00 |

| | A | B | C | D | E | F | G | H |
|---|---|---|---|---|---|---|---|---|
| 1 | LOCATION | TIMESTAMP | PRODUCT | PRICE | COUNTRY | CURRENCY | USD | STD_TIMESTAMP |
| 2 | ON | 2018-08-27 19:05:55+00:00 | 12346 | 3.99 | CANADA | CAD | 3 | 2018-08-27T18:05:55+00:00 |
| 3 | ON | 2018-08-27 20:05:55+00:00 | 12346 | 3.99 | CANADA | CAD | 3 | 2018-08-27T19:05:55+00:00 |
| 4 | ON | 2018-08-27 21:05:55+00:00 | 12346 | 3.99 | CANADA | CAD | 3 | 2018-08-27T20:05:55+00:00 |
| 5 | ON | 2018-08-27 22:05:55+00:00 | 12345 | 10.5 | CANADA | CAD | 8 | 2018-08-27T21:05:55+00:00 |
| 6 | ON | 2018-08-27 23:05:55+00:00 | 12346 | 3.99 | CANADA | CAD | 3 | 2018-08-27T22:05:55+00:00 |
| 7 | ON | 2018-08-28 00:05:55+00:00 | 12346 | 3.99 | CANADA | CAD | 3 | 2018-08-27T23:05:55+00:00 |
| 8 | ON | 2018-08-28 01:05:55+00:00 | 12346 | 3.99 | CANADA | CAD | 3 | 2018-08-28T00:05:55+00:00 |
| 9 | ON | 2018-08-28 02:05:55+00:00 | 12346 | 3.99 | CANADA | CAD | 3 | 2018-08-28T01:05:55+00:00 |
| 10 | ON | 2018-08-28 03:05:55+00:00 | 12346 | 3.99 | CANADA | CAD | 3 | 2018-08-28T02:05:55+00:00 |
| 11 | ON | 2018-08-28 04:05:55+00:00 | 12346 | 3.99 | CANADA | CAD | 3 | 2018-08-28T03:05:55+00:00 |
| 12 | ON | 2018-08-28 05:05:55+00:00 | 12345 | 10.5 | CANADA | CAD | 8 | 2018-08-28T04:05:55+00:00 |
| 13 | ON | 2018-08-28 06:05:55+00:00 | 12346 | 3.99 | CANADA | CAD | 3 | 2018-08-28T05:05:55+00:00 |
| 14 | ON | 2018-08-28 07:05:55+00:00 | 12346 | 3.99 | CANADA | CAD | 3 | 2018-08-28T06:05:55+00:00 |
| 15 | ON | 2018-08-28 08:05:55+00:00 | 12345 | 13.5 | CANADA | CAD | 10 | 2018-08-28T07:05:55+00:00 |
| 16 | ON | 2018-08-28 09:05:55+00:00 | 12346 | 3.99 | CANADA | CAD | 3 | 2018-08-28T08:05:55+00:00 |
| 17 | ON | 2018-08-28 10:05:55+00:00 | 12345 | 10.5 | CANADA | CAD | 8 | 2018-08-28T09:05:55+00:00 |
| 18 | ON | 2018-08-28 11:05:55+00:00 | 12346 | 3.99 | CANADA | CAD | 3 | 2018-08-28T10:05:55+00:00 |
| 19 | ON | 2018-08-28 12:05:55+00:00 | 12346 | 3.99 | CANADA | CAD | 3 | 2018-08-28T11:05:55+00:00 |
| 20 | ON | 2018-08-28 13:05:55+00:00 | 12346 | 3.99 | CANADA | CAD | 3 | 2018-08-28T12:05:55+00:00 |
| 21 | ON | 2018-08-28 14:05:55+00:00 | 12346 | 3.99 | CANADA | CAD | 3 | 2018-08-28T13:05:55+00:00 |
| 22 | ON | 2018-08-28 15:05:55+00:00 | 12346 | 3.99 | CANADA | CAD | 3 | 2018-08-28T14:05:55+00:00 |
| 23 | ON | 2018-08-28 16:05:55+00:00 | 12346 | 3.99 | CANADA | CAD | 3 | 2018-08-28T15:05:55+00:00 |
| 24 | ON | 2018-08-28 17:05:55+00:00 | 12346 | 3.99 | CANADA | CAD | 3 | 2018-08-28T16:05:55+00:00 |
| 25 | ON | 2018-08-28 18:05:55+00:00 | 12345 | 13.5 | CANADA | CAD | 10 | 2018-08-28T17:05:55+00:00 |
| 26 | ON | 2018-08-28 19:05:55+00:00 | 12346 | 3.99 | CANADA | CAD | 3 | 2018-08-28T18:05:55+00:00 |
| 27 | ON | 2018-08-28 20:05:55+00:00 | 12346 | 3.99 | CANADA | CAD | 3 | 2018-08-28T19:05:55+00:00 |
| 28 | ON | 2018-08-28 21:05:55+00:00 | 12345 | 10.5 | CANADA | CAD | 8 | 2018-08-28T20:05:55+00:00 |
| 29 | ON | 2018-08-28 22:05:55+00:00 | 12345 | 10.5 | CANADA | CAD | 8 | 2018-08-28T21:05:55+00:00 |
| 30 | ON | 2018-08-28 23:05:55+00:00 | 12345 | 13.5 | CANADA | CAD | 10 | 2018-08-28T22:05:55+00:00 |

*Figure 7.3: Screenshots of consistent standardized timestamps*

Notice how the times in the **STD_TIMESTAMP** column are formatted in the same way, while those in the **TIMESTAMP** column are not.

> **Tip**
>
> Be careful as Excel will tend to interpret values as dates, which may cause trouble. A famous case is the renaming by the Human Genome Organization of the names of the genes SEPT1 and MARCH1 to SEPTIN1 and MARCHF1 to avoid problems when opening files with Excel. See for more details `https://revistapesquisa.fapesp.br/en/automatic-conversion-in-excel-changed-to-prevent-errors-in-genetic-studies/`.

## How it works...

Let's take a look at the `standard_date.py` script, used in *step 3*.

The end of the script deals with the parsing of arguments, which was described in detail in *Chapter 2, Automating Tasks Made Easy*.

The main function reads the input CSV and calls the `add_std_timestamp` function for each of the rows. It then writes the results in the output file:

```
def main(input_file, output_file):
    reader = csv.DictReader(input_file)
    result = [add_std_timestamp(row) for row in reader]

    # Save into csv format
    header = result[0].keys()
    writer = csv.DictWriter(output_file, fieldnames=header)
    writer.writeheader()
    writer.writerows(result)
```

The script uses the CSV `DictReader` class to transform each of the rows into a dictionary, which is then passed for processing. The output CSV file stores the resulting rows using `DictWriter`. The output file field headers are obtained from the keys in the dictionary of the first output row.

The usage of `DictReader` and `DictWriter` was described in *Chapter 6, Fun with Spreadsheets*.

Each of the rows is modified in the `add_std_timestamp` function, depending on the country the log was written in. Let's take a look:

```
def add_std_timestamp(row):
    country = row['COUNTRY']
    if country == 'USA':
        row['STD_TIMESTAMP'] = to_isotime(row['TIMESTAMP'], AMERICAN_FORMAT)
    elif country == 'CANADA':
        row['STD_TIMESTAMP'] = to_isotime(row['TIMESTAMP'], CANADIAN_FORMAT)
    else:
        raise ValueError(f'Country not found: {country}')

    return row
```

Based on the country of origin, this function transforms the date and creates a new standardized timestamp.

> **Tip**
>
> Note that the country has been inserted into the data in the previous recipe, having been derived from the location codes. Storing the country explicitly in the previous stage of processing allows us to simplify the script for the date, as the data has been

> already calculated. This may look straightforward in this example, but separating operations in different stages while processing data is quite common as the focus while developing is generally on only a small part of the code.
>
> This process of cascading steps, each one adding more information, is very useful as it allows each step to be run independently with clear inputs and outputs.

The function adds a new key to the dictionary with a standard timestamp in ISO 8601 format. The logs produced in Canada already have this format, but the ones generated in the United States need a deeper transformation. The translation is performed by the `to_isotime` function:

```
# Timestamp formats
AMERICAN_FORMAT = '%m-%d-%Y %H:%M:%S'
CANADIAN_FORMAT = '%Y-%m-%d %H:%M:%S+00:00'

def to_isotime(timestamp, time_format):
    parsed_tmp = datetime.strptime(timestamp, time_format)
    time_with_tz = parsed_tmp.replace(tzinfo=timezone.utc)
    isotimestamp = time_with_tz.isoformat()

    return isotimestamp
```

The American timestamp is parsed using the standard Python library with `datetime.strptime` with the format `"%m-%d-%Y %H:%M:%S"`, which corresponds to `MM-DD-YYYY HH:MM:SS`. The resulting `datetime` object, which at that time doesn't have a specific timezone, is then attached the UTC time zone, transformed into an ISO 8601 valid string, and then returned.

> **Note**
>
> Remember that in Python, dictionaries preserve the insertion order.

For Canadian timestamps, the format is almost correct, but it's parsed in a similar way.

> **Tip**
>
> Note that we are expecting to receive all the Canadian timestamps in UTC format, with a time offset of +00:00. We are hard-coding it in our code. But if we are expecting differences there, we can instead parse it with '%Y-%m-%d %H:%M:%S%z' which will

> parse different time offsets. See all the possible time variables available in the docs at `https://docs.python.org/3/library/time.html#time.strftime`.

The resulting file allows us to compare times in the same format.

## There's more...

In some cases, detection of the timestamp format may be dependent on parameters such as the country or application that produced the logs, and may require you to try several formats to see which one fits. When working with many sources, this can become a problem, as a single row may not contain enough information. For example, a date string of *05-06-2019* could mean June 5th in international format, or May 6th in US format. An analysis of the whole file may be required, or it may be necessary to take a guess and validate it afterward.

> **Tip**
>
> Our GenAI friend can also help here producing an informed guess about a particular file or part of it, but typically the best solution is to check with the people in charge of the data source.

In all the log files for the recipe time is stored in UTC time, but this cannot be assumed in general. Time can be stored in different time zones.

In our example, the time zones for Ohio and Ontario are the same, but time zones may differ for other location pairs. Depending on the logs, this may require an adjustment. Check your assumptions in your specific project.

> **Tip**
>
> The ISO 8601 format may include the time zone. For example, the ending +00:00 shows the time zone is UTC. Don't assume that the time format will always include time zone information. If it's not present, it may lead to inconsistent times in your data. Always include the time zone or use the times in UTC when combining different sources to avoid confusion.

If different time zones are used, the `pendulum` module introduced in *Chapter 1* can help with defining the times and matching equivalent times in an easy way:

```
>>> import pendulum
>>> timestamp = pendulum.parse('2025-08-28 20:05:55+00:00')
```

```
>>> timestamp_EST = timestamp.in_timezone('US/Eastern')
>>> timestamp_EST.isoformat()
'2025-08-28T16:05:55-04:00'
```

The full Pendulum documentation can be found online at `https://pendulum.eustace.io`.

Notice how the old timestamps are still present in the CSV file, instead of being overwritten by the new timestamp column. Unless there's a clear need to save space, it's best to keep it for reference and to detect possible problems later. It also allows us to easily check whether or when this stage has been applied to the given CSV file.

## See also

- The *Appending currency based on location* recipe in the previous section.
- The *Reading CSV files recipe in Chapter 4, Searching and Reading Local Files.*
- The *Preparing a task recipe in Chapter 2, Automating Tasks Made Easy.*

# Transforming and validating data in JSON

While we can use CSV as a format, it is very common to use JSON instead. JSON is another standard data format. As part of the transformation to JSON of data in CSV, we will validate that the contents of the data are correct and as expected, by using the `pydantic` module.

## Getting ready

We will use the CSV file resulting from the previous recipe, which receives and transforms logs in the following format:

```
[<Timestamp>] - SALE - PRODUCT: <product id> - PRICE: <price>
```

Each line will represent a sale log.

We will use the `parse`, as in the previous recipes, but will also add `pydantic`. We install these modules by adding them to our `requirements.txt` file as follows:

```
$ echo "parse==1.20.2" >> requirements.txt
$ echo "pydantic==2.12.5" >> requirements.txt
$ uv pip install -r requirements.txt
```

The GitHub repository contains some log files to process, which have the following structure:

```
sale_logs/
  OH
```

```
    logs.txt
  ON
    logs.txt
```

The code can be found in the GitHub repository at https://github.com/PacktPublishing/Python-Automation-Cookbook-Third-Edition/tree/main/ch07.

## How to do it...

1. Import the data and transform it into a CSV file using the logs_to_csv.py script. The script takes the location as input. Create the files for both the OH and OT logs:

```
$ uv run logs_to_csv.py sale_logs/OH/logs.txt output_1_OH.csv -l OH
$ uv run logs_to_csv.py sale_logs/ON/logs.txt output_1_ON.csv -l ON
```

2. Process both resulting files using the location_price.py script:

```
$ uv run location_price.py output_1_OH.csv output_2_OH.csv
$ uv run location_price.py output_1_ON.csv output_2_ON.csv
```

3. Process both files using the standard_date.py script:

```
$ uv run standard_date.py output_2_OH.csv output_3_OH.csv
$ uv run standard_date.py output_2_ON.csv output_3_ON.csv
```

4. Now that we have prepared the data, run the transform_into_json.py script.

```
$ uv run transform_into_json.py output_3_OH.csv output_4_OH.json
$ uv run transform_into_json.py output_3_ON.csv output_4_ON.json
```

5. Check that the values of the .json files are easy to retrieve back into the Python interpreter by loading the JSON file.

```
>>> import json
>>> with open('output_4_ON.json') as fp:
...     data = json.load(fp)
...
>>> data[0]
{'LOCATION': 'ON', 'TIMESTAMP': '2018-08-27 19:05:55+00:00', 'PRODUCT':
```

```
'12346', 'PRICE': '3.99', 'COUNTRY': 'CANADA', 'CURRENCY': 'CAD', 'USD':
'3.0', 'STD_TIMESTAMP': '2018-08-27T18:05:55+00:00'}
```

## How it works...

Let's take a look at the `transform_into_json.py` script, used in *step 4*.

The end of the script file deals with the parsing of arguments, which was described in detail in *Chapter 2, Automating Tasks Made Easy*.

The `main` function reads the input CSV, then reads and verifies each of the logs with `verify_log` before storing the file in JSON format by calling `json.dump`. Note the `importjson` at the top of the file, which is a standard library included in Python by default.

```
def main(input_file, output_file):
    reader = csv.DictReader(input_file)
    # Go for each of the rows and verify that is correct
    # Only correct rows will be added to the saved data
    data = [row for row in reader if verify_log(row)]
    json.dump(data, output_file)
```

Importantly, note that both `input_file` and `output_file` are open files with the right permissions.

We perform validation in the `verify_log` function and associated `Log` class. Let's take a look first at the function:

```
def verify_log(log):
    try:
        Log.model_validate(log)
        return True
    except ValidationError as err:
        print(f'Error validating log: {log}, {err}. \nSkipping')
        return False
```

It calls `Log.model_validate` for each log, returning `True`. If there's a `ValidationError` it will return `False` and print an error message. The `False` value will cause the list comprehension in `main` to skip the bad log and not store it.

The Log class is a pydantic class that defines how the input data should be:

```
class Log(BaseModel):
    LOCATION: Literal['ON', 'OH']
    TIMESTAMP: str
    PRODUCT: int
    PRICE: Decimal
    COUNTRY: Literal['USA', 'CANADA']
    CURRENCY: Literal['USD', 'CAD']
    USD: Decimal
    STD_TIMESTAMP: datetime
```

We define in the class the accepted kinds of values for the different fields. For example, `TIMESTAMP` is fine with any string as this is the source timestamp which has multiple formats, but we define `STD_TIMESTAMP` to be a valid `datatime`.

> **Note**
>
> The way `pydantic` defines requirements is by using Python **annotations**. This is a Python extension that allows us to define the expected type for a value by adding to its definition a type after a colon, e.g. `USD: float` means that the value of the `USD` field is expected to be a `float`. While optional in Python, `pydantic` uses this to enforce definitions when type checking is present, as we are seeing. See more about annotations in the Python documentation `https://typing.python.org/en/latest/spec/annotations.html`.

For values that should be one of a fixed list, we use the Literal annotation, as in `LOCATION: Literal['ON', 'OH']`. That means that we only accept values for `LOCATION` that are be either `ON` or `OH`.

In our data all our logs are correct, but we will see errors in the next section.

> **Note**
>
> Note that we are storing all our JSON data as a single file, in a single list. For relatively small amounts of data that's perfectly fine, but if the amount of data grows it may be a good idea to create smaller chunks. Compared with CSV processing, note that we are loading everything into memory. For large numbers of elements that will be inefficient. Typically, you create multiple files, each one dealing with a particular period of time

> (e.g. a set of files containing data for individual hours) so that each can be loaded and processed independently.

## There's more...

We are reading and storing JSON data from files, but it is very common to want to transform Python dictionaries into JSON strings and vice versa. For that we can use the `json.dumps` and `json.loads` functions:

```
>>> import json
>>> my_dict = {'COUNTRY': 'CANADA', 'LOCATION': 'ON'}
>>> json_string = json.dumps(my_dict)
>>> json_string
'{"COUNTRY": "CANADA", "LOCATION": "ON"}'
>>> json.loads(json_string)
{'COUNTRY': 'CANADA', 'LOCATION': 'ON'}
```

> **Note**
>
> The representation of a dictionary in Python and a JSON string are very similar, but while `json_string` is a string, `my_dict` is a dictionary that you can access via its keys.

To see what happens with different errors, we will use a specific file containing bad logs, `bad_output_3_ON.csv`.

```
$ uv run transform_into_json.py bad_output_3_ON.csv bad_output_4_ON.json
Error validating log: {'LOCATION': 'NY', 'TIMESTAMP': '2025-08-27 19:05:55+00:00',
'PRODUCT': '12346', 'PRICE': '3.99', 'COUNTRY': 'CANADA', 'CURRENCY': 'CAD',
'USD': '3.0', 'STD_TIMESTAMP': '2025-08-27T18:05:55+00:00'}, 1 validation error
for Log
LOCATION
  Input should be 'ON' or 'OH' [type=literal_error, input_value='NY',
input_type=str]
    For further information visit https://errors.pydantic.dev/2.12/v/
literal_error.
--- Skipping ---
Error validating log: {'LOCATION': 'ON', 'TIMESTAMP': '2025-08-27 20:05:55+00:00',
'PRODUCT': '12346', 'PRICE': 'BAD_PRICE', 'COUNTRY': 'CANADA', 'CURRENCY': 'CAD',
'USD': '3.0', 'STD_TIMESTAMP': '2025-08-27T20:05:55+00:00'}, 1 validation error
```

```
for Log
PRICE
  Input should be a valid number, unable to parse string as a number
[type=float_parsing, input_value='BAD_PRICE', input_type=str]
    For further information visit https://errors.pydantic.dev/2.12/v/
float_parsing.
--- Skipping ---
Error validating log: {'LOCATION': 'ON', 'TIMESTAMP': '27-08-2025 21:05:55+00:00',
'PRODUCT': '12346', 'PRICE': '3.99', 'COUNTRY': 'CANADA', 'CURRENCY': 'CAD',
'USD': '3.0', 'STD_TIMESTAMP': '27-08-2025T20:05:55+00:00'}, 1 validation error
for Log
STD_TIMESTAMP
  Input should be a valid datetime or date, invalid character in year
[type=datetime_from_date_parsing, input_value='27-08-2025T20:05:55+00:00',
input_type=str]
    For further information visit https://errors.pydantic.dev/2.12/v/
datetime_from_date_parsing.
--- Skipping ---
Error validating log: {'LOCATION': 'ON', 'TIMESTAMP': '2025-08-27 22:05:55+00:00',
'PRODUCT': '12346', 'PRICE': '3.99', 'COUNTRY': 'CANADA', 'CURRENCY': 'USD',
'USD': '3.0', 'STD_TIMESTAMP': '2025-08-27T20:05:55+00:00'}, 1 validation error
for Log
  Value error, For COUNTRY=CANADA, CURRENCY should be CAD [type=value_error,
input_value={'LOCATION': 'ON', 'TIMES...5-08-27T20:05:55+00:00'}, input_type=dict]
    For further information visit https://errors.pydantic.dev/2.12/v/value_error.
--- Skipping ---
Error validating log: {'LOCATION': 'ON', 'TIMESTAMP': '2025-08-27 23:05:55+00:00',
'PRODUCT': '12346', 'PRICE': '3.99', 'COUNTRY': 'USA', 'CURRENCY': 'CAD', 'USD':
'3.0', 'STD_TIMESTAMP': '2025-08-27T19:05:55+00:00'}, 1 validation error for Log
  Value error, For COUNTRY=USA, LOCATION should be a valid state
[type=value_error, input_value={'LOCATION': 'ON', 'TIMES...
5-08-27T19:05:55+00:00'}, input_type=dict]
    For further information visit https://errors.pydantic.dev/2.12/v/value_error.
--- Skipping ---
```

There are five errors reported in this result (and the output file `bad_output_4_ON.json` is empty):

- The first log has an unrecognized `LOCATION` (`NY`, when the allowed ones are `ON` and `OH`)

- The second log has as `PRICE` a non-numerical value (it has `'BAD_PRICE'` instead)
- The third has an invalid `STD_TIMESTAMP`; note that it doesn't complain about `TIMESTAMP` as that doesn't need to be a valid `datetime`.

The last two errors are, respectively, because the `CURRENCY` is not valid for `CANADA` and the `LOCATION` `'ON'` is not located in `USA`. These two checks are implemented in our own method `check_location_and_currency` in the Log class:

```
    @model_validator(mode='after')
    def check_location_and_currency(self):
        # Check location and country match
        if self.COUNTRY == 'USA' and self.LOCATION not in US_STATES:
            raise ValueError('For COUNTRY=USA, LOCATION should be a valid state')
        elif self.COUNTRY == 'CANADA' and self.LOCATION not in CA_PROVINCES:
            raise ValueError('For COUNTRY=CANADA, LOCATION should be a valid
province')

        # Check currency match
        if self.COUNTRY == 'CANADA' and self.CURRENCY != 'CAD':
            raise ValueError('For COUNTRY=CANADA, CURRENCY should be CAD')
        elif self.COUNTRY == 'USA' and self.CURRENCY != 'USD':
            raise ValueError('For COUNTRY=USA, CURRENCY should be USD')
    return self
```

The `@model_validator(mode='after')` decorator causes the check to take place after the other checks have been carried out, providing our own extra validation. If there's something wrong, we raise a `ValueError` exception with a descriptive message.

`Pydantic` is not only checking the value, but also parsing it.

```
>>> from transform_into_json import Log
>>> log =  {"LOCATION": "ON", "TIMESTAMP": "2018-09-09 05:05:55+00:00", "PRODUCT": 
"12346", "PRICE": "3.99", "COUNTRY": "CANADA", "CURRENCY": "CAD", "USD": "3.0", 
"STD_TIMESTAMP": "2018-09-09T04:05:55+00:00"}
>>> result = Log.model_validate(log)
>>> result
Log(LOCATION='ON', TIMESTAMP='2018-09-09 05:05:55+00:00', PRODUCT=12346, 
PRICE=3.99, COUNTRY='CANADA', CURRENCY='CAD', USD=3.0, 
STD_TIMESTAMP=datetime.datetime(2018, 9, 9, 4, 5, 55, tzinfo=TzInfo(0)))
```

Note how it has transformed the timestamp into a `datetime` object, and prices to `float` values. `TIMESTAMP`, though, remains as a string value.

> **Tip**
>
> Remember that we talked in *Chapter 1* about the risks of working with prices in `float` format. Refer to the recipe *Extracting data from structured strings* for a longer discussion about that.

In this example, we are storing the result from `.model_validate()` in the `result` variable. Note that this parses the result and provide you with an object that contains the parsed values of the log.

> **Tip**
>
> A very common usage of `pydantic` is not just to validate, but to parse the text into structured objects, following the rules of the spec.

If we want to enforce stronger validations when using `pydantic`, we can use `strict=True`. This avoids making explicit conversions and `pydantic` won't transform strings into other types automatically.

```
>>> Log.model_validate(log, strict=True)
...
pydantic_core._pydantic_core.ValidationError: 4 validation errors for Log
PRODUCT
  Input should be a valid integer [type=int_type, input_value='12346',
input_type=str]
    For further information visit https://errors.pydantic.dev/2.12/v/int_type
PRICE
  Input should be a valid number [type=float_type, input_value='3.99',
input_type=str]
    For further information visit https://errors.pydantic.dev/2.12/v/float_type
USD
  Input should be a valid number [type=float_type, input_value='3.0',
input_type=str]
    For further information visit https://errors.pydantic.dev/2.12/v/float_type
STD_TIMESTAMP
  Input should be a valid datetime [type=datetime_type,
```

```
input_value='2018-09-09T04:05:55+00:00', input_type=str]
    For further information visit https://errors.pydantic.dev/2.12/v/datetime_type
```

If you are using `pydantic` to parse data, being stricter can be limiting, but the strict mode can be helpful in situations where you need to be very careful about accepting data.

> **Tip**
>
> `pydantic` is a very powerful and flexible module, allowing plenty of configurational flexibility in how you define your validation schema, but it can require some work to make it work correctly. GenAI can be very helpful helping you define the proper schema validation for your usage.
>
> The important point is that it is highly optimized for checks and parsing, making it very fast for transforming high amounts of data.

The full `pydantic` documentation can be found here `https://docs.pydantic.dev/latest/`.

## See also

- The *Standardizing the data format* recipe in the previous section.
- The *Reading CSV files* recipe in *Chapter 4, Searching and Reading Local Files.*
- The *Preparing a task* recipe in *Chapter 2, Automating Tasks Made Easy.*

# Aggregating results

Once the data is cleaned we can process the results. For our example, we will calculate the average sale price by both location and day, as well as the total sales by location and day in the data range. As our data is stored by location, this will be done in two steps. First, we'll create the files per location, and then by date, using the date on the location results.

## Getting ready

We will use the JSON file from the previous recipe that receives and transforms logs in the following format:

```
[<Timestamp>] - SALE - PRODUCT: <product id> - PRICE: <price>
```

Each line will represent a sale log.

We will use the parse and pydantic modules. Install the modules by adding them to requirements.txt:

```
$ echo "parse==1.20.2" >> requirements.txt
$ echo "pydantic==2.12.5" >> requirements.txt
$ uv pip install -r requirements.txt
```

The GitHub repository contains some log files to process with the following structure:

```
sale_logs/
  OH
    logs.txt
  ON
    logs.txt
```

The code can be found in the GitHub repository, at https://github.com/PacktPublishing/Python-Automation-Cookbook-Third-Edition/tree/main/ch07.

## How to do it...

1. Import the data and transform it into a CSV file using the logs_to_csv.py script. The script takes the location as input. Create the files for both the OH and OT logs:

```
$ uv run logs_to_csv.py sale_logs/OH/logs.txt output_1_OH.csv -l OH
$ uv run logs_to_csv.py sale_logs/ON/logs.txt output_1_ON.csv -l ON
```

2. Process both resulting files using the location_price.py script:

```
$ uv run location_price.py output_1_OH.csv output_2_OH.csv
$ uv run location_price.py output_1_ON.csv output_2_ON.csv
```

3. Process both files using the standard_date.py script:

```
$ uv run standard_date.py output_2_OH.csv output_3_OH.csv
$ uv run standard_date.py output_2_ON.csv output_3_ON.csv
```

4. Transform the result into JSON:

```
$ uv run transform_into_json.py output_3_OH.csv output_4_OH.json
$ uv run transform_into_json.py output_3_ON.csv output_4_ON.json
```

5. Process both resulting files using the `aggregate_by_location.py` script:

```
$ uv run aggregate_by_location.py output_4_ON.json aggregate_ON.csv
$ uv run aggregate_by_location.py output_4_OH.json aggregate_OH.csv
```

6. Check the resulting CSV files in a spreadsheet application. In the following screenshots, the files are displayed using the LibreOffice software:

| | A | B | C | D | E |
|---|---|---|---|---|---|
| 1 | LOCATION | DATE | TOTAL USD | NUMBER | AVERAGE |
| 2 | OH | 2025-08-27 | 32.93 | 7 | 4.7 |
| 3 | OH | 2025-08-28 | 114.76 | 24 | 4.78 |
| 4 | OH | 2025-08-29 | 111.76 | 24 | 4.66 |
| 5 | OH | 2025-08-30 | 113.76 | 24 | 4.74 |
| 6 | OH | 2025-08-31 | 135.76 | 24 | 5.66 |
| 7 | OH | 2025-09-01 | 112.76 | 24 | 4.7 |
| 8 | OH | 2025-09-02 | 126.76 | 24 | 5.28 |
| 9 | OH | 2025-09-03 | 114.76 | 24 | 4.78 |
| 10 | OH | 2025-09-04 | 115.76 | 24 | 4.82 |
| 11 | OH | 2025-09-05 | 100.76 | 24 | 4.2 |
| 12 | OH | 2025-09-06 | 119.76 | 24 | 4.99 |
| 13 | OH | 2025-09-07 | 112.76 | 24 | 4.7 |
| 14 | OH | 2025-09-08 | 97.76 | 24 | 4.07 |
| 15 | OH | 2025-09-09 | 102.76 | 24 | 4.28 |
| 16 | OH | 2025-09-10 | 111.76 | 24 | 4.66 |
| 17 | OH | 2025-09-11 | 107.76 | 24 | 4.49 |
| 18 | OH | 2025-09-12 | 105.76 | 24 | 4.41 |
| 19 | OH | 2025-09-13 | 114.76 | 24 | 4.78 |
| 20 | OH | 2025-09-14 | 88.76 | 24 | 3.7 |
| 21 | OH | 2025-09-15 | 119.76 | 24 | 4.99 |
| 22 | OH | 2025-09-16 | 139.76 | 24 | 5.82 |
| 23 | OH | 2025-09-17 | 98.76 | 24 | 4.12 |
| 24 | OH | 2025-09-18 | 111.76 | 24 | 4.66 |
| 25 | OH | 2025-09-19 | 107.76 | 24 | 4.49 |

| | A | B | C | D | E |
|---|---|---|---|---|---|
| 1 | LOCATION | DATE | TOTAL USD | NUMBER | AVERAGE |
| 2 | ON | 2025-08-27 | 23 | 6 | 3.83 |
| 3 | ON | 2025-08-28 | 113 | 24 | 4.71 |
| 4 | ON | 2025-08-29 | 120 | 24 | 5 |
| 5 | ON | 2025-08-30 | 120 | 24 | 5 |
| 6 | ON | 2025-08-31 | 120 | 24 | 5 |
| 7 | ON | 2025-09-01 | 108 | 24 | 4.5 |
| 8 | ON | 2025-09-02 | 124 | 24 | 5.17 |
| 9 | ON | 2025-09-03 | 161 | 24 | 6.71 |
| 10 | ON | 2025-09-04 | 107 | 24 | 4.46 |
| 11 | ON | 2025-09-05 | 134 | 24 | 5.58 |
| 12 | ON | 2025-09-06 | 94 | 24 | 3.92 |
| 13 | ON | 2025-09-07 | 111 | 24 | 4.62 |
| 14 | ON | 2025-09-08 | 122 | 24 | 5.08 |
| 15 | ON | 2025-09-09 | 25 | 6 | 4.17 |

*Figure 7.4: Screenshots of aggregated results*

## How it works...

Let's take a look at the `aggregate_by_location.py` script used in *step 5*.

The final part of the script file deals with the parsing of arguments, which was described in detail in *Chapter 2, Automating Tasks Made Easy.*

The main function reads the input CSV and calls the `calculate_results` function to generate the aggregated reports. It then writes the results to the output file. Loading of the input data is done with the module `json`, as described in the previous recipe. The use of `DictWriter` was described in *Chapter 6, Fun with Spreadsheets.*

The aggregation takes place In the `calculate_results` function. Each line of the log is analyzed to check its date, and all the entries with the same date are aggregated:

```
def calculate_results(reader):
    result = []
    last_date = None
    total_usd = 0
    number = 0

    for row in reader:
        location = row['LOCATION']
```

```
        date = parse_iso(row['STD_TIMESTAMP'])
        if not last_date:
            last_date = date

        if last_date < date:
            # New day!
            result.append(line(location, last_date, total_usd, number))
            total_usd = 0
            number = 0
            last_date = date

        number += 1
        total_usd += Decimal(row['USD'])

    # Final results
    result.append(line(location, date, total_usd, number))
    return result
```

The code takes note of the latest date and keeps aggregating until it changes. Every time there's a change in date, the line is appended to the result array.

> **Tip**
>
> Note that this takes advantage of the fact that the data is sorted by timestamp. In this example, the timestamps in the logs are sorted by origin, but there may be scenarios where it is necessary to perform some ordering and/or filtering. Use the techniques described in this chapter, and create an extra step with the sorting process if necessary.

To obtain the date, the input ISO format is parsed using the standard `datetime` module:

```
def parse_iso(timestamp):
    # Parse the ISO format
    total = datetime.fromisoformat(timestamp)
    # Keep only the date
    return total.date()
```

We don't need to specify anything to the parser as we are using ISO format, which is the first format the module tries for decoding.

Each newline is configured in a dictionary format on the `line` function, which is as follows:

```
def line(location, date, total_usd, number):
    data = {
        'LOCATION': location,
        'DATE': date,
        'TOTAL USD': total_usd,
        'NUMBER': number,
        # Round to two decimal places
        'AVERAGE': round(total_usd / number, 2),
    }
    return data
```

Each of the lines has the location, the date, the total USD from sales, the number of sales, and average price per item.

> **Tip**
>
> Storing the aggregate total and the number of events comprising this total allows us to aggregate the values further and calculate the average. Just the average on its own cannot be aggregated further, but the aggregated total and the number of events can, and the average can easily be calculated from them.

The aggregated file is stored in CSV format, after `calculate_results` has returned the value to `main`.

> **Tip**
>
> We use CSV as the final format because it's likely to be read by a business analyst, but the most appropriate format will depend on your particular use case. Perhaps you'll need to store the result as an Excel spreadsheet, or further integrate it with a system.

## There's more...

The average price per sale is rounded to two decimal places, which keeps it up to the penny and makes sense in this specific case. This is done using the built-in `round` function that can accept an extra parameter specifying the number of decimal places to round to:

```
>>> round(3.14159)
3
```

```
>>> round(3.14159, 4)
3.1416
```

If you need more control to round either up or down to the next integer, you can use the `math.ceil` and `math.floor` functions:

```
>>> import math
>>> math.ceil(3.14159)
4
>>> math.floor(3.14159)
3
```

For additional general statistical operators besides average, the Python `statistics` module in the standard library includes functions such as `median()` and `quantiles()`. Check the documentation at `https://docs.python.org/3/library/statistics.html`.

While not required for computing the average, some of these quantities (such as mode or median) may require working with the full data set in memory. This limits the amount of data that can be processed, especially for very big sets of data.

Tip

The debate over what exactly *big data* is is difficult, as there's no single point at which regular data becomes *big*. While an in-depth discussion about big data is out of scope for this book, for sure we can determine that data which cannot be contained in a single computer is indeed big, requiring distributed processing by multiple computers. This complicates the operation a lot, to the point of requiring specialized skills to deal with it. Before moving to that area, think about whether the data could fit onto a specific server with as much memory as possible and if that could be helpful. This approach of 'throwing hardware at a problem' can go a long way, and it's typically cheaper than the work involved in re-architecting the code.

Data that can be treated in smaller chunks, even when the amount of data is huge, can be dealt with in increments, which simplifies greatly processing. For example, think about whether you can treat each day or each hour independently. If you can, you can greatly simplify the processing task.

Please note that calculating statistics can be a difficult challenge requiring specific knowledge to avoid particular problems, such as outliers modifying the average, or more subtle issues such as unrepresentative sampling of the data. When calculating something complicated, double check your assumptions and verify that the result correctly represents the desired measure. This may seem like an easy task, but it can be trickier than expected.

## See also

- The previous recipe, *Transforming and validating data in JSON*.
- The *Reading CSV files* recipe in *Chapter 4, Searching and Reading Local Files*.
- The *Preparing a task* recipe in *Chapter 2, Automating Tasks Made Easy*.

# Process data in parallel

The processing presented in the previous recipe works well, but it processes each file one by one. When we have a small number of files this may be fine, but when there are huge numbers of files to handle this will not be efficient. For most file processing we typically use a single CPU core, which is not the best approach for this type of number-crunching task. Instead, we can use multiple CPUs to process more than one chunk of data at a time.

In this recipe we will see how to process the files in parallel, making use of all the cores of the computer to speed up the process and greatly increase the throughput.

> **Tip**
>
> Remember what we said in the previous recipe about treating data in smaller chunks? In this case, we will chunk the data by location.

## Getting ready

We will use the CSV file resulting from the previous recipe that receives and transforms logs in the following format:

```
[<Timestamp>] - SALE - PRODUCT: <product id> - PRICE: <price>
```

Each line will represent a sale log.

We will use the `parse` and `pydantic` modules, installing them by adding them to our `requirements.txt` file as follows:

```
$ echo "parse==1.20.2" >> requirements.txt
$ echo "pydantic==2.12.5" >> requirements.txt
$ uv pip install -r requirements.txt
```

The GitHub repository contains some log files to process which have the following structure:

```
sale_logs/
  OH
    logs.txt
  ON
    logs.txt
```

The code can be found in the GitHub repository, at `https://github.com/PacktPublishing/Python-Automation-Cookbook-Third-Edition/tree/main/ch07`.

## How to do it...

1. Import the data and transform it into a CSV file using the `logs_to_csv.py` script. The script takes the location as input. Create the files for both the `OH` and `OT` logs:

```
$ uv run logs_to_csv.py sale_logs/OH/logs.txt output_1_OH.csv -l OH
$ uv run logs_to_csv.py sale_logs/ON/logs.txt output_1_ON.csv -l ON
```

2. Process both resulting files using the `location_price.py` script:

```
$ uv run location_price.py output_1_OH.csv output_2_OH.csv
$ uv run location_price.py output_1_ON.csv output_2_ON.csv
```

3. Process both files using the `standard_date.py` script:

```
$ uv run standard_date.py output_2_OH.csv output_3_OH.csv
$ uv run standard_date.py output_2_ON.csv output_3_ON.csv
```

4. Transform the result into JSON:

```
$ uv run transform_into_json.py output_3_OH.csv output_4_OH.json
$ uv run transform_into_json.py output_3_ON.csv output_4_ON.json
```

5. Process all the files in a single call to `aggregate_by_location_parallel.py`, specifying the files to process:

```
$ uv run aggregate_by_location_parallel.py "output_4_*.json"
Processing output_4_ON.json
Processing output_4_OH.json
```

```
Done with output_4_ON.json => aggregate_ON.csv
Done with output_4_OH.json => aggregate_OH.csv
```

6. Check the resulting CSV files in a spreadsheet application. In the following screenshots, the files are displayed using LibreOffice:

| | A | B | C | D | E |
|---|---|---|---|---|---|
| 1 | LOCATION | DATE | TOTAL USD | NUMBER | AVERAGE |
| 2 | OH | 2025-08-27 | 32.93 | 7 | 4.7 |
| 3 | OH | 2025-08-28 | 114.76 | 24 | 4.78 |
| 4 | OH | 2025-08-29 | 111.76 | 24 | 4.66 |
| 5 | OH | 2025-08-30 | 113.76 | 24 | 4.74 |
| 6 | OH | 2025-08-31 | 135.76 | 24 | 5.66 |
| 7 | OH | 2025-09-01 | 112.76 | 24 | 4.7 |
| 8 | OH | 2025-09-02 | 126.76 | 24 | 5.28 |
| 9 | OH | 2025-09-03 | 114.76 | 24 | 4.78 |
| 10 | OH | 2025-09-04 | 115.76 | 24 | 4.82 |
| 11 | OH | 2025-09-05 | 100.76 | 24 | 4.2 |
| 12 | OH | 2025-09-06 | 119.76 | 24 | 4.99 |
| 13 | OH | 2025-09-07 | 112.76 | 24 | 4.7 |
| 14 | OH | 2025-09-08 | 97.76 | 24 | 4.07 |
| 15 | OH | 2025-09-09 | 102.76 | 24 | 4.28 |

| LOCATION | DATE | TOTAL USD | NUMBER | AVERAGE |
|---|---|---|---|---|
| ON | 2025-08-27 | 23 | 6 | 3.83 |
| ON | 2025-08-28 | 113 | 24 | 4.71 |
| ON | 2025-08-29 | 120 | 24 | 5 |
| ON | 2025-08-30 | 120 | 24 | 5 |
| ON | 2025-08-31 | 120 | 24 | 5 |
| ON | 2025-09-01 | 108 | 24 | 4.5 |
| ON | 2025-09-02 | 124 | 24 | 5.17 |
| ON | 2025-09-03 | 161 | 24 | 6.71 |
| ON | 2025-09-04 | 107 | 24 | 4.46 |
| ON | 2025-09-05 | 134 | 24 | 5.58 |
| ON | 2025-09-06 | 94 | 24 | 3.92 |
| ON | 2025-09-07 | 111 | 24 | 4.62 |
| ON | 2025-09-08 | 122 | 24 | 5.08 |
| ON | 2025-09-09 | 25 | 6 | 4.17 |

*Figure 7.5: The results of the recipe*

## How it works...

Let's take a look at the `aggregate_by_location_parallel.py` script, used in *step 5*.

The final part of the script file deals with the parsing of arguments, which was described in detail in *Chapter 2, Automating Tasks Made Easy*.

The `main` function identifies the input files to be aggregated and then processes them in parallel:

```
def main(input_glob):
    input_files = glob.glob(input_glob)
    with concurrent.futures.ProcessPoolExecutor(max_workers=4) as executor:
        futures = [executor.submit(aggregate_filename, filename)
                   for filename in input_files]
        concurrent.futures.wait(futures)
```

The function first uses the input glob to filter the related files and store them in the `input_files` variable. This is done through the `glob.glob` function, which returns the filenames that match the glob.

> Note
>
> Globs are patterns commonly encountered to match groups of filenames with wildcard characters, normally `*`. For example, glob `*.txt` will match any filename that has the extension `txt`.
>
> Python includes a glob module as part of its standard library. You can check out the full documentation at `https://docs.python.org/3/library/glob.html`.

The glob pattern by default searches in the current working directory. Keep this in mind in case it requires tweaking.

The next step is to make a call using a parallel executor for each of the files to the `aggregate_filename` function. We will describe this function shortly, but let's look at the executor first:

```
    with concurrent.futures.ProcessPoolExecutor(max_workers=4) as executor:
        futures = [executor.submit(aggregate_filename, filename)
                   for filename in input_files]
        concurrent.futures.wait(futures)
```

First, we define the executor using a `with` statement and a call to `ProcessPoolExecutor`. `ProcessPoolExecutor` creates a number of process workers that will run the submitted calls to the executor in the background.

> **Tip**
>
> `ProcessPoolExecutor` uses independent processes created in the background, instead of threads. You can use `ThreadPoolExecutor` as well.
>
> Due to some limitations arising from how Python is structured internally, using threads is not optimal for workloads that are CPU intensive, such as numerical operations. Threads are adequate for I/O operations, including calling external APIs and reading from disk. This limitations are being improved in later versions of Python, which shows a lot of promise, but it's still not the default state.
>
> For this particular workload that relies on crunching numbers, for optimal processing the number of processes (and therefore workers) should be the same as the number of cores in the CPU used. We used four for this example, as we are processing only two files in any case. By default Python will default to the number of cpus.
>
> Of course, the best solution is to use specialized modules like Pandas that are optimized for this work. We will see a bit more about Pandas later in the next recipe.

The next step is to create a `future` for each filename. The `future` is an object that references the call that will be executed in the background by the executor. When it's done, the `future` object will store the result.

> **Tip**
>
> You can think of a future object as a ticket for a valet car cleaning. You submit the task, get a ticket, and go do other things. When you're done, you hand back the ticket. If the cleaning is finished, which most likely it is, fantastic. If not, you will need to wait.

The last step is to wait until all `futures` are completed by calling `concurrent.futures.wait`. Note that there's no result returned in the execution of `aggregate_filename`, so we don't need to check any `future` result.

We introduced futures and executors in the *Speeding up web scraping* recipe in *Chapter 3, Building Your First Web Scraping Application*. In that recipe we used a thread-based future.

The task to be executed wraps the aggregation of the file. Let's take a look:

```
from aggregate_by_location import main as main_by_file
def aggregate_filename(filename):
    try:
        print(f'Processing {filename}')
        # Obtain the location
        match = re.match(r'output_\d_(.*)\.json', filename)
        location = match.group(1)
        output_file = f'aggregate_{location}.csv'
        with open(filename) as in_file, open(output_file, 'w') as out_file:
            main_by_file(in_file, out_file)
        print(f'Done with {filename} => {output_file}', flush=True)
    except Exception as exc:
        print(f'Unexpected exception {exc}')
```

At the core of it there's a call to `main_by_file`. This method is imported directly from the *Aggregating results* recipe from the previous section. It receives an input file and produces an output file. These files are opened with read and write access using the `with` statement.

The names of the files are determined beforehand. The input file is a parameter of the function, but the output file is obtained from it. It uses the regex `output_\d_(.*)\.json` file to extract the location from the filename in a match group:

```
        match = re.match(r'output_\d_(.*)\.json', filename)
        location = match.group(1)
        output_file = f'aggregate_{location}.csv'
```

Note that the `\d` part of the regex matches a single digit, but it's not captured as a group, as it's not within brackets.

The input filename and the resulting output file are printed to provide feedback while they are executing.

Working with regexes was described in more detail in the *Introducing regular expressions* and *Going deeper with regular expressions* recipes in *Chapter 1, Let's Begin Our Automation Journey*.

The resulting file is the same as the one produced in the previous *Aggregating results* recipe, but in this case we process the files in parallel, up to four at the same time. This speeds up the process significantly.

## There's more...

Working with parallel tasks has multiple advantages, but there are also some caveats to take into account.

While executing multiple tasks, errors may raise `Exceptions` that can interfere with the execution of the whole script, as would happen with single-task runs. An error on a single file may stop all processing if not managed properly. In our example, the `aggregate_filename` function contains a `try/except` block that will capture any possible issues and log the error. The rest of the files will continue, but at least the error can be noticed and won't be silently ignored.

> **Note**
>
> This is actually part of the Zen of Python, available by calling `import this`.
>
> Errors should never pass silently.
>
> Unless explicitly silenced.

The script could also include an extra check to see whether a particular file has already been created, after determining the output filename. This can be checked with the `os.path.isfile` function:

```
import os.path
...
output_file = f'aggregate_{location}.csv'
if os.path.isfile(output_file):
    # File already exists, do not overwrite
    return
with open(filename) as in_file ...
```

When dealing with large numbers of files, to repeat the execution of the script without starting from the beginning is a great advantage. A common problem is to process a gigantic amount of data, to have an error when processing is 80% complete, and then have to restart the script from the beginning, redoing all the work.

If possible, invest a bit of time in saving partial results to disk or other storage places, so they can be skipped over, thereby speeding up the processing.

Tip

Keep the working dataset small for the purposes of development. It will allow you to iterate quickly and limit distractions. Also, store already-processed data on disk.

One of the print statements to produce feedback adds the flush parameter:

```
print(f'Done with {filename} => {output_file}', flush=True)
```

The flush parameter will use the `print` statement to display the message immediately. If `flush` is not set, or if it's set to `False`, the message won't be printed instantly on screen, but into an intermediate buffer. The buffer will be printed when the operating system decides to, usually after a newline.

This buffer may cause a small delay from the call to `print` to the actual displaying of the information. That delay can be noticeable in certain cases, such as in the last task executed. In that case, the print buffer might hold information, but the program exits before the information is printed. In a single-task program, before exiting, the buffer is printed, but that's not guaranteed in multitask applications.

The parallel nature of the multitask application may also mean that the order of the files being processed is not consistent from one run to the next. To avoid problems, each of the tasks should be independent of the others.

To learn more about futures and executors, check the Python documentation at `https://docs.python.org/3/library/concurrent.futures.html`.

## See also

- The *Aggregating Results* recipe from the previous section.
- The *Reading CSV files* recipe in *Chapter 4, Searching and Reading Local Files.*
- The *Preparing a task* recipe in *Chapter 2, Automating Tasks Made Easy.*
- The *Speeding up web scraping* recipe in *Chapter 3, Building Your First Web Scraping Application.*

# Process data with Pandas

For some operations, simple calculations are not enough. Some complex operations may have nuances in the way they work, and/or problems with precision due to using certain data types. For example, calculating the statistical variance of float numbers can produce problems due to precision issues, as described in this article `https://leimao.github.io/blog/Compute-Variance-One-Pass-Naive-Algorithm/`.

> **Note**
>
> Python allows us to use arbitrarily big integers automatically, but floats present challenges in precision. Adapting code to handle big numbers can be a challenge. Numbers in computing have limitations such as limited precision or restricted ranges over which they are accurate. These limitations may not be obvious at first glance.

Moreover, straight Python is known not to have an amazing number-crunching performance. Complicated mathematical operations will take longer when compared to a compiled language such as C++ or even Java.

That's why using a specialized library can greatly help. They deal with many of the complexities involved in the handling of data, and produce better performance as a result of being highly optimized.

In this recipe we will see how to process files using Pandas, which is an easy-to-use data analysis library for Python that's widely used by the scientific community. Related to the initial example, Pandas has native support to calculate the variance.

> **Note**
>
> Note that `pandas` has recently, at the time of writing this book, released a new major version with `pandas` 3. This has some backwards incompatible changes, in case you are upgrading older code, check the official documentation https://pandas.pydata.org/community/blog/pandas-3.0.html

## Getting ready

We will use the CSV file resulting from the previous recipe that receives and transforms logs in the following format:

```
[<Timestamp>] - SALE - PRODUCT: <product id> - PRICE: <price>
```

Each line will represent a sale log.

In addition to the parse and pydantic modules, we will use pandas. Install the modules by adding them to requirements.txt as follows:

```
$ echo "parse==1.20.2" >> requirements.txt
$ echo "pydantic==2.12.5" >> requirements.txt
$ echo "pandas==3.0.0" >> requirements.txt
$ uv pip install -r requirements.txt
```

The GitHub repository contains some log files to process which have the following structure:

```
sale_logs/
  OH
    logs.txt
  ON
    logs.txt
```

The code can be found in the GitHub repository at https://github.com/PacktPublishing/Python-Automation-Cookbook-Third-Edition/tree/main/ch07.

## How to do it...

1. Import the data and transform it to a CSV file using the logs_to_csv.py script. The script takes the location as input. Create the files for both the OH and OT logs:

```
$ uv run logs_to_csv.py sale_logs/OH/logs.txt output_1_OH.csv -l OH
$ uv run logs_to_csv.py sale_logs/ON/logs.txt output_1_ON.csv -l ON
```

2. Process both resulting files using the location_price.py script:

```
$ uv run location_price.py output_1_OH.csv output_2_OH.csv
$ uv run location_price.py output_1_ON.csv output_2_ON.csv
```

3. Process both files using the standard_date.py script:

```
$ uv run standard_date.py output_2_OH.csv output_3_OH.csv
$ uv run standard_date.py output_2_ON.csv output_3_ON.csv
```

4. Transform the result into JSON:

```
$ uv run transform_into_json.py output_3_OH.csv output_4_OH.json
$ uv run transform_into_json.py output_3_ON.csv output_4_ON.json
```

5. Process all the files in a single call to `aggregate_by_location_by_pandas.py`, specifying the files to process:

```
$ uv run aggregate_by_location_by_pandas.py output_3_OH.csv
aggregate_pd_OH.csv
$ uv run aggregate_by_location_by_pandas.py output_3_ON.csv
aggregate_pd_ON.csv
```

6. Check the resulting CSV files, `aggregate_pd_OH.csv` and `aggregate_pd_ON.csv`, in a spreadsheet application. In the following screenshots, the files are displayed using LibreOffice:

| | A | B | C | D | E |
|---|---|---|---|---|---|
| 1 | DATE | TOTAL USD | NUMBER | AVERAGE | LOCATION |
| 2 | 2025-08-27 | 32.93 | 7 | 4.7 | OH |
| 3 | 2025-08-28 | 114.76 | 24 | 4.78 | OH |
| 4 | 2025-08-29 | 111.76 | 24 | 4.66 | OH |
| 5 | 2025-08-30 | 113.76 | 24 | 4.74 | OH |
| 6 | 2025-08-31 | 135.76 | 24 | 5.66 | OH |
| 7 | 2025-09-01 | 112.76 | 24 | 4.7 | OH |
| 8 | 2025-09-02 | 126.76 | 24 | 5.28 | OH |
| 9 | 2025-09-03 | 114.76 | 24 | 4.78 | OH |
| 10 | 2025-09-04 | 115.76 | 24 | 4.82 | OH |
| 11 | 2025-09-05 | 100.76 | 24 | 4.2 | OH |
| 12 | 2025-09-06 | 119.76 | 24 | 4.99 | OH |
| 13 | 2025-09-07 | 112.76 | 24 | 4.7 | OH |
| 14 | 2025-09-08 | 97.76 | 24 | 4.07 | OH |
| 15 | 2025-09-09 | 102.76 | 24 | 4.28 | OH |
| 16 | 2025-09-10 | 111.76 | 24 | 4.66 | OH |
| 17 | 2025-09-11 | 107.76 | 24 | 4.49 | OH |
| 18 | 2025-09-12 | 105.76 | 24 | 4.41 | OH |
| 19 | 2025-09-13 | 114.76 | 24 | 4.78 | OH |
| 20 | 2025-09-14 | 88.76 | 24 | 3.7 | OH |
| 21 | 2025-09-15 | 119.76 | 24 | 4.99 | OH |

*Figure 7.6: Checking the results of the recipe*

## How it works...

Let's take a look at the `aggregate_by_location_by_pandas.py` script, used in *step 5*.

> **Note**
>
> This recipe is equivalent to the *Aggregating results* recipe in this chapter.

The final part of the script file deals with the parsing of arguments, which was described in detail in *Chapter 2, Automating Tasks Made Easy*.

In Pandas, the basic data model is called a `DataFrame`, which in essence is a representation of a table with rows and columns. Most operations in Pandas are related to mutating the `DataFrame`.

The `main` function reads the input CSV and calls the `calculate_results` function to generate the aggregated reports.

We extract the location using a regex. The `r'_(\D*?).json'` pattern matches as few (`*?`) non-digits (`\D`) as possible after an underscore (`_`) and before the string `.json`. (Working with regexes was described in more detail in the *Introducing regular expressions* and *Going deeper with regular expressions* recipes in *Chapter 1, Let's Begin Our Automation Journey*.)

The use of `json.load` was described in the *Transforming and validating data in JSON* recipe in this chapter. The `calculate_results` function returns a `DataFrame`:

```
def main(input_file, output_file):
    # Find the location from the input_file
    match = re.search(r'_(\D*?)\.json', input_file.name)
    location = match.group(1)
    reader = json.load(input_file)
    result = calculate_results(reader, location)

    # Save into csv format
    output_file.write(result.to_csv())
```

The write operation to the output file uses Panda's `.to_csv()` function to generate from the `DataFrame` a text result that's equivalent to the CSV format. The data is written using the low-level `output.write()` call.

The aggregation takes place in the `calculate_results` function, in three phases. First, the data is imported into a `DataFrame`, then the values are aggregated, and finally the data is rounded to two decimal positions for compatibility. Let's take a look at the code:

```
def pandas_format(row):
    row['DATE'] = pd.to_datetime(row['STD_TIMESTAMP'])
    row['USD'] = pd.to_numeric(row['USD'])
    return row
def calculate_results(reader, location):
    # Load the data, formatting
    data = pd.DataFrame(pandas_format(r) for r in reader)
    by_usd = data.groupby(data['DATE'].dt.date)['USD']
    result = by_usd.agg(['sum', 'count', 'mean'])
    # Round to 2 digital places
    result = result.round(2)
    # Rename columns
    result = result.rename(columns={
        'sum': 'TOTAL USD',
        'count': 'NUMBER',
        'mean': 'AVERAGE',
    })
    result['LOCATION'] = location
    return result
```

The first line imports the data into a Pandas `DataFrame`. The `pandas_format` function adds the `DATE` column, transforming the standard timestamp into a `datetime` object, and transforms the `USD` column into a numeric format. This is all laying the groundwork to allow Pandas to work with these columns.

The core of the aggregation happens in these two lines:

```
    by_usd = data.groupby(data['DATE'].dt.date)['USD']
    result = by_usd.agg(['sum', 'count', 'mean'])
```

The first line transforms the `DataFrame` to group the results by the `DATE` column (which is a full `datetime` object), but only by date, i.e. without hour information. This aggregates the results by whole days. The grouped values are only presented for the `USD` column.

The second line aggregates the results, in three different ways: `sum` is used to get the total results, `count` to get the number of events, and `mean` for the average value. They all refer to the `USD` column, selected previously.

The rest of the `calculate_results` function is more straightforward. It first rounds the results to two decimal places with `.round(2)`. It then changes the names of the columns to be consistent with previous recipes. The `.rename` function uses a dictionary to define the input and output results.

To keep track of the `LOCATION` we add it as a constant column.

The resulting CSV file is equivalent to the one presented in the *Aggregating results* recipe, except for minimal format differences, such as the location of the `LOCATION` column.

## There's more...

The pattern shown in `calculate_results` when applying changes and overwriting the results is very common in Pandas:

```
result = by_usd.agg(['sum', 'count', 'mean'])
result = result.round(2)
result = result.rename(...)
```

This process can also be concatenated easily into the following:

```
result = by_usd.agg(['sum', 'count', 'mean']).round(2).rename(...)
```

> **Note**
>
> Before version 3 of `pandas`, this generated by default a copy of the data, which was not efficient for big amounts of data. Now copy-on-write is the default mode, which avoids unnecessary copies while still providing predictable behavior.
>
> You can learn more about the implications in the documentation, at `https://pandas.pydata.org/docs/user_guide/copy_on_write.html`.

Pandas is a big, complex package that has a lot of uses, from statistical analysis to plotting to complex mathematical applications. It is widely used in the data science community.

> **Tip**
>
> It's also well understood by GenAI, which can greatly assist you in shaping code for the operation you're trying to perform.

Pandas uses the approach of describing the desired result, instead of the operations that need to be performed.

> **Note**
>
> This approach is described as **declarative**, as opposed to imperative. Declarative languages aim at describing the result, the 'what', while imperative languages describe the 'how'. The most common example of a declarative language is SQL, used to interact with databases. Python is mainly an imperative language, but as we see in Pandas, the declarative approach can be used as well.
>
> Defining the result allows the use internally of low-level operations to produce great results.

Pandas is very commonly used with Jupyter Notebook. This application allows users to create rich Python sessions that mix code execution, documentation, and graphs for a rich environment in the form of notebooks that can be accessed via a web browser. It's capable of automatically presenting data from modules such as `pandas` or `matplotlib`.

The aim of this project is to allow the exploration of data, instead of following a more repetitive process as when using an automated tool, but Jupyter Notebook is a fantastic tool to know how to use.

The notebook can be tested online at `https://jupyter.org/try`. Go to the main web page at `https://jupyter.org/` to check how to install it locally and read the complete documentation.

Here is an example session displaying some data:

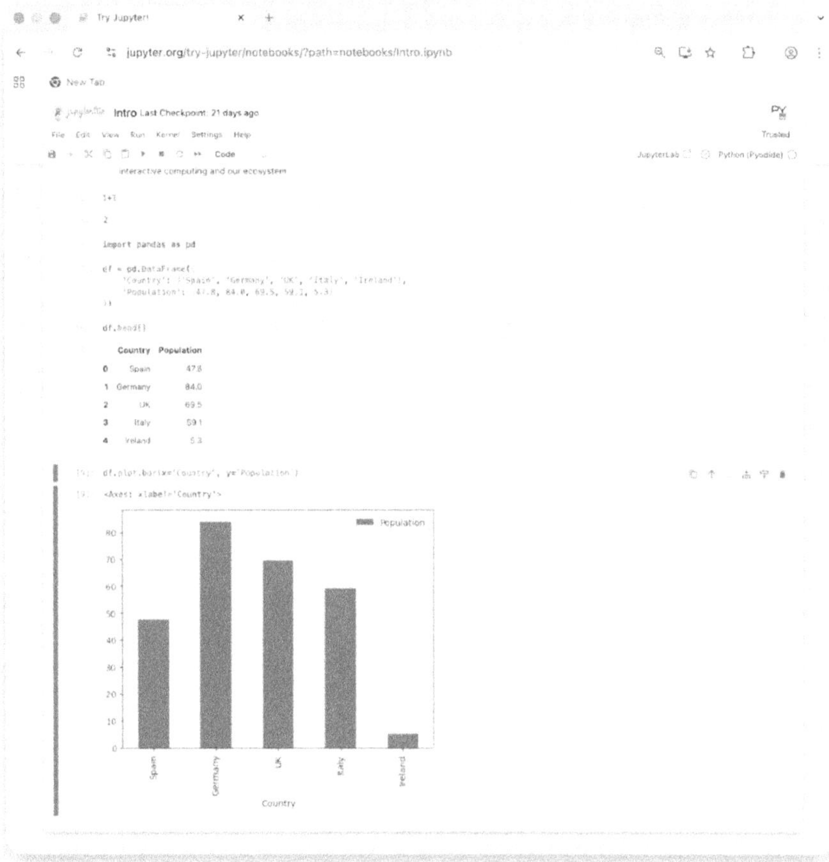


*Figure 7.7: The Jupyter Notebook*

You can find the complete Pandas documentation at `https://pandas.pydata.org/docs/user_guide/index.html`.

**Tip**

Another alternative, out of scope for this book, is to perform these kinds of operations in a SQL database, where the SQL code can express the operations. Python has library support to connect to most available databases, and it's even able to work locally with SQLite (`https://sqlite.org`), a SQL database that works against a local file. This makes it possible to create a local database, import all your data into it, and then query it.

Documentation for the standard library module for working with SQLite is available at `https://docs.python.org/3/library/sqlite3.html`.

## See also

- The *Aggregating results* recipe, earlier in this chapter.
- The *Reading CSV files* recipe in *Chapter 4, Searching and Reading Local Files.*
- The *Preparing a task* recipe in *Chapter 2, Automating Tasks Made Easy.*

# Get this book's PDF version and more

Scan the QR code (or go to `packtpub.com/unlock`). Search for this book by name, confirm the edition, and then follow the steps on the page.

UNLOCK NOW

*Note: Keep your invoice handy. Purchases made directly from Packt don't require an invoice.*

# 8

# Developing Stunning Graphs

Graphs and images are fantastic ways of presenting complex data in an easy-to-understand way. In this chapter, we will make use of powerful Python libraries to learn how to create all kinds of graphs. We will mainly use `matplotlib`, a library aimed at displaying data in multiple ways and which can create stunning plots that help transmit and display information, but we will also use `plotly`.

> **Note**
>
> `matplotlib` is well known and interacts well with other tools in the Python ecosystem. For `example`, `matplotlib` graphs can also be automatically displayed by Jupyter Notebooks as introduced in *Chapter 7, Cleaning and Processing Data*.

The graphs we'll cover will go from simple bar graphs to line graphs, and combine multiple plots in the same graph, annotate them, and even draw geographical maps.

The following recipes will be covered in this chapter:

- Plotting a simple sales graph
- Drawing stacked bars
- Displaying multiple lines
- Drawing a scatter plot
- Visualizing map info
- Adding legends and annotations
- Combining graphs

- Saving charts
- Plotting a chart with plotly

Let's start by creating our first graph.

# Technical requirements

You can check the code presented in the chapter in the GitHub URL `https://github.com/PacktPublishing/Python-Automation-Cookbook-Third-Edition/tree/main/ch08`.

# Plotting a simple sales graph

In this recipe we'll see how to draw a sales chart by drawing bars proportional to sales in different periods.

## Getting ready

We can install `matplotlib` in our environment using the following commands:

```
$ echo "matplotlib==3.10.8" >> requirements.txt
$ uv pip install -r requirements.txt
```

## How to do it...

1. Import `matplotlib`:

```
>>> import matplotlib.pyplot as plt
```

2. Prepare the data to be displayed on the graph:

```
>>> DATA = (
...     ('Q1 2025', 100),
...     ('Q2 2025', 150),
...     ('Q3 2025', 125),
...     ('Q4 2025', 175),
... )
```

3. Split the data into usable formats for the graph. This is a preparation step:

```
>>> POS = list(range(len(DATA)))
>>> VALUES = [value for label, value in DATA]
>>> LABELS = [label for label, value in DATA]
```

4. Create a bar graph with the data:

```
>>> plt.bar(POS, VALUES)
<BarContainer object of 4 artists>
>>> plt.xticks(POS, LABELS)
([<matplotlib.axis.XTick object at 0x111350c20>, <matplotlib.axis.XTick
object at 0x1113ace10>, <matplotlib.axis.XTick object at 0x1113ad1d0>,
<matplotlib.axis.XTick object at 0x1113ad590>], [Text(0, 0, 'Q1 2025'),
Text(1, 0, 'Q2 2025'), Text(2, 0, 'Q3 2025'), Text(3, 0, 'Q4 2025')])
>>> plt.ylabel('Sales')
Text(76.31944444444443, 0.5, 'Sales')
```

5. Display the graph:

```
>>> plt.show()
```

The result will be displayed as follows in a new window:

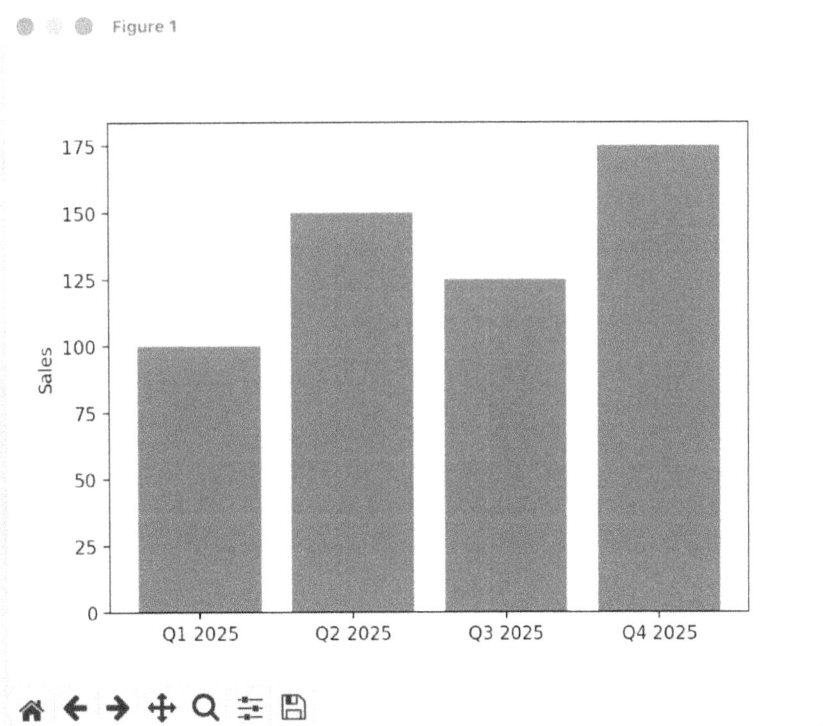


*Figure 8.1: Displayed graph*

## How it works...

After importing the module, the data is presented in *step 2* of the *How to do it...* section in a useable structure.

Because of the way `matplotlib` works, the graph requires an *X* component, as well as a *Y* component. In this case, our *X* component is just a sequence of increasing numbers, as many as there are data points. We store that in the variable `POS`. This positions each of the *Y* values and works as a temporal series. In `VALUES`, we store the numeric value of the sales as a sequence, and in `LABELS`, we store the associated label for each data point. All that preparation work is done in *step 3*.

*Step 4* creates the bar graph with the sequences *X* (`POS`) and *Y* (`VALUES`). These define our bars. To specify the period it refers to, we put labels on the *x-axis* for each value with `.xticks` in the same way. To clarify the meaning, we add a label with `.ylabel`.

To display the resulting graph, *step 5* calls `.show`, which opens a new window with the result.

> **Tip**
>
> Calling `.show` blocks the execution of the program. The program will resume when the window is closed.

## There's more...

You may want to change the format in which the values are presented. In our example, maybe the numbers represent millions of dollars. To do so, you can add a formatter to the *y-axis*, so the values represented there will have it applied to them:

```
>>> from matplotlib.ticker import FuncFormatter
>>> def value_format(value, position):
...     return '$ {}M'.format(int(value))
>>> axes = plt.gca()
>>> axes.yaxis.set_major_formatter(FuncFormatter(value_format))
```

`value_format` is a function that returns a value based on the value and position of the data. Here, it will return the value 100 as $100M.

> **Tip**
>
> Values will be retrieved as floats, requiring you to transform them into integers for display.

To apply the formatter, we need to retrieve the axis object with `.gca` (get current axes). Then, the `.yaxis` attribute sets up the formatter for the *y-axis* labels.

Even though using default colors can be good enough in many situations, you can define the color of the bars with the `color` parameter. Colors can be specified in multiple formats, including the common hexadecimal color code (e.g. vivid red as `#FF1A1A`), as described at `https://matplotlib.org/stable/api/colors_api.html`, but my favorite method is to follow the XKCD color survey using the `xkcd:` prefix (no space after the colon):

```
>>> plt.bar(POS, VALUES, color='xkcd:moss green')
```

The full survey can be found at `https://xkcd.com/color/rgb/`; it provides codes for many go-to colors.

> **Tip**
>
> Most common colors, such as blue and red, are also available for quick tests. They tend to be a little too bright and harsh to be used in good-looking reports, though. They also don't print properly on paper.
>
> Remember that GenAI can help in picking colors on the basis of descriptions you give in the prompt, e.g. '*get me, in hexadecimal code, a dark green for a graph that looks professional*'.

Combining the color with formatting the axis gives us the following result:

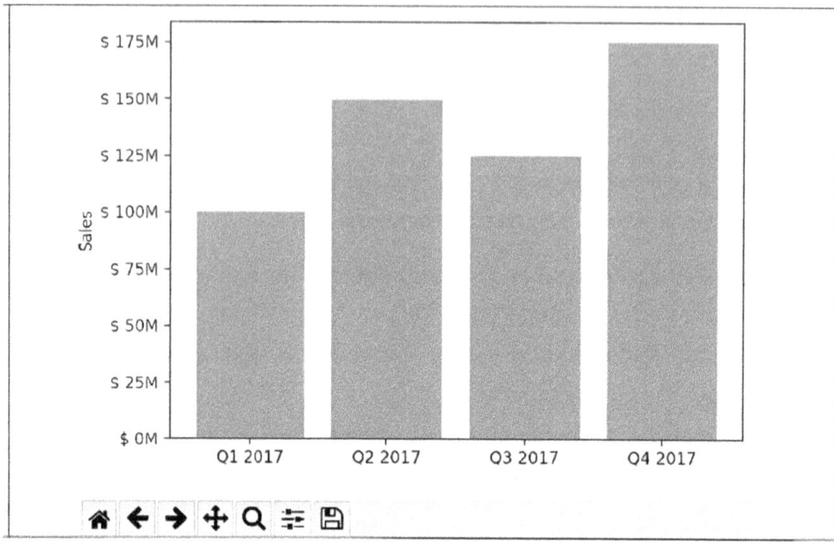


*Figure 8.2: Graph with a different color*

Bar graphs don't need to display information in a temporal way. As we've seen, `matplotlib` requires us to specify the *X* parameter of each bar.

> **Tip**
>
> For example, the bars can be arranged to display a histogram, e.g. for displaying the distribution of people's heights. The bars will start at a low height, increase to the average size, and then drop back. Don't limit yourself to just time information charts!

The full matplotlib documentation can be found here: `https://matplotlib.org/`.

## See also

- The *Drawing stacked bars* recipe, next in this chapter, to learn how to plot more accumulated information on each bar.
- The *Adding legends and annotations* recipe, later in this chapter, to learn how to add context information to a graph.
- The *Combining graphs* recipe, later in this chapter, to learn how to combine multiple plots into a single graph.

# Drawing stacked bars

A powerful way of displaying different categories is to present them as stacked bars so that each of the categories and the total are displayed. We'll see how to do that in this recipe.

## Getting ready

We can install `matplotlib` in our environment using the following commands:

```
$ echo "matplotlib==3.10.8" >> requirements.txt
$ uv pip install -r requirements.txt
```

## How to do it...

1. Import `matplotlib`:

```
>>> import matplotlib.pyplot as plt
```

2. Prepare the data. This represents the sales of two products, an established product and a new one:

```
>>> DATA = (
...     ('Q1 2025', 100, 0),
...     ('Q2 2025', 105, 15),
...     ('Q3 2025', 125, 40),
...     ('Q4 2025', 115, 80),
... )
```

3. Process the data to prepare the expected format:

```
>>> POS = list(range(len(DATA)))
>>> VALUESA = [valueA for label, valueA, valueB in DATA]
>>> VALUESB = [valueB for label, valueA, valueB in DATA]
>>> LABELS = [label for label, value1, value2 in DATA]
```

4. Create the bar plot. Two plots are required:

```
>>> plt.bar(POS, VALUESB)
<BarContainer object of 4 artists>
>>> plt.bar(POS, VALUESA, bottom=VALUESB)
<BarContainer object of 4 artists>
```

```
>>> plt.ylabel('Sales')
Text(93.94444444444443, 0.5, 'Sales')
>>> plt.xticks(POS, LABELS)
([<matplotlib.axis.XTick object at 0x117d39d10>, <matplotlib.axis.XTick
object at 0x117d3b610>, <matplotlib.axis.XTick object at 0x117d3b9d0>,
<matplotlib.axis.XTick object at 0x117d3bd90>], [Text(0, 0, 'Q1 2025'),
Text(1, 0, 'Q2 2025'), Text(2, 0, 'Q3 2025'), Text(3, 0, 'Q4 2025')])
```

5. Display the graph:

```
>>> plt.show()
```

6. The result will be displayed in a new window, as follows:

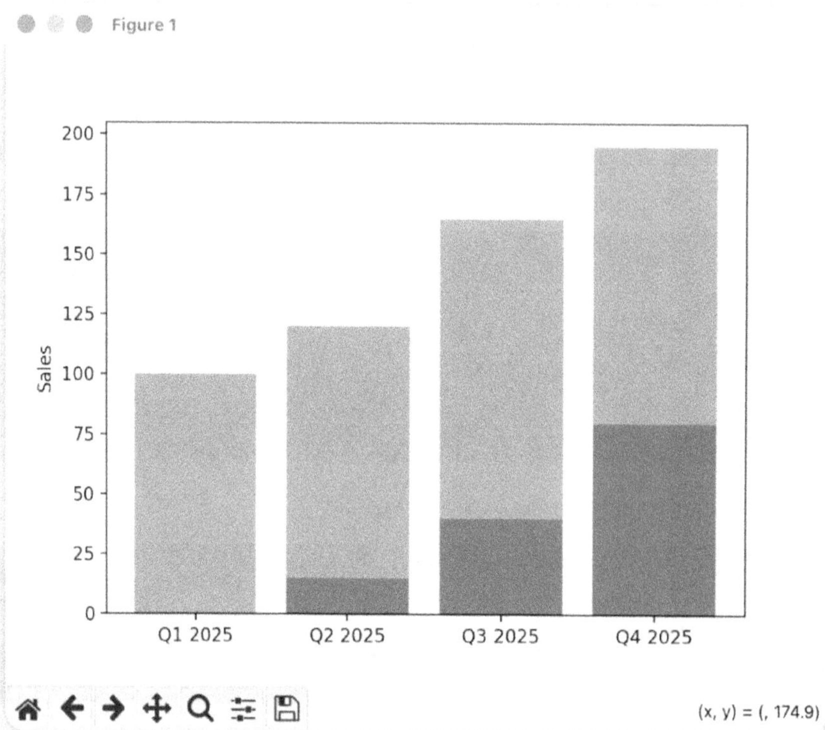


Figure 8.3: Stacked bars

## How it works...

After importing the module, the data is presented in *step 2* in a useable structure.

In *step 3* the data is prepared in three sequences: `VALUESA`, `VALUESB`, and `LABELS`. A `POS` increasing sequence is added so that the bars are positioned over the *x-axis*, one after the other.

*Step 4* creates the bar graph with the sequences *X* (`POS`) and *Y* (`VALUESB`). The second bar sequence, `VALUESA`, is added on top of the previous sequence using the `bottom=VALUESB` argument. This process stacks both bars, positioning the full `VALUESA` bar on top of the `VALUESB` bar.

> **Tip**
>
> Notice that we stack the second value, `VALUESB`, first. The second value represents a new product that was introduced to the market. `VALUESA` represents the established product and is more stable. This graph puts the emphasis on the growth of the new product.
>
> Drawing graphs is an exercise in presenting information in a way that's easy to understand. That may require you to experiment until you find the best approach. Don't be afraid to do so.

Each of the periods is labeled on the *x-axis* with `.xticks`. To clarify the meaning, we add a label with `.ylabel`.

To display the resulting graph, *step 5* calls `.show`, which opens a new window with the result.

> **Tip**
>
> Calling `.show` blocks the execution of the program. The program will resume when the window is closed.

## There's more...

> **Note**
>
> For this section we present alternative ways of displaying the information. Be sure to repeat the previous steps to define the data available as well as to display the '*Sales*' labels, etc.

Another way of presenting stacked bars is by adding them as percentages so that the total doesn't change, only their relative sizes compared to each other.

To do that, VALUESA and VALUEB need to be calculated relative to the percentages in this way:

```
>>> VALUESA = [100 * valueA / (valueA + valueB) for label, valueA, valueB in DATA]
>>> VALUESB = [100 * valueB / (valueA + valueB) for label, valueA, valueB in DATA]
```

This makes each value equal to the percentage of the total, and the total always adds up to 100. This produces the following graphic:

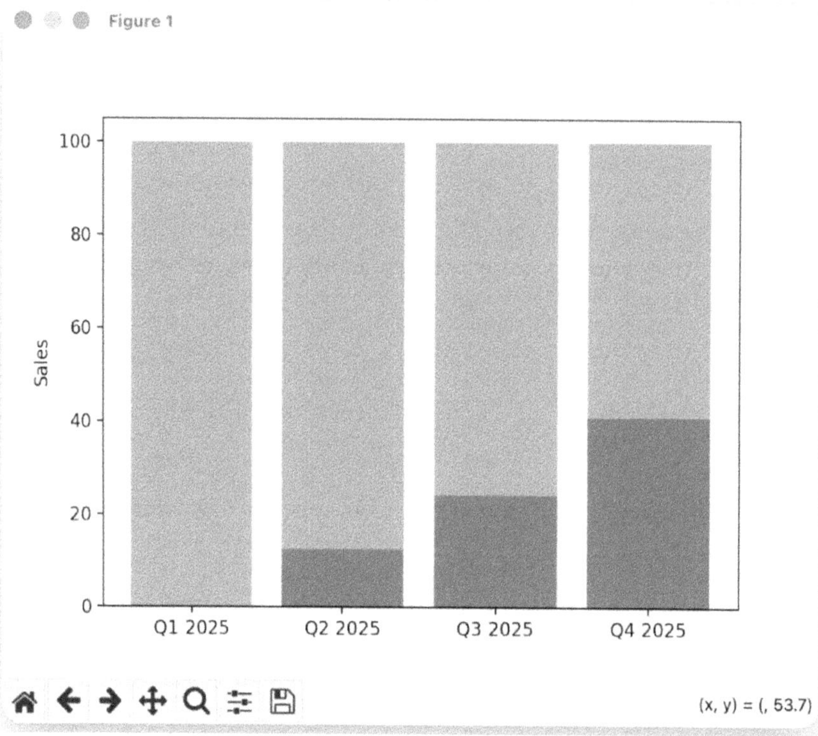


Figure 8.4: Stacking percentages

The bars don't necessarily need to be stacked. Sometimes, it may be interesting to present the bars side-by-side for comparison.

To do that, we need to move the position of the second bar sequence. We'll also need to set thinner bars to allow space:

```
>>> WIDTH = 0.3
>>> plt.bar([p - WIDTH / 2 for p in POS], VALUESA, width=WIDTH)
>>> plt.bar([p + WIDTH / 2 for p in POS], VALUESB, width=WIDTH)
```

Note how the width of the bar is set to a third of the space, since our reference space is 1 unit between the bars. This space is adjusted automatically depending on the size of the chart. The first bar is moved to the left, while the second bar is moved to the right to center them. The bottom argument has been deleted so that the bars aren't stacked:

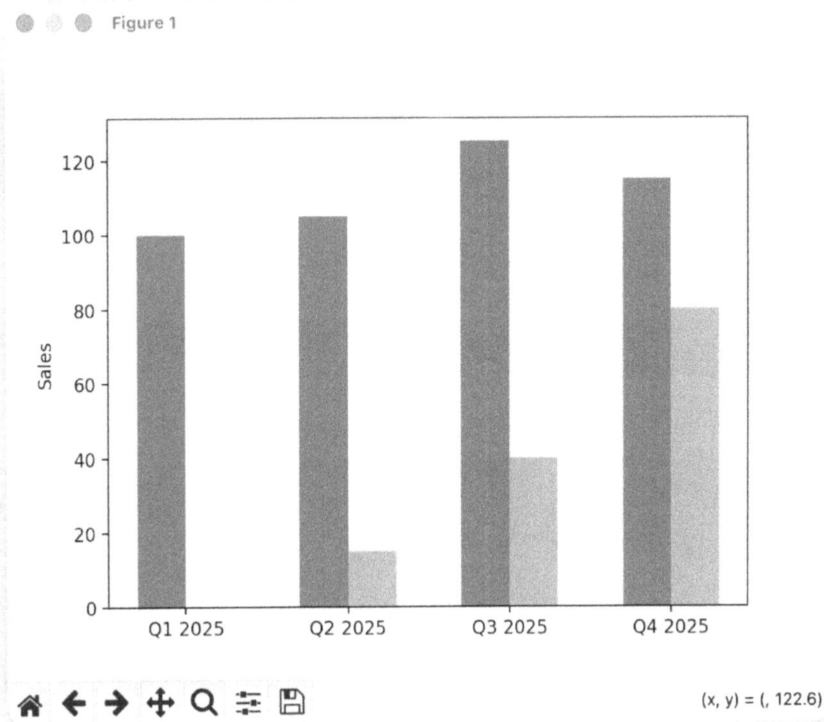


*Figure 8.5: Independent bars*

The full `matplotlib` documentation can be found here: `https://matplotlib.org/`.

## See also

- The previous recipe, *Plotting a simple sales graph* recipe, to learn the basics of drawing bar graphs.
- The *Adding legends and annotations* recipe, later in this chapter, to learn how to add context information to a graph.
- The *Combining graphs* recipe, later in this chapter, to learn how to add multiple plots to a single graph.

# Displaying multiple lines

This recipe will show you how to display multiple lines in a graph.

## Getting ready

First we install `matplotlib` in our environment using the following commands:

```
$ echo "matplotlib==3.10.8" >> requirements.txt
$ uv pip install -r requirements.txt
```

## How to do it...

1. Import `matplotlib`:

```
>>> import matplotlib.pyplot as plt
```

2. Prepare the data. This represents two products' sales:

```
>>> DATA = (
...     ('Q1 2025', 100, 5),
...     ('Q2 2025', 105, 15),
...     ('Q3 2025', 125, 40),
...     ('Q4 2025', 115, 80),
... )
```

3. Process the data to prepare the expected format:

```
>>> POS = list(range(len(DATA)))
>>> VALUESA = [valueA for label, valueA, valueB in DATA]
>>> VALUESB = [valueB for label, valueA, valueB in DATA]
>>> LABELS = [label for label, value1, value2 in DATA]
```

4. Create the line plot. Two lines are required:

```
>>> plt.plot(POS, VALUESA, 'o-')
[<matplotlib.lines.Line2D object at 0x118338980>]
>>> plt.plot(POS, VALUESB, 'o-')
[<matplotlib.lines.Line2D object at 0x1183906e0>]
>>> plt.ylabel('Sales')
Text(76.31944444444443, 0.5, 'Sales')
```

```
>>> plt.xticks(POS, LABELS)
([<matplotlib.axis.XTick object at 0x1182ffd90>, <matplotlib.axis.XTick
object at 0x118329450>, <matplotlib.axis.XTick object at 0x118329810>,
<matplotlib.axis.XTick object at 0x118329bd0>], [Text(0, 0, 'Q1 2025'),
Text(1, 0, 'Q2 2025'), Text(2, 0, 'Q3 2025'), Text(3, 0, 'Q4 2025')])
```

5. Display the graph:

```
>>> plt.show()
```

6. The result will be displayed in a new window:

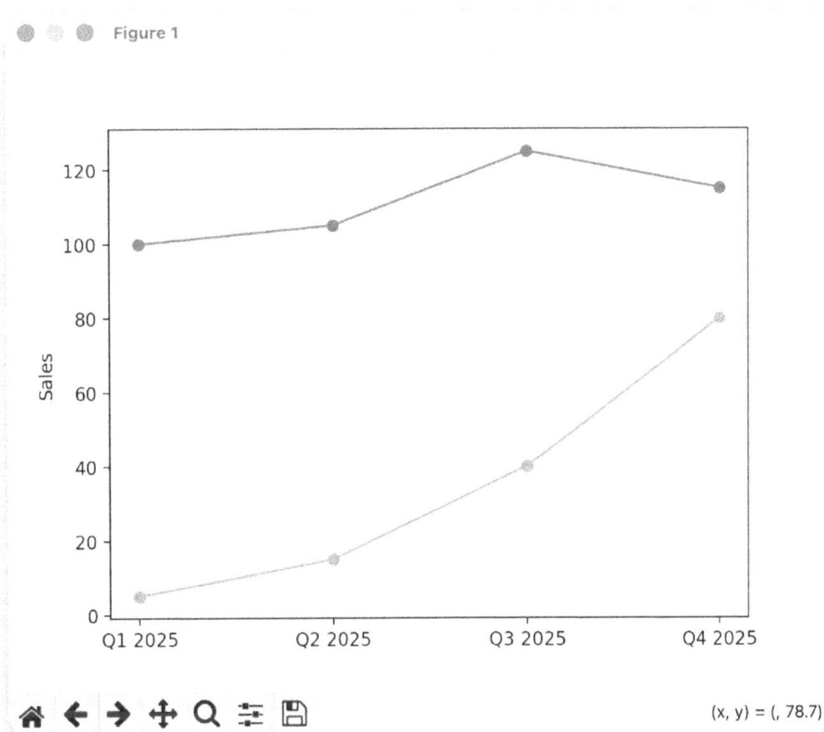


Figure 8.6: Line chart

## How it works...

In the *How to do it...* section, *step 1* imports the module and *step 2* shows the data to be plotted in a formatted way.

In *step 3* the data is prepared in three sequences: `VALUESA`, `VALUEB`, and `LABELS`. A `POS` increasing sequence is used to locate each of the points along the *x-axis*.

*Step 4* creates the graph with the sequences *X* (`POS`) and *Y* (`VALUESA`), and then `POS` and `VALUESB`. The value `'o-'` is added to draw a circle on each of the data points and a full line between them.

> **Tip**
>
> By default, the plot will display a solid line, with no marker on each point. If only the marker is used (that is, 'o'), there'll be no line.

Each of the periods is labeled on the *x-axis* with `.xticks`. To clarify the meaning, we add a label with `.ylabel`.

To display the resulting graph, *step 5* calls `.show`, which opens a new window containing the result.

> **Note**
>
> Calling `.show` blocks execution of the program. The program will resume when the window is closed.

## There's more...

Graphs with lines are deceptively simple and using them it is possible to create a variety of interesting representations. It is probably the most convenient option when showing mathematical graphs. For example, we can display a graph showing **Moore's Law** in a few lines of code.

> **Tip**
>
> Moore's Law is an observation by Gordon Moore that the number of components in an integrated circuit doubles every 2 years. It was first described in 1965 and then corrected in 1975. It seems to be quite close to the historic rate of technological advancement over the last 50 years.

The code is available in `https://github.com/PacktPublishing/Python-Automation-Cookbook-Third-Edition/tree/main/ch08/moores.py`.

We first create a line that describes the theoretical line, with data points from 1970 to 2025. Starting with 1,000 transistors, we double it every 2 years, up to 2025:

```
import matplotlib.pyplot as plt

POS = [year for year in range(1970, 2025)]
MOORES = [1000 * (2 ** (i * 0.5)) for i in range(len(POS))]
plt.plot(POS, MOORES)
```

Using readily available information (`https://en.wikipedia.org/wiki/Microprocessor_chronology.`), we extract a few examples of commercial CPUs, with year of release and number of integrated components.

As the numbers are very large, we'll use the notation of 1_000_000 for 1 million, available in Python 3:

```
DATA = (
    ('Intel 4004', 2_250, 1971),
    ('Motorola 68000', 68_000, 1979),
    ('Intel Pentium', 3_100_000, 1993),
    ('Intel Itanium', 25_000_000, 2001),
    ('Intel Core i7', 730_000_000, 2008),
    ('AMD Zen', 4_800_000_000, 2017),
    ('Apple M1', 16_000_000_000, 2020),
    ('Apple M4', 28_000_000_000, 2024),
)
```

Draw a line with markers to display those points at the proper places. The 'v' mark will display a triangle:

```
data_x = [x for label, y, x in DATA]
data_y = [y for label, y, x in DATA]
plt.plot(data_x, data_y, 'v')
```

For each data point, append a label in the proper place with the name of the CPU. We increase the *X* and *Y* position by one point to slightly separate the label from the marker:

```
for label, y, x in DATA:
    plt.text(x + 1, y + 1, label)
```

Finally, this level of growth doesn't make sense displayed in a linear graph, so we change the scale to be logarithmic, which makes exponential growth look like a straight line. But, to give a sense of dimension, we add a grid. Finally, we call `.show` to display the graph:

```
plt.gca().grid()
plt.yscale('log')

plt.show()
```

Running

```
$ uv run moores.py
```

Shows the graph. As usual, exit the window to close the execution of the script.

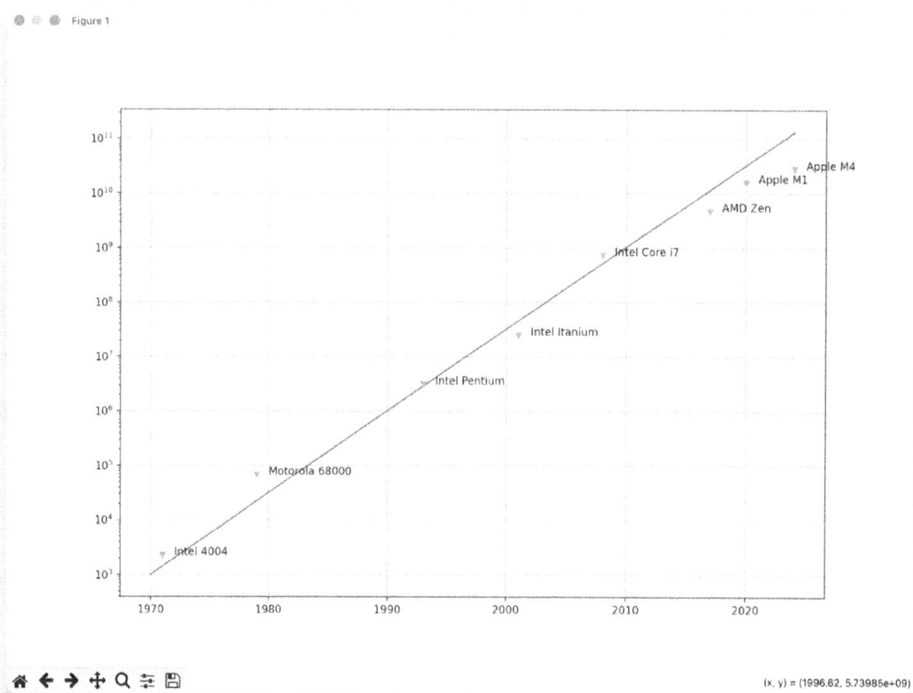


*Figure 8.7: Moore's Law graph*

Even if in the last decade the rate of growth has been a bit lower than expected, you can see that the transistor counts of real processors still conform pretty closely to the Moore's Law predictions!

The full matplotlib documentation can be found at `https://matplotlib.org/`. In particular, check the available formats for lines (solid, dashed, dotted, and so on) and markers (dot, circle, triangle, star, and so on) here: `https://matplotlib.org/stable/api/_as_gen/matplotlib.pyplot.plot.html`.

## See also

- The *Adding legends and annotations* recipe, later in this chapter, to learn how to add context information to a graph.
- The *Combining graphs* recipe, later in this chapter, to learn how to add multiple plots to a single graph.

# Drawing a scatter plot

A scatter plot is one where the information is displayed as dots with *X* and *Y* values. They are very useful when presenting data with two dimensions (not necessarily a time series as seen previously) and to see whether there's any relationship between two variables. In this recipe we'll plot time spent on a website against money spent, to see whether we can see a pattern.

## Getting ready

We can install `matplotlib` in our environment using the following commands:

```
$ echo "matplotlib==3.10.8" >> requirements.txt
$ uv pip install -r requirements.txt
```

As we're going to be working with data points, we'll use the `scatter.csv` file as the source of our data. This file is available on GitHub at `https://github.com/PacktPublishing/Python-Automation-Cookbook-Third-Edition/blob/main/ch08/scatter.csv`.

## How to do it...

1. Import `matplotlib`, `csv`, and `FuncFormatter` (to format the axes later):

```
>>> import csv
>>> import matplotlib.pyplot as plt
>>> from matplotlib.ticker import FuncFormatter
```

2. Prepare the data, reading from the file using the `csv` module:

```
>>> with open('scatter.csv') as fp:
...     reader = csv.reader(fp)
...     data = list(reader)
```

3. Prepare the data for plotting:

```
>>> data_x = [float(x) for x, y in data]
>>> data_y = [float(y) for x, y in data]
```

4. Plot the data:

```
>>> plt.scatter(data_x, data_y)
<matplotlib.collections.PathCollection object at 0x11022f8c0>
```

5. Improve the context by formatting the axes:

```
>>> def format_minutes(value, pos):
...     return '{}m'.format(int(value))
>>> def format_dollars(value, pos):
...     return '${}'.format(value)
>>> plt.gca().xaxis.set_major_formatter(FuncFormatter(format_minutes))
>>> plt.xlabel('Time in website')
Text(0.5, 47.04444444444444, 'Time in website')
>>> plt.gca().yaxis.set_major_formatter(FuncFormatter(format_dollars))
>>> plt.ylabel('Spending')
Text(76.31944444444443, 0.5, 'Spending')
```

6. Show the graph:

```
>>> plt.show()
```

The result will be displayed in a new window:

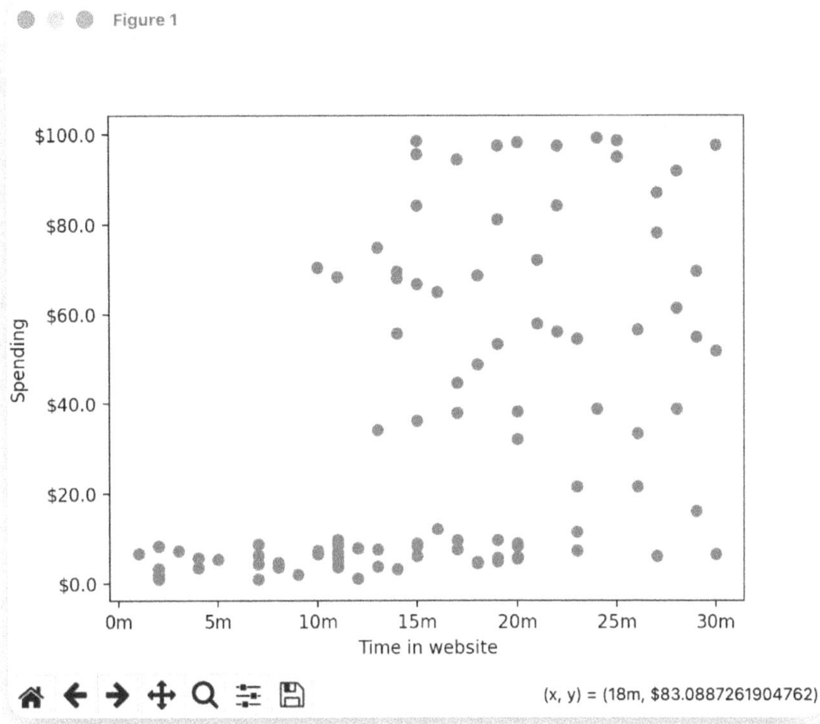


*Figure 8.8: Scatter plot*

## How it works...

*Step 1* of the *How to do it...* section imports the modules we'll use later.

*Step 2* reads the data from the CSV file. The data is transformed into a list to allow us to iterate through it several times, as that's necessary for *step 3*.

*Step 3* prepares the data in two arrays and then uses `.scatter` to plot them. The parameters for `.scatter`, as with other methods of `matplotlib`, include an array of *X* and *Y* values. They both need to be the same size. The data is converted into a `float` from the file format to ensure the number format.

*Step 4* refines the way the data is presented on each axis. For each axis, a function is created that defines how the values on that axis should be displayed (in dollars or in minutes). The function accepts as inputs the value to display and the position. Typically, the position will be ignored. The axis formatter will be overwritten with `.set_major_formatter`. Notice that both axes are returned with `.gca` (get current axes).

Labels are added to the axes with `.xlabel` and `.ylabel`.

Finally, *step 5* displays the graph in a new window. Analyzing the result, we can say that there seem to be two kinds of user: those who spend less than 10 minutes and never spend more than $10, and users who spend more time and also have a higher chance of spending up to $100.

> **Tip**
>
> Note that the data presented is synthetic, and it has been generated with the result in mind with two visible clusters to make the technique easier to learn. Real-life data will probably look more spread out. Statistical analysis can be used to determine trends and patterns with a higher degree of sophistication.

## There's more...

A scatter plot can display not only points in two dimensions but can also add a third (via area) and even a fourth dimension (via color).

> **Tip**
>
> Technically is possible to show scatter plots with three dimensions with a Z axis, but those graphs are difficult to read

To add those elements, use the parameters `s` for size and `c` for color.

> **Note**
>
> `size` is defined as the diameter of a ball in points squared. So, for a ball of diameter 10, 100 will be used. `color` can use any of the usual definitions of color in `matplotlib`, such as hex color, RGB, and so on. See the documentation for more details: `https://matplotlib.org/stable/users/explain/colors/colors.html`.
>
> Remember that you can use XKCD colors or ask GenAI to generate a palette.

For example, we can generate a random graph using the four dimensions in the following way:

```
>>> import matplotlib.pyplot as plt
>>> import random
>>> NUM_POINTS = 100
>>> COLOR_SCALE = [
```

```
...     '#8B1E1E',  # darkest - muted red
...     '#1F6F43',  # dark green
...     '#B36A00',  # amber
...     '#4F8F6A',  # mid green
...     '#C9B458'   # brightest - muted gold
... ]
>>> data_x = [random.random() for _ in range(NUM_POINTS)]
>>> data_y = [random.random() for _ in range(NUM_POINTS)]
>>> size = [(50 * random.random()) ** 2 for _ in range(NUM_POINTS)]
>>> color = [random.choice(COLOR_SCALE) for _ in range(NUM_POINTS)]
>>> plt.scatter(data_x, data_y, s=size, c=color, alpha=0.5)
<matplotlib.collections.PathCollection object at 0x115920a50>
>>> plt.show()
```

`COLOR_SCALE` goes from red to green to yellow, and the size of each of the points will be between 0 and 50 points in diameter. The result should be something like this:

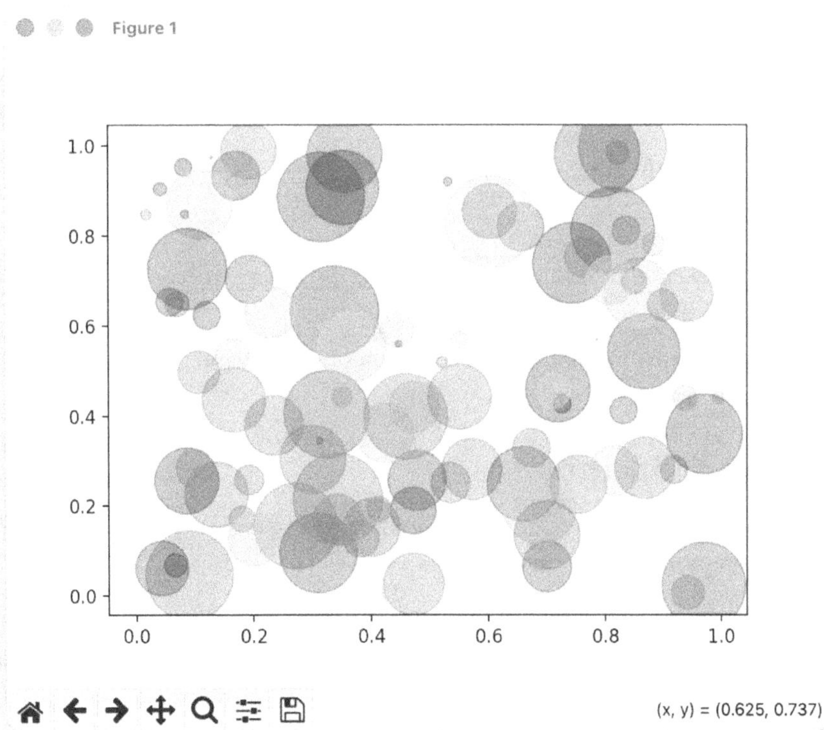


*Figure 8.9: Displaying points, sizes, and colors*

Note that the values are random, so each time the code is run it will generate a different plot.

The alpha value makes each of the points semi-transparent, allowing us to see where they overlap. The higher this value is, the less transparent the points will be. This parameter will affect the displayed color as it will blend the point in with the background.

> Tip
>
> Even though it's possible to display independent values via the size and color of plots, they can also be related. For example, making the color dependent on the size will make all the points of the same size the same color, which may help us distinguish between different components of the data, reinforcing the information. Remember that the ultimate goal of a graph is to make data easy to understand. Try different approaches to achieve this.
>
> You can also get recommendations using GenAI tools to see what's the best way to present certain data and quickly iterate solutions. For example, changing the range of colors is very easy with GenAI, but you can be more ambitious and get ideas through prompts like '*what is the best plot style to display this data representing power vs energy consumption for different kinds of machine?*'

The full `matplotlib` documentation can be found here: `https://matplotlib.org/`.

## See also

- The *Displaying multiple lines* recipe, earlier in this chapter, to learn how to plot multiple lines that follow a temporal series.
- The *Adding legends and annotations* recipe, later in this chapter, to learn how to add context information to a graph.

# Visualizing map info

To best way to show information that changes from region to region is to create a map that presents the information in a way that provides a sense of geographic location.

In this recipe, we'll make use of the `Geopandas` module to import GIS information, as well as `matplotlib` to display it. We will display a map of Western Europe and show the population of each country with a color grade. The darker the color, the larger the population.

## Getting ready

We need to install `matplotlib` and `geopandas` in our virtual environment:

```
$ echo "matplotlib==3.10.8" >> requirements.txt
$ echo "geopandas==1.1.2" >> requirements.txt
$ uv pip install -r requirements.txt
```

The map data needs to be downloaded. Fortunately there's a lot of freely available geographic information. A search on Google should quickly return almost everything you need, including detailed information on regions, counties, rivers, or any other kind of data.

> **Note**
>
> GIS information is available in different formats from a lot of public organizations. `geopandas` can handle most common formats and is able to treat them in equivalent ways, but there are small differences. Read the documentation for more details: `https://geopandas.org/en/stable/docs.html`.

The data we'll use in this recipe, covering all European countries, is available on GitHub at the following URL: `https://github.com/leakyMirror/map-of-europe/blob/master/GeoJSON/europe.geojson`. Note that it is in GeoJSON, which is an easy standard to work with.

## How to do it...

1. Import the modules:

```
>>> import matplotlib.pyplot as plt
>>> import geopandas
```

2. Load the population of the countries to display:

```
>>> COUNTRIES_POPULATION = {
...     'Spain': 47.8,
...     'Portugal': 10.4,
...     'United Kingdom': 69.5,
...     'Ireland': 5.3,
...     'France': 66.6,
...     'Italy': 59.1,
...     'Germany': 84.0,
...     'Netherlands': 18.3,
```

```
...     'Belgium': 11.7,
...     'Denmark': 6.0,
...     'Slovenia': 2.1,
...     'Austria': 9.1,
...     'Luxembourg': 0.7,
...     'Andorra': 0.082,
...     'Switzerland': 8.9,
...     'Liechtenstein': 0.040,
... }
```

3. Open the file and read the data, filtering by the countries for which we defined the populations in *step 1*:

```
>>> full_europe_map = geopandas.read_file('europe.geojson')
>>> weurope_map =
full_europe_map[full_europe_map['NAME'].isin(COUNTRIES_POPULATION)]
```

4. Map the population of each country:

```
>>> weurope_map['POPULATION'] =
weurope_map['NAME'].map(COUNTRIES_POPULATION)
```

5. Plot the map, showing the POPULATION column, in a range of greens:

```
>>> weurope_map.plot(column='POPULATION', cmap='Greens')
<Axes: >
```

6. Display the result:

```
>>> plt.show()
```

The result will be displayed in a new window, as follows:

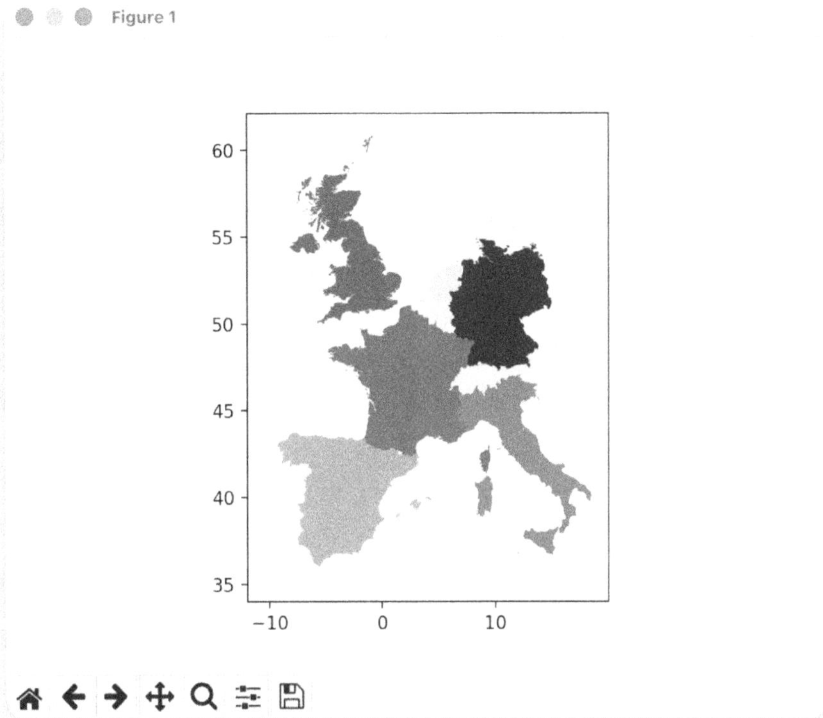


*Figure 8.10: Displaying a map*

## How it works...

After importing the modules in *step 1* from the *How to do it...* section, the data to be displayed is defined in *step 2*. Note that the names need to be in the same format as they'll be in the GEO file.

> **Note**
>
> The population has been rounded to a significant number, and it's defined in millions. Only a few countries have been defined for this recipe, but more are available in the GIS file.

The GIS information is then retrieved in *step 3*. `geopandas` reads the `europe.geojson` file and the data is copied so we can use it in the next steps.

> **Note**
>
> GIS information is stored as points represented by coordinates for latitude and longitude. Areas, such as countries, are defined by lists of coordinates delimiting the area within them. Some maps are more precise and use more points to define areas. Multiple polygons may be required to define a country, as some parts may be separated from others, with islands being the most obvious case, but there are also exclaves. Exclaves are regions of countries detached from the main body, like Alaska.

The data is returned in a `DataFrame` object, as with the `panda` module. We call it `full_europe_map`, because it contains all the countries available in the GIS file. But immediately we filter out the ones that are not in the `COUNTRIES_POPULATION`, using this command:

```
weurope_map = full_europe_map[full_europe_map['NAME'].isin(COUNTRIES_POPULATION)]
```

We filter the `full_europe_map` by `NAME` to just the keys present in `COUNTRIES_POPULATION`, by using `.isin`.

> **Tip**
>
> Notice that we operate on a `DataFrame` by applying operations to the whole of it, not by creating loops or iterating. This is the expected way of working with `DataFrames`.

In *step 4* we create a new column, `POPULATION`, for the `DataFrame` to store the population information. We use `.map` to assign each key in `COUNTRIES_POPULATION` to the matching `NAME` row.

In *step 5*, we plot the map value for `POPULATION`, using a color range that is a scale of `Greens`. This is one standard `colormap` in `matplotlib`, but we can use others, such as `Oranges`, `Reds`, or `plasma` for a more cold-to-hot approach. More details are available in the documentation: `https://matplotlib.org/stable/users/explain/colors/colormaps.html`.

Finally, the data is displayed by calling `.show` in *step 6*.

## There's more...

Taking advantage of the information contained in the GIS file, we can add extra information to the map. The properties object contains information about the name of the country, but also its

ISO name, FID code, and geographical center in terms of longitude (LON) and latitude (LAT). We can use this information to display the name of the country using `.text`, but we need to add one label per country, requiring us to iterate over the `DataFrame`. We can use the `.iterrows()` to get each row in the `DataFrame`. For each row, returned as a dictionary, we create a `.text` call located at the `LON` and `LAT` position, using the `ISO3` code of the country (the standardized 3 letter code for the country). With the `ha` and `va` parameters we center the label and set the size of the text with `fontsize`.

```
>>> for index, row in weurope_map.iterrows():
...     plt.text(row['LON'], row['LAT'], row['ISO3'],
...              ha='center', va='center', fontsize=7)
```

**Tip**

If you analyze the file, you'll see that the properties object contains old information about the population, stored as `POP2005`. Different map files contain different information, so be sure to play around to unleash all the possibilities.

Also, you may notice that the map may be distorted in some cases. `matplotlib` will try to present it in a square box, and if the map is not roughly square, this will be evident. For example, try to display only Spain, Portugal, Ireland, and the UK. We can force the graph to present 1 point of latitude with the same space as 1 point of longitude, which is a good approach if we are not drawing something near the poles and the map is small enough.

This is achieved by calling `.set_aspect` in the axes. Current axes can be obtained through `.gca` (get current axes):

```
>>> axes = plt.gca()
>>> axes.set_aspect('equal', adjustable='box')
```

Also, to improve the look of the map, we can set up a background color that helps to differentiate between the background and the foreground, and remove the labels on the axes, as printing the latitude and longitude is probably distracting. Removing the labels on the axes is done by setting empty labels with `.xticks` and `.yticks`. The background color is mandated by the foreground color of the axes:

```
>>> plt.xticks([])
([], <a list of 0 Text major ticklabel objects>)
>>> plt.yticks([])
```

```
([], <a list of 0 Text major ticklabel objects>)
>>> axes = plt.gca()
>>> axes.set_facecolor('xkcd:light blue')
```

Finally, to better differentiate between the different regions, a line surrounding each area can be added at the time of the map plot. You can use the parameters `edgecolor` and `linewidth`:

```
>>> weurope_map.plot(column='POPULATION', cmap='Greens',
...                  edgecolor="black", linewidth=0.2)
```

After applying all these elements to the map, it now looks like this:

*Figure 8.11: Map with colored countries and background color*

The resulting code is available on GitHub: `https://github.com/PacktPublishing/Python-Automation-Cookbook-Third-Edition/blob/main/ch08/visualising_maps.py`.

Maps are drawn as general polygons. You can see the polygons in column `geometry`. They are stored in either a `Polygon` object (if it's a single `Polygon`) or `MultiPolygon` (if there are several).

For example, to see all the line segments that make up the contour of the map of Ireland, you can pick the 7$^{th}$ element of the full GIS information. Each map can be composed of multiple polygons, each defining an independent part of the country (for example, different islands)

```
>>> ireland = full_europe_map.loc[7]
>>> ireland['geometry']
<MULTIPOLYGON (((-9.656 53.222, -9.663 53.221, -9.689 53.223, -9.696 53.223,...>
>>> ireland['geometry'].geoms[0]  # First polygon of the multipolygon
<POLYGON ((-9.656 53.222, -9.663 53.221, -9.689 53.223, -9.696 53.223, -9.70...>
```

Each Polygon stores a list of coordinates (`.coords`) that make up each segment.

```
>>> first_polygon = ireland['geometry'].geoms[0]
>>> list(first_polygon.exterior.coords)
[(-9.65639, 53.222221), (-9.663334, 53.221382), (-9.68861, 53.222771), (-9.695557,
53.223328), (-9.70389, 53.22694400000012), (-9.709723, 53.232498000000135),
(-9.72556, 53.263885), (-9.72472, 53.26805), (-9.67056, 53.28166), (-9.664446,
53.281944), (-9.660833, 53.279999), (-9.64194, 53.25193800000011), (-9.64861,
53.22694400000012), (-9.65639, 53.222221)]
```

You can manually print each of the forms with `.fill`. For example, to print the main part of the map of Ireland, which is defined as the last polygon of the list, you can use the following code. Notice how we need to define the *X* and *Y* values in two lists, as usual with `matplotlib`.

```
>>> last_polygon = ireland['geometry'].geoms[4]
>>> data_x = [x for x, y in last_polygon.exterior.coords]
>>> data_y = [y for x, y in last_polygon.exterior.coords]
>>> plt.fill(data_x, data_y, c='xkcd:emerald')
[<matplotlib.patches.Polygon object at 0x12425ec10>]
>>> plt.show()
```

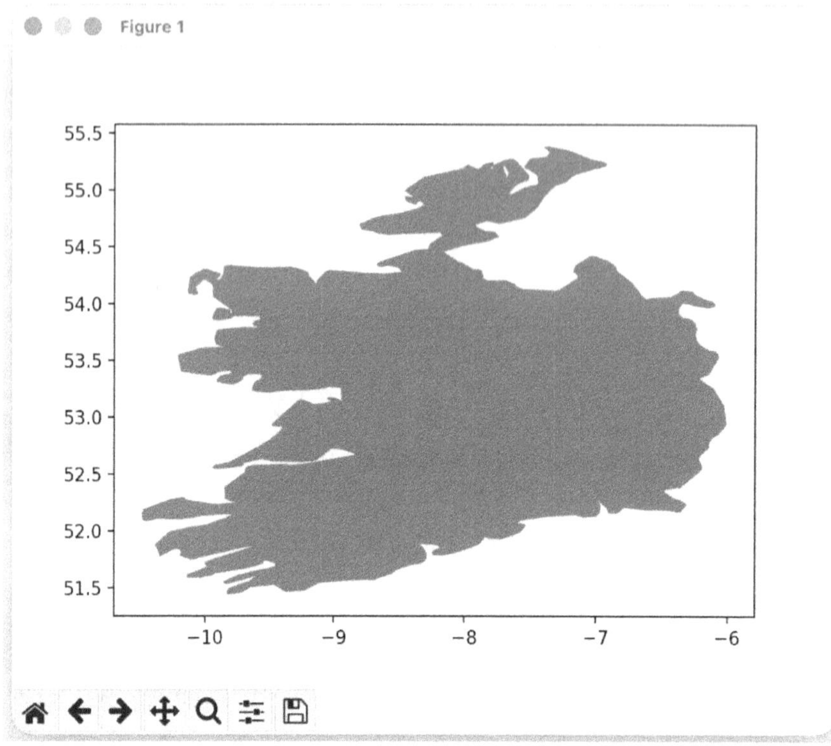


*Figure 8.12: Simplified map of Ireland*

With that information, you can add more elements to your map! Don't be afraid to include other geometrical forms. You can define your own polygons. For example, far away regions, like islands far from the mainland, may need to be moved or reduced to avoid having too large a map. Or rectangles can be used to frame and print extra information on top of parts of the map.

> **Tip**
>
> You can ask GenAI for help in creating the proper coordinates for a geometrical form on a map, or to move one part of the map to a different location.

The full geopandas documentation can be found here: `https://geopandas.org/en/stable/docs.html`. The full `matplotlib` documentation is here: `https://matplotlib.org/`.

## See also

- The next recipe, *Adding legends and annotations* recipe, to learn how to add context information to a graph.
- The *Combining graphs* recipe, later in this chapter, to learn how to add multiple plots to a single graph.

# Adding legends and annotations

When drawing graphs with dense information, a legend may be required to display information that makes the data more understandable, for example to explain what color is assigned to what concept. In `matplotlib` legends can be pretty rich, and there are multiple ways of presenting them. Annotations to draw attention to specific points are also useful in helping the reader understand the information displayed on the graph.

In this recipe, we'll create a graph with three different components and display a legend with information that helps to understand it, and we'll also annotate the most interesting points of our graph.

## Getting ready

We can install `matplotlib` in our environment using the following commands:

```
$ echo "matplotlib==3.10.8" >> requirements.txt
$ uv pip install -r requirements.txt
```

## How to do it...

1. Import `matplotlib`:

```
>>> import matplotlib.pyplot as plt
```

2. Prepare the data to be displayed on the graph and the legends that should be shown. Each line of data consists of the time label, sales of `ProductA`, sales of `ProductB`, and sales of `ProductC`:

```
>>> LEGEND = ('ProductA', 'ProductB', 'ProductC')
>>> DATA = (
...     ('Q1 2025', 100, 30, 3),
...     ('Q2 2025', 105, 32, 15),
...     ('Q3 2025', 125, 29, 40),
```

```
...     ('Q4 2025', 115, 31, 80),
... )
```

3. Split the data into usable formats for the graph. This is a preparation step:

```
>>> POS = list(range(len(DATA)))
>>> VALUESA = [valueA for label, valueA, valueB, valueC in DATA]
>>> VALUESB = [valueB for label, valueA, valueB, valueC in DATA]
>>> VALUESC = [valueC for label, valueA, valueB, valueC in DATA]
>>> LABELS = [label for label, valueA, valueB, valueC in DATA]
```

4. Create a bar graph with the data:

```
>>> WIDTH = 0.2
>>> plt.bar([p - WIDTH for p in POS], VALUESA, width=WIDTH)
<BarContainer object of 4 artists>
>>> plt.bar([p for p in POS], VALUESB, width=WIDTH)
<BarContainer object of 4 artists>
>> plt.bar([p + WIDTH for p in POS], VALUESC, width=WIDTH)
<BarContainer object of 4 artists>
>>> plt.ylabel('Sales')
Text(76.31944444444443, 0.5, 'Sales')
>>> plt.xticks(POS, LABELS)
<REDACTED>
```

5. Add an annotation displaying the maximum growth in the chart:

```
>>> plt.annotate('400% growth', xy=(1.2, 18), xytext=(1.3, 40),
...                  horizontalalignment='center',
...                  arrowprops=dict(facecolor='black', shrink=0.05))
...
Text(1.3, 40, '400% growth')
```

6. Add the legend:

```
>>> plt.legend(LEGEND)
<matplotlib.legend.Legend object at 0x1127d7a10>
```

7. Display the graph:

```
>>> plt.show()
```

8. The result will be displayed in a new window:

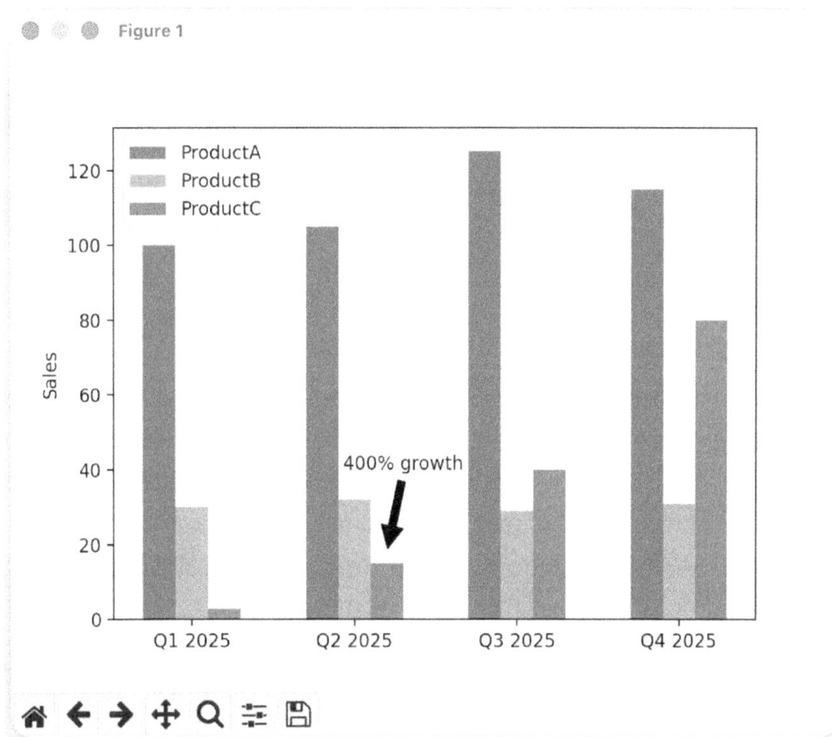


*Figure 8.13: Pointing to interesting parts of the graph*

## How it works...

*Steps 1* and *2* of the *How to do it...* section prepare the imports and the data to be displayed by the chart. In *step 3*, the data is split into different arrays to prepare the input for `matplotlib`. Each data sequence is stored in a different array.

*Step 4* draws the data. Each data sequence gets a call to `.bar`, specifying its position and values. Labels do the same as `.xticks`. To separate each of the bars around the labels, the first is displaced to the left and the third to the right.

An annotation is added above the bar for `ProductC` in the second quarter in *step 5*, using `.annotate`. Note that the annotation includes the point in `xy` and the text location in `xytext`. The `arrowprops` parameter specifies an arrow pointing to the data.

In *step 6* the legend is added. Note that the labels need to be added to the data in the same order as the data was inputted. The legend is located automatically in an area that doesn't cover any data.

Finally, the graph is drawn in *step 7* by calling `.show`.

> Note
>
> Calling `.show` blocks the execution of the program. The program will resume when the window is closed.

## There's more...

Legends will be displayed automatically in most cases with just a call to `.legend`. If you need to customize the order in which they appear, you may refer each label to a specific bar. For example (note how the labels follow a different order as above, calling `Product A`, defined in the first slot of the LEGEND, the `valueC` series):

```
>>> valueA = plt.bar([p - WIDTH for p in POS], VALUESA, width=WIDTH)
>>> valueB = plt.bar([p for p in POS], VALUESB, width=WIDTH)
>>> valueC = plt.bar([p + WIDTH for p in POS], VALUESC, width=WIDTH)
>>> plt.legend((valueC, valueB, valueA), LEGEND)
<matplotlib.legend.Legend object at 0x112273fa0>
```

The location of the legend can also be changed manually, through the `loc` parameter. By default, it will draw the legend over an area where there's the least overlap of data (ideally none). But values such as right, upper, left, and so on can be used, or a specific `(X, Y)` tuple.

Another option is to plot the legend outside of the graph using the `bbox_to_anchor` option. In this case, the legend is attached to the (*X*, *Y*) of the bounding box, where 0 is the bottom-left corner of the graph and 1 is the upper-right corner. This may cause the legend to be clipped by the external border (see *Figure 8.14*), so you may need to adjust where the graph starts and ends with `.subplots_adjust`:

```
>>> plt.legend(LEGEND, title='Products', bbox_to_anchor=(1, 0.8))
<matplotlib.legend.Legend object at 0x11963b910>
>>> plt.subplots_adjust(right=0.80)
```

> **Tip**
>
> Adjusting the `bbox_to_anchor` and `.subplots_adjust` parameters may require a little bit of trial and error to produce the desired result.

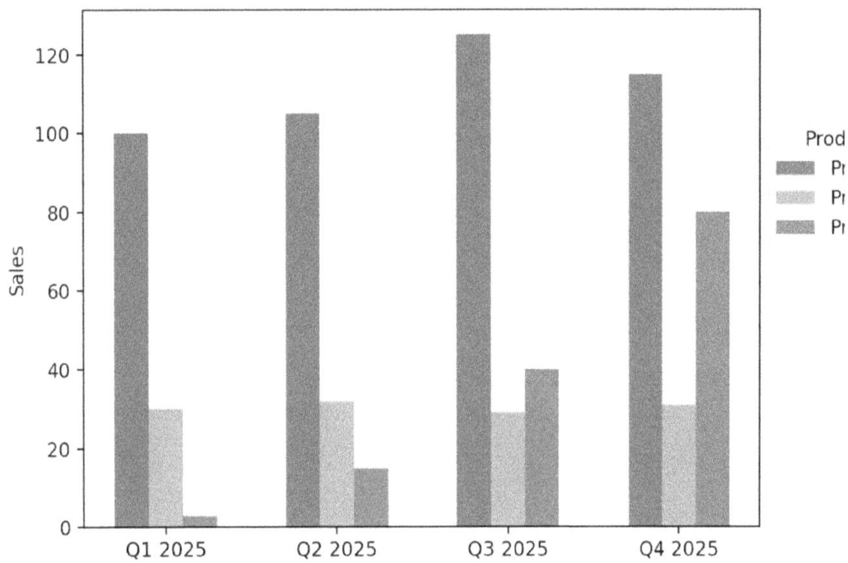


*Figure 8.14: Clipped legend if the subplots are not adjusted*

`.subplots_adjust` references the position of the chart in relation to the position of the axis. This means that `right=0.80` will leave 20% of the screen on the right of the plot, while the default for left is `0.125`, meaning it leaves 12.5% of the space on the left of the plot. See the documentation for further details: `https://matplotlib.org/stable/api/_as_gen/matplotlib.pyplot.subplots_adjust.html`.

The annotations can be done in different styles and can be tweaked with different options for connecting the text with the data. For example, this code will create an arrow with the fancy style connecting with a curve; the result is displayed in *Figure 8.15*:

```
plt.annotate('400% growth', xy=(1.2, 18), xytext=(1.3, 40),
             horizontalalignment='center',
             arrowprops={'facecolor': 'black',
                         'arrowstyle': "fancy",
                         'connectionstyle': "angle3",
                         })
```

In our recipe, we did not annotate to the end of the bar (point (1.2, 15)), but slightly above it, to give a little bit of breathing space.

> **Tip**
>
> Adjusting the exact point at which to annotate and locate the text will require a bit of testing. Position the text by looking for the best place to not overlap the text with the bars. The font size and color can be changed using the `fontsize` and color parameters in both the `.legend` and `.annotate` calls.
>
> The annotation should display the information so that it's easily understood and does not distract. Try a couple of options and tweak it until it feels correct.

Applying all these elements, the graph may look similar to the following graph. This graph can be replicated by calling the `adding_legend_and_annotation.py` script (available on GitHub at `https://github.com/PacktPublishing/Python-Automation-Cookbook-Third-Edition/blob/main/ch8/adding_legend_and_annotations.py`):

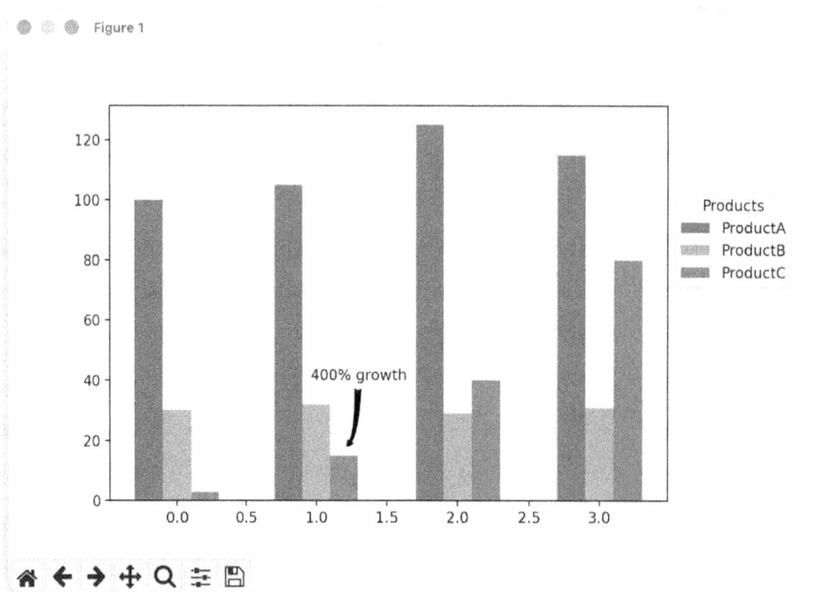


*Figure 8.15: Legend adding context to each bar*

The full matplotlib documentation can be found at `https://matplotlib.org/`. The guide for legends is at `https://matplotlib.org/stable/users/explain/axes/`

`legend_guide.html` and the guide for annotations is at `https://matplotlib.org/stable/users/explain/text/annotations.html`.

## See also

- The *Drawing stacked bars* recipe, earlier in this chapter, to learn how to plot accumulated values as bars that will benefit from a legend.
- The next recipe, *Combining graphs*, to learn how to add multiple plots to a single graph.

# Combining graphs

More than one plot can be combined in the same figure. In this recipe, we'll see how to present data in the same plot, on two different axes, and how to add more plots to the same figure.

## Getting ready

We can install `matplotlib` in our environment using the following commands:

```
$ echo "matplotlib==3.10.8" >> requirements.txt
$ uv pip install -r requirements.txt
```

## How to do it...

1. Import `matplotlib`:

```
>>> import matplotlib.pyplot as plt
```

2. Prepare the data to be displayed on the graph, and also the legends. Each of the lines is composed of the time label, sales of `ProductA`, and sales of `ProductB`. Notice how `ProductB` has a much higher value than A:

```
>>> DATA = (
...     ('Q1 2025', 100, 3000, 3),
...     ('Q2 2025', 105, 3200, 5),
...     ('Q3 2025', 125, 2900, 7),
...     ('Q4 2025', 115, 3100, 3),
... )
```

3. Prepare the data in independent arrays:

```
>>> POS = list(range(len(DATA)))
>>> VALUESA = [valueA for label, valueA, valueB, valueC in DATA]
```

```
>>> VALUESB = [valueB for label, valueA, valueB, valueC in DATA]
>>> VALUESC = [valueC for label, valueA, valueB, valueC in DATA]
>>> LABELS = [label for label, valueA, valueB, valueC in DATA]
```

Note that this expands and creates a list for each of the values.

> **Note**
>
> The values can also be expanded with this: `LABELS, VALUESA, VALUESB, VALUESC = zip(*DATA)`.

4. Create the first subplot:

```
>>> plt.subplot(2, 1, 1)
<Axes: >
```

5. Create a bar graph with information about `VALUESA`:

```
>>> valueA = plt.bar(POS, VALUESA)
>>> plt.ylabel('Sales A')
Text(85.06944444444443, 0.5, 'Sales A')
```

6. Create a different *y-axis*, and add information about `VALUESB` as a line plot:

```
>>> plt.twinx()
<Axes: >
>>> valueB = plt.plot(POS, VALUESB, 'o-', color='red')
>>> plt.ylabel('Sales B')
Text(0, 0.5, 'Sales B')
>>> plt.xticks(POS, LABELS)
<REDACTED>
```

7. Create another subplot and fill it with `VALUESC`:

```
>>> plt.subplot(2, 1, 2)
<Axes: >
>>> plt.plot(POS, VALUESC)
[<matplotlib.lines.Line2D object at 0x115b28ec0>]
>>> plt.gca().set_ylim(ymin=0)
(0.0, 7.2)
```

```
>>> plt.xticks(POS, LABELS)
<REDACTED>
```

8. Display the graph:

```
>>> plt.show()
```

The result will be displayed in a new window:

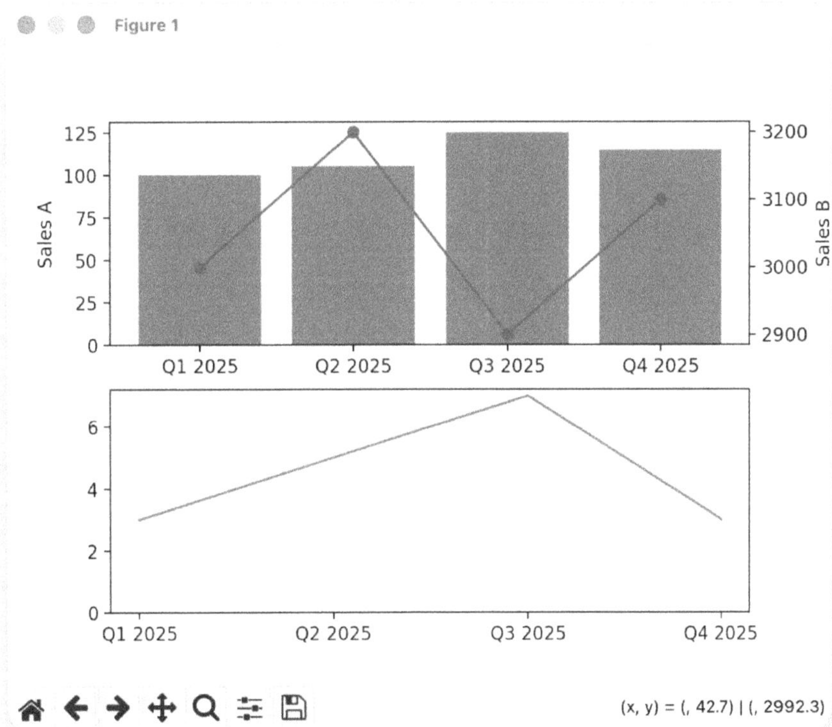


*Figure 8.16: Multiple plots in the same figure*

## How it works...

In *Step 1* of the *How to do it...* section, all the required imports for the module are called.

*Step 2* presents the data in a usable format.

*Step 3* is a preparation step that splits the data into different arrays for the subsequent steps.

*Step 4* creates a new `.subplot`. This splits the full drawing into two elements. The parameters are number of rows, columns, and the selected subplot. So, we create two subplots, each effectively on a row of a single column, and draw in the first one.

*Step 5* prints a `.bar` plot in this subplot using `VALUESA` data, and labels the *y-axis* with Sales A using `.ylabel`.

*Step 6* creates a new *y-axis* with `.twinx`, drawing `VALUESB` as a line plot through `.plot`. The label is marked with `.ylabel` as Sales B. The *x-axis* is labeled using `.xticks`.

> **Note**
>
> The `VALUESB` plot is set to red to avoid both plots having the same color. By default, the first color is the same in both cases, and that will lead to confusion. The data points are marked with the 'o' option.

In *step 7*, we changed to the second subplot using `.subplot`. We select the second element for a two rows, one column configuration, matching the previous subplot. The plot prints `VALUESC` as a line, and again puts the labels on the *x-axis* with `.xticker` and sets the minimum of the *y-axis* to 0. The full, data-rich figure is then displayed in *step 8*.

## There's more...

Plots with multiple axes are complicated to read as a general rule. Use them only when there's a good reason to do so and the data is highly correlated.

> **Tip**
>
> By default, the *y-axis* in line plots will try to present information between the minimum and maximum Y values. Truncating the axis is normally not the best way to present information, as it can distort the perceived differences. For example, changing values in the range from 10 to 11 can look like a huge deal if the graph goes only from 10 to 11, but in reality the change is less than 10%. Setting the *y-axis* minimum to 0 with `plt.gca().set_ylim(ymin=0)` is a good idea, especially with two different axes, so you don't lose sense of perspective.

The call to select the subplot will first go by row, then by column, so `.subplot(2, 2, 3)` will select the subplot in the first column, second row.

The divided subplot grid can be changed. A first call to `.subplot(2, 2, 1)` (two rows, two columns, first subplot) and `.subplot(2, 2, 2)` (two rows, two columns, second subplot), and then calling `.subplot(2, 1, 2)` (two rows, one column, second plot) will create a structure with two small plots in the first row and a wider one in the second. Going back will overwrite previously drawn subplots.

> **Tip**
>
> Try to avoid making extremely complex graphs, as they can be difficult to read. If you need help with determining how to position different values in multiple axis or subplots you can ask GenAI for advice, but ultimately trust in your judgement when you see the graph. Allow yourself to see the final graph and tweak it so that it works correctly.

The full `matplotlib` documentation can be found at `https://matplotlib.org/`, and the guide for subplots with multiple examples is at `https://matplotlib.org/stable/gallery/subplots_axes_and_figures/index.html`.

## See also

- The *Drawing multiple lines* recipe, earlier in this chapter, which shows alternatives to displaying multiple values in a single graph.
- The *Visualizing map info* recipe, earlier in this chapter, to learn how to display other kinds of rich graphs with multiple data.

# Saving charts

Once a chart is ready we can store it on the hard drive so that it can be referenced in other documents. In this recipe, we'll see how to save charts in different formats.

## Getting ready

We can install `matplotlib` using the following commands:

```
$ echo "matplotlib==3.10.8" >> requirements.txt
$ uv pip install -r requirements.txt
```

## How to do it...

1. Import `matplotlib`:

```
>>> import matplotlib.pyplot as plt
```

2. Prepare the data to be displayed on the graph and split it into different arrays:

```
>>> DATA = (
...     ('Q1 2025', 100),
...     ('Q2 2025', 150),
...     ('Q3 2025', 125),
...     ('Q4 2025', 175),
... )
>>> POS = list(range(len(DATA)))
>>> VALUES = [value for label, value in DATA]
>>> LABELS = [label for label, value in DATA]
```

3. Create a bar graph with the data:

```
>>> plt.bar(POS, VALUES)
<BarContainer object of 4 artists>
>>> plt.xticks(POS, LABELS)
<REDACTED>
>>> plt.ylabel('Sales')
Text(76.31944444444443, 0.5, 'Sales')
```

4. Save the graph to the hard drive:

```
>>> plt.savefig('data.png')
```

5. Open the new file `data.png` to show the graph, as follows:

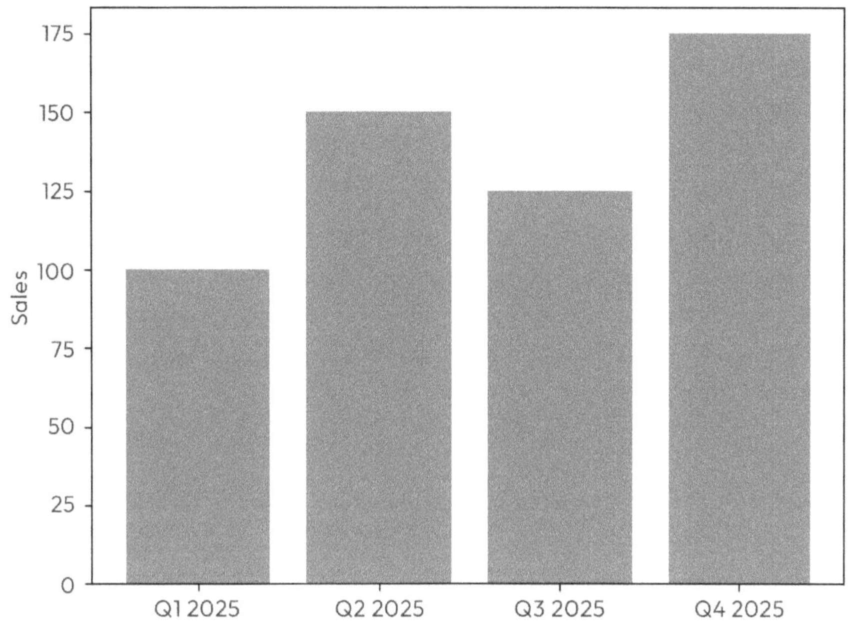


*Figure 8.17: Graph saved in PNG format*

## How it works...

After importing and preparing the data in *steps 1* and *2* in the *How to do it...* section, the graph is generated in *step 3* by calling `.bar`. A `.ylabel` is added and the *x-axis* is labelled with the proper time description through `.xticks`.

*Step 4* saves the file to the hard drive with the name `data.png`.

## There's more...

The resolution of the image can be determined through the `dpi` parameter (dpi = dots per inch – how many individual points are printed within an inch). This will affect the size of the file. Use resolutions between 72 and 300. Lower ones will be difficult to read, while higher ones won't make sense unless the graph is enormous:

```
>>> plt.savefig('data.png', dpi=72)
```

`matplotlib` understands how to store the most common file formats, such as JPEG, PDF, and PNG. The file extension will be used automatically to store the data is the expected format.

> **Tip**
>
> Unless you have a specific requirement, use PNG. It is very efficient at storing graphs with limited colors compared to other formats and, compared with JPG, it doesn't loose resolution, meaning that lines will appear crisp. If you need to find all the supported file types, you can call `plt.gcf().canvas.get_supported_filetypes()`.
>
> An interesting option is SVG, which is a vector-based format. That means that it doesn't have resolution, but it stores every element of the graph (lines, curves) as mathematical elements. This allows it to replicate a graphic precisely at any size and resize it without losing quality. It's a viable option for big graphs that need to be zoomed greatly. Most browsers can properly represent SVG files.

The full `matplotlib` documentation can be found here: `https://matplotlib.org/`.

## See also

- The *Plotting a simple sales graph* recipe, earlier in this chapter, to learn the basics of plotting a bar graph.
- The *Adding legends and annotations* recipe, earlier in this chapter, to learn how to add context information to graphs.

# Plotting a chart with plotly

While `matplotlib` is a well-known module to plot graphs in Python, it's not the only option. In this recipe, we will see an example using `plotly`.

> **Note**
>
> While `matplotlib` is mostly aimed at static images and has been very popular in academic environments, `plotly` is more oriented towards interactive, web-based graphs. `matplotlib` is also very big and allows for many different options.

## Getting ready

We can install `plotly`, `kaleido` and `pandas` in our environment using the following commands:

```
$ echo "plotly==6.5.2" >> requirements.txt
$ echo "kaleido==1.2.0" >> requirements.txt
$ echo "pandas==3.0.0" >> requirements.txt
$ uv pip install -r requirements.txt
```

> **Note**
>
> In *Chapter 7* we mentioned that the recently released version of pandas 3 has some differences with respect to previous versions. Check there for more info.

## How to do it...

1. Import `plotly` and `pandas`:

```
>>> import plotly.express as px
>>> import pandas as pd
```

2. Prepare the data to display:

```
>>> DATA = (
...     ('Q1 2025', 100, 0),
...     ('Q2 2025', 105, 15),
...     ('Q3 2025', 125, 40),
...     ('Q4 2025', 115, 80),
... )
```

3. Prepare a `DataFrame` specifying the columns:

```
>>> data_frame = pd.DataFrame(DATA, columns=["Period", "ProductA",
"ProductB"])
```

4. Create a bar chart with the prepared data:

```
>>> fig = px.bar(data_frame, x="Period", y=["ProductA", "ProductB"],
...              title="Sales")
```

5. Add a description for the legend:

```
>>> fig.update_layout(legend_title_text="Products")
```

6. Display the chart, which will open in your default browser:

```
>>> fig.show()
```

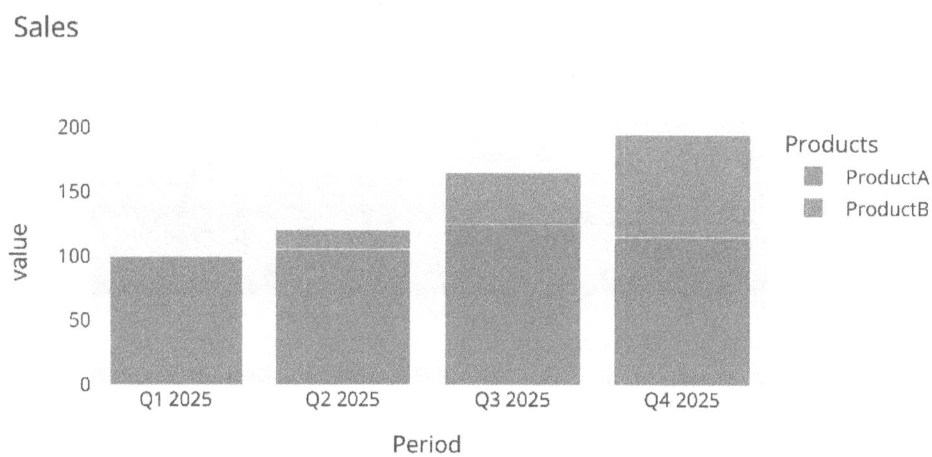


*Figure 8.18: The bar chart*

The chart is interactive, allowing for clicking around to find out the different values. You can also see that there's a tools bar in the right top part of the graph offering different actions, like zooming or saving the plot as a PNG file.

## How it works...

After importing and preparing the data in *steps 1* and *2* in the *How to do it...* section, the data is prepared in *step 3* by transforming it into a `pandas DataFrame` object. We define what are the columns that correspond to the raw `DATA` list.

> **Tip**
>
> `pandas` is a well-known module and `DataFrames` is a very flexible, very powerful interface by which to manipulate data. It's very likely that any data manipulation is done way more efficiently by using `DataFrame` interface than by doing it manually. It's common for data scientists to use it extensively.
>
> Because of that it's also very well understood by GenAI, making it easy to obtain insights into how to manipulate data to obtain the desired results.

*Step 4* creates the bar chart, calling `px.bar` and specifying the data, the column to be used as `x`, the column(s) that will be used for `y`, and a `title`.

We update the layout in *step 5* to label properly the legend. Finally, we display the plot by calling `.show`.

## There's more...

Though the default is to show stacked bars, we can also present the chart as non-stacked bars using the `barmode` parameter. The default for this parameter is `stack`, but it accepts other options like `group` (showing the bars one close to the other), `relative` for bars that can go down as well (e.g. profit) or `overlay`, which shows both bars overlapping. Let's draw the bars grouped:

```
>>> fig = px.bar(data_frame, x="Period", y=["ProductA", "ProductB"],
...              title="Sales", barmode="group")
>>> fig.show()
```

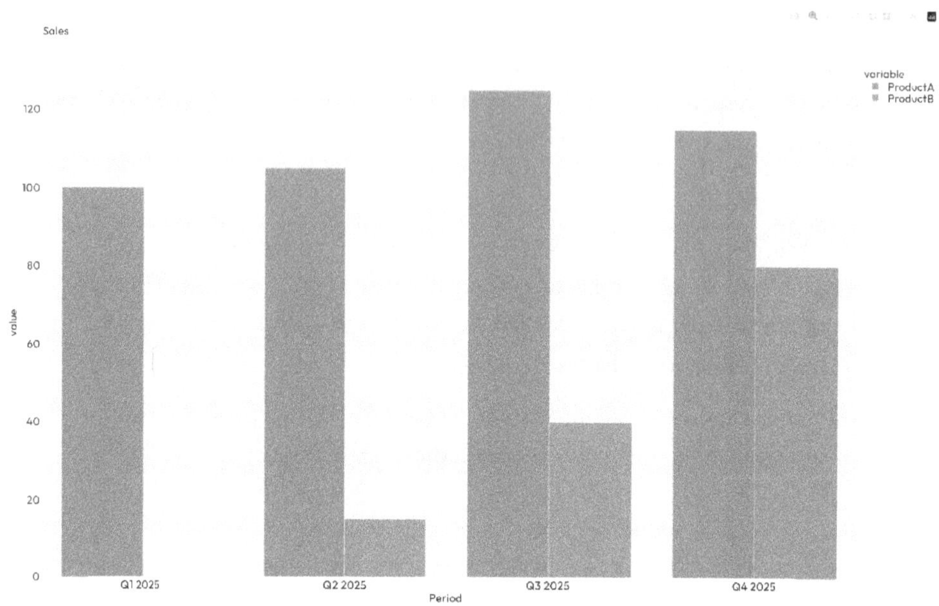


*Figure 8.19: Grouped bars*

There are also many more ways to show the data – check out the documentation at `https://plotly.com/python/bar-charts/` to see all the possibilities for bar charts.

While `DataFrame` is the most natural container for data in `plotly`, you can also define the graphs using raw data. For that we need to use `plotly.graph_objects`, which is a lower-level way of working.

> **Note**
>
> Note that previously we used `plotly.express`. This module makes the drawing process easier, but works only with `DataFrames`. There are certain features that are only available outside of `plotly.express`, but in general it is easier to use it.

For example, we can plot the same stacked bar diagram with this code:

```
# Import graph objects
import plotly.graph_objects as go
# Prepare the data
LABELS = [label for label, pA, pB in DATA]
PRODUCTA = [pA for label, pA, pB in DATA]
```

```
PRODUCTB = [pB for label, pA, pB in DATA]
# Start the chart
fig = go.Figure()
# Add two bars with the values of ProductA and ProductB
fig.add_bar(x=LABELS, y=PRODUCTA, name='Product A')
fig.add_bar(x=LABELS, y=PRODUCTB, name='Product B')
# Set the mode to stack and add the title
fig.update_layout(barmode='stack', title='Sales')
# Show the chart
fig.show()
```

This produces a chart very similar to *Figure 8.18*.

When saving your graph, you have two options. You can save it as an HTML file, which will retain interactivity, using `.write_html`:

```
>>> fig.write_html('graph.html')
```

It's also possible to write it as a plain image file, for better compatibility or to embed it into other documents or presentations. For that, use `.write_image` method:

```
>>> fig.write_image('graph.png')
```

**Note**

To be able to write the image, you need to have installed the `kaleido` package.

You can write to the usual image file formats: JPG, PNG, PDF, SVG, etc. A good default format for writing charts is PNG, which enables you to preserve good image definition while keeping the image files relatively small.

`plotly` is very powerful and has a wealth of features. Check the complete documentation at `https://plotly.com/python`.

**Tip**

GenAI also understands `plotly` very well, so don't be afraid to ask it how to do something.

## See also

- The *Drawing stacked bars* recipe, earlier in this chapter, to learn how to generate the same kind of graphs using `matplotlib`.
- The *Visualizing maps* recipe, earlier in this chapter, to see other uses of `DataFrames` objects.

# 9

# Dealing with Communication Channels

Dealing with communication channels is where automation can produce big gains. In this chapter, we'll see how to work with two of the most common communication channels – emails (including newsletters), and sending and receiving text messages by phone.

Over the years there has been a fair amount of abuse of both channels, in the form of spam or unsolicited marketing messages, and this makes it necessary for senders to use external applications that handle message validation and abuse to avoid messages being rejected by automated filters.

> Note
>
> For example, if you send many marketing emails from your own Gmail account, it is likely that the account will be blocked as it will detect this as possible spam. Instead, using a specialized tool for marketing emails will ensure that proper validation and spam protections are in place.

When presenting those tools, we will comment on the common pitfalls (rate limits, getting blocked, anti-spam rules) where they apply. The tools presented have numerous features to help you with specific tasks, and they also have excellent documentation, so do not be afraid to read it.

The chapter covers the following recipes:

- Working with email templates
- Sending an individual email

- Reading an email
- Adding subscribers to an email newsletter
- Sending notifications via email
- Producing SMS messages
- Receiving SMS messages
- Creating a Telegram bot

We will start by understanding how to use templates to generate well-formatted emails.

# Technical requirements

The code presented in this chapter is available in the GitHub repository, at `https://github.com/PacktPublishing/Python-Automation-Cookbook-Third-Edition/tree/main/ch09`.

# Working with email templates

To send an email we first need to generate its content. In this recipe, we'll see how to generate a proper template, in both text-only style and as HTML.

## Getting ready

We start by installing the `mistune` module, which will compile Markdown documents into HTML. We will also use the `jinja2` module to combine HTML with our text:

```
$ echo "mistune==3.2.0" >> requirements.txt
$ echo "jinja2==3.1.6" >> requirements.txt
$ uv pip install -r requirements.txt
```

In the GitHub repository are a couple of templates we will use: `email_template.md` at `https://github.com/PacktPublishing/Python-Automation-Cookbook-Third-Edition/blob/main/ch09/email_template.md`, and for styling, the template `email_styling.html` at `https://github.com/PacktPublishing/Python-Automation-Cookbook-Third-Edition/blob/main/ch09/email_styling.html`.

## How to do it...

1. Import the modules:

```
>>> import mistune
>>> import jinja2
```

2. Read both templates from disk:

```
>>> with open('email_template.md') as md_file:
...     markdown = md_file.read()
>>> with open('email_styling.html') as styling_file:
...     styling = styling_file.read()
```

3. Define the data to include in the template. The template is quite simple and accepts only a single `name` parameter:

```
>>> data = {'name': 'Seamus'}
```

4. Render the Markdown template. This produces the text-only version of the data:

```
>>> text = markdown.format(**data)
```

5. For the HTML version, render the Markdown and add the styling:

```
>>> html_content = mistune.html (text)
>>> html = jinja2.Template(styling).render(content=html_content)
```

6. Save the text and HTML versions to disk to check them:

```
>>> with open('text_version.txt', 'w') as fp:
...     fp.write(text)

>>> with open('html_version.html', 'w') as fp:
...     fp.write(html)
```

7. Exit the interpreter and check the text version:

```
$ cat text_version.txt
Hi Seamus:

This is an email talking about **things**

### Very important info

1. One thing
2. Other thing
3. Some extra detail
```

```
Best regards,

   *The email team*
```

8. Check the HTML version in a browser:

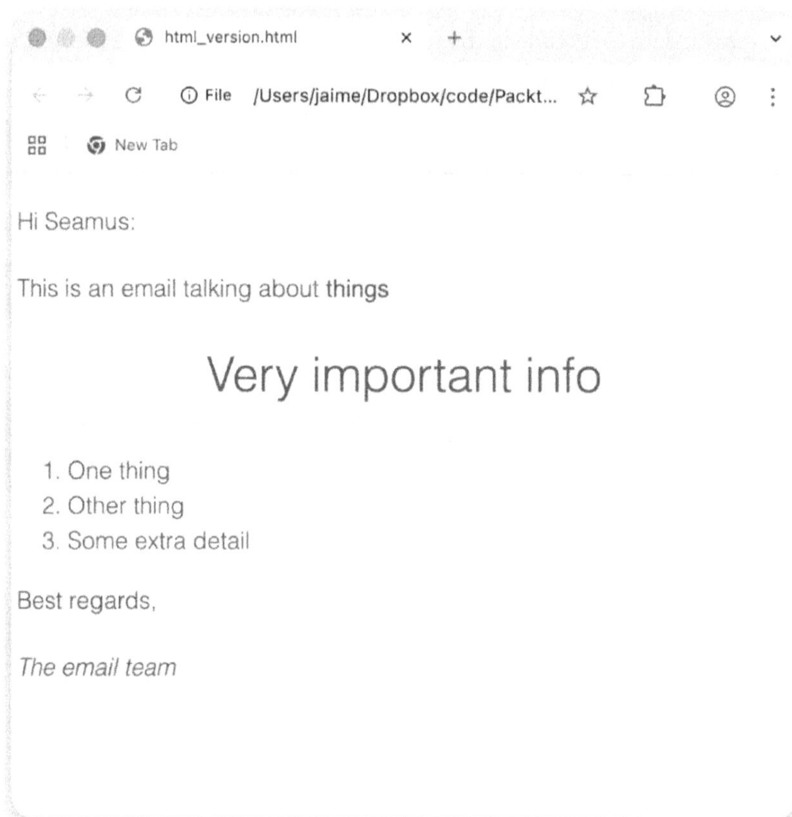


*Figure 9.1: Rendered image of the HTML file*

## How it works...

*Step 1* imports the modules that will be used later, and *step 2* reads the two templates that will be rendered. `email_template.md` is the basis of the content, and it's a Markdown template. `email_styling.html` is an HTML template that contains the basic HTML scaffolding and CSS styling information.

**Tip**

The basic strategy is to create the content in Markdown format. This is a readable plain text file which can be sent as part of the email. That content can then be converted into HTML and wrapped with some styling to assemble the complete, styled HTML file. The styling file `email_styling.html` has a content area where we can put the rendered HTML from Markdown.

*Step 3* defines the data that will be rendered in `email_template.md`. It is a very simple template that requires only a parameter called `name`.

**Note**

Notice that the template contains placeholders for the variables that will be printed, in Python `format` data, using curly brackets. That requires the template not to contain other curly brackets that are part of the text to be present. For long or complex templates, you may want to render the Markdown also with a `jinja` template.

In *step 4* the Markdown template gets rendered with the data. This produces the plain text version of the email.

The HTML version is rendered in *step 5*. The plain text version is rendered to HTML using `mistune`, and then wrapped by `email_styling.html` using a `jinja2` template. The final version is a self-contained HTML document.

Finally, we save both versions, plain text (as text) and HTML (as html), to file in *step 6*. *Steps 7* and *8* check the stored values. The information is the same in both versions, but in the HTML version it is better styled.

## There's more...

Using Markdown makes it easy to generate emails in both plain text and HTML versions. Markdown is a quite readable text format which renders very naturally into HTML. That said, it is possible to generate totally different HTML versions, allowing for more customization and greater advantage to be taken of HTML's features.

The full Markdown syntax can be found at `https://daringfireball.net/projects/markdown/syntax`, and a good cheat sheet covering the most commonly used elements can be found at `https://www.markdownguide.org/cheat-sheet`.

While making a plain text version of an email is not strictly necessary, it is a good practice and shows you care about who reads the email. Most email clients accept and display HTML, but it's not universal.

> **Tip**
>
> For an HTML email, the complete stylesheet information should be contained in the email. This means that the CSS needs to be embedded into the HTML. Avoid making external references to resources that could lead the email to not render properly in some email clients or even be classified as spam.

The styling in `email_styling.html` is based on the *modest* stylesheet, which can be found here: `http://markdowncss.github.io/`. There are other CSS stylesheets that can be used, and a search using Google should find more. Remember to remove any external references, as discussed previously.

> **Tip**
>
> Alternatively, generate a new stylesheet or modify an existing one using GenAI tools.

Images can be included in HTML by encoding them in `base64` format, so they can be embedded directly into HTML `img` tags, instead of by adding references.

The template includes an img tag that displays only if the base64img variable is defined when rendering the HTML. See this part of the template email_styling.html, which renders this info conditionally:

```
{% if base64img %}
<div>
    <p>This presents an image</p>
    <img alt="image" src='data:image/png;base64,{{base64img}}'/>
</div>
{% endif %}
```

Check the image.png file in the directory https://github.com/PacktPublishing/Python-Automation-Cookbook-Third-Edition/tree/main/ch09

```
>>> import base64
>>> with open("image.png",'rb') as file:
...     encoded_data = base64.b64encode(file.read())
>>> print("<img src='data:image/png;base64,{data}'/>".format(data=encoded_data))
```

You can now include the image in the template, by adding the encoded_data , which contains the data in base64, to the HTML template in the variable base64img.

```
>>> html = jinja2.Template(styling).render(content=html_content,
base64img=encoded_data)
>>> with open('html_version.html', 'w') as fp:
...     fp.write(html)
```

**Note**

You can find more information about this technique in this article: https://css-tricks.com/data-uris/.

The rendered template, using `image.png`, looks like this:

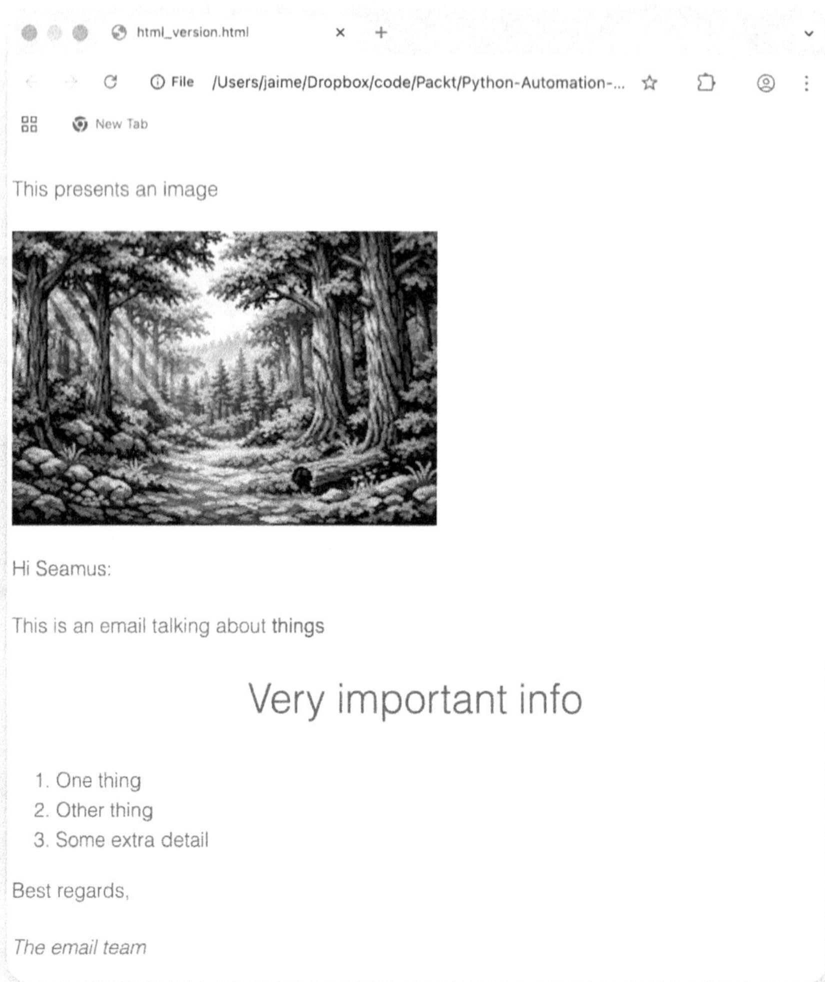


*Figure 9.2: HTML result including the image*

> **Note**
>
> The image in *Figure 9.2* has been generated with GenAI (ChatGPT) using the prompt: *Generate, in pixelart, a banner showing a forest with high trees. It should look like a 16-bit image from the 90s.*

The full documentation for `mistune` is available at `http://mistune.readthedocs.io/en/latest/`, while the `jinja2` documentation can be found at `https://jinja.palletsprojects.com/en/stable/`.

## See also

- The *Formatting text in Markdown* recipe in *Chapter 5, Generating Fantastic Reports*, to learn more about Markdown
- The *Using templates for reports* recipe in *Chapter 5, Generating Fantastic Reports*, to learn more about Jinja2 templates
- The *Sending an individual email* recipe, next in this chapter, to learn how to send the composed email

# Sending an individual email

The most basic way of sending an email is by using the **Simple Mail Transfer Protocol** (**SMTP**). SMTP is one of the oldest protocols on the Internet. Although newer proprietary protocols exist, SMTP is the standard used by all email providers to communicate with each other and is one of the pillars of electronic communications.

SMTP allows you to send rich emails with multiple sections containing different kinds of data. These sections can be used to add attachments, or to generate alternative sections, such as a plain text and HTML version of the same message, for display on compatible email clients.

SMTP is easy to use, and virtually all languages and operating systems support it. But this ease of use is also a weakness, as the amount of spam email that can be generated is huge, and big players in the email domain have strong incentives to disallow emails coming from non-verified sources, such as Python scripts.

For this reason it is recommended that SMTP is used only sparingly, and for simple purposes, such as sending a few emails a day to controlled addresses.

> **Tip**
>
> Do not use this method to send emails in bulk to distribution lists or to customers from random email addresses. You risk being banned by your service provider due to anti-spam rules.

## Getting ready

For this recipe, we'll need an email account with a service provider. There are small differences based on the provider you use, but we'll be using a Gmail account as these are very common and are free to access.

Gmail blocks SMTP sign-ins with your regular account password, so we'll create a specific app password for mail access. Follow the instructions at `https://support.google.com/accounts/answer/185833` to generate a password for the purposes of implementing this recipe. Remember to create it for mail access. You can delete the password afterwards.

We'll use the `smtplib` module, which is part of Python's standard library.

## How to do it...

1. Import the `smtplib` and `email` modules:

```
>>> import smtplib
>>> from email.mime.multipart import MIMEMultipart
>>> from email.mime.text import MIMEText
```

2. Set up the credentials, replacing these with your own ones. For the password, we use the standard library `getpass` that will require you to interactively fill in the password. For testing purposes, we'll send to the address we're sending from, but feel free to use a different address:

```
>>> import getpass
>>> USER = 'your.account@gmail.com'
>>> PASSWORD = getpass.getpass()
Password:
>>> sent_from = USER
>>> send_to = [USER]
```

3. Specify the data to be sent. Notice the two alternatives: plain text and HTML:

```
>>> text = "Hi!\nThis is the text version linking to https://
www.packtpub.com/\nCheers!"
>>> html = """<html><head></head><body>
... <p>Hi!<br>
... This is the HTML version linking to <a href="https://
www.packtpub.com/">Packt</a><br>
... </p>
```

```
... </body></html>
"""
```

4. Compose the message as a MIME multipart, including `Subject`, `To`, and `From` fields:

```
>>> msg = MIMEMultipart('alternative')
>>> msg['Subject'] = 'An interesting email'
>>> msg['From'] = sent_from
>>> msg['To'] = ', '.join(send_to)
```

5. Fill in the data content parts of the email:

```
>>> part_plain = MIMEText(text, 'plain')
>>> part_html = MIMEText(html, 'html')
>>> msg.attach(part_plain)
>>> msg.attach(part_html)
```

6. Send the email using the SMTP secure protocol, using `SMTP_SSL`:

```
>>> with smtplib.SMTP_SSL('smtp.gmail.com', 465) as server:
...     server.login(USER, PASSWORD)
...     server.sendmail(sent_from, send_to, msg.as_string())
```

The email should have been sent. Check your email account (or whatever destination account you specified) for the message. Checking the original email, you will see the full raw email, with elements in both HTML and plain text. Parts of the email have been redacted in the following screenshot:

Original message

| | |
|---|---|
| Message ID | @mx.google.com> |
| Created on: | 14 February 2026 at 18:15 (Delivered after 0 seconds) |
| From: | @gmail.com |
| To: | @gmail.com |
| Subject: | An interesting email |

Download original

Copy to clipboard

```
Return-Path: <@gmail.com>
Received: from 1.0.0.0.0.0.0.0.0.0.0.0.0.0.0.0.0.0.0.0.0.0.0.0.0.0.0.0.0.0.0.0.ip6.arpa
([2a02:8086:d68:9a80:4ba:6035:5970:acca])
        by smtp.gmail.com with ESMTPSA id 5b1f17b1804b1-
4835d92267bsm427300095e9.0.2026.02.14.10.15.20
        for <@gmail.com>
        (version=TLS1_3 cipher=TLS_AES_256_GCM_SHA384 bits=256/256);
        Sat, 14 Feb 2026 10:15:20 -0800 (PST)
Message-ID: <@mx.google.com>
Date: Sat, 14 Feb 2026 10:15:20 -0800 (PST)
Content-Type: multipart/alternative; boundary="===============7931778091581627904=="
MIME-Version: 1.0
Subject: An interesting email
From: @gmail.com
To: @gmail.com

--===============7931778091581627904==
Content-Type: text/plain; charset="us-ascii"
MIME-Version: 1.0
Content-Transfer-Encoding: 7bit

Hi!
This is the text version linking to https://www.packtpub.com/
Cheers!
--===============7931778091581627904==
Content-Type: text/html; charset="us-ascii"
MIME-Version: 1.0
Content-Transfer-Encoding: 7bit

<html><head></head><body>
<p>Hi!<br>
This is the HTML version linking to <a href="https://www.packtpub.com/">Packt</a><br>
</p>
</body></html>

--===============7931778091581627904==--
```

Figure 9.3: Email in both plain text and HTML format

## How it works...

After *step 1*, making the pertinent imports from `smtplib` and `email`, *step 2* defines the credentials obtained from Gmail.

*Step 3* shows the HTML and text that are going to be sent. They are alternatives, so they should present the same information, but in different formats.

The basic message information is set up in *step 4*. It specifies the subject of the email, as well as the `From` and `To` fields. *Step 5* adds multiple parts, each with the proper `MIMEText` type.

> **Tip**
>
> The last part that's added is the preferred alternative, according to the MIME format, so we add the HTML part last. Be sure that both formats have the same content. If not, you are effectively sending two different messages.

*Step 6* sets up the connection with the server, logs in using the credentials, and sends the message. It uses a `with` context to get the connection. Note that the address `smtp.gmail.com` and port 465 are specific for Gmail.

If there's an error with the credentials, an exception will be raised indicating that the username and password are not accepted.

## There's more...

Note that `send_to` is a list of addresses. You can send an email to more than one address. The only caveat is in *step 4*, where a list of comma-separated values for all addresses needs to be specified.

> **Tip**
>
> Although it is possible to label `sent_from` as a different address than the address used to send the email, it is ***not recommended***, as it can be interpreted as an indication of trying to fake the origin of the email and may cause the email to be labeled as spam.

You should only use secure SMTP (SMTPS protocol) as it's encrypted and cannot be read by intermediaries on the network across the internet. Gmail requires you to always use it. If you use port 587, which is the standard SMTP port, Gmail requires you to call `.starttls` to produce a secure session, as shown in the following code:blue

```
with smtplib.SMTP('smtp.gmail.com', 587) as server:
    server.starttls()
    server.login(USER, PASSWORD)
    server.sendmail(sent_from, send_to, msg.as_string())
```

If you are interested in learning more about these differences and about both protocols, check out this article: `https://www.fastmail.help/hc/en-us/articles/360058753834-SSL-TLS-and-STARTTLS`.

The full `smtplib` documentation can be found at `https://docs.python.org/3/library/smtplib.html`, and that for the `email` module, with information on the different email formats (including information on MIME types), can be found here: `https://docs.python.org/3/library/email.html`. MIME types can be used to add binary attachments to emails.

In the next recipe we will interact with the email server from the opposite position, reading the emails.

## See also

- The *Working with email templates* recipe, previously in this chapter, to see how to compose the body of the email
- The *Sending notifications via email* recipe, later in this chapter, to learn how to send bulk emails

# Reading an email

In this recipe we'll see how to read emails from an account. We'll use the IMAP4 standard, which is the most commonly used standard for reading emails.

Once read, the email can be processed and analyzed automatically to generate actions such as smart automated responses, forwarding the email to a different target, aggregating the results for monitoring, and so on. The options are unlimited!

## Getting ready

For this recipe, we'll need an email account with a service provider. There are small differences based on the provider you use, but we'll use a Gmail account, as it is well-known, common, and free to access.

Gmail blocks IMAP access with your regular account password, so we'll create a specific app password for mail access. Follow the instructions here: `https://support.google.com/accounts/answer/185833`. This will generate a password for the purpose of this recipe. Remember to create it for mail. You can delete the password afterward.

We'll use the `imaplib` module, which is part of Python's standard library.

This recipe will read the last received email, so you can use it for better control over what's going to be read. We'll send a short email that looks like it was sent to the support team.

## How to do it...

1. Import the `imaplib` and `email` modules:

```
>>> import imaplib
>>> import email
>>> from email.parser import BytesParser, Parser
>>> from email.policy import default
```

2. Set up the credentials, replacing the following with your own details:

```
>>> USER = 'your.account@gmail.com'
>>> PASSWORD = 'YourPassword'
```

3. Connect to the email server:

```
>>> mail = imaplib.IMAP4_SSL('imap.gmail.com')
>>> mail.login(USER, PASSWORD)
('OK', [b'USER@gmail.com authenticated (Success)'])
```

4. Select the `inbox` folder:

```
>>> mail.select('inbox')
```

5. Read all email UIDs and retrieve the latest received email:

```
>>> result, data = mail.uid('search', None, 'ALL')
>>> latest_email_uid = data[0].split()[-1]
>>> result, data = mail.uid('fetch', latest_email_uid, '(RFC822)')
>>> raw_email = data[0][1]
```

6. Parse the email into a Python object:

```
>>> email_message = BytesParser(policy=default).parsebytes(raw_email)
```

7. Display the subject and sender of the email:

```
>>> email_message['subject']
'[Ref ABCDEF] Subject: Product A'
```

```
>>> email.utils.parseaddr(email_message['From'])
('Sender name', 'sender@gmail.com')
```

8. Retrieve the payload of the text:

```
>>> email_type = email_message.get_content_maintype()
>>> payload = ''
>>> if email_type == 'multipart':
...     for part in email_message.get_payload():
...         if part.get_content_type() == 'text/plain':
...             payload = part.get_payload()
... elif email_type == 'text':
...     payload = email_message.get_payload()
>>> print(payload)
Hi:
  I'm having difficulties getting into my account. What was the URL, again?
  Thanks!
    A confused customer
```

## How it works...

After importing the modules that will be used and defining the credentials, we connect to the server in *step 3*.

*Step 4* connects to `inbox`. This is a default folder in Gmail that contains the received email.

> **Tip**
>
> Of course, you may need to read a different folder. You can get a list of all folders by calling `mail.list()`.

In *step 5*, a list of UIDs is first retrieved for all the emails in the inbox by calling `.uid('search', None, "ALL")`. The list of emails is returned as a single string with all the email IDs concatenated, so we need to split the string and keep the latest email with the line.

```
latest_email_uid = data[0].split()[-1]
```

The last email received is then retrieved again from the server through a fetch action with `.uid('fetch', latest_email_uid, '(RFC822)')`. This retrieves the email in RFC822 format, which is the standard. Note that retrieving the email marks it as read.

> **Tip**
>
> The `.uid` command allows us to call IMAP4 commands, returning a tuple with the result (OK or NO) and the data. If there's an error, it raises the proper exception.

The `BytesParser` module is used to transform the raw RFC822 email into a Python object. This is done in *step 6*.

The metadata, including details such as the subject, the sender, and the timestamp, can be accessed like a dictionary, as shown in *step 7*. The addresses can be parsed from raw text format to separate the part with `email.utils.parseaddr`.

Finally, the content can be unfolded and extracted. If the type of the email is multipart, each of the parts can be extracted by iterating through `.get_payload()`. The one that's easier to deal with is `plain/text`, so assuming it is present, the code in *step 8* will extract it.

> **Tip**
>
> Note that we set up a default empty `payload` variable in case we cannot find plain text content. If a plain text version is not available, you may need to read and process the content in HTML.

The email's body is stored in the `payload` variable.

## There's more...

In *step 5* we retrieved all the emails from the inbox, but that's not necessary. The search command can be parameterized with filter criteria, for example, by retrieving only the last day's emails:

```
import datetime
since = (datetime.date.today() - datetime.timedelta(days=1)).strftime("%d-%b-%Y")
result, data = mail.uid('search', None, f'(SENTSINCE {since})')
```

This will search according to the date of the email. Notice that the resolution is in days.

There are more actions that can be done through IMAP4. See RFC 9051 at `https://datatracker.ietf.org/doc/html/rfc3501` for the latest protocol revision and further details.

Tip

The preceding RFCs describing the IMAP4 protocol can be a little arid. Checking the available commands in the RFCs' indexes will give you an idea of the capabilities of the protocol, and then you can search for examples on how to implement the specific command. You can also enlist the help of GenAI to explain particular points you are interested in, such as the protocol implementation, or to generate code that behaves in accordance with your specifications.

The subject and body of the email, as well as other metadata fields such as `date`, `to`, `from`, and so on, can be parsed and processed. For example, the subject retrieved in this recipe can be processed in the following way:

```
>>> import re
>>> re.search(r'\[Ref (\w+)] Subject: (\w+)', '[Ref ABCDEF] Subject: Product
A').groups()
('ABCDEF', 'Product')
```

## See also

- *Chapter 1, Let's Begin Our Automation Journey*, for more information about regular expressions and other ways of parsing information

# Adding subscribers to an email newsletter

Newsletter emails are a common marketing tool, since they are a convenient way of sending information to multiple targets. A good newsletter system is difficult to implement, and the recommended way is to use one of the solutions already available on the market. A well-known one is **MailChimp** (`https://mailchimp.com/`).

MailChimp has a lot of possibilities, but the interesting feature for your purposes is its API, which can be scripted to allow tool automation. This RESTful API can be accessed through Python, and in this recipe we will see how to add more subscribers to an existing list.

## Getting ready

To use MailChimp, we need to have an account. You can create a free account at `https://login.mailchimp.com/signup/`.

After creating the account, you need an audience that we can add subscribers to. As part of the registration process, it may have been created for you. It will appear under **Audience** -> **More Options** -> **Audience Settings**:

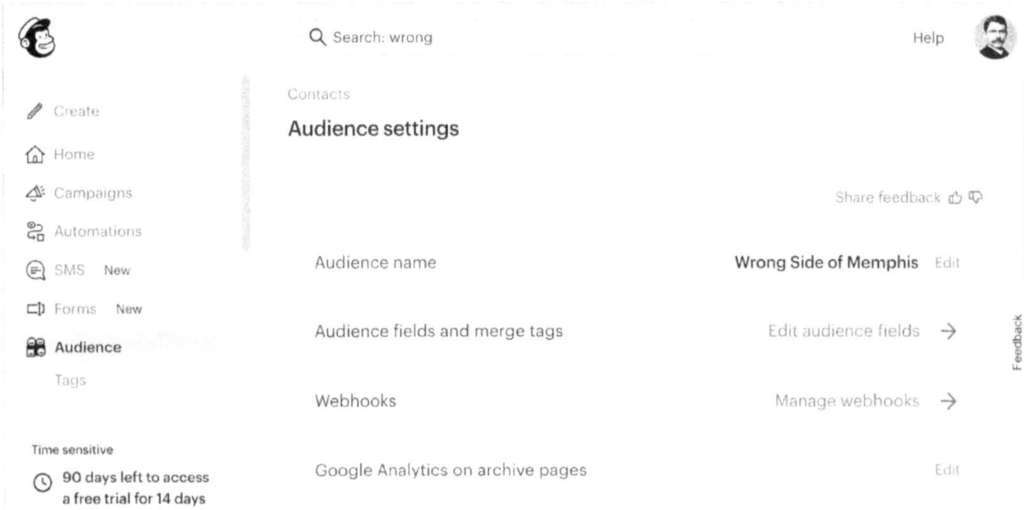


*Figure 9.4: Audiences in MailChimp*

The audience will contain the subscribed users. We will need the audience name later.

For the API, we'll need an API key. Go to your avatar, and select **Account & Billing** -> **Extras** -> **API keys** and create a new one:

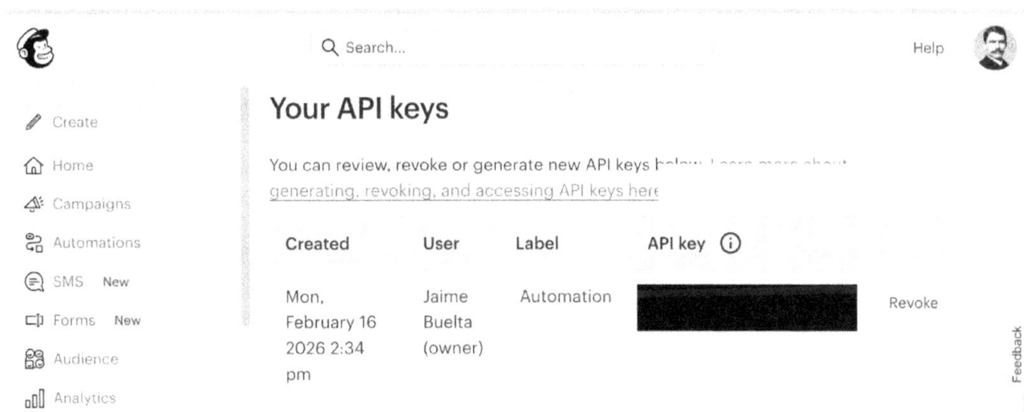


*Figure 9.5: A screenshot of API keys in MailChimp*

We will use the `requests` module to access the API. Add it to your environment:

```
$ echo "requests==2.32.5" >> requirements.txt
$ uv pip install -r requirements.txt
```

The MailChimp API uses the concept of the data center (DC) that your account uses. This can be obtained from the last 4 digits of your API key or from the start of the URL from the MailChimp admin site. For example, `us19`.

## How to do it...

1. Import the `requests` module:

```
>>> import requests
```

2. Define the authentication and base URLs. The base URL requires your DC at the start (such as `us19`):

```
>>> API_KEY = 'your secret key'
>>> BASE = 'https://<dc>.api.mailchimp.com/3.0'
>>> auth = ('user', API_KEY)
```

3. Check that the calls are correct:

```
>>> url = f'{BASE}/ping'
>>> response = requests.get(url, auth=auth)
>>> response.json()
{'health_status': "Everything's Chimpy!"}
```

4. Obtain all your lists (audiences). In this example, there should be only one audience.

```
>>> url = f'{BASE}/lists'
>>> response = requests.get(url, auth=auth)
>>> result = response.json()
```

5. Filter your lists to obtain the `href` for the required list:

```
>>> LIST_NAME = 'Your audience name'
>>> this_list = [link for link in result['lists']
                 if link['name'] == LIST_NAME][0]
```

```
>>> list_url = [link['href'] for link in this_list['_links']
                if link['rel'] == 'self'][0]
```

6. With the list URL, you can obtain the URL for the members of the list:

```
>>> response = requests.get(list_url, auth=auth)
>>> result = response.json()
>>> result['stats']
{'member_count': 2, 'unsubscribe_count': 0, 'cleaned_count': 0, ...}

>>> members_url = [link['href'] for link in result['_links']
                   if link['rel'] == 'members'][0]
```

7. The list of members can be retrieved through a GET request to `members_url`:

```
>>> response = requests.get(members_url, auth=auth)
>>> result = response.json()
>>> len(result['members'])
2
```

8. Append a new member to the list. Note that the new email address should be a valid one. A fake one like `test@test.com` may be rejected.

```
>>> new_member = {
    'email_address': 'new_member@domain.com',
    'status': 'subscribed',
}
>>> response = requests.post(members_url, json=new_member, auth=auth)
>>> response.status_code
200
```

9. Retrieving the list of users with a GET obtains all users:

```
>>> response = requests.get(members_url, auth=auth)
>>> result = response.json()
>>> len(result['members'])
3
>>> [m['email_address'] for m in result['members']]
['member1@domain.com', 'member2@domain.com', 'new_member@domain.com']
```

## How it works...

After importing the requests module in *step 1*, we define the basic values to connect in *step 2*: the base URL and the credentials. Note that for authentication, we only require the API key as the password, and any user (as described by the MailChimp documentation: `https://mailchimp.com/developer/marketing/docs/fundamentals/`). We use `user`.

*Step 3* tests that the authentication and connection are correct, by calling the `/ping` endpoint. The result is returned in JSON format. The call includes the `auth` parameter with the defined credentials. All subsequent calls will be made with this `auth` parameter for authentication purposes.

*Step 4* retrieves all the lists, calling the proper URL. *Step 5* shows how to filter the returned list to grab the URL of the list of interest. Each of the returned calls includes a list of `_links` with related information, making it possible to walk through the API.

The URL for the list is called in *step 6*. This returns information for the list, including the basic stats. By applying similar filtering to that used in *step 5*, we retrieve the URL for the members.

> **Note**
>
> Due to size constraints and to show relevant data, not all of the retrieved elements have been displayed. Feel free to analyze them interactively. The data is well constructed and follows the RESTful principles of discoverability. Python's introspection makes it quite readable and understandable.

*Step 7* retrieves the list of members by making a GET request to `members_url`. This can be seen in the *Getting ready* section in the web interface.

*Step 8* creates a new user and posts on `members_url` with the information passed in the `json` parameter so that it gets translated into JSON format. The updated data is retrieved in *step 8*, showing that there's a new user in the list.

## There's more...

The full MailChimp API is quite powerful and can perform a large number of tasks. Go to the full MailChimp documentation to discover all the possibilities: `https://developer.mailchimp.com/`.

Even though the calls that we are presenting here are done directly through the REST interface, a module is available that wraps them up in a convenient Python style, called `mailchimp-marketing`.

You can install it as usual:

```
$ uv pip install mailchimp-marketing==3.0.80
```

And then use it like this:

```
>>> from mailchimp_marketing import Client
>>> mailchimp = Client()
>>> mailchimp.set_config(
  {'api_key':API_KEY,
  'server': DC}
)
>>> response = mailchimp.lists.get_all_lists()
```

While using an API with the specific library is convenient and clear, the response is the same as that you'd get with the equivalent `request` call.

> **Tip**
>
> As a brief note, and a little outside the scope of this book, be aware of the legal implications of adding subscribers to an automated list. Spam is a serious concern and there are new regulations in place to protect the rights of customers, such as GDPR. Make sure that you have the permission of users to email them. The good thing is that MailChimp automatically implements tools to help with this, such as automatic unsubscribe buttons.

The general MailChimp documentation is also quite interesting and shows some of the possibilities. MailChimp is capable of managing newsletter and general distribution lists, but it can also be tailored to generate flows, schedule the sending of emails, and automatically send messages to your audience based on parameters such as their birthday.

## See also

- The *Sending an individual email* recipe, earlier in this chapter, to see the differences between sending an email directly without this kind of tool
- The *Sending notifications via email* recipe, next, to learn how to send emails tailored to a specific user for an action

# Sending notifications via email

In this recipe, we will cover how to send emails to customers. Transactional emails, such as confirmation or alert emails, are sent in response to actions by users and addressed to them. Due to spam protection and other limitations, it is better to implement this kind of email with the help of external tools. In this recipe, we will use Mailgun (`https://www.mailgun.com`), which is able to send these kinds of emails as well as communicate responses.

## Getting ready

We'll need to create an account with Mailgun. Go to `https://signup.mailgun.com/new/signup` to create one. Notice that the credit card information is optional.

Once registered, go to **Send** -> **Sending** -> **Domains** to see that there's a sandbox environment. We can use it to test Mailgun's functionality, although it will only send emails to registered test email accounts.

You need to add a test email recipient in the sandbox **Domain settings** -> **Setup**. To do so, it will send an email to the recipient account, asking the account holder to agree to receive test emails from Mailgun.

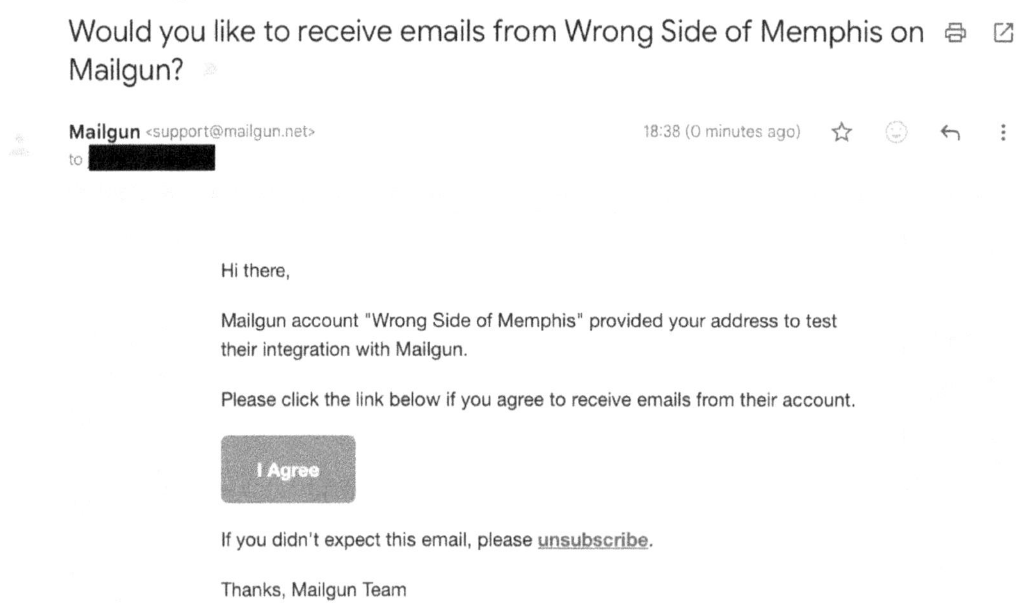


*Figure 9.6: Received email to approve that we are fine receiving test emails*

Once the **I Agree** button is clicked, you'll see in the interface that the email is approved for testing.

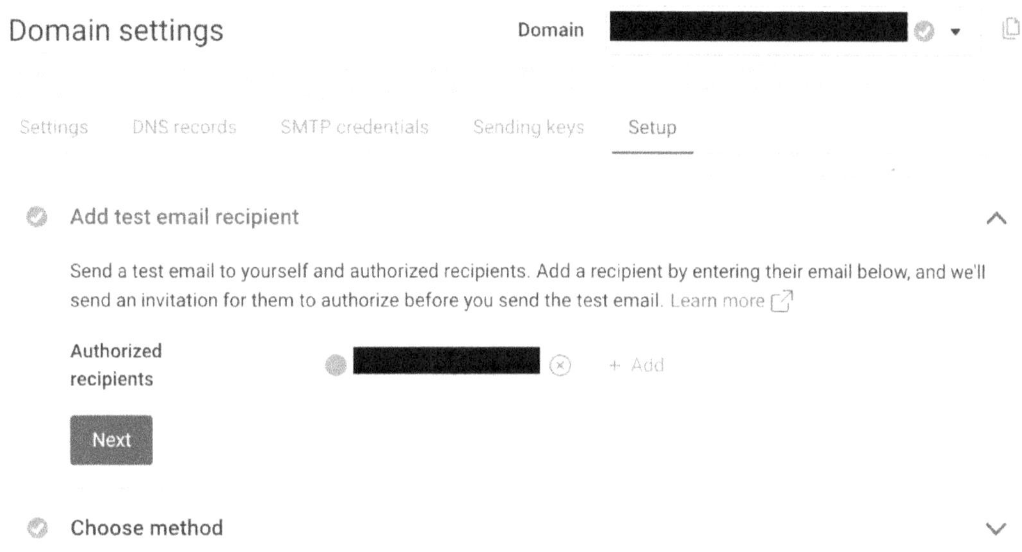


*Figure 9.7: Verified email for testing. Your email will appear in the authorized recipients*

You'll need to create API credentials (sending key) on the same screen:

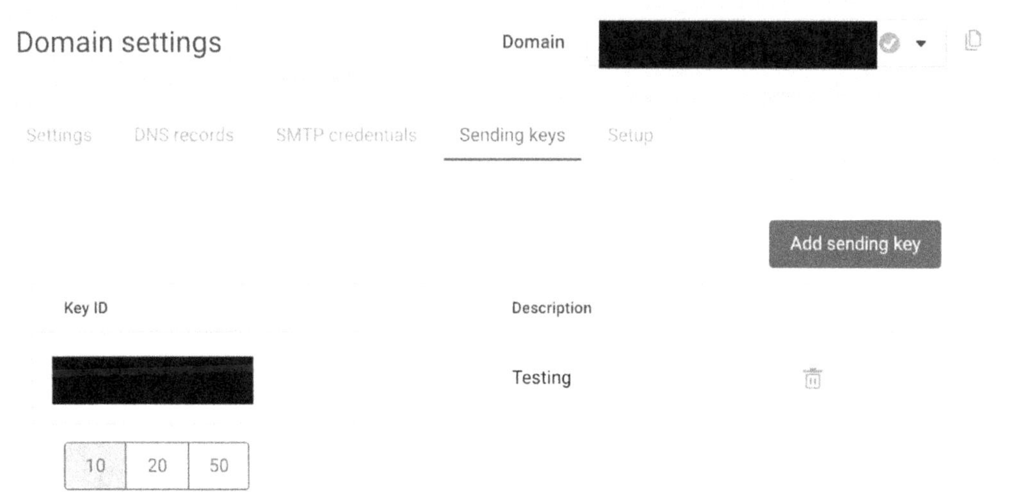


*Figure 9.8: Key created*

As is typical with these services, the API will only be seen once, so be sure to store it securely.

We will use the `requests` module to connect to the Mailgun API. Install it in the virtual environment:

```
$ echo "requests==2.32.5" >> requirements.txt
$ uv pip install -r requirements.txt
```

Everything is ready to send emails, but notice that you can only send emails to authorized recipients. Being able to send emails everywhere requires us to set up a domain. Follow the Mailgun documentation for that: `https://documentation.mailgun.com/docs/mailgun/user-manual/domains/domains-custom`.

## How to do it...

1. Import the `requests` module:

```
>>> import requests
```

2. Prepare the credentials, as well as the 'to' and 'from' email addresses. Note we're using a mock 'from' address:

```
>>> KEY = 'YOUR-SECRET-KEY'
>>> DOMAIN = 'sandboxYOUR-DOMAIN.mailgun.org'
>>> TO = 'YOUR-AUTHORISED-RECEIVER'
>>> FROM = f'sender@{DOMAIN}'
>>> auth = ('api', KEY)
```

3. Prepare the email to be sent. Here, there is an HTML version and a plain text one alternative:

```
>>> text = "Hi!\nThis is the text version linking to https://
www.packtpub.com/\nCheers!"
>>> html = '''<html><head></head><body>
...     <p>Hi!<br>
...         This is the HTML version linking to <a href="https://
www.packtpub.com/">Packt</a><br>
...     </p>
...   </body></html>'''
```

4. Set up the data to send to Mailgun:

```
>>> data = {
...     'from': f'Sender <{FROM}>',
...     'to': f'Recipient <{TO}>',
...     'subject': 'An interesting email!',
...     'text': text,
...     'html': html,
... }
```

5. Make the API call:

```
>>> response = requests.post(f"https://api.mailgun.net/v3/{DOMAIN}/
messages", auth=auth, data=data)
>>> response.json()
{'id': '<YOUR-ID.mailgun.org>', 'message': 'Queued. Thank you.'}
```

6. Retrieve the events and check the email has been delivered:

```
>>> response_events = requests.get(f'https://api.mailgun.net/v3/{DOMAIN}/
events', auth=auth)
>>> response_events.json()['items'][0]['recipient'] == TO
True
>>> response_events.json()['items'][0]['event']
'delivered'
```

7. The email should appear in your inbox. As it was sent through the sandbox environment, be sure to check your spam folder if it doesn't show up directly.

## How it works...

*Step 1* imports the requests module to be used later. The credentials and the basic information in the message are specified in *step 2* and should be extracted from the Mailgun web interface, as shown previously.

*Step 3* defines the email that will be sent. *Step 4* structures the information in the way Mailgun expects. Notice the `html` and `text` fields. By default, it will set HTML as the preferred option and the plain text option as an alternative. The format for `TO` and `FROM` should be in the `Name <address>` format. You can use commas to separate multiple recipients in `TO`.

The call to the API is made in *step 5*. It is a `POST` call to the `/messages` endpoint. The data is transferred in the standard way, and basic authentication is used with the `auth` parameter.

Notice the definition in *step 2*. All calls to Mailgun should include this `auth` parameter. It returns a message, notifying you that it was successful, and then the message is queued.

In *step 6*, a call to retrieve the events through a `GET` request is made. This will show the latest actions performed, the last of which will be the most recent send. Information about delivery status can also be found here.

## There's more...

To send emails outside of the sandbox environment, you'll need to set up the DNS domain with which to send them. You can find the instructions on how to do this here: `https://documentation.mailgun.com/docs/mailgun/user-manual/domains/domains-verify`. You'll need to change your DNS records to verify that you are the legitimate owner of the domain. Then you'll be able to deliver emails beyond just test use cases.

You can include email attachments in the following way:

```
attachments = [
    ("attachment",
        ("attachment1.jpg", open("image.jpg","rb").read())
    ),
    ("attachment",
        ("attachment2.txt", open("text.txt","rb").read())
    )]
response = requests.post(f"https://api.mailgun.net/v3/{DOMAIN}/messages",
                                 auth=auth, files=attachments, data=data)
```

Notice the structure of `("attachment", (<filename>, <binary data>))`.

The data can include the usual information such as *cc* or *bcc*, but you can also delay the delivery for up to three days with the `o:deliverytime` parameter:

```
import datetime
import email.utils
delivery_time = datetime.datetime.now() + datetime.timedelta(days=1)
data = {
    ...
    'o:deliverytime': email.utils.format_datetime(delivery_time),
}
```

Mailgun can also be used to receive emails and to trigger processes when they arrive; for example, forwarding them based on rules. Check the Mailgun documentation to find out more:

https://documentation.mailgun.com/docs/mailgun. Be sure to check the *Best Practices* section at https://documentation.mailgun.com/docs/mailgun/email-best-practices/best_practices to understand more about sending emails and how to avoid them being labeled as spam.

## See also

- The *Working with email templates* recipe, earlier in this chapter, to learn how to style emails using templates
- The *Sending an individual email* recipe, earlier in this chapter, to learn how to send emails directly from Python instead of using an external service
- The *Adding subscribers to an email newsletter* recipe to learn about the Mailchimp interface. Mailchimp also allows for transactional email

# Producing SMS messages

Text messages constitute one of the most widely available communication channels, being very convenient as a means of distributing information.

> Note
>
> SMS messages can be used for marketing purposes, but also as a way of alerting or sending notifications, or as a way of implementing two-factor authentication systems.

We will use **Twilio**, a service that exposes APIs to send SMS easily.

> Tip
>
> Twilio also has an API to interact through WhatsApp. The API is very similar.

to the SMS one, though for professional usage (outside of a sandbox for testing) you'll need a verified account. For more information, check the Twilio docs at https://www.twilio.com/docs/whatsapp.

## Getting ready

We need to create an account for Twilio at https://www.twilio.com/. Go to the page and register a new account.

You'll need to follow the instructions and set up a phone number to receive messages. You will need to input a code sent to this phone or receive a call to verify that the phone line is correct.

> **Note**
>
> Twilio also generates a recovery code to use in case you lose access to your phone. Store it safely.

Create a new project and check the dashboard. You can create a trial account for testing. From there, you'll be able to create your first phone number so that you can receive and send SMS.

From the creation page you can test that it sends SMS text messages either to your phone (the one you set up when configuring your account) or the newly created phone number produced as part of the project (essentially sending messages to itself). Once the number has been configured, it will appear in the **Phone Numbers** -> **Active numbers** section.

On the account dashboard, check `ACCOUNT SID` and `AUTH TOKEN` in **Account info**. They'll be used later. Note that you'll need to copy the auth token to use it later.

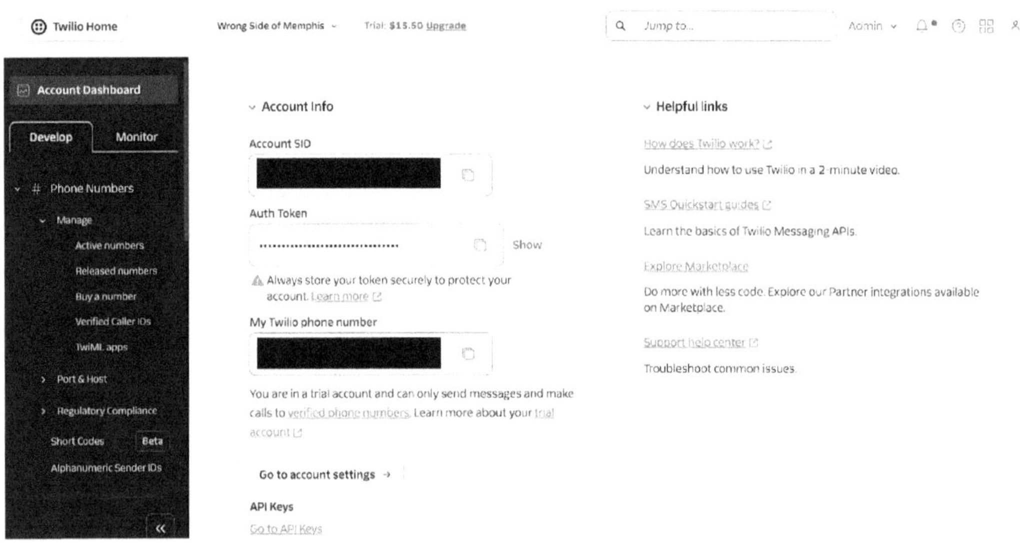


*Figure 9.9: Your Account SID , Auth Token and Twilio Phone number*

We'll also need to install the `twilio` module. Add it to your virtual environment:

```
$ echo "twilio==9.10.2" >> requirements.txt
$ uv pip install -r requirements.txt
```

Notice that the receiver phone number can only be a verified number with a trial account. You can verify more than one number; follow the documentation at `https://help.twilio.com/articles/223180048-How-to-Add-and-Remove-a-Verified-Phone-Number-or-Caller-ID-with-Twilio`.

# How to do it...

1. Import `Client` from the twilio module:

```
>>> from twilio.rest import Client
```

2. Set up the authentication credentials obtained from the dashboard previously, and also set your Twilio phone number:

```
>>> ACCOUNT_SID = 'Your account SID'
>>> AUTH_TOKEN = 'Your secret token'
>>> FROM = 'YOUR TWILIO PHONE NUMBER'
```

3. Start the client to access the API:

```
>>> client = Client(ACCOUNT_SID, AUTH_TOKEN)
```

4. Send a message to your authorized phone number. (Note the underscore at the end of `from_`, which is required because Python reserves the word `from` for loops):

```
>>> message = client.messages.create(
...     body='This is a test message from Python!',
...     from_=FROM,
...     to='+YOUR AUTHORIZED NUMBER')
```

5. You'll receive an SMS on your phone:

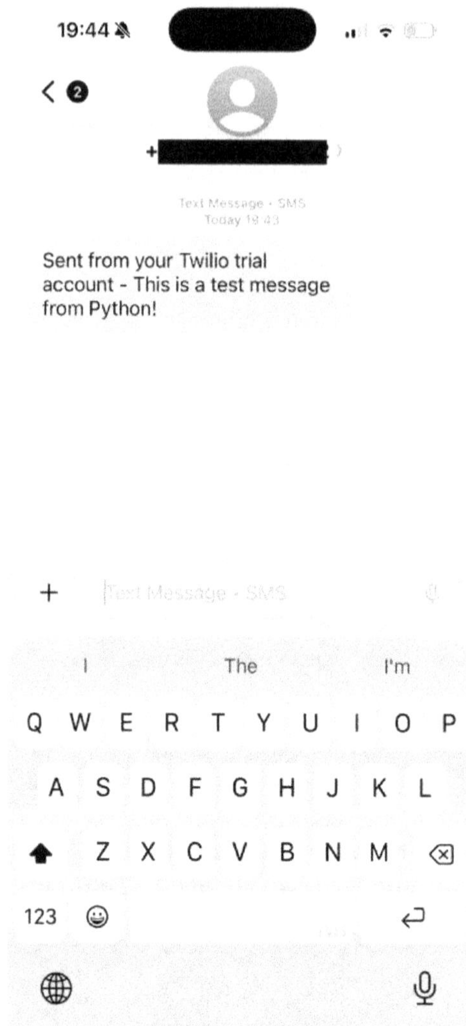


*Figure 9.10: Test message from Python*

## How it works...

The use of the Twilio client to send messages is very straightforward.

In *step 1* we import `Client`. We prepare the credentials and configure the phone number in *step 2*.

*Step 3* creates the client with the proper authentication, and the message is sent in *step 4*.

> **Note**
>
> Note that the *to* number needs to be one of the authenticated numbers while you're working in a trial account, or an error will occur.

All messages sent from a trial account will say that they are from a trial account, as you can see in *step 5*.

## There's more...

In certain regions (mainly the US and Canada), SMS numbers have the ability to send MMS messages, including images. To attach images to a message, add the `media_url` parameter and the URL of the image to send:

```
client.messages.create(body='An MMS message',
                       media_url='http://my.image.com/image.png',
                       from_=FROM,
                       to='+your authorised number')
```

Outside supported regions, the `media_url` will appear as a link.

The client is based on a RESTful API and allows you to perform multiple operations, such as creating a new phone number or obtaining an available number first and then purchasing it:

```
available_numbers = client.available_phone_numbers("IE").local.list()
number = available_numbers[0]
new_number =
client.incoming_phone_numbers.create(phone_number=number.phone_number)
```

> **Note**
>
> Check the documentation for more available actions; most of the dashboard point-and-click actions can be performed programmatically.

Twilio is also capable of performing other phone services, such as phone calls and text-to-speech. Check them out in the full documentation, available here: `https://www.twilio.com/docs/`.

We will see next the other part of texting, receiving messages.

## See also

- The *Receiving SMS messages* recipe, next, to learn how to receive messages, as well as send them
- The *Creating a Telegram bot* recipe, later in this chapter, to further your knowledge

# Receiving SMS messages

SMS messages can also be received and processed automatically. This enables services such as delivery of information on request (for instance, send INFO GOALS to receive Soccer League results), but also more complex flows such as in bots, which can have simple conversations with users to enable rich services such as remotely configuring a thermostat.

> **Tip**
>
> Each time Twilio receives an SMS to one of your registered phone numbers, it performs a request to a publicly available URL. This is configured in the Twilio service, meaning the code to execute when accessing the URL should be under your control. This creates the problem of having this URL available on the internet, meaning that just your local computer won't work, as it's very unlikely that it is addressable externally from your local network. We will use Railway (`http://railway.com`) to make the service available, but there are other alternatives. The Twilio documentation provides examples of using ngrok, which allows for local development by creating a tunnel between a public address and your local development environment. See here for more details: `https://www.twilio.com/en-us/blog/test-your-webhooks-locally-with-ngrok-html`.

This way of operating is common in communication APIs. It should be noted that Twilio has an API for WhatsApp, which works in a similar way. Check the docs for more information at `https://www.twilio.com/docs/sms/whatsapp/quickstart/python`.

## Getting ready

We need to create an account for Twilio at `https://www.twilio.com/`. Refer to the *Getting ready* section in the *Producing SMS messages* recipe for detailed instructions.

For this recipe, we'll also need to set up a web service in Railway (`https://www.railway.com/`) in order to create a webhook capable of receiving SMS addressed to Twilio. Because the main objective of this recipe is the SMS part, we will be concise when setting up Railway, but you can refer to its excellent documentation at `https://docs.railway.com`.

1. Create an account in Railway. You can use your GitHub account or create one with your email.
2. Download the web application from `https://github.com/PacktPublishing/Python-Automation-Cookbook-Third-Edition/tree/main/ch09/railway`.
3. Verify that the application works correctly by running it. You'll need to first install the dependencies and then run the application:

```
$ uv venv
$ uv pip install -r requirements.txt
$ uv run gunicorn main:app
[2026-02-19 18:45:34 +0100] [51542] [INFO] Starting gunicorn 25.1.0
[2026-02-19 18:45:34 +0100] [51542] [INFO] Listening at: http://
127.0.0.1:8080 (51542)
[2026-02-19 18:45:34 +0100] [51542] [INFO] Using worker: sync
[2026-02-19 18:45:34 +0100] [51543] [INFO] Booting worker with pid: 51543
```

   Once running, open a browser and go to `http://127.0.0.1:8080`. It should display 'All working!'. After that, you can exit the dev server with `CTRL+C`.

4. You'll need to install the command-line interface for Railway (instructions for all platforms can be found at `https://docs.railway.com/cli#installing-the-cli`) and then run to log in (it will open the browser to log you into the service):

```
$ railway login
```

5. Verify that the code to log in is the same as presented in the console, and proceed to be logged in
6. Run `init` to start the project:

```
$ railway init
> Select a workspace My Projects
> Project Name <randomly generated>
```

```
Created project perfect-learning on My Projects
https://railway.com/project/XXXXXXXXX
```

7. We have now an empty project, but we need to add our code. Do so with the `up` command:

```
$ railway up
Indexed
  Compressed [====================] 100%
  Uploaded
…
Build time: 27.27 seconds
Deploy complete
```

8. You will see, if you have a browser open at the address returned before, that the project is building and deploying:

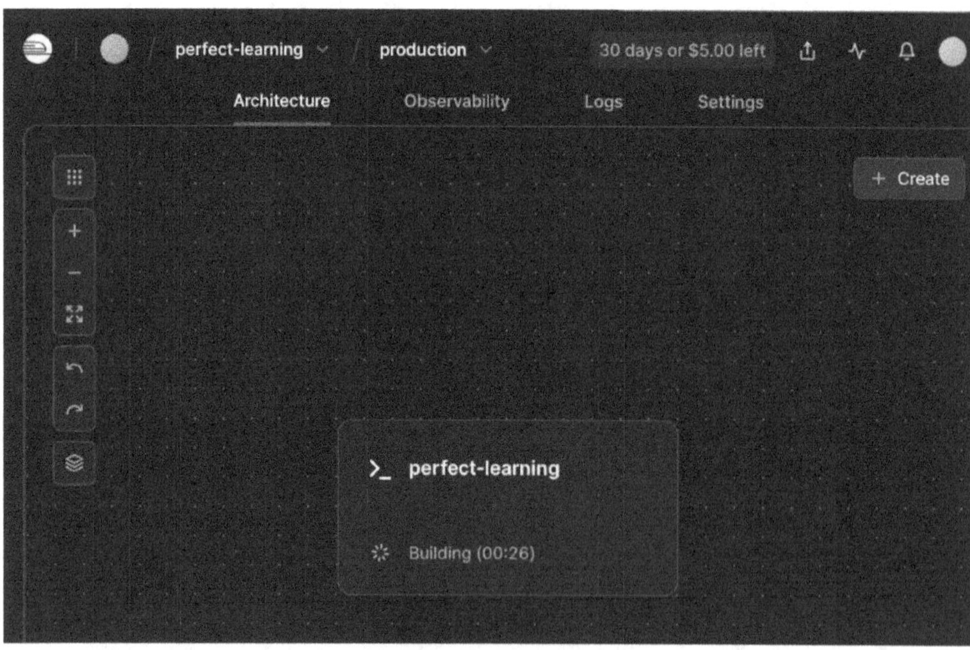


*Figure 9.11: Project building in Railway*

9. Once the project is deployed, we need to give it an accessible URL. Go to **Settings** (clicking on the box) -> **Networking**, and generate a domain:

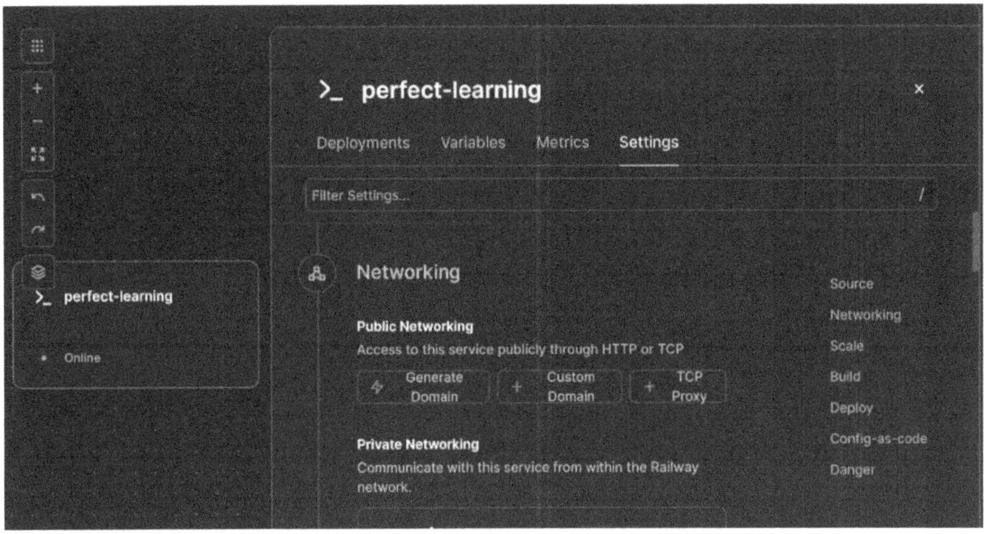


*Figure 9.12: Generate a domain to allow contact with the service*

10. Verify that the detected port is the one you are using. You should see in your command line a log similar to this:

```
[2026-02-19 18:18:19 +0100] [48976] [INFO] Starting gunicorn 25.1.0
[2026-02-19 18:18:19 +0100] [48976] [INFO] Listening at: http://
127.0.0.1:8080 (48976)
[2026-02-19 18:18:19 +0100] [48976] [INFO] Using worker: sync
```

Which means that you are serving the content on port 8080. *Verify in your networking configuration that this is the port being served.* If it is not, you may get a 502 error when accessing.

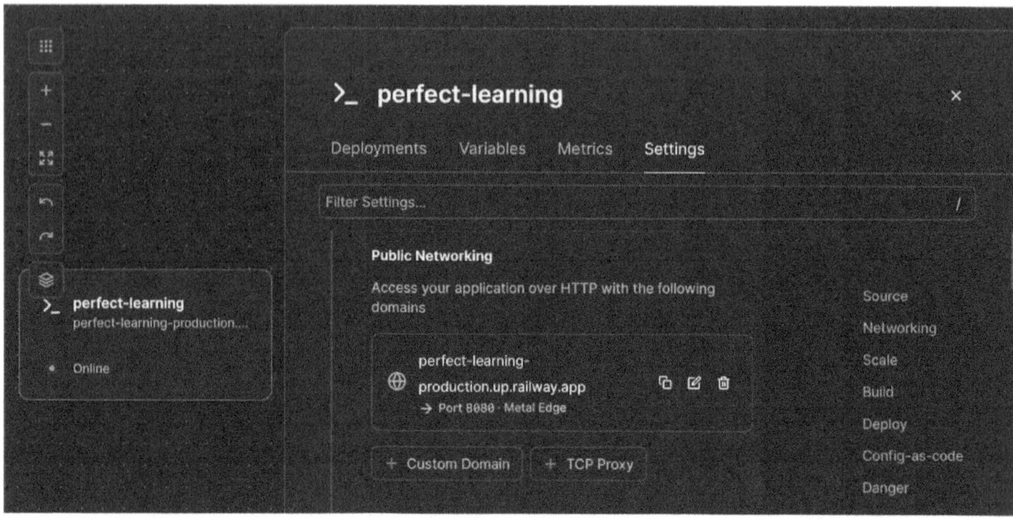


*Figure 9.13: Public networking port*

11. Access now your public networking URL; you should see the message. You can also check it in a browser.

Check that the service is up and running at the webhook URL. Note it is displayed as output in the previous step. You can also check it in a browser:

```
$ curl https://perfect-learning-production.up.railway.app
All working!
```

## How to do it...

1. Go to Twilio and access the **Phone Numbers** section and **Manage** -> **Active numbers** inside that. Go to the **Messaging Service** configuration to configure the webhook URL. The webhook should be your URL as above, plus the path `/sms`. Click on **Save configuration**:

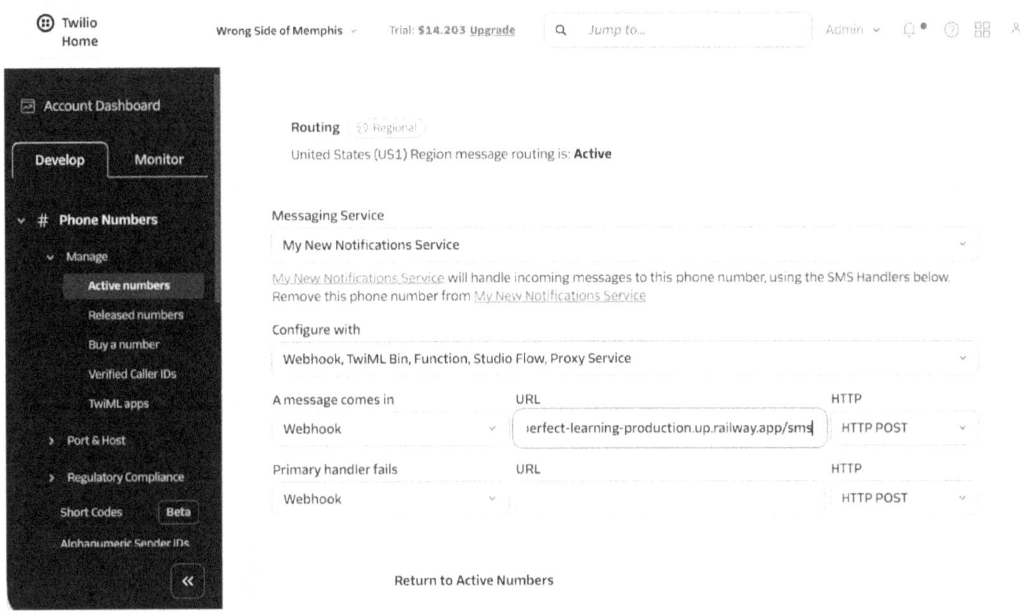


*Figure 9.14: Configuring phone numbers in Twilio*

2. The service is now up and running and can be used. Send an SMS to your Twilio phone number; you should get an automated response:

*Figure 9.15: SMS from Twilio trial account*

Note the redacted parts should be replaced with your information.

> **Note**
>
> If you have a trial account, you can only send messages back to one of your authorized phone numbers, so you'll need to send the text from them.

## How it works...

*Step 1* sets up the webhook, so Twilio calls your Railway app when it receives an SMS on the phone line.

Let's take a look at the code in `main.py` to see how this works. Here it is, edited for clarity; check the full file at `https://github.com/PacktPublishing/Python-Automation-Cookbook-Third-Edition/blob/main/ch09/railway/main.py`:

```
from flask import Flask, request
from twilio.twiml.messaging_response import MessagingResponse
app = Flask(__name__)
@app.route('/')
def homepage():
    return 'All working!'
@app.route("/sms", methods=['GET', 'POST'])
def sms_reply():
    from_number = request.form['From']
    body = request.form['Body']
    resp = MessagingResponse()
    msg = (f'Awwwww! Thanks so much for your message {from_number}, '
           f'"{body}" to you too.')
    resp.message(msg)
    return str(resp)
if __name__ == '__main__':
    app.run()
```

`main.py` can be divided into three parts:

- The Python imports at the start of the file and startup of the Flask app at the end, which is just setting up Flask
- The function `homepage`, configured to be served at `/`, which is generated to test that the server is working
- `sms_reply`, which is where the magic happens

The `sms_reply` function obtains the phone number that sends the SMS, as well as the body of the message, from the `request.form` dictionary. Then, compose a response in `msg`, attach it to a new `MessagingResponse`, and return it.

Tip

We are using the complete message from the user, but remember all the techniques to parse text mentioned in *Chapter 1, Let's Begin Our Automation Journey*. They are all applicable here for detecting predefined actions or performing any other text processing.

With GenAI, we can understand and produce better responses than ever before! Check *Chapter 11* for more information about techniques.

The value returned will be sent back to the sender by Twilio, producing the result seen in *step 2*.

## There's more...

To be able to generate automated conversations, the state of the conversation should be stored. For simple cases, storing information in `session` may be enough. The `session` is able to store information in cookies that are persistent between the same combination of *to* and *from* phone numbers, allowing you to retrieve it between messages.

Tip

If the conversation is more complex, it may require storing the state of the conversation in a database and generating a conversation flow with the different states that a conversation can take. Check *Chapter 11* and later regarding how to use AI models to produce more complex conversations. If you go that route, you'll need to store the context.

For example, this modification will return not only the sent body, but the previous one as well. Only the relevant parts have been included:

```
app = Flask(__name__)
app.secret_key = b'somethingreallysecret!!!!'
...
@app.route("/sms", methods=['GET', 'POST'])
def sms_reply():
    from_number = request.form['From']
    last_message = session.get('MESSAGE', None)
    body = request.form['Body']
    resp = MessagingResponse()
    msg = (f'Awwwww! Thanks so much for your message {from_number}, '
```

```
        f'"{body}" to you too. ')
    if last_message:
        msg += f'Not so long ago you said "{last_message}" to me..'
    session['MESSAGE'] = body
    resp.message(msg)
    return str(resp)
```

The previous body is stored in the `MESSAGE` key of the session, which is carried over. Notice the requirement to define a secret key to be able to use the session data. For more information about this, read `https://flask.palletsprojects.com/en/stable/quickstart/#sessions`. More information about the handling of cookies in Twilio can be found at `https://help.twilio.com/articles/223136287-How-do-Twilio-cookies-work-`.

> **Note**
>
> To deploy the new version in Railway, make your changes and run the `railway up` command again.

Because the main objective of this recipe is to demonstrate how to receive an SMS message, Railway and Flask are not described in detail, but they both have excellent documentation. That for Railway can be found at `https://docs.railway.com/`, while the documentation for Flask is here: `http://flask.pocoo.org/docs/`.

> **Note**
>
> Remember, the use of Railway and Flask is just a convenience for this recipe. They're great and easy tools to use, but there are multiple alternatives to them, as long as you are able to expose a URL that Twilio can call. Also, check the security measures to ensure that requests to this endpoint come from Twilio: `https://www.twilio.com/docs/usage/security#validating-requests`.

On top of connecting through SMS, you can also use Twilio for WhatsApp communication, in similar ways. Check their documentation here `https://www.twilio.com/docs/whatsapp`.

We have only scratched the possibilities for Twilio. Its full documentation can be found here: `https://www.twilio.com/docs/`.

## See also

- The *Producing SMS messages* recipe, earlier in this chapter, to get to grips with the fundamentals of Twilio and how to receive messages
- The *Creating a Telegram bot* recipe, next

# Creating a Telegram bot

Telegram Messenger is an instant messaging app that has strong support for creating bots. Chatbots are small applications that aim to produce automatic conversational responses. The big promise of bots is that, as machines, they can create any kind of conversation, indistinguishable from human conversation, and pass the **Turing Test**. With the latest improvements in GenAI, this objective is actually closer than ever, though it still presents challenges.

> Note
>
> The Turing Test was proposed by Alan Turing in 1950, in what he called the "imitation game," involving three participants communicating only via text (like in an instant messaging app). The first is a human judge who can ask questions, and the other two are a human and a machine/software program. The judge needs to find out, through asking them questions, which one is human and which one is not. If the judge can only guess correctly 50% of the time, it can't be easily determined, and therefore the AI passes the test. This was one of the first attempts to measure AI.

We will improve our dialog abilities using GenAI in *Chapter 11*, but chatbots can still be very useful in more limited contexts, for example phone systems where traditionally you have needed to (say) press 2 to check your account and press 3 to report a missing card. In this recipe we'll see how to generate a simple chatbot to display offers and events for a company.

## Getting ready

We need to create a new bot for Telegram. This is done through an interface called the **BotFather**, which is a special Telegram channel that allows us to create a new bot. You can access it here: `https://telegram.me/botfather`. Access it through your Telegram account.

Run `/start` to start the interface and then create a new bot with `/newbot`. The interface will ask you for the name of the bot and a username, which should be unique.

Once set up it will give you the following:

- The Telegram channel of your bot: `https://t.me/<yourusername>`.
- A token to allow access to the bot. Copy it as it will be used later.

> **Note**
>
> You can generate a new token if you lose an existing token. Read the BotFather documentation for more information.

We also need to install the Python module `python-telegram-bot`, which wraps the RESTful interface from Telegram:

```
$ echo "python-telegram-bot==22.6" >> requirements.txt
$ uv pip install -r requirements.txt
```

Download the `telegram_bot.py` script from GitHub at `https://github.com/PacktPublishing/Python-Automation-Cookbook-Third-Edition/blob/main/ch09/telegram_bot.py`.

## How to do it...

1. Set up your generated token in the `telegram_bot.py` script's TOKEN constant in line 6:

    ```
    TOKEN = '<YOUR TOKEN>'
    ```

2. Start the bot:

    ```
    $ uv run telegram_bot.py
    ```

3. Open the Telegram channel on your phone using the URL and start it. You can use the help, offers, and events commands:

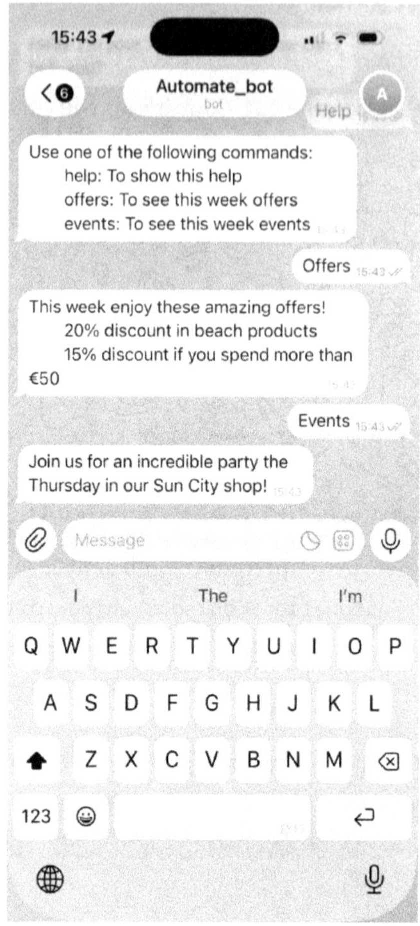


Figure 9.16: Marketing offers sent by Telegram

## How it works...

*Step 1* sets the token to use for your specific channel. In *step 2*, we start the bot locally.

Let's see how `telegram_bot.py` is structured:

```
# IMPORTS
# TOKEN
# Commands
async def start(update, context):
async def help_command(update, context):

# Define the information to return per message
```

```
def get_help():
def get_offers():
def get_events():
COMMANDS = {
    'help': get_help,
    'offers': get_offers,
    'events': get_events,
}
# Handle the messages
async def chat_message(update, context):
...
```

Taking a look at `main`:

```
# Create and start the bot
def main():
    application = ApplicationBuilder().token(TOKEN).build()
    application.add_handler(CommandHandler("start", start))
    application.add_handler(CommandHandler("help", help_command))
    application.add_handler(MessageHandler(filters.TEXT & ~filters.COMMAND,
                                           chat_message))
    application.run_polling()
```

```
The main function starts the application using the TOKEN, and then sets up three
different handlers:
```

- Handler for the command `start`, called by `/start`
- Handler for the command `help`, called using `/help`
- Handler for messages (regular text with no / start). We apply a filter to say that we only accept `TEXT` messages that are 'no' commands.

> **Tip**
>
> Telegram bots need to support the `start` and `help` command. `start` will be triggered at the start of a conversation with the bot.
>
> Note that Telegram defines commands as actions starting with `/`. You can create more actions if you want.

A message that has no handler (e.g. an image in our example) will be ignored.

The start and help commands are straightforward; now let's take a look at `chat_message`:

```
async def chat_message(update, context):
    # Detect the message and return the proper response
    message = update.message.text.lower()
    if message not in COMMANDS:
        await update.message.reply_text('Sorry, I did not catch that. Type "help"
to see all options.')
        return

    message_back = COMMANDS[message]()
    await update.message.reply_text(message_back)
```

First of all, we notice the `async def` in the definition of the function. This is to indicate that the function is asynchronous. That also explains the `await` calls.

> **Note**
>
> Asynchronous programming is a form of multitasking where the code releases control when waiting for an operation – hence `await`. It is suitable for communication-heavy processes, as a single process will be able to handle multiple concurrent conversations.
>
> The main disadvantage of async programming is that the code can become more difficult to understand, and you cannot generally call an `async` function from a regular function.

The code detects the message, and if it's one of the understood ones, it calls the proper `get_message` function in order to obtain the message that's to be returned. It sends the message back to the user with

```
await update.message.reply_text(message_back)
```

Note the `await` code word there.

*Step 3* shows how this works from the point of view of the user who is interacting with the bot.

## There's more...

You can add more information, an avatar picture, and so on to your Telegram channel using the *BotFather* interface.

To simplify our interface, we can create an inline keyboard to simplify the options and allow users to click on them directly. To do that, we need to create a new function `show_options` for the display and `press_button` for capturing the action by the user. Let's first see `show_options`:

```
async def show_options(update, context):
    keyboard = [
        [
            InlineKeyboardButton('Offers', callback_data='offers'),
            InlineKeyboardButton('Events', callback_data='events'),
            InlineKeyboardButton('Help', callback_data='help'),
        ]
    ]

    reply_markup = InlineKeyboardMarkup(keyboard)
    await update.message.reply_text('Available Options:',
reply_markup=reply_markup)
```

This creates an `InlineKeyboard` with three buttons, one for each option. When the user clicks on one of them, the event is captured by the `press_button` function:

```
async def press_button(update, context):
    query = update.callback_query
    await query.answer()
    option = query.data
    await query.edit_message_text(text=f'Selected option: {option}')
    message_back = COMMANDS[option]()
    await context.bot.send_message(chat_id=update.effective_chat.id,
text=message_back)
```

The displayed button is edited into the selected option.

> **Note**
>
> You can see this in Figure 9.17. The last line shows the available options in independent boxes (Offers, Events, Help). Above, at 16:31, there was a previous selection that was edited into text showing the selection.

Then it gets the message back for the selected option and sends another message.

Note that there's no text to reply to, so we need to use the `context.bot.send_message` call, which requires the `chat_id`.

This makes the available options very obvious:

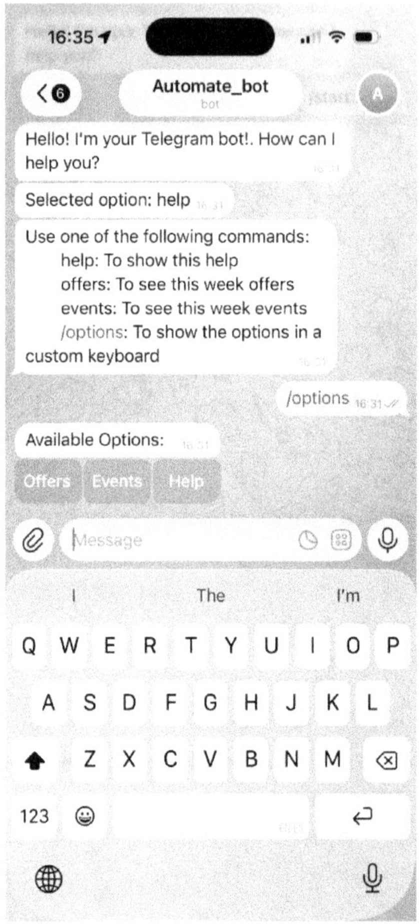


*Figure 9.17: Telegram messages with buttons*

These changes can be downloaded from the `telegram_bot_custom_keyboard.py` file, available in GitHub here: `https://github.com/PacktPublishing/Python-Automation-Cookbook-Third-Edition/blob/main/ch09/telegram_bot_custom_keyboard.py`.

You can create other kinds of custom interfaces, including a platform for creating games! Check the Telegram API docs for more information.

To have the system working in production, you will likely require your bot to be deployed, for which the documentation of `python-telegram-bot` provides some recommendations – see `https://github.com/python-telegram-bot/python-telegram-bot/wiki/Where-to-host-Telegram-Bots`.

Railway, which we introduced in the previous recipe, also has an example at `https://railway.com/deploy/a0ln90`.

The full Telegram API for bots can be found at `https://core.telegram.org/bots`, while the documentation for the `python-telegram-bot` module can be found at `https://docs.python-telegram-bot.org/en/stable/`.

## See also

- The *Producing SMS messages* recipe, earlier in this chapter, to learn about the fundamentals of Twilio and how to receive SMS messages
- The *Receiving SMS messages* recipe, previously in this chapter, to learn how to receive SMS messages using Twilio

# Get this book's PDF version and more

Scan the QR code (or go to `packtpub.com/unlock`). Search for this book by name, confirm the edition, and then follow the steps on the page.

UNLOCK NOW

*Note: Keep your invoice handy. Purchases made directly from Packt don't require an invoice.*

# 10

# Why Not Automate Your Marketing Campaign?

In this chapter, we will create a marketing campaign and go through each of the multiple automatic steps we'll take. We will draw on concepts and recipes taken from earlier in this book.

Let's look at an example. For our project, our company wishes to set up a marketing campaign to improve engagement and sales – a laudable objective. We can divide it into several sub-tasks:

1. We want to detect the best moment to launch the campaign, so we will be notified from different sources about keywords that will help us make an informed decision about when to launch the campaign and its characteristics
2. The campaign will include the generation of individual promotional codes to be sent to potential customers. At the end of this step, we will have a file with a list of promotional codes.
3. We will send these codes directly to users over their preferred channel, whether that is text message or email. We will first use a list of users and mix it with the codes generated in the previous step to prepare a list of messages, and then send all the messages.
4. We will compile sales information to monitor the success of the campaign, creating a spreadsheet with all the sales information
5. Finally, a sales report will be generated based on that spreadsheet

This chapter will go through each of these tasks and present a combined solution based on the modules and techniques that have been introduced in the book.

> **Tip**
>
> While these examples have been created with real-life requirements in mind, your specific environment can always surprise you. Don't be afraid to experiment, tweak, and improve your system as you learn more about it. Iterating is the way to create great systems.
>
> This chapter will use techniques that don't rely heavily on GenAI. There's plenty of automation that can be done 'the old-fashioned way', but in the following chapters we will expand on GenAI use in ways that mean it could well be worth revisiting this chapter later.

In this chapter, we will cover the following recipes related to each of the steps of our marketing campaign:

1. Detecting opportunities
2. Creating personalized coupon codes
3. Sending a notification to a customer on their preferred channel
4. Preparing sales information
5. Generating a sales report

Let's get started!

# Technical requirements

The code presented in this chapter can be found in the GitHub repo at `https://github.com/PacktPublishing/Python-Automation-Cookbook-Third-Edition/tree/main/ch10`.

# Detecting opportunities

This recipe covers *step 1* on the list of tasks, detecting the best moment when to launch our campaign.

Our first task is to detect the best time to launch a campaign. To do so, we will monitor a list of news sites and search for news containing one of our defined keywords. We add any article that matches these keywords to a report and send it in an email.

> **Note**
>
> This task can be expanded using agentic flows, as we will see in *Chapters 11* to *14*. Check there to expand on this recipe.

## Getting ready

In this recipe, we will use several external modules previously presented in this book: pendulum, jinja2, and mistune. We need to add them to our virtual environment if they're not already there:

```
$ echo "pendulum==3.3.0" >> requirements.txt
$ echo "feedparser==6.0.12" >> requirements.txt
$ echo "jinja2==3.1.6" >> requirements.txt
$ echo "mistune==3.2.0" >> requirements.txt
$ uv pip install -r requirements.txt
```

You need to make a list of RSS feeds from which to retrieve data.

For this example, we'll be using the technology feeds of some well-known news sites:

1. https://techcrunch.com/feed/
2. https://rss.nytimes.com/services/xml/rss/nyt/Technology.xml
3. https://feeds.bbci.co.uk/news/science_and_environment/rss.xml

Download the search_keywords.py script, which will perform the actions, from GitHub at https://github.com/PacktPublishing/Python-Automation-Cookbook-Third-Edition/blob/main/ch10/search_keywords.py. You'll also need to download the email templates, which can be found at the subdirectory ch10 as email_styling.html and email_template.md. There is a config template called config-opportunity.ini.

You need to have a valid username and password for an email service. Check the *Sending an individual email* recipe in *Chapter 9, Dealing with Communication Channels.*

## How to do it...

1. Create a config-opportunity.ini file, which should be in the following format. Remember to fill it with your details:

```
[SEARCH]
keywords = keyword,
           keyword
feeds = feed,
        feed
[EMAIL]
user = <YOUR EMAIL USERNAME>
password = <YOUR EMAIL PASSWORD>
```

```
from = <EMAIL ADDRESS FROM>
to = <EMAIL ADDRESS TO>
```

You can use the template from GitHub at `https://github.com/PacktPublishing/Python-Automation-Cookbook-Third-Edition/blob/master/ch10/config-opportunity.ini` to search for the keywords 'crypto', 'AI' and 'artificial intelligence', and some test feeds. Remember to fill in the `EMAIL` fields with your own account details in the `.ini` file.

2. Call the script to produce the email and report:

```
$ uv run search_keywords.py config-opportunity.ini
```

3. Check the email defined in the `to` field; you should receive a report listing the articles found. Keep in mind that its exact composition will depend on the daily news, but it should be something similar to this:

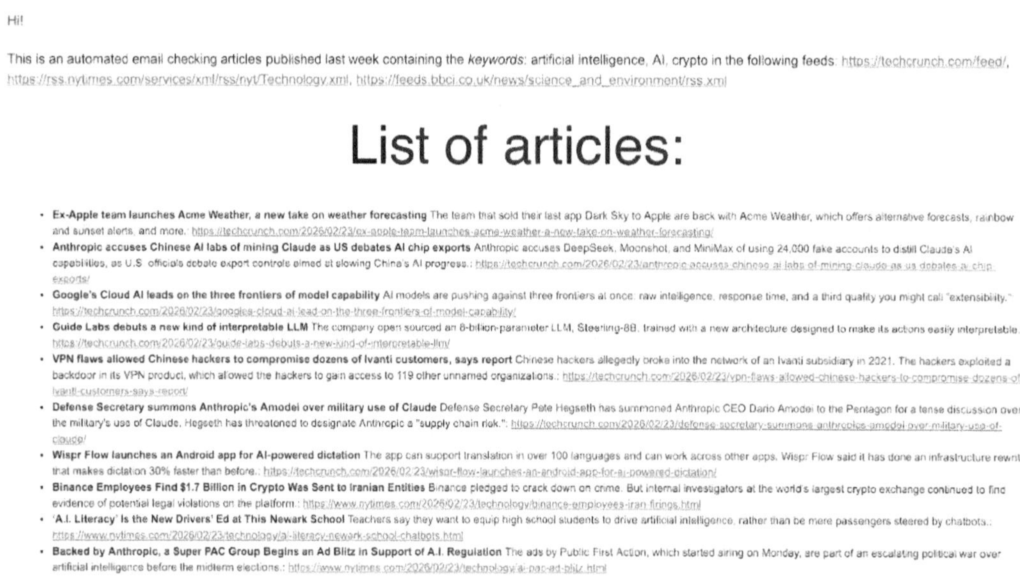

Hi!

This is an automated email checking articles published last week containing the *keywords*: artificial intelligence, AI, crypto in the following feeds: https://techcrunch.com/feed/, https://rss.nytimes.com/services/xml/rss/nyt/Technology.xml, https://feeds.bbci.co.uk/news/science_and_environment/rss.xml

List of articles:

- **Ex-Apple team launches Acme Weather, a new take on weather forecasting** The team that sold their last app Dark Sky to Apple are back with Acme Weather, which offers alternative forecasts, rainbow and sunset alerts, and more.: https://techcrunch.com/2026/02/23/ex-apple-team-launches-acme-weather-a-new-take-on-weather-forecasting/
- **Anthropic accuses Chinese AI labs of mining Claude as US debates AI chip exports** Anthropic accuses DeepSeek, Moonshot, and MiniMax of using 24,000 fake accounts to distill Claude's AI capabilities, as U.S. officials debate export controls aimed at slowing China's AI progress.: https://techcrunch.com/2026/02/23/anthropic-accuses-chinese-ai-labs-of-mining-claude-as-us-debates-ai-chip-exports/
- **Google's Cloud AI leads on the three frontiers of model capability** AI models are pushing against three frontiers at once: raw intelligence, response time, and a third quality you might call "extensibility.": https://techcrunch.com/2026/02/23/googles-cloud-ai-lead-on-the-three-frontiers-of-model-capability/
- **Guide Labs debuts a new kind of interpretable LLM** The company open sourced an 8-billion-parameter LLM, Steerling-8B, trained with a new architecture designed to make its actions easily interpretable.: https://techcrunch.com/2026/02/23/guide-labs-debuts-a-new-kind-of-interpretable-llm/
- **VPN flaws allowed Chinese hackers to compromise dozens of Ivanti customers, says report** Chinese hackers allegedly broke into the network of an Ivanti subsidiary in 2021. The hackers exploited a backdoor in its VPN product, which allowed the hackers to gain access to 119 other unnamed organizations.: https://techcrunch.com/2026/02/23/vpn-flaws-allowed-chinese-hackers-to-compromise-dozens-of-ivanti-customers-says-report/
- **Defense Secretary summons Anthropic's Amodei over military use of Claude** Defense Secretary Pete Hegseth has summoned Anthropic CEO Dario Amodei to the Pentagon for a tense discussion over the military's use of Claude. Hegseth has threatened to designate Anthropic a "supply chain risk.": https://techcrunch.com/2026/02/23/defense-secretary-summons-anthropics-amodei-over-military-use-of-claude/
- **Wispr Flow launches an Android app for AI-powered dictation** The app can support translation in over 100 languages and can work across other apps. Wispr Flow said it has done an infrastructure rewrite that makes dictation 30% faster than before.: https://techcrunch.com/2026/02/23/wispr-flow-launches-an-android-app-for-ai-powered-dictation/
- **Binance Employees Find $1.7 Billion in Crypto Was Sent to Iranian Entities** Binance pledged to crack down on crime. But internal investigators at the world's largest crypto exchange continued to find evidence of potential legal violations on the platform.: https://www.nytimes.com/2026/02/23/technology/binance-employees-iran-firings.html
- **'A.I. Literacy' Is the New Drivers' Ed at This Newark School** Teachers say they want to equip high school students to drive artificial intelligence, rather than be mere passengers steered by chatbots.: https://www.nytimes.com/2026/02/23/technology/ai-literacy-newark-school-chatbots.html
- **Backed by Anthropic, a Super PAC Group Begins an Ad Blitz in Support of A.I. Regulation** The ads by Public First Action, which started airing on Monday, are part of an escalating political war over artificial intelligence before the midterm elections.: https://www.nytimes.com/2026/02/23/technology/ai-pac-ad-blitz.html

*Figure 10.1: A list of articles containing the keywords 'crypto', 'AI' or 'artificial intelligence'*

## How it works...

After creating the proper script configuration in *step 1*, web scraping and sending an email with the results are carried out in *step 2* by calling `search_keywords.py`.

Let's take a look at the search_keywords.py script.

```
# IMPORTS #
import argparse
import sys
import configparser

import feedparser
import pendulum
import mistune
import jinja2
from collections import namedtuple

import smtplib
import calendar
from email.mime.multipart import MIMEMultipart
from email.mime.text import MIMEText

# READ TEMPLATES #

# Group the email configuration parameters
# Note the 'from_' to avoid using a reserved Python keyword (from)
EmailConfig = namedtuple('EmailConfig', ['user', 'password', 'from_', 'to'])


# Get the email templates from hard disk
EMAIL_TEMPLATE_FILE = 'email_template.md'
EMAIL_STYLING_FILE = 'email_styling.html'

with open(EMAIL_TEMPLATE_FILE) as md_file:
    EMAIL_TEMPLATE = md_file.read()

with open(EMAIL_STYLING_FILE) as html_file:
    EMAIL_STYLING = html_file.read()


def get_articles(keywords, feeds):
    '''
    Retrieve a list of articles from the feeds that contain the keywords

    Each article is returned in the format:
```

```
    (title, summary, link)
    '''
    articles = []

    for feed in feeds:
        rss = feedparser.parse(feed)
        updated_raw = rss.get('updated_parsed')
        # Use as base time either the last update time or now
        if updated_raw is None:
            updated_at = pendulum.now()
        else:
            updated_at = pendulum.from_timestamp(calendar.timegm(updated_raw))

        # Calculate the oldest article we will check, 7 days ago
        time_limit = updated_at.subtract(days=7)
        for entry in rss.entries:
            # Normalise the time
            entry_time = entry.published_parsed
            if not entry_time:
                # No time for this entry, skip
                continue
            entry_time = pendulum.from_timestamp(calendar.timegm(entry_time))
            if entry_time < time_limit:
                # Skip this entry
                continue

            # Get the article reference
            title = entry.title.strip()
            summary = entry.summary.strip()
            article_reference = (title, summary, entry.link)

            for keyword in keywords:
                summary_found = keyword.lower() in summary.lower()
                title_found = keyword.lower() in title.lower()
                if summary_found or title_found:
                    articles.append(article_reference)
                    break

    return articles
```

```
def compose_email_body(articles, keywords, feed_list):
    '''
    From the list of articles, keywords and feeds, fill the email template

    Set the list in the adequate format for the template
    '''
    # Compose the list of articles
    ARTICLE_TEMPLATE = '* **{title}** {summary}: {link}'
    article_list = [ARTICLE_TEMPLATE.format(title=title, summary=summary,
                                            link=link)
                    for title, summary, link in articles]

    data = {
        'article_list': '\n'.join(article_list),
        'keywords': ', '.join(keywords),
        'feed_list': ', '.join(feed_list),
    }
    text = jinja2.Template(EMAIL_TEMPLATE).render(**data)

    html_content = mistune.html(text)
    html = jinja2.Template(EMAIL_STYLING).render(content=html_content)

    return text, html


def send_email(email_config, text_body, html_body):
    '''
    Send an email with the text and html body, using the parameters
    configured in email_config
    '''
    msg = MIMEMultipart('alternative')
    msg['Subject'] = 'Weekly report'
    msg['From'] = email_config.from_
    msg['To'] = email_config.to

    part_plain = MIMEText(text_body, 'plain')
    part_html = MIMEText(html_body, 'html')

    msg.attach(part_plain)
    msg.attach(part_html)
```

```
    with smtplib.SMTP('smtp.gmail.com', 587) as server:
        server.starttls()
        server.login(email_config.user, email_config.password)
        server.sendmail(email_config.from_, [email_config.to], msg.as_string())


def main(keywords, feeds, email_config):
    articles = get_articles(keywords, feeds)
    text_body, html_body = compose_email_body(articles, keywords, feeds)
    send_email(email_config, text_body, html_body)


if __name__ == '__main__':
    parser = argparse.ArgumentParser()
    parser.add_argument(type=argparse.FileType('r'), dest='config',
                        help='config file')
    parser.add_argument('-o', dest='output', type=argparse.FileType('w'),
                        help='output file',
                        default=sys.stdout)

    args = parser.parse_args()
    config = configparser.ConfigParser()
    config.read_file(args.config)
    keywords = config['SEARCH']['keywords'].split(',')
    feeds = [feed.strip() for feed in config['SEARCH']['feeds'].split(',')]

    email_user = config['EMAIL']['user']
    email_password = config['EMAIL']['password']
    email_from = config['EMAIL']['from']
    email_to = config['EMAIL']['to']
    email_config = EmailConfig(email_user, email_password, email_from,
                               email_to)

    main(keywords, feeds, email_config)
```

As you can see, the code is structured into the following parts:

- The `IMPORTS` section includes all the Python modules to be used later. It also defines `EmailConfignamedtuple` to help with handling the email parameters.

- `READ TEMPLATES` retrieves the email templates and stores them for later use in the `EMAIL_TEMPLATE` and `EMAIL_STYLING` constants.
- The `__main__` block starts the process by getting the configuration parameters, parsing the config file, and then calling the main function.
- The `main` function combines the other functions. First, it retrieves the articles, and then it obtains the body and sends the email.
- `get_articles` walks through all the feeds and discards any article over a week old. For the remaining articles, it searches for a match on the keywords. All the matched articles are returned, including information about the *link* and a *summary*.
- `compose_email_body` uses the email templates to – unsurprisingly – compile the email body. Notice that the template is in Markdown and it gets parsed into HTML, to yield the same information in plain-text and in HTML.
- `send_email` gets the body information, as well as required information such as username and password, and sends the email.

## There's more...

One of the main challenges in retrieving information from different sources is to parse the text successfully in all cases. Some feeds may return information in different formats.

For instance, in our example, you can see that the Reuters feed summary includes HTML information that gets rendered in the resulting email. If you have that kind of problem, you may need to process the returned data further, until it becomes consistent. This can be highly dependent on the desired quality of the resulting report.

> **Tip**
>
> When developing automatic tasks, especially when dealing with multiple input sources, expect to spend a lot of time cleaning the input to make it consistent. However, find a balance and keep the final recipient in mind. If the email is to be received, for example, by yourself or a friend, you can probably be a little more permissive than with an important client.

Another possibility is to increase the complexity of the match. In this recipe, the check is done with a simple `in` operator against the parameters in the feed. Remember that all the techniques in *Chapter 1, Let's Begin Our Automation Journey*, are available for you to use, including all the capabilities of regular expressions.

This script is automatable through a cron job, as described in *Chapter 2, Automating Tasks Made Easy*. Try to run it every week!

Another possibility is to retrieve the full page (and not just the feed summary) using the techniques in *Chapter 3* and perhaps download the pages with Playwright to properly parse them.

## See also

- The *Adding command-line arguments recipe* in *Chapter 1, Let's Begin Our Automation Journey*, to learn the details about command-line arguments
- The *Preparing a task recipe* in *Chapter 2, Automating Tasks Made Easy*, to check the structure for a good automated task
- The *Setting up a cron job recipe* in *Chapter 2, Automating Tasks Made Easy*, to learn how to repeat a job automatically
- The *Subscribing to feeds recipe* in *Chapter 3, Building Your First Web Scraping Application*, to learn the basics about dealing with RSS feeds
- The *Sending an individual email* recipe in *Chapter 9, Dealing with Communication Channels*, to learn how to send emails using Python

# Creating personalized coupon codes

This recipe handles *step 2* of the campaign, generating the individual codes to send to potential customers.

After an opportunity has been detected, we decide to generate a campaign for all customers. To direct promotions and avoid duplication we will generate 1 million unique coupons, divided into three batches:

- Half of the coupon codes will be printed and distributed in a marketing action
- 300,000 codes will be reserved to be used later if the campaign hits particular goals
- The remaining 200,000 will be directed to customers through SMS and email

These coupons can be redeemed in the online system. Our task will be to generate the proper codes, which should meet the following requirements:

- The codes need to be unique.
- The codes need to be printable and easy to read, as some customers will be dictating them over the phone.

- There should be a quick way to discard fake codes. This will avoid attacks with random codes that could overload the system.
- The codes should be presented in CSV format for the next steps.

> **Tip**
>
> CSV format will allow us to easily share the coupon codes if necessary. While in this example we are assuming that we will be sending them in individual notifications over channels, this is not the only possibility. We could, for example, print them physically in scratch cards or similar. CSV format is a standard easy to share with any external service.

## Getting ready

Download the `create_personalised_coupons.py` script, which will generate the coupons in CSV files, from GitHub `ch10` subdirectory.

## How to do it...

1. Call the `create_personalised_coupons.py` script. It will take a minute or two to run, depending on your processor speed. It will display the generated codes on screen:

```
$ uv run create_personalised_coupons.py
Code: F9GA-GP7GR-TR
Code: JGYA-UTP7A-AT
Code: WKKV-UJYLL-HN
...
```

2. Check that it has created three CSV files, `codes_batch_1.csv`, `codes_batch_2.csv`, and `codes_batch_3.csv`, each with the proper number of codes:

```
$ wc -l codes_batch_*.csv
  500000 codes_batch_1.csv
  300000 codes_batch_2.csv
```

```
  200000 codes_batch_3.csv
 1000000 total
```

3. Verify that each of the batch files contains unique codes. Your codes will be unique and different from the ones displayed here:

```
$ head codes_batch_2.csv
FEYE-WU7PF-NA
EU7M-PWNUA-PM
YFTT-TNV3W-AF
...
```

## How it works...

*Step 1* calls the script that generates all the codes, and *step 2* checks that the results are correct. *Step 3* shows the format in which the codes are stored and allows us to verify that they are indeed unique. It is worth analyzing the `create_personalised_coupons.py` script. It has the following overall structure:

```
# IMPORTS
...
# FUNCTIONS
def random_code(digits)
    ...
def checksum(code1, code2)
    ...
def check_code(code)
    ...
def generate_code()
    ...
# SET UP TASK
...
# GENERATE CODES
...
# CREATE AND SAVE BATCHES
...
```

The different functions work together to create a code. `random_code` generates a combination of random letters and numbers taken from the string `CHARACTERS`, which contains all the valid characters available to choose from.

**Tip**

The selection of characters includes just those that are easy to print and which cannot be mistaken for each other. For example, it can be difficult to distinguish between a letter O and the number 0, or the number 1 and the letter I, depending on the font. This may depend on the specifics of the typeface if digitally displayed (like on a phone screen) and the printing process (if physically printed), so verification and/or printing tests are encouraged to adjust the character selection. Increase the code length if necessary; for example, if many more codes are required or if the number of easily recognizable symbols is smaller.

The checksum function generates, based on two codes, an extra digit derived from the two codes. This process is called **hashing**, and it's a well-known process in computing, especially for cryptography.

**Note**

The basic aim of hashing is to produce an output that has a defined length, via a process that is not reversible, meaning that it's very difficult to guess unless the input is known. Hashing has a lot of common applications in computing, normally hidden away under the hood. For example, Python dictionaries make extensive use of hashing.

In our recipe we'll use SHA256, a well-known fast hashing algorithm included in the Python `hashlib` module:

```
def checksum(code1, code2):
    m = hashlib.sha256()
    m.update(code1.encode())
    m.update(code2.encode())
    checksum = int(m.hexdigest()[:2], base=16)
    digit = CHARACTERS[checksum % len(CHARACTERS)]
    return digit
```

Both codes are concatenated as input, and the two hex digits of the resulting hash string are used to pick the corresponding character from `CHARACTERS`.

The hash digits get transformed into a base 10 number (from base 16) and we apply the modulo operator to obtain the corresponding available character.

The objective of this checksum is to be able to quickly check whether a code looks like it is correct and discard possible input errors. We can perform the operation again over a code to see whether the checksum is as expected, detecting possible typos or mistakes. Note that this is not a cryptographic hash, as no secret is required at any point in the operation. Given this specific use case, this (low) level of security is probably fine for our purposes. The hashing strategy is common when working with long numbers that can be easily confused, like bank accounts or credit card numbers.

> **Tip**
>
> Cryptography is a much bigger theme and ensuring that security is strong can be difficult. The main strategy in cryptography involving hashing is probably hash storage to avoid storing passwords in a readable format. You can read a quick introduction to that technique here: `https://crackstation.net/hashing-security.html`.

The `generate_code` function then produces a random code, composed of four digits, then five digits, and then two digits of the checksum, divided by dashes. The first checksum digit is generated with the first nine digits in right-to-left order (using the four-character block as `code1` and the five-character block as `code2`). The second checksum digit is generated by reversing them (the five-character block as `code1` and the four-character block as `code2`).

The `check_code` function reverses the process and returns `True` if the code is correct and `False` otherwise.

With the basic elements in place, the script starts by defining the required batches: 500,000, 300,000, and 200,000.

All the codes are generated in the same pool, called `codes`. This is to avoid duplicates between batches. Note that, due to the randomness of the process, we can't rule out the possibility of generating a duplicated code, though such a possibility is small. We are allowed to retry up to three times to avoid generating a duplicated code. The codes are stored in a set accumulator to guarantee their uniqueness and to speed up the process of checking whether a code is already there.

> **Note**
>
> `Sets` is another of the places where Python uses hashing under the hood, so it hashes the element to be added and compares it with the hashes of the elements already there. This makes checking in sets a very quick operation.

To be sure that the process is correct, each code is verified and printed to display progress while generating the code. This also allows us to see that everything is working as expected.

Finally, the codes are divided into the proper number of batches and each batch is saved in an individual `.csv` file. The codes are removed one by one from `codes` using `.pop()` until the batch is the proper size:

```
batch = [(codes.pop(),) for _ in range(batch_size)]
```

Note how the previous line creates a batch of the proper number of rows with a single code on each. Each row is still a list, as it should be for a CSV file.

Then a file is created and, using `csv.writer`, the codes are stored as rows.

As a final test, the `codes` list is verified to make sure that it's empty and there are no more codes to assign to batches with an `assert` statement.

```
assert 0 == len(codes)
```

## There's more...

In this recipe, a direct approach was used in the file structure, not wrapping the execution of the code in a `main` function. This is in opposition to the principles presented in the *Preparing a task to run* recipe in *Chapter 2, Automating Tasks Made Easy*. Notice that, compared with the tasks presented there, this script is intended to be run a single time to produce the codes, and that's it. It also uses defined constants, such as `BATCHES`, for configuration, instead of command-line parameters or config files.

Given that it is a unique task, designed to be run once, spending time structuring it into a reusable component is probably not the best use of our time.

> **Tip**
>
> Over-engineering is definitely possible, and choosing between a pragmatic design and a more future-facing approach may not be easy. Be realistic about maintenance costs and try to find your own balance.

In the same way, the design in this recipe of the checksum is intended to provide a minimal way to check whether a code is totally made up or looks legitimate. Given that codes will be checked against a system this seems like a sensible approach, but consider your particular use case.

Our code space is made up of 22 possible characters raised to the power of 9 for each random position, which gives 1,207,269,217,792 possible codes, meaning the probability of guessing one of the million generated is very small. It's also not very likely that we produce the same code twice, but nevertheless we've protected our code against that with up to three retries.

Verifying each code as it's generated in `check_code`, and the final verification that there are no remaining codes, are very useful when developing this kind of script. It ensures that we are going in the right direction and things are going according to plan. The `assert` statements will produce an `Exception` if there's a problem.

> **Note**
>
> As described in the Python documentation, `assert` commands are ignored if the Python code is optimized (run with the `-O` command). See the documentation here: `https://docs.python.org/3/reference/simple_stmts.html#the-assert-statement`. The usage of the `-O` argument is rare, but can be confusing. Avoid depending heavily on `assert` statements.

Learning the basics of cryptography is not as difficult as you may think. There are a small number of basic schemes that are well-known and can be easily learned. A good introductory article is `https://thebestvpn.com/cryptography/`. Python also has a good number of cryptographic functions; see the documentation at `https://docs.python.org/3/library/crypto.html`. The best approach is to find a good book and know that, while it's a difficult subject to truly master, it is definitely approachable.

## See also

- The *Introducing regular expressions* recipe in *Chapter 1, Let's Begin Our Automation Journey*, to learn how to use regular expressions
- The *Reading CSV files* recipe in *Chapter 4, Searching and Reading Local Files*, to learn how to work with CSV files

# Sending a notification to a customer on their preferred channel

This recipe shows *step 3* of the campaign, sending the codes directly to users over their preferred channel, either a text message or an email.

Once our codes have been created for direct marketing, we need to distribute them to our customers.

For this recipe, we take a CSV file of customer information, including their preferred contact methods, fill the CSV file with the codes generated previously, and then send a notification through the proper method. This will include the promotional code.

## Getting ready

In this recipe we will use several modules already presented: `pendulum`, `requests`, and `twilio`. We need to add them to our virtual environment if they're not already there:

```
$ echo "pendulum==3.2.0" >> requirements.txt
$ echo "requests==2.32.5" >> requirements.txt
$ echo "twilio==9.10.2" >> requirements.txt
$ uv pip install -r requirements.txt
```

We need to define a `config-channel.ini` file with our credentials for the services to use, Mailgun and Twilio. A template of this file can be found on GitHub here: `https://github.com/PacktPublishing/Python-Automation-Cookbook-Third-Edition/blob/master/ch10/config-channel.ini`.

For information on how to obtain the credentials, refer to the *Sending notifications via emails* and *Producing SMS messages* recipes in *Chapter 9*, *Dealing with Communication Channels*.

The file has the following format:

```
[MAILGUN]
KEY = <YOUR KEY>
DOMAIN = <YOUR DOMAIN>
FROM = <YOUR FROM EMAIL>
[TWILIO]
ACCOUNT_SID = <YOUR SID>
AUTH_TOKEN = <YOUR TOKEN>
FROM = <FROM TWILIO PHONE NUMBER>
```

For a description of all the contacts to target, we need to generate a CSV file, `notifications.csv`, in the following format:

| Name | Contact Method | Target | Status | Code | Timestamp |
|---|---|---|---|---|---|
| John Smith | PHONE | +1-555-12345678 | NOT-SENT | | |

| Name | Contact Method | Target | Status | Code | Timestamp |
|---|---|---|---|---|---|
| Paul Smith | EMAIL | paul.smith@test.com | NOT-SENT | | |

*Table 10.1: Format of notifications.csv*

Note that the Code column is empty and that all the statuses should be `NOT-SENT` or empty.

If you are using test accounts in Twilio and Mailgun, be aware of the limitations. For example, Twilio only allows you to send messages to authenticated phone numbers. You can create a small CSV file with only two or three contacts to test the script.

The coupon codes to be used should be ready in a CSV file. You can generate several batches with the `create_personalised_coupons.py` script, available on GitHub at `https://github.com/PacktPublishing/Python-Automation-Cookbook-Third-Edition/blob/master/ch10/create_personalised_coupons.py`.

Download the script to be used, `send_notifications.py`, from GitHub at `https://github.com/PacktPublishing/Python-Automation-Cookbook-Third-Edition/blob/master/ch10/send_notifications.py`.

## How to do it...

1. Run `send_notifications.py` to see its options and usage:

```
$ uv run send_notifications.py --help
usage: send_notifications.py [-h] [-c CODES] [--config CONFIG_FILE]
notif_file

positional arguments:
  notif_file            notifications file

options:
  -h, --help            show this help message and exit
  -c, --codes CODES     Optional file with codes. If present, the file will
be populated with
                        codes. No codes will be sent
  --config CONFIG_FILE  config file (default config.ini)
```

2. Check the `notifications.csv` file showing empty codes:

```
$ head notifications.csv
Name,Contact Method,Target,Status,Code,Timestamp
John Smith,PHONE,+1-555-12345678,NOT-SENT,,
Paul Smith,EMAIL,paul.smith@test.com,NOT-SENT,,
...
```

3. Add the codes to the `notifications.csv` file:

```
$ uv run send_notifications.py --config config-channel.ini
notifications.csv -c codes_batch_3.csv
$ head notifications.csv
Name,Contact Method,Target,Status,Code,Timestamp
John Smith,PHONE,+1-555-12345678,NOT-SENT,CFXK-U37JN-TM,
Paul Smith,EMAIL,paul.smith@test.com,NOT-SENT,HJGX-M97WE-9Y,
...
```

4. Finally, send the notifications:

```
$ uv run send_notifications.py --config config-channel.ini
notifications.csv
$ head notifications.csv
Name,Contact Method,Target,Status,Code,Timestamp
John Smith,PHONE,+1-555-12345678,SENT,CFXK-U37JN-TM,
2026-02-26T18:30:02.975892+00:00
Paul Smith,EMAIL,paul.smith@test.com,SENT,HJGX-M97WE-9Y,
2026-02-26T18:30:06.980951+00:00
...
```

5. Check the emails and phones to verify the messages were received

## How it works...

*Step 1* shows the use of the script. The general idea is to call it several times; the first time to fill it with codes, and the second time to send the messages. If there's an error, the script can be executed again, and only messages not previously sent will be retried.

The `notifications.csv` file gets the codes that will be injected in *step 2*. The codes are finally sent in *step 3*.

Let's analyze the code of `send_notifications.py`. Only the most relevant bits are shown here:

```
# IMPORTS
def send_phone_notification(...):
def send_email_notification(...):
def send_notification(...):
def save_file(...):
def main(...):
if __name__ == '__main__':
    # Parse arguments and prepare configuration
    ...
```

The `main` function goes through the file line by line and analyzes what to do in each case. If the entry is `SENT`, it skips it. If it has no code, it tries to fill it. If it tries to send it, it will attach the timestamp to record when it was sent or tried to be sent.

For each entry, the whole file is rewritten by the function `save_file`. Notice how the file cursor is positioned at the start of the file. The file is written and then flushed to disk:

```
def save_file(notif_file, data):
    '''
    Overwrite the file with the new information
    '''
    # Start at the start of the file
    notif_file.seek(0)
    header = data[0].keys()
    writer = csv.DictWriter(notif_file, fieldnames=header)
    writer.writeheader()
    writer.writerows(data)
    # Be sure to write to disk
    notif_file.flush()
```

This overwrites the file on each entry operation, without us having to close and open the file again.

> **Note**
>
> Why write the whole file for each entry? Because it's an easy way to store each of the operations and it allows you to retry the sending process. For example, if an entry produces an unexpected error or a timeout, or even if there's a general failure, all the progress and previous codes will be marked as `SENT` already and won't be sent a second

time. This means the operation can be retried as needed. For a large number of entries, this is a good way of ensuring that a problem in the middle of the process doesn't make us resend messages to our customers.

This convenience has problems, though. For a huge number of rows, we risk having a problem with saving the file. This may cause the file to get corrupted by an unexpected error while writing or take too long to save. In our planned original amount of 200,000 codes, saving this big file at least 200,000 times may create problems and delays.

If that's the case, split the file into smaller independent batches that can be treated independently, for example, dividing the problem into 400 independent batches of 500 rows. For very big processes, a system that guarantees the data won't get corrupted, such as a database, may be required.

For each code to be sent, the `send_notification` function decides whether to call `send_phone_notification` or `send_email_notification`. It appends the current time in both cases.

Both send functions return an error if they can't send a message. This allows you to mark it in the resulting `notifications.csv` file and retry later.

**Tip**

The `notifications.csv` file can also be changed manually. For example, imagine there's a typo in an email and that's the reason for the error. It can be changed and retried.

`send_email_notification` sends the message based on the Mailgun interface. For more information, refer to the *Sending notifications via emails* recipe in *Chapter 9*, *Dealing with Communication Channels*. Note that the email sent here is text only.

**Tip**

Our simple example email template may be detected as spam by email providers. Be sure to expand it and create a more substantive message to avoid that.

`send_phone_notification` sends the message based on the Twilio interface. For more information, refer to the *Producing SMS recipe in Chapter 9*, *Dealing with Communication Channels*.

## There's more...

Timestamps have been deliberately written in ISO format, as it is a parsable format. This means that we can get back a proper object in an easy way, like this:

```
>>> import datetime
>>> timestamp = datetime.datetime.now(datetime.timezone.utc).isoformat()
>>> timestamp
'2026-02-26T20:30:02.975892+00:00'
>>> datetime.datetime.fromisoformat(timestamp)
datetime.datetime(2026, 2, 26, 20, 30, 2, 975892, tzinfo=datetime.timezone.utc)
```

This allows you to easily parse the timestamp back and forth.

> **Tip**
>
> The ISO 8601 time format is well supported in most programming languages and defines the time precisely as it includes the time zone. It is an excellent choice for recording times, if you can use it.

The strategy used in `send_notification` to route the notifications is an interesting one:

```
# Route each of the notifications
METHOD = {
    'PHONE': send_phone_notification,
    'EMAIL': send_email_notification,
}
try:
    method = METHOD[entry['Contact Method']]
    result = method(entry, config)
except KeyError:
    result = 'INVALID_METHOD'
```

The `METHOD` dictionary assigns each of the possible `Contact Method` entries to a function that has the same definition, accepting both an entry and a config.

Then, based on the specific method, the function is retrieved from the dictionary and called. Note that the method variable contains the correct function to call.

> **Note**
>
> This acts in a similar way to the switch operation that is available in other programming languages. It is also possible to achieve this through `if` … `else` blocks. For simple cases like this code, the dictionary method makes the code very readable.

If `Contact Method` is not one of the available options (`PHONE` or `EMAIL`), then a `KeyError` will be raised and captured, and the result will be defined as `INVALID_METHOD`.

## See also

- The *Sending notifications via emails* recipe in *Chapter 9*, *Dealing with Communication Channels*, to learn how to send emails through Mailgun
- The *Producing SMS messages* recipe in *Chapter 9*, *Dealing with Communication Channels*, to learn how to send text messages using Twilio

# Preparing sales information

This recipe shows *step 4* of the campaign: collecting the results of the campaign.

After sending the information to users, we need to collect the sales logs from the shops to monitor how big the campaign's impact is.

The sales logs are reported as individual files from each of the associated shops, so in this recipe we'll see how to aggregate the information from those files into a spreadsheet, so that we can process the information as a whole.

> **Note**
>
> In our example promotion, we allow only the "Single item" product to use the redeemable code and obtain a discount of 15%, while the "Family pack" cannot use the code, but already has another campaign with a 20% discount. We will use this information in a later recipe to present the results of the campaigns.

## Getting ready

For this recipe, we need to install the following modules:

```
$ echo "openpyxl==3.1.5" >> requirements.txt
$ echo "parse==1.20.2" >> requirements.txt
```

```
$ echo "pendulum==3.2.0" >> requirements.txt
$ uv pip install -r requirements.txt
```

We can obtain a test structure and test logs for this recipe from GitHub from `https://github.com/PacktPublishing/Python-Automation-Cookbook-Third-Edition/tree/master/ch10/sales`. Please download the full sales directory, which contains numerous test logs. To display the structure, we'll use the tree command (`http://mama.indstate.edu/users/ice/tree/`), which is installed by default in Linux and can be installed using brew in macOS (`https://brew.sh/`). You can use a graphical tool to inspect the directory as well.

We'll also need the `sale_log.py` module and the `parse_sales_log.py` script, available from GitHub at `https://github.com/PacktPublishing/Python-Automation-Cookbook-Third-Edition/blob/master/ch10/parse_sales_log.py`.

## How to do it...

1. Check the structure of the sales directory. Each subdirectory represents a shop that has submitted its sales logs for the specified period:

```
$ tree sales
sales
├── 345
│   └── logs.txt
├── 438
│   ├── logs_1.txt
│   ├── logs_2.txt
│   ├── logs_3.txt
│   └── logs_4.txt
└── 656
 └── logs.txt
```

2. Check the log files:

```
$ head sales/438/logs_1.txt
[2025-08-27 19:05:55+00:00] - SALE - PRODUCT: 12346 - PRICE: $02.99 - NAME:
Single item - DISCOUNT: 0% - CODE: -
[2025-08-27 20:05:55+00:00] - SALE - PRODUCT: 12346 - PRICE: $02.54 - NAME:
Single item - DISCOUNT: 15% - CODE: GLP7-AYKCV-A9
[2025-08-27 21:05:55+00:00] - SALE - PRODUCT: 12346 - PRICE: $02.99 - NAME:
Single item - DISCOUNT: 0% - CODE: -
[2025-08-27 22:05:55+00:00] - SALE - PRODUCT: 12345 - PRICE: $07.99 - NAME:
```

```
Family pack - DISCOUNT: 20% - CODE: -
...
```

3. Call the `parse_sales_log.py` script to generate the repository:

```
$ uv run parse_sales_log.py sales -o report.xlsx
```

4. Check the generated Excel file, `report.xlsx`:

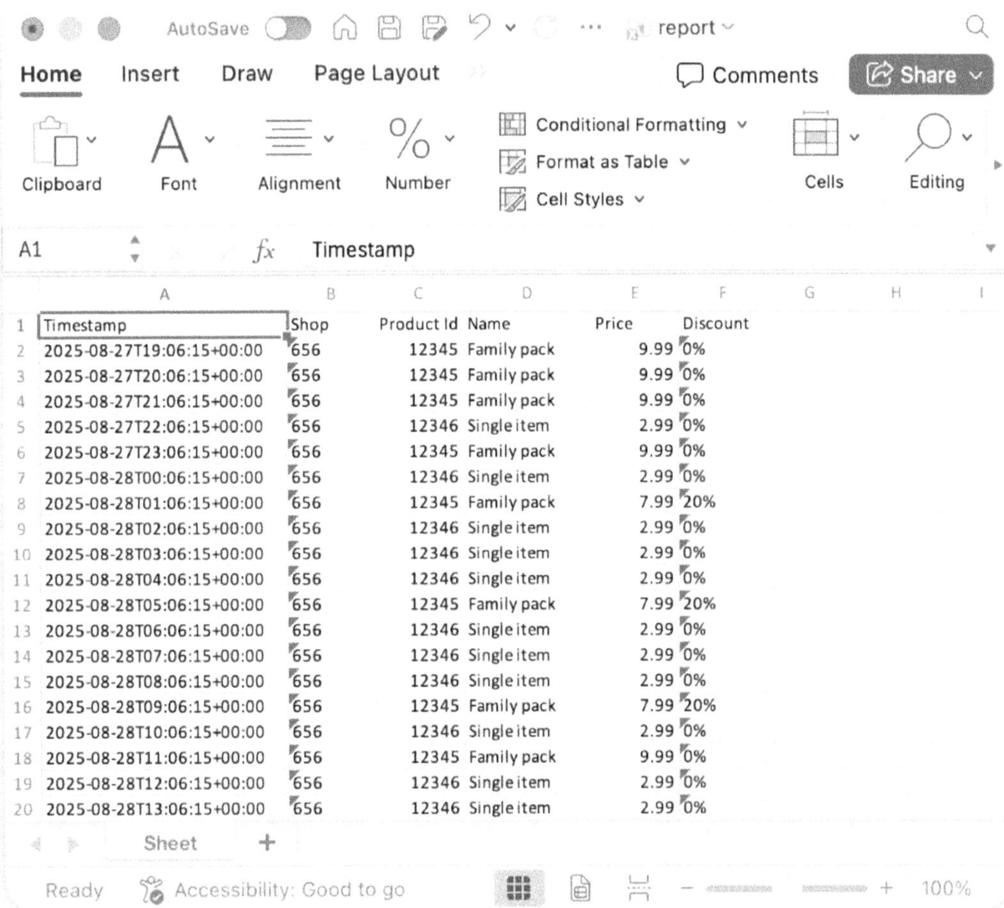


*Figure 10.2: Screenshot of report.xlsx*

## How it works...

*Steps 1* and *2* show how the data is structured. *Step 3* calls `parse_sales_log.py` to read all the log files and parse them, and then stores them in an Excel spreadsheet. The contents of the spreadsheet are displayed in *step 4*.

Let's see how *parse_sales_log.py* is structured:

```
# IMPORTS
from sale_log import SaleLog
def get_logs_from_file(shop, log_filename):
    with open(log_filename) as logfile:
        logs = [SaleLog.parse(shop=shop, text_log=log)
                for log in logfile]
    return logs
def main(log_dir, output_filename):
    logs = []
    for dirpath, dirnames, filenames in os.walk(log_dir):
        for filename in filenames:
            # The shop is the last directory
            shop = os.path.basename(dirpath)
            fullpath = os.path.join(dirpath, filename)
            logs.extend(get_logs_from_file(shop, fullpath))
    # Create and save the Excel sheet
    xlsfile = openpyxl.Workbook()
    sheet = xlsfile['Sheet']
   sheet.append(SaleLog.row_header())
    for log in logs:
        sheet.append(log.row())
    xlsfile.save(output_filename)
if __name__ == '__main__':
   # PARSE COMMAND LINE ARGUMENTS AND CALL main()
```

The command-line arguments are explained in *Chapter 1, Let's Begin Our Automation Journey*. Note that the imports include `SaleLog`.

The `main` function walks through the whole directory and grabs all the files through `os.walk`. You can find out more about `os.walk` in *Chapter 2, Automating Tasks Made Easy*. Each file is then passed to `get_logs_from_file` to parse its logs and add them to the global logs list.

Note that the specific shop is stored in the last subdirectory, so it is extracted with `os.path.basename`.

Once the list of logs has been completed, a new Excel sheet is created using the openpyxl module. The SaleLog module has a .row_header method to add the first row, and then all the logs are converted into row format using .row. Finally, the file is saved.

To parse the logs, we have a module called sale_log.py, which abstracts parsing and dealing with rows.

Note

Note that, compared with the previous parse_log.py scripts in the book, this includes an optional section to store the code used to purchase if present.

We will focus here on the parse method:

```
@classmethod
def parse(cls, shop, text_log):
    '''
    Parse from a text log with the format
    ...
    to a SaleLog object
    '''
    def price(string):
        return Decimal(string)
    def isodate(string):
        return pendulum.parse(string)
    FORMAT = ('[{timestamp:isodate}] - SALE - PRODUCT: {product:d} '
              '- PRICE: ${price:price} - NAME: {name:D} '
              '- DISCOUNT: {discount:d}% '
              '- CODE: {code:S}')
    formats = {'price': price, 'isodate': isodate}
    result = parse.parse(FORMAT, text_log, formats)
    return cls(timestamp=result['timestamp'],
               product_id=result['product'],
               price=result['price'],
               name=result['name'],
               discount=result['discount'],
               shop=shop)
```

sale_log.py is a classmethod, meaning that it can be used by calling SaleLog.parse. It returns a new element of the class.

> **Note**
>
> `Classmethods` are called with a first argument that stores the class, instead of the object normally stored in `self`. The convention is to name the argument `cls`. Calling `cls(...)` at the end is equivalent to `SaleFormat(...)`, so it calls the `__init__` method.

The method uses the `parse` module to retrieve the values from the template. Note how two elements, `timestamp` and `price`, have custom parsing. The `pendulum` module helps us with parsing the date, and the `price` is better described as a `Decimal` to keep the proper resolution. The custom filters are applied in the `formats` argument.

## There's more...

- The `Decimal` type is described in detail in the Python documentation here: `https://docs.python.org/3/library/decimal.html`.
- The full `openpyxl` documentation can be found here: `https://openpyxl.readthedocs.io/en/stable/`. Also, check *Chapter 6, Fun with Spreadsheets*, for more examples on how to use the module.
- The full `parse` documentation can be found here: `https://github.com/r1chardj0n3s/parse`. *Chapter 1, Let's Begin Our Automation Journey*, also describes this module in greater detail.

## See also

- The *Using a third-party tool – parse* recipe in *Chapter 1, Let's Begin Our Automation Journey*, to learn more about the `parse` module
- The *Crawling and searching directories* recipe in *Chapter 4, Searching and Reading Local Files*, to learn about how to walk and find all the files in a directory
- The *Reading text files* recipe in *Chapter 4, Searching and Reading Local Files*, to learn how to open text files
- The *Updating an Excel spreadsheet* recipe in *Chapter 6, Fun with Spreadsheets*, to learn how to write Excel spreadsheets using Python

Now that we have compiled the information, we can analyze the results of the campaign

# Generating a sales report

This recipe shows *step 5* of the campaign, the final one, generating a sales report with an analysis of the results.

As the final step, the information about all the sales is aggregated and displayed in a sales report.

In this recipe, we'll see how to read from spreadsheets, create PDFs, and produce graphs to generate a comprehensive report automatically in order to analyze the performance of our campaign.

## Getting ready

In this recipe, we'll require the following modules in our virtual environment:

```
$ echo "openpyxl==3.1.5" >> requirements.txt
$ echo "fpdf2==2.8.5" >> requirements.txt
$ echo "pendulum==3.2.0" >> requirements.txt
$ echo "pypdf==6.6.0" >> requirements.txt
$ echo "matplotlib==3.10.8" >> requirements.txt
$ pip install -r requirements.txt
```

We'll need the `sale_log.py` module, which is available on the GitHub `ch10` subdirectory.

The input spreadsheet was generated in the previous recipe, *Preparing sales information*. Refer to that recipe for more information.

You can download the script to generate the input spreadsheet, `parse_sales_log.py`, from the GitHub `ch10` subdirectory.

Download the raw log files from GitHub at `https://github.com/PacktPublishing/Python-Automation-Cookbook-Third-Edition/tree/master/ch10/sales`. Please download the full sales directory.

Download the `generate_sales_report.py` script from the GitHub `ch10` subdirectory.

## How to do it...

1. Call the `parse_sales_log.py` script to generate the input file:

```
$ uv run parse_sales_log.py sales -o report.xlsx
```

2. Check the input file and the use of `generate_sales_report.py`:

```
$ ls report.xlsx
report.xlsx
$ uv run generate_sales_report.py --help
usage: generate_sales_report.py [-h] input_file output_file
positional arguments:
  input_file
  output_file
optional arguments:
  -h, --help show this help message and exit
```

3. Call the `generate_sales_report.py` script with the input file and an output file:

```
$ uv run generate_sales_report.py report.xlsx output.pdf
```

4. Check the `output.pdf` output file. It will contain three pages, the first a brief summary and the second and third with graphs showing sales by day and by shop.

## How it works...

*Step 1* shows how to use the script and *step 2* calls it on the input file. Let's take a look at the basic structure of the `generate_sales_report.py` script:

```
# IMPORTS
def generate_summary(logs):
def aggregate_by_day(logs):
def aggregate_by_shop(logs):
def graph(...):
def create_summary_brief(...):
def main(input_file, output_file):
  # open and read input file
  # Generate each of the pages calling the other calls
  # Group all the pdfs into a single file
  # Write the resulting PDF
if __name__ == '__main__':
  # Compile the input and output files from the command line
  # call main
```

There are two key elements – the aggregation of the logs in different ways (by shop and by day) and the generation of a summary in each case. The summary is generated with `generate_summary`, which, from a list of logs, generates a dictionary containing its aggregated information. The aggregation of the logs is performed in different styles in the `aggregate_by` functions.

> **Note**
>
> `generate_summary` produces a dictionary with the aggregated information, including start and end time, total income of all logs, total units, average discount, and a breakdown of the same data by product.
>
> To better show the impact of the sales that applied the code, they are presented as a different product, adding `"- code"` to the product name.

The script is better understood by starting at the end. The `main` functions join all the different operations. Read each of the logs and transform them into native `SaleLog` objects.

Then, it generates each of the pages as intermediate PDF files:

- A brief generated by `create_summary_brief` provides a general summary of all the data.
- Information by day, as created by the method `aggregate_by_day`. A summary is created, and a graph is produced.
- Information by shop, using `aggregate_by_shop`. A summary is created and a graph is produced.

All the intermediate PDF pages are joined, using `pypdf`, into a single file. Finally, the intermediate pages are deleted.

Both `aggregate_by_day` and `aggregate_by_shop` return a list with a summary of the relevant data. In `aggregate_by_day`, we detect when a day ends by using `.end_of_day` to differentiate one day from another.

The graph function does the following:

1. Prepares all the data that is going to be displayed. That includes the number of units per tag (day or shop) and the total income per tag.
2. Creates a top graph with the total income, split by product into stacked bars. To be able to do this, at the same time as the total income is calculated the baseline (the position where the next stack is located) is calculated.
3. It divides the bottom part of the graph into as many graphs as there are products and displays the number of units sold on each one, per tag (day or shop)

> **Note**
>
> For a better display, the graph is defined to be the size of an A4 sheet. It also allows us, using `skip_labels`, to print one of each `skip_label` label on the second graph on the *X* axis to avoid overlapping. You can see what this means in Figure 10.4, in the bottom graphs, where we label only one day per week. This approach makes the graph easier to read, as labelling every single day would make it appear cluttered.

The resulting graph is saved to a file.

`create_summary_brief` uses the `fpdf` module to save a text PDF page containing the total summary information.

The template and information in `create_summary_brief` have been left deliberately simple to avoid complicating this recipe, but they can be enhanced with better descriptive text and formatting. Refer to *Chapter 5, Generating Fantastic Reports*, for more details about how to use `fpdf`.

As shown previously, the `main` function groups all the PDF pages and joins them into a single document, removing the intermediate pages later:

Report generated at 2026-02-26T21:42:53.859747+00:00
Covering data from 30 Aug to 08 Oct

Summary

-------

TOTAL INCOME: $ 14225.00
TOTAL UNIT: 3000 units
AVERAGE DISCOUNT: 2.71%

*Figure 10.3: Sales summary*

The second page shows a graph of sales by day:

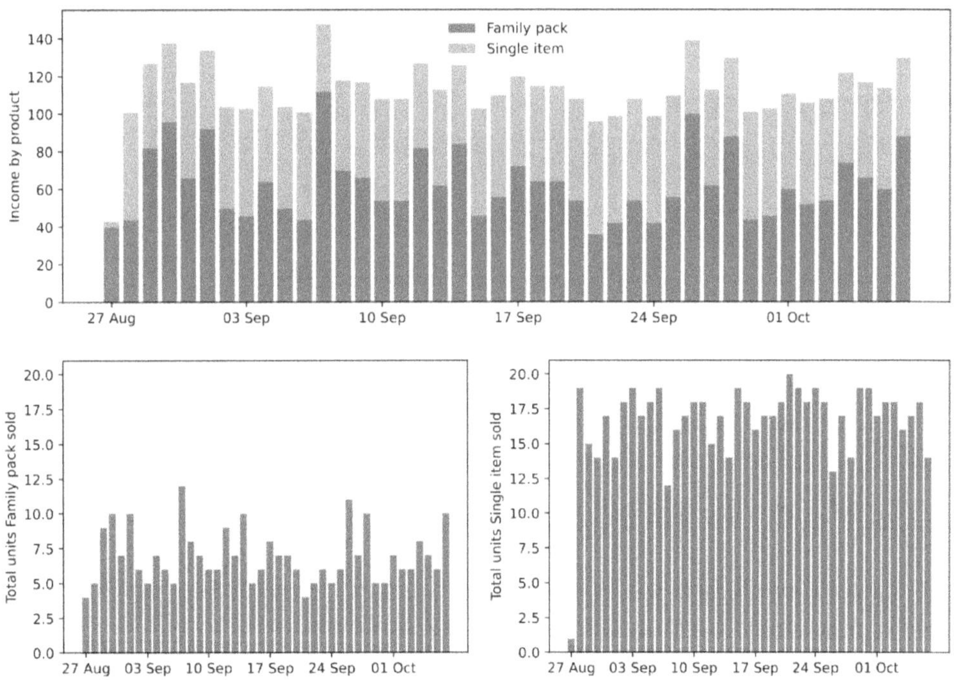


*Figure 10.4: Graphical display of daily sales. Notice the sales that used a code*

The third page divides the sales by shop:

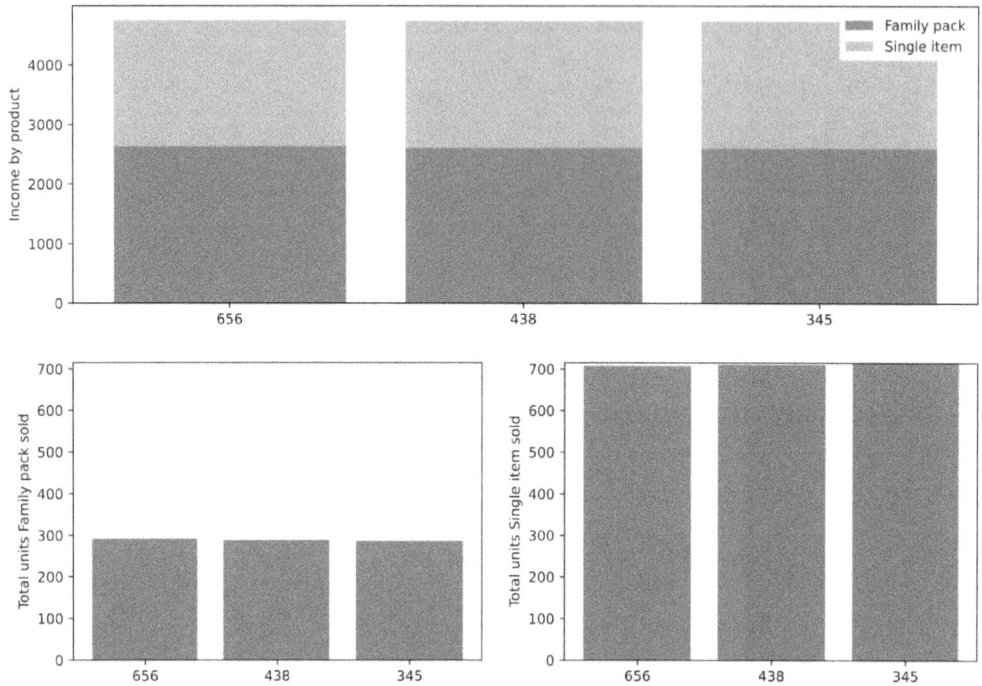


*Figure 10.5: Graphical display of sales by shop*

## There's more...

The reports included in this recipe can be expanded. For example, the average discount could be calculated on each page and displayed as a line:

```
# Generate a data series with the average discount
discount = [summary['average_discount'] for _, summary in full_summary]
....
# Print the legend
# Plot the discount in a second axis
plt.twinx()
plt.plot(pos, discount,'o-', color='green')
plt.ylabel('Average Discount')
```

Be careful not to put too much information in a single graph, however, as it may reduce readability. In this case, another graph is probably a better way of displaying it.

**Tip**

Be careful to print the legend before creating the second axis, or the graph will display only the information on the second axis.

The size and orientation of the graphs can determine whether to use more labels or fewer so that they are clear and readable. This is demonstrated in the use of `skip_labels` to avoid clutter. Keep an eye on the resulting graphics and try to adapt to possible problems by changing sizes or limiting labels in some cases.

**Tip**

For example, one possible limit is to have no more than three products, since printing four graphs on the second row in our graphs would probably make the text illegible. Feel free to experiment and check the limits of the code.

As you can see in the script, we are already reducing the size of the font to be sure that we can read three graphs in the bottom row.

You can also present the information in multiple ways to better see the impact of the campaign, like a more detailed comparison between sales using the code or not using the code. Because we are tracking the code usage, we can also follow up with targeted marketing actions to the customers who used the codes.

The complete `matplotlib` documentation can be found at `https://matplotlib.org/`, while the `pendulum` documentation is at https://pendulum.eustace.io.

All the documentation for `openpyxl` is available at `https://openpyxl.readthedocs.io/en/stable/`. The full documentation for the PDF manipulation modules can be found for `pypdf` at `https://pypdf.readthedocs.io/en/stable/` and for `pyfdf2` at `https://py-pdf.github.io/fpdf2/`.

This recipe makes use of different concepts and techniques that are discussed in *Chapter 5, Generating Fantastic Reports* (PDF creation and manipulation), *Chapter 6, Fun with Spreadsheets* (spreadsheet reading), and *Chapter 8, Developing Stunning Graphs* (graph creation). Check them out to learn more.

## See also

- The *Aggregating PDF reports* recipe in *Chapter 5, Generating Fantastic Reports*, to learn how to join multiple PDF files
- The *Reading an Excel spreadsheet* recipe in *Chapter 6, Fun with Spreadsheets*, to learn how to get information from Excel spreadsheets
- The *Drawing stacked bars* recipe in *Chapter 8, Developing Stunning Graphs*, to find out more about how to draw stacked bar graphs
- The *Displaying multiple lines* recipe in *Chapter 8, Developing Stunning Graphs*, to learn how to get a single graph with multiple information lines
- The *Adding legends and annotations* recipe in *Chapter 8, Developing Stunning Graphs*, for more information about adding legends and extra annotations to graphs
- The *Combining graphs* recipe in *Chapter 8, Developing Stunning Graphs*, to learn how to combine different graphs into a single image
- The *Saving charts* recipe in *Chapter 8, Developing Stunning Graphs*, to find out more about how to store graphs in different formats

# 11

# Calling AI Models

GenAI is taking the software world by storm. Each month there are new models being released that are increasingly capable and allow us to automate many tasks that would have seemed impossible before. Tools are now available that leverage GenAI capabilities to write code, analyze documents, generate images, and assist in complex decision-making.

But the real power of the models is unlocked when they are used programmatically. We can use them to power our automation recipes and create very capable automation workflows.

In this chapter, we will see how to create simple interactions with AI models, which will become the foundation for the next chapters.

> **Note**
>
> This is a very fast-developing area. For simplicity, we will mostly use models from OpenAI, famous for its ChatGPT application. But check that the models available at the time of writing this book are still available for you. You can see the currently available models at this URL: `https://developers.openai.com/api/docs/models`.

While there are other competing companies with other models, like Claude from Anthropic or Gemini from Google, the models behave in a very similar way. You can quickly learn how to call them and replace them in all the recipes in this book.

- Creating your own chatbot
- Using a local model
- Generating images
- Describe images

Let's start by making a simple chatbot that will call an LLM model to answer questions.

# Technical requirements

For most of our recipes, we will use OpenAI models. We need to set up an API key to allow connecting to their services. You'll need to set up an account capable of calling their API by going to `https://platform.openai.com/` and creating an account.

You'll need to go to **Billing** and add your payment details.

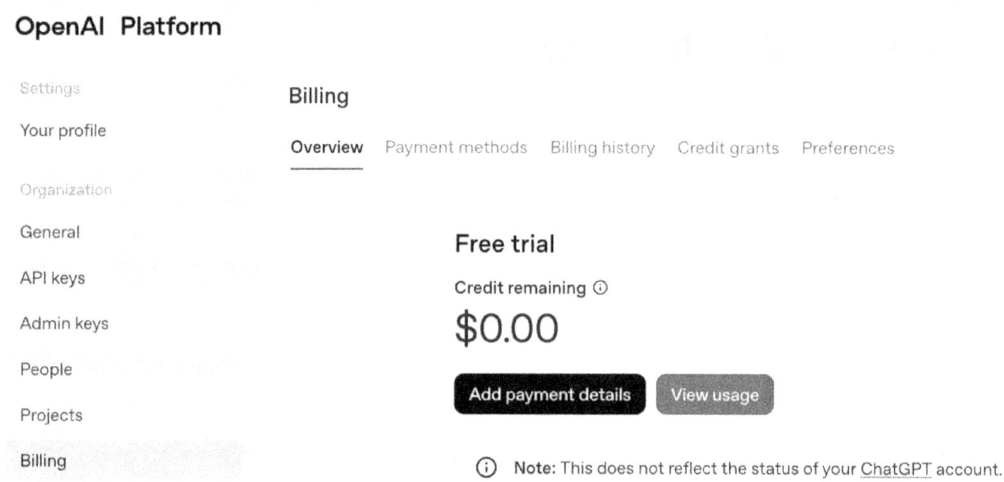


*Figure 11.1: Enter your payment details*

> **Tip**
>
> Note that this is independent of your ChatGPT account. You may have a paying ChatGPT account and not be able to make API calls.

After you set some credit (for example, $10), you'll see your credit reflected on the page.

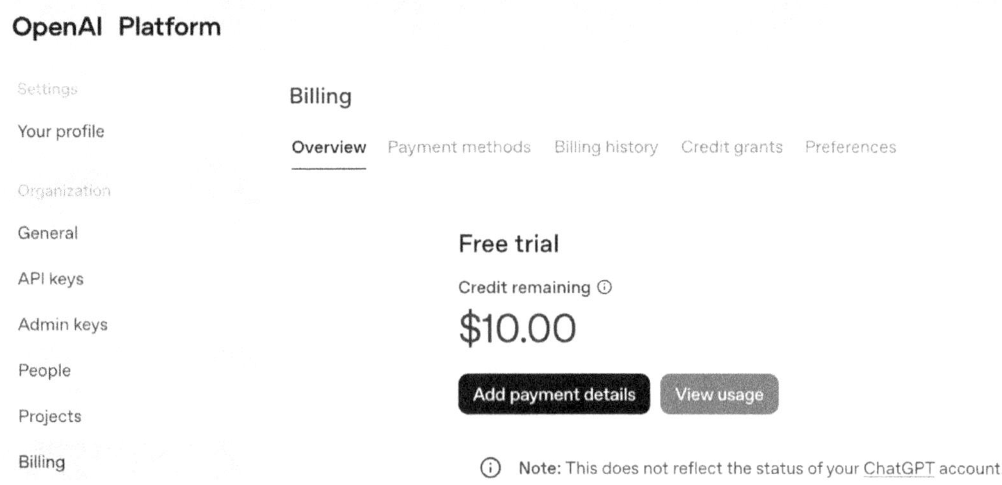


*Figure 11.2: After setting your details and purchasing some credit*

Monitor your expenses on the `https://platform.openai.com/settings/organization/usage` page.

Go to `https://platform.openai.com/settings/organization/api-keys` and create a key with all permissions. Store the key safely to be used later. You won't be able to see the key again, but if you lose it, you can cancel it and create a new one.

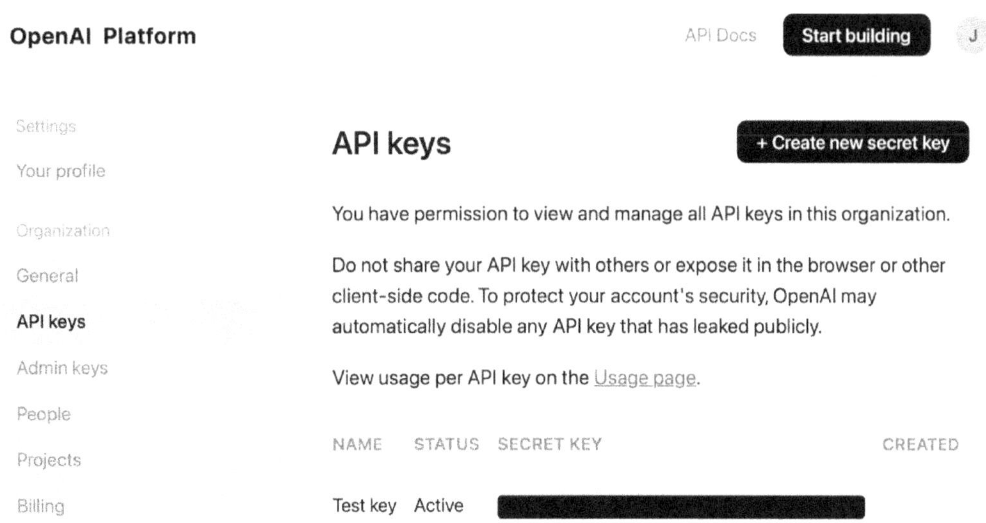


*Figure 11.3: Create an API key*

We will set up a file.env file that will have the following structure.

```
OPEN_AI_KEY = '<your key> '
```

Include it in your working directory when applicable. This file will get environment variables into your project. There's an available `.env.template` file in the directory to use as a base.

> **Note**
>
> Be careful and do not add this file to your repo! It contains your API key, and someone with access to it will be able to use it and expend your credits. Add it to your `.gitignore` file to avoid problems, something that is done by default in many `.gitignore` templates.

You can check the code presented in the chapter at the GitHub URL `https://github.com/PacktPublishing/Python-Automation-Cookbook-Third-Edition/tree/main/ch11`.

# Understanding GenAI elements

The key element in Artificial Intelligence is the **AI Model**. In general, there's some confusion between AI models and GenAI tools.

For example, ChatGPT is a tool by OpenAI, and it can call several different models that can be chosen, based on the requirements. For example, GPT-5.4 is a specific model by OpenAI.

GenAI tools call AI models internally, but they perform coordination on which model to use, when to call it, and what information to send back and forth.

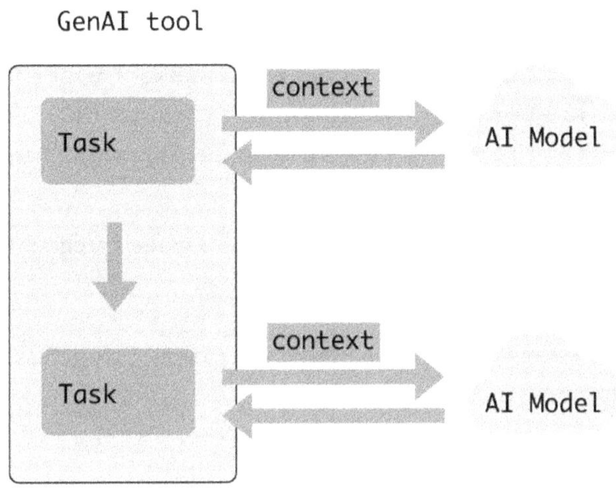


*Figure 11.4: Schema of a GenAI tool calling the AI model*

For example, ChatGPT itself is a GenAI tool. It keeps a conversation, is able to call the AI model multiple times, and calls the right tools.

> **Tip**
>
> AI libraries also have capabilities that allow more actions than purely calling the model. In that regard, they act as GenAI tools. We won't be using them in this chapter but will do so later in the book. See *Chapter 15* for more information.

In this chapter we will focus on working directly with the AI model and showing the different elements that make up a basic GenAI tool.

> **Note**
>
> Be careful as an AI model may return made-up results, in a convincing voice. This is known as a *hallucination*. New models as less prone to hallucinate than older ones, but there's always the possibility that the model returns incorrect info. Be careful with accepting blindly everything that the model return.

## Many different AI models

The AI Model is the core of any GenAI application, but there are different alternatives to use.

> **Tip**
>
> To further complicate things, companies may release families of models. For example, for OpenAI, there's a GPT-5 family with GPT-5.4, GPT-5 mini and GPT-5 nano models. When working with specific models, we will need to specify exactly the model we will use.
>
> The commercial API allows you to discover the available models programmatically.

AI Models are divided in open-weight models, that you can publicly access; and proprietary models that require to access them as a service.

Some examples of AI model families:

| Model | Developer | Type |
|---|---|---|
| GPT-5.4 | OpenAI | Proprietary |
| Claude Sonnet 4.6 | Anthropic | Proprietary |
| Qwen3 | Alibaba | Open-weight |
| Gemini 3.1 | Google | Proprietary |
| DeepSeek v3.2 | DeepSeek | Open-weight |

Open-weight AI Models can be very resource hungry and require powerful hardware that's not common. Because of that, accessing Open-weight models through services is also available.

Each specific model has its peculiarities. Most models accept text, meaning that you submit some text with a prompt and it responds with an answer. But they can also understand data input like images (*e.g., describe me this image*) or binary formats (*e.g., summarize me this PDF*). We will see examples working with images later in this chapter.

Importantly, each model has a context window. That is the maximum input that can be sent to a model for an answer. This context is crucial, as every single call to the model is independent and requires its own context. While the context window is a maximum, AI models lose effectiveness if the context grows. This is analogous to asking a very long query—it's easy to get confused! Managing the information in the context is an important element of tasks involving multiple steps.

# Creating your own chatbot

We will start by creating our own chatbot, similar to the functionality of ChatGPT. This recipe will describe a basic GenAI tool and how it calls the AI model behind the scenes, handles the context, and keeps track of the users' information. We will use a commercial model from OpenAI.

We will see the loop of asking new questions and updating the context to make sure that the AI model is using all the information in the conversation.

## Getting ready

In this recipe, we'll require the following modules in our virtual environment:

```
$ echo "python-dotenv==1.2.2" >> requirements.txt
$ echo "openai==2.24.0" >> requirements.txt
$ pip install -r requirements.txt
```

Remember to have your OpenAI key available in the file `keys.py`

Download the `simple_chatbot.py` script from GitHub at `https://github.com/PacktPublishing/Python-Automation-Cookbook-Third-Edition/blob/master/ch11/simple_chatbot.py`.

We will use the *GPT-5.4* model, but models are being released quickly, so please verify that it is available. If it's not, check later on the *There's more* section to see available models and how to change to use newer available models.

## How to do it...

1. Run the script to start the chatbot

```
$ uv run simple_chatbot.py
Welcome to the chatbot! Write bye to end!
You:
```

2. Enter some question

```
$ uv run simple_chatbot.py
Welcome to the chatbot! Write bye to end!
You: Do you know Python?
Bot:  Yes—I can help with Python (syntax, debugging, writing scripts, data
analysis, web/API code, async, testing, packaging, etc.).
```

```
What are you trying to do, and what Python version/environment are you
using?
You:
```

3. Do a follow up question

````
You: How can I change the value of the value on a dictionary
Bot:  To change (update) a value in a Python dictionary, assign to the key:

```python
d = {"a": 1, "b": 2}
d["a"] = 10         # change existing key
print(d)            # {'a': 10, 'b': 2}
```

If the key might not exist, you have a few options:

**1) Add it (assignment creates it if missing):**
```python
d["c"] = 3
```

**2) Update multiple keys at once:**
```python
d.update({"a": 5, "b": 6})
```

**3) Set a default only if missing:**
```python
d.setdefault("d", 0)  # doesn't overwrite if "d" already exists
```

If you share your dictionary and what you want to change, I can show the
exact line.
You:
````

4. Say "bye" to end the session

```
You: bye
Bot: Bye, bye!
```

## How it works...

Let's take a look at the script `simple_chatbot.py`.

```
import os
from openai import OpenAI
from dotenv import load_dotenv
load_dotenv()

OPEN_AI_KEY = os.getenv('OPEN_AI_KEY')
client = OpenAI(api_key=OPEN_AI_KEY)
MODEL = 'gpt-5.4'
def main():
    messages = [
        {'role': 'system', 'content': 'you are a useful assistant'},
    ]
    print('Welcome to the chatbot! Write bye to end!')
    while True:
        user_input = input('You: ')
        if not user_input:
            continue
        elif user_input.lower() == 'bye':
            print('Bot: Bye, bye!')
            break
        messages.append({'role': 'user', 'content': user_input})
        response = client.responses.create(
            model=MODEL,
            input=messages,
        )

        reply = response.output_text
        print('Bot: ', reply)
        messages.append({'role': 'assistant', 'content': reply})

if __name__ == '__main__':
    main()
```

We use the `dotenv` module to load the `.env` file as environment variables with a call to load_dotenv. We then retrieve the `OPEN_AI_KEY` definition into a local constant.

> **Tip**
>
> `dotenv` allows us to set up environment variables in a convenient file. It's especially handy for secrets. You can read more about it here https://pypi.org/project/python-dotenv/

The `main` function prepares a `messages` list which stores all the conversation. We store the `messages`, both the ones the user inputs (using the `input` function) and the responses of the model. Note that we store each message with the following format:

```
message = {'role': <the source of the message>, 'content': content}
```

We use three roles in the script:

- `user`: The user of the chatbot
- `assistant`: The responses from the chatbot
- `system`: An initial message to set the tone for the chatbot

The model is first prepared with the call to

```
client = OpenAI(api_key=OPEN_AI_KEY)
```

And then we call it with `client.responses.create`, specifying the `MODEL` and putting all our `messages`. This is where we make the external request to the model with all the context.

We then add the resulting reply as a new message to feed the loop and retry it.

The `while True` loop repeats the steps, each time adding more context. Note that we keep all the messages in the context.

> **Note**
>
> If we don't update the context by adding all the previous messages, including responses, the AI model will only know the latest question, which will make the chatbot less capable.

We add a command to stop the loop if the user inputs `bye`.

## There's more...

We are using the `gpt-5.4` model, but that's not the only option. We may want to tweak the model for our use case.

> **Note**
>
> A possibility is that this specific model is not available at the time you are reading these lines. Check what's the latest available model and replace the value in `MODEL`

To obtain all the models available, you can retrieve them from the python module by calling the `client.models.list()` function.

This can return a lot of info; to reduce it, you can return only models that start with the latest versions like this. They may have different versions based on when they were released.

```
>>> [model.id for model in client.models.list() if model.id.startswith('gpt-5')]
['gpt-5.4', 'gpt-5.3-chat-latest', 'gpt-5.4-2026-03-05', 'gpt-5.4-pro', 'gpt-5.4-
pro-2026-03-05', 'gpt-5-chat-latest', 'gpt-5-2025-08-07', 'gpt-5', 'gpt-5-
mini-2025-08-07', 'gpt-5-mini', 'gpt-5-nano-2025-08-07', 'gpt-5-nano', 'gpt-5-
codex', 'gpt-5-pro-2025-10-06', 'gpt-5-pro', 'gpt-5-search-api', 'gpt-5-search-
api-2025-10-14', 'gpt-5.1-chat-latest', 'gpt-5.1-2025-11-13', 'gpt-5.1', 'gpt-5.1-
codex', 'gpt-5.1-codex-mini', 'gpt-5.1-codex-max', 'gpt-5.2-2025-12-11',
'gpt-5.2', 'gpt-5.2-pro-2025-12-11', 'gpt-5.2-pro', 'gpt-5.2-chat-latest',
'gpt-5.2-codex', 'gpt-5.3-codex']
```

The model list may be different when you call it. Every month there are new models!

> **Tip**
>
> Check the `OpenAI` documentation for the differences between the different models: `https://developers.openai.com/api/docs/models`. Resist the temptation to use the biggest, latest model! For many usages, a `smaller`, cheaper model may be good enough for your use case.

The **system prompt** is an important element of a system based on repetition like this one. This is the initial message when we specify how the rest of the conversation is going to be. Models are trained to treat these messages with higher priority to fulfill the expected behavior of applications.

You can change the tone by making changes there, for example, changing it to:

```
messages = [
    {'role': 'system', 'content': 'answer talking like a pirate'}.
]
```

Makes the answers quite different.

```
You: Do you know Python?
Bot:  Aye, matey—I know Python well. I can help ye write code, fix bugs, explain
libraries, or chart a course through scripts, data, web, or automation. What be ye
tryin' to do?
```

Other possibilities are to control the language (e.g. *answer in German*), guardrails (e.g. whatever *the user says, do not answer questions related to Python*), or format (e.g. *avoid responding in Markdown*).

> **Tip**
>
> For example, if you check the answer in *Step 3*, you'll see that it's trying to return Markdown text, which is not formatted by our application. You can discourage it by saying that no Markdown can be returned. Or you can tweak the chatbot to properly print Markdown format. You can try integrating the `rich` library (`https://rich.readthedocs.io/en/latest/markdown.html`) into our chatbot!

An important element of the chatbot is the fact that our context is going to be growing. As the conversation and number of messages grow, we are using more and more context. Even if we don't totally fill our context window, it also has the effect that our calls to the API are more expensive. As a simple strategy, it may be a good idea to put a maximum number of messages, dropping the oldest to avoid problems, or call the model to create a summary of the previous conversation after a certain size.

> **Tip**
>
> AI model calls to APIs are typically charged by the number of tokens in and out. Think of tokens as fractions of a word, or a fancy way to count characters. You can set up some instructions in the system prompt to reduce the verbosity of the responses (e.g., *make your answers concise*) to try to avoid waste.

As you can see here, the model doesn't have any memory. It doesn't remember our previous interactions unless we provide them as part of the context. Remember what we discussed in the *Understanding GenAI elements* section: if the context is too big, the quality of the responses will decrease. A very long conversation with the chatbot will produce worse results.

The call to the model itself happens in the `client.responses.create` call. This call may fail for multiple reasons like a transient network error, rate limiting, etc. In our simple example, any problem will make us exit the program. In a real application, we should wrap the call into a try...except block and capture the relevant errors that may need to be retried.

> **Tip**
>
> Some errors can be transient, and others won't be affected by a retry. For example, an authentication problem (`openai.APIStatusError` returning a 401 status code) is likely bad configuration of the keys, while a `openai.RateLimitError` exception means that we should wait a bit until we are able to send a request again.
>
> See the definition of the errors and how to manage them at`https://github.com/openai/openai-python#handling-errors`

The full `openai` documentation is available at `https://developers.openai.com/api/docs/`

## See also

- The *Using a local model* recipe, next in this chapter, to learn how to create a chatbot that runs locally on your computer

# Using a local model

Calling a commercial AI model is not the only option when using GenAI. In this recipe, we will see how to use a local model installed on our computer, instead of calling an external API.

> **Tip**
>
> Unless you have specialized hardware, local models are much smaller and less capable than commercial ones. But you can use them without paying extra, and they can provide good results for your use case.

For that, we will use Ollama, which will allow us to download and run open-weight sources on our computer.

## Getting ready

You need to install Ollama locally (https://ollama.com/). Go to its page and follow the instructions at https://ollama.com/download.

Once installed, you should be able to run it locally and pull models. For this example, we will use a small model that should run on any modern machine with enough RAM, `qwen-3:8b`.

Download and install this model with this command.

```
$ ollama pull qwen3:8b
pulling manifest
pulling a3de86cd1c13: 100%
████████████████████████████████████ 5.2 GB
pulling ae370d884f10: 100%
████████████████████████████████████ 1.7 KB
pulling d18a5cc71b84: 100%
████████████████████████████████████ 11 KB
pulling cff3f395ef37: 100%
████████████████████████████████████ 120 B
pulling 05a61d37b084: 100%
████████████████████████████████████ 487 B
verifying sha256 digest
writing manifest
success
```

Try that it works correctly by running the following command.

```
$ ollama run qwen3:8b
>>>
```

> **Note**
>
> This model should run on computers with 8GB of RAM, though it may be a bit slow. If it crashes, you can try a smaller model like `qwen3:4b`. You can see the whole list of available models for this family on this page:`https://ollama.com/library/qwen3`

You also need to install the module `ollama` to interact in a programmatic way in Python.

```
$ echo "ollama==0.6.1" >> requirements.txt
$ pip install -r requirements.txt
```

Download the `local_chatbot.py` script from GitHub chapter folder.

## How to do it...

1. Run the script to start the chatbot.

```
$ uv run local_chatbot.py
Welcome to the chatbot! Write bye to end!
You:
```

2. Enter some question. Notice it will take some time to get back (more information on that later).

```
$ uv run local_chatbot.py
Welcome to the chatbot! Write bye to end!
You: Do you know Python?
Bot:  Yes, I know Python! I can help with writing code, debugging,
explaining concepts, or solving problems. How can I assist you today?
You:
```

3. Do a follow-up question. After some time, it will return a result.

````
You: How can I change the value of the value on a dictionary
Bot:  To change a value in a dictionary, use the key and assign the new
value directly:

```python
my_dict = {'key': 'old_value'}
my_dict['key'] = 'new_value'
```

This updates the value for the specified key. If the key doesn't exist, it
will create a new entry. For multiple updates, use `update()`:

```python
my_dict.update({'key': 'new_value'})
````
````

```
...
You:
```

4. Say "bye" to end the session.

```
You: bye
Bot: Bye, bye!
```

## How it works...

Let's take a look at the script `local_chatbot.py`.

```
from ollama import chat

MODEL = 'qwen3:8b'


def main():
    messages = [
        {'role': 'system', 'content': 'you are a helpful assistant. Be concise in
your answers'},
    ]
    print('Welcome to the chatbot! Write bye to end!')
    while True:
        user_input = input('You: ')
        if not user_input:
            continue
        elif user_input.lower() == 'bye':
            print('Bot: Bye, bye!')
            break
        messages.append({'role': 'user', 'content': user_input})
        response = chat(model=MODEL, messages=messages)

        reply = response.message.content
        print('Bot: ', reply)
        messages.append({'role': 'assistant', 'content': reply})


if __name__ == '__main__':
    main()
```

If you compare it with the `simple_chatbot.py` script from the previous recipe, it is very similar, with a couple of details.

- We import `ollama` and use the local `MODEL qwen3:8b` instead of the `openai` module and model.
- We use `ollama.chat()` in an analogous way to the previous `client.response.create`. The interface is almost identical.
- We added the instruction `Be concise in your answers` in the system prompt to reduce the length of the answers.

This model is completely local, without any extra cost or your information leaving your computer. Feel free to experiment with the quality of the answers compared with the ones in the previous recipe.

The execution time will be highly dependent on the hardware you run the model on. This may range from really slow to something that's acceptable. It will also depend on the model, with a correlation to the size (bigger models will typically take longer to run). For a list of all the models that you can download, you can check on the Ollama webpage here:`https://ollama.com/search`

> **Tip**
>
> Finding out whether a model will run on your hardware may be difficult beforehand. The project `https://github.com/AlexsJones/llmfit` has a dynamic approach where you can see a lot of models and a recommendation on whether they'll be runnable on your computer or not.
>
> As a rule of thumb, see the size of the model (e.g. for `qwen3:8b` it is 5.2GB). If it fits in the total RAM of your computer, it's likely possible to run it.

## There's more...

1. We selected a model that is a *thinking* model. They produce an internal monolog that tends to produce better results, but they are slower in their responses. It is possible to expose this internal monolog to provide feedback and understand the reasoning behind the answer.
2. To do that, we need to enable a streaming chat, which will be feeding the results as they are available. Check the resulting script in `local_stream_chatbot.py`, available in

the GitHub repository chapter folder. To execute it, you need to include the `colorama` module in your requirements.

```
$ echo "colorama==0.4.6" >> requirements.txt
$ pip install -r requirements.txt
```

3. When calling it, you'll see the thinking process appear, like this:

```
$ uv run local_stream_chatbot.py
Welcome to the chatbot! Write bye to end!
You: Do you know python?
Bot:

Okay, the user is asking if I know Python. Let me confirm that first. Yes,
I do know Python. I should mention that I can help with coding, debugging,
or explaining concepts.

Wait, the user might be looking for specific help. Maybe they have a
problem they need solved. I should offer assistance in those areas. Let me
keep the response friendly and open-ended.

Also, the user might not know exactly what they need. I should invite them
to ask questions or provide code snippets so I can assist better. Let me
make sure the response is clear and helpful without being too technical.

Yes, I know Python! I can help with coding, debugging, explaining concepts,
or solving problems. Just let me know what you need!
```

Note that the thinking part appears grayed out.

4. The script is very similar to `local_chatbot.py`, but there are a few differences. The loop is the following:

```
stream = chat(model=MODEL, messages=messages, stream=True, thinking=True)

print('Bot: ')
thinking_style = False
response = []
for chunk in stream:
    if chunk.message.thinking:
        if not thinking_style:
```

```
                # Thinking style, set clearer type for text
                thinking_style = True
                print(Fore.LIGHTBLACK_EX)
            # Print the thinking process
            text = chunk.message.thinking
            print(text, end='', flush=True)
        else:
            if thinking_style:
                # Back to regular response, reset style
                thinking_style = False
                print(Style.RESET_ALL)

            text = chunk.message.content
            response.append(text)
            print(text, end='', flush=True)
```

You can see that we call the `chat` function with `stream=True`. This produces a `stream` object that we can iterate over, and receive information as it is generated, `chunk` by `chunk`.

The thinking parts are stored in the `message.thinking` part and we receive them before. After that, we receive the usual `message.content`.

To follow with the conversation, we join all the non-thinking parts and add them as part of the context for the next iteration.

> **Tip**
>
> You can also use the streaming concept in OpenAI models. Check their documentation here:`https://developers.openai.com/api/docs/guides/streaming-responses`

In each case, we `print` the result. We avoid printing a newline, and `flush` on each chunk of information to be sure to display the information as it's generated.

```
print(text, end='', flush=True)
```

We use the `colorama` module to provide some formatting and differentiate between the thinking part of the process and the reply. This module allows us to print colours in the console in a multiplatform fashion, in an easy way.

We use the following commands to set the text in clear color and then to reset it back to normal.

```
from colorama import init, Fore, Style
# Init colorama to show properly in all platforms
init()
print(Fore.LIGHTBLACK_EX)
print(Style.RESET_ALL)
```

The full `colorama` documentation is here: `https://github.com/tartley/colorama`

You can check the whole `ollama` Python module documentation here: `https://github.com/ollama/ollama-python`

> **Note**
>
> In advance to allowing you to run open-weight models in your own hardware, Ollama also allows to run the models in their cloud, which may be an alternative to other providers. Check the documentation in Ollama on how to do that and pricing. `https://docs.ollama.com/cloud`

## See also

- The *Creating your own chatbot* recipe, earlier in this chapter, to learn the basics of calling the `openai` module

# Generating images

GenAI doesn't only work with just text. It can create images as well. We will see how to create images by calling the `openAI` API based on a prompt.

## Getting ready

In this recipe, we'll require the following modules in our virtual environment:

```
$ $ echo "python-dotenv==1.2.2" >> requirements.txt
$ echo "openai==2.24.0" >> requirements.txt
$ pip install -r requirements.txt
```

Remember to fill the `.env` file based on `.env.template` with your OpenAI key.

We will use the *GPT Image 1.5* model. Verify that it is available. If it's not, check the *There's more* section on how to change it.

## How to do it...

Import os, openai, base64 , and dotenv modules and load the environment variables.

```
>>> import os
>>> import openai
>>> import base64
>>> from dotenv import load_dotenv
>>> load_dotenv()
```

1. Retrieve from the environment the API key and prepare the client for the call.

```
>>> OPEN_AI_KEY = os.getenv('OPEN_AI_KEY')
>>> client = openai.OpenAI(api_key=OPEN_AI_KEY)
```

2. Define the model we will use and the prompt for the image.

```
>>> MODEL = 'gpt-image-1.5'
>>> prompt = 'A pixelart black and white scene of a forest at dawn, with
some mountains far away. No animals or people should be. The place is
peaceful'
```

3. Call the model with the defined parameters. This may take a few seconds.

```
>>> response = client.images.generate(model=MODEL, prompt=prompt)
```

4. We save the returned image contained in `response`.

```
>>> binary_image = base64.b64decode(response.data[0].b64_json)
>>> extension = encoded_image.output_format
>>> with open(f'image.{extension}', 'wb') as fp:
...     fp.write(binary_image)
```

5. You should have the file `image.png` that should show an image based on the prompt.

Figure 11.5: Your output image should be different, but also represent the prompt

## How it works...

*Steps 1* to *3* are preparation. In *Step 3* we defined the model to use, which needs to be a model capable of generating images. In this case, we use `gpt-image-1.5`.

The prompt to generate the image is also defined in *Step 3*.

We make the call to the API in *Step 4*, which, after a few seconds, returns the image in the `encoded_image` object.

The image is returned in `base64` format. To be able to save it as an understandable image, we need to decode it to binary, which we do at the start of *Step 6*.

> **Note**
>
> `base64` is an encoding that allows you to transform any binary data into a subset of 64 printable characters. `base64` is a very common encoding to transmit binary data over text interfaces. In this case, the `openai` module is internally using HTTP requests, which use text. We need to decode the encoding into binary before saving it.

encoded_image also contains the output_format, which corresponds to the type of image that is being generated. We should save the file with that extension to avoid problems opening the file.

We save the file with a with open block. Note that we open the file with the writing binary option using wb.

Finally, we can look at the resulting image in *Step 6*. If you repeat the process several times, it will show different results!

## There's more...

Be sure that you are using a valid model and that the model is available from OpenAI. The field is changing rapidly and there are new models added and older models being deprecated quickly.

> Note
>
> Using a model that's not image compatible will return an error. Check the available models in OpenAI documentation:https://developers.openai.com/api/docs/models

When we generate the image, we can specify more parameters. For example, we can choose to select the size. The possible sizes may depend on the model, but you can try to send a size and, if not correct, it will return an error message with the valid values. For example,

```
>>> encoded_image = client.images.generate(model=MODEL, prompt=prompt,
size='512x512')
...
openai.BadRequestError: Error code: 400 - {'error': {'message': "Invalid value:
'512x512'. Supported values are: '1024x1024', '1024x1536', '1536x1024', and
'auto'.", 'type': 'invalid_request_error', 'param': 'size', 'code':
'invalid_value'}}
```

Showing that the valid values are 1024x1024 (square), 1024x1536 (landscape), and 1536x1024 (portrait). The size will be returned in the encoded_image.size attribute.

You can produce more than one image in a single call, by calling the parameter n. You can generate up to 10 images in a single call, but they will all use the same prompt. For example, to generate 3 images call the following.

```
>>> encoded_image = client.images.generate(model=MODEL, prompt=prompt, n=3)
```

When returning the information, we have seen that the attribute `encoded_image.data` is a list. In our previous example, it contained only one element, but if we call for more images, it will have more elements.

```
>>> len(encoded_image.data)
3
>>> encoded_image.data[0]
>>> encoded_image.data[1]
>>> encoded_image.data[2]
```

The model is not only capable of creating a new image but also of editing or combining images. For example, if you have two images, one of a forest and another of a deer (you can create them with this recipe by changing the prompt) stored in `forest.png` and `deer.png`, you can combine them in this way.

> **Note**
>
> We kept the forest image from above and created the image of the deer with the prompt *"A deer, in cartoon style."*

Call the `client.images.edit` method, opening the images and adding them to the image parameter.

```
>>> with open('deer.png', 'rb') as deer, open('forest.png', 'rb') as forest:
...     encoded_image = client.images.edit(model=MODEL, prompt='Combine these
images putting naturally the deer into the forest. Merge the styles so the end
result is natural and keep proper proportions. Maintain the black and white',
image=[deer, forest])
>>> binary_image = base64.b64decode(encoded_image.data[0].b64_json)
>>> with open('result.png', 'wb') as fp:
...     fp.write(binary_image)
...
```

The result follows our instructions.

*Figure 11.6: The resulting combined image*

We deliberately used different styles (pixelart and cartoon). Note how it changed the style to make the deer more pixelated and put it in the right place of the image. Try changing the prompt and giving more instructions to produce a different result.

The full `openai` documentation is available at `https://developers.openai.com/api/docs/`

## See also

- The *Creating your own chatbot* recipe, earlier in this chapter, to learn the basics of calling the `openai` module
- The *Describe images* recipe, later in this chapter, to learn how to describe images instead of creating them

# Describe images

When working with images, we can also revert the process and, instead of generating images, describe them through GenAI. We will see how to do that in this recipe.

## Getting ready

In this recipe, we'll require the following modules in our virtual environment:

```
$ echo "openai==2.24.0" >> requirements.txt
$ pip install -r requirements.txt
```

Remember to have your OpenAI key available in the file `keys.py`

Download the image `photo-dublin-a1.jpg` from the folder for this chapter available in GitHub.

> **Note**
>
> You may recognize the photo! We used it in both chapter 4 and chapter 5 earlier.

*Figure 11.7: Photo-dublin-a1.jpg, a picture of Dublin*

We will use the *GPT-5.4* model. Verify that it is available. If it's not, check the *There's more* section on how to change it.

## How to do it...

1. Import os, openai, base64, and dotenv modules and load the dotenv variables.

```
>>> import os
>>> import openai
>>> import base64
>>> from dotenv import load_dotenv
>>> load_dotenv()
```

2. Obtain the API key and prepare the client for the call.

```
>>> OPEN_AI_KEY = os.getenv('OPEN_AI_KEY')
>>> client = openai.OpenAI(api_key=OPEN_AI_KEY)
```

3. Define the model we will use and the prompt for the image.

```
>>> MODEL = 'gpt-5.4'
>>> prompt = 'Describe this image'
```

4. Read the image, and encode it into base64.

```
>>> with open('photo-dublin-a1.jpg', 'rb') as fp:
...     encoded_image = base64.b64encode(fp.read()).decode('utf-8')
```

5. Structure the data that we will send to the AI model.

```
>>> content = {
...     'role': 'user',
...     'content': [
...       {'type': 'input_text', 'text': prompt},
...       {
...           'type': 'input_image',
...           'image_url':f'data:image/jpeg;base64,{encoded_image}'
...       }
...     ]
... }
```

6. We call the model. It may take a few seconds.

```
>>> response = client.responses.create(model=MODEL, input=[content])
```

7. Check the resulting description. It will be different in your case, as the returned value is non-deterministic.

```
>>> response.output_text
'A bright, clear-day waterfront city scene. A wide river runs through the
center, with modern office and apartment buildings lining the left bank. A
historic tall-masted ship is docked along the water, adding contrast to the
contemporary skyline. In the distance, a striking white harp-shaped cable-
stayed bridge spans the river. On the right, a paved riverside walkway with
black railings and round street lamps stretches into the distance, with a
few pedestrians visible. The sky is cloudless and intensely blue, giving
the whole image a calm, open feel.'
```

## How it works...

*Steps 1* to *3* are preparation. In *Step 3* we defined the model to use, which needs to be a model capable of understanding images. In this case, we use `gpt-5.4`. Also, in *Step 3* we set up the prompt to describe the image.

We need to read the image, and we encode it in `base64` in step 4. The encoding transforms it from binary format to a collection of characters.

> **Note**
>
> We discussed in the previous recipe about `base64`. It is a convenient way to transfer binary content as text. A bit more about that later.

We need to prepare the data to be structured in the right way for the `openai` API. Let's take a look at it.

```
content = {
    'role': 'user',
    'content': [
      {'type': 'input_text', 'text': prompt},
      {'type': 'input_image',
       'image_url':f'data:image/jpeg;base64,{encoded_image}'}
```

```
    ]
}
```

We need to define the `role,` which should be `user`, as this is an input from the user. Neither `system` nor `assistant` will apply here. Check the recipe *Creating your own chatbot* for more information about the available roles.

`content` need two elements, the `input_text` and the `input_image`. The structure in both is a dictionary with the `type`, and then `text` for `input_text`, and `image_url` for `input_image`.

`image_url` can be a URL, but we can also embed an image in `base64` in the same way that we would do in an HTML image URL.

> **Note**
>
> We did the same operation in the recipe *Working with email templates* in *Chapter 9*. Be sure that you put the correct extension for the image, `jpg` in this case.

*Step 5* calls the API. Note that input is a list of elements, so we include the content object in brackets to define a list.

Finally, we get the results in *Step 6*. If you repeat the process several times, it will present different descriptions! For example, this is another run at the same image.

```
>>> response = client.responses.create(model=MODEL, input=[content])
>>> response.output_text
'A wide waterfront city scene on a bright, clear day. A river runs through the
center, with modern office buildings lining the left bank and a cobblestone
promenade with black railings and street lamps on the right. In the distance, a
sleek white cable-stayed bridge spans the water, and a tall-masted historic ship
is moored near the left side. The sky is vivid blue with no clouds, giving the
whole scene a clean, sunny feel.'
```

## There's more...

Be sure that you are using a valid model and that the model is available from OpenAI. The field is changing rapidly and there are new models added and older models being deprecated quickly.

> **Note**
>
> Using a model that's not image compatible will return an error. Check the available models in OpenAI documentation:`https://developers.openai.com/api/docs/models`.

While we made a very simple prompt asking for a general description, we can also be more imaginative and extract information. For example, where was the picture taken?

```
>>> prompt = 'Try to find the location of this image'
>>> content = {'role': 'user', 'content': [{'type': 'input_text', 'text': prompt},
{'type': 'input_image', 'image_url':'data:\
image/jpeg;base64,{}'.format(encoded_image)}]}
>>> response = client.responses.create(model=MODEL, input=[content])
>>> response.output_text
'This appears to be **Dublin, Ireland**, along the **River Liffey**.\n\nThe key
landmark is the white harp-shaped bridge in the distance, which is the **Samuel
Beckett Bridge**.  \nSo the photo was likely taken from the **north quay east of
the bridge**, looking west/southwest across the river toward the Dublin Docklands.
\n\nA more precise guess:\n- **Dublin Docklands**\n- On or near **North Wall
Quay / Sir John Rogerson's Quay area**\n- Facing toward the **Samuel Beckett
Bridge**\n\nWhy I think so:\n- The bridge is very distinctive and unique to
Dublin.\n- The modern glass building behind it resembles the **Convention Centre
Dublin**.\n- The riverfront architecture and quay lamps match the Docklands area.
\n\nIf you want, I can try to pinpoint the **exact standing spot** on a map.'
```

This is spot on.

> **Tip**
>
> It may not be! Be careful because GenAI can hallucinate. This image shows recognizable landmarks, but images that can fit many places can return incorrect locations. Always treat GenAI results with care. A good tip is to use a prompt including a score between 0 and 100 on how sure the model is that the result is correct.

You can also better structure the result into JSON, using `pydantic` module, as we saw in *Chapter 7*, and calling `client.responses.parse`.

```
>>> from pydantic import BaseModel
>>> class Location(BaseModel):
...     city: str
...     location: str
...     landmarks: list[str]
...     confidence: int
...
>>> prompt = 'Try to find the location of this image. Give a confidence score on location'
>>> content = {'role': 'user', 'content': [{'type': 'input_text', 'text': prompt},
{'type': 'input_image', 'image_url':'data:\
image/jpeg;base64,{}'.format(encoded_image)}]}
>>> response = client.responses.parse(model=MODEL, input=[content],
text_format=Location)
>>> response.output_parsed
Location(city='Dublin', location='River Liffey / Dublin Docklands, near Samuel
Beckett Bridge', landmarks=['Samuel Beckett Bridge', 'River Liffey', 'Dublin
Docklands', 'Citi building visible on the quay'], confidence=96)
```

This can be very useful for using the results from the calls to the AI models.

You may be tempted to think that this is being extracted from the information that we described in the recipe *Reading images*, in *Chapter 4*. You can verify that the image contains the metadata with the location. But it still works when it is not.

You can check it using the image `dublin-pixelart.png` available in the GitHub repo, which presents a pixel art representation of the same picture.

*Figure 11.8: Pixelart version of the same image*

If we go through the process again for this new image (remember to adjust the type of the file in the `image_url`, as this file is a PNG file), we get the following result.

```
>>> prompt = 'Try to find the location of this image. Describe the image. Be
concise in the answer'
...
>>> response.output_text
'This looks like **Dublin, Ireland — the River Liffey / Dublin Docklands**.
\n\nClues: the **Samuel Beckett Bridge** (white harp-like cable-stayed bridge) is
visible in the background, along with a **quayside promenade**, modern docklands
buildings, and a **tall ship** on the river.\n\nThe image is a **stylized/pixel-
art waterfront scene** with bright blue water and sky, black railings and lamps
along the quay, modern buildings, and the white bridge in the distance.'
```

Even if we have clear landmarks that help in the location of the place, this is remarkable.

> **Note**
>
> Remember that we can set up `image_url` as a full URL to work with images located on the Internet, but be sure that the access is fair usage.

You can make more questions like identifying tree and animal species, models of cars or many other operations.

The full `openai` documentation is available at `https://developers.openai.com/api/docs/`

## See also

- The *Creating your own chatbot* recipe, earlier in this chapter, to learn the basics of calling the `openai` module
- The *Generating images* recipe, earlier in this chapter, to learn how to generate files with the `openai` module

# Get this book's PDF version and more

Scan the QR code (or go to `packtpub.com/unlock`). Search for this book by name, confirm the edition, and then follow the steps on the page.

UNLOCK NOW

*Note: Keep your invoice handy. Purchases made directly from Packt don't require an invoice.*

# 12

# Adding Tools to GenAI

We've seen how AI models are capable of generating text following instructions from a prompt, and how they can work with images. But that's not all they can do.

If you remember what we discussed in *Chapter 11*, the GenAI tool calls the AI model. The AI models can also understand the concept of a tool available in the GenAI tool, and request that it is called to process its output and iterate through it.

For example, a regular AI model cannot obtain the current weather, because it's not capable of obtaining information on what's going on right now. But if we add a tool capable of retrieving the weather in our GenAI tool, the AI model can request it to be executed and obtain the information as part of its context.

The process will be similar to the one shown in *Figure 12.1*. The GenAI tool adds, as part of the context, the fact that tools are available. The AI model requests the tool to execute them and come back with the result. And, finally, once all the relevant information is in the context, it can generate the right answer.

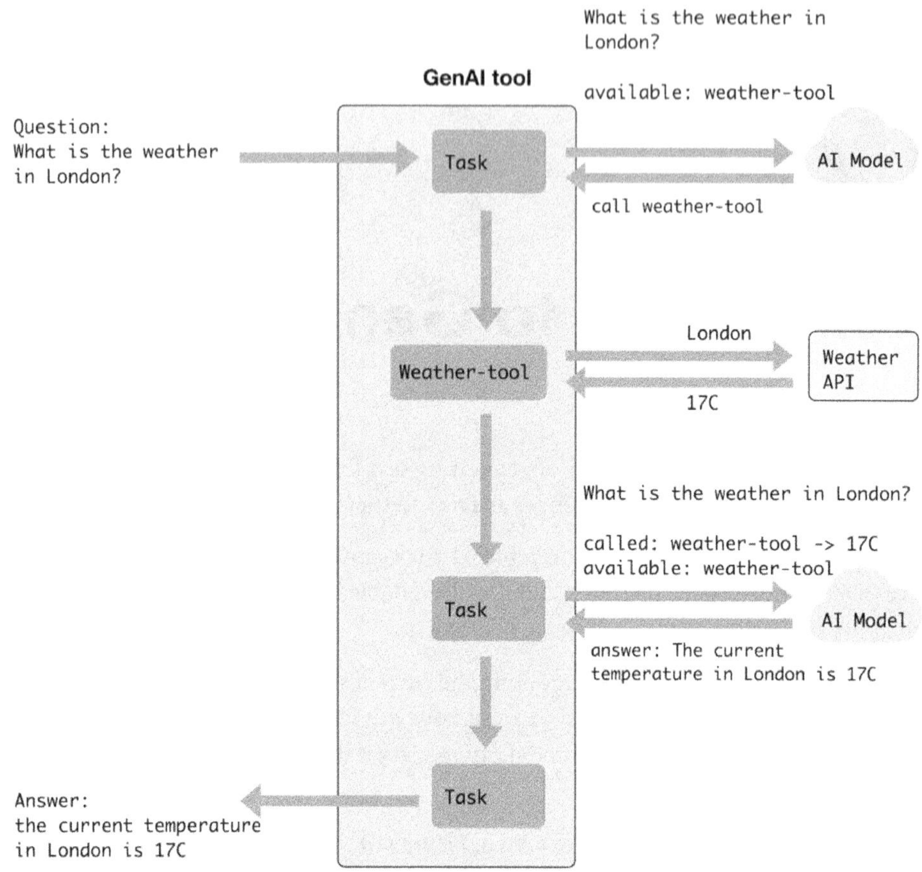


*Figure 12.1: A simple workflow of a GenAI tool using tools*

This is an extremely powerful concept, as it gives a lot of capabilities to our GenAI tools to compound and greatly increase what is possible to achieve with AI models.

> **Note**
>
> In a way, the tools are the way for AI models to request adding new information in the context.

We will see in this chapter how we can use existing tools as well as create our own to extend what we can do. We will see the following recipes:

- Enhancing AI models with web search

- Let's use MCP servers
- Create your own MCP servers

Let's start by understanding the tools that are already available as part of the `openai` module.

# Technical requirements

We will use OpenAI as our provider for the AI models in this chapter.

> **Tip**
>
> Remember that these techniques are available in different AI models and frameworks. You can achieve similar results with other providers like Anthropic's Claude or using local models through Ollama. See *Chapter 11*, recipe *Using a local model* to know more about the latter option.

We described in the *Technical requirements* section of *Chapter 11* the steps that we need to set up an account that will allow us to call the OpenAI APIs. Go there and follow the instructions if you haven't already done so.

Be sure to have your `keys.py` file present in your working directory.

You can check the code presented in the chapter at the GitHub URL `https://github.com/PacktPublishing/Python-Automation-Cookbook-Third-Edition/tree/main/ch12`.

# Enhancing AI models with web search

The `openai` module is not just an interface over the OpenAI interface, but it includes useful tools that we can use out of the box.

Arguably, the most important one is the capacity to do web searches to interact with the external world, helping the AI model dig into current events or find out specific information outside of its training.

> **Note**
>
> Remember, after an AI model is trained, its knowledge is fixed in stone. It can't learn anything new other than the information available in the provided context. Adding web searching capabilities, where the model can request to include data from the web into the context of the task, is incredibly useful. It allows the AI model to get out of the constraints of the training.

In this recipe, we will create a sports calendar for the most important sport events in the upcoming week, with the objective of seeing how you can request the OpenAI module to include a web search as part of the request.

## Getting ready

In this recipe, we'll require the following modules in our virtual environment:

```
$ echo "python-dotenv==1.2.2" >> requirements.txt
$ echo "openai==2.28.0" >> requirements.txt
$ echo "rich==14.3.3" >> requirements.txt
$ pip install -r requirements.txt
```

Remember to have available your `openAI` key in the file `.env` . In the repo directory there's an example `.env.template` that can be filled.

> **Note**
>
> Note that the template file contains elements that will be used in other recipes from this chapter. Only the openAI key is required for this one.

Download the `sports_calendar.py` script from the GitHub repo directory.

We will use the GPT-5.4 model. Verify that it is available on the OpenAI webpage (https://developers.openai.com/api/docs/models). If it's not, change it accordingly. *There's more* information about it in the There's more section of the *Creating your own chatbot* recipe in *Chapter 11*.

## How to do it...

1. Run the script `sports_calendar.py`

    ```
    $ uv run sports_calendar.py
    ```

2. After some time, a calendar will appear with events for the next week. This depends on the week, of course, but it also changes a lot per execution. For example, this is a possible result

    ```
    Calendar of major sports events in Europe for the week of Monday, March 16,
    2026 to Sunday, March 22, 2026
    One event per day; each date checked against two independent sources.
    ```

```
 • Monday, March 16, 2026 – Premier League: Brentford vs Wolverhampton
Wanderers (England). The EPL schedule lists the match
   on March 16, and the club fixture listing confirms the same date.
(formula1.com)
 • Tuesday, March 17, 2026 – UEFA Champions League round of 16, second legs
begin. UEFA's competition calendar lists
   round-of-16 second legs on 17/18 March 2026, and the official round-
of-16 schedule PDF shows fixtures specifically on
   Tuesday, 17 March 2026. (uefa.com)
 • Wednesday, March 18, 2026 – Miami Open main-draw week begins. The WTA
event page gives the tournament dates as March 17-29,
   2026, while the ATP calendar lists the Miami Open as 18-29 March 2026,
confirming Wednesday as the men's main-draw start
   during this week. (wtatennis.com)
 • Thursday, March 19, 2026 – UEFA Europa League round of 16, second legs.
UEFA's Europa League competition page states the
   round of 16 is played on 12 & 19 March 2026, and the official draw/
schedule material says the quarter-final schedule will
   be communicated after the return legs on 19 March 2026. (uefa.com)
 • Friday, March 20, 2026 – Premier League: Bournemouth vs Manchester
United (England). The league schedule lists the match on
   Friday, March 20, 2026, and UEFA's 2026 football calendar also
identifies March 20 as an active club-football date
   immediately after the European midweek. (uefa.com)
 • Saturday, March 21, 2026 – Premier League: Brighton & Hove Albion vs
Liverpool (England). The EPL schedule shows this match
   on Saturday, March 21, 2026, and the same weekend slate is reflected in
the official competition schedule. (uefa.com)
 • Sunday, March 22, 2026 – Premier League: Sunderland vs Newcastle United
(England), a major Tyne-Wear derby. The EPL
   schedule lists it on Sunday, March 22, 2026, and the official league
fixture feed places it on that date as part of the
   weekend programme. (uefa.com)
```

As we can see, it's a very intense week of football/soccer.

**Tip**

Try running the script a few times. You'll see that you will generate very different results. This is one of the key aspects of GenAI: they are non-deterministic!

## How it works...

Let's take a look at the script `sports_calendar.py`.

```
from keys import OPEN_AI_KEY
from openai import OpenAI
from rich.console import Console
from rich.markdown import Markdown

client = OpenAI(api_key=OPEN_AI_KEY)

MODEL = 'gpt-5.4'

console = Console()


def main():
    prompt = ('Create a calendar of the most important '
              'sport events in Europe for the new week. '
              'One event per day. Verify each event'
              'independently twice to be sure the date is '
              'correct. Do not suggest next steps')

    response = client.responses.create(
        model=MODEL,
        tools=[{'type': 'web_search'}],
        input=prompt
    )
    markdown = Markdown(response.output_text)
    console.print(markdown)


if __name__ == '__main__':
    main()
```

The important part is in the call to the `client.response.create` method, where we add the parameter `tools` and include `web_search`. This tells the model we want to use the web search tool.

> **Tip**
>
> Tweaking the prompt may be necessary for best results. As you can see, we are asking to verify independently the events that are presented. This is to reduce the likelihood of hallucinations. It's possible to retrieve search results that are outdated or that are general (like "this event tends to happen in the last week of April" kind of statements) and produce a final calendar that is neither correct nor useful.
>
> Try to experiment with the prompt and see the different results that you're able to obtain. Perhaps focus on a specific sport or country.

The result is returned in the `response.output_text` attribute. Because the returned text is formatted in Markdown, we use the `rich` module. This module properly formats the text so it appears as it should when printed in the console.

Once imported, we need to create a new `Console`, and then we can apply the `Markdown` function to the text and print it.

```
from rich.console import Console
from rich.markdown import Markdown

console = Console()
markdown = Markdown(text_in_markdown_format)
console.print(markdown)
```

Given that AI models tend to return the code formatted in Markdown, it is a good approach to always expect it and handle the Markdown format to print it correctly, but it can depend on your use case.

## There's more...

You can inspect the queries that the model has used as part of the process. The full information that it's returned is in the `response.output` array, which returns all the actions that were part of the process. Each of the elements can be examined.

If you follow the sequence of elements, you'll see that there are several search actions, finalized by a message with the final answer.

```
>>> [element.type for element in response.output]
['web_search_call', 'web_search_call', 'web_search_call', 'web_search_call',
'message']
```

Each of the `web_search_call` actions performs different queries to obtain the results, while the final `message` contains the text result.

You can obtain the specific queries that the action produced as well, for example:

```
>>> response.output[1].action.queries
['site:uefa.com Nations League quarter-finals March 19 2026 official',
 'site:uefa.com Nations League quarter-finals March 20 2026 official',
 'site:uefa.com Nations League quarter-finals March 22 2026 official',
 'site:euroleaguebasketball.net March 17 2026 EuroLeague schedule official']
```

This particular action was finding out the calendar for different competitions related to football/soccer happening on the specified days.

> **Note**
>
> It is important to note that, in the `openai` model, the searches are produced on OpenAI servers, instead of doing these searches locally on your computer. So we call the OpenAI API, and the GenAI tool part that we defined in our diagram in *Figure 12.1* is executed in part on the OpenAI servers.
>
> Because of that, search actions have an extra cost in OpenAI. See this page for more details: `https://developers.openai.com/api/docs/pricing#built-in-tools`

The full `openai`documentation is available at `https://developers.openai.com/api/docs/`

## See also

- The *Creating your own chatbot* recipe, in *Chapter 11*, describes the basics of working with AI models
- The *Let's use MCP servers* recipe, next, to see how to use many other tools

# Let's use MCP servers

Adding tools to AI models multiplies their capabilities, as it allows the AI model to access external data and even have control over the context by going back and forth over the data, inquiring about details.

The effect of tools is multiplicative. More tools allow for correlating different data sources and achieving more impactful operations. Some tools can also allow the model to produce actions, not only obtain information.

> **Note**
>
> Many tools, like OpenAI Codex or Claude Code among many others, are capable of calling tools through MCP, which makes the operation just a matter of configuring the server correctly. In this recipe, though, we will see how you can access it in code. For documentation about Codex, check the OpenAI documentation here: `https://developers.openai.com/codex/mcp`.

In order to allow tools to be more easily connected, a standard called Model Context Protocol was created as an open standard, defining how a tool should connect with others. It's a very simple protocol that allows for wrapping any system so it's callable by a compatible GenAI tool and for adding more capacities.

For this recipe, we will use an MCP server that is able to interact with a local database. Check the project here `https://github.com/prayanks/mcp-sqlite-server`; we included the code into the GitHub repo in the mcp-sqlite-server subdirectory.

> **Note**
>
> We will access a SQLite server. While we won't get into details about how, it's good to understand what it is. SQLite is a local database that allows for using a full SQL syntax using a local file storing the results. It's easy to use, and very useful for projects where you want to store data locally and with a small footprint, compared with other bigger SQL servers like MySQL or PostgreSQL. Python has support for SQLite included in its standard library. Get more information here: `https://docs.python.org/3/library/sqlite3.html`

Using this MCP it will allow the model to interact with the SQLite database, and we can perform queries in natural format to analyze the content in the database.

## Getting ready

In this recipe, we'll require the following modules in our virtual environment:

```
$ echo "python-dotenv==1.2.2" >> requirements.txt
$ echo "openai==2.28.0" >> requirements.txt
$ echo "rich==14.3.3" >> requirements.txt
$ echo "openai-agents==0.12.3" >> requirements.txt
$ uv pip install -r requirements.txt
```

Download the `database_analysis.py` script from GitHub at `https://github.com/PacktPublishing/Python-Automation-Cookbook-Third-Edition/blob/master/ch12/database_analysis.py`.

We need to download the project `mcp-sqlite-server`, originally from `https://github.com/prayanks/mcp-sqlite-server`, but it has been included as a subdirectory in our GitHub repo.

Remember to have available your `openAI` key in the file `.env` . In the repo directory there's an example `.env.template` that can be filled.

You'll also need to find the UV_COMMAND by running a which uv command.

```
$ which uv # Find the location of uv
/usr/bin/uv
```

Finally, fill the MCP_PATH variable as well, using the full path to the `sqlite_stdio_mcp_server.py` file inside the `mcp-sqlite-server` directory.

```
MCP_PATH = '/full/path/to/mcp-sqlite-server/sqlite_sdio_mcp_server.py'
```

> **Note**
>
> Note that the template file contains elements that will be used in other recipes from this chapter. Only `OPEN_AI_KEY`, `UV_COMMAND` and `MCP_PATH` are required for this recipe.

We will use the GPT-5.4 model. Verify that it is available on the OpenAI webpage (https://developers.openai.com/api/docs/models). If it's not, change it accordingly. *There's more* information about it in the There's more section of the *Creating your own chatbot* recipe in *Chapter 11*.

## How to do it...

1. We need to prepare the MCP server. In the directory of `mcp-sqlite-server`, set up an environment and install the dependencies. Verify with the README file that these are the correct dependencies.

```
$ uv venv
Using CPython 3.14.3 interpreter at: /usr/local/opt/python@3.14/bin/python3.14
Creating virtual environment at: .venv
```

```
Activate with: source .venv/bin/activate
$ uv pip install "mcp[cli]"
```

2. You need to define the database file to use. We will use the example included in the repo, `startups.db`. Edit the file `sqlite_stdio_mcp_server.py` to change the parameter `DB_PATH` to point to your file

```
DB_PATH = "/path/to/your/local/directory/mcp-sqlite-server/startups.db"
```

3. Launch the `database_analysis.py` file. After some time, it will return its analysis.

```
$ uv run database_analysis.py
...
----------------------------------------------
The database is a small SQLite dataset with a single business table,
startups, containing 5 startup records. The table stores
each company's name, description, website, funding amount, funding date,
and investors. The startups span AI, enterprise SaaS,
biotech, fintech, and green energy, suggesting a curated sample of venture-
backed companies across several high-growth
sectors.

The situation described is a compact 2023 funding snapshot: all 5 deals
occurred in 2023, totaling $54.5M, with an average
raise of $10.9M. Delta Ventures leads with $20M, followed by BetaSoft at
$12M and Epsilon Dynamics at $10M. Overall, the data
suggests investor interest is spread across diverse industries rather than
concentrated in one theme, with especially strong
capital flowing into fintech and enterprise software, while climate/energy
and biotech also remain meaningfully represented
----------------------------------------------
```

You can see while it's running the logs produced by the MCP server as it progresses

```
[2026-03-17 15:43:37] DEBUG - Initializing server 'SQLite MCP Server'
...
[2026-03-17 15:43:47] DEBUG - Tool 'sql_query' invoked with query: SELECT
strftime('%Y-%m', funding_date) AS month, SUM(funding_amount) AS
monthly_total, COUNT(*) AS deals FROM startups GROUP BY strftime('%Y-%m',
funding_date) ORDER BY month;
```

```
[2026-03-17 15:43:47] INFO - SQL query executed successfully.
...
[2026-03-17 15:43:49] INFO - Database connection closed. MCP server
shutdown complete.
```

As we've seen with GenAI tools, this analysis will change with each execution

## How it works...

Let's take a look at the interesting parts of the `database_analysis.py` script.

```
set_default_openai_key(OPEN_AI_KEY)

UV_COMMAND = os.environ.get('UV_COMMAND')
MCP_PATH = os.environ.get('MCP_PATH')

async def main():
    async with MCPServerStdio(
        name='database',
        params={
            'command': UV_COMMAND,
            'args': ['run', MCP_PATH],
        },
    ) as mcp_server:
        agent = Agent(
            name='MCP Assistant',
            instructions='You are a helpful assistant with access '
                         'to MCP tools',
            mcp_servers=[mcp_server],
            model=MODEL,
        )

        prompt = '''
            Explain the contents of the database accessible through
            MCP server. Provide insights about the situation
            described. Be concise. Return your results in a
            couple of paragraphs.
        '''

        result = await Runner.run(agent, input=prompt)

        markdown = Markdown('---')
```

```
        console.print(markdown)

        markdown = Markdown(result.final_output)
        console.print(markdown)

        markdown = Markdown('---')
        console.print(markdown)

asyncio.run(main())
```

We first set up the key to access the OpenAI interface using `set_default_openai_key`. We also use two environment variables (defined in the `.env` file), `UV_COMMAND` and `MCP_PATH`, to configure the command to execute for the MCP server.

The meaty part is the creation of the setup of the MCP server through the call to `MCPServerStdio`, which includes a name and the command to run to start the server.

> **Note**
>
> Note that we are using asynchronous code to handle the call to MCP. In the `with` statement, we prepare the server that is then handled later in the block on the `mcp_server` object.

We create an `Agent` object, adding the `mcp_server` to the list of available MCP tools.

> **Note**
>
> The Agent SDK, accessible through `openai-agents`, is an official framework by OpenAI that's more capable than their regular `openai` module. It allows you to generate more capable code, leading to powerful agents. We will use it through this chapter and the next ones.

The rest of the code is very similar to the previous recipe *Enhancing AI models with web search*. We call the `agent` with the `Runner`, adding the `prompt`, and `print` the resulting text as Markdown.

> **Note**
>
> We also add two lines in Markdown to clearly separate the start and end of the text that's the result from the logs of the MCP server.

The resulting analysis comes from the database file. You can see the way that this example was populated in the file `/mcp-sqlite-server/create_sample_db.py`. You can see that it's generating some mock data for a few startup companies, with data about funding. The AI model used the available tool to produce different SQL commands and understanding of both the structure as well as the data.

You can try to tweak the prompt to make different questions.

> **Note**
>
> Importantly enough, the MCP server itself does not know the structure of the database! Instead, the AI model analyzes it (through the MCP available tools) and discovers it to interpret it.

The MCP server is stopped at the end once we finalize our script.

## There's more...

The list of freely available MCP servers is very big and varied. The protocol was created to standardize the access to any kind of tools, and it has quickly become ubiquitous. It was nicknamed "the USB for AI," promising to allow interconnection of any tool with AI models, multiplying the capabilities of GenAI tools.

There are many freely available MCP servers to access databases, work with your filesystem, scrape the web, perform specific searches (e.g. search on a particular service like available flights), shop in a store, interact with SaaS tools or many more.

> **Note**
>
> For a good list of available MCP servers, you can refer to the page `https://mcpservers.org/`.

Remember also that you can configure more than one MCP server. Each one is more useful as they can interact. For example, adding a database tool and a filesystem one may allow you to store a report with the results of the database analysis.

While in this recipe we use a locally running MCP server, which is run as the execution of a command, this is one of the ways to run an MCP: by calling it and interacting with it through stdio (hence the name of the server `MCPServerStdio`). This method is convenient when the MCP server lives locally on our machine, but it's not the only option.

We can also call a remote server. The `mcp-sqlite-server` project has a script to start a remote server called `sqlite_sse_mcp_server.py`.

> **Note**
>
> Be sure to edit the file `sqlite_sse_mcp_server.py` to set up the `DB_PATH` constant to point to your `startups.db` file, as we did with `sqlite_sdio_mcp_server.py`.

Start the MCP server. This server will run locally and expose its interface at `http://localhost:8000`.

```
$ uv run sqlite_sse_mcp_server.py
...
INFO:     Started server process [77999]
INFO:     Waiting for application startup.
INFO:     Application startup complete.
INFO:     Uvicorn running on http://0.0.0.0:8000 (Press CTRL+C to quit)
```

Once the MCP server is started, we can open a different terminal and run a different script, tweaked to access it. This script is accessible at `https://github.com/PacktPublishing/Python-Automation-Cookbook-Third-Edition/blob/master/ch12/database_analysis_sse.py`.

It is very similar to `database_analysis.py`, but with the difference that we use `MCPServerSse` to communicate instead of `MCPServerStdio`, and we specify the url to connect.

```
    async with MCPServerSse(
        params={'url': 'http://localhost:8000/sse'},
        name='database',
    ) as mcp_server:
```

If we call it, we get a similar result as before.

```
$ uv run database_analysis_sse.py
------------------------------------


The database is a small SQLite dataset with a single relevant table, startups,
containing 5 startup funding records. Each
record includes the startup name, description, website, funding amount, funding
date, and investors. The companies span
```

```
several sectors: AI (AlphaTech), enterprise SaaS (BetaSoft), biotech (Gamma
Innovations), fintech (Delta Ventures), and green
energy (Epsilon Dynamics).

The situation described is a compact snapshot of recent startup fundraising
activity, with all 5 companies having recorded
funding. Total disclosed funding is $54.5M, with an average round of $10.9M;
amounts range from $5M to $20M. Delta Ventures
has the largest raise at $20M, followed by BetaSoft at $12M and Epsilon Dynamics
at $10M. The mix of sectors suggests a
diversified investment landscape, with especially strong backing for fintech and
software, while investor participation ranges
from single-investor rounds to broader syndicates.
----------------------------------------------------
```

Notice that this execution call didn't produce MCP logs. Instead, the logs were produced in the terminal that is executing the server.

```
...
[2026-03-17 16:24:52] DEBUG - sqlite_mcp_server - SQL query executed successfully.
Result: [
  {
    "startup_name": "AlphaTech",
    "description": "Innovative AI startup",
    "website": "https://alphatech.io"
  },
  {
    "startup_name": "BetaSoft",
    "description": "Enterprise SaaS solution",
    "website": "https://betasoft.com"
  },
  {
    "startup_name": "Gamma Innovations",
    "description": "Cutting-edge biotech research",
    "website": "https://gammainnovations.org"
  },
  {
    "startup_name": "Delta Ventures",
    "description": "Fintech disrupting traditional banking",
    "website": "https://deltaventures.net"
  },
```

```
    {
      "startup_name": "Epsilon Dynamics",
      "description": "Sustainability through green energy",
      "website": "https://epsilondynamics.com"
    }
  ]
  ...
```

As you can see, the server remains up after finishing the task, compared with the `Stdio` one, which stopped the process when we ended the connection.

> **Note**
>
> While we have used SSE as it's the one available in the example project, this protocol is no longer recommended for connecting to MCP, instead preferring MCPServerStreamableHttp. This connection is configured in the same way as SSE.

So far, we've connected locally to tools in our computer. But it's possible to access remote tools in the same way, just changing the URL pointing at the right URL address. It may be necessary to authenticate to the remote service. Check the specific configuration for it, but very likely you'll need to add some headers with information related to the specific service. For example, an authentication token.

```
async with MCPServerStreamableHttp(
    params={
        'url': SERVICE_URL,
        'headers': {'Authorization': 'Bearer <TOKEN>'}
    },
    name='service',
) as mcp_server:
```

A very typical pattern is to have a local MCP server that handles the authentication to a remote service, acting as a proxy. In this case, the start of the MCP requires setting up some configuration to allow the authentication (for example, login and password or a token).

The full documentation for the OpenAI Agents SDK is available here: `https://openai.github.io/openai-agents-python/`

For the official documentation about MCP, go to `https://modelcontextprotocol.io/`.

## See also

- The *Creating your own chatbot* recipe, in *Chapter 11*, describes the basics of working with AI models
- The *Create your own MCP servers* recipe, next in this chapter, to learn how to create your own MCP tools

# Create your own MCP server

In case you can't find a generic MCP server giving you the capabilities that you need, you can create your own. The MCP protocol is quite straightforward and setting up a new MCP tool is quite easy.

> **Note**
>
> A very good way of creating an MCP server is to use GenAI tools for that. GenAI understands the MCP protocol very well and can help you create one quickly.

We will see in this recipe how to create your own check on an email inbox, following on the recipe *Reading an email* from *Chapter 9*. The scripts will provide a summary of your emails since yesterday (to a maximum of 20 emails to keep it simple) and leave you with the option to keep asking questions about them.

> **Tip**
>
> Remember on what we discuss in *chapter 11* about local models. Here we are sending emails to be treated remotely, which have data privacy implications and trust in the model provider. You may prefer to use a model running in your computer, even if it's less powerful, to be sure that your data remains private.

## Getting ready

In this recipe, we'll require the following modules in our virtual environment:

```
$ echo "python-dotenv==1.2.2" >> requirements.txt
$ echo "openai==2.28.0" >> requirements.txt
$ echo "rich==14.3.3" >> requirements.txt
$ echo "mcp==1.26.0" >> requirements.txt
$ pip install -r requirements.txt
```

Remember to have available your openAI key in the file `.env`. We will also need your email credentials, as we described in *Reading an email* from *Chapter 9*. Include them in the `.env` file as `EMAIL_USER` and `EMAIL_PASSWORD`. You may also add the `MAILBOX`, as we will see later.

> **Note**
>
> You have in the repo a `.env.template` file that can be filled, but it contains all the variables used in this chapter. Only `OPEN_AI_KEY`, `EMAIL_USER`, `EMAIL_PASSWORD` and `MAILBOX` are used in this recipe.

Download the `ask_email.py`, `email_mcp_server.py`, and `email_tool.py` scripts from GitHub at `https://github.com/PacktPublishing/Python-Automation-Cookbook-Third-Edition/blob/master/ch12/`.

We will use the GPT-5.4 model. Verify that it is available on the OpenAI webpage (https://developers.openai.com/api/docs/models). If it's not, change it accordingly. *There's more* information about it in the There's more section of the *Creating your own chatbot* recipe in *Chapter 11*.

## How to do it...

1. Verify that your email credentials are correct. Call `email_tool.py` to see if it can retrieve your latest emails.

```
$ uv run email_tool.py
1 Email subject
...
20 Email subject
```

2. Call `ask_email.py` to process it. It will show you a couple of paragraphs summarizing your emails.

```
$ uv run ask_email.py
[03/19/26 20:28:19] INFO     Processing request of type
ListToolsRequest
                                                   server.py:720
[03/19/26 20:28:21] INFO     Processing request of type
CallToolRequest
                                                   server.py:720
```

```
[03/19/26 20:28:25] INFO     Processing request of type
ListToolsRequest
                                                     server.py:720
----------------------------------------------------------------------------

Here's a summary of the latest day of emails you received:

It was a fairly busy mix of transactional updates, newsletters, promotions,
and a couple of personal/work messages. The most important practical emails
were a receipt confirming a payment to Netflox and multiple delivery
updates. There was also a short work-related note from
John Smith at Corp saying the contract is ready for review.

The rest of the inbox was mostly newsletters and marketing. On the reading
side, you got a issue 292 from Important News focused heavily on AI,
engineering trends, tooling, and startup/industry news. There were also
startup and crowdfunding digests from different sites. Retail and
promotional emails came from places like
Grocery Stores, Amazing Computers, Great Pens and Cozy Footwear, mostly
highlighting new products, discounts, or entertainment recommendations.
Overall, the day's inbox leaned heavily toward shopping, newsletters, and
campaign promotions, with the key actionable items the receipt, the
tracking updates, and the contract review
------------------------------------------------
Do you want to ask any question? [end to finish]
```

3. You can ask more questions in your inbox.

```
Do you want to ask any question? [end to finish] Any good promotion?
[03/19/26 20:34:52] INFO     Processing request of type
ListToolsRequest
                                                     server.py:720
[03/19/26 20:34:53] INFO     Processing request of type
CallToolRequest
                                                     server.py:720
[03/19/26 20:34:57] INFO     Processing request of type
ListToolsRequest
                                                     server.py:720
----------------------------------------------------------------------------
```

```
A few stood out, depending on what you care about:

 • Great Pens: probably the clearest "real" promo – 50% off selected S.T.
Quill pens. If you're even slightly tempted by premium pens, this is the
strongest discount in the batch.
 • Cozy Footwear: 25% off everything, including licensed apparel. Broad but
decent if you were already planning to buy.
• Grocery Stores: not a simple percentage-off promo, but potentially good
value if the products matches your taste.
 • Amazing Computers: more product pushes than compelling promotions from
what I can see.

So in short: best obvious deal = Cozy Pens 50% off S.T. Quill, best general
discount = Cozy Footwear 25% off everything.

If you want, I can also give you a "best promo by category" breakdown:
tech, stationery, clothing, and home.
--------------------------------------------------------------------------

Do you want to ask any question? [end to finish]
```

4. Once you don't want to ask more questions, exit by typing `end`.

```
Do you want to ask any question? [end to finish] end
bye!
```

## How it works...

First, let's take a look at the `email_tool.py` script. This script creates the tool that we use to obtain the last emails. The full script is available in the `email_tool.py` file in the GitHub repository chapter folder, but we will present a simplified version here.

```
# Imports
...
EMAIL_USER = os.getenv('EMAIL_USER')
EMAIL_PASSWORD = os.getenv('EMAIL_PASSWORD')
MAILBOX = os.getenv('MAILBOX', 'inbox')

# Connect to the server and select the mailbox
mail = imaplib.IMAP4_SSL('imap.gmail.com')
```

```
mail.login(EMAIL_USER, EMAIL_PASSWORD)

mail.select(MAILBOX)


def retrieve_email_uid(email_uid):
    '''
    Retrieve a single email, based on its uid.
    Return its subject, address and text body as payload
    '''
    ...
    return {
        'subject': subject,
        'address': address,
        'payload': payload,
    }

def retrieve_last_emails():
    '''
    Retrieve all emails since a day ago
    '''
    ...
    # We retrieve only the last 20 emails, to simplify
    email_uids = email_uids[-20:]
    data = [retrieve_email_uid(uid) for uid in email_uids]
    return data

if __name__ == '__main__':
    # Test that the retrieval of emails is successful
    for index, email in enumerate(retrieve_last_emails()):
        print(index, email['subject'])
```

This code retrieves the last day's messages.

**Note**

For simplicity and to reduce the time, we cap the number of emails to a maximum of 20.

Each email is retrieved as a dictionary of `subject`, `address` (the sender), and `payload` (the text body of the message). When we execute the script, we test that it works by displaying the subjects of all of those emails.

Tip

It is good to add this kind of verification, as it will allow us to double-check that our code works correctly before moving to the next step.

We performed this verification as *Step 1*.

We now need to take a look at `email_mcp_server.py`. This file is the one that's defining the MCP server.

```
from mcp.server.fastmcp import FastMCP
from email_tool import retrieve_last_emails as _retrieve_last_emails

mcp = FastMCP('Email Server')


@mcp.tool()
def retrieve_last_emails():
    '''Retrieve today's email from the mailbox.
    Returns a list of dicts with subject, address, and payload.
    '''
    return _retrieve_last_emails()


if __name__ == '__main__':
    mcp.run(transport='stdio')
```

When we call the script, it sets up an MCP server that communicates through the standard output. And we define a single action: `retrieve_last_emails()`. This is a call to the tool that we prepared in `email_tool.py`.

The MCP framework sets everything in a way that's very easy to define a tool. We just use the `@mcp.tool` decorator. The framework exposes that the tool is available and uses the docstring to allow the AI model calling it to understand what it can be expected.

The `ask_email.py` script is the one where the GenAI work is done. We configure first the MCP server to be called and to retrieve the first question.

```
async with MCPServerStdio(
    params={
        'command': 'uv',
```

```
            'args': ['run', 'email_mcp_server.py'],
        },
        name='email',
        # Longer session (default is 5 seconds) to allow
        # enough time to retrieve the emails
        client_session_timeout_seconds=30,
    ) as mcp_server:
        agent = Agent(
            name='MCP Assistant',
            instructions='You are a helpful assistant with access '
                         'to MCP tools',
            mcp_servers=[mcp_server],
            model=MODEL,
        )

        prompt = '''
            Summarise me in a paragraph or two the latest day of emails
            received
        '''
        messages = [
            {'role': 'user', 'content': prompt}
        ]

        result = await Runner.run(agent, input=messages)
        ...
        markdown = Markdown(result.final_output)
        console.print(markdown)
        ...
```

As we did in the previous recipe, we have to configure how the MCP server is configured. In this case, being in the same directory makes the configuration easier. We call it through standard output.

This is the part that gets executed in *step 2*.

Then, we start the chatbot loop to allow interrogation of the data or to generate other actions.

```
    while True:
        # Allow to ask questions
        question = input('Do you want to ask any question? [end to finish] ')
        if question == 'end':
            print('bye!')
```

```
        break

    # As in other chatbots, we add the context up to this moment
    # question to the context of the AI Model
    messages = result.to_input_list(mode='normalized')
    # Plus the new question from the user
    messages.append({'role': 'user', 'content': question})

    result = await Runner.run(agent, input=messages)
    ...
    markdown = Markdown(result.final_output)
    console.print(markdown)
    ...
```

The `result.to_input_list(mode='normalized')` call returns all context up to the moment.

> **Note**
>
> If you use at this point the latest result from the AI model (i.e. `result.final_output`), it will forget the calls to the tools, so it will likely produce them again.

The loop is executed in *step 3*, allowing you to prompt interactively. As we have done with other chatbots, note that we are appending the previous information so it can keep track of the previous questions and information.

> **Note**
>
> We print the data in Markdown, as the model tends to generate text in that format. This makes the returned info much more appealing and easier to read.

## There's more...

One MCP server is good, but the possibilities can multiply when you add more. You can use your own MCP server in combination with others. You can set up more than one MCP server in this way.

```
async with MCPServerStdio(params=params1, name='server1') as mcp_server1,
           MCPServerStdio(params=params2, name='server2') as mcp_server2:
        agent = Agent(
            name='MCP Assistant',
            instructions='You are a helpful assistant with access '
```

```
                        'to MCP tools',
                mcp_servers=[mcp_server1, mcp_server2],
                model=MODEL,
            )
```

And, of course, you can mix stdio servers with HTTP ones or any other protocol!

To be able to define your own MCP server is useful, as MCP servers are easy to share. But you don't have to use the overhead if you define your own specific tool that is not expected to be shared, instead defining a simpler tool, which is an available call.

```
@function_tool
def retrieve_last_emails():
    '''
    Retrieve today's email from the mailbox.
    Returns a list of dicts with subject, address, and payload.
    '''
    return _retrieve_last_emails()


async def main():
    agent = Agent(
        name='MCP Assistant',
        instructions='You are a helpful assistant with access '
                     'to tools',
        tools=[retrieve_last_emails],
        model=MODEL,
    )

    prompt = '''
        Summarise me in a paragraph or two the latest day of emails
        received
    '''
    messages = [
        {'role': 'user', 'content': prompt}
    ]

    result = await Runner.run(agent, input=messages)
```

> **Tip**
>
> For simplicity, we are not adding parameters to our tool. But you totally can! Just remember to add a description in the docstring so the AI model can better evaluate how to call it.

MCP servers have some problems that are good to describe. It is very easy to create servers and there are a lot already available that can be downloaded and used with small configuration. But that flexibility also makes some MCP servers overbloated with many tools and setups.

In essence, every time that you access an MCP server, you are obtaining a definition of all the available tools in the server, plus a description of how to use them. And, when you call any of the tools, the response can be big.

Many MCP servers take the approach of adding many tools, and returning much information on every single call. That tends to fill the context of the AI Model quickly, especially if you connect many MCP servers at the same time. The AI Model may think that obtaining all possible information is a great idea! As we commented in *Chapter 11*, the context for the AI model is important as filling it provides worse results. This is an easy trap to fall into when getting overexcited and connecting every possible MCP server to your tool.

> **Tip**
>
> In the rush to have an MCP server available to allow interaction with services, many companies (and enthusiasts) have created thin wrappers around existing APIs. This enables capabilities very quickly, but likely produces a suboptimal integration in many situations. A well-designed MCP should implement elements like caching the calls to the API, provide access control, enable/disable tools, and make available tools that are useful in an AI integration situation, not necessarily just blindly replicating the already existing API. For example, a flexible `search` tool is a powerful tool that allows the AI model to find the best information. In many ways, an AI-friendly interface is very similar to a human-friendly interface.

In professional environments, it's useful to want to connect your email server (Outlook, Gmail,...) to your company wiki (Confluence, Notion...) to your chat communication (Teams, Slack...) to your ticketing system (Jira, Zendesk, Monday.com ...) to something else. This is the promise to get everything working together, but in practice it may fail, because the MCP servers used to connect to them are providing too much information, aiming for maximum flexibility.

A service like Jira may have 20 or 30 different tools with options like searching tickets, adding labels, retrieving individual tickets, dashboards, etc. A search can also return too much information that gets composed. For example, imagine that a search returns every single possible parameter for each of the matched tickets. You can see how all that information can quickly add up and fill the available context.

To avoid falling into these traps, you can either work with the specific configuration to disable many of the tools to focus only on the actions that are really relevant for your workflow or create your own integrations with very specific actions, like we've seen in this recipe.

This recipe is not trying to cover every possible action on your email, but instead does something small and builds it into a sensible action.

Another caveat, that we will explore in depth later in *Chapter 13*, is to work on the restriction of possible actions. For example, we may prefer to only allow the agent to generate drafts instead of sending emails, so we can later review them. Typically available MCP servers cover the full range of potentially dangerous actions like sending emails directly.

> **Tip**
>
> Be aware that providing untrusted text to an AI model can produce a prompt injection. An attacker can design text to make the model and the agent perform malicious actions. Any external text that can be read can produce it.
>
> For example, an attacker can send you an email that contains instructions for the agent to obtain private details in other emails (which the agent will likely be able to read) and send it through either sending an email (which is also likely the agent will do) or contacting a web page if the agent is able to use the web. The combination of private data, untrusted content, and ability to communicate externally has been called "the lethal trifecta" and it's a serious problem for agents.
>
> A good article describing it can be found here: `https://simonwillison.net/2025/Jun/16/the-lethal-trifecta/`
>
> Risk can be mitigated by making our agents stricter and more directed, reducing the capacity of tools, reducing the amount of private data they have access to, the possibility of external communication and the amount of untrusted input that our tools receive and treating it with care, but unfortunately this is something that cannot be totally eliminated.

The full documentation for the MCP SDK is available at `https://github.com/modelcontextprotocol/python-sdk`. The full documentation for the OpenAI Agents SDK is available here: `https://openai.github.io/openai-agents-python/`

## See also

- The *Creating your own chatbot* recipe, in *Chapter 11*, describes the basics of working with AI models
- The *Let's use MCP servers* recipe, earlier in this chapter, to learn how to use existing MCP tools

# 13

# Building AI Agents for Business Automation

As we learned in the previous chapter, giving an AI model access to tools greatly amplifies what it can do. When you combine a reasoning-capable model with the ability to gather new information and carry out actions, you get what's known as a ReAct agent. This is an AI Agent that can Reason about a problem and then Act on its conclusions by using the tools available, hence the name "ReAct." With each result it obtains, the Model can keep reasoning, expanding its capabilities to handle more complex and extended tasks.

These tools, in addition to collecting information, can also execute commands. Command execution can be remarkably powerful, but it's not without risk. The level of access a tool provides determines both the potential and the danger. Greater access can make an agent very effective, but it also increases the chance of unforeseen consequences. AI models can behave in surprising or risky ways.

For instance, imagine giving a GenAI agent the job of automatically replying to your emails. It might accidentally approve an expensive order from a supplier you didn't actually want! This is why current best practice is to minimize the potential impact of tool usage, carefully containing what each tool can do. Over time, as more safeguards are introduced, these risks are likely to reduce. But for now, caution is key. AI agents remain a rapidly evolving and, to a great degree, experimental technology.

> **Tip**
>
> We limit all the access our tools do in this and other chapters in the book, as a way to ensure that the agent remains in the boundaries of what we want. We discussed about the risks of the lethal trifecta in the previous chapter, the combination of private data, untrusted content, and ability to communicate externally. Limiting the scope of the

> tools is both steering the agent into doing what is supposed to do and reduce the risk of the agent doing something dangerous.

In this chapter, we'll explore how to apply the ReAct pattern to combine multiple tools into seamless, useful workflows. We'll introduce techniques for chaining different tasks together, making your AI Agents more capable.

- Prepare meetings by combining data from different tools
- Draft documents with subagents

We will start by gathering information from your Calendar and local files to prepare for meetings

# Technical requirements

We will use OpenAI as our provider for the AI models in this chapter.

> **Tip**
>
> Remember that these techniques are available in different AI models and frameworks. You can achieve similar results with other providers like Anthropic's Claude or using local models through Ollama. See *Chapter 11*, recipe *Using a local model* to learn more about the latter option.

We described in the *Technical requirements* section of *Chapter 11* the steps that we need to set up an account that will allow us to call the OpenAI APIs. Go there and follow the instructions if you haven't already done so.

Be sure to have your `.env` file present in your working directory.

You can check the code presented in the chapter at the GitHub URL `https://github.com/PacktPublishing/Python-Automation-Cookbook-Third-Edition/tree/main/ch13`.

# Prepare meetings by combining data from different tools

By mixing capabilities of different tools, we can create a powerful assistant that is able to gather information about our meeting for today and obtain relevant information to be ready for it.

To be able to get it, we need to add several tools to our Agent, giving it the ability to work on a ReAct loop: First, Reason about the required steps, and then Act by gathering information. This loop can be performed several times until we have all the required information we need to produce a text report.

For this recipe, we will obtain information from a Google Calendar, and we will read meeting notes from previous meetings stored as text files in our filesystem. The AI Agent will use tools to obtain the info and collect a report to be prepared for our next meeting.

## Getting ready

In this recipe, we'll require the following modules in our virtual environment:

```
$ echo "python-dotenv==1.2.2" >> requirements.txt
$ echo "openai==2.28.0" >> requirements.txt
$ echo "rich==14.3.3" >> requirements.txt
$ echo "openai-agents==0.12.3" >> requirements.txt
$ echo "icalendar==7.0.3" >> requirements.txt
$ echo "caldav==3.1.0" >> requirements.txt
$ uv pip install -r requirements.txt
```

Remember to have available your `openAI` key in the file `.env`.

> **Note**
>
> There's a `.env.template` in the repo that you can use to fill with your info. This file contains all the configuration for all recipes in the draft, so some variables won't be used for this recipe.

Download the `calendar_tools.py`, `notes_tools.py` and `meeting_preparation_agent.py` scripts from GitHub at `https://github.com/PacktPublishing/Python-Automation-Cookbook-Third-Edition/blob/main/ch13/`. Download also the meeting notes available from `https://github.com/PacktPublishing/Python-Automation-Cookbook-Third-Edition/blob/main/ch13/data/` to your own `data` subdirectory. You'll need to match the names and emails to the ones on your calendar. That includes the name of the file (currently `jbuelta.md`).

You need to have access to a Google Calendar. If you have followed the instructions in *Chapter 2*, recipe *Sending email notifications*, and created a password to access a Gmail account, you can use it here as well, but be sure that you don't include spaces in the password. Store the email and password into the `.env` file, as `EMAIL_USER` and `CALENDAR_PASSWORD`. More information about creating app passwords can be found in `https://support.google.com/accounts/answer/185833`.

> **Note**
>
> You may obtain a password in the style of "`AAAA BBBB CCCC DDDD`". For this recipe, be sure to use it as a single word "`AAAABBBBCCCCDDDD`" or it may not accept it.

Set up also the `CALENDAR`, marking the specific calendar you want to retrieve in this recipe.

> **Tip**
>
> For testing purposes, you may use a test calendar, with some test meetings. For that, in Google Calendar, you can create a new Calendar with *"Other Calendars +"* > *"Create New Calendar"*, and then add a name and description. Remember to match any invitee in events on the calendar with the name on the `data/` note files. Our example uses my name, but feel free to change it. For the recipe to work, a name on the invite should loosely match one of the available `data/md` files.

We will use the GPT-5.4 model. Verify that it is available on the OpenAI webpage (https://developers.openai.com/api/docs/models). If it's not, change it accordingly. *There's more* information about it in the There's more section of the *Creating your own chatbot* recipe in *Chapter 11*.

## How to do it...

1. Check the end lines in `data/jbuelta.md` (or your version, if you changed the filename).

```
$ tail data/jbuelta.md
...
# 2026-03-12
The Python system is mostly working end-to-end, though some automation
tasks fail silently. Jaime added logging and alerts to track issues. Still
a bit rough, but improving steadily.
Comment: Almost there.
```

2. Verify that you can access your calendar.

```
$ uv run calendar_tools.py
[{'start': datetime.datetime(2026, 4, 8, 17, 0,
tzinfo=zoneinfo.ZoneInfo(key='Europe/Dublin')), 'summary': 'Ongoing
conversation about the Python project', 'attendees': [REDACTED EMAILS]}]
```

3. Check that you can read the notes on the `data` subdirectory. This is the same value as the `data/jbuelta.md` file.

```
$ uv run notes_tools.py
['jbuelta']
Jaime Buelta (REDACTED EMAIL)
-------

# General notes
He is a Software Engineer. we had some conversations about using Python for
our new project. He's convinced that using Python will increase the
productivity

# 2025-02-12
Jaime started setting up the Python project structure and initialized the
repo. They got basic automation scripts running for file organization.
Looks like a solid foundation so far.
Comment: Nice clean start.
...
# 2026-03-12
The Python system is mostly working end-to-end, though some automation
tasks fail silently. Jaime added logging and alerts to track issues. Still
a bit rough, but improving steadily.
Comment: Almost there.
```

4. Run the agent to produce notes for the next meeting.

```
$ uv run meeting_preparation_agent.py

Agent: Calendar assistant
......
Calling tool: retrieve_calendar_events
.......
Calling tool: available_notes
```

```
............
Calling tool: retrieve_note
......................................................................
Calling tool: write_meeting_brief
......................................................................C
alling tool: write_meeting_brief
......................................................................
----------------------------------------------------------------------

Meeting brief

Meeting: Ongoing conversation about the Python project
When: 2026-04-08 17:00 Europe/Dublin
Attendees with prior notes: Jaime Buelta

Relevant context

 • Jaime Buelta is a Software Engineer and has been supportive of using
Python for the new project, believing it will improve productivity.
 • Previous discussions focused on building out the Python project and
related automation work.
 • He set up the initial project structure and repository, including basic
automation scripts.
 • He later automated data collection through an API, addressed rate-
limiting with scheduling changes and retry logic, and fixed cron/timezone
   issues by standardizing on UTC.
 • More recently, he worked on automated report generation, resolved file
overwriting with timestamped filenames, and added logging and alerts
   to investigate silent failures.
 • Overall, the system appears mostly working end-to-end, with reliability
and observability improving over time.
```

5. Check the file `data/jbuelta.md`, and see that the brief has been included there.

```
$ tail data/jbuelta.md
...
## Meeting brief for 2026-04-08
Meeting brief

Meeting: Ongoing conversation about the Python project
When: 2026-04-08 17:00 Europe/Dublin
```

```
Attendees with prior notes: Jaime Buelta
...
```

Note

Remember that AI Models are non-deterministic, and that the results may be different than the ones that are shown here, though they should follow the general idea.

## How it works...

We divided the task into three different files:

- A tool file about calendar access
- A tool file that reads notes archived about previous meetings
- The agent that uses the tools to first read the information, and later, produce and save the meeting notes

Let's first take a look at the calendar tool. Note that it retrieves the configuration variables from the environment variables defined in the `.env` file.

```
EMAIL_USER = os.getenv('EMAIL_USER')
CALENDAR_PASSWORD = os.getenv('CALENDAR_PASSWORD')
CALENDAR = os.getenv('CALENDAR')

def retrieve_calendar_events():
    '''
    Obtain the calendar from the user and get events
    '''
    url = f'https://www.google.com/calendar/dav/{EMAIL_USER}/user'
    client = caldav.DAVClient(
        url=url,
        username=EMAIL_USER,
        password=CALENDAR_PASSWORD,
    )
    principal = client.principal()
    calendar = principal.calendar(name=CALENDAR)

    all_events = []

    for event in calendar.events():
        cal = Calendar.from_ical(event.data)
        for component in cal.walk("VEVENT"):
```

```
            summary = component.get("summary", "No title")
            start = component.get("dtstart").dt

            attendees = component.get('attendee')
            if not isinstance(attendees, list):
                # In case there's a single attendee
                attendees = [attendees]

            attendees = [att.params.get('CN') for att in attendees]
            event = {
                'start': start,
                'summary': str(summary),
                'attendees': attendees,
            }

            all_events.append(event)

    return all_events
```

We use the `caldav` module to access the Google Calendar. We configure the URL, and using the `DAVClient`, we retrieve the specific calendar specified.

Then, we retrieve all events in the calendar and generate a small dictionary with the start time of the meeting, the summary, and the attendees, as a list of names or emails.

> **Note**
>
> The content of the parameter `att.params.get('CN')` will be emails or names if they are available.

The `notes_tools.py` file contains more tools to deal with the notes on the data subdirectory. There are three tools:

```
def available_notes():
    ''' Retrieve all available notes '''

    notes = []
    for filename in os.listdir(NOTES_DIR):
        if filename.endswith('.md'):
            notes.append(filename.removesuffix('.md'))
```

```
    return notes
```

`available_notes` allows you to retrieve all the different notes that are in the directory. It understands the notes as files ending in `.md`. Markdown files. The name of the file is understood as the name of the note, which is related to the person the note refers to. In our example, we use `jbuelta`.

```
def retrieve_note(user):
    '''
    Retrieve the note from a user
    '''
    filename = os.path.join(NOTES_DIR, f'{user}.md')
    with open(filename) as fp:
        note = fp.read()

    return note
```

`retrieve_note` reads the content from an existing note on the filesystem.

```
def write_meeting_brief(user, date, text):
    '''
    Append into the note for the user the brief for the
    next meeting
    '''
    filename = os.path.join(NOTES_DIR, f'{user}.md')

    # Check that the file exists
    if not os.path.exists(filename):
        return f'ERROR: NOTE FOR {user} DOES NOT EXIST. USE AN EXISTING NOTE'

    with open(filename, 'a') as fp:
        data = f'''## Meeting brief for {date}
        {text}
        '''
        fp.write(data)

    return 'SUCCESS'
```

`write_meeting_brief` saves text into an existing note. If there's no note by that name, it returns an error message. If it's correct, it just returns `SUCCESS`.

> **Tip**
>
> Note that we are opening the file with the `'a'` parameter to append data to the end of the file. This limits the capacity of the agent to overwrite existing data.

Finally, the `meeting_preparation_agent.py` script is the one that orchestrates everything.

We first import and give information about the different tools that we will use.

```
from notes_tools import available_notes as _available_notes
from notes_tools import retrieve_note as _retrieve_note
from notes_tools import write_meeting_brief as _write_meeting_brief
from calendar_tools import retrieve_calendar_events as _retrieve_calendar_events


@function_tool
def available_notes():
    '''
    Retrieve all available notes from people from previous meetings
    '''
    return _available_notes()


@function_tool
def retrieve_note(user: str):
    '''
    Retrieve the note for a person to check information on previous meetings
    It returns Markdown text with the general notes and specifics about
    previous meetings
    '''
    return _retrieve_note(user)


@function_tool
def retrieve_calendar_events():
    '''
    Obtain the next calendar events
    '''
```

```
    return _retrieve_calendar_events()


@function_tool
def write_meeting_brief(user: str, date: str, text: str):
    '''
    Write a meeting brief for a person.

    Returns:
        SUCCESS
        ERROR: Error Description
    '''
    return _write_meeting_brief(user, date, text)
```

We wrap each of the tools that we created in the other files in a descriptive function, with a `docstring`, and annotating the elements so the agent can understand their types. In all these cases, the input parameters are str objects, strings.

In the `main` function, we run the agent with our prepared prompt and add all the tools that we will use.

```
async def main():

    agent = Agent(
        name='Calendar assistant',
        instructions='You are a helpful assistant preparing meetings',
        tools=[available_notes, retrieve_note, write_meeting_brief,
               retrieve_calendar_events],
        model=MODEL,
    )

    prompt = '''
    Check the calendar events for meetings. Only for the next one,
    check if there are meeting notes for any of the participants
    (name will be related to the email in the calendar, but it
    will likely not match completely), and provide a summary of the
    relevant information for the meeting. Format it as a short
    meeting brief. Do not suggest follow up. Write the meeting
    brief.
    '''
    result = Runner.run_streamed(agent, input=prompt)
```

```
    async for event in result.stream_events():
        event_type = event.type

        # Lifecycle
        if event_type == "agent_updated_stream_event":
            console.print(f"\nAgent: {event.new_agent.name}")

        # Show progress
        elif event_type == 'raw_response_event':
            print('.', end='', flush=True)

        # Tool calls
        elif event_type == "run_item_stream_event":
            item = event.item

            if item.type == "tool_call_item":
                console.print(f"\nCalling tool: {item.raw_item.name}")

            elif item.type == "message_output_item":
                # Final message chunks
                for content in item.raw_item.content:
                    if content.type == "output_text":
                        print()
                        markdown = Markdown('---')
                        console.print(markdown)
                        markdown = Markdown(content.text)
                        console.print(markdown)
```

To obtain more information about the process, we call it with `run_streamed` to retrieve stream events as they are happening. This happens in the `async for` loop.

This is a loop that iterates through a `async` generator.

We identify each of the events that we return, and we print some feedback depending on the type of event:

- Display any new agent. Only one should run here.
- For tool calls (`tool_call_item`), we identify the call and the tool. This allows us to show how the tools are used. We will discuss this later.

- The final result (`message_output_item`) is printed in Markdown.
- For other, less important events (`raw_response_event`), we just print a dot (`.`) to show progress. This is printed with no newline at the end and the buffer is flushed each time, so we present progress while the agent is processing.

Let's analyze how the agent worked, by looking at the presented log.

```
Agent: Calendar assistant
......
Calling tool: retrieve_calendar_events
.......
Calling tool: available_notes
...........
Calling tool: retrieve_note
...............................................................................
Calling tool: write_meeting_brief
...............................................................................Calling
tool: write_meeting_brief
...............................................................................
```

It first creates an agent, then calls `retrieve_calendar_events` to obtain the calendar events, `available_notes` to understand the notes available, and `retrieve_note` for the match in `jbuelta`.

Then we have two calls to `write_meeting_brief`. But there are not two writes on the file! What happens here is that the name for the note was not correct the first time, when the model likely used the email address present on the calendar event, and that didn't match the file name. The agent, after the `ERROR` message by the tool, corrected it and wrote again, this time successfully.

The generation of the brief happened between the call to `retrieve_note` and the first `write_meeting_brief`.

> **Note**
>
> Note how the access pattern follows the ReAct pattern. It first Reasons thinks what it should do next, then Act by calling tools, and repeat the process until the task is complete. It's able to understand the nuances of matching the email address with the note name, for example. It can adjust to problems like the `ERROR` when writing the note.

Our prompt is also detailed and steers the AI model into specific details.

```
Check the calendar events for meetings. Only for the next one,
check if there are meeting notes for any of the participants
(name will be related to the email in the calendar, but it
will likely not match completely), and provide a summary of the
relevant information for the meeting. Format it as a short
meeting brief. Do not suggest follow up. Write the meeting
brief.
```

We help the model by saying that the name on the meeting notes may not be exact to the one on the calendar, but it's a match. It correctly understands this, and is able to understand that the email address corresponds to the `jbuelta` note.

We also define that we want a small brief to be on point. AI Models can be a bit wordy.

## There's more...

You may have issues with your calendar, if you have multiple events. We described to the model that we want the next event, but if there are multiple, it may not understand very well which one is that. There's a small detail... The AI model doesn't know what date and time it is at the moment!

For that, we need to add another tool and tweak the prompt a bit.

```
from datetime import datetime


@function_tool
def current_time():
    '''
    Return current date time
    '''
    return datetime.datetime.now(datetime.UTC)
...
async def main():
    agent = Agent(
        name='Calendar assistant',
        instructions='You are a helpful assistant preparing meetings',
        tools=[available_notes, retrieve_note, write_meeting_brief,
               retrieve_calendar_events, current_time],
        model=MODEL,
    )
...
```

```
prompt = '''
Check the calendar events for meetings. Only for the next one,
verifying with the current time, check if there are meeting
notes for any of the participants (name will be related to the
email in the calendar, but it will likely not match completely),
and provide a summary of the relevant information for the meeting.
Format it as a short meeting brief. Do not suggest follow up.
Write the meeting brief.
'''
```

These changes are available in the `meeting_preparation_agent_time.py` script located in the chapter folder of the GitHub repository.

> **Note**
>
> We are being deliberately specific with our tools (append only, checking only a single calendar) to limit the scope of our task. While being broader allows the AI model to be freer and access more, it also risks overreaching and doing something that we don't want. Also, having strong guardrails allows steering the model and achieving better replicability of tasks.
>
> A risk with AI models is to produce wildly different results than the ones you expected initially. Also, remember what we discussed in *Chapter 12* about prompt injection.

Check the full documentation for OpenAI Agents SDK at `https://openai.github.io/openai-agents-python/`.

A note about Google access to Calendar. For simplicity, we maintain the app password access that we introduced in *Chapter 9*. This is still valid, but it's no longer recommended by Google. The recommended version is to use their new API, which requires more dedicated setup. Check their documentation here: `https://developers.google.com/workspace/calendar/api/quickstart/python?utm_source=chatgpt.com`.

Remember that you can use GenAI to help you during the process.

## See also

- The *Creating your own chatbot* recipe, in *Chapter 11*, describing the basics of working with AI models
- The *Create your own MCP servers* recipe, in *Chapter 12*, introducing the usage of direct tools and showing how to create your own tools using the MCP protocol

# Draft documents with subagents

In this recipe, we will grab information from the notes stored in the filesystem defined in the previous recipe and use it to prepare a project proposal.

To create a stronger and more coherent document, we will rely on two subagents to draft and review the proposal, passing the content between them alternately until the reviewer subagent is satisfied. Their work will be coordinated by the main agent, which we call orchestrator, which manages the full workflow and ensures that all steps are completed in the right order.

> **Tip**
>
> Subagents are specialized agents with individual tasks, contexts, and goals, allowing them to focus more effectively on their specific part of the work. This division of labor avoids the challenge of forcing a single agent to handle a large, complex task with one prompt trying to fit everything. The orchestrator oversees these subagents, ensuring smooth collaboration and combining their outputs into a cohesive result.

Once the subagents have refined the proposal, we will use an MCP server to save the final document as a Word file.

## Getting ready

In this recipe, we'll require the following modules in our virtual environment:

```
$ echo "python-dotenv==1.2.2" >> requirements.txt
$ echo "openai==2.28.0" >> requirements.txt
$ echo "rich==14.3.3" >> requirements.txt
$ echo "openai-agents==0.12.3" >> requirements.txt
$ pip install -r requirements.txt
```

Remember to have available your `openAI` key in the file `.env`.

> **Note**
>
> There's a `.env.template` in the repo that you can use to fill with your info. This file contains all the configuration for all recipes in the draft, so some variables won't be used for this recipe.

Download the `notes_tools.py` and `draft_document_agent.py` scripts from GitHub at `https://github.com/PacktPublishing/Python-Automation-Cookbook-Third-Edition/blob/main/ch13/`. Download also the notes available in the `/data/` subdirectory into your own `data` subdirectory.

Please download the `Office-Word-MCP-Server`, originally from `https://github.com/GongRzhe/Office-Word-MCP-Server`, that has been included in our GitHub repo as a subdirectory in this chapter. This MCP will allow the GenAI tool to save the resulting proposal as a `.docx` Word document.

For the `.env` file, you'll also need to find the `UV_COMMAND` by running a which uv command.

```
$ which uv # Find the location of uv
/usr/bin/uv
```

Finally, fill the MCP_DIR_PATH variable as well, using the full path to the directory `Office-Word-MCP-Server`.

```
MCP_DIR_PATH = ' /full/path/to/Office-Word-MCP-Server'
```

We will use the GPT-5.4 model. Verify that it is available on the OpenAI webpage (https://developers.openai.com/api/docs/models). If it's not, change it accordingly. *There's more* information about it in the There's more section of the *Creating your own chatbot* recipe in *Chapter 11*.

## How to do it...

1. We need to prepare the MCP server. In the directory of `Office-Word-MCP-Server`, set up an environment and install the dependencies.

```
$ uv venv
Using CPython 3.14.3 interpreter at: /usr/local/opt/python@3.14/bin/
python3.14
Creating virtual environment at: .venv
Activate with: source .venv/bin/activate
$ uv pip install -r requirements.txt
Resolved 73 packages in 325ms
Prepared 1 package in 103ms
Installed 73 packages in 106ms
...
```

2. Launch the script `draft_document_agent.py` to generate our draft document. The following is just an example, as it will depend on the particular execution. The logs have been adjusted to avoid repetition.

```
$ uv run draft_document_agent.py


╭──────────────────────────────────────────────────────────────────────╮
│                                                                      │
│                                                                      │
│                                                                      │
│                                                                      │
│                                                                      │
│                                                                      │
│                           FastMCP 3.2.3                              │
│                       https://gofastmcp.com                          │
│                                                                      │
│            🖥 Server:      Word Document Server, 3.2.3               │
│            🚀 Deploy free: https://horizon.prefect.io                │
│                                                                      │
╰──────────────────────────────────────────────────────────────────────╯


[04/11/26 17:31:30] INFO     Starting MCP server 'Word Document Server'
```

```
with transport 'stdio'                                    transport.py:209

Agent: Orchestrator
......
Calling tool: available_notes
....
Calling tool: retrieve_note
............
Calling tool: retrieve_note
.............................................................................
.........................
Calling tool: writer_subagent
.............................................................................
......................................................................
Calling tool: reviewer_subagent
.............................................................................
....................
Calling tool: writer_subagent
.................................
Calling tool: create_document
....................................
Calling tool: add_heading
..................................
Calling tool: add_heading
.......................................
Calling tool: add_paragraph
........................
...
Calling tool: insert_numbered_list_near_text
..........................................
Calling tool: add_paragraph
................................
Done — I created the document:

**`jaime_buelta_javascript_collaboration_proposal.docx`**
```

3. Check the created document (which may have a different name, as it's generated by the model)

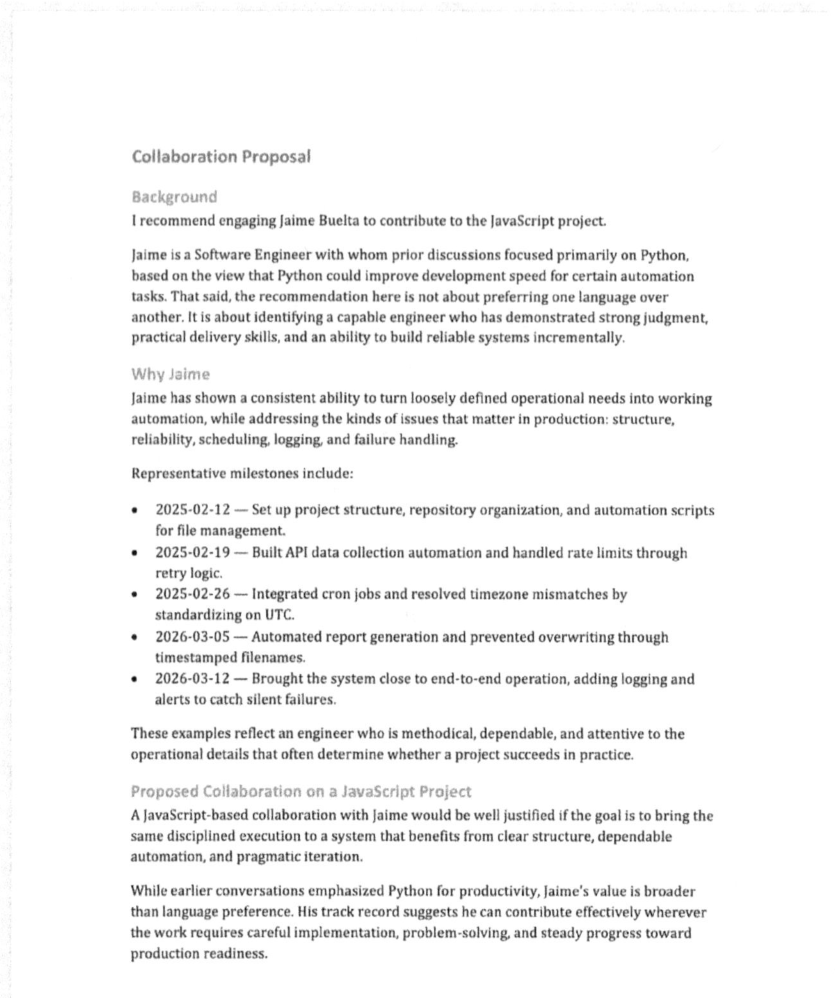

Collaboration Proposal

Background

I recommend engaging Jaime Buelta to contribute to the JavaScript project.

Jaime is a Software Engineer with whom prior discussions focused primarily on Python, based on the view that Python could improve development speed for certain automation tasks. That said, the recommendation here is not about preferring one language over another. It is about identifying a capable engineer who has demonstrated strong judgment, practical delivery skills, and an ability to build reliable systems incrementally.

Why Jaime

Jaime has shown a consistent ability to turn loosely defined operational needs into working automation, while addressing the kinds of issues that matter in production: structure, reliability, scheduling, logging, and failure handling.

Representative milestones include:

- 2025-02-12 — Set up project structure, repository organization, and automation scripts for file management.
- 2025-02-19 — Built API data collection automation and handled rate limits through retry logic.
- 2025-02-26 — Integrated cron jobs and resolved timezone mismatches by standardizing on UTC.
- 2026-03-05 — Automated report generation and prevented overwriting through timestamped filenames.
- 2026-03-12 — Brought the system close to end-to-end operation, adding logging and alerts to catch silent failures.

These examples reflect an engineer who is methodical, dependable, and attentive to the operational details that often determine whether a project succeeds in practice.

Proposed Collaboration on a JavaScript Project

A JavaScript-based collaboration with Jaime would be well justified if the goal is to bring the same disciplined execution to a system that benefits from clear structure, dependable automation, and pragmatic iteration.

While earlier conversations emphasized Python for productivity, Jaime's value is broader than language preference. His track record suggests he can contribute effectively wherever the work requires careful implementation, problem-solving, and steady progress toward production readiness.

*Figure 13.1: Resulting Word document*

**Tip**

Remember that AI Models are non-deterministic, and that the results may be different than the ones that are shown here, though they should follow the general idea.

## How it works...

For this recipe we mix different tools, including an MCP server, to perform the task. You can see that we use the following tools:

- Read notes tools (`available_notes` and `retrieve_note`) from the previous recipe.
- The Office Word server MCP. This MCP server allows you to read and write Word `.docx` documents.
- Other agents that act as tools. These are the *subagents*, that we create with different prompts to fill different roles. They get smaller context from the main agent, the *orchestrator*, and focus on specific aspects.

In the code from `draft_document_agent.py`, we mix all these elements. Let's check some sections of it. You can see the whole code at `https://github.com/PacktPublishing/Python-Automation-Cookbook-Third-Edition/blob/main/ch13/draft_document_agent.py`.

The key elements are the different prompts and the definition of the subagents. Let's see how they are defined.

```
writer_subagent = Agent(
    name='Writer subagent',
    model=MODEL,
    instructions=(
        '''
        You are a writer agent that produces professional documents.
        You use a formal tone, but keeping a warm tone, without being
        too close. You keep things short and to the point, but without
        becoming too direct.
        '''
    ),
)

reviewer_subagent = Agent(
    name='Reviewer subagent',
    model=MODEL,
    instructions=(
        '''
        You are a reviewer and editor subagent focused on professional
        documents.  You proofread the documents and propose changes,
        improving the readability of the result. You try to maintain
        the voice of the author, but clarify points and remove cliches.
```

```
        Once a version is deemed good to go, say that it is approved.
        '''
    )
)
```

As you can see, each agent has its own set of instructions, that defines its objective. We provide each one with a different point of view for the task at hand. Remember that each subagent will look at a smaller context than if you tried to integrate all these behaviors into the same prompt, which could make it more difficult to balance. In this case, we make them work in a team to write and review the document.

The orchestrator agent requires a different prompt, making it work with all the tools.

```
        ORCHESTRATOR_PROMPT = '''
        You are the orchestrator of a multi-agent system. Your task is to
        take the user's request and generate a proper document draft based
        on their request by passing it to the appropriate agent tools. Be
        sure to see if we have any notes relevant for the document. Go
        to the tool to write something, and then pass it to the reviewer
        tools to get comments, iterating on the result.
        You may need to do the process multiple times, as well as calling
        multiple agents to get all of the information you need. Once
        the draft is approved, write it as an MS Word file using the MCP
        server tools.  Do not mention or draw attention to the fact that
        this is a multi-agent system. Do not propose follow up.
    '''
```

We define the different tools and start the agent in the `main` function.

```
async def main():

    async with MCPServerStdio(
        name='ms_word_writer',
        params={
            'command': UV_COMMAND,
            'args': ['run', '-w', MCP_DIR_PATH, MCP_SERVER_PATH],
        }
    ) as mcp_server:
        orchestrator = Agent(
            name='Orchestrator',
            model=MODEL,
```

```
            instructions=ORCHESTRATOR_PROMPT,
            mcp_servers=[mcp_server],
            tools=[
                writer_subagent.as_tool(
                    tool_name='writer_subagent',
                    tool_description='Writes documents'
                ),
                reviewer_subagent.as_tool(
                    tool_name='reviewer_subagent',
                    tool_description='Reviews documents'
                ),
                available_notes,
                retrieve_note,
            ]
        )

        result = Runner.run_streamed(
            starting_agent=orchestrator,
            input=('Make a document about the notes for user Jaime Buelta'
                ' to propose a collaboration for a new project that will '
                'use JavaScript'),
            max_turns=50,
        )
```

Note how we can use agent objects as subagents using the `.as_tool` method and allow the orchestrator to call them as tools.

> **Tip**
>
> When running the MCP server with uv, we need to specify the directory to run with the `-w` parameter to be sure to use the right virtual environment. We create the `MCP_SERVER_PATH` constant by appending the name of the MCP script to the directory.
>
> ```
> MCP_SERVER_PATH = os.path.join(MCP_DIR_PATH, 'word_mcp_server.py')
> ```

The instructions for the task are described in the `input` parameter of the agent run.

> **Note**
>
> Notice the `max_turns` parameter. This parameter limits the number of times that the agent can perform a new call to the AI Model. When working with subagents, this number may need to be higher. If the execution reaches the limit, it will stop, raising a `agents.exceptions.MaxTurnsExceeded` exception. You can use this parameter to protect against unexpected long tasks. Each AI Model call has a cost.

We present constant feedback by showing the different tools that are being called. As you can see in the logs, there are many calls while generating the Word document.

## There's more...

For simplicity, we have used the same AI Model in all agents (`gpt-5.4`), but that's not a requirement. You can tweak the model on each one, so you can use a less powerful one for some of the subagents if that makes sense, saving time and money. Or the other way around, you may want to write some part that requires a more sophisticated model, but the rest of the document will be ok with a smaller one.

Each agent has its own `model` parameter that can be adjusted.

While using an MCP server to write a Word document may seem to replace the recipes presented on *Chapter 5*, each approach fill a different role and can be used at different needs. A MCP server is a tool controlled by an AI Model which will always generate different structures and results, as it's non-deterministic. Meanwhile, the techniques in *Chapter 5* allow you to generate deterministic documents, that will always follow the same structure. Both techniques are useful.

> **Tip**
>
> Of course, you can use a GenAI tool to help you generate code that will produce deterministic results. In the same way, you can attach deterministic code as a GenAI tool to write in the format of your choosing. You can combine all the techniques in the best way to achieve your goals.

Check the full documentation for Office Word MCP server at `https://github.com/GongRzhe/Office-Word-MCP-Server`.

Check the full documentation for OpenAI Agents SDK here: `https://openai.github.io/openai-agents-python/`.

## See also

- The *Creating Your Own Chatbot* recipe, in *Chapter 11*, describing the basics of working with AI models
- The *Let's use MCP servers* and *Create your own MCP servers* recipes in *Chapter 12*, introducing the usage of MCP servers and direct tools

# 14

# Real-World AI Example

In this chapter, we will apply the GenAI concepts introduced in the previous chapters and combine them into a complete, automatable task that can help us every day.

We will rely on the definition and use of tools, as well as the ReAct architecture, to create a task that will analyze our emails, draft responses for actionable messages in a style consistent with our usual tone, and provide a summary of everything received in the past 24 hours.

> **Note**
>
> For handling email, we will use a Gmail account. While the concepts are compatible with any IMAP and SMTP server, some folder names will follow Gmail conventions.

When developing the tools that we will use to communicate with email, we will take into account the limitations of each tool's scope, carefully managing the AI model's capabilities and implementing guardrails to ensure reliable results.

> **Tip**
>
> AI models are extremely powerful and capable of making informed guesses. With generalist tools like MCPs, they can explore freely multiple options and try to fix a problem from very different points of view. While this can be useful in certain contexts, for an automated task that needs to run repeatedly, this variability and exploration can lead to inconsistent outputs and increased costs. To achieve consistency, we must provide clear direction and limit the scope available for the AI model. Therefore, in this chapter, we code our own function tools designed for our exact requirements.

Throughout the chapter, we will discuss important elements of creating automated GenAI tasks, including security, cost management, and data reusability.

> **Note**
>
> Don't underestimate the cost management part! For an automation that will run often, keeping costs at a reasonable level is key. We will discuss it in depth at the end of the chapter.

# Technical requirements

We will use OpenAI as our provider for the AI models in this chapter.

> **Tip**
>
> Remember that these techniques are available in different AI models and frameworks. You can achieve similar results with other providers like Anthropic's Claude or using local models through Ollama. See *Chapter 11, Using a local model,* to learn more about the latter option.

We described in the *Technical requirements* section of *Chapter 11* the steps that we need to set up an account that will allow us to call the OpenAI APIs. Go there and follow the instructions if you haven't already done so.

You can check the code presented in the chapter at the GitHub URL `https://github.com/PacktPublishing/Python-Automation-Cookbook-Third-Edition/tree/main/ch14`.

Be sure to have your `keys.py` file present in your working directory. There's a template for the required fields in the GitHub repo directory called `keys.py.template`.

# Summarize your email and draft responses agentically

We all receive a lot of emails every day. Managing it with traditional ways, like creating folders and rules, is difficult and doesn't allow us to get a good grip on the dynamic nature of emails. Also, many of the emails require a response that, in most cases, feels pretty standard. In this recipe, we will see how to create a task that will run and:

- Read your last day of emails and produce a summary email in your inbox.
- Provide a draft for any of those emails that require a response, following the style of your own emails. These drafts can be reviewed and approved.

We will produce an agentic script that will iterate through different tools and fulfill those tasks.

## Getting ready

For this recipe, we will need the following modules in our virtual environment:

```
$ echo "python-dotenv==1.2.2" >> requirements.txt
$ echo "openai==2.28.0" >> requirements.txt
$ echo "rich==14.3.3" >> requirements.txt
$ echo "openai-agents==0.12.3" >> requirements.txt
$ uv pip install -r requirements.txt
```

There's a template file in `.env.py.template` that you'll need to fill with your information and copy into `.env`.

- Your `openAI` key
- Email user and password

We will need your email credentials, as we described in *Reading an email* from *Chapter 9*. Include them in the `.env` file as `EMAIL_USER` and `EMAIL_PASSWORD`. You may also add the `MAILBOX`, which is by default `"inbox"`, as we will see later.

We will use the GPT-5.4 model. Verify that it is available on the OpenAI webpage (https://developers.openai.com/api/docs/models). If it's not, change it accordingly. *There's more* information about it in the There's more section of the *Creating your own chatbot* recipe in *Chapter 11*.

Download `email_tool.py` and `email_agent.py` from GitHub `ch14` subdirectory.

## How to do it...

1. Run first the `email_tool.py` script to recover the last 90 days of sent emails on the account and store them locally. You'll see a progress bar.

```
$ uv run email_tool.py
Retrieve and store sent emails for later access
Found 125
Processing emails ━━━━━━━━━━━━━━━━━━━━━━━━━━━━━━━━━━━━━━━━ 100% 0:03:04
```

2. Run the agent `email_agent.py`.

```
$ uv run email_agent.py
retrieve_last_emails
Retrieve email 275722
```

```
...
Retrieve email 275842
creating a draft reply for 275727
Retrieve email 275727
Creating a draft reply for 275760
Retrieve email 275760
Sending a summary email
------------------------------------------------------------------------
Done – reviewed the latest day's emails, checked prior sent mail for reply
style and existing summaries, created one draft reply for the project
request and a reply for CorpCo and sent a new summary email covering these
elements.
------------------------------------------------------------------------
```

3. Check your inbox in Gmail, which should present the mentioned draft replies. Here is one example:

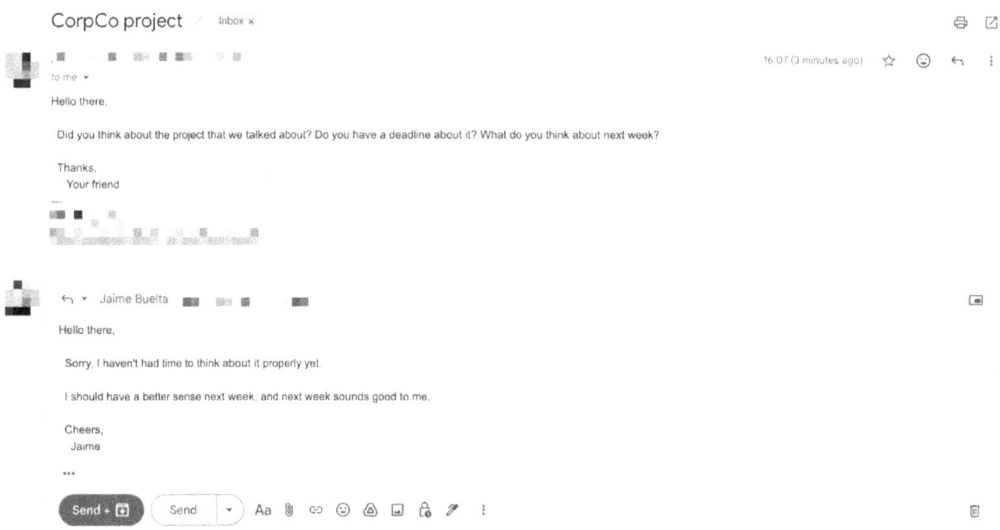


*Figure 14.1: A sample Gmail response*

4. There's also a summary that describes the last day of received emails:

```
The latest day of email was mostly a mix of transactional notifications, shipping
and delivery updates, account/security notices, and promotional newsletters. The
main practical items were Packt follow-ups that needed responses, a personal
follow-up about a project and timing for next week, several delivery updates, and
```

```
an SaaSApp temporary login code. Most other messages were informational or
marketing-related and did not require action.

- Draft created for Packt on gave a short status update that Chapter 14 is in
progress.
- Draft created on "CorpCo project": apologized for not having thought about it
properly yet, said there should be a better sense next week, and agreed that next
week sounds good.
```

## How it works...

We use the `email_tool.py` script to encapsulate the access to email and prepare the different tools that we will allow the agent to use. These tools are defined as functions.

The functions that are expected to be called by the agent are:

- `read_stored_sent_emails`, which returns a list of bodies of sent emails to provide context on what's expected for the draft emails' styles and tone.
- `retrieve_last_emails`, which will retrieve all received emails since one day ago.
- `create_a_draft_reply`, to produce a reply to an email that demands one. This reply is stored as a draft, so it can be reviewed later.
- `send_a_summary_email`, to send the email with the summary of the received emails.

There are more functions, but they are marked as internal for the module by adding an underscore (_) at the start.

> **Tip**
>
> This is a Python convention that declares the function, module, or variable as internal and not expected to be accessed externally.

We added some print statements to provide some feedback on the access to the different tools, for demonstration purposes.

### Interact with the email service

At the start of the script, we define basic variables that we will be using throughout the whole script:

```
from dotenv import load_dotenv
load_dotenv()
```

```
EMAIL_USER = os.getenv('EMAIL_USER')
EMAIL_PASSWORD = os.getenv('EMAIL_PASSWORD')

MAILBOX = os.getenv('MAILBOX', 'inbox')
DRAFT_FOLDER = '"[Gmail]/Drafts"'
SEND_FOLDER = '"[Gmail]/Sent Mail"'
IMAP_SERVER = 'imap.gmail.com'
SMTP_SERVER = 'smtp.gmail.com'
SMTP_PORT = 465
```

They allow the script to connect to the Gmail account and access the different folders that we will check.

> **Note**
>
> Note that the keys are imported from the `.env` file. You should fill them with your details. Note that `MAILBOX` is optional; by default, it will use `"inbox"`.

The connection with the Gmail account is handled through the `_mail_select` function.

```
def _mail_select(folder):
    mail = imaplib.IMAP4_SSL(IMAP_SERVER)
    mail.login(EMAIL_USER, EMAIL_PASSWORD)
    mail.select(folder)
    return mail
```

This creates a new connection to the server and logs in, and it's done at the start of all the tools to create a new connection. Note that it requires to `select` a particular folder, which will be used when we perform our next operations.

The handling and interaction with emails are described in the three functions:

- `_mail_select`, as we described
- `_retrieve_email_message`, to make a call and return a raw version of the email
- `_parse_email`, which returns a more manageable dictionary with only the parts of the email that we care about

Let's see the code for each.

```
def _retrieve_email_message(mail, email_uid):
    result, data = mail.uid('fetch', email_uid, '(RFC822)')
```

```
    raw_email = data[0][1]
    email_message = BytesParser(policy=default).parsebytes(raw_email)
    return email_message
```

In `imaplib`, you can access the `.uid` of the emails in the selected folder. With the `fetch` operation, you grab one email identified by its `uid`. The UID of an email is a unique identifier.

> **Tip**
>
> We will see a bit later the operation `search` that will allow us to retrieve a list of email `uids`.

We retrieve the `raw_email`, and parse it into an `EmailMessage` object. This object contains much information, so to simplify it, we will normally proceed with a `_parse_email` call.

```
def _parse_email(email_uid, email_message):
    subject = email_message['subject']
    address = parseaddr(email_message['From'])

    # Walk the entire MIME tree, collect text parts
    text_plain = None
    text_html = None
    for part in email_message.walk():
        content_type = part.get_content_type()
        if content_type == 'text/plain' and text_plain is None:
            text_plain = part.get_content()
        elif content_type == 'text/html' and text_html is None:
            text_html = part.get_content()

    # Prefer plain text, fall back to HTML
    payload = text_plain or text_html or ''

    # We need this information for replies
    message_id = email_message['Message-Id']
    email_references = email_message.get('References', '')
    references = (email_references + ' ' + message_id).strip()
    reply_to = email_message['Reply-To'] or email_message['From']

    result = {
        'email_uid': email_uid,
```

```
            'message-id': message_id,
            'references': references,
            'reply_to': reply_to,
            'subject': subject,
            'address': address,
            'payload': payload,
        }
        return result
```

The objective of `_parse_email` is to return an accessible dictionary with the key elements of it. Some information gets extracted from the `EmailMessage` object like a dictionary (for example `subject` or `From`), but it also walks through the different parts that an email may have to return either the text or (if not present) the HTML version of the content.

> **Tip**
>
> For our goals of understanding the email content, it's better to default to the text version.

Note also that we collect the `Reply-To` to understand who to send a reply to. If the Reply-To is not present, this should be the `From` field.

Finally, we create a dictionary with all this information and return it.

## Retrieve sent emails

At the end of the file, if we call `email_tool.py` on its own, we are calling the `_retrieve_and_store_sent_emails()`, which downloads and stores the last sent emails from the last 90 days locally.

> **Tip**
>
> We use the last 90 days as a sample, that should be relatively good, of the style, and tone that the emails are written. We want to prepare a draft reply that it's not too far away from the usual ones. Providing the agent with an example of what is expected will help it to adequately know what to aim for.

```
if __name__ == '__main__':
    # Store the last SENT_EMAILS_DAYS days of sent emails
    # to be sure to cover the style of replies
    _retrieve_and_store_sent_emails()
```

This prepares the data for `read_stored_sent_emails`. Let's take a look at the function.

```
from rich.progress import track

SENT_EMAILS_FILE = './sent_emails.json'
SENT_EMAILS_DAYS = 90

def _retrieve_and_store_sent_emails():
    '''
    Retrieve messages that have been sent to
    get data on the tone and style of responses
    '''
    print('Retrieve and store sent emails for later access')
    mail = _mail_select(SEND_FOLDER)

    since = (datetime.now() - timedelta(days=SENT_EMAILS_DAYS)).strftime("%d-%b-
%Y")

    result, data = mail.uid('search', None, f'(SINCE "{since}")')
    sent_uids = data[0].split()
    # Check all sent emails from the last SENT_EMAILS_DAYS days
    contents = []
    print(f'Found {len(sent_uid})')
    for sent_uid in track(sent_uids, description='Processing emails'):
        email = _retrieve_sent_message(sent_uid)
        payload = email['payload']
        contents.append(payload)

    # Store all contents in a file
    with open(SENT_EMAILS_FILE, 'w') as json_file:
        json.dump(contents, json_file)
```

This function selects emails from `SEND_FOLDER` folder and retrieves the last 90 days (defined as `SENT_EMAIL_DAYS`) `uids` with the call to

```
result, data = mail.uid('search', None, f'(SINCE "{since}")')
```

Then, it iterates through the returned `uids` to retrieve each of them and append their contents (stored in `payload`) to a list. Finally, we store the content in the `SENT_EMAILS_FILE` JSON file.

> **Note**
>
> We provide feedback on the progress by using the `rich` library, with a `track` function that automatically shows the progress on a loop, including the ETA.
>
> When performing operations that can take some time, it's good to add some visual feedback to give certainty that it's moving on.

The tool that will be called by the agent, `read_stored_sent_emails`, retrieves the data from the file; it's straightforward.

```
def read_stored_sent_emails():
    '''
    Retrieve the stored sent emails from the file.
    This function will be exposed as a tool.
    '''
    # Retrieve the contents from the file
    with open(SENT_EMAILS_FILE) as json_file:
        result = json.load(json_file)

    return result
```

We are storing the sent emails in a file to avoid having to make all the independent calls while operating the agent. For our purposes, we don't require the very latest emails or to be constantly updating them. There could even be a curated selection of emails to provide a good reference for what we are looking for. Preparing the data in advance helps us reduce the time and cost it takes to run the agent, and storing the data over a longer time span reduces the load on the email server as well.

## Obtain the last day of received emails

To retrieve the last day of emails, our process is very similar to the one to retrieve the sent ones, with the difference that we use the folder MAILBOX, which corresponds to the general inbox.

```
def retrieve_last_emails():
    '''
    Retrieve all emails since a day ago
    '''
    print('retrieve_last_emails')
    mail = _mail_select(MAILBOX)
```

```
    since = (datetime.now() - timedelta(days=1)).strftime("%d-%b-%Y")

    result, data = mail.uid('search', None, f'(SINCE "{since}")')
    email_uids = data[0].decode().split()
    data = [_retrieve_email_uid(uid) for uid in email_uids]
    return data
```

The delta is one day, but the rest is very similar to the first part of `_retrieve_and_store_sent_emails`. We also keep the whole data in the email, instead of only the `payload`.

> **Tip**
>
> In this case, we need to be making the calls at the time when the agent is calling, as we require the full information and the up-to-date information of the last emails. That is not a requirement in `_retrieve_and_store_sent_emails`

## Create draft replies

When allowing the agent to create a draft reply to our emails, we use the following code:

```
def create_a_draft_reply(email_uid, content):
    '''
    This tool creates a draft as response to the specified email
    '''
    print(f'creating a draft reply for {email_uid}')

    # Retrieve the original email to get the relevant values for
    # reply
    source_email = _retrieve_email_uid(email_uid)

    # Check first that a draft reply is not already present
    if _check_draft_for_email(email_uid):
        return 'Draft already exists'

    reply = EmailMessage()
    reply['From'] = EMAIL_USER
    reply['To'] = source_email['reply_to']
    reply['Subject'] = 'Re: ' + source_email['subject'].replace('Re: ', '')
    reply['Date'] = formatdate(localtime=True)
    reply['Message-ID'] = make_msgid()
```

```
    reply['In-Reply-To'] = source_email['message-id']
    reply['References'] = source_email['references']

    reply.set_content(content)

    mail = _mail_select(DRAFT_FOLDER)
    mail.append(DRAFT_FOLDER,
                '\\Draft',
                imaplib.Time2Internaldate(time.time()),
                reply.as_bytes())

    return 'draft created'
```

We first retrieve the email to reply to, and we validate that there's not already a draft reply to it. If it exists, we return a descriptive text, that the agent will be able to understand.

Next, we create a new `EmailMessage` and fill all the required fields, like the `To` and `Date`. Importantly, we add the `In-Reply-To` field with the id of the source message, which is what makes the email to be a reply.

We add the content that the agent has prepared and we add the reply to the `DRAFT_FOLDER` to ensure that it's a draft.

**Tip**

We could go an extra step and send the email directly, but that would be granting too much power to the AI agent. With only the limited context of the most recent day's emails, the agent may misunderstand what the appropriate next steps are or misread the tone of an ongoing conversation. Mistakes can easily cause confusion or even harm.

Instead, the approach here is to have the agent only prepare a rough draft for us. This saves time while ensuring you keep ultimate control: you can review, approve, or adjust the message before it goes out. Reviewing the draft allows you to catch errors and add relevant details.

In the end, every email you send remains truly yours.

On top of that, it also minimizes risk from possible abuses and malicious intent. We are using untrusted content in the process, like the text from emails and addresses to reply to, which can be sent to you by a bad source. Check the discussion about the security risks, prompt injection, and the lethal trifecta in *Chapter 12*.

To check if a draft is already present, we check the drafts folder and see if there's already a draft there that is written in response to the email.

```
def _check_draft_for_email(email_uid):
    '''
    Verify if there's already a draft email responding to this email,
    and return True if it is
    '''
    source_email = _retrieve_email_uid(email_uid)

    # Retrieve all emails from draft folder
    mail = _mail_select(DRAFT_FOLDER)

    result, data = mail.uid('search', None, 'ALL')
    draft_uids = data[0].split()
    # Check all existing drafts
    for draft_uid in draft_uids:
        draft = _retrieve_draft(draft_uid)
        # Check if it responds to this email
        if draft['In-Reply-To'] == source_email['message-id']:
            return True

    return False
```

For that, we retrieve the email first, and then we iterate through the emails in drafts to see if there's one that has its `In-Reply-To` that coincides with the `message-id` of the `source_email`.

> **Tip**
>
> We are making here the assumption that there's a small number of drafts in our `DRAFT_FOLDER`, and therefore, retrieving them is not a big operation. That's a reasonable assumption in general, but if it's not in your case (you tend to keep many drafts around), this code may be inefficient if called multiple times.
>
> It can be improved by storing each draft on local disk and then checking if there are new drafts from the local copy. That will require less external costs, but it may be an overoptimization if the number of drafts is typically small.

To retrieve a draft, we use code that's very similar to retrieving it from the inbox, but targeting the `DRAFT_FOLDER`

```
def _retrieve_draft(draft_uid):
    '''
    Return a draft email
    '''
    mail = _mail_select(DRAFT_FOLDER)
    draft_email = _retrieve_email_message(mail, draft_uid)
    return draft_email
```

There's a difference with `_retrieve_email_uid`, though. Here we are not parsing the email, as we are only interested in the `In-Reply-To` parameter, which is easily accessible directly in the `EmailMessage` object.

## Send the summary email

To create the summary email, we only need to create a `EmailMessage` with all the required parameters and send it.

```
def send_a_summary_email(summary, content):
    '''
    Send an email to yourself from your Agent with a summary of emails
    '''
    print('Sending a summary email')

    email = EmailMessage()
    email['From'] = EMAIL_USER
    email['To'] = EMAIL_USER
    email['Subject'] = summary

    email['Date'] = formatdate(localtime=True)
    email['Message-ID'] = make_msgid()

    email.set_content(content)

    # Connect to the SMTP server and send the email

    with smtplib.SMTP_SSL(SMTP_SERVER, SMTP_PORT) as smtp_server:
        smtp_server.login(EMAIL_USER, EMAIL_PASSWORD)
        smtp_server.send_message(email)
```

In this case, we need to send the email through the `smtplib` library, as the `imaplib` only covers the reading of email, not sending.

> **Tip**
>
> Note that we are explicitly deciding the `To` field of the email, ensuring it can only be sent to the `EMAIL_USER`. We are not making the email destination dependent on the AI agent in any way, only the content and subject. This approach follows the same rationale as before with draft emails, maintaining strict control to limit what the AI agent can do. By doing so, we reduce uncertainty, avoid potential errors, and ensure that any summaries or messages remain securely in our own inbox. Even if a summary is incorrect, only we will see it, and there is no risk of a mistaken or hallucinated email containing private information being sent to the wrong recipient.

With all the agents defined, we move to define how the AI agent calls them.

## The agent that calls the tools

This is defined in the script `email_agent.py`. The general structure is the same as we've seen already before.

First, we import the libraries that we will use, set up which model to use (GPT-5.4), and prepare a `console` object to use `rich` for the output.

```
import asyncio
from keys import OPEN_AI_KEY
from agents import Agent, Runner, set_default_openai_key
from agents import ModelSettings
from agents import function_tool, retry_policies
from agents.model_settings import ModelRetrySettings, ModelRetryBackoffSettings
from rich.console import Console
from rich.markdown import Markdown

from email_tool import retrieve_last_emails as _retrieve_last_emails
from email_tool import create_a_draft_reply as _create_a_draft_reply
from email_tool import send_a_summary_email as _send_a_summary_email
from email_tool import read_stored_sent_emails as _read_stored_sent_emails

MODEL = 'gpt-5.4'

console = Console()
```

```
set_default_openai_key(OPEN_AI_KEY)
```

We import all the tools, adding an underscore at the start of each to indicate that they'll be used internally, wrapped by a `function_tool` decorator, as we do next.

```
@function_tool
def retrieve_last_emails():
    '''
    Retrieve today's email from the mailbox.
    Returns a list of dicts with subject, address, and payload.
    '''
    return _retrieve_last_emails()


@function_tool
def create_a_draft_reply(email_uid: str, content: str):
    '''
    Create a draft reply to an email, given its email_uid
    and the content will be the response.
    If there's already a draft responding to the email, it
    won't create a new one.
    '''
    return _create_a_draft_reply(email_uid, content)


@function_tool
def send_a_summary_email(summary: str, content: str):
    '''
    Send a summary email
    '''
    return _send_a_summary_email(summary, content)


@function_tool
def read_stored_sent_emails():
    '''
    Read stored sent emails content
    '''
    return _read_stored_sent_emails()
```

This allows the agent to call and understand what the tools can do.

> **Note**
>
> The docstring on the tools defined with `function_tool` is what the AI agent will use to guide and understand it better. You don't need to write something lengthy; all the tools here are relatively simple, but be sure to include the key details for the agent to understand what to expect from them.
>
> For example, it may be necessary to add more context about an input parameter, like an expected format for a string. The agent will also understand errors, so remember to provide proper context on those in case it needs to retry. But any extra call that the agent needs to do trying is extra cost. Better to provide good tools that can be understood from the beginning.

The next element is the `main` function, which starts the agent and provides instructions.

```
async def main():

    # Create retry settings that will help us if there's
    # a problem, like a rate-limit or error
    retry_settings = ModelRetrySettings(
        max_retries=6,
        policy=retry_policies.provider_suggested(),
        backoff=ModelRetryBackoffSettings(initial_delay=1.0,
                                          multiplier=2.0,
                                          max_delay=60.0,
                                          jitter=True)
    )

    agent = Agent(
        name='Assistant',
        instructions='You are a helpful assistant with access '
                     'to tools',
        tools=[retrieve_last_emails, create_a_draft_reply,
               send_a_summary_email, read_stored_sent_emails],
        model=MODEL,
        model_settings=ModelSettings(retry=retry_settings),
    )
```

On top of defining all the tools that are going to be used, we also add the `model_settings` parameter, that allows to setup the retry mechanism defined in the `ModelRetrySettings`.

When doing a task that may take some time, we may have to retry problems communicating with the GenAI model. For example, there could be a transient problem on the connection that will stop the execution of the script and require us to start from scratch. That's quite wasteful in terms of tokens spent.

Another common problem that can be handled through retries is that we can be rate-limited by OpenAI (or any other provider), meaning that we are sending too many tokens over a short period of time, and they return a message saying that the script must wait. If this is not captured, it will raise a `RateLimitError` exception that will stop the execution of your program. For example

```
openai.RateLimitError: Error code: 429 - {'error': {'message': 'Rate limit reached
for gpt-5.4 (for limit gpt-5.4-long-context) in organization org-XXXXX on tokens
per min (TPM): Limit 400000, Used 154039, Requested 358172. Please try again in
16.831s. Visit https://platform.openai.com/account/rate-limits to learn more.',
'type': 'tokens', 'param': None, 'code': 'rate_limit_exceeded'}}
```

The initial rate limits for a new account are quite low, and it can be limiting. See the OpenAI documentation for more details at `https://developers.openai.com/api/docs/guides/rate-limits`.

The retry `policy` defined will make the agent try a few times in case there's an error. We use the `retry_policies.provider_suggested()` to determine when to retry, using the suggestion by the provider. For example, certain errors should not be retried, like an explicit abort or an authentication error. We defer that to the provider instead of controlling that ourselves. More information is available in the OpenAI documentation, including how to use other policies here `https://openai.github.io/openai-agents-python/models`.

We also define that we will retry a maximum of 6 times, in an exponential backoff fashion. We define the parameters for that with an initial delay of 1 second, a multiplier of 2, and a maximum of 60 seconds. That means that we will retry in the following way:

| Retry | Time since last try | Time since start |
|---|---|---|
| First | 1 second | 1 second |
| Second | 2 seconds | 3 seconds |

| Retry | Time since last try | Time since start |
|---|---|---|
| Third | 4 seconds | 7 seconds |
| Fourth | 8 seconds | 15 seconds |
| Fifth | 16 seconds | 31 seconds |
| Sixth | 32 seconds | 63 seconds |

Note that we are not reaching the maximum delay; the highest that we reach is 32 seconds, while we set the maximum to the next, seventh retry, which will be 64. But we are also adding some jitter to the mix. The jitter is an extra random time that gets added to the base time, to allow variability. This makes the retry times less predictable and, if several elements are retrying, less synchronized. That means that instead of adding 32 seconds, we may add sometimes 37, others 40, etc., to a maximum of 60, as we described.

**Tip**

It's anyway good practice to add a maximum to the retry time to ensure that we won't be endlessly retrying. At some point, if there's an error that gets repeated, we cannot assume that it's transient and we will have to stop the execution.

We now get to the prompt to command the AI agent on its task.

```
prompt = '''
    Review all emails received in the last 24 hours. Provide a clear,
    concise summary in one or two paragraphs, giving a high-level
    overview of the correspondence.

    For any emails that require a response:
      * Draft a reply in the style of previous sent emails.
      * Ensure the draft includes only relevant elements from the
      original email and maintains the established tone.
      * Save each draft using the proper tool.

    If no existing summary covers the same content, create and send
    a new summary email with the subject starting with "Summary :".
    The summary should have:
      * An opening paragraph with a high-level overview of all emails.
      * Each draft reply listed as a bullet point.
```

```
        * A separator line, followed by bullet points with detailed
        notes about each email.

      Conclude by reporting the completion of the task with a brief
      message.
  '''
```

Here, we explain to the agent what we want it to do. We provide a clear description of the actions we want, helping the agent understand its task. We don't need to specify exactly which tools must be used at every step, but we can point to their use to guide the result.

We can also use typographical elements such as quotes, bullet points, and Markdown formatting to better communicate our expectations.

> **Tip**
>
> Don't be afraid to be imaginative when writing prompts. You can even create diagrams in ASCII art or other formats, like Mermaid diagrams (a text-based diagram description; see `https://mermaid.ai/`), which AI models can interpret.

There are many unusual recommendations for prompt-writing, such as adding phrases like "do not make mistakes", "you are an expert email writer with 20 years of experience," or writing the prompt in JSON. While different models may respond differently, the truth is that with modern AI, the most effective approach is to write clear instructions, provide context, and focus on describing the outcome you want.

We've discussed the importance of context. That's why, in this recipe, we include examples of previous emails, so the AI Model knows our tone and style, and can provide similar draft responses. While AI models can generally make guesses at what you want, without proper context the results can differ significantly from your expectations. Instead, focus on providing clarity and compiling information that gives the AI model strong hints about your goal, and you'll achieve better results. Lack of context will make the prompt likely go in the wrong direction.

> **Tip**
>
> An interesting element: AI models are actually quite good at writing prompts. You can use a GenAI tool like ChatGPT to help you with your draft prompt and iterate on it. You can ask for weak spots or elements where it leaves space for ambiguity.

After the definition of the prompt, we just call the Agent runner, as usual, and print the result.

```
    messages = [
        {'role': 'user', 'content': prompt}
    ]

    result = await Runner.run(agent, input=messages)

    markdown = Markdown('---')
    console.print(markdown)

    markdown = Markdown(result.final_output)
    console.print(markdown)

    markdown = Markdown('---')
    console.print(markdown)
```

Note that in the prompt we ask to print a final message, but it can be something quite minimal.

The final line of the script just runs the async main function, as in previous recipes.

## There's more...

This recipe is thought to be run periodically, likely every day. For example, it could be run very early in the morning and have the summary and draft ready for the moment that you start your day.

For that, we can use the concepts introduced in *Chapter 2, Setting up a cron job recipe* and prepare a cron job to execute at a particular time of the day.

For this, the best is to create a new script, `execute_agent.sh`, that encapsulates everything necessary to execute our agent. You need to provide the local path of the directory where the agent script is located and the path for `uv`.

```
#!/bin/bash
cd "/YOUR/FULL/PATH/HERE" || exit 1
</YOUR/FULL/PATH/TO/UV/HERE>/uv run email_agent.py
```

Grant execute permissions using `chmod` and run the script to check it works correctly. Verify that you can run it from anywhere using the full path to the file.

```
$ chmod +x execute_agent.sh
$ /YOUR/FULL/PATH/HERE/execute_agent.sh
...
```

Once this is correct, we can prepare the execution. For example, if we want to run the agent once a day at 5:30 AM, we can configure the following:

```
$ crontab -e
30 5 * * * /YOUR/FULL/PATH/HERE/execute_agent.sh
```

See in *Chapter 2* recipe *Setting up a cron job* for more details.

There is an important detail to take into account if you are planning to run an agent regularly: **cost**.

An agent can become relatively expensive to run, depending on how frequently the AI model is called. This cost can be difficult to manage, as it depends heavily on the specific model and amount of context. In the examples provided in this book, we mainly use GPT-5.4, which, at the time of writing, is not OpenAI's latest model but offers solid performance without being the most expensive option.

Even so, in our tests, each execution of `email_agent.py` costs roughly a couple of dollars.

> **Note**
>
> Keep in mind that AI model pricing may have changed. Verify the current costs to ensure your estimates are accurate.

While a few dollars per run may seem reasonable, the expense can add up over time. Running the agent daily could amount to around $60 per month. For cost efficiency, you might explore smaller models. For instance, GPT-5.4-mini is about one-third the cost of the full GPT-5.4 model, and GPT-5.4-nano is roughly ten times cheaper. These models may still deliver results that are "good enough" for many use cases.

Tip

Although it can be tempting to use the latest frontier models as the default, they are expensive in agentic flows because they typically tend to consume larger contexts using more tokens, which are also more expensive than in smaller models.

Be careful and keep an eye on costs.

Remember also that AI model providers like OpenAI include some tools to keep costs under control, like setting budgets. Explore those options.

Tip

It's very difficult to get a good estimation of costs in advance. Remember to check often and especially at the start of a project on the evolution of costs, and adjust accordingly, to avoid surprises.

Alternatively, to commercial providers, you can consider using local models via tools such as Ollama, as discussed in *Chapter 11*. Running a model locally on your machine is effectively free and can get good results for your use case.

Note

Though we haven't made it the focus, there is an important element in relation to the cost: the amount of context. In our script, we use a lot of context to provide the AI model with examples of our emails in order to produce a more accurate draft. Depending on the number of emails, that can increase the amount of context. Instead of the naïve approach we took, you can either reduce the number of emails or, even better, curate a small selection of emails manually and then only use that. That should bring down the cost.

Another alternative in the same direction, left as an exercise, is to reduce the stored raw emails to a description of their content, using a GenAI tool. Using a prompt like: "generate a prompt that will produce messages using the same style and tone as these emails," generate some text that can replace the `sent_emails.json` and is much smaller, while containing the information to produce good drafts. Try it yourself!

## See also

- The *Sending Email Notifications* recipe, in *Chapter 2*, describing how to send an email
- The *Creating your own chatbot* recipe, in *Chapter 11*, describing the basics of working with AI models
- The *Let's use MCP servers* and *Create your own MCP servers* recipes, in *Chapter 12*, introducing the usage of MCP servers, function tools and how to read email using `imaplib`

# 15

# Automatic Testing Routines

When the code and the complexity of your software grow, generating tests to ensure your program does what it is supposed to do is the best tool to provide you with a firm footing over rocky terrain.

Tests are, in essence, double-checking that the code is valid and doing what it is supposed to do. This is a deceptively simple statement. In practice, testing can be difficult.

> **Note**
>
> Mastering the ability to test is a difficult task and is worth a book or two. The tasks introduced in this chapter move from business-oriented tasks to software engineering tasks, which is a different approach. The objective of this chapter is to present some practical aspects of testing to introduce the subject.
>
> We have a great help in GenAI tools to generate and maintain tests. GenAI will quickly generate tests to check that the behavior of the code follows the expectations. But those expectations can be wrong! It is good to verify that tests generated by AI are actually checking the right assumptions.
>
> Another common problem with GenAI is the overeagerness to add more tests, which can generate a lot of boilerplate without real merit, as well as the generation of spurious tests that don't really test anything, like just writing and reading values in mocks. Validate the generated tests and keep GenAI on track.

The most important thing about a test is that it tries to check the code that is being tested independently. This involves a mindset of looking at the code and the inputs and outputs and approaching the task with a fresh look, and to not be influenced by the internal implementation. In some cases, the people testing the software may be different from the people writing the code in the first place, to ensure that there's a good understanding of what the code should and should not do. Try to design your tests with this approach and create well-defined interfaces to work with.

Note that GenAI can fall into this trap in the same way that a developer will do, and require effort in validating that the tests are checking the right behavior. In many cases, it is easier to understand the meaning of the code from tests than from the code directly.

> **Note**
>
> In summary, testing checks that the code does what it is supposed to do, and doesn't do what it is not supposed to do.
>
> The first part of the sentence is easier, but the second part is very difficult or even impossible. Writing tests has a cost, both in time and in maintenance. Only in highly critical software is code tested extensively to ensure that nothing unexpected happens. Try to find your balance in how many tests are adequate for your needs.

Tests are typically classified depending on how many different parts of the software they test. A test that only covers a small part of the code, like a function, is normally called a unit test, while a test that covers the whole system is called a system test. A test that covers the integration of different software elements is called an integration test. This is a very fluid definition, as not everyone agrees on what the system is, or how big a unit test can be before it becomes an integration test, or whether there's a significant difference between integration and system tests. But it helps to understand that different tests cover different areas of software – some are bigger, some are smaller – and have different requirements.

> **Tip**
>
> To have a team of developers working on the same software, ensuring it is of high quality, the discipline of adding and running tests continuously is crucial. That's why there are lots of types of tests to help with that task. Continuous integration, or CI, includes the practice of running tests for each change to the software and before merging them with changes by other developers. CI tools allow you to run tests in the background automatically and notify developers of any problem, ensuring that there are no unexpected failures.
>
> This test loop is also useful for GenAI tools, which will be able to understand problems and fix them. AI models are very good at working on reinforcement models, meaning that they have a way to validate that what they are producing is correct. This validation is provided by tests.

In this chapter, we will cover the usage of pytest as a tool to run various tests. This is one of the most complete Python test frameworks. pytest enables the easy setup of tests and provides a lot of useful options to run subsets of tests, run tests quickly, and detect problems when tests fail.

It also has an extensive ecosystem of plugins that allows you to integrate with other systems, like databases and web services, and to extend pytest with additional features, such as code coverage, running tests in parallel, and performance benchmarking.

In this chapter we will cover

- Writing and executing test cases
- Testing external code
- Testing using dependency mocking
- Testing using HTTP call mocking
- Preparing testing scenarios
- Running tests selectively
- Understand the coverage of your tests

Let's start by writing and running some simple tests.

# Technical requirements

You can check the code presented in the chapter at the GitHub URL https://github.com/PacktPublishing/Python-Automation-Cookbook-Third-Edition/tree/main/ch15

For all the tests, we need to install pytest. We should install the module, adding it to our requirements.txt file as follows:

```
$ echo "pytest==9.0.3" >> requirements.txt
$ uv pip install -r requirements.txt
```

You can call pytest directly in uv with

```
$ uv run pytest
```

# Writing and executing test cases

In this recipe, we will learn how to define and run tests using the pytest library.

## Getting ready

We will use the file `test_case.py`. You can download it from the GitHub repository at `https://github.com/PacktPublishing/Python-Automation-Cookbook-Third-Edition/tree/main/ch15/tests`.

## How to do it...

1. Check the file `tests/test_case.py`, which contains the definition of four tests:

```
LIST = [1, 2, 3]
def test_one():
    # Nothing happens
    pass
def test_two():
    assert 2 == 1 + 1
def test_three():
    assert 3 in LIST
def test_fail():
    assert 4 in LIST
```

2. Run `pytest` to run the test file:

```
$ uv run pytest tests/test_case.py
=====================. test session starts ======================
platform darwin -- Python 3.14.4, pytest-9.0.3, pluggy-1.6.0
rootdir: Python-Automation-Cookbook/ch15
collected 4 items
tests/test_case.py ...F
[100%]
============================ FAILURES ===========================
_____________________________ test_fail __________________________
    def test_fail():
>       assert 4 in LIST
E       assert 4 in [1, 2, 3]
tests/test_case.py:18: AssertionError
==================== short test summary info =====================
FAILED tests/test_case.py::test_fail - assert 4 in [1, 2, 3]
=================== 1 failed, 3 passed in 0.06s ==================
```

3. Fantastic! You've run your first suite of tests. Notice how one of the tests has failed.

## How it works...

pytest allows you to define tests simply as functions.

> **Tip**
>
> Not every function will be interpreted as a test. By default, only functions starting with the string "test" will be treated as such. This is a very handy default configuration, but it can be changed if needed. The documentation can be found at https://docs.pytest.org/en/latest/explanation/goodpractices.html#test-discovery.

Each function in tests/test_case.py defines a test, as we saw in *step 1.*

The four tests defined in the file tests/test_case.py define the basis of a pytest test: code that executes and contains one or more assertions verifying the code is correct. Note that these first tests are very simple. We will see more complicated tests later in the chapter:

- test_one doesn't have any assertions, so it can only pass.
- test_two checks that the addition is correct with an == operator.
- test_three uses the in operator to check whether a value is contained in a list.
- test_fail uses the in operator to check whether a value is contained in a list. It is not, so this test will fail, as seen in *step 2.*

In *step 2*, pytest collects all the tests at the start and then runs them:

```
collected 4 items
tests/test_case.py ...F                                              [100%]
```

Each passing test is represented by a dot, while each failed test shows an F.

> **Note**
>
> If color is available in the terminal, failures will be marked in red and passes marked in green.

For failed tests, the details of the exact line where an assertion failed are shown:

```
________________________________ test_fail ________________________________
    def test_fail():
```

```
>       assert 4 in LIST
E       assert 4 in [1, 2, 3]
tests/test_case.py:18: AssertionError
======================== short test summary info =========================
FAILED tests/test_case.py::test_fail - assert 4 in [1, 2, 3]
```

A brief summary of failed tests, total tests, and time taken is displayed later. This information is very useful for being able to act and fix the code to make the tests pass.

Tip

For GenAI, this information can be input to find out why a particular test is failing.

## There's more...

The displayed information shows almost nothing on passing tests by default. This allows you to focus on the failing tests. If you want to display every single test, you can call `pytest` with the verbose flag (`-v` or `-verbose`) activated:

```
$ uv run pytest -v tests/test_case.py
============================= test session starts ==============================
platform darwin -- Python 3.14.4, pytest-9.0.3, pluggy-1.6.0 -- Python-Automation-
Cookbook/ch15/.venv/bin/python3
cachedir: .pytest_cache
rootdir: Python-Automation-Cookbook/ch15
collected 4 items

tests/test_case.py::test_one PASSED                                      [ 25%]
tests/test_case.py::test_two PASSED                                      [ 50%]
tests/test_case.py::test_three PASSED                                    [ 75%]
tests/test_case.py::test_fail FAILED                                     [100%]

================================= FAILURES =================================
_______________________________test_fail__________________________________

    def test_fail():
>       assert 4 in LIST
E       assert 4 in [1, 2, 3]

tests/test_case.py:18: AssertionError
======================= short test summary info ==========================
```

```
FAILED tests/test_case.py::test_fail - assert 4 in [1, 2, 3]
====================== 1 failed, 3 passed in 0.06s =======================
```

The usage of the `assert` keyword in Python is very flexible and easy to understand. The test needs to be defined in a way that it asserts that something evaluates as `True`.

`pytest` will not only show the line that's failing but also give some context, as shown in our example, making it easy to see the problem.

Try to fix the error to make all the tests pass.

You can access the full `pytest` documentation at the following link: `https://docs.pytest.org/en/stable/`.

## See also

- The *Running tests selectively* recipe, later in this chapter, explains how to run only a subsection of the tests
- The *Testing external code* recipe, next up in this chapter, teaches how to test code in other modules

# Testing external code

The main objective of testing is to be able to check code that's out of the boundaries of the test files. We can import code easily in the tests, and then verify whether it is working as expected. Let's see how to do it.

## Getting ready

We will use the test files `tests/test_external.py` and `external_code/external.py`. You can download them from the GitHub repository at `https://github.com/PacktPublishing/Python-Automation-Cookbook-Third-Edition/tree/main/ch15/` under the subdirectories `tests` and `external_code`.

The tree should contain these files:

```
├── external_code
│   ├── __init__.py
│   └── external.py
├── conftest.py
└── tests
    └── test_external.py
```

## How to do it...

1. The `__init__.py` file and `conftest.py` are empty but define the structure of the modules
2. Check the file `external_code/external.py`, which contains the definition of a division function:

```
def division(a, b):
    return a / b
```

3. The test file `tests/test_external.py` contains some tests about the division function:

```
import pytest
from external_code.external import division
def test_int_division():
    assert 4 == division(8, 2)
def test_float_division():
    assert 3.5 == division(7, 2)
def test_division_by_zero():
    with pytest.raises(ZeroDivisionError):
        division(1, 0)
```

4. Run `pytest` on `tests/test_external.py` to see all the tests pass:

```
$ uv run pytest tests/test_external.py
====================== test session starts ======================
platform darwin -- Python 3.14.4, pytest-9.0.3, pluggy-1.6.0
rootdir: Python-Automation-Cookbook/ch15
collected 3 items
tests/test_external.py ...                                  [100%]
======================= 3 passed in 0.01s =======================
```

## How it works...

The tree structure allows `pytest` to detect the different modules in the structure:

- The `__init__.py` file defines that the subdirectory `external_code` contains a Python module. This is a standard Python definition.
- The file `conftest.py` contains specific information for `pytest`. Even if it's empty, it defines the root directory for the tests.

- The files starting with `test` are detected as containing tests. Inside these files, the functions prefixed with `test` are detected and run.
- The `external_code` module content is defined in *step 1*. The file `external.py` contains the function `division`.

In *step 3*, the test file is defined. Note the import:

```
from external_code.external import division
```

That allows you to use external code defined outside of the boundaries of the test file. The function is then verified in three situations:

- `test_int_division` checks that division divides two integers and returns the correct `integer` result
- `test_float_division` verifies that dividing two integers can produce a `float` result
- `test_division_by_zero` checks that the correct exception is raised if trying to divide by zero

The first two tests contain a simple assertion checking the result of the function call, but `test_division_by_zero` requires that you verify that the code raises an exception. This is done through a `with` block using `pytest.raises`:

```
def test_division_by_zero():
    with pytest.raises(ZeroDivisionError):
        division(1, 0)
```

This block will generate an assertion error if the call doesn't generate the exception, allowing you to check the behavior. Note that the specific exception needs to be passed as an argument.

*Step 4* runs the tests, checking that all tests are correct and that the code does what it is supposed to do.

## There's more...

To be able to define the exceptions to be captured, you'll need to import the exception definitions from the module code or the relevant library.

Raising an exception in any part inside of the `with` block will capture it. Try to include the smallest possible call that is expected to raise the exception to avoid capturing spurious exceptions. For the same reason, the most precise exception should be declared.

When running `pytest` without specifying a file, it will try to detect possible test files and capture all the tests in the subdirectory. Be sure that the modules are properly defined as specified by `__init__.py` and `conftest.py`.

We will see more of `conftest.py` later in this chapter.

## See also

- The *Writing and executing test cases* recipe, in the previous section, to learn the basics of how to define tests
- The *Testing using HTTP call mocking* recipe, later in this chapter, to learn how to use testing modules that mock specific libraries

# Testing using dependency mocking

One of the biggest advantages of using Python is having a rich library of resources at our disposal. That includes modules in the standard library, like the `csv` module to `re` and write CSV files or the re library to use regexes.

Others can be external, like `Beautiful Soup` to parse HTML or `matplotlib` to generate graphs. We can also create our own libraries or structure our code in different files and encapsulate the functionality in a way that's reusable and improves readability.

When creating tests, sometimes using external elements and library calls in the core of the test is not advisable. For example, to test that a report is correctly processed, it may be necessary to read a CSV file that contains the report. But preparing the test by preparing a file, in this case, becomes cumbersome and can lose focus on the actual objective of the test.

In these cases, it can be convenient to simulate those dependencies to simplify the tests or to avoid external calls such as calls to network access or other kinds of hardware. This kind of simulation, which replaces the external dependencies during testing, is known as a *mock*.

> Note
>
> Mocks are closely related to unit tests, in that they are small focused tests that cover a single unit of code, like a function, a class, or even a small module. This allows you to test such units of code in isolation from external elements, or, more precisely, fully controlling the external elements the code accesses. Exactly how big a unit test can get before it is no longer a unit test is up for debate in the industry. Don't let that stop you from doing something that works for you.

This can be done through the library `mock` in the Python standard library, which allows you to replace the behavior of external dependencies.

## Getting ready

We will use the test files `tests/test_dependencies.py` and `external_code/dependencies.py`. You can download them from the GitHub repository at `https://github.com/PacktPublishing/Python-Automation-Cookbook-Third-Edition/tree/main/ch15/` under the subdirectories `tests` and `external_code`.

The tree should contain these files:

```
├── external_code
│   ├── __init__.py
│   └── dependencies.py
├── conftest.py
└── tests
    └── test_dependencies.py
```

## How to do it...

1. The `__init__.py` file and `conftest.py` are empty, but define the structure of the modules
2. Check the file `external_code/dependencies.py`, which contains the definition of calculating areas for certain shapes:

```
PI = 3.14159
def rectangle(sideA, sideB):
    return sideA * sideB
def circle(radius):
    return 2 * PI * radius
def calculate_area(shape, sizeA, sizeB=0):
    if sizeA <= 0:
        raise ValueError('sizeA needs to be positive')
    if sizeB < 0:
        raise ValueError('sizeB needs to be positive')
    if shape == 'SQUARE':
        return rectangle(sizeA, sizeA)
    if shape == 'RECTANGLE':
        return rectangle(sizeA, sizeB)
    if shape == 'CIRCLE':
```

```
        return circle(sizeA)
    raise Exception(f'Shape {shape} not defined')
```

3. Check the tests in the file `tests/test_dependencies.py`, validating the calculations of the function `calculate_area`:

```
from unittest import mock
from external_code.dependencies import calculate_area
def test_square():
    result = calculate_area('SQUARE', 2)
    assert result == 4
def test_rectangle():
    result = calculate_area('RECTANGLE', 2, 3)
    assert result == 6
def test_circle_with_proper_pi():
    result = calculate_area('CIRCLE', 2)
    assert result == 12.56636
@mock.patch('external_code.dependencies.PI', 3)
def test_circle_with_mocked_pi():
    result = calculate_area('CIRCLE', 2)
    assert result == 12
@mock.patch('external_code.dependencies.rectangle')
def test_circle_with_mocked_rectangle(mocked_rectangle):
    mocked_rectangle.return_value = 12
    result = calculate_area('SQUARE', 2)
    assert result == 12
    mocked_rectangle.assert_called()
```

Run pytest to run the test file:

```
$ uv run pytest tests/test_dependencies.py
======================= test session starts ======================
platform darwin -- Python 3.14.4, pytest-9.0.3, pluggy-1.6.0
rootdir: Python-Automation-Cookbook/ch15
collected 5 items
tests/test_dependencies.py .....                              [100%]
======================== 5 passed in 0.01s =======================
```

## How it works...

The code module content is defined in *step 1*. The file dependencies.py contains the following elements:

- The definition of the variable `PI`.
- Two internal functions that calculate the areas of rectangles (based on two sides) and circles (based on the radius)
- The `calculate_area` function, which accepts several kinds of shapes and channels the request to the correct internal one. It understands that a square is a kind of rectangle with four equal sides, for example.

In *step 3*, the test file is defined. Note the imports, both of the `mock` module and the function to test:

```
from unittest import mock
from external_code.dependencies import calculate_area
```

The first three tests (`test_square`, `test_rectangle`, and `test_circle_with_proper_pi`) are straightforward.

The test `test_circle_with_mocked_pi` uses a `mock.patch` decorator to replace the `PI` variable with 3 in the `external_code.dependencies` module:

```
@mock.patch('external_code.dependencies.PI', 3)
def test_circle_with_mocked_pi():
    result = calculate_area('CIRCLE', 2)
    assert result == 12
```

This changes the `PI` constant while the test is running, affecting the result. Once the test is done, the mock is disabled and the variable is again set to the previously defined value.

The test `test_circle_with_mocked_rectangle` mocks the rectangle function. As a replacement is not defined in the decorator, it is passed as a parameter to the function `mocked_rectangle`:

```
@mock.patch('external_code.dependencies.rectangle')
def test_circle_with_mocked_rectangle(mocked_rectangle):
    mocked_rectangle.return_value = 12
    result = calculate_area('SQUARE', 2)
```

```
    assert result == 12
    mocked_rectangle.assert_called()
```

The function, during the test, is replaced with a `MagicMock` object. To specify the value returned when this object is called as a function, use the `attribute .return_value`. As we see in the result, it replaces the area calculation. The mock can also be checked to see whether it has been called with `.assert_called()`.

> **Note**
>
> If the mock tested with `.assert_called()` hasn't been called, it will raise an `AssertionError`.

In step 4, the tests are called to see if all tests are working as expected.

## There's more...

Mocks are very flexible, and there are different ways of checking whether they have been called and how. A few possibilities are listed here:

- `.assert_called_once()`: Raises an error if not called or called more than once.
- `.assert_called_with(args)`: Raises an error if not called or called with different arguments. The arguments will be checked against the last call of the mock.
- `.call_count`: Counts the number of times it has been called.

A `Mock` object will create another `mock` automatically if any attribute is accessed or called. For example:

```
>>> from unittest.mock import Mock
>>> mock = Mock()
>>> mock.attribute
<Mock name='mock.attribute' id='4337292000'>
>>> mock.other_attribute
<Mock name='mock.other_attribute' id='4337292144'>
>>> mock.other_attribute()
<Mock name='mock.other_attribute()' id='4337353728'>
```

This means mocks have a flexible API that adapts easily to most calls of a module.

In our example, we mocked a function and a constant in our code, but you can also mock any library, either in the Python standard library or any other installed package.

> **Note**
>
> Keep in mind that you need to mock in the correct path. You need to mock the object where it's imported to, not where it's originally defined. For example, if you're importing `from extpck import extfunction` into your package `external_code.module`, you need to mock it as follows:
>
> ```
> @mock.patch('external_code.module.extfunction')
> ```
>
> It's an easy mistake to make, even for seasoned mocking users. Remember that you need to mock *where it's used, not where it's defined.*

If you need to raise an exception when a mock is called, you can do so using the `.side_effect` attribute. This is very useful for testing error conditions in external libraries and making sure your code can correctly handle them:

```
>>> from unittest.mock import Mock
>>> mock = Mock()
>>> mock.side_effect = Exception('Custom error')
>>> mock()
Traceback (most recent call last):
  File "<python-input-7>", line 1, in <module>
    mock()
    ~~~~^^
  File "/usr/local/Cellar/python@3.14/3.14.4_1/Frameworks/Python.framework/
Versions/3.14/lib/python3.14/unittest/mock.py", line 1176, in __call__
    return self._mock_call(*args, **kwargs)
           ~~~~~~~~~~~~~~~^^^^^^^^^^^^^^^^^
  File "/usr/local/Cellar/python@3.14/3.14.4_1/Frameworks/Python.framework/
Versions/3.14/lib/python3.14/unittest/mock.py", line 1180, in _mock_call
    return self._execute_mock_call(*args, **kwargs)
           ~~~~~~~~~~~~~~~~~~~~~~~^^^^^^^^^^^^^^^^^
  File "/usr/local/Cellar/python@3.14/3.14.4_1/Frameworks/Python.framework/
Versions/3.14/lib/python3.14/unittest/mock.py", line 1241, in _execute_mock_call
    raise effect
Exception: Custom error
```

The same `.side_effect` attribute, assigning an iterator, can be used if the mock needs to return different results for multiple calls:

```
>>> from unittest.mock import Mock
>>> mock = Mock()
>>> mock.side_effect = (1, 2, 3)
>>> mock()
1
>>> mock()
2
>>> mock()
3
```

We mentioned that `mock.patch` can be used as a decorator. This is a Python concept that, in essence, modifies the function it is decorating, usually by adding extra functionality before and/or after the function processes.

Decorators are a very useful concept and, in essence, they replace the function with a modified version. You can gain a deeper understanding of how decorators work from this article: `https://realpython.com/primer-on-python-decorators/`.

> **Note**
>
> We've also used decorators in *Chapters 7* and *14*.

`patch` can also be used as a `with` block. If that's the case, the module is mocked while inside the block:

```
>>> from unittest.mock import patch
>>> from external_code.dependencies import circle
>>> with patch('external_code.dependencies.PI', 2):
...   print(circle(2))
...
8
>>> circle(2)
12.56636
```

You can read the full documentation for mocks at `https://docs.python.org/3/library/unittest.mock.html`.

## See also

- The *Testing external code* recipe, earlier in this chapter, to learn how to test code in other modules
- The *Testing using HTTP call mocking* recipe is up next, to learn how to use testing modules that mock specific libraries

# Testing using HTTP call mocking

Working with mocks is a common operation when testing. Some dependencies are typically mocked in most tests.

One common dependency to be mocked is external HTTP calls. Performing these calls while running tests is costly, slow, and can produce unreliable results if the network connection fails.

Though external calls can be mocked through the library `mock` in the Python standard library, as shown in the previous recipe, *Testing using dependency mocking*, there are specific testing modules that allow you to simulate HTTP calls and responses. Also, there are specific libraries that mock other specific libraries. This produces easier and better mocks, as they are adapted to the behavior of the mock.

We have previously used the fantastic `requests` library (introduced in the *Installing third-party packages* recipe from *Chapter 1, Let's Begin Our Automation Journey*, but also used throughout the book). We will look at how to mock this library specifically. We will use the testing library `responses`, which allows us to generate expected requests and their responses.

> **Note**
>
> Note that this testing library doesn't mock general HTTP access, but specifically the `requests` module.

## Getting ready

We will use the `pytest` module, along with the requests and responses libraries. We should install the modules, adding them to our `requirements.txt` file as follows:

```
$ echo "requests==2.33.1" >> requirements.txt
$ echo "responses==0.26.0" >> requirements.txt
$ uv pip install -r requirements.txt
```

We will use the test files tests/test_requests.py and external_code/code_requests.py. You can download them from the GitHub repository at https://github.com/PacktPublishing/Python-Automation-Cookbook-Third-Edition/tree/main/ch15/ under the subdirectories tests and external_code.

The file tree should contain these files:

```
├── external_code
│   ├── __init__.py
│   └── code_requests.py
├── conftest.py
└── tests
    └── test_requests.py
```

## How to do it...

1. The __init__.py file and conftest.py are empty but define the structure of the modules.
2. Check the file external_code/code_requests.py, which contains a call to an external form in https://httpbin.org/post to order a pizza:

```
import requests
from datetime import datetime, timedelta
RECIPES = {
    'DEFAULT': {
        'size': 'small',
        'topping': ['bacon', 'onion'],
    },
    'SPECIAL': {
        'size': 'large',
        'topping': ['bacon', 'mushroom', 'onion'],
    }
}
def order_pizza(recipe='DEFAULT'):
    delivery_time = datetime.now() + timedelta(hours=1)
    delivery = delivery_time.strftime('%H:%M')
    data = {
        'custname': "Sean O'Connell",
        'custtel': '123-456-789',
        'custemail': 'sean@oconnell.ie',
```

```
        # Indicate the time
        'delivery': delivery,
        'comments': ''
    }
    extra_info = RECIPES[recipe]
    data.update(extra_info)
    resp = requests.post('https://httpbin.org/post', data)
    return resp.json()['form']
```

3. Check the tests in the file `tests/test_requests.py`, checking that the code behaves correctly:

```
import pytest
import requests
import responses
import urllib.parse
from external_code.code_requests import order_pizza
@responses.activate
def test_order_pizza():
    body = {
        'form': {
            'size': 'small',
            'topping': ['bacon', 'onion']
        }
    }
    responses.add(responses.POST, 'https://httpbin.org/post',
                  json=body, status=200)
    result = order_pizza()
    assert result['size'] == 'small'
    # Decode the sent data
    encoded_body = responses.calls[0].request.body
    sent_data = urllib.parse.parse_qs(encoded_body)
    assert sent_data['size'] == ['small']
@responses.activate
def test_order_pizza_timeout():
    responses.add(responses.POST, 'https://httpbin.org/post',
                  body=requests.exceptions.Timeout())
```

```
    with pytest.raises(requests.exceptions.Timeout):
        order_pizza()
```

4. Run pytest to run the test file:

```
$ uv run pytest tests/test_requests.py
===================== test session starts ======================
platform darwin -- Python 3.14.4, pytest-9.0.3, pluggy-1.6.0
rootdir: Python-Automation-Cookbook/ch15
collected 2 items
tests/test_requests.py ..                                 [100%]
====================== 2 passed in 0.17s =======================
```

## How it works...

The code module content is defined in *step 1*. The file code_requests.py contains the following elements:

- A section of imports
- The definition of two kinds of pizzas in the RECIPES constant
- The order_pizza function selects the pizza, composes the form data, and then POSTs it to https://httpbin.org/post

> **Note**
>
> The form rendered in https://httpbin.org/forms/post and its POSTing URL https://httpbin.org/post were introduced in the Interacting with forms recipe from Chapter 3, Building Your First Web Scraping Application. It presents a form to order a pizza and returns the same information that is posted in the form in JSON format.

Let's take a closer look at the order_pizza function.

The code uses the current time to calculate the delivery time, adding an hour. The time is described in the format HH:MM using delivery_time.strftime('%H:%M'). . The function strftime formats the time and the string '%H:%M' prints only the hours and minutes of the time:

```
delivery_time = datetime.now() + timedelta(hours=1)
delivery = delivery_time.strftime('%H:%M')
```

The full data is composed of both a predefined data dictionary and the recipe information. The recipe information gets selected from the `RECIPE` dictionary and is then added to the data dictionary using `.update()`:

```
data = {
    'custname': "Sean O'Connell",
    'custtel': '123-456-789',
    'custemail': 'sean@oconnell.ie',
    # Indicate the time
    'delivery': delivery,
    'comments': ''
}
extra_info = RECIPES[recipe]
data.update(extra_info)
```

Finally, the information is sent to the URL using `requests.post`. The response data, once decoded from JSON, is returned by the function:

```
resp = requests.post('https://httpbin.org/post', data)
return resp.json()['form']
```

In *step 3*, the test file is defined. Note the import of the `responses` module. The first test, `test_order_pizza`, starts by activating the responses module with the decorator `@responses.activate`:

```
@responses.activate
def test_order_pizza():
    body = {
        'form': {
            'size': 'small',
            'topping': ['bacon', 'onion']
        }
    }
    responses.add(responses.POST, 'https://httpbin.org/post',
                  json=body, status=200)
    result = order_pizza()
    assert result['size'] == 'small'
    # Decode the sent data
    encoded_body = responses.calls[0].request.body
```

```
    sent_data = urllib.parse.parse_qs(encoded_body)
    assert sent_data['size'] == ['small']
```

The first thing it does is define the expected HTTP request as `https://httpbin.org/post` and the response that should be returned:

```
    body = {
        'form': {
            'size': 'small',
            'topping': ['bacon', 'onion']
        }
    }
    responses.add(responses.POST, 'https://httpbin.org/post',
                  json=body, status=200)
```

The call to `responses.add` specifies the method (`POST`), the URL, the response in JSON format, and the status code. When our code makes a request to the given URL, it will receive this information instead of making an external call to the network.

The next block is the call to `order_pizza()` and the assertion of the result, which is straightforward.

After that, the following block checks the data sent and captured by responses:

```
# Decode the sent data
    encoded_body = responses.calls[0].request.body
    sent_data = urllib.parse.parse_qs(encoded_body)
    assert sent_data['size'] == ['small']
```

The responses library keeps track of all the captured requests. We retrieve the body of the first request and store it in the `encoded_body` variable. This data has been encoded and sent as part of the POST in `application/x-www-form-urlencoded` format, which is the default for POST requests. We decode it using the default library, `urllib`, and `parse_qs()` to transform it into a dictionary.

> **Note**
>
> The full documentation for `urllib.parse` can be found in the Python official documentation: `https://docs.python.org/3/library/urllib.parse.html`.

The second test, `test_order_pizza_timeout`, shows how to raise an exception when requesting a particular URL:

```
@responses.activate
def test_order_pizza_timeout():
    responses.add(responses.POST, 'https://httpbin.org/post',
                  body=requests.exceptions.Timeout())
    with pytest.raises(requests.exceptions.Timeout):
        order_pizza()
```

The `responses.add` call, in this case, specifies an `Exception` in the body that will be raised when the URL is requested with the defined method.

> **Note**
>
> Because the exception is raised instantly when the request is done, this speeds up the generation of a `Timeout` exception, which normally would require seconds or minutes to be generated.

*Step 4* runs the tests to check that the code works as expected.

## There's more...

The responses library is very useful for generating error conditions and preparing your code for them. The `STATUS` argument can be used to generate error codes in external systems, such as `"403 Forbidden"`, `"404 Not Found"`, `"500 Internal Server error"`, and `"503 Service Unavailable"`. Properly handling the different situations that can be produced and reacting to them will improve the reliability of your code.

> **Tip**
>
> Notice that some of these errors can happen at the server level, without any changes at your end, like 503, meaning the service is temporarily unavailable. In some cases, a wait-and-retry strategy can be adequate, and in others, the proper notification of "external service unavailable" can be better. Don't assume that external services will always behave perfectly, as they can (and will) have problems.

Once you enable `responses.activate` to capture all the HTTP requests, any request to an unexpected URL will raise an error:

```
E           requests.exceptions.ConnectionError: Connection refused by Responses - the call doesn't match any registered mock.
E
E           Request:
E           - POST https://httpbin.org/otherurl
E
E           Available matches:
E           - POST https://httpbin.org/post
```

This makes every test that uses responses self-contained and means they won't leak any external calls due to mistakes or changes.

The full documentation of the responses library can be found here: `https://github.com/getsentry/responses`.

`responses` is not the only example of a library created to mock some specific aspects when testing. Another example is `freezegun`, which allows you to set the time. Take this test, for example:

```
import responses
import urllib.parse
from freezegun import freeze_time
from external_code.code_requests import order_pizza
@responses.activate
@freeze_time("2020-03-17T19:34")
def test_order_time():
    body = {
        'form': {
            'size': 'small',
            'topping': ['bacon', 'onion']
        }
    }
    responses.add(responses.POST, 'https://httpbin.org/post',
                  json=body, status=200)
    order_pizza()
    # Decode the sent data
    encoded_body = responses.calls[0].request.body
```

```
    sent_data = urllib.parse.parse_qs(encoded_body)
    assert sent_data['delivery'] == ['20:34']
```

This test uses the `freeze_time` decorator to set the time to `19:34`, no matter when the test is run. Note that it also sets the date.

> **Tip**
>
> The test is available on GitHub as `tests/test_requests_time.py`. Remember to install the package `freezegun` using `uv pip`.

The full documentation of `freezegun` can be accessed here: https://github.com/spulec/freezegun.

## See also

- The *Testing external code* recipe, earlier in this chapter, to learn how to test code in other modules
- The *Testing using dependency mocking* recipe, from the previous section, to learn how to mock any kind of package or function

# Preparing testing scenarios

Tests are typically prepared in batches. Similar tests require a similar setup and cleanup, and they only differ on small details. Repeating the same preparation over and over generates boilerplate code and is less readable.

> **Tip**
>
> The term boilerplate comes from 19th-century local newspapers printing already-prepared news stamped onto metal plates by distribution companies. This meant the same news, in the same format, was repeated all across different newspapers. Boilerplate code is reused code that presents little or no variation and, in most cases, mainly adds clutter. When creating tests, it is easy to fall into this pattern, which makes the code cumbersome.
>
> At the moment, a common trap is to repeat the code quickly through the usage of GenAI tools, which will produce boilerplate and won't get tired of adding it over and over. While this is good from the point of view of generation, it makes the tests more difficult to read and to understand. Easily understandable tests will help you verify that the behavior of the code is the expected one.

In this recipe, we will see how to prepare setup scenarios to run tests using `pytest` fixtures.

## Getting ready

We will use the test files `tests/test_fixtures.py` and `external_code/code_fixtures.py`. You can download them from the GitHub repository at `https://github.com/PacktPublishing/Python-Automation-Cookbook-Third-Edition/tree/main/ch15/` under the subdirectories `tests` and `external_code`.

The file tree should contain the following:

```
├── external_code
│   ├── __init__.py
│   └── code_fixtures.py
├── conftest.py
└── tests
    └── test_fixtures.py
```

## How to do it...

1. The `__init__.py` file and `conftest.py` are empty, but define the structure of the modules.
2. Check the file `external_code/code_fixtures.py`, which contains the code to store data in a zip file and retrieve it:

```
from zipfile import ZipFile
INTERNAL_FILE = 'internal.txt'
def write_zipfile(filename, content):
    with ZipFile(filename, 'w') as zipfile:
        zipfile.writestr(INTERNAL_FILE, content)
def read_zipfile(filename):
    with ZipFile(filename, 'r') as zipfile:
        with zipfile.open(INTERNAL_FILE) as intfile:
            content = intfile.read()
    return content.decode('utf8')
```

3. Check the tests in the file `tests/test_fixtures.py`, checking that the code behaves correctly:

```
import os
import random
```

```
import string
from pytest import fixture
from zipfile import ZipFile
from external_code.code_fixtures import write_zipfile, read_zipfile
@fixture
def fzipfile():
    content_length = 50
    content = ''.join(random.choices(string.ascii_lowercase,
k=content_length))
    fnumber = ''.join(random.choices(string.digits, k=3))
    filename = f'file{fnumber}.zip'
    write_zipfile(filename, content)
    yield filename, content
    os.remove(filename)
def test_writeread_zipfile():
    TESTFILE = 'test.zip'
    TESTCONTENT = 'This is a test'
    write_zipfile(TESTFILE, TESTCONTENT)
    content = read_zipfile(TESTFILE)
    assert TESTCONTENT == content
def test_readwrite_zipfile(fzipfile):
    filename, expected_content = fzipfile
    content = read_zipfile(filename)
    assert content == expected_content
def test_internal_zipfile(fzipfile):
    filename, expected_content = fzipfile
    EXPECTED_LIST = ['internal.txt']
    # Verify only a single file exist in the zipfile
    with ZipFile(filename, 'r') as zipfile:
        assert zipfile.namelist() == EXPECTED_LIST
```

4. Run `pytest` to run the test file:

```
$ pytest tests/test_fixtures.py
======================== test session starts =====================
platform darwin -- Python 3.14.4, pytest-9.0.3, pluggy-1.6.0
rootdir: Python-Automation-Cookbook/ch15
collected 3 items
```

```
tests/test_fixtures.py ...                                    [100%]
========================= 3 passed in 0.01s ======================
```

5. Check that a new file called `test.zip` has been created in the directory:

```
$ ls test.zip
test.zip
```

We will see how this file was created and how to avoid keeping files related to tests.

## How it works...

The code module content is defined in *step 1*.

As described in *step 2*, the file `code_fixtures.py` contains two functions to store and save information in a zip file. This uses the standard Python `zipfile` module to deal with zip files:

- `write_zipfile` creates a zip file with an internal compressed file, `internal.txt`, which contains the data passed as an argument. This is written using the method `.writestr()`:

```
def write_zipfile(filename, content):
    with ZipFile(filename, 'w') as zipfile:
        zipfile.writestr(INTERNAL_FILE, content)
```

- `read_zipfile` reads the file and extracts the content from the internal file:

```
def read_zipfile(filename):
    with ZipFile(filename, 'r') as zipfile:
        with zipfile.open(INTERNAL_FILE) as intfile:
            content = intfile.read()
    return content.decode('utf8')
```

`read_zipfile` follows the same pattern as the write. It searches for the defined internal file inside the zip file and reads its content. The content needs to be decoded as it's encoded in `UTF-8`.

Zip files are a collection of files that are compressed. We need to define at least one file to store information inside a zip file. You can learn more about the `zipfile` module here: `https://docs.python.org/3/library/zipfile.html`

The tests are defined in *step 3*. The test `test_writeread_zipfile` first generates a file and then reads it, testing the whole lifecycle and ensuring that a file can be written, then read:

```
def test_writeread_zipfile():
    TESTFILE = 'test.zip'
    TESTCONTENT = 'This is a test'
    write_zipfile(TESTFILE, TESTCONTENT)
    content = read_zipfile(TESTFILE)
    assert TESTCONTENT == content
```

This test works correctly but doesn't perform any cleanup, which leaves the file `test.zip` in the working directory.

For the other two tests, use the declared fixture `fzipfile`. Note the `@fixture` decorator. Let's take a look at it:

```
import os
import random
import string
from pytest import fixture
@fixture
def fzipfile():
    content_length = 50
    content = ''.join(random.choices(string.ascii_lowercase, k=content_length))
    fnumber = ''.join(random.choices(string.digits, k=3))
    filename = f'file{fnumber}.zip'
    write_zipfile(filename, content)
    yield filename, content
    os.remove(filename)
```

The fixture generates some random content in the shape of a string of 50 lowercase characters. It also generates a random filename. It then writes this file and `yields` both the generated filename and the content. Finally, it removes the file with a call to `os.remove`.

The `yield` keyword in Python allows us to pause the execution of code, return a value, and then resume the code. In a `fixture`, everything that goes before `yield` will be executed before the start of a test, and everything after `yield` will be executed at the end of the test.

**Note**

`yield` is typically used within generator functions that act as iterators, but each time a new value is requested, the code keeps executing until another `yield` is found; for example:

```
>>> def generator():
...   yield 1
...   yield 2
...   for _ in range(3):
...     yield 3
...
>>> list(generator())
[1, 2, 3, 3, 3]
```

You can learn more about generators at `https://realpython.com/introduction-to-python-generators/`.

The `fixture` then performs some setup (creates a zip file), returns the values (randomly generated name and content) to work with, and finally cleans up (deletes the file).

The other two tests use this fixture to set up the test. `test_readwrite_zipfile` is very straightforward; it reads the file created by the fixture:

```
def test_readwrite_zipfile(fzipfile):
    filename, expected_content = fzipfile
    content = read_zipfile(filename)
    assert content == expected_content
```

Note that the value returned by the fixture `fzipfile` is a tuple with two elements: the filename and the content.

`test_internal_zipfile` uses the fixture to then check that there's only one file inside the zip file and that it has the correct name. It opens the zip file and uses `.namelist()` to get a list of the files inside to verify them:

```
def test_internal_zipfile(fzipfile):
    filename, expected_content = fzipfile
    EXPECTED_LIST = ['internal.txt']
    # Verify only a single file exist in the zipfile
```

```
    with ZipFile(filename, 'r') as zipfile:
        assert zipfile.namelist() == EXPECTED_LIST
```

## There's more...

Fixtures can be shared across multiple test files. You don't need to import them. Add them instead to the `conftest.py` file. You can generate local conftest.py files in the subdirectory for fixtures that are local to that directory only.

> **Note**
>
> To use a `fixture`, the name of the parameter in the test needs to have the name of the `fixture`. Be careful not to overwrite these names unintentionally.

`pytest` provides some built-in fixtures available for common operations. For example, the fixture `caplog` captures the logs emitted while running tests, and `tmp_path` creates a temporary subdirectory that's unique to each test. Go to the `fixture` documentation for more details.

There are a lot of `pytest` plugins that include fixtures to deal with a lot of common scenarios or tools; for example, connecting to databases, web frameworks, external APIs, and so on. It's worth running a search on `pypi.org` before creating a fixture.

`pytest` also adds context for the specific data on fixtures when there's a failing test. This helps with understanding behavior and debugging problems, either on the fixture or in the code that's being tested:

```
$ pytest tests/test_fixtures.py
======================== test session starts ========================
platform darwin -- Python 3.14.4, pytest-9.0.3, pluggy-1.6.0
rootdir: Python-Automation-Cookbook/ch15
collected 3 items
tests/test_fixtures.py ..F                                     [100%]
============================= FAILURES ==============================
_______________________ test_internal_zipfile _______________________
fzipfile = ('file989.zip', 'ldrnfqwqodcwmkxkehfcaaxzaocxasbduixouchvrzqyfgaaxv')
...
FAILURE
```

Remember to perform a cleanup stage in your fixtures. As we've seen in the example of `test_writeread_zipfile`, not cleaning up can lead to spurious data being stored on the hard drive or any other place where the fixture created spurious data. Putting code in the fixture after the `yield` keyword will be called even if there's an exception or some other kind of error.

The full `pytest` fixture documentation is available here: `https://docs.pytest.org/en/latest/fixture.html`.

## See also

- The *Writing and executing test cases* recipe, earlier in this chapter, to learn the basics of how to define tests
- The *Testing external code* recipe, earlier in this chapter, to learn how to test code in other modules

# Running tests selectively

Detecting and running all the defined tests in a project is good to verify that everything is working. But most of the development work done while dealing with tests benefits from executing only a subset of all tests.

When adding new code or new tests, it is crucial to iterate quickly through a specific part of the tests and code to narrow your focus.

In this recipe, we will see how to run a subset of available tests with `pytest` and which parameters to use in different scenarios.

## Getting ready

We will use the `pytest` module among others. We should install the modules by adding them to our `requirements.txt` file as follows:

```
$ echo "requests==2.33.1" >> requirements.txt
$ echo "responses==0.26.0" >> requirements.txt
$ echo "freezegun==1.5.5" >> requirements.txt
$ uv pip install -r requirements.txt
```

We will use the test files introduced in the previous recipes of the chapter. You can download them from the GitHub repository at `https://github.com/PacktPublishing/Python-Automation-Cookbook-Third-Edition/tree/main/ch15/`, under the subdirectories `tests` and `external_code`:

```
├── external_code
│   ├── __init__.py
│   ├── code_fixtures.py
```

```
│   ├── code_requests.py
│   ├── dependencies.py
│   └── external.py
├── conftest.py
└── tests
    ├── test_case.py
    ├── test_dependencies.py
    ├── test_external.py
    ├── test_fixtures.py
    ├── test_requests.py
    └── test_requests_time.py
```

## How to do it...

1. Run all the tests with `pytest`:

```
$ uv run pytest
====================== test session starts =======================
platform darwin -- Python 3.14.5, pytest-9.0.3, pluggy-1.6.0
rootdir: Python-Automation-Cookbook/ch15
collected 18 items

tests/test_case.py ...F                                    [ 22%]
tests/test_dependencies.py .....                           [ 50%]
tests/test_external.py ...                                 [ 66%]
tests/test_fixtures.py ...                                 [ 83%]
tests/test_requests.py ..                                  [ 94%]
tests/test_requests_time.py .                              [100%]

============================ FAILURES ============================
____________________________ test_fail ___________________________

    def test_fail():
>       assert 4 in LIST
E       assert 4 in [1, 2, 3]

tests/test_case.py:18: AssertionError
===================== short test summary info ====================
FAILED tests/test_case.py::test_fail - assert 4 in [1, 2, 3]
================== 1 failed, 17 passed in 0.34s ==================
```

Note that `test_fail` is failing.

2. Run `pytest --collect-only`:

```
$ uv run pytest --collect-only
======================== test session starts =====================
platform darwin -- Python 3.14.4, pytest-9.0.3, pluggy-1.6.0
rootdir: Python-Automation-Cookbook/ch15
collected 18 items
<Module tests/test_case.py>
  <Function test_one>
  <Function test_two>
  <Function test_three>
  <Function test_fail>
<Module tests/test_dependencies.py>
  <Function test_square>
  <Function test_rectangle>
  <Function test_circle_with_proper_pi>
  <Function test_circle_with_mocked_pi>
  <Function test_circle_with_mocked_rectangle>
<Module tests/test_external.py>
  <Function test_int_division>
  <Function test_float_division>
  <Function test_division_by_zero>
<Module tests/test_fixtures.py>
  <Function test_writeread_zipfile>
  <Function test_readwrite_zipfile>
  <Function test_internal_zipfile>
<Module tests/test_requests.py>
  <Function test_order_pizza>
  <Function test_order_pizza_timeout>
<Module tests/test_requests_time.py>
  <Function test_order_time>
====================== no tests ran in 0.20s =====================
```

3. Run `pytest -v -k time`:

```
$ uv run pytest -v -k time
======================= test session starts ======================
platform darwin -- Python 3.14.4, pytest-9.0.3, pluggy-1.6.0
rootdir: Python-Automation-Cookbook/ch15
```

```
cachedir: .pytest_cache
rootdir: Python-Automation-Cookbook/ch15
collected 18 items / 16 deselected / 2 selected
tests/test_requests.py::test_order_pizza_timeout PASSED              [ 50%]
tests/test_requests_time.py::test_order_time PASSED                  [100%]
================ 2 passed, 16 deselected in 0.24s ===============
```

4. Run `pytest -v -k time tests/test_requests.py`:

```
$ uv run pytest -v -k time tests/test_requests.py
====================== test session starts ===================
platform darwin -- Python 3.14.4, pytest-9.0.3, pluggy-1.6.0
cachedir: .pytest_cache
rootdir: Python-Automation-Cookbook/ch15
collected 2 items / 1 deselected / 1 selected
tests/test_requests.py::test_order_pizza_timeout PASSED             [100%]
================ 1 passed, 1 deselected in 0.18s =============
```

5. Run `pytest -v tests/test_requests_time.py::test_order_time`:

```
$ uv run pytest -v tests/test_requests_time.py::test_order_time
====================== test session starts ===================
platform darwin -- Python 3.14.4, pytest-9.0.3, pluggy-1.6.0
cachedir: .pytest_cache
rootdir: Python-Automation-Cookbook/ch15
collected 1 item
tests/test_requests_time.py::test_order_time PASSED                 [100%]
======================== 1 passed in 0.38s ===================
```

6. Run `pytest -v --lf`:

```
$ uv run pytest -v --lf
====================== test session starts ===================
platform darwin -- Python 3.14.4, pytest-9.0.3, pluggy-1.6.0
cachedir: .pytest_cache
rootdir: Python-Automation-Cookbook/ch15
collected 1 item
run-last-failure: rerun previous 1 failure (skipped 5 files)
tests/test_case.py::test_fail FAILED                                [100%]
============================ FAILURES ========================
____________________________ test_fail _______________________
```

```
    def test_fail():
>       assert 4 in LIST
E       assert 4 in [1, 2, 3]
tests/test_case.py:18: AssertionError
==================== short test summary info =================
FAILED tests/test_case.py::test_fail - assert 4 in [1, 2, 3]
================ 1 failed in 0.06s ===========
```

## How it works...

In *step 1*, the call to `pytest` is done with no arguments. This runs all the tests defined under the subdirectory.

Note that it displays how many tests it collects:

```
collected 18 items
```

*Step 2* shows how to get the list of tests collected, but without running them. This is done through the `the --collect-only` parameter. It presents them all but doesn't run them.

To run only certain tests, *step 3* shows how to generate a matching string that will limit the tests to run. Using `-k` allows matching by string, so all the tests that match the string time will be executed.

> **Note**
>
> The option `-v` makes the output verbose and displays a line per test instead of a line per test file.

Note how the total number of tests is still present. `pytest` collects them all, but then only runs the ones that match the `-k` parameter:

```
collected 18 items / 16 deselected / 2 selected
```

To limit the number of collected tests, a file path can be specified, as done in *step 4*, where the path of a specific file is added to the command. In this case, the number of collected tests is only the ones located in the file path:

```
$ uv run pytest -v -k time tests/test_requests.py
...
collected 2 items / 1 deselected / 1 selected
```

*Step 5* shows how to specify a single test, using the full file path and descriptor. This is easy to copy from the output when using the `-v` argument:

```
$ uv run pytest -v tests/test_requests_time.py::test_order_time
...
collected 1 item
```

Finally, in step 6, a different argument is used: `--lf`. This runs only the last failed tests:

```
$ uv run pytest -v --lf
...
collected 1 item
run-last-failure: rerun previous 1 failure (skipped 5 files)
```

If no test has failed in the last run, `--lf` will run all the tests.

## There's more...

Keep in mind that all these parameters can be combined. For example, `--collect-only` can be used with `-k` to check whether the selected tests are correct.

In the same way, multiple file paths and tests can be added. For example:

```
$ uv run pytest -v tests/test_external.py::test_int_division tests/
test_requests.py
========================== test session starts ==========================
platform darwin -- Python 3.14.4, pytest-9.0.3, pluggy-1.6.0
cachedir: .pytest_cache
rootdir: Python-Automation-Cookbook/ch15
collected 3 items
tests/test_external.py::test_int_division PASSED                   [ 33%]
tests/test_requests.py::test_order_pizza PASSED                    [ 66%]
tests/test_requests.py::test_order_pizza_timeout PASSED            [100%]
========================== 3 passed in 0.11s ==========================
```

Collecting tests, when the number of tests grows, can take a significant amount of time. When the number of tests is in the hundreds or thousands, collecting and filtering using `-k` can take so much time as to delay the execution of tests (by half a minute or more). This makes it important to know how to reduce the number of collected tests by specifying the files to collect tests from.

To stop the execution of tests when a failure is detected, use the parameter -x:

```
$ uv run pytest -v -x
========================= test session starts ==========================
platform darwin -- Python 3.14.4, pytest-9.0.3, pluggy-1.6.0
cachedir: .pytest_cache
rootdir: Python-Automation-Cookbook/ch15
collected 18 items
tests/test_case.py::test_one PASSED                                [  5%]
tests/test_case.py::test_two PASSED                                [ 11%]
tests/test_case.py::test_three PASSED                              [ 16%]
tests/test_fail FAILED                                             [ 22%]
=============================== FAILURES ===============================
______________________________ test_fail _______________________________
    def test_fail():
>       assert 4 in LIST
E       assert 4 in [1, 2, 3]
tests/test_case.py:18: AssertionError
======================= short test summary info ========================
FAILED tests/test_case.py::test_fail - assert 4 in [1, 2, 3]
!!!!!!!!!!!!!!!!!!!!!!! stopping after 1 failures !!!!!!!!!!!!!!!!!!!!!!!!!
===================== 1 failed, 3 passed in 0.26s ======================
```

When developing, it's common to iterate through a test or a small number of tests to fix them. In these situations, , --lf can greatly help to run the whole test suite at once, and then repeat with only the failing tests. As the code is fixed, tests that pass will be removed from the execution group, until finally the last test passes. Then, --lf will run all the tests again.

Tip

With small numbers of tests in a test suite, most of this advice won't be necessary, as tests will be very quick. As the number of tests increases, using these parameters becomes more important so as to not waste time executing tests that are not directly related to the specific part of the code being developed. Just remember to run the whole suite once at the end to ensure that your changes didn't have a disruptive effect on an unexpected part of the code. This is something that happens more times than developers would like!

GenAI tools that work by iterating through running tests and adjusting the code also benefit from shorter execution times.

## See also

- The *Writing and executing test case* recipe, earlier in this chapter, to learn the basics of how to define tests
- The *Testing external code* recipe, earlier in this chapter, to learn how to test code in other modules

# Understand the coverage of your tests

On top of the features that `pytest` have, it has a vibrant ecosystem of plugins that allows to expand its capabilities. One of them allows to check what is the coverage of our tests, understanding if there's some area of our code that it's not being exercised by our test cases and addressing gaps.

## Getting ready

As usual, we will use the `pytest` module, and add the plugin `pytest-cov`. We should install the modules by adding them to our `requirements.txt` file as follows:

```
$ echo "requests==2.33.1" >> requirements.txt
$ echo "responses==0.26.0" >> requirements.txt
$ echo "freezegun==1.5.5" >> requirements.txt
$ echo "pytest-cov==7.1.0" >> requirements.txt
$ uv pip install -r requirements.txt
```

We will use the test files introduced in the previous recipes of the chapter. You can download them from the GitHub repository, under the subdirectories `tests` and `external_code`:

```
├── external_code
│   ├── __init__.py
│   ├── code_fixtures.py
│   ├── code_requests.py
│   ├── dependencies.py
│   └── external.py
├── conftest.py
└── tests
    ├── test_case.py
    ├── test_dependencies.py
    ├── test_external.py
    ├── test_fixtures.py
```

```
├── test_requests.py
└── test_requests_time.py
```

## How to do it...

1. Run all test with the -cov argument. This will display the coverage as a table at the end of the test run.

```
$ uv run pytest --cov
======================== test session starts ========================
...
========================= tests coverage ==========================
_________ coverage: platform darwin, python 3.14.5-final-0 __________

Name                               Stmts   Miss  Cover
------------------------------------------------------
conftest.py                            0      0   100%
external_code/__init__.py              0      0   100%
external_code/code_fixtures.py        10      0   100%
external_code/code_requests.py        11      0   100%
external_code/dependencies.py         17      3    82%
external_code/external.py              2      0   100%
tests/test_case.py                     9      0   100%
tests/test_dependencies.py            21      0   100%
tests/test_external.py                 9      0   100%
tests/test_fixtures.py                30      0   100%
tests/test_requests.py                19      0   100%
tests/test_requests_time.py           13      0   100%
------------------------------------------------------
TOTAL                                141      3    98%
====================== short test summary info ======================
FAILED tests/test_case.py::test_fail - assert 4 in [1, 2, 3]
=================== 1 failed, 17 passed in 0.51s ====================
```

2. Generate a more detailed HTML report:

```
$ uv run pytest --cov --cov-report=html
======================== test session starts ========================
...
========================= tests coverage ==========================
_________ coverage: platform darwin, python 3.14.5-final-0 __________
```

```
Coverage HTML written to dir htmlcov
===================== short test summary info ======================
FAILED tests/test_case.py::test_fail - assert 4 in [1, 2, 3]
================== 1 failed, 17 passed in 0.50s ===================
```

3. Check the generated HTML, which is created locally in the dir `htmlcov/index.html` and open it in your browser.

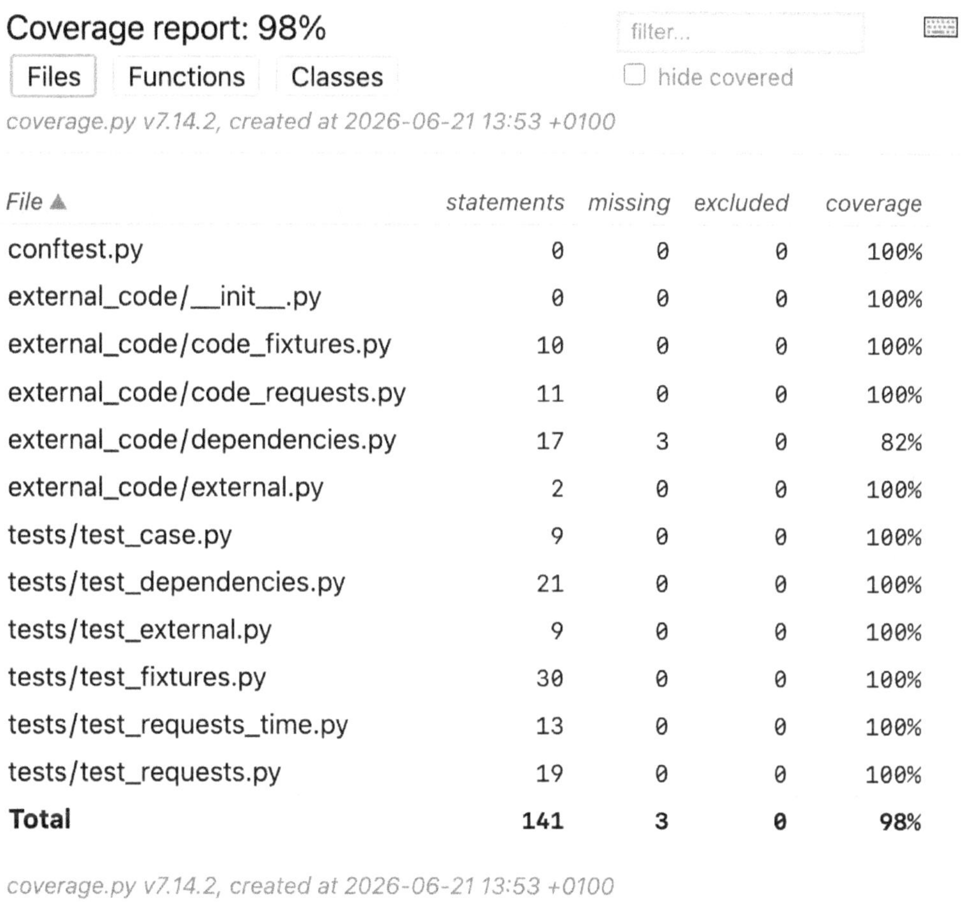

Coverage report: 98%

filter...

Files | Functions | Classes

hide covered

coverage.py v7.14.2, created at 2026-06-21 13:53 +0100

| File ▲ | statements | missing | excluded | coverage |
|---|---|---|---|---|
| conftest.py | 0 | 0 | 0 | 100% |
| external_code/__init__.py | 0 | 0 | 0 | 100% |
| external_code/code_fixtures.py | 10 | 0 | 0 | 100% |
| external_code/code_requests.py | 11 | 0 | 0 | 100% |
| external_code/dependencies.py | 17 | 3 | 0 | 82% |
| external_code/external.py | 2 | 0 | 0 | 100% |
| tests/test_case.py | 9 | 0 | 0 | 100% |
| tests/test_dependencies.py | 21 | 0 | 0 | 100% |
| tests/test_external.py | 9 | 0 | 0 | 100% |
| tests/test_fixtures.py | 30 | 0 | 0 | 100% |
| tests/test_requests_time.py | 13 | 0 | 0 | 100% |
| tests/test_requests.py | 19 | 0 | 0 | 100% |
| **Total** | **141** | **3** | **0** | **98%** |

coverage.py v7.14.2, created at 2026-06-21 13:53 +0100

*Figure 15.1: Full coverage report*

4. Go to the `external_code/dependencies.py` report to see the missing lines:

Coverage for **external_code/dependencies.py**: 82%

17 statements | 14 run | 3 missing | 0 excluded

« prev ^ index » next coverage.py v7.14.2, created at 2026-06-21 13:53 +0100

```python
PI = 3.14159


def rectangle(sideA, sideB):
    return sideA * sideB


def circle(radius):
    return 2 * PI * radius


def calculate_area(shape, sizeA, sizeB=0):
    if sizeA <= 0:
        raise ValueError('sizeA needs to be positive')

    if sizeB < 0:
        raise ValueError('sizeB needs to be positive')

    if shape == 'SQUARE':
        return rectangle(sizeA, sizeA)

    if shape == 'RECTANGLE':
        return rectangle(sizeA, sizeB)

    if shape == 'CIRCLE':
        return circle(sizeA)

    raise Exception(f'Shape {shape} not defined')
```

*Figure 15.2: Detailed report for dependencies.py file*

## How it works...

In *step 1*, we call the coverage plugin in pytest. This runs all the tests defined under the subdirectory and produces the final short report, which presents a view of all the tests and the lines that are executed in our test run.

Most of the files are running completely, as we produce 100% of the lines of code.

The only one that is not is `external_code/dependencies.py`. To get into the details on what are the missing lines, we produce a detailed HTML report in *step 2*. This allows us to better visualize the execution in our tests.

There we can see what the gaps in our tests are, identified with red blocks in the HTML report. We are not checking that the input sizes may be negative and should produce an error! We are also not testing the case where a shape is not defined.

For that, we can create new tests that check all these eventualities.

```
def test_negative_dimensionA():
    with pytest.raises(ValueError):
        calculate_area('RECTANGLE', -1, 1)


def test_negative_dimensionB():
    with pytest.raises(ValueError):
        calculate_area('RECTANGLE', 1, -1)


def test_unkown_shape():
    with pytest.raises(Exception):
        calculate_area('TRIANGLE', 1, 1)
```

If we add them to `test_dependencies.py` and run again, we will see that the coverage is now 100%!

```
$ uv run pytest tests/test_dependencies.py --cov
======================= test session starts =======================
…
========================= tests coverage ==========================
_________ coverage: platform darwin, python 3.14.5-final-0 __________

Name                              Stmts   Miss  Cover
-----------------------------------------------------
conftest.py                           0      0   100%
external_code/__init__.py             0      0   100%
external_code/dependencies.py        17      0   100%
tests/test_dependencies.py           31      0   100%
-----------------------------------------------------
```

```
TOTAL                                   48      0   100%
========================= 8 passed in 0.07s =========================
```

Having a good coverage without big gaps is a great way of ensuring that your code is not missing any obvious checks, and the code is enabled, and therefore behaving appropriately, but it's not the solution for everything.

While coverage shows that a particular line of code is exercised, the different combinations of the paths code can take may not be (what is known as code branches). And, even worse, there could be situations that are not covered in your tests, like an unexpected error raised by a library that you are mocking for your tests. A code with 100% coverage in the tests doesn't guarantee that it's bug-free.

Tip

In general, in projects it is also not good to try to set the bar to 100% coverage. This creates bad incentives to structure code more to pass the tests than to fulfill the function. It also requires significant investment, which may not be worth it. While very low coverage is not good, do not obsess with having a perfect percentage everywhere.

## There's more...

Instead of adding three different tests, we can structure the tests to use parameters, using a `pytest` capability to parametrize tests. In essence, these three tests are the same one, changing the shape, two dimensions, and the expected error.

Instead of defining three tests, you can define one to be executed with different parameters like this.

```
import pytest

@pytest.mark.parametrize(
    "shape,dimensionA,dimensionB,exc",
    [
        ('RECTANGLE', -1, 1, ValueError),
        ('RECTANGLE', 1, -1, ValueError),
        ('TRIANGLE', 1, 1, Exception),
    ],
)
def test_error_conditions(shape, dimensionA, dimensionB, exc):
```

```
    with pytest.raises(exc):
        calculate_area(shape, dimensionA, dimensionB)
```

Note the first parameter of the parametrization needs to be the same parameter that the test will accept. Then we have a list with each of the individual executions for all parameters.

When running it, it will treat them as different tests, showing the different parameters, like this.

```
$ uv run pytest tests/test_dependencies.py -v
======================= test session starts ========================
platform darwin -- Python 3.14.5, pytest-9.0.3, pluggy-1.6.0 --
cachedir: .pytest_cache
rootdir: Python-Automation-Cookbook /ch15
plugins: cov-7.1.0
collected 8 items

tests/test_dependencies.py::test_square PASSED                  [ 12%]
tests/test_dependencies.py::test_rectangle PASSED               [ 25%]
tests/test_dependencies.py::test_circle_with_proper_pi PASSED [ 37%]
tests/test_dependencies.py::test_circle_with_mocked_pi PASSED [ 50%]
tests/test_dependencies.py::test_circle_with_mocked_rectangle PASSED [ 62%]
tests/test_dependencies.py::test_error_conditions[RECTANGLE--1-1-ValueError]
PASSED [ 75%]
tests/test_dependencies.py::test_error_conditions[RECTANGLE-1--1-ValueError]
PASSED [ 87%]
tests/test_dependencies.py::test_error_conditions[TRIANGLE-1-1-Exception] PASSED
[100%]

========================= 8 passed in 0.04s =========================
```

Parametrizing tests is a great way to cover more cases while keeping the definition of tests small and understandable.

Read more about the possibilities of parametrizing in the `pytest` configuration at `https://docs.pytest.org/en/7.1.x/example/parametrize.html`.

## See also

- The *Writing and executing test case* recipe, earlier in this chapter, to learn the basics of how to define tests
- The *Testing external code* recipe, earlier in this chapter, to learn how to test code in other modules

# Get this book's PDF version and more

# 16

# Debugging Techniques

Writing code is not easy. Actually, it is very hard. Even the best programmer in the world can't foresee every possible alternative and flow of the code.

This means that executing our code will always produce surprises and unexpected behaviors. Some will be very evident, while others will be very subtle, but the ability to identify and remove these defects in the code is critical to building solid software.

These defects in software are known as **bugs**, and therefore removing them is called **debugging**.

Inspecting the code just by reading it and reasoning about its execution image will never be enough to cover all the possible outcomes on non-trivial code. That's true even with the more advanced AI models. There are always surprises, complex code is difficult to follow in all possible combinations and also there are likely external elements, like a call to an external service, that are out of your control. That's why the ability to debug by observing the actual flow of the code is so important.

> **Note**
>
> Everyone, and I mean *EVERYONE*, introduces bugs in the code, only to be surprised by them later. Some people have described debugging as *being the detective in a crime movie where you are also the murderer*.
>
> This is even true with GenAI tools! AI models will both introduce bugs in their code and not detect bugs when reviewing. Don't blindly trust them.

Any debugging process roughly follows this path:

1. You realize there's a problem

2. You understand what the correct behavior should be
3. You discover why the current code produces the bug
4. You change the code to produce the proper result

95% of the time, everything but *step 3* is straightforward. *Step 3* is the bulk of the debugging process.

Realizing the *why* of a bug, at its core, follows a scientific methodology:

1. Measure and observe what the code is doing
2. Produce a hypothesis on why that is
3. Validate or disprove the hypothesis, through either a specifically designed experiment (for example, a test) or the examination of the execution of a test (which can be considered a natural experiment)
4. Use the resulting information to fix the bug or iterate the process

Debugging is a *skill*, and as such, it will improve over time. Practice plays an important role in developing intuition on what paths look promising to identify an error. Even if you use GenAI to help you in the process, there are always strategies that you can use to help the process:

- **Divide and conquer**: Isolate small parts of the code so that it is possible to understand the code. Simplify the problem as much as possible.

  > **Tip**
  >
  > There's a format of this method called the **Wolf fence algorithm**, described by Edward J. Gauss in 1982.
  >
  > *"There's one wolf in Alaska; how do you find it? First, build a fence down the middle of the state, wait for the wolf to howl, and determine which side of the fence it is on. Repeat this process on that side only, until you get to the point where you can see the wolf."*

- **Move backward from the error**: If there's a clear error at a specific point, the bug is likely located in the surroundings. Move progressively backward from the error, following the track until the source of the error is found.
- **You can assume anything you want, as long as you prove your assumption is true**: Code is very complex to keep in your head all at once. You need to validate small assumptions that, when combined, will provide solid ground to move forward with detecting and fixing the problem. Make small experiments that allow you to rule out parts of the code that work and focus on untested ones.

Tip

Or, in the words of Sherlock Holmes:

Once you eliminate the impossible, whatever remains, no matter how improbable, must be the truth.

Remember to prove any assumption you make. Avoid unproven assumptions, as they'll distract you from the location of the bug. It's very easy to think that the error happens in one part of the code and look at another.

Note

All of this may sound a bit scary, but most bugs are pretty evident. Maybe a typo, or a piece of code not ready for a particular value. GenAI will help greatly with many problems given the right description.

Try to keep things simple. Simple code is easier to analyze and debug.

Check out *Chapter 15, Automatic Testing Routines*, to learn how to work with tests. Tests are excellent tools to help you debug, find problems, and add validation points. Debugging the code in a defined test allows you to create a small environment where you can focus on the expected inputs and outputs and search for bugs.

In this chapter, we will look at several tools and techniques for debugging and apply them specifically to Python scripts. The scripts will contain some bugs that we will fix as part of the recipe.

Tip

In this chapter, we will try to develop your skills in debugging and will go over details that can be easily detected by a GenAI tool. The objective here is not to present the most complicated bugs, but rather to present the techniques available to you and the mindset to use.

GenAI is fantastic at helping with the process, but being able to discover how your program is working is a critical tool for long-term success. Some defects in software are about what is the right process, which can be open to interpretation and require a human decision.

In this chapter we're going to cover the following main topics:

- Learning Python interpreter basics
- Debugging through logging
- Debugging with breakpoints
- Improving your debugging skills

# Technical requirements

You can check the code presented in the chapter at the GitHub URL `https://github.com/PacktPublishing/Python-Automation-Cookbook-Third-Edition/tree/main/ch16`.

# Learning Python interpreter basics

In this recipe, we'll cover some of Python's built-in capabilities to examine code, investigate what's going on, and detect when things are not behaving properly.

> **Tip**
>
> We can also verify when things are working as expected. Remember that being able to rule out part of the code as the source of a bug is incredibly important.

While debugging, we typically need to analyze unknown elements and objects that come from an external module or service. Code in Python is highly discoverable at any point in its execution. This ability to examine the types and properties of the code while it is being executed is called *introspection*.

Everything in this recipe is included by default in Python's interpreter.

## How to do it...

1. Import `pprint`:

```
>>> from pprint import pprint
```

2. Create a new dictionary called `dictionary`:

```
>>> dictionary = {'example': 1}
```

3. Display `globals` in this environment:

```
>>> globals()
{...'pprint': <function pprint at 0x10c52c880>,
...'dictionary': {'example': 1}}
```

4. Print the `globals` dictionary in a readable format with `pprint`:

```
>>> pprint(globals())
{'__builtins__': <module 'builtins' (built-in)>,
 '__doc__': None,
 '__loader__': <class '_frozen_importlib.BuiltinImporter'>,
 '__name__': '__main__',
 '__package__': None,
 '__spec__': None,
 'dictionary': {'example': 1},
 'pprint': <function pprint at 0x10c52c880>}
```

5. Display all of the attributes of `dictionary`:

```
>>> dir(dictionary)
['__class__', '__class_getitem__', '__contains__', '__delattr__',
'__delitem__', '__dir__', '__doc__', '__eq__', '__format__', '__ge__',
'__getattribute__', '__getitem__', '__getstate__', '__gt__', '__hash__',
'__init__', '__init_subclass__', '__ior__', '__iter__', '__le__',
'__len__', '__lt__', '__ne__', '__new__', '__or__', '__reduce__',
'__reduce_ex__', '__repr__', '__reversed__', '__ror__', '__setattr__',
'__setitem__', '__sizeof__', '__str__', '__subclasshook__', 'clear',
'copy', 'fromkeys', 'get', 'items', 'keys', 'pop', 'popitem', 'setdefault',
'update', 'values']
```

6. Show the help for the `dictionary` object:

```
>>> help(dictionary)
Help on dict object:

class dict(object)
 |  dict() -> new empty dictionary
 |  dict(mapping) -> new dictionary initialized from a mapping object's
```

```
    |      (key, value) pairs
...
```

## How it works...

After importing `pprint` (pretty print) in *step 1*, we create a new dictionary to work in as shown in *step 2*.

*Step 3* shows how the `global` namespace contains, among other things, the defined `dictionary` and the module. `globals()` displays all imported modules and other global variables.

> **Note**
>
> There's an equivalent `locals()` for local namespaces.

`pprint` helps display the `globals` in a more readable format in *step 4*, adding more space and separating the elements by line.

*Step 5* shows how to use `dir()` to obtain all the names of the attributes of a Python object. Note that this includes all the double underscore values, such as `__len__`.

The use of the built-in `help()` function will display relevant information for objects.

## There's more...

dir(), in particular, is extremely useful for inspecting unknown objects, modules, or classes. If you need to filter out the default attributes and clarify the output, you can filter the output using a list comprehension:

```
>>> [att for att in dir(dictionary) if not att.startswith('__')]
['clear', 'copy', 'fromkeys', 'get', 'items', 'keys', 'pop', 'popitem',
'setdefault', 'update', 'values']
```

In the same way, you can do this if you're searching for a particular method (such as something that starts with `set`).

`help()` will display the `docstring` of a function or class. `docstring` is the string defined just after the definition to document the function or class:

```
>>> def something():
...     '''
...     This is help for something
```

```
...     '''
...     pass
...
>>> help(something)
Help on function something in module __main__:
something()
    This is help for something
```

Notice how the "This is help for something" string is displayed just after the definition of the function.

> **Tip**
>
> docstring is normally enclosed in triple quotes to allow writing strings with multiple lines. Python will treat everything inside triple quotes as a big string, even if there are newlines. You can use either ' (single quote) or " (double quote) characters, as long as you use three of them. You can find more information about docstrings at https://www.python.org/dev/peps/pep-0257/.

The documentation for the built-in functions can be found at https://docs.python.org/3/library/functions.html#built-in-functions, while the full documentation for pprint can be found at https://docs.python.org/3/library/pprint.html.

## See also

- The *Improving your debugging skills* recipe, later in this chapter, to pick up more debugging tools
- The *Debugging through logging* recipe, next in this chapter, teaches how to debug elements by setting traces

# Debugging through logging

Debugging is, after all, detecting what's going on inside our program and finding out what unexpected or incorrect effects may be happening. A simple, yet very effective, approach is to output variables and other information at strategic parts of your code to allow the programmer to follow the flow of the program.

The simplest form of this approach is called **print debugging**. This technique consists of inserting print statements at certain points to print the value of variables or points while debugging.

But taking this technique a little further and combining it with the logging techniques presented in *Chapter 2, Automating Tasks Made Easy*, allows us to create a trace of the execution of the program. This tracing information can be really useful when detecting issues in a running program. Logs are also typically displayed when running tests using a test framework.

> **Note**
>
> `pytest`, introduced in *Chapter 15, Automatic Testing Routines*, automatically shows logs of failed tests. Other test frameworks may need to be configured. Logging is presented in this book in *Chapter 2, Automating Tasks Made Easy*.

## Getting ready

Download the `debug_logging.py` file from GitHub: `https://github.com/PacktPublishing/Python-Automation-Cookbook-Third-Edition/blob/main/ch16/debug_logging.py`.

This contains an implementation of the bubble sort algorithm(`https://www.studytonight.com/data-structures/bubble-sort`), which is one of the simplest ways to sort a list of elements. It iterates several times over the list, and within each iteration, two adjacent values are checked and interchanged so the bigger one comes after the smaller. This makes the bigger values ascend like bubbles in the list.

> **Tip**
>
> Bubble sort is a simple but naive way of implementing a sort, and there are better alternatives. Unless you have an extremely good reason not to, rely on the standard `.sort` method in lists.

When run, it checks the following list to verify that the sort works correctly:

```
assert [1, 2, 3, 4, 7, 10] == bubble_sort([3, 7, 10, 2, 4, 1])
```

We have a bug in this implementation, so we can fix it as part of the recipe!

> **Tip**
>
> You can "cheat" and ask a GenAI tool to read the code and explain what the problem is. But no spoilers here! Keep reading!

## How to do it...

1. Run the `debug_logging.py` script and check whether it fails:

```
$ uv run debug_logging.py
INFO:Sorting the list: [3, 7, 10, 2, 4, 1]
INFO:Sorted list:      [2, 3, 4, 7, 10, 1]
Traceback (most recent call last):
  File "debug_logging.py", line 17, in <module>
    assert [1, 2, 3, 4, 7, 10] == bubble_sort([3, 7, 10, 2, 4, 1])
AssertionError
```

2. Enable debug logging by changing the second line of the `debug_logging.py` script:

```
logging.basicConfig(format='%(levelname)s:%(message)s', level=logging.INFO)
```

Change the preceding line to the following one:

```
logging.basicConfig(format='%(levelname)s:%(message)s',
level=logging.DEBUG)
```

Note the different level.

3. Run the script again, with more information inside:

```
$ uv run debug_logging.py
INFO:Sorting the list: [3, 7, 10, 2, 4, 1]
DEBUG:alist: [3, 7, 10, 2, 4, 1]
DEBUG:alist: [3, 7, 10, 2, 4, 1]
DEBUG:alist: [3, 7, 2, 10, 4, 1]
DEBUG:alist: [3, 7, 2, 4, 10, 1]
DEBUG:alist: [3, 7, 2, 4, 10, 1]
DEBUG:alist: [3, 2, 7, 4, 10, 1]
DEBUG:alist: [3, 2, 4, 7, 10, 1]
DEBUG:alist: [2, 3, 4, 7, 10, 1]
DEBUG:alist: [2, 3, 4, 7, 10, 1]
DEBUG:alist: [2, 3, 4, 7, 10, 1]
INFO:Sorted list : [2, 3, 4, 7, 10, 1]
Traceback (most recent call last):
  File "debug_logging.py", line 17, in <module>
```

```
    assert [1, 2, 3, 4, 7, 10] == bubble_sort([3, 7, 10, 2, 4, 1])
AssertionError
```

4. After analyzing the output, we realize that the last element of the list is not sorted. We analyze the code and discover an off-by-one error in line 7. Do you see it? Let's fix it by changing the following line:

   ```
   for passnum in reversed(range(len(alist) - 1)):
   ```

   Change the preceding line to the following one:

   ```
   for passnum in reversed(range(len(alist))):
   ```

   Notice the removal of the `-1` operation.

Run it again and you will see that it works as expected. The debug logs are not displayed here:

```
$ uv run debug_logging.py
INFO:Sorting the list: [3, 7, 10, 2, 4, 1]
...
INFO:Sorted list     : [1, 2, 3, 4, 7, 10]
```

## How it works...

*Step 1* presents the script and shows that the code is faulty, as it's not sorting the list properly.

The script already has some logs to show the start and end result, as well as some debug logs that show each intermediate step. In *step 2*, we activate the display of the `DEBUG` logs, as in *step 1* only the `INFO` ones were shown.

> **Note**
>
> Note that the logs are displayed by default in the standard error output. This is displayed by default in the terminal. If you need to direct the logs somewhere else, such as a file, you can configure a different handler. See the logging configuration in Python for more details: `https://docs.python.org/3/howto/logging.html`.

*Step 3* runs the script again, this time displaying extra information, showing that the last element in the list is not sorted.

The bug is an off-by-one error, a very common kind of error, as it should iterate through the whole size of the list. This is fixed in *step 4*.

Note

Check the code to understand why there's an error. The whole list should be compared, but we made the mistake of reducing the size by one.

If necessary, you can ask a GenAI tool to explain the problem and ask questions. GenAI is also a good learning tool.

*Step 5* shows that the fixed script runs correctly.

## There's more...

In this recipe, we have strategically located the debug logs beforehand, but that may not be the case in a real-life debugging exercise. You may need to add more or change the location as part of the bug investigation.

The biggest advantage of this technique is that we're able to see the flow of the program, being able to inspect the output of one block of the code execution to the next and make sense of the flow. The disadvantage is that we can end up with a wall of text that doesn't provide specific information about our problem. You need to find a balance between too much and too little information.

Be verbose if you have to, but to reduce clutter, try to avoid long and confusing logs. Keep the text as short and as descriptive as possible. Keep each log concise, as you can always create more logs if you have to.

Remember to turn down the logging level after fixing the bug. You may need to delete some logs afterward as they won't be useful in the long term.

Tip

The quick and dirty version of this technique is to add print statements instead of debug logs. While some people are resistant to this, it is a valuable technique to use for debugging purposes. But remember to clean them up when you're done.

All the introspection tools are available while generating logs, so you can create logs that display, for example, all the results of a call to a `dir(object)` object:

```
logging.debug(f'object {dir(object)}')
```

Anything that can be displayed as a string can be presented in a log.

## See also

- The *Learning Python interpreter basics* recipe, earlier in this chapter, to learn the basics of Python introspection tools
- The *Improving your debugging skills* recipe, later in this chapter, shows a whole example of debugging covering different problems

# Debugging with breakpoints

Python has a built-in debugger called `pdb`. Stopping the execution of the code at any point is possible by setting a breakpoint. A breakpoint will stop the execution and jump into command-line mode. From the command line, the current status can be analyzed using any introspection available. Given that Python is interpreted, any new code can be executed from this stage. This is very flexible and allows you to create flexible breakpoints and change the current state to analyze the behavior of the program.

Let's see how to do it.

## Getting ready

Download the `debug_algorithm.py` script, available from GitHub: `https://github.com/PacktPublishing/Python-Automation-Cookbook-Third-Edition/blob/main/ch16/debug_algorithm.py`.

In the next section, we will analyze the execution of the code in detail. The code checks whether numbers fulfill certain criteria:

```
def valid(candidate):
    if candidate <= 1:
        return False
    lower = candidate - 1
    while lower > 1:
        if candidate / lower == candidate // lower:
            return False
        lower -= 1
    return True
assert not valid(1)
assert valid(3)
assert not valid(15)
assert not valid(18)
assert not valid(50)
assert valid(53)
```

It is possible that you recognize (or ask a GenAI tool) what the code is doing, but bear with me so that we can analyze it interactively.

## How to do it...

1. Run the code to see that all the assertions are valid:

```
$ uv run debug_algorithm.py
```

2. Add `breakpoint()`, after the while statement, just before line 7, resulting in the following:

```
    while lower > 1:
        breakpoint()
        if candidate / lower == candidate // lower:
```

3. Execute the code again, and see that it stops at the `breakpoint`, entering into the interactive `Pdb` mode:

```
$ uv run debug_algorithm.py
> .../debug_algorithm.py(7)valid()
-> breakpoint()
(Pdb)
```

4. Continue to the next instruction with `n`

```
(Pdb) n
> .../debug_algorithm.py(8)valid()
-> if candidate / lower == candidate // lower:
```

5. Check the value of the candidate and the two operations. This line is checking whether dividing candidate by lower is an integer (float and integer division are the same):

```
(Pdb) candidate
3
(Pdb) candidate / lower
1.5
(Pdb) candidate // lower
1
```

6. Check that it ends the `while` loop and returns `True`:

```
(Pdb) n
> ...debug_algorithm.py(10)valid()
-> lower -= 1
(Pdb) n
> ...debug_algorithm.py(6)valid()
-> while lower > 1:
(Pdb) n
> ...debug_algorithm.py(12)valid()
-> return True
(Pdb) n
--Return--
> ...debug_algorithm.py(12)valid()->True
-> return True
```

7. Continue the execution until another breakpoint is found with `c`. Note that this is the next call to `valid()`, which has `15` as an input:

```
(Pdb) c
> ...debug_algorithm.py(7)valid()
-> breakpoint()
> ...debug_algorithm.py(8)valid()
-> if candidate / lower == candidate // lower:
(Pdb) candidate
15
(Pdb) lower
14
```

8. Continue running and inspecting the numbers until what the `valid` function is doing makes sense. Are you able to find out what the code does? (If you can't, don't worry and check the next section.) When you're done, exit with `q` and confirm. This stops the execution:

```
(Pdb) q
Quitting pdb will kill the process. Quit anyway? [y/n] y
```

## How it works...

The code is, as you probably know already, checking whether a number is a prime number. It tries to divide the number by all integers lower than it. If at any point the number is exactly divisible by any of them, it returns `False`, because it's not a prime number.

This code has two problems.

First of all, it contains another bug that doesn't show up in our investigation. It will produce wrong results for big numbers, as the float division of big numbers will lose precision.

For example, checking a large enough prime will show the problem.

```
>>> candidate = 47769131098520414182480566228824883l9
>>> lower = candidate - 1
>>> candidate / lower
1.0
```

That 1.0 should be greater than 1 (as a number is divided by a slightly smaller number), but it is exactly 1, which will make the code discard it.

> **Note**
>
> 4776913109852041418248056622882488319 is a known prime; you can check at `https://oeis.org/A050918`.

That problem can be fixed by using a modulo operation (%), providing precision on divisibility. A `numberA % numberB` equal to zero means that `numberA` is divisible by `numberB`.

```
def valid(candidate):
    if candidate <= 1:
        return False

    lower = candidate - 1
    while lower > 1:
        if candidate % lower == 0:
            return False
        lower -= 1

    return True
```

But secondly, it is also an extremely inefficient way of checking for a prime number, as it will take a very long time to deal with large numbers. It is fast enough for our teaching purposes, but it will take a long time to run on 4776913109852041418248056622882488319, if we ever need to.

> **Tip**
>
> If you're interested in finding primes, you can take a look at math packages such as SymPy (`https://docs.sympy.org/latest/modules/ntheory.html?highlight=prime#sympy.ntheory.primetest.isprime`).

After checking the general execution in *step 1*, in *step 2*, we introduced a `breakpoint` in the code.

When you execute the code in *step 3*, it will stop at the breakpoint position and enter interactive mode.

In the interactive mode, we can inspect the values of any variable, as well as perform any kind of operation. As demonstrated in *step 4*, sometimes, a line of code can be better analyzed by reproducing its parts.

The code can be inspected, and regular operations can be executed in the command line. The next line of code can be executed by calling `n(next)`, as implemented in *step 5* several times, to see the flow of the code.

*Step 6* shows how to resume the execution with the `c(continue)` command, in order to stop in the next breakpoint. All these operations can be iterated to see the flow and values, and to understand what the code is doing at any point.

The execution can be stopped with `q(quit)`, as demonstrated in *step 7*.

## There's more...

To see all the available operations, you can call `h(help)` at any point.

You can check the surrounding code at any point using the `l(list)` command. For example, in *step 4*:

```
(Pdb) l
  2         if candidate <= 1:
  3             return False
  4
  5         lower = candidate - 1
  6         while lower > 1:
```

```
  ->          breakpoint()
            if candidate / lower == candidate // lower:
                return False
            lower -= 1

        return True
```

The other two main debugger commands are `s(step)`, which will execute the next step, including entering a new call (as in *stepping into*), and `r(return)`, which will continue the execution of the current function until it executes a `return` statement and then stops. Note that at the end of any Python function, there's an implicit `return None`.

> **Tip**
>
> You can set up (and disable) more breakpoints using the `pdb` command `b(break)`. You need to specify the file and line for the `breakpoint`, but it's typically more straightforward and less error-prone to just change the code and run it again.

You can overwrite variables as well as read them. Or create new variables. Or make extra calls. Or anything else you can imagine. The full power of the Python interpreter is at your service! Use it to check how something works or verify whether something is happening.

> **Tip**
>
> Avoid creating variables with names that are reserved for the debugger, such as calling a list `l`. It will make things confusing and interfere with `pdb` commands, sometimes in non-obvious ways.

You can read more about the new breakpoint call in the official PEP at `https://www.python.org/dev/peps/pep-0553/`.

The full `pdb` documentation can be found here: `https://docs.python.org/3/library/pdb.html`. It includes all the debug commands.

> **Note**
>
> Remember to remove any breakpoints once debugging is done, especially when committing to a version control system such as Git.

## See also

- The *Learning Python interpreter basics* recipe, earlier in this chapter, to learn the basics of Python introspection tools
- The *Improving your debugging skills* recipe, next in this chapter, to see an example of debugging covering different problems

# Improving your debugging skills

In this recipe, we will analyze and fix some bugs using a small script that replicates a call to an external service. We will show different techniques to improve your debugging skills.

The script will send some personal names to an internet server (`httpbin.org`, a test site) to get them back, simulating their retrieval from an external server. It will then split them into first and last names and prepare them to be sorted by surname. Finally, it will sort them.

> Note
>
> We used this test site previously in the Interacting with forms recipe, *Chapter 3, Building Your First Web Scraping Application*. Note that the URL `https://httpbin.org/forms/post` renders the form but internally calls the URL `https://httpbin.org/post` to send the information. We only need to use the second URL for this recipe.

The script contains several bugs that we will detect and fix.

## Getting ready

For this recipe, we will use the requests and parse modules and include them in our virtual environment:

```
$ echo "requests==2.34.2" >> requirements.txt
$ echo "parse==1.22.0" >> requirements.txt
$ uv pip install -r requirements.txt
```

The `debug_skills.py` script is available from GitHub: `https://github.com/PacktPublishing/Python-Automation-Cookbook-Third-Edition/blob/main/ch16/debug_skills.py`. Note that it contains bugs that we will fix as part of this recipe.

## How to do it...

1. Run the script, which will generate an error:

```
$ uv run debug_skills.py
Traceback (most recent call last):
 File "debug_skills.py", line 26, in <module>
 raise Exception(f'Error accessing server: {result}')
Exception: Error accessing server: <Response [405]>
```

2. Analyze the status code. We get **405**, which means that the method we sent is not allowed. We inspect the code and realize that for the request on line 24, we used GET when we should have used POST (as described in the URL). Replace the code with the following:

```
# ERROR Step 2. Using .get when it should be .post
# (old) result = requests.get('http://httpbin.org/post', json=data)
result = requests.post('http://httpbin.org/post', json=data)
```

   We keep the old buggy code commented with (old) for clarity about the changes that we made.

3. Run the code again, which will produce a different error:

```
$ uv run debug_skills.py
Traceback (most recent call last):
  File "debug_skills.py", line 34, in <module>
    first_name, last_name = full_name.split()
ValueError: too many values to unpack (expected 2)
```

4. Insert a breakpoint at line 33, one preceding the error. Run it again and enter debugging mode:

```
$ uv run debug_skills.py
..debug_skills.py(34)<module>()
-> breakpoint()
(Pdb) n
..debug_skills.py(35)<module>()
-> first_name, last_name = full_name.split()
(Pdb) n
> ...debug_skills.py(36)<module>()
```

```
-> ready_name = f'{last_name}, {first_name}'
(Pdb) c
> ...debug_skills.py(34)<module>()
-> breakpoint()
```

Running n does not produce an error, meaning that it's not the first value. After a few runs on c, we realize that this is not the correct approach, as we don't know what input is the one generating the error.

5. Instead, wrap the line with a `try...except` block and produce a `breakpoint` at that point:

```
try:
    first_name, last_name = full_name.split()
except:
    breakpoint()
```

6. We run the code again. This time, the code stops at the moment the data produces an error:

```
$ uv run debug_skills.py
> ...debug_skills.py(37)<module>()
-> breakpoint()
(Pdb) n
> ...debug_skills.py(38)<module>()
-> ready_name = f'{last_name}, {first_name}'
(Pdb) full_name
'John Paul Smith'
```

7. The cause is now clear; line 35 only allows us to split two words, but raises an error if a middle name is added. After some testing, we settle on this line to fix it:

```
# ERROR Step 6 split only two words. Some names have middle names
# (old) first_name, last_name = full_name.split()
first_name, last_name = full_name.rsplit(maxsplit=1)
```

8. We run the script again. Be sure to remove breakpoint and the `try..except` block. This time, it generates a list of names! And they are sorted alphabetically by surname. However, a few of the names look incorrect:

```
$ uv run debug_skills.py
['Berg, Keagan', 'Cordova, Mai', 'Craig, Michael', 'Garc\\u00eda, Roc\
\u00edo', 'Mccabe, Fathima', "O'Carroll, S\\u00e9amus", 'Pate, Poppy-Mae',
'Rennie, Vivienne', 'Smith, John Paul', 'Smyth, John', 'Sullivan, Roman']
```

Who's called `O'Carroll, S\\u00e9amus`?

9. To analyze this particular case but skip the rest, we must create an if condition to break only for that name in line 33. Notice the in to avoid having to be totally correct:

```
full_name = parse.search('"custname": "{name}"', raw_result)['name']
if "O'Carroll" in full_name:
    breakpoint()
```

10. Run the script once more. The breakpoint stops at the proper moment:

```
$ uv run debug_skills.py
> debug_skills.py(37)<module>()
-> breakpoint()
(Pdb) n
> debug_skills.py(38)<module>()
-> first_name, last_name = full_name.rsplit(maxsplit=1)
(Pdb) full_name
"S\\u00e9amus O'Carroll"
```

11. Move upward in the code and check the different variables:

```
(Pdb) full_name
"S\\u00e9amus O'Carroll"
(Pdb) raw_result
'{"custname": "S\\u00e9amus O\'Carroll"}'
(Pdb) result.json()
{'args': {}, 'data': '{"custname": "S\\u00e9amus O\'Carroll"}', 'files':
{}, 'form': {}, 'headers': {'Accept': '*/*', 'Accept-Encoding': 'gzip,
deflate', 'Connection': 'close', 'Content-Length': '37', 'Content-Type':
'application/json', 'Host': 'httpbin.org', 'User-Agent': 'python-requests/
```

```
2.34.2'}, 'json': {'custname': "Séamus O'Carroll"}, 'origin': 'X.X.X.X',
'url': 'http://httpbin.org/post'}
```

12. In the `result.json()` dictionary, there's actually a different field that seems to be rendering the name properly, which is called `'json'`. Let's look at it in detail; we can see that it's a dictionary:

```
(Pdb) result.json()['json']
{'custname': "Séamus O'Carroll"}
(Pdb) type(result.json()['json'])
<class 'dict'>
```

13. Now, we need to change the code. Instead of parsing the raw value in '`data`', use the '`json`' field directly from the result. This simplifies the code, which is great!

```
# ERROR Step 11. Obtain the value from a raw value. Use
# the decoded JSON instead
# raw_result = result.json()['data']
# Extract the name from the result
# full_name = parse.search('"custname": "{name}"', raw_result)['name']
raw_result = result.json()['json']
full_name = raw_result['custname']
```

14. Run the code again. Remember to remove the `breakpoint`:

```
$ uv run  debug_skills.py
['Berg, Keagan', 'Cordova, Mai', 'Craig, Michael', 'García, Rocío',
'Mccabe, Fathima', "O'Carroll, Séamus", 'Pate, Poppy-Mae', 'Rennie,
Vivienne', 'Smith, John Paul', 'Smyth, John', 'Sullivan, Roman']
```

This time, it's all correct! You have successfully debugged the program!

## How it works...

The structure of this recipe is divided into three different problems. Let's analyze it in small blocks:

1. First error—Wrong call to the external service
   After showing the first error in *step 1*, we read the resulting error with care, noting that the server is returning a 405 status code.

This corresponds to a method not allowed error, indicating that our calling method is not correct.

Inspect the following line:

```
result = requests.get('http://httpbin.org/post', json=data)
```

This gives us the indication that we are sending a GET request to one URL that accepts only POST requests, so we make the change in *step 2*.

> **Note**
>
> Notice that no specific debug steps have been required to detect this error, only a careful reading of the error message and the code. Remember to pay attention to error messages and logs. Often, this is enough to discover the issue or at least a very important piece of the puzzle.
>
> As always, GenAI can help you understand what a particular error means.

We run the code in *step 3* to find the next problem.

2. Second error—Wrong handling of middle names
   In *step 3*, we get an error of too many values to unpack. We can create a breakpoint to analyze the data in *step 4* at this point but discover that not all the data produces this error. The analysis done in *step 4* shows that it may be very confusing to stop the execution when an error is not produced, thus having to continue until it does. We know that the error is produced at this point, but only for specific data.

   As we know that the error is being produced at some point, we capture it in a `try..except` block in *step 5*. When the exception is produced, we trigger the breakpoint.

   This causes the *step 6* execution of the script to stop when `full_name` is `'John Paul Smith'`. This produces an error as the split expects two elements, not three.

   This is fixed in *step 7*, allowing everything except the last word to be part of the first name, grouping any middle name(s) into the first element. This fits our purpose for this program: to sort by last name.

> **Tip**
>
> Names are actually quite complex to handle. Check out this article if you want to be delighted by the vast numbers of incorrect assumptions one can make

> regarding names: `https://www.kalzumeus.com/2010/06/17/falsehoods-programmers-believe-about-names/`.

The following line does that with `rsplit`:

```
first_name, last_name = full_name.rsplit(maxsplit=1)
```

It divides the text by words, starting from the right and making a maximum of one split, guaranteeing that only two elements, at most, will be returned.

> **Note**
>
> This may produce an error if a name with no surname is defined, for example. We may need to amend the code if the input data change.

When the code is changed, *step 8* runs the code again to discover the next error.

3. Third error—Using an incorrect return value from the external service
Running the code in *step 8* displays the list and does not produce any errors. However, by examining the results, we can see that some names are incorrectly processed.

We pick one example in *step 9* and create a conditional breakpoint. We only activate the breakpoint if the data fulfills the if condition.

> **Note**
>
> The if condition, in this case, stops at any time the `"O'Carroll"` string appears, not having to make it stricter with an equal statement. Be pragmatic about this code, as you'll need to remove it after the bug is fixed anyway.

The code is run again in *step 10*. Once we've validated the data is as expected, we work backward to find the root of the problem. *Step 11* analyzes previous values and the code up to that point, trying to find out what led to the incorrect value.

We then discover that we used the wrong field of the server response. The value in the `json` field is better for this task and it's already parsed for us. *Step 12* checks the value and sees how it should be used.

In *step 13*, we change the code to properly decode the JSON content using the existing `.json()` method. Notice that the parse module is no longer needed and that the code is cleaner using the `json` method.

> **Tip**
>
> This outcome, using already existing tools, is more common than it looks, especially when dealing with external interfaces. We may use it in a way that works, but maybe it's not the best. Take a little bit of time to read the documentation to keep an eye on improvements and learn how to better use the tools.

Once this is fixed, the code is run again in *step 14*. Finally, the code is doing what's expected, sorting the names alphabetically by surname. Notice that the other name that contained strange characters is fixed as well.

## There's more...

The fixed script is available from GitHub: `https://github.com/PacktPublishing/Python-Automation-Cookbook-Third-Edition/blob/main/ch16/debug_skills_fixed.py`. You can download it and see the differences.

There are other ways of creating conditional breakpoints. There's actually support from the debugger to create breakpoints that stop, but only if some conditions are met. When possible, I find it easier to work directly with code, as it is persistent between runs and easier to remember and operate. You can check how to create it in the Python `pdb` documentation: `https://docs.python.org/3/library/pdb.html#pdbcommand-break`.

The kind of breakpoint that catches an exception, as shown in the first error, is a demonstration of how making breaking conditions in code is flexible and easy to do. Just be careful to remove them afterward!

In addition to `pdb`, there are other debuggers available that have an increased set of features; for example:

- `ipdb` (`https://github.com/gotcha/ipdb`): Adds tab completion and syntax highlights
- `pudb` (`https://documen.tician.de/pudb/`): Displays an old-style, semi-graphical, text-based interface, in the style of early 90s tools that displays the local scope variables automatically
- Web-pdb (`https://github.com/romanvm/python-web-pdb`): Opens a web server to access a graphical interface with the debugger

Read the debuggers' documentation to learn how to install and run them.

> **Tip**
>
> There are more debuggers available. A search on the Internet will give you more options, including Python IDEs. In any case, be aware of adding dependencies. It is always good to be able to use the default debugger.

The new breakpoint commands allow us to change easily between debuggers using the `PYTHONBREAKPOINT` environment variable; for example:

```
$ PYTHONBREAKPOINT=ipdb.set_trace python my_script.py
```

This starts `ipdb` on any breakpoint in the code. You can learn more about this in the `breakpoint()` documentation, which can be found here: `https://www.python.org/dev/peps/pep-0553/#environment-variable`.

> **Tip**
>
> An important effect on this is to disable all breakpoints by setting `PYTHONBREAKPOINT=0`, which is a great tool to ensure that code in production is never interrupted by a `breakpoint()` left by mistake.

The Python pdb documentation can be found here: `https://docs.python.org/3/library/pdb.html`. The entire documentation regarding the `parse` module can be found at `https://github.com/r1chardj0n3s/parse`, while the whole `requests` documentation can be found at `https://requests.readthedocs.io/en/master/`.

## See also

- The *Learning Python interpreter basics* recipe, earlier in this chapter, to learn the basics of code introspection in Python
- *The Debugging with breakpoints* recipe, from the previous section, to learn the basics of setting up breakpoints

# Final thoughts

As we reach the end of the book, I'd like to share a few final comments.

First and foremost, I hope you enjoyed the journey and that it has sparked exciting new ideas for automations that can support your work or hobbies. One of the aims of this book has been to present a variety of scenarios and options to stimulate your imagination, encouraging you to adapt the different recipes to your own specific challenges. It's not feasible to cover every possibility in a single volume, but I tried to showcase representative Python modules and libraries that highlight the breadth of the ecosystem. There are many more to explore, and the number keeps growing. I encourage you to do so.

We are in the early days of a significant change in programming with the rise of GenAI. It lowers the barrier to producing high-quality code at a speed that was not possible before, and it's a tool you can leverage to achieve excellent results.

Traditionally, tasks could be divided into two categories:

- **Tasks ripe for automation**, where it was worthwhile to invest significant resources to code and automate them. These are mostly already automated and supported by professional teams.
- **Less automatable tasks**, where the cost of automation outweighed the value. These might require human judgment or worse, occur too infrequently to justify the effort, remaining as minor annoyances.

GenAI is now making many previously complex tasks far easier to automate, raising the bar for what is achievable. While not everything will be feasible to automate, many of those annoyances can now be addressed.

Some believe the future lies in fully autonomous, agentic GenAI models completing tasks on their own from vague instructions, but I find that unrealistic. As we've discussed, granting an AI model too much freedom is risky, costly, and produces wildly inconsistent results. Instead, the key is to guide the AI model with clear context, using deterministic code to enable the agent to understand and fulfill the task reliably.

> Note
>
> Of course, that code may be written with the help of GenAI.

Automating a task remains hard work. Even with high-level libraries and GenAI support, there are numerous steps, corner cases, real-world challenges, and subtleties. To successfully implement a task, you require deep knowledge of all the aspects of it. And remember that

GenAI can also greatly help with learning! You can discuss and bounce ideas with a chatbot to get insights on a piece of code, bugs, or any other topic. Keep learning!

> Tip
>
> **GenAI is a multiplier**. It allows you to leverage your existing knowledge, but it equally increases any gaps in your understanding. As previously discussed in the book, if the context isn't focused, the AI model can drift in all sorts of directions, producing inconsistent and unfocused results. Learning is crucial to steer the AI models into success.

Don't be afraid to start with a partial automation with manual steps and gradually work toward a more complete solution. Be realistic and always consider ROI (return on investment); some tasks are simply not frequent or burdensome enough to justify the work for full automation.

I hope you enjoyed the book and found it both informative and helpful. Now, go on and automate some task that's annoying you!

# 17

# Unlock Your Exclusive Benefits

Your copy of this book includes the following exclusive benefits:

### DRM-Free PDF Version

Download DRM-free PDF and ePub copies of this book.

### 7-Day Packt Library Access

Get 7-day unlimited access to 8,000+ books and videos. No credit card required.

Available for first-time Packt+ trial users only.

### Next-Gen Reader Access

Read this book on Packt Reader with progress sync, dark mode and note-taking.

Follow the guide below to unlock them. The process takes only a few minutes and needs to be completed once.

# Unlock this Book's Free Benefits in 3 Easy Steps

## Step 1

Keep your purchase invoice ready for *Step 3*. If you have a physical copy, scan it using your phone and save it as a PDF, JPG, or PNG.

For more help on finding your invoice, visit `https://www.packtpub.com/en-us/unlock?step=1`.

> Note
>
> **Note**: If you bought this book directly from Packt, no invoice is required. After *Step 2*, you can access your exclusive content right away.

## Step 2

Scan the QR code or go to `packtpub.com/unlock`.

On the page that opens (similar to *Figure 17.1* on desktop), search for this book by name and select the correct edition.

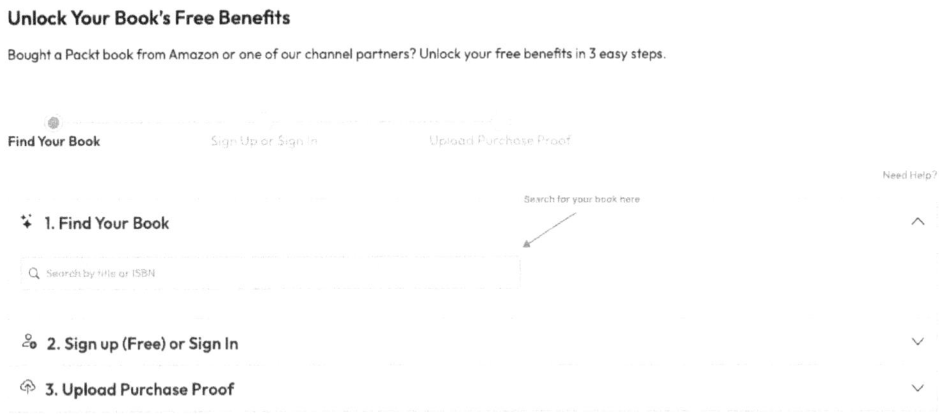


Figure 17.1: Packt unlock landing page on desktop

## Step 3

After selecting your book, sign in to your Packt account or create one for free. Then upload your invoice (PDF, PNG, or JPG, up to 10 MB). Follow the on-screen instructions to finish the process.

## Need Help

If you get stuck and need help, visit `https://www.packtpub.com/unlock-benefits/help` for a detailed FAQ on how to find your invoices and more. This QR code will take you to the help page.

Note

**Note**: If you are still facing issues, reach out to `customercare@packt.com`.

packtpub.com

Subscribe to our online digital library for full access to over 7,000 books and videos, as well as industry leading tools to help you plan your personal development and advance your career. For more information, please visit our website.

## Why subscribe?

- Spend less time learning and more time coding with practical eBooks and Videos from over 4,000 industry professionals
- Improve your learning with Skill Plans built especially for you
- Get a free eBook or video every month
- Fully searchable for easy access to vital information
- Copy and paste, print, and bookmark content

At www.packtpub.com, you can also read a collection of free technical articles, sign up for a range of free newsletters, and receive exclusive discounts and offers on Packt books and eBooks.

# Other Books You May Enjoy

If you enjoyed this book, you may be interested in these other books by Packt:

**Python Illustrated**

Maaike van Putten, Imke van Putten

ISBN: 9781836646334

- Set up Python and write your first program
- Understand variables, data types, and conditional statements
- Use loops, lists, dictionaries, and tuples to handle data efficiently
- Write and use functions to create reusable code
- Manage files and understand object-oriented programming and inheritance
- Debug your Python code to ensure it works flawlessly
- Discover how you can keep learning and building beyond this book

**Hands-On Software Engineering with Python**

Brian Allbee

ISBN: 9781835888018

- Distinguish software engineering from general programming
- Break down and apply each phase of the SDLC to Python systems
- Create system models to plan architecture before writing code
- Apply Agile, Scrum, and other modern development methodologies
- Use dataclasses, pydantic, and schemas for robust data modeling
- Set up CI/CD pipelines with GitHub Actions and cloud build tools
- Write and structure unit, integration, and end-to-end tests
- Evaluate and integrate tools like Poetry, pytest, and Docker

## Packt is searching for authors like you

If you're interested in becoming an author for Packt, please visit `authors.packt.com` and apply today. We have worked with thousands of developers and tech professionals, just like you, to help them share their insight with the global tech community. You can make a general application, apply for a specific hot topic that we are recruiting an author for, or submit your own idea.

## Share your thoughts

Now you've finished *Python Automation Cookbook, Third Edition*, we'd love to hear your thoughts! Scan the QR code below to go straight to the Amazon review page for this book and share your feedback or leave a review on the site that you purchased it from.

`https://packt.link/r/1806702894`

Your review is important to us and the tech community and will help us make sure we're delivering excellent quality content.

# Index

## H



## I



## J



## L



## M



## N



## O



## P

# U



# V



# W

www.ingramcontent.com/pod-product-compliance
Lightning Source LLC
LaVergne TN
LVHW060010210926
848481LV00013B/3682
*9781806702893*